PARALEGAL
HANDBOOK

PARALEGAL HANDBOOK

Theory, Practice, and Materials

American Institute for Paralegal Studies, Inc.

Mahwah, New Jersey

Charles P. Nemeth

St. Joseph's University, Philadelphia, Pennsylvania
Member of the Pennsylvania Bar Association

PRENTICE HALL, *Englewood Cliffs, NJ* 07632

Library of Congress Cataloging-in-Publication Data
Main entry under title:

Paralegal handbook.

   Includes bibliographies and index.
   1. Legal assistants—United States.   2. Law—
United States—Outlines, syllabi, etc.   I. Nemeth,
Charles P. (date)   II. American Institute for
Paralegal Studies.
KF320.L4P38   1986   340′.023   85-16898
ISBN   0-13-648593-6

Editorial/production supervision and
   interior design: Maureen Wilson
Cover design: Edsal Enterprises
Manufacturing buyer: Ed O'Dougherty

Printed in the United States of America

ISBN 0-13-648593-6   01

PRENTICE-HALL INTERNATIONAL (UK) LIMITED, *London*
PRENTICE-HALL OF AUSTRALIA PTY. LIMITED, *Sydney*
PRENTICE-HALL CANADA INC., *Toronto*
PRENTICE-HALL HISPANOAMERICANA, S.A., *Mexico*
PRENTICE-HALL OF INDIA PRIVATE LIMITED, *New Delhi*
PRENTICE-HALL OF JAPAN, INC., *Tokyo*
PRENTICE-HALL OF SOUTHEAST ASIA PTE. LTD., *Singapore*
EDITORA PRENTICE-HALL DO BRASIL, LTDA., *Rio de Janeiro*

To
Jean Marie, Eleanor, Stephen, Anne Marie,
and Those Yet to Come

CONTENTS

PREFACE

Much can be said about the field of paralegalism—in terms of practice, theory, and the influence the profession has on society. This book is testimony to that influence. Also testimony to that influence is the fact that by the year 1990, job opportunities in the field are expected to be the greatest of any occupation, according to U.S. government data.

The American Institute for Paralegal Studies has been a believer in the field of paralegalism since 1978, when it incorporated in the state of New Jersey and opened its first campus at Felician College in Lodi. Since then, the Institute has developed rapidly and now offers services in thirteen states. There are presently eighty-five campuses where the Institute conducts classes, and more are in the offing.

Along with the interest in the field has come the need for a series of works or a single text that will prepare students for the multiskilled demands paralegals face in the profession. This book is designed to fill that need.

I have tried to accomplish an almost impossible task—that is, the synthesis of all major topics in American law with an eye to the practical aspects of legal practice. I have tried also not to offend localities, states, and other interests where parochial views sometimes make them feel that one way is the only way. More important, I view this text as a tool of education and learning.

REASONS FOR THE GROWTH OF THE PROFESSION

Why is the profession growing at such a pace—with the concurrent growth of the American Institute? A variety of factors are involved. First of all, changing trends in our society have contributed to the increased complexity of law and regulation; to the recognition and advocacy of human and corporate rights; and to a heightened demand by citizens for participation in a wide spectrum of corporate, governmental, and social activities—all once the province of select groups.

Another factor is the changing face of American labor and industry. Traditional industries such as automobile and steel no longer offer good career opportunities, dependent as they are on supply, import quotas, taxes, and tariffs. Paralegalism, on the other hand, does not have to be overly concerned with these variables.

A third point is that paralegalism is a highly accessible occupation because of the opportunity to pursue studies in adult and continuing education classes. The Institute, for instance, offers a basic program that requires a commitment for two nights a week for about thirty weeks or, alternatively, Saturday classes.

The American Institute has achieved marked success owing to its plan of instruction and curricular presentation. The Institute's staff and faculty are all skilled practitioners in the field of law, and many also are professional educators. The Institute commits itself to academic excellence by its emphasis on faculty development, institutional research and scholarship, and high standards for acceptance and graduation. Courses are not simply mechanical, technical recitations but are imbued with theory, common sense, and ethics. The Institute is dedicated to the proposition that a good paralegal must also be a rational, inquisitive thinker and not simply a robot who performs technical tasks.

PROGRAM OF THE AMERICAN INSTITUTE FOR PARALEGAL STUDIES

The Institute has formally aligned itself with divisions or departments of continuing education in many colleges and has also worked out departmental alliances or institutional agreements. The major characteristics of those agreements include:

1. College credit for Institute course work.
2. Institute exemptions for collegiate credits earned at specific institutions.
3. The Institute's specific course of instruction located within a given department, such as law, criminal justice, business, or social work.

Most important, the Institute's program has been thoroughly reviewed by Thomas Edison State College in New Jersey, which is the host institution for the Program of Non-Collegiate Sponsored Instruction (PONSI) in New Jersey and has made college credit equivalency recommendations totaling sixteen college credits. These sixteen college credits have been formally approved by the American Council on Education in Washington, D.C., and are fully transferable to over forteen hundred collegiate institutions throughout the United States, subject to institutional guidelines.

FUTURE DIRECTIONS

The Institute has no plans of halting its expansion or service to the national community and has embarked on a variety of upcoming projects including:

1. *Advanced Independent Study Course:* The Institute has announced an advanced study course that can be performed on a part-time, correspondence basis. The program is quite intensive and features sophisticated review of real estate practice, personal injury litigation, legal research and writing, and estates and trusts. Students who complete the program will qualify for an advanced paralegal certificate and continuing education credits. The entire advanced study course has also been reviewed by PONSI and been awarded a total of seven college credits.
2. The Institute also hopes to market its basic course of instruction in some state prison systems, but much of that success will depend on state, federal, and private funding.
3. The Institute will participate in vocational training programs that can be funded under the Job Training Partnership Act.
4. The Institute is also exploring videotaped instruction.
5. The Institute is currently preparing advanced and specialized materials for national publication and marketing through a nationally known law publisher.

It is my hope and wish that students who journey through these pages will know the law very generally yet very comprehensively; that they will have those very essential concepts of law—elements, rules, traditions, and legal customs firmly implanted; that students will also realize that law is merely the product of men and women, nothing all too amazing or mysterious. Finally, I hope that students will take seriously their vocation, adhere to ethical principles, and rigidly uphold all that is good in the law and endeavor to discard the bad. If I can help to make that happen, then this work is worth far more than the paper and pages of print. Be paralegals at all cost, but be men and women of good will first.

ACKNOWLEDGMENTS

So many forces contribute to a project as demanding as a textbook of this nature. It would be nice for me to simply pat myself on the back and take full credit for the finished product, but that is plainly not the truth. I owe so much to so many, and my order of thanks is no reflection on priorities.

First, I thank my teachers, every one of them from kindergarten all the way past law school. I am deeply indebted to all of you who planted those sparks, ideas, and dreams. Secondly, I am deeply indebted to the founder and president of the American Institute, Thomas W. Williams, and its vice president, Michael Manna, who clearly believed in me. Their varied means and methods of support provided the bases for this endeavor. Many other industrious and talented employees of the Institute, including the vice president of operations, Edward Schwartz; the administrative vice president, Julie Clark; and all the regional directors and faculty, provided insightful advice and commentary. Others to be acknowledged are the many, many inspirational students, paralegals, and law practitioners. To my secretary, Donna Reuter, goes the greatest thanks for her unflinching determination to complete requested tasks and to outperform even the best in their fields. Great appreciation also goes to Maureen Wilson, a truly masterful writer and editor for Prentice-Hall, who made this task easier, and also to my brother, James Nemeth, for his suggestions and encouragement; and to Bart Brizée, a man who makes his love of language contagious. Finally, a thank you to my family, who truly mean more to me than anything and whose love makes my mind, my thoughts, my purpose so clear and meaningful.

CHARLES P. NEMETH
Chadds Ford, Pennsylvania

PARALEGAL HANDBOOK

CHAPTER ONE

THE NATURE OF LAW, THE JUDICIAL SYSTEM, AND LEGAL ETHICS

CHAPTER DESCRIPTION

In this chapter, we examine the nature of law, its philosophical and legal foundations; and its modern challenges and demands. We also present an overview of the American judicial system including the federal courts and selected state courts. The concepts of jurisdiction are also analyzed. Lastly, we review the ethical dilemmas and challenges in the practice of law and review specifically the ABA's Model Rules of Professional Conduct.

PARALEGAL FUNCTIONS

Choose the appropriate type of law for a given case.

Analyze jurisdictional questions.

Determine the professional and ethical responsibilities of the paralegal or attorney in the practice of law.

Become familiar with the appropriate judicial forum for a case.

Gain insight into the basis for law in our society.

I. THE PARALEGAL AND THE LAW

Why is it that paralegals exist? How did the paralegal profession—a quite recent phenomenon—come into the limelight? What forces made this profession an integral player in the delivery of legal services? To the astonishment of many, paralegals and legal assistants are now essential to the administration of justice, indispensable in legal investigation and management, and readily accepted professionals in the traditionally stodgy world of lawyering. What policies, social forces, and legal realities made this possible? A variety of reasons have been posed.

First, the entire field of law has been revolutionized in the last thirty years, becoming so complex that no lawyer is capable of functioning without some assistance. Initial calls for legal assistants, similar to dental or medical assistants, were viewed favorably, and the legal assistant is now the professional's valued aide, vital to a lawyer besieged by multiple clients and myriad rules, regulations, forms, and filings. The complexity of even a very small law practice requires more energy and intellect than even the keenest lawyer can provide alone.

Complexity is a key word here, especially in light of how all fundamental law in our society has rapidly developed, matured, and expanded. In this sense, historical comparisons are illuminating. Think back thirty years (if you can) or even twenty or less. How complex was the tax law of the United States? Was environmental law a topic of much litigation or popular discussion? Were lawyers active participants in administrative-law cases relating to Social Security, welfare, and other entitlement programs? How about toxic-chemical litigation on such issues as agent orange injuries or asbestos-related diseases? Historically, legal or practical analysis on equal pay, sexual rights, fair housing, and age discrimination was very uncommon twenty years ago. All these legal topics are essentially modern-day applications of law but certainly evidence of legal and social complexity. Within this context, individuals can make their own judgments on whether this complexity has brought the American scene a better way of a living. To say the least, life is more confusing by anyone's standards.

Second, driven by complex issues and relationships, the modern lawyer is crying out for assistance. He or she is ardently endeavoring to be professional, diligent, and all knowing in all these areas of law, or at least in a few of them, but that goal is unattainable. This complexity can make the lawyer feel inefficient, unproductive, and generally beleaguered. In bygone days wills were easy to do, crime was less rampant and a real estate settlement was a piece of cake. Today the lawyer needs an assistant to work cooperatively with and to rely on as a lifesaver in a sea of legal turbulence. Paralegals serve both lawyers and the public alike by their promotion of efficiency and productivity. Paralegals can tackle a multitude of tasks, from preparation of the settlement sheet in real estate to the filing of proper documents. Without any doubt, paralegals free the lawyer from the shackles of bureaucracy, technical legal applications, and administrative demands. In every chapter of this text, suggestions and insights will come forth that demonstrate the importance of paralegals in every common practice of law.

Third, the paralegal profession has come into the forefront because of the economic realities of the legal profession itself. Gone are the days when simple, exclusive, cushy law firms dominated an entire geographic region. To say that a particular firm has a "lock" on a company or a specific institution is not reflective of a modern public shopping around for legal services. In the past the expenses incurred by the general public in receiving legal services were commonly painful and exorbitant, primarily because there was no competition in the marketplace. A variety of deregulatory moves—for instance, allowing lawyers to advertise—have provided the public with a wider spectrum of legal services with an even wider range of prices for those services. Incredibly, costs for a simple real estate settlement can run from two hundred to one thousand dollars and up, depending on choice of firm or lawyer. If general trends are discernible in the delivery of legal services, it would appear that prices are going down. The free and open market seems to be forcing the cheaper delivery of legal services, and in the midst of this economic fury stands the paralegal. No other party is as responsible for the reduction in legal services costs, for it is the paralegal profession that makes the lawyer productive, efficient, and capable of handling diverse issues, cases, and clients.

While proponents of paralegalism are proud of this cost-efficiency role, critics claim that paralegals have taken much of the dignity and professionalism out of the practice of law. Some critics contend that the delivery of legal services has become no more than wholesale mass marketing. Equally vocal are lawyers who claim paralegals have ruined the job market for the now-graduating law classes and make a career in law almost an impossibility. Those criticisms have some wide support in legal circles, and the paralegal must prepare for that type of confrontation.

Whatever the case, critics and proponents alike can do little to stop this vocation from rolling along. Unstoppable as a speeding train, the paralegal has gone beyond the law-firm station and now is bound for hospitals, public defenders' offices, real estate companies, and other points.

The lawyer, in a crazy kind of way, has really very little to say about where this profession eventually winds up. Society, institutions, agencies, and other nontraditional law firms have already made their judgment that paralegals are an effective, productive, and necessary cog in the wheels of justice.

In sum, paralegals serve the law in a most honorable fashion by making it accessible. When prisoners with appellate or habeas corpus issues need assistance, they frequently receive assistance from paralegals employed by the prison or by publicly or privately funded prison-legal-assistance projects. When food stamps are arbitrarily cut, or other entitlements denied capriciously, legal-aid offices regularly employ paralegals to counsel, console, and investigate. Other duties might include investigating a criminal case for a public defender's or DA's office, searching titles for a title company, handling all secondary issues related to a real estate closing for a real estate company, or investigating accident cases for insurance companies. By no means are these examples exhaustive, only illustrative of how the law and the society itself has made the decision that paralegals are essential. There's no stopping this train.

II. THE NATURE OF LAW

Many paralegals feel that theory as it relates to law is a wasted exercise because it is too general. This shortsighted and blurred perspective assumes that "nuts and bolts" legal application is taught or learned in a vacuum with no conceptual understanding or mastery needed. The paralegal's maxim should be: *To apply the law requires understanding of the law*. So critics of theory really invite error and misapplication with their call for an army of trained paralegals functioning robotically with little or no understanding of the conceptual or foundational aspects of law. Technical drudgery is not what makes this profession interesting! It is my intention to provide the student with both theory and practical knowledge, a blending that will more appropriately produce a thinking and reasoning paralegal instead of an automaton of rules and process.

Thus our first general question emerges, highly theoretical in scope but essential to practical application: *Why does society have laws?*

A. The Necessity of Law

Isn't it possible to have a society with no laws? Wouldn't all people voluntarily pay taxes and behave in an orderly fashion, never trespass on another's property, or commit other offensive acts? Since people are basically good, can't they work out all their problems amicably without assistance from courts, judges, and lawyers? Wouldn't all companies keep the environment clean, charge fair prices, and treat their employees equitably? If any of your answers to the above questions are affirmative, then the reader is either awfully optimistic, unflinchingly idealistic, or just plain crazy. While all of us dream of such a world, reality crushes those fantasies quickly and gives credence to the *necessity* argument; that is, law exists because it is necessary and essential to the orderly flow of life. Acknowledgment of this necessity rationale is found in a variety of philosophical traditions with much consideration of why law exists, and some of those considerations are discussed briefly below.

B. Law as a Result of Morality or Religion

Of great topical interest today is the relationship law has with moral values, religion, and other beliefs. To most civil libertarians, the mix of religion, morality, and values with law is an improper formula guided by sectarian and nonpluralistic principles. Since there are so many religious and moral points of view in modern society, the use of religion and morality in the law-making process is an affront to minority points of view. In essence, the libertarians argue, there really is no common morality, only a plurality of moral positions influenced by ethical relativism.

On the other hand, proponents of morality as an integral part of the law call our attention to the most basic, the most fundamental values of our society, which do in fact rest in religion and moral values. In the purest sense, each law promulgated in the society is a value judgment. Every law adopted seems to have some moral overtone. Think of the Ten Commandments and how they might relate to a criminal code or divorce act. Think of English common law, the English tradition, and the British government's more closely aligned church and state.

Truly, this topic is controversial, with both sides probably overexuberant in their righteousness. In the final analysis, neither side wants a state religion, a state prayer, or a state code of ethics. Both sides want tranquillity, respect for life, and recognition of the dignity of the person and the necessity for general order. Neither can really deny the other, but in the modern secular world, religion has been given a total, thorough downgrading in its influence in the making of law. To say our culture should give no value to religious and moral principles in the making of laws is to deny reality and the community consensus. If law is the result of community consensus, how can religion and morality be excluded from the general population's mind set?

C. Positivism and Law

While proponents of religion and morality hope the passage of law reflects their concerns, a true *positivist* has little or no regard for religion and morality. Under a positivist's system, law is simply the product of the state, a legislative consensus passed on to the general public. There is no room for moral or religious choices since the law is the product of the state. Individualized issues are irrelevant. Positivism's basic rationale and justification is that law is a necessity for order and the prevention of chaos. Positive law is strictly the invention of the people, the human institutions operating in the particular society. As can be easily envisioned, positivism's scientific, nonsupernatural flavor has brought it into direct conflict with natural-law proponents as discussed below.

D. Law as a Product of the Natural Law

The *natural law* is a philosophical, religious and rational school of thought more than three thousand years old. Since the early Greeks, philosophers have pointed out the "natural" order of things in the universe. Simplistically, any nature observer can see this natural order operating. Bees have sex with other bees, always the opposite sex. Tides come in, the tides go out. When it rains, the water comes down, not up, and so on. These are all orderly events that happen with such regularity that they are obviously natural. Ergo, a natural law, or a law of nature, must exist!

Natural-law theorists go a good bit further in applying these natural rules and principles to human interaction. In short, they argue that people naturally interact in certain ways. For example, members of the opposite sex marry; most people choose to love others rather than kill them, to respect another's property rather than take it. At all costs, the natural law gives us evidence that society needs to promote and adopt rules that offer peace, harmony, and tranquillity to mankind.

Lastly, and certainly of tremendous value, we have the religious application of natural law. Natural-law philosophers such as St. Thomas Aquinas and Jacques Maritain avidly support the notion that all law should be a reflection of the eternal law of God, the supreme player in the natural order of things. God, as first cause of all, provides human beings with the knowledge and insight to discern the eternal rule of God, the right and wrong of deeds and actions. Manmade laws should not be contrary to the eternal laws of God. Do you see why the pure positivist would be upset with the religious natural-law theorist?

E. Law and Social Forces

As in all sociological analysis, institutions, individuals, agencies, trends, mores, habits, and customs must be reviewed before an explanation of law is possible or even likely. To the empirical social scientist, law is fundamentally a product of social and cultural evolution. To paraphrase, one might say: *The more evolved the society, the more laws it has*. While this thought may be true, evolution is a judgmental term. Is the United States really more evolved than Ireland? Technologically it is. Industrially it is. Medically it is. But are these the variables by which the society is measured as being evolved? Maybe so, for certainly this country really has a ton of laws, far more than Ireland could ever imagine. Is this a fact worth bragging about? Is it a reflection of our own inability to deal amicably in our relationships or to resolve problems efficiently?

Equally important in the sociological explanation of law is how social forces, trends, or influences affect our law-making decisions. In the sociological context, the community consensus is critical, for it is a mirror image of those social influences. Accordingly, law is less than a fixed, infallible principle and more an elastic variable ideal reflecting the mood, trends, and social influences operating at any particular stage in history. Could a natural-law theorist easily be in conflict with a sociological theorist?

III. TYPES OF LAW

One of the eternal fascinations with the field of law is its extraordinary diversity. Law in a generous sense is a combination of a hundred forms or types of law. The paralegal may spend a whole lifetime working with only a few areas of law. This text will cover the following types of law:

□ Criminal law (Chapter 2)
□ Criminal procedure (Chapter 2)
□ Legal investigation (Chapter 3)
□ Family law (Chapter 4)
□ Tort law (Chapter 5)
□ Civil procedure and evidence (Chapter 6)
□ Corporations, partnership/agency (Chapter 7)
□ Commercial law (Chapter 8)
□ Real estate law (Chapter 9)
□ Estates and trusts (Chapter 10)

This list contains some of the main categories of law in which a paralegal will practice regularly and consistently. The list will expand as the role of the paralegal becomes more widely accepted and supported. Already paralegals are engaging in significant efforts in the following emerging fields: administrative law, tax law, social security law, environmental law, and worker's compensation law.

Believe it or not, a paralegal, or a lawyer or judge for that matter, could spend an entire lifetime on one or two of these areas of law and never really totally master them. This thought brings to mind another maxim worth pondering: *The more you learn, the less you really know*.

A. Sources of Law

Imperative in the understanding of law is a recognition of the law's chief sources. As discussed thus far, it is clear that the roots of law are a mixture of social forces, community consensus, religion, positivism, and values, but how does the society make its laws? How does it draw inward and promulgate, refer to, and rely on law? What are the laws' support systems, or roots?

1. Common law or tradition

Our legal heritage springs from various historical periods including the Greco-Roman period, the Anglo-Saxon age, and the colonial period, when the colonies followed English tradition as well as American colonial law. In fact our nation's common law is a product of both England and our own traditions. Speaking in the most basic terms, our common law is our common thread, our heritage of law, legal reasoning, and application throughout the centuries. *Common law* is mostly a body of ideas and principles, extremely broad in construction and grounded in rational fairness, equity, justice, and common sense. Black's Law Dictionary defines the common law as follows:

> **COMMON LAW.** As distinguished from the Roman law, the modern civil law, the canon law, and other systems, the common law is that body of law and juristic theory which was originated, developed, and formulated and is administered in England, and has obtained among most of the states and peoples of Anglo-Saxon stock.

This common theme or thread poignantly finds its way into our next two sources of law: *cases and statutes*.

2. Case law

Ever see the following type of designation?

State v. *Jonesy*

This short term lists the parties to a case, the complainant or plaintiff—*the state*—versus the defendant—*Jonesy*. The parties to such an action are simple evidence of a dispute of some kind, whether criminal or civil. The citation further typifies that the parties could not informally resolve this dispute and as a result turned it into a case. This case has to be resolved in the courts by either a judge or a jury. No matter what the decision by the judge or jury in this particular case, the finding of the court is defined as *case law*. It may be an interpretation so odd that it has no support in any other setting and hence has little or no *precedent*. Even if no precedent exists, the decision is still law until overturned. Again, the term *case law*.

3. Statutes

The most prolific source of law in modern society consists of statutory materials. Statutes are laws passed by state legislatures or Congress. Statutes cover a broad gamut of topics including traffic laws, criminal codes, tax laws, environmental laws and so forth. A statute might read as follows:

> U.S.C.A. §1717. **Letters and writings as nonmailable; opening letters** (b) Whoever uses or attempts to use the mails or Postal Service for the transmission of any matter declared by this section to be nonmailable, shall be fined not more than $5,000 or imprisoned not more than ten years or both.

As can be discerned, statutes must be passed by the proper majorities and withstand constitutional inquiry, public opposition or wrath, and judicial inquiry. Statute law frequently becomes the subject matter of a case decided by a judge, particularly at the appellate level. A case decision may result in the overturning or forced repeal of a statute. Think of all the possibilities.

4. Other sources of law

No effort has been made to cover everything on the following list, but the paralegal should be aware that there are many secondary sources of law including:

1. Constitution—Federal. American law is particularly affected by the constitutional dimensions of law including the separation of powers in the legislative, executive, and judicial branches and the Bill of Rights. The Constitution is reprinted in chapter 2, appendix 2A.

2. Constitutions—State. While in some respects mere repetitions of the federal design, they differ significantly in some areas, such as the ERA and police powers.

3. Administrative Regulations. The burgeoning federal bureaucracy, although not purposely, has inevitably overwhelmed the population with a massive load of regulations, rules, and administrative codes. The Code of Federal Regulations (CFR) is the publisher of these federal rules.

4. Treaties

5. Other Foreign Agreements

6. International Law

IV. THE COURT SYSTEM

The arena for legal inquiry and decision making fundamentally rests with the *courts*! Courts are places of civilized behavior, or at least we hope so, where the law is put to the test. Which court handles the law? The answer to this question depends on the jurisdiction of the court and the type of law to be resolved or decided.

A. Jurisdiction

To arrive at the proper jurisdiction, the paralegal must consider these varied forms of jurisdictions:

1. Subject matter

A court will be competent to hear a particular case if the legislature has granted it a particular power or capability to review specific areas, such as divorce or criminal cases.

2. Exclusive jurisdiction

Federal or state legislatures may also devise a court for a solitary purpose—for instance, for resolving housing, trademark, or patent claims. That court has the exclusive right to jurisdiction in its particular subject matter.

3. Concurrent jurisdiction

Many actions in law can possibly be heard in more than one forum. Especially illustrative are the many federal lawsuits that can also be competently brought before a state court. This equal access is deemed concurrent.

4. Appellate jurisdiction

Beyond the trial stage, a defendant must seek a remedy from the next highest court with powers over his or her subject matter. That next court is usually appellate in nature, signifying the appeal process.

5. Pendent jurisdiction

This is a form of jurisdiction of the federal courts in which there is a problem that has a federal claim *and* a state claim. If both federal and state claims arise out of a common event or the same operative facts, the federal court has pendent jurisdiction.

6. Federal jurisdiction

Federal jurisdiction obviously rests in the federal courts with cases that have a federal problem or, to put it more aptly, a "federal question." The ease at proving a "federal question" is discussed in chapter 6. Also discussed in detail are the other requirements for jurisdiction. For clarity's sake, the following elements are required to insure federal jurisdiction: (1) federal question or (2) diversity of citizenship parties from differing states and (3) damages of $10,000 or more.

B. An Overview of American Courts

1. The federal court system

The federal system of courts is quite expansive. Owing to the proliferation of federal law and legislation, many supporters of the federal judiciary are begging for increased funding for judgeships and improved conditions for employees in the federal judiciary. Like all court systems, the federal system follows a fundamental hierarchy beginning with:

a. THE UNITED STATES SUPREME COURT

Little doubt exists that the Supreme Court is the final arbiter of law in American jurisprudence. The decisions of the Court can really be reversed only by the Court itself, or by congressional legislation, both very unlikely events. The Supreme Court is fascinating historically and has had its share of media attention, personalities, and political pressure in recent years. It is composed of nine judges appointed for life by the president subject to congressional approval. It has been proven time and time again that the politics of the presidency has little influence on the decision-making trends of the Court. While the Court has some *original* jurisdiction in some state/federal disputes as well as diplomatic concerns, the overwhelming thrust of the Court's work is in the *appellate* area. In its appellate capacity, the Court has the main duty of reviewing decisions of lower trial courts and lower, inferior appellate tribunals. Appellate process before the Supreme Court is certainly not a right in any sense and will be granted only by a grant of a writ of *certiorari*. The Court considers the following factors in its decision to hear a case: timeliness, special or important reasons, urgent national issue, lower-court inconsistency, and major constitutional dilemma.

b. UNITED STATES CIRCUIT COURTS OF APPEAL

Under authority granted to the federal government in article III of the Constitution, Congress has the powers to form "such inferior Courts" as it "may from time to time ordain and establish." Congress has continually responded under the Judiciary Act of 1789 and funded this intermediate appeals court in eleven different circuits. (See figure 1.1.) Within these circuits are one or several federal district courts, which are the basic trial courts.

FIGURE 1.1

The Eleven Federal Judicial Circuits

See 28 U.S.C.A. § 41

c. FEDERAL DISTRICT COURTS

Under the same authority of article III and the Judiciary Act of 1789, Congress established the first-level trial network in the federal court system—the federal district courts. At last count there were ninety-two districts served by these federal courts, with each state having at least one and larger states such as New York, Texas, and California having four districts each. The allocation of districts and the necessary judgeships has been the subject of intense federal lobbying and political patronage.

d. SPECIALIZED FEDERAL COURTS

A variety of inferior courts with exclusive subject-matter jurisdiction have been authorized by Congress. Among them are the U.S. Court of Military Appeals, the U.S. Tax Court, the U.S. Court of Customs and Patents, and the U.S. Court of Claims (dealing with claims against the U.S. by persons or other legal entities).

2. The state court system

The diversity of state systems of courts is absolutely mind boggling. In appendix 1B is an overview of all fifty state court systems, entitled *Jurisdiction of Trial Courts, 1980*. The table graphically illustrates court characteristics by name of court, level, geographic jurisdiction, number of districts, number of judges, subject-matter jurisdiction, and appellate jurisdiction. Review in depth and notice the following general trends in state court structure.

First, all states distinguish *trial courts* from *appellate courts*. Lower courts, which hear the cases and try to resolve the disputes, are generally deemed trial courts. Higher courts, which hear appeals from the decisions of the trial courts, are known as appellate courts. Appellate courts generally do not do anything but review the record of the lower courts and affirm, reverse, or remand the decisions.

Second, state courts are generally divided up into districts or other geographic regions: common placement of state courts is in each county, parish, or major city of a state. For example, Pennsylvania has a court of common pleas, a basic trial court.

Third, state courts are further functionalized by subject-matter jurisdiction. Some state courts, such as Surrogate's Court or Probate Court, handle matters relating only to estates and trusts. Other subject-matter examples might include a specific court for domestic relations, housing, or traffic offenses.

Fourth, every state has a court of last resort, its highest court. Generally that court is termed the Supreme Court, but variations are not uncommon. In New York, the Court of Appeals is the highest court, while the Supreme Court is a trial court. Again, this type of diversity, while perplexing, is quite common.

Fifth, state courts are usually further broken down into more regional divisions. As noted, these courts can be called State District Courts but often take on the following common names: magistrate's court, justice of the peace courts, municipal court, town justice, village court, and alderman's court.

These are really indicative of the people's courts—the places where small disputes are resolved, traffic offenses are disposed of, and parking tickets paid. Again, refer to the table in appendix 1B for the multiple approaches taken by the American states. See also figure 1.2, the New York court chart.

V. ETHICAL ISSUES IN THE PRACTICE OF LAW

Critically important to the paralegal is an understanding of the ethical and moral dilemmas common in the practice of law. Governed by traditional habits and mores as well as noble professional principles, the legal profession has struggled long and hard to abide by a strong, viable credo. At the state level, the profession has adopted, of its own volition, Codes of Professional Responsibility. Some state law associations have adopted the ABA's Model Rules of Professional Conduct passed on August 10, 1982. (See table 1.1.) These Model Rules serve as a guide for the self-policing of the profession and pose recurring ethical dilemmas with commentary. Portions of this set of Rules will be referred to in this section in hopes that the paralegal will learn the pitfalls in the practice of law.[1]

To be sure, all professional behavior has many difficult questions to solve and dreadful "gray" areas where no appropriate response is possible, but the bulk of what lawyers do unethically is just plain and simple corruption. Paralegals will have to come to grips with these issues since they will often be the intermediary between client and

[1]The Model Rules following in sections V-A—V-D are excerpted from Model Rules of Professional Conduct, copyright August 1983 by the American Bar Association. All rights reserved. Reprinted with permission.

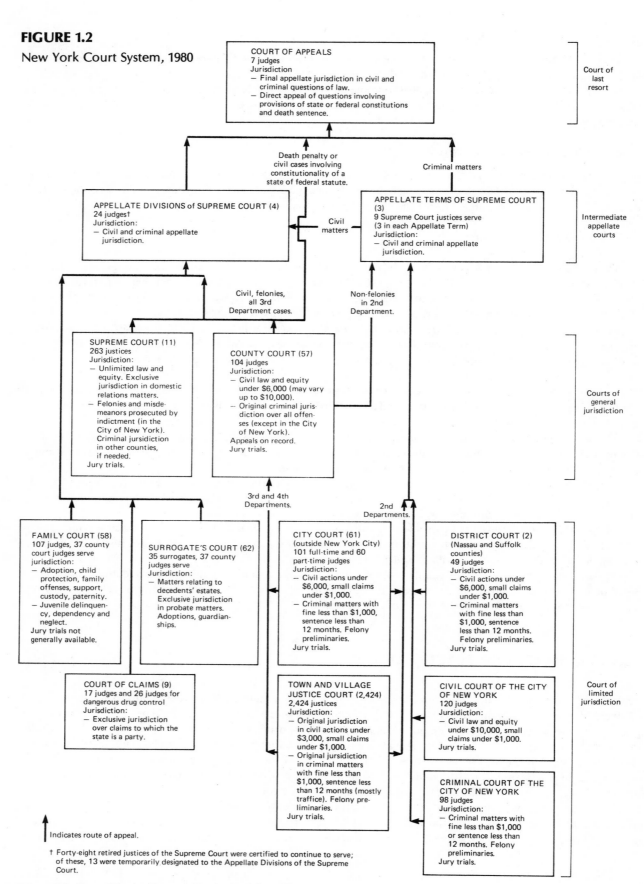

FIGURE 1.2

New York Court System, 1980

COURT OF APPEALS
7 judges
Jurisdiction
— Final appellate jurisdiction in civil and criminal questions of law.
— Direct appeal of questions involving provisions of state or federal constitutions and death sentence.

Court of last resort

Death penalty or civil cases involving constitutionality of a state of federal statute.

Criminal matters

APPELLATE DIVISIONS of SUPREME COURT (4)
24 judges†
Jurisdiction:
— Civil and criminal appellate jurisdiction.

Civil matters

APPELLATE TERMS OF SUPREME COURT (3)
9 Supreme Court justices serve (3 in each Appellate Term)
Jurisdiction:
— Civil and criminal appellate jurisdiction.

Intermediate appellate courts

Civil, felonies, all 3rd Department cases.

Non-felonies in 2nd Department.

SUPREME COURT (11)
263 justices
Jurisdiction:
— Unlimited law and equity. Exclusive jurisdiction in domestic relations matters.
— Felonies and misdemeanors prosecuted by indictment (in the City of New York). Criminal jursidiction in other counties, if needed.
Jury trials.

COUNTY COURT (57)
104 judges
Jurisdiction:
— Civil law and equity under $6,000 (may vary up to $10,000).
— Original criminal jurisdiction over all offenses (except in the City of New York).
Appeals on record.
Jury trials.

Courts of general jurisdiction

3rd and 4th Departments.

2nd Departments.

FAMILY COURT (58)
107 judges, 37 county court judges serve jurisdiction:
— Adoption, child protection, family offenses, support, custody, paternity.
— Juvenile delinquency, dependency and neglect.
Jury trials not generally available.

SURROGATE'S COURT (62)
35 surrogates, 37 county judges serve
Jurisdiction:
— Matters relating to decedents' estates. Exclusive jurisdiction in probate matters. Adoptions, guardianships.

CITY COURT (61)
(outside New York City)
101 full-time and 60 part-time judges
Jurisdiction:
— Civil actions under $6,000, small claims under $1,000.
— Criminal matters with fine less than $1,000, sentence less than 12 months. Felony preliminaries.
Jury trials.

DISTRICT COURT (2)
(Nassau and Suffolk counties)
49 judges
Jurisdiction:
— Civil actions under $6,000, small claims under $1,000.
— Criminal matters with fine less than $1,000, sentence less than 12 months. Felony preliminaries.
Jury trials.

Court of limited jurisdiction

COURT OF CLAIMS (9)
17 judges and 26 judges for dangerous drug control
Jurisdiction:
— Exclusive jurisdiction over claims to which the state is a party.

TOWN AND VILLAGE JUSTICE COURT (2,424)
2,424 justices
Jurisdiction:
— Original jurisdiction in civil actions under $3,000, small claims under $1,000.
— Original jursidiction in criminal matters with fine less than $1,000, sentence less than 12 months (mostly traffice). Felony preliminaries.
Jury trials.

CIVIL COURT OF THE CITY OF NEW YORK
120 judges
Jursidiction:
— Civil law and equity under $10,000, small claims under $1,000.
Jury trials.

CRIMINAL COURT OF THE CITY OF NEW YORK
98 judges
Jurisdiction:
— Criminal matters with fine less than $1,000 or sentence less than 12 months. Felony preliminaries.
Jury trials.

Indicates route of appeal.

† Forty-eight retired justices of the Supreme Court were certified to continue to serve; of these, 13 were temporarily designated to the Appellate Divisions of the Supreme Court.

Source: U.S. Dept. of Justice, Bureau of Justice Statistics, 1980.

attorney and can even be viewed as the moral buffer that exculpates the attorney from his or her wrongdoing. Paralegals clearly have an obligation to stand firmly and courageously against conduct they perceive as violative of professional conduct.

With the growth of paralegalism, standards for professional conduct have evolved. Refer to appendix I A for an example of a paralegal ethical code.

TABLE 1.1

Schematic Overview of the ABA Model Rules of Professional Conduct

RULE

CLIENT-LAWYER RELATIONSHIP

1.1 Competence
1.2 Scope of representation
1.3 Diligence
1.4 Communication
1.5 Fees
1.6 Confidentiality of information
1.7 Conflict of interest: General rule
1.8 Conflict of interest: Prohibited transactions
1.9 Conflict of interest: Former client
1.10 Imputed disqualification: General rule
1.11 Successive government and private employment
1.12 Former judge or arbitrator
1.13 Organization as the client
1.14 Client under a disability
1.15 Safekeeping property
1.16 Declining or terminating representation

COUNSELOR

2.1 Advisor
2.2 Intermediary
2.3 Evaluation for use by third person

ADVOCATE

3.1 Meritorious claims and contentions
3.2 Expediting litigation
3.3 Candor toward the tribunal
3.4 Fairness to opposing party and counsel
3.5 Impartiality and decorum of the tribunal
3.6 Trial publicity
3.7 Lawyer as witness
3.8 Special responsibilities of a prosecutor
3.9 Advocate in nonadjudicative proceedings

TRANSACTIONS WITH PERSONS OTHER THAN CLIENTS

4.1 Truthfulness in statements to others
4.2 Communication with person represented by counsel
4.3 Dealing with unrepresented person
4.4 Respect for rights of third persons

LAW FIRMS AND ASSOCIATIONS

5.1 Responsibilities of a partner or supervisory lawyer
5.2 Responsibilities of a subordinate lawyer
5.3 Responsibilities regarding nonlawyer assistants
5.4 Professional independence of a firm

An in-depth analysis of particular provisions of the model rule follows.

A. Client-Lawyer Relationship

1. *Rule 1.1:* *Lawyer competence*

A lawyer should provide competent representation to a client. Competent representation requires the legal knowledge, skill, thoroughness, and preparation reasonably necessary for the representation.

The paralegal should be thoroughly prepared and dedicated to his or her client's case. Competency entails a variety of issues, which the model rules attempt to clarify. Competency does not mean pure expertise or specialized training. In fact the rules make clear that all attorneys who are thoroughly prepared, have done their research, and are conceptually oriented can provide competent services. The level of intellectual complexity in a given case is also relevant to the issues of competency and is directly relevant when evaluating a reasonable lawyer's competence.

2. *Rule 1.2:* *Scope of representation*

(*a*) A lawyer shall abide by a client's decisions concerning the objectives of representation, subject to paragraphs *c*, *d*, and *e*, and shall consult with the client as to the means by which they are to be pursued. A lawyer shall abide by a client's decision whether to accept an offer of settlement of a matter. In a criminal case, the lawyer shall abide by the client's decision, after consultation with the lawyer, as to a plea to be entered, whether to waive jury trial, and whether the client will testify.
(*b*) A lawyer's representation of a client, including representation by appointment, does not constitute an endorsement of the client's political, economic, social, or moral views or activities.
(*c*) A lawyer may limit the objectives of the representation if the client consents after consultation.
(*d*) A lawyer shall not counsel or assist a client in conduct that the lawyer knows is criminal or fraudulent, or in the preparation of a written instrument containing terms the lawyer knows are expressly prohibited by law, but a lawyer may counsel or assist a client in a good faith effort to determine the validity, scope, meaning, or application of the law.
(*e*) When a lawyer knows that a client expects assistance not permitted by the Rules of Professional Conduct or other law, the lawyer shall consult with the client regarding the relevant limitations on the lawyer's conduct.

Again, numerous issues come under this rule. In particular, rule 1.2 advises the lawyer that the client, not the lawyer, has the ultimate decision-making power of the case. If a lawyer does not agree, he or she does not have to continue on the case. Section *d* specifies that no lawyer can possibly ethically support the behavior of his client if he or she knows it is criminal, fraudulent, or prohibited by law.

3. Rule 1.3: Diligence

A lawyer shall act with reasonable diligence and promptness in representing a client.

Be aware that a client's perception of diligence is often influenced by the feeling that his or her case is the only case the lawyer has. Past interpretation of the term *diligence* has been realistic and required lawyers to be punctual, deliberate, courteous, and forthright. Endless procrastination is not only bad for lawyer productivity but generally resented by clients.

4. Rule 1.4: Communication

(*a*) A lawyer shall keep a client reasonably informed about the status of a matter and promptly comply with reasonable requests for information.
(*b*) A lawyer shall explain a matter to the extent reasonably necessary to permit the client to make informed decisions regarding the representation.

If only lawyers would communicate with their clients more regularly, the bulk of their public relations problems would dissipate. A short note, a quick call, or even a visit to an elderly client serves not only to keep the client apprised but also to generate good will. Paralegals have an obligation and duty to keep in touch with all assigned cases. (See exhibit 1.1.)

EXHIBIT 1.1

CLIENT NOTIFICATION LETTERS*

RE: State v. _____
Dear _____:
The pre-trial conference in your case was held today. As we discussed, this conference was for the purpose of plea negotiation.
After discussing the case, the District Attorney would make the following recommendation in your case: _____.
You are scheduled to appear on_____.
Please call me immediately to decide whether to have a trial or to accept the negotiated plea offer.
I look forward to hearing from you.
Sincerely,

Attorney at Law

RE: State v. _____
Dear _____:
Your case has been set for jury trial on _____. We will not know the exact time and room number until the day before trial, so you will need to call us then to get that information.

It is important that you maintain contact so that we can provide the best possible defense. Keep us advised of any changes in your situation, particularly any change of address. If we have lost contact with you and you fail to show at the time of trial, the court will issue a warrant for your arrest.

If you have any questions, contact either myself or your attorney.
Sincerely,

Trial Assistant
for _____, Attorney at Law

---

*Excerpted from *Working with Legal Assistants: A Team Approach for Lawyers and Legal Assistants*, Paul G. Ulrich and Robert S. Mucklestone, eds. Reprinted with permission of the American Bar Association.

Date: _____

STATE v. _____

Dear _____ :

It is imperative that you contact this office *immediately!*

Your attorney has been unable to reach you, and he must plan for your case, which is now set for _____ on _____.

Call your attorney or his trial assistant at _____ as soon as possible. If they are not in, leave a phone number and a time at which we can reach you.

Sincerely,

Trial Assistant
for_____, Attorney at Law

Address mailed to: _____

_____

Dear _____ :

Your case is set for a pre-trial conference on _____, at _____.

This is the time when your attorney gets together with the district attorney to find out what they would be recommending if you plead guilty to the charge. That doesn't mean that you will plead guilty to the charge. It just gives us an idea what would happen if you decided you wanted to plead guilty.

We would like you to give us a call a couple of days before your pre-trial conference so we can talk to you and find out how you're doing as this helps in our negotiations at the pre-trial conference. Then it will be your responsibility to call us the day after your pre-trial conference so we can tell you what the offer was. At that point, we will decide whether we want to accept the pre-trial offer or whether we want to go to trial.

Therefore, we expect to hear from you a few days before the pre-trial conference. Hope things are going well with you.

Sincerely,

Trial Assistant
for _____, Attorney at Law

---

5. Rule 1.5: Fees

(a) A lawyer's fee shall be reasonable. The factors to be considered in determining the reasonableness of a fee include the following:

1. the time and labor required, the novelty and difficulty of the question involved, and the skill requisite to perform the legal service properly;

2. the likelihood, if apparent to the client, that the acceptance of the particular employment will preclude other employment by the lawyer;

3. the fee customarily charged in the locality for similar legal services;

4. the amount involved and the results obtained;

5. the time limitations imposed by the client or by the circumstances;

6. the nature and length of the professional relationship with the client;

7. the experience, reputation, and ability of the lawyer or lawyers performing the services;

8. whether the fee is fixed or contingent. A lawyer shall not enter into an arrangement for, charge, or collect a contingent fee for representing a defendant in a criminal case.

(b) When the lawyer has not regularly represented the client, the basis or rate of the fee shall be communicated to the client, preferably in writing, before or within a reasonable time after commencing the representation.

(c) A fee may be contingent on the outcome of the matter for which the service is rendered, except in a matter in which a contingent fee is prohibited by law or by these rules. A contingent fee agreement shall be in writing and shall state the method by which the fee is to be determined, including the percentage or percentages that shall accrue to the lawyer in the event of settlement, trial or appeal, litigation and other expenses to be deducted from the recovery, and whether such expenses are to be deducted before or after the contingent fee is calculated. Upon conclusion of a contingent fee matter, the lawyer shall provide the client with a written statement stating the outcome of the matter and, if there is a recovery, showing the remittance to the client and the method of its determination.

(*d*) A lawyer shall not enter into an arrangement to charge or collect any fee in a domestic relations matter, the payment or amount of which is contingent upon the amount of alimony or support or property settlement in lieu thereof.

(*e*) A division of fee between lawyers who are not in the same firm may be made only if:

1. the division is in proportion to the services performed by each lawyer, or, by written agreement with the client, each lawyer assumes joint responsibility for the representation; and

2. the client consents to the participation of all the lawyers involved; and

3. the total fee is reasonable.

Little imagination is required to see the plethora of disputes that arise from this Rule of Conduct. Of course, both lawyers and clients alike are at fault in this area. So the suggestions of rule 1.5 are preventive in scope.

Particular issues are most difficult to define precisely. When is a fee *reasonable*? The Rule gives us eight criteria or factors to consider in assessing the reasonableness of a fee. By those criteria, can $220 an hour ever be considered reasonable? Who is worth that? Paralegals will frequently be affronted by bills from neighboring lawyers or firms or even by bills from their own firms that are far more devastating than "sticker" shock! By whose standards do we measure?

The Rule also provides excellent advice on putting that bill in writing and enunciating the terms of payment and any appropriate divisions between parties other than the hired attorney. (See exhibit 1.2.)

6. Rule 1.6:   Confidentiality of information

(*a*) A lawyer shall not reveal information relating to representation of a client unless the client consents after consultation, except for disclosures that are impliedly authorized in order to carry out the representation, and except as stated in paragraph *b*.

(*b*) A lawyer may reveal such information to the extent the lawyer reasonably believes necessary:

EXHIBIT 1.2

EMPLOYMENT CONTRACT FOR CRIMINAL DEFENSE REPRESENTATION

THIS AGREEMENT, made and entered into this _____ day of _____, 19____, by and between _____, party of the first part, and _____, Attorney at Law, party of the second part;

WITNESSETH: That the party of the first part hereby employs, engages and retains _____, Attorney at Law, to represent him/her/them in a criminal action pending in the _____ Court, and in consideration thereof, the first party hereby promises and agrees to pay to the second party as an attorney fee a sum equal to _____, payable as follows:

_____

_____

_____

The first party agrees to pay all court costs incurred and all expenses incident to the investigation and prosecution of the case, such as medical and other records, cost of photographs, maps, diagrams, costs of investigation such as mileage, services of investigator, etc.

The second party accepts the employment under the conditions set forth herein, but it is understood and agreed that if first party fails to honor this employment agreement, the second party may declare this contract null and void and may proceed to officially withdraw from said case.

_____
Party of the first part

_____
Party of the second part

_____
Witness

1. to prevent the client from committing a criminal or fraudulent act that the lawyer reasonably believes is likely to result in death or substantial bodily harm, or in substantial injury to the financial interests or property of another;

2. to rectify the consequences of a client's criminal or fraudulent act in the furtherance of which the lawyer's services had been used;

3. to establish a claim or defense on behalf of the lawyer in a controversy between the lawyer and the client, or to establish a defense to a criminal charge, civil claim, or disciplinary complaint against the lawyer based upon conduct in which the client was involved; or

4. to comply with other law.

To foster a lawyer/client relationship, confidentiality must be not only assured but guaranteed. Confidentiality insures full and free-flowing communication of highly personal and often obviously damaging and incriminating matter. Of course, if the client grants permission to disclose privileged communications, then a waiver has occurred. Other well-defined exceptions exist, including (a) when a lawyer forsees that his or her client intends to seriously injure another person, or (b) to undo previous advice innocently given to a client that furthered a criminal act. Much argument took place in ABA convention hearings on when a lawyer is obliged to divulge information to protect another. However, when does a lawyer really know another may be the victim of his client's conduct? Is it talk? Bluffing? (See exhibit 1.3.)

EXHIBIT 1.3

MODEL CLIENT INFORMATION SHEET

Criminal

Office Docket # _____

Attorney _____

CONFIDENTIAL

Client's Name _____ D.O.B. _____ Age _____

Address _____ How Long _____

Phone _____

If Married, Name of Spouse _____ How Long _____

Address/phone # if other than above _____

Children (if adults give address/phone #) _____

_____

_____

Occupation _____ How Long _____

Employer _____ How Long _____

Previous Employer _____ How Long _____

Community, Church, Social Involvement _____

_____

_____

Other Interested Relatives or Friends: _____

Name _____ Address _____ Phone _____ How Long _____

Name _____ Address _____ Phone _____ How Long _____

Name _____ Address _____ Phone _____ How Long _____

Offense _____ Statute _____

Where _____ When _____ Time _____

Others Charged

Name _____ Address _____

Phone _____ Attorney _____

Name _____ Address _____

Phone _____ Attorney _____

Is Client Incarcerated? _____ Where _____

Bail _____ Cash _____ Bond _____ Bondsman _____

Indicted? _____ Where _____ Indictment # _____

Issues _____

Search _____ Warrant _____ No Warrant _____

Where _____ When _____

Statement _____ Miranda given _____

Where _____ When _____

Identification _____ On Scene _____ Photo _____

   Line-Up _____ Police Station _____

   Other _____

Witnesses: Names, Addresses, Phones
Friendly: _____

_____

_____

Adverse: _____

_____

_____

Defenses:
   Motions _____

   Alibi _____

   Misidentification _____

   Insanity—Incompetence _____

   Others _____

Evidence:
   Real _____

   Medical _____

   Expert _____

Log of Investigation (Note time involved in each)

DATE	TYPE	PLACE

7. Rule 1.7: Conflict of interest

(*a*) A lawyer shall not represent a client if the representation of that client will be directly adverse to another client, unless:

1. the lawyer reasonably believes the representation will not adversely affect the relationship with the other client; and
2. each client consents after consultation.

(*b*) A lawyer shall not represent a client if the representation of that client may be materially limited by the lawyer's responsibilities to another client or to a third person, or by the lawyer's own interests, unless

1. the lawyer reasonably believes the representation will not be adversely affected; and
2. the client consents after consultation. When representation of multiple clients in a simple matter is undertaken, the consultation shall include explanation of the implications of the common representation and the advantages and risks involved.

Another bevy of ethical dilemmas trudge forth under this Rule. At its base, the Rule mandates unswerving loyalty to the client first. Any conflicts between the client and any other party or entity must be resolved in favor of the client. As a result the lawyer should turn over representation to another attorney as long as any conflict is possible. Other conflict situations are possible in the following contexts:

☐ A lawyer representing opposing parties in a contract dispute
☐ A lawyer representing opposing parties in a divorce action
☐ A lawyer of a corporation who is also a member of its board of directors
☐ A lawyer related to another lawyer representing opposing parties known to both

B. The Lawyer as Advocate

1. Rule 3.1: Meritorious claims and contentions

A lawyer shall not bring or defend a proceeding, or assert or controvert an issue therein, unless there is a basis for doing so that is not frivolous, which includes a good faith argument for an extension, modification, or reversal of existing law. A lawyer for the defendant in a criminal proceeding, or the respondent in a proceeding that could result in incarceration, may nevertheless so defend the proceeding as to require that every element of the case be established.

A common moral qualm faced by attorneys is the substance of this Rule. When is a claim really meritorious, or is the lawyer simply trying to make money? What is a frivolous case, and by whose standards do those measurements take place?

2. Rule 3.2: Expediting litigation

A lawyer shall make reasonable efforts to expedite litigation consistent with the interests of the client.

Lawyers are incessantly criticized for the slow pace at which cases progress and are sometimes viewed as prolonging a case for their own economic gains. More often than not the drudgeries of negotiation and the tortoiselike pace of the machinery of justice more than exonerate the lawyer.

3. Rule 3.3: Candor toward the tribunal

(*a*) A lawyer shall not knowingly:

1. make a false statement of material fact or law to a tribunal;
2. fail to disclose a material fact to a tribunal when disclosure is necessary to avoid assisting a criminal or fraudulent act by the client;
3. fail to disclose to the tribunal legal authority in the controlling jurisdiction known to the lawyer to be directly adverse to the position of the client and not disclosed by opposing counsel; or

4. offer evidence that the lawyer knows to be false. If a lawyer has offered material evidence and comes to know of its falsity, the lawyer shall take reasonable remedial measures.

(b) The duties stated in paragraph (a) continue to the conclusion of the proceeding, and apply even if compliance requires disclosure of information otherwise protected by Rule 1.6.

(c) A lawyer may refuse to offer evidence that the lawyer reasonably believes is false.

(d) In an ex parte proceeding, a lawyer shall inform the tribunal of all relevant facts known to the lawyer that should be disclosed to permit the tribunal to make an informed decision, whether or not the facts are adverse.

Clearly a lawyer is obliged to insure that his or her arguments are correct and viable recitations of law and fact. No tribunal should be responsive or amenable to evidence that is false or misleading. Hence, the Rules demand an attorney disclosure of any false evidence. Most troubling is the lawyer's client who clearly sits before the tribunal and continuously perjures himself or herself. The Rules have been interpreted to require disclosure of the perjury after repeated attempts by the attorney to dissaude the client from further perjury. This is an extremely controversial area.

C. Information about Legal Services

1. Rule 7.1:   Communications concerning a lawyer's services

A lawyer shall not make false or misleading communication about the lawyer or the lawyer's services. A communication is false or misleading if it:

a. contains a material misrepresentation of fact or law, or omits a fact necessary to make the statement considered as a whole not materially misleading;

b. is likely to create an unjustified expectation about results the lawyer can achieve or states or implies that the lawyer can achieve results by means that violate the Rules of Professional Conduct or other law; or

c. compares the lawyer's services with other lawyer's services, unless the comparison can be factually substantiated.

In an age of advertising, the Rule attempts to curb "Have I got a deal for you" forms of advertising. A lawyer's services can only be presented factually, with no puffing tolerated.

2. Rule 7.2:   Advertising

a. Subject to the requirements of Rules 7.1 and 7.3(b), a lawyer may advertise services through public media, such as a telephone directory, legal directory, newspaper or other periodical, radio or television, or through written communication not involving personal contact.

b. A copy or recording of an advertisement or written communication shall be kept for [one year] after its dissemination along with a record of when and where it was used.

c. A lawyer shall not give anything of value to a person for recommending the lawyer's services, except that a lawyer may pay the reasonable cost of advertising or written communication permitted by this Rule and may pay the usual charges of a not-for-profit lawyer referral service or other legal service organization.

Recent state and federal rulings have opened up the frontier when it comes to legal advertising. Critics argue that the profession, already reeling from a bad image, has been demeaned even more. Proponents argue that advertising opens up the once forbidding world of "law," and provides services to a broader base of people.

D. Integrity of the Profession

1. Rule 8.4:   Misconduct

It is professional misconduct for a lawyer to:

(a) violate or attempt to violate the Rules of Professional Conduct, knowingly assist or induce another to do so, or do so through the acts of another;

(b) commit a criminal or fraudulent act that reflects adversely on the lawyer's honesty, trustworthiness, or fitness as a lawyer in other respects;

(c) state or imply an ability to influence improperly a government agency or official;

(d) practice law in a jurisdiction where doing so violates the regulation of the legal profession in that jurisdiction;

(e) assist a person who is not a member of the bar in the performance of activity that constitutes the practice of law:

(f) knowingly assist a judge or judicial officer in conduct that is a violation of applicable Rules of Judicial Conduct or other law.

All the above rules attempt to delineate both moral and ethical obligations in the profession. Rule 8.4 denounces any violations of those promulgations and defines a violation as professional misconduct. A lawyer is subject to a wide array of disciplinary action for that misconduct, including disbarment.

In conclusion, while the above exemplary rules hope to codify behavior on an ethical plane, no set of rules can delineate what most people plainly recognize as right and wrong. Lacking any better way of expressing it, the paralegal must realize that IF IT LOOKS OR FEELS WRONG, IT PROBABLY IS. All of us have some appreciation for equity, fairness, and general ethics. Keeping to those virtues is an uphill battle all through life, especially in a profession so tempted with power.

DISCUSSION QUESTIONS AND PRACTICAL EXERCISES

Discussion Questions and Short Exercises

1. Dan Ward, a resident of State X is involved in an accident in State X with Suzy Cox, a resident of State Y. Dan Ward is seriously injured (his medical bills exceed $20,000), and he wants to bring suit. In what court can he institute an action?

2. Irv Letter is injured when he trips on a piece of torn carpet in his local post office. His lawyer, Jim Rogers, brings a suit in federal court. The amount in controversy must exceed
   (a) $ 1,000
   (b) $10,000
   (c) $ 5,000
   (d) $15,000

3. There is a statute in State X that requires all reporters to divulge his or her sources. Joe Martin is arrested and convicted under the statute for not divulging his sources. If the state court holds the State X statute valid under the state constitution and valid under the U.S. Constitution and defendant appeals, will the Supreme Court review, and if so, how?
   (a) Supreme Court will not hear case because issue is moot.
   (b) Supreme Court will hear case by certiori.
   (c) Supreme Court will hear case by appeal.
   (d) None of the above.

4. Clarice Jones represents Carmine Smith, who is out on bail for armed robbery. Smith disappears before her trial, and Smith's mother informs Clarice as to her whereabouts. It is proper for the attorney to:
   (a) contact Carmine and urge her surrender but not inform the police if she does not give herself up;
   (b) inform the police of Carmine's whereabouts;
   (c) withdraw from the case;
   (d) permit Carmine to relocate before informing police.

5. Attorney represents client in a matter involving a claim by the United States Internal Revenue Service (IRS) for unpaid income taxes for the years 1971–1973. Client informs attorney that before consulting attorney, client gave IRS false financial statements for the years in question. It is proper for attorney to:
   (a) continue to represent client and make no disclosure;
   (b) inform IRS concerning the false financial statements;
   (c) immediately withdraw from the case;
   (d) advise client that attorney will withdraw from the case unless client makes a full disclosure to IRS.

6. Larry Davis is a member of the bar. He does not practice law but operates a licensed investment-counseling business. Investor consults Davis, who persuades investor to invest $10,000 in a business venture. Davis does not reveal to investor that he, Larry Davis, owns 100 percent of the business venture. Is Davis subject to discipline?

7. During cross-examination, Carol Bates denied that she hated the utilities and denied she ever stated she wanted

her attorney to "squeeze every penny out of their pockets." Andy Attorney knows that this testimony is false. What is Andy Attorney's obligation?

8. Joe Morgan was visiting his neighborhood butcher shop, and while waiting for his pork chops, slipped and fell on what appeared to be chicken fat, severely injuring his neck and back. He hired Barry Barrister, who instituted the proper action in the superior court. The jury returned a verdict for the defendant, and Morgan appealed. To which court did he appeal?

9. Andy Attorney is the majority shareholder of a collection agency, incorporated as SHARKO. If SHARKO's efforts are not successful, Andy has authorized SHARKO's manager, who is not a member of the bar, to write any needed collection letters to the debtor on the attorney's letterhead. The letter contains a statement that the matter has been referred to Andy Attorney and that a suit will be filed in ten days if payment is not received. The manager is authorized to sign Andy's name to the letter. Is Andy Attorney subject to discipline?

10. Attorney is on an annual retainer by a client to handle its litigation. The client consults the attorney on a complex tax matter. The attorney has had no training or experience to handle such matters. How should the attorney handle this situation?

Practical Exercises

Use the paralegal ethical code in appendix 1A to solve the following problems.

You are a legal assistant in the law firm of Hummel & Howe, P.C. The receptionist answers the telephone. (You don't.) There is a young attorney in your firm, Shirley Newby, a graduate who passed the bar three weeks ago. These facts are common to all the questions below.

1. Mr. Howe comes to you with a great idea. You are going to take over the routine family-law cases. He tells you what he thinks you should do. Circle the number of the correct response.

   (I) He wants you to do the opening interview with each prospective client, using an information checklist.
   - *a.* You cannot do this because a legal assistant may not interview clients.
   - *b.* You can do this if the client understands that you are a legal assistant and not a lawyer.
   - *c.* You can do this because everybody does it anyway.

   (II) He wants you to prepare draft pleadings to be filed in routine cases.
   - *a.* You can do this but only if you sign the pleadings.
   - *b.* You cannot do this because drafting a pleading involves the independent judgment of a lawyer.
   - *c.* You can do this if he supervises your work and he signs the pleadings.

   (III) He wants you to go to the homes of clients and investigate child-custody conditions.
   - *a.* You cannot do this because contact with the client without an attorney present is unethical for a legal assistant.
   - *b.* You can do this if the client is aware that you are a legal assistant.
   - *c.* You cannot do this because a legal assistant must be directly supervised by an attorney.

   (IV) He wants you to go to court for him and attend pretrials and handle routine court matters.
   - *a.* You can do this if the judge approves.
   - *b.* You can do this because paralegals regularly appear in court.
   - *c.* You can do this if the client consents.
   - *d.* None of the above

2. Mr. Hummel told Judge Holmes that he would like Ms. Newby to handle some court appointments "to get her feet wet."

   Ms. Newby is off in court on a motion. The phone rings. Ms. Newby's client Paul Lyer calls from the county jail. When you tell him that Ms. Newby is in court, Lyer asks for your opinion. He asks you for a complicated analysis of a recent Supreme Court ruling.

   Check only the appropriate response.

   ☐ You heard Ms. Newby discussing this case, and they said that this ruling would be helpful.
   ☐ You read this Supreme Court case, and you think that it would be helpful.

□ You will leave a message for Ms. Newby.

□ You are not an attorney.

□ This is a matter that requires the independent judgment of an attorney.

□ You are a legal assistant.

□ You can advise him if he consents and Ms. Newby directs you to do so.

□ You can go to talk with him at the jail, to interview him about the facts, if an attorney directs you to do so.

□ You and Ms. Newby will split the fee fifty-fifty.

ENRICHMENT ACTIVITY

By interviewing an officer of your local or regional bar association or similar organization, gain an understanding of its professional expectations and ethical demands of its members. In what manner does the organization enforce its regulations? What disciplinary actions are exercised upon violations? Does a need exist to regulate the professional activity of paralegals? In what ways could this regulation be accomplished?

SUGGESTED READING

ATIYAH, P. S. *Promises, Morals, and Law*. New York: Oxford University Press, 1981.

BODENHEIMER, EDGAR. *Jurisprudence: The Philosophy and Method of Law*. Cambridge, Mass.: Harvard University Press, 1981.

COHN, MORRIS M. *An Essay on the Growth of Law*. Littleton, Colo.: F. B. ROTHMAN, 1983.

DETMOLD, M. J. *The Unity of Law and Morality: A Refutation of Legal Positivism*. Boston: Routledge & Kegan Paul, 1984.

DWORKIN, R. M. *Taking Rights Seriously*. Cambridge, Mass.: Harvard University Press, 1977.

HARRIS, J. W. *Law and Legal Science: An Inquiry into the Concepts of Legal Rule and Legal System*. New York: Oxford University Press, 1979.

HEXNER, ERVIN P. *Studies in Legal Terminology*. Littleton, Colo.: F. B. ROTHMAN, 1981.

JENKINS, IREDELL. *Social Order and the Limits of Law: A Theoretical Essay*. Princeton, N.J.: Princeton University Press, 1980.

PATTEE, WILLIAM S. *The Essential Nature of Law: Or, the Ethical Basis of Jurisprudence*. Littleton, Colo.: F. B. ROTHMAN, 1982.

PERRY, THOMAS D. *Moral Reasoning and Truth: An Essay in Philosophy and Jurisprudence*. Oxford: Clarendon Press, 1976.

APPENDIX 1A

Code of Ethics and Professional Responsibility

Preamble

It is the responsibility of every legal assistant to adhere strictly to the accepted standards of legal ethics and to live by general principles of proper conduct. The performance of the duties of the legal assistant shall be governed by specific canons as defined herein in order that justice will be served and the goals of the profession attained.

The canons of ethics set forth hereafter are adopted by the National Association of Legal Assistants, Inc., as a general guide, and the enumeration of these rules does not mean there are not others of equal importance although not specifically mentioned.

Canon 1. A legal assistant shall not perform any of the duties that lawyers only may perform nor do things that lawyers themselves may not do.

Canon 2. A legal assistant may perform any task delegated and supervised by a lawyer so long as the lawyer is responsible to the client, maintains a direct relationship with the client, and assumes full professional responsibility for the work product.

Canon 3. A legal assistant shall not engage in the practice of law by accepting cases, setting fees, giving legal advice or appearing in court (unless otherwise authorized by court or agency rules).

Canon 4. A legal assistant shall not act in matters involving professional legal judgment as the services of a lawyer are essential in the public interest whenever the exercise of such judgment is required.

Canon 5. A legal assistant must act prudently in determining the extent to which a client may be assisted without the presence of a lawyer.

Canon 6. A legal assistant shall not engage in the unauthorized practice of law and shall assist in preventing the unauthorized practice of law.

Canon 7. A legal assistant must protect the confidences of a client, and it shall be unethical for a legal assistant to violate any statute now in effect or hereafter to be enacted controlling privileged communication.

Canon 8. It is the obligation of the legal assistant to avoid conduct which would cause the lawyer to be unethical or even appear to be unethical, and loyalty to the employer is incumbent upon the legal assistant.

Canon 9. A legal assistant shall work continually to maintain integrity and a high degree of competency throughout the legal profession.

Canon 10. A legal assistant shall strive for perfection through education in order to better assist the legal profession in fulfilling its duty of making legal services available to clients and the public.

Canon 11. A legal assistant shall do all other things incidental, necessary, or expedient for the attainment of the ethics and responsibilities imposed by statute or rule of court.

Canon 12. A legal assistant is governed by the American Bar Association Code of Professional Responsibility.

APPENDIX 1B

JURISDICTION OF TRIAL COURTS, 1980

Level and name of court, geographic jurisdiction, number of districts, number of judges, civil, criminal, traffic, juvenile, and appellate jurisdiction

STATE, COURT LEVEL, AND COURT NAME	GEOGRAPHIC BOUNDS OF COURT	NUMBER OF COURT DISTRICTS OR LOCATIONS	NUMBER OF JUDGES
ALABAMA:			
General—Circuit Court	Multi-county	39	113
Limited—District Court	County	88	88
Probate Court	County	67	67
Municipal Court	Municipality	215	215
ALASKA:			
General—Superior Court	Multi-county	4	21
Limited—District Court	Multi-county	4	69
ARIZONA:			
General—Superior Court	County	14	80
Limited—Justice of the Peace Court	Precinct	84	84
City Magistrate Court	City	74	94
ARKANSAS:			
General—Circuit Court	Multi-county	19	33
Chancery Court	Multi-county	22	30
Probate Court	Multi-county	22	(d)
Limited—Municipal Court	County	98	98
County Court	County	75	75
Court of Common Pleas	County	12	
Justice of the Peace Court	Varies	3	2
Police Court	City	1	3
City Court	City	82	76
CALIFORNIA:			
General—Superior Court	County	58	607
Limited—Municipal Court	Combinations of municipalities	83	472
Justice Court	Judicial district	100	96
COLORADO:			
General—District Court	Multi-county	22	106
Limited—Denver Superior Court	Denver City and County	1	1
Denver Juvenile Court	Denver City and County	1	3*
Denver Probate Court	Denver City and County	1	1
County Court	County	63	108
Municipal Court	Municipality	210	240
CONNECTICUT:			
General—Superior Court	Judicial district	11	110
Limited—Probate Court	Probate district	130	130
DELAWARE:			
General—Superior Court	County	3	11
Court of Chancery	County	3	3
Limited—Court of Common Pleas	County	3	5
Family Court	County	3	12
Municipal Court of Wilmington	Wilmington	1	3
Alderman's Court**	Town	14	20
Justice of the Peace Court	Part of a county	16	54

SUBSTANTIVE JURISDICTION

CIVIL						CRIMINAL				APPELLATE		
ESTATE	DOMESTIC RELATIONS	LAW	OTHER CIVIL	MINIMUM $-AMOUNT JURISDICTION	MAXIMUM $-AMOUNT JURISDICTION	FELONY	MISDEMEANOR	TRAFFIC	JUVENILE	CIVIL	CRIMINAL	ADMINISTRATIVE AGENCY
X	X	X	X	$ 500		X	X		X	X	X	
	X	X	X		$ 5,000	X	X	X	X			
X							X	X				
X	X	X	X			X	X	X		X	X	X
		X	X		$10,000		X	X		X	X	X
X	X	X	X			X	X	X	X	X	X	
		X	X		$ 2,500		X	X				
							X	X				
		X	X	$ 100		X	X			X	X	X
	X		X									
X			X									
		X	X		$ 300		X	X				
	X								X			
		X	X		$ 500							
		X	X		$ 300		X	X				
		X	X		$ 300		X	X				
		X	X		$ 300		X	X				
X	X	X	X	$15,000		X				X	X	X
		X	X		$15,000		X	X				
		X	X		$15,000		X	X				
X	X	X	X			X	X		X	X	X	X
		X	X	$ 1,000	$ 5,000					X	X	
	X		X						X			
X		X	X									
		X	X		$ 1,000		X	X			X	
							X	X				
	X	X	X			X	X	X	X	X	X	X
X	X	X	X									
	X	X	X			X	X			X	X	X
X	X	X	X									
		X	X		$ 5,000		X					
	X		X				X		X			
							X	X				
		X	X				X	X				
		X	X		$ 1,500		X	X				

STATE, COURT LEVEL, AND COURT NAME	GEOGRAPHIC BOUNDS OF COURT	NUMBER OF COURT DISTRICTS OR LOCATIONS	NUMBER OF JUDGES
FLORIDA:			
General—Circuit Court	Multi-county	20	302
Limited—County Court	County	67	198
GEORGIA:			
General—Superior Court	Multi-county	42	110
Limited—Probate Court**	County	159	159
Juvenile Court	County	55	48
Justice of the Peace Court	Militia district	1,774	1,531
State Court	County	60	77
Small Claims Court**	Varies	97	97
Municipal Court (located in Savannah and Columbus)	County	2	2
Magistrate Court	County	4	5
County Court	County	3	2
Civil Court	County	2	3
Criminal Court, Municipal Court (other locations), Recorder's Court, Mayor's Court, City Council Court, and Police Court**	Varies	383	NA
HAWAII:			
General—Circuit Court	County	4	25
Land Court	State	1	
Tax Appeal Court	State	1	
Limited—District Court	County	4	18
IDAHO:			
General—District Court	Multi-county	7	99
ILLINOIS:			
General—Circuit Court	Multi-county	21	677
INDIANA:			
General—Circuit Court	Multi-county	88	88
Superior Court	County	35	83
Limited—County Court	Multi-county	65	65
Probate Court	County	1	1
Municipal Court of Marion County	County	1	15
Small Claims Court of Marion County	County	8	8
City Court	City	47	47
Town Court	Town	19	19
IOWA:			
General—District Court	Multi-county	8	300
KANSAS:			
General—District Court	Multi-county	29	211
Limited—Municipal Court	City	369	356
KENTUCKY:			
General—Circuit Court	Multi-county	56	91
Limited—District Court	Multi-county	56	123

SUBSTANTIVE JURISDICTION

CIVIL — (ESTATE, DOMESTIC RELATIONS, LAW, OTHER CIVIL, MINIMUM $-AMOUNT JURISDICTION, MAXIMUM $-AMOUNT JURISDICTION) · CRIMINAL — (FELONY, MISDEMEANOR) · TRAFFIC · JUVENILE · APPELLATE — (CIVIL, CRIMINAL, ADMINISTRATIVE AGENCY)

ESTATE	DOMESTIC RELATIONS	LAW	OTHER CIVIL	MINIMUM $-AMOUNT JURISDICTION	MAXIMUM $-AMOUNT JURISDICTION	FELONY	MISDEMEANOR	TRAFFIC	JUVENILE	CIVIL	CRIMINAL	ADMINISTRATIVE AGENCY
X	X	X	X	$ 5,000		X	X		X	X	X	X
		X	X		$ 5,000		X					
	X	X	X			X	X		X	X		X
X			X				X			X		X
								X		X		
		X	X		$ 200					X		
		X	X				X	X				
		X	X		$ 400							
		X	X		$ 1,500		X	X				
		X	X		$ 1,000		X	X				
		X	X		$ 500		X					
			X		$ 3,000							
							X	X				
X	X	X	X	$ 1,000		X	X	X	X	X	X	X
			X									X
		X										X
		X	X		$ 5,000		X	X				
X	X	X	X			X	X	X	X	X	X	X
X	X	X	X			X	X	X	X			
X	X	X	X			X	X	X	X	X	X	X
X	X	X	X			X	X	X	X	X	X	
		X	X		$ 3,000		X	X				
X		X	X							X		
		X	X		$12,500	X	X	X				
		X	X		$ 1,500							
		X	X		Varies		X	X				
							X	X				
X	X	X	X			X	X	X	X			
X	X	X	X			X	X	X	X	X	X	X
							X	X				
	X	X	X	$ 1,500		X	X			X	X	
X			X		$ 1,500		X	X	X			

STATE, COURT LEVEL, AND COURT NAME	GEOGRAPHIC BOUNDS OF COURT	NUMBER OF COURT DISTRICTS OR LOCATIONS	NUMBER OF JUDGES
LOUISIANA:			
General—District Court	Multi-parish	41	161
Limited—Juvenile Court	Parish	3	9
Family Court	Parish	1	3
City Court	Ward	49	60
Parish Court	Part or all of a parish	3	5
Municipal Court of New Orleans	City	1	4*
Traffic Court of New Orleans	Parish	1	4*
Justice of the Peace Court	Single or multi-wards	376	376*
Mayor's Court	Municipality	250	250
MAINE:			
General—Superior Court	County	16	14
Limited—District Court		33	20
Probate Court	County	16	16
Administrative Court	State	1	2
MARYLAND:			
General—Circuit Court	Multi-county	8	97
Limited—District Court	Multi-county	12	87
Orphans' Court	County	22	66*
MASSACHUSETTS:			
General—Trial Court of the Commonwealth:			
Superior Court Department	County	14	56
Housing Court Department	County	2	3
Land Court Department	State	1	3
Probate and Family Court Department	County	14	33
Boston Municipal Court Department	City	1	9
Juvenile Court Department	Divisions	4	7
District Court Department	Divisions	69	153
MICHIGAN:			
General—Circuit Court	Multi-county	52	147
Recorder's Court of Detroit	City of Detroit	1	26
Limited—District Court	Combinations of cities and counties	98	214
Probate Court	County	83	106
Municipal Court	Varies	8	8
Common Pleas Court of Detroit	Wayne County	1	13
MINNESOTA:			
General—District Court**	Multi-county	10	72
Limited—Probate Court	County	2	2
County Court	County	67	136
County Municipal Court	County	2	28
Conciliation Court	County	69	

SUBSTANTIVE JURISDICTION

CIVIL						CRIMINAL				APPELLATE		
ESTATE	DOMESTIC RELATIONS	LAW	OTHER CIVIL	MINIMUM $-AMOUNT JURISDICTION	MAXIMUM $-AMOUNT JURISDICTION	FELONY	MISDEMEANOR	TRAFFIC	JUVENILE	CIVIL	CRIMINAL	ADMINISTRATIVE AGENCY
X	X	X	X			X	X	X		X	X	X
	X						X		X			
	X						X		X			
		X	X		$ 3,000		X	X				
		X	X		$ 5,000		X	X				
							X					
								X				
		X	X		$ 750							
							X	X				
	X	X	X			X				X	X	
	X	X	X		$20,000	X	X	X	X			
X	X		X									
		X										
X	X	X	X	$ 2,500		X	X		X	X	X	X
		X	X		$ 5,000	X	X	X	X			
X												
	X	X	X			X	X			X	X	X
		X	X				X					
			X									
X	X		X									
	X	X	X			X	X	X		X	X	X
							X		X			
	X	X	X			X	X	X	X	X	X	
	X	X	X	$10,000		X	X			X	X	X
						X	X	X				
		X	X		$10,000		X	X				
X		X	X						X			
		X	X		$ 1,500		X	X				
		X	X		$10,000							
	X	X	X			X	X		X	X	X	X
X			X									
X	X	X	X		$ 5,000		X	X	X	X		
		X	X		$ 5,000		X	X		X		
		X	X		$ 1,000							

STATE, COURT LEVEL, AND COURT NAME	GEOGRAPHIC BOUNDS OF COURT	NUMBER OF COURT DISTRICTS OR LOCATIONS	NUMBER OF JUDGES
MISSISSIPPI:			
General—Circuit Court	Multi-county	20	30
Chancery Court	Multi-county	20	35
Limited—County Court	County	16	20
Family Court	County	1	1
Municipal Court**		NA	150*
Justice Court	Justice court district	410	420
MISSOURI:			
General—Circuit Court	Judicial circuit	43	300
MONTANA:			
General—District Court	Multi-county	19	32
Limited—Justice of the Peace Court	County	90	90
City Court	City	100	100
Municipal Court	Municipality	2	2
Water Court	Water division	4	
NEBRASKA:			
General—District Court	Multi-county	21	45
Limited—County Court	Multi-county	21	43
Separate Juvenile Court	County	3	4
Municipal Court	City	2	13
Workmen's Compensation Court	State	1	5
NEVADA:			
General—District Court	Judicial district	9	29
Limited—Justices' Court	Township	60	60
Municipal Court	City or town	21	21
NEW HAMPSHIRE:			
General—Superior Court	County	10	15
Limited—Probate Court	County	10	10*
District Court	Judicial district	41	84
Municipal Court	Town	15	20
NEW JERSEY:			
General—Superior Court	Multi-county	21	214
Limited—County District Court	County	21	39
Juvenile and Domestic Relations Court	County	21	33
Surrogate's Court	County	21	21
Municipal Court	Municipality	526	372
Tax Court	State	1	9
NEW MEXICO:			
General—District Court	Multi-county	13	44
Limited—Magistrate Court	County	32	72
Municipal Court	Municipality	96	96
Probate Court	County	32	32
Metropolitan Court of Bernalillo County	County	1	11
Small Claims Court of Albuquerque	Municipality	1	1

SUBSTANTIVE JURISDICTION

ESTATE	DOMESTIC RELATIONS	LAW	OTHER CIVIL	MINIMUM $-AMOUNT JURISDICTION	MAXIMUM $-AMOUNT JURISDICTION	FELONY	MISDEMEANOR	TRAFFIC	JUVENILE	CIVIL (appellate)	CRIMINAL (appellate)	ADMINISTRATIVE AGENCY
		CIVIL				*CRIMINAL*				*APPELLATE*		
		X	X			X	X			X	X	X
X	X	X	X						X	X	X	X
X	X	X	X		$10,000		X		X	X	X	
	X						X		X	X		
							X	X	X			
		X	X		$ 500		X	X				
X	X	X	X			X	X	X	X			
X	X	X	X	$ 50		X	X			X	X	X
		X	X		$ 1,500		X	X					
		X	X		$ 300		X					
		X	X		$ 300		X	X				
			X									
	X	X	X	$ 5,000		X	X			X	X	X
X	X	X	X		$ 5,000		X	X	X			
	X								X			
		X	X		$ 5,000		X	X	X			
												X
X	X	X	X	$ 300		X	X			X	X	X
			X		$ 750		X	X				
		X	X		$ 750		X	X				
	X	X	X	$ 500		X	X				X	
X	X		X									
		X	X		$ 5,000		X	X	X			
		X	X		$ 500		X	X				
X	X	X	X			X	X	X			X	X
		X	X		$ 3,000		X	X				
	X								X			
X												
							X	X				
												X
X	X	X	X			X	X			X	X	X
			X		$ 2,000		X	X				X
							X	X				
X												
		X	X		$ 5,000		X					
		X	X		$ 2,000		X					

STATE, COURT LEVEL, AND COURT NAME	GEOGRAPHIC BOUNDS OF COURT	NUMBER OF COURT DISTRICTS OR LOCATIONS	NUMBER OF JUDGES
NEW YORK:			
General—Supreme Court	Multi-county	11	263
County Court	County	57	104
Limited—Surrogate's Court	County	62	35
Family Court	County	58	107
Civil Court of the City of New York	City of New York	1	120
Criminal Court of the City of New York	City of New York	1	98
District Court	Varies	2	49
City Court**	City	61	161
Court of Claims	Multi-county	9	43
Town Justice Court and Village Justice Court	Municipality	2,424	2,424
NORTH CAROLINA:			
General—Superior Court	Multi-county	33	66
Limited—District Court	Multi-county	33	136
NORTH DAKOTA:			
General—District Court	Multi-county	7	24
Limited—County Court	County	36	36
County Court with Increased Jurisdiction	County	17	17
County Justice Court	County	36	36
Municipal Court	Municipality	187	190
OHIO:			
General—Court of Common Pleas	County	88	313
Limited—Municipal Court	Varies	110	189
County Court	Varies	59	59
Mayor's Court	Municipality	700	690
Court of Claims	State	1	
OKLAHOMA:			
General—District Court	Judicial district	26	198
Limited—Municipal Criminal Court of Record	City	2	19
Municipal Court Not of Record	City	167	534
Workers' Compensation Court	State	1	
Court of Tax Review	State	1	
Court of Bank Review	State	1	
OREGON:			
General—Circuit Court	Multi-county	20	75
Tax Court	State	1	1
Limited—District Court**	Multi-county	24	55
Justice Court	Portion of county	40	40
County Court**	County	9	9
Municipal Court	City	165	193
PENNSYLVANIA:			
General—Court of Common Pleas	Multi-county	59	285
Limited—District Justice Court	Magisterial district	555	555
Community Court			0
Philadelphia Municipal Court	Philadelphia County	1	22
Philadelphia Traffic Court	Philadelphia County	1	6
Pittsburgh Magistrates Court	City of Pittsburgh	1	6

| | CIVIL | | | | | CRIMINAL | | | | APPELLATE | | |
ESTATE	DOMESTIC RELATIONS	LAW	OTHER CIVIL	MINIMUM $-AMOUNT JURISDICTION	MAXIMUM $-AMOUNT JURISDICTION	FELONY	MISDEMEANOR	TRAFFIC	JUVENILE	CIVIL	CRIMINAL	ADMINISTRATIVE AGENCY
	X	X	X		$ 6,000	X	X					
	X	X	X		$ 6,000	X	X			X	X	
X	X	X	X									
X	X								X			
		X	X		$10,000							
							X					
		X	X		$ 6,000		X	X				
		X	X				X	X				
		X	X									X
		X	X		$ 3,000		X	X				
X		X	X	$ 5,000		X	X				X	X
	X	X	X		$ 5,000		X	X	X			
	X	X	X			X	X		X	X	X	X
X												
X		X	X		$ 1,000		X	X			X	
		X	X		$ 200		X	X	X			
X	X	X	X	$ 500		X			X			X
		X	X		$10,000		X	X			X	
		X	X		$ 3,000		X	X			X	
							X	X				
		X	X									X
X	X	X	X			X	X	X	X		X	
								X				
								X				
			X									X
												X
												X
X	X	X	X	$ 3,000		X			X	X	X	X
												X
X		X	X		$ 3,000		X	X				
		X	X		$ 2,500		X	X				
X									X			
X	X	X	X			X	X		X	X	X	X
		X	X		$ 2,000		X	X				
			X		$ 2,000		X	X				
		X	X		$ 1,000	X	X					
									X			
			X				X	X				

STATE, COURT LEVEL, AND COURT NAME	GEOGRAPHIC BOUNDS OF COURT	NUMBER OF COURT DISTRICTS OR LOCATIONS	NUMBER OF JUDGES
RHODE ISLAND:			
General—Superior Court	County	4	19
Limited—Family Court	State	1	11
District Court	Judicial district	8	13
Probate Court	City or town	39	39*
Municipal Court	City or county	3	5*
SOUTH CAROLINA:			
General—Circuit Court	Multi-county	16	31
Limited—Family Court	Multi-county	16	46
Probate Court	County	46	46
Magistrate's Court	Magisterial District	322	330
Municipal Court	Municipality	82	250
SOUTH DAKOTA:			
General—Circuit Court	Multi-county	8	141
TENNESSEE:			
General—Circuit Court	Multi-county	31	58
Criminal Court	Multi-county	13	26
Chancery Court	Multi-county	18	27
Law and Equity Court	County	4	5
Limited—County Court	County	68	68
General Sessions Court**	County	92	92
Probate Court	County	3	2
Juvenile Court	County	16	6
Trial Justice Court	County	2	2
Municipal Court	Municipality	300	192
TEXAS:			
General—District Court**	Varies	310	310
Limited—County Court:			
County Court Constitutional	County	254	254
County Court at Law**	County	98	98
Probate Court	County	8	8
Justice of the Peace Court	Precinct	972	972
Municipal Court	Municipality	863	863
UTAH:			
General—District Court	Judicial district	7	24
Limited—Circuit Court	Judicial circuit	12	33
Justice Court	Municipality	210	170
Juvenile Court	State	5	9
VERMONT:			
General—Superior Court	County	14	38
Limited—District Court	Multi-county	16	14
Probate Court	All or part of a county	19	19*
VIRGINIA:			
General—Circuit Court	Multi-county	31	111
Limited—General District Court	Multi-county	32	98
Juvenile and Domestic Relations District Court	Multi-county	32	65

SUBSTANTIVE JURISDICTION

	CIVIL					CRIMINAL				APPELLATE		
ESTATE	DOMESTIC RELATIONS	LAW	OTHER CIVIL	MINIMUM $-AMOUNT JURISDICTION	MAXIMUM $-AMOUNT JURISDICTION	FELONY	MISDEMEANOR	TRAFFIC	JUVENILE	CIVIL	CRIMINAL	ADMINISTRATIVE AGENCY
		X	X	$ 5,000		X	X			X	X	X
	X		X				X	X	X			
		X	X		$ 5,000		X	X				X
X							X	X				
X		X	X			X	X			X	X	X
	X		X					X	X			
X			X						X			
		X	X		$ 1,000		X	X				
		X	X		$ 1,000		X	X				
X	X	X	X			X	X	X	X	X	X	X
	X	X	X	$ 50		X	X			X	X	X
						X	X				X	X
X	X	X	X	$ 50								X
X	X	X	X	$ 50						X	X	X
X	X		X						X			
X	X	X	X		$10,000		X		X			
X												
	X						X		X			
	X	X	X		$10,000		X					
							X	X				
X	X	X	X	$ 500		X	X		X	X		X
X		X	X	$ 200	$ 1,000		X	X	X	X	X	
X		X	X	$ 200	$ 5,000		X	X	X	X	X	
X			X									
		X	X		$ 500		X	X				
							X	X				
X	X	X				X	X			X	X	
			X		$ 5,000		X	X				
		X	X		$ 750		X	X				
							X	X	X			
	X	X	X	$ 200		X	X			X		X
	X	X	X		$ 5,000	X	X	X	X			
X	X		X									
X		X	X	$ 1,000		X	X			X	X	X
		X	X		$ 5,000		X	X				
	X						X	X	X			

STATE, COURT LEVEL, AND COURT NAME	GEOGRAPHIC BOUNDS OF COURT	NUMBER OF COURT DISTRICTS OR LOCATIONS	NUMBER OF JUDGES
WASHINGTON:			
General—Superior Court	Multi-county	28	118
Limited—Justice of the Peace Court	Columbia County	1	2
District Court	Part or all of a county	73	94
Municipal Court	Municipality	225	206
WEST VIRGINIA:			
General—Circuit Court	Multi-county	31	60
Limited—Magistrate Court	County	55	150
Municipal Court	Municipality	54	54
WISCONSIN:			
General—Circuit Court	Multi-county	69	190
Limited—Municipal Justice Court	Municipality	216	216
WYOMING:			
General—District Court	Multi-county	9	15
Limited—County Court	County	2	4
Justice of the Peace Court	County	38	43*
Municipal Court	Municipality	74	77*
AMERICAN SAMOA:			
General—High Court of American Samoa	Territory	1	7
Limited—District Court	Territory	1	1
Village Court	Village		
DISTRICT OF COLUMBIA:			
General—Superior Court	District	1	44
GUAM:			
General—Superior Court	Territory	1	5
PUERTO RICO:			
General—Superior Court	Court district	12	92
Limited—District Court	Municipality	38	99
Municipal Court	Municipality		60
VIRGIN ISLANDS:			
Limited—Territorial Court of the Virgin Islands	Judicial division	2	5

Source: U.S. Dept. of Justice, Bureau of Justice Statistics, 1980

NA = not available
* Judges in this court serve part-time.
** Jurisdiction in this court varies from location to location.

| | CIVIL | | | | | CRIMINAL | | | | APPELLATE | | |
ESTATE	DOMESTIC RELATIONS	LAW	OTHER CIVIL	MINIMUM $-AMOUNT JURISDICTION	MAXIMUM $-AMOUNT JURISDICTION	FELONY	MISDEMEANOR	TRAFFIC	JUVENILE	CIVIL	CRIMINAL	ADMINISTRATIVE AGENCY
X	X	X	X	$ 3,000		X	X			X	X	X
		X	X		$ 1,000		X	X				
		X	X		$ 3,000		X	X				
								X				
	X	X	X	$ 100		X	X			X	X	X
		X	X		$ 1,500		X	X				
							X					
X	X	X	X			X	X		X	X	X	X
									X			
X	X	X	X	$ 500		X	X			X	X	X
		X	X		$ 7,000		X					
		X	X		$ 4,000		X		X			
							X		X			
X	X	X	X	$ 3,000		X				X	X	X
	X	X	X		$ 3,000		X	X			X	
							X					
X	X	X	X			X	X	X	X	X		X
X	X	X	X			X	X	X	X	X		X
X	X	X	X	$10,000		X	X			X	X	X
		X	X	X		$10,000		X	X			
			X									
X	X	X	X		$50,000	X	X			X		

CHAPTER TWO

CRIMINAL LAW AND PROCEDURE

CHAPTER DESCRIPTION

Crimes against both the person and property are defined and their elements explained in this chapter. Constitutional safeguards and procedures necessary from arrest through trial, sentencing, and punishment are reviewed.

PARALEGAL FUNCTIONS

Investigate facts of criminal case.

Assist in bail proceedings.

Assemble necessary evidence.

Interview potential witnesses and obtain statements.

Prepare witnesses for trial.

Assist in trial proceedings.

Gather necessary evidence to assist in sentencing.

I. THE ROLE OF THE PARALEGAL IN THE ADMINISTRATION OF JUSTICE

The development of the role of the paralegal in the administration of justice has been quite phenomenal. The steady, almost unparalleled growth in this occupation was not predicted, though continued growth is certainly projected for the future. The job of paralegal, or legal assistant, in some circles is considered a profession, similar to a teacher, police officer, or other public-service occupation. Paralegal work has also become a popular career choice for a wide variety of people, who differ in educational level, gender, and overall career aspirations. In a sense, this emerging "player" in the field of law is the most radical change to take place in many years in a traditional, standard field. Paralegals are effectively leading a cultural revolution or reformation in delivery of legal services. As is so often said, the paralegal's work allows the attorney to do what is expected of him or her—to think about and interpret law. The fact that paralegals excel in the private sector is no secret. But what about the public sector, particularly the fields of criminal law and procedure? Is it possible for the paralegal to operate productively within a governmental agency or body? The Civil Service Commission of the United States government thinks so. In particular, the commission delineates a paralegal's functions in the following settings:

1. The police department—investigation
2. Public Defender's/ District Attorney's offices
3. Trial preparation
4. Correctional departments
5. Parole and probation
6. Presentence investigation
7. Community relations
8. Internal review agencies

On the whole, career opportunities in this public sector offer the trained paralegal a bright future with stimulating work and solid civil-service security and renumeration.

II. THE NATURE OF CRIME

Every society has reached some consensus on what it considers "bad" or evil. A few cultures seem to have difficulty differentiating between good and evil, and others appear far too tolerant. Essentially, the law of crime exists to outlaw conduct that is distasteful and abhorrent to general social, moral, and political principles. Defining the appropriate consensus is not always easy, as evidenced by the wide variance of opinion on whether acts such as drug usage, gambling, prostitution, and sodomy should be deemed criminal behavior. Historical analysis does demonstrate that attitudes, norms, and mores are subject to change, vacillation, or maturity. What was a crime two hundred years ago might now be considered a harmless social exercise.

On the whole, the law of crimes has historical permanence since most people and their nations have regularly agreed that certain behaviors are *wrong*—murder, incest, theft, and rape. In our times, though, even these traditionally accepted violations are being tested by all sorts of bizarre defenses. However, a safe guess would be that three thousand years from now a criminal code will exist with much of the same subject matter as today, though probably reflective of more creative ways of bending age-old principles and with descriptions of criminal aberrations even today's criminal would never dream of. We hope that the criminal code book will be smaller, testifying to a better, simpler world.

To label behavior *crime*, the act must be injurious to the society as a whole or so significant that the peace of the community as a whole is disrupted. That "peace" supposedly assures the citizen of freedom from arrogant deeds and disturbances and prevents the disintegration of the social unit of which he or she is a member. In this sense, the law of crimes requires a less individualized, more communal analysis on the part of the criminal law theoretician, a difficult task in an age of individualism. Whether an act is a crime does not simply depend on whether an individual chooses freely to perform the act, or on whether the act is consensual, or on whether a minority of citizens enjoy the behavior. The definition of a crime requires a more global inquiry, one in which individual desires become subservient to the greater good of all members of the community. In short, acts that negatively influence the collective conscience or good of a community can be described as crimes.

III. ESSENTIAL ELEMENTS IN EVERY CRIME

A. Introductory Questions

Every single crime, no matter how insignificant, requires proof of two elements: (1) Actus reus: *act committed*; and (2) Mens rea: *criminal intent*. All criminal-law analysis demands that two fundamental questions be asked before criminal liability can be imposed. First, has some act been done, such as a theft of a record, an assault or battery on someone in a barroom fight, or a death by use of a weapon? Always, always, always be sure that an act was done because our system of law does not punish people for what they think, only for what they do. Second, what was the mental state or reasoning process of the actor when doing the act? What was in his or her mind? What desires, emotions, motives, logic, or strategy? The mind of the actor must be made accountable for the deed since our adjudicatory system does not hold responsible those parties who are not mentally in control. Again, these two fundamental questions lay the proper groundwork in the analysis of every single act suspected of being a crime.

B. Problems with the Actus Reus

A general tenet in criminal law is that criminal intent unaccompanied by a criminal act is not punishable. To think of killing, maiming, burning, torturing, kidnapping another person is never going to be a crime unless some affirmative steps are taken to put in motion those desires. As a result, the actus reus is the mental by-product of the mens rea. As a policy, no criminal liability is imposed unless these two elements concur in point of time or are substantially simultaneous. At first glance, proof of the actus reus appears a simple task, but the following issues attest to its conceptual difficulty.

1. Is the questioned behavior simply a function of a status or condition?

Many statutes, especially those in the public-safety and health realm, attempt to give enforcement powers to the police system as it deals with vagrants, "bag" people, loiterers, or other displaced individuals. What crimes are these unfortunates really committing? Statutes that punish a condition or a status cannot be deemed on a par with normal criminal behavior. Consider these definitions of a vagrant:

- Looking unemployed
- A person who wanders aimlessly
- A person who meanders without purpose
- A person with no apparent means of subsistence

Are these descriptions indicative of criminal behavior or simply a status or condition? The law requires the actus reus to be a volitional deed, not an inherent or acquired trait.

2. Who actually commits the actus reus?

The law does not require actual perpetration of an act in order for a person to be liable for the conduct. A person is basically responsible for any conduct he or she originates, sets in motion, solicits, supports, or incites. Equally true is the relationship of the parties involved in the proscribed conduct, namely whether the parties can be described as principals, accessories, aiders, abettors, and agents. All of these interlocking relationships can hold accountable all the parties even though there may be only one lone perpetrator.

3. Does the accused's conduct or act really cause the injury or harm?

This section appropriately delves into causation. The state or other prosecuting authorities are obligated to demonstrate that a causal relationship exists between the act done and the harm resulting therefrom. Defendants always pose insightful arguments that break this chain of liability. Just as in the law of torts, the criminal law must effectively prove that (1) defendants acted, and (2) the act caused the result. Defense counters usually include these arguments:

- Defendant is not responsible for the end result because there was an *intervening cause*.
- Defendant is not responsible for the end result because there were other *concurrent causes*.
- Defendant is not responsible for the end result because there was an *independent intervening cause*.
- Defendant is not responsible for the end result because there was a *superseding cause*.

The complexities of this causal analysis and the defense counters are well documented and certainly not this short course's main purpose, but it is essential that the student of criminal law pose theories that break the causal chain. If a break is found, so too is a good, viable defense. For example, consider a thug who beats up someone and throws the victim in the street. That victim is eventually run over by a car. Is the thug liable for murder? Has there been a break in the chain of responsibility? Is the death of the victim caused by totally independent forces or causes? And when do third parties become partially responsible? When does the contributory negligence of the victim affect the criminal liability of the actor? These and other queries provide intelligent insight into this area of criminal responsibility.

4. When is an attempted act a legally complete actus reus?

Finding the accused guilty does not require the successful completion of a crime. An attempt is an unfinished crime, yet just as serious and injurious to the society. While the law does not punish the ideas of individuals, it does not take lightly conduct, characterized as overt or affirmative, that sets in motion the eventual criminal conduct. Just when conduct is viewed as overt, and hence constituting an actus reus, has been the subject of major intellectual inquiry. A confusing distinction exists between what is *mere preparation* for the crime and an *overt act* that sets in motion the intended crime. In most basic terms, an attempt consists of three elements: intent to commit the crime, performance of an overt act, and failure to complete the crime.

Since attempts are equally as serious offenses as completed crimes, the rules for proof of an overt act are quite rigid and place a heavy burden on the state. While a variety of definitions exist, all generally document the need for dangerous proximity or closeness to success in the crime. The overt act must be sufficiently proximate to the intended crime. Once this proof is met, the actus reus of attempt is demonstrated. In its law of attempts the actus reus is not a completed crime.

5. Is it impossible to commit the actus reus?

A variety of arguments on impossibility emerge in the analysis of actus reus.

First, is it *physically impossible* to commit the act? Consider the pickpocket who attempts to steal from a person with no wallet. How about the drug buyer who wishes to purchase narcotics when the dealer has none? Both scenarios manifest a physical impossibility to formulate the actus reus. Do these factual patterns result in no liability? A majority of jurisdictions would charge attempted offenses,

Second, what if the intended actus reus is *factually impossible* to commit? Examples could include an assault on a mannequin, an abortion on a nonpregnant woman, or shooting a pillow thought to be a human body. While all of these acts manifest an intent of a criminal nature, can the law punish a party with the same level of severity as it would an actual perpetrator of murder, criminal abortion, or assault? Do we not distinguish the end result? Since an underlying hallmark of our system is not to punish people for what they think, how can an actus reus be inferred from these facts?

As problematic as these inquiries are, it is little wonder that a majority of jurisdictions are totally perplexed as to an appropriate solution. Generally, if the offense could be effected and is not inherently impossible, the charge of attempt may be posited.

Third, can the accused be held responsible when by operation of law the actus reus committed was *legally impossible*? As further examples:

☐ Can perjury be committed outside a legal proceeding?
☐ Can a juvenile commit an adult crime?
☐ Can a defendant be convicted of rape when the party consented?
☐ Can a person be found guilty of larceny for retaking his or her own property?

All impossibility arguments are highly subtle but geared to issues revolving around the actus reus. If the act is impossible to commit, whether by legal definition, physical reality, or actual truth, the actus reus may not be properly proven for the purposes of establishing criminal liability.

C. Mens Rea: An Analysis

Regardless of what society thinks of criminals, their mental processes are fascinating. Criminals certainly provide the professional and the community with a continual challenge. To ascertain and prove a mind set is the most demanding aspect in the proof of a crime. For as many ways as there are to commit criminal behavior, there are also ways of reasoning, thinking, pondering and plotting. That is why criminal codes abound with terms that are descriptive of intent. How about these:

1. Knowingly	*9.* With evil purpose
2. Maliciously	*10.* Negligently
3. Willfully	*11.* With gross disregard
4. Fraudulently	*12.* With mischief
5. With malice aforethought	*13.* With depraved indifference to human life
6. With guilty knowledge	*14.* Capriciously
7. Recklessly	*15.* Perversely
8. With felonious intent	*16.* Wantonly

17. Intentionally
18. Carelessly
19. Complete disregard
20. Deliberately
21. Designedly

22. With evil mind or design
23. Unconscionably
24. Without due care
25. Deceptively

Consider the above descriptive words. Each addresses a way of thinking or doing. Remember, the actus reus must be accompanied by a mental state, an intent reflective of these mental characterizations. It is also obvious that there are varying levels of evil thought. In turn, the term *willfully* is a far cry more serious than *negligently*. A person who kills another negligently is likely to be punished less severely than one who does so willfully. Accordingly, these intent levels or gradations, which can be inferred from the terms themselves, have great bearing on the choice of charge and overall nature of the offense. As will be seen shortly, the mind of a criminal is critical to the nature, description, and grade of the offense charged.

1. Basic types of intent in the law of crimes

The intent element is further reduced with states of consciousness, or the lack thereof, by this three-tiered gradation:

a. SPECIFIC INTENT

The more serious crimes involve the proof of specific intent. For specific intent, proof must be posed that illuminates the true mental state of the accused. Proof must come forth on how the accused wanted to *specifically* murder, rape, or whatever. Proof of this type cannot be automatically inferred, since specific-intent crimes are generally extremely serious and as a result carry very heavy penalties. To support the gravity of these offenses requires the highest evidentiary standards in proof of intent. In general, the majority of specific-intent crimes can be remembered by the following anagram:

L	A	B	R	E	A	K	E	M
A	R	U	A	X	S	I	S	U
R	S	R	P	T	S	D	C	R
C	O	G	E	O	A	N	A	D
E	N	L	/	R	U	A	P	E
N		A	R	T	L	P	E	R
Y		R	O	I	T	P	F	
		Y	B	O		I	R	
			B	N		N	O	
			E			G	M	
			R				P	
			Y				R	
							I	
							S	
							O	
							N	

A quick review of our descriptive terms on intent provides insight into terms relating to specific intent, such as *knowingly, willfully, with malice aforethought, with gross disregard, and wantonly.* Levels of mental clarity and purpose become more obvious when the law of crimes moves to the lower-intent forms.

So unless the prosecution comes forth with evidence as to how the accused specifically intended to perform any of the above acts, it has not met its burden.

b. GENERAL INTENT

Some advocates of revised criminal codes have argued for a middle ground between specific-intent crimes and strict-liability offenses. Some critics say that the *general-intent* definition is nothing more than a watered-down version of specific-intent analysis. They may be right, but for intellectual simplicity it may be best to accept the fact that gray areas do exist in the evaluation of the mental state. Again, refer to the descriptive terms above and consider which designations are compromises of sorts. How does *recklessly* measure mental state? Does *capriciously, gross disregard,* or *with mischief* connote the same level of evil-mindedness or deliberation as other mental states reviewed thus far? Plainly these descriptions are less severe and generally are utilized in the lower degrees of offenses in the specific-intent categories, such as assault in the third degree or manslaughter in the second or third. Other offenses that fall into this lower-intent description include the negligent behaviors such as criminally negligent homicide, that is deaths resulting from DWI (driving while under the influence).

c. Strict Liability

Contradictory though it might appear from the lessons learned thus far, an accused can be found guilty of an offense even if the intent is minimal or nonexistent. Hence the term *strict liability*, the attributing of guilt to a party who simply commits the act. Conceptually, strict liability is so easy no student ever believes the result. That is because the student generally does not fathom the policy and rationale for the strict-liability offense.

The meting out of punishment for crimes is a message from the community, a result of a community consensus, that certain acts will not be tolerated under any circumstances. Certain behaviors such as drunk driving, improper nuclear disposal, environmental violations, and government trespass and other defense issues are so difficult to regulate that the criminal's mens rea is inferred from the act itself. While this is a generalization, it is clear that the society does not want to hear every excuse imaginable from people who say, "I never intended to be drunk," or "I didn't think that nuclear waste would hurt anyone," and so on. Some behaviors are just plain inexcusable. I'm sure the IRS has little sympathy for a taxpayer who says, "I forgot all about those taxes."

As a result, strict-liability crimes emerge because of enforcement realities, public-health and safety issues, and the society's overwhelming interest in control of these matters.

See exhibits 2.1 and 2.2 for helpful reports.

IV. SPECIFIC TYPES OF CRIMES

A. Crimes against the Person

1. Homicide

Little doubt exists on the multitude of approaches criminals select in the perpetration of murder. As a reminder, never lose sight of those differing mental states or intents because they so inextricably relate to the proof of the degrees of murder.

Not all homicides are crimes. They can be *justifiable*, as in self-defense, or *excusable*, as in time of war. Our only concern is the unlawful form of homicide, namely, murder and manslaughter.

a. Murder

Most states attempt to define murder in the most serious terms. A typical definition follows.

MURDER IN THE FIRST DEGREE.   A homicide that is purposely or knowingly done or is committed recklessly, manifesting extreme indifference to human life.

The ramifications of this language are quite demanding in terms of proof. First, note the descriptive states of mind, all of which show conscious mental processes, for instance, *knowingly* and *purposely*. Or if there was no malice aforethought, the statute paints a picture of a perpetrator so warped, so lacking in human compassion that he or she is capable only of exhibiting a reckless disregard of human life. From a tactical standpoint, a district attorney has to weigh long and hard the quality of his or her case before proceeding with this charge. The DA's evaluation must be done with comparison statutes in mind—murder in the second and third degrees, if they exist in the jurisdiction, or a higher level of manslaughter. See exhibit 2.3.

b. Manslaughter

While murder is often typified as a conscious, premeditated act, manslaughter is more commonly viewed as an act of passion. Generalized as this distinction is, it is essentially correct everywhere. As the level of intent decreases, the society views the act more tolerantly. Empathy goes out to an individual who kills as a result of stress, emotion, or

EXHIBIT 2.1

INVESTIGATION REPORT

1. Department	2. Mun. Code	3. Phone Number and Ext.	4. UCR	21. Prosecutor's Case No.	22. Dept. File No	☐ Co-op
						☐ Original

5. Crime/Incident	6. NJS	23. Victim (First, Middle, Last)

	Social Security Number	24. D.O.B.	25. Sex	26. Race

| DATE AND TIME | 7. Between ☐ | 8. Hour | 9. Day | 10. Mo. | 11. Date | 12. Yr | 27. Victim's Address (City, State, Zip) | Phone and Ext. No. |
| | At ☐ | | | | | | |

13. Crime/Incident Location	28. Employer/Address	Phone and Ext. No.

14. Municipality	15. County	16. Code	29. Person Reporting Crime/Incident	30. Date and Time

17. Type of Premises	18. Code	19. Weapons—Tools	20. Code	31. Address	Phone and Ext. No

32. Modus Operandi/How Committed

33. Vehicle	34. Year	35. Make	36. Body Type	37. Color	38. Registration Number and State	39. Serial Number or Identification

VALUE STOLEN PROPERTY	40. Currency	41. Jewelry	42. Furs	43. Clothing	44. Auto	45. Miscellaneous

46. Total Value Stolen	47. Total Value Recovered	48. Teletype Alarm	49. Technical Services	50. Technician and Agency

51. Weather	52.	53.	54.	55. Evidence None	56. Disposition
				YES NO	YES NO
				☐ ☐ NJSBI	☐ ☐ Arrest Pending
57. Chem. Lab. No	58. Ballistics Lab. No	59. MV Summ	60.	☐ ☐ Retained	
				☐ ☐ Returned	☐ ☐ Teletype Pending
				☐ ☐ Destroyed	☐ ☐ Evidence Pending

List arrested/summoned—List and identify additional victims—Describe perpetrators or suspects—Date action taken include findings and observations of investigator—Physical evidence found—Where, by whom—Disposition and technical services performed—Interview of Victims—Witnesses—Persons contacted—Suspects—Attach Victim Property Loss Report—Attach Statements—Court Action—All NCIC Entry/Inquiries—Prisoner Disposition. Use continuation page if additional space is needed, attach to this report

61. No. Arrested	62. Adult	63. Juvenile	64. Status Crime	65. Status Case	66. UCR Status	67. Date Cleared

68. Name	ADDRESS OF ARRESTED/SUMMONED	69. Age	70. Sex	71. Race	72. D.O.B

73. Rank/Name (Type)	74. Badge No	75. Page ___ of ___ Pages	76. Date of Report
Signature _____	78. Unit	79.	77. Reviewed By

EXHIBIT 2.2

6. Dept. File No. _____

ARREST REPORT

FBI Identification Number

SBI Identification Number

SPN Identification Number

| 1. Department | 2. Mun. Code | 3. Phone Number | 4. UCR | Municipal B.C.I. Numbers |
| | | | | 5. Prosecutor's Case Number |

| 7. Name (First) | (Middle) | (Last) | 8. Phone No. (Area) | 9. Alias/Nickname |

| 10. Full Address (No.) (Street) | 10A. Municipality | 10B. County | 10C. State | 10D. Zip | 11. Place of Birth (City) | (State) |

| 12. Date of Birth | 13. Age | 14. Sex | 15. Race | 16. Ht. (Ft./In.) | 17. Weight | 18. Hair | 19. Eyes | 20. Complexion | 21. Marital Status |

| 22. Other Descriptive Information—Marks—Scars—Tatoos | 23. Driver's License Number |

| 24. Employer/School | 25. Occupation | 26. Social Security Number |

| 27. Employer's/School Address | 28. Business Phone (Area) (Extension) |

DETAILS OF ARREST

| 29. Arrest Date | 30. Time | 31. Loc of Arrest (No.-Street) | 31A. Municipality | 31B. County | 31C. State | 32. Mun. Code |

| 33. Crime | 33A. Total Crimes | 34. NJ Statue | 35. Warrant Docket Number |

| 36. Complainant's Name and Address—Zip Code | 37. Phone Number (Area) |

| 38. Crime Date | 39. Time | 40. Loc. of Crime (No. Street) | 40A. Municipality | 40B. County | 40C. State | 41. Mun. Code |

| 42. Arrest ☐ W/Warrant ☐ W/O Warrant ☐ On View ☐ Summ. ☐ Juv. ☐ P.R.A. | 43. Juv. Code | 44. Constitutional Rights ☐ Yes ☐ No | 45. Constitutional Rights—By Whom | 46. How Responded |

| 47. Own | 48. Multiple | 49. Other | 50. Fingerprinted/By ☐ Yes ☐ No | 51. Photographed/By ☐ Yes ☐ No | 52. NCIC ☐ Yes ☐ No ☐ Wanted ☐ No Record | 53. Previous Record ☐ Yes ☐ No |

| 54. Vehicle Information ☐ Owned ☐ Used | Year | Make | Body Type | Color | Reg. Number and State | Other Discription Information—VIN |

BAIL HEARING

| 55. Date | 56. Court | 57. Judge Setting Bail |

| 58. Amount Bail | 59. Results of Hearing ☐ Released on Bail ☐ R.O.R. ☐ Committed in Default ☐ Committed W/O Bail | 60. Code | 61. Place Committed/Detained |

FINAL DISPOSITION

| 62. Date | 63. Court | 64. Judge |

| 65. Disposition ☐ Gulty ☐ Dismissed ☐ Lesser Offense ☐ Acquitted | 66. Code | 67. T.O.T. | 68. Sentence | 69. Code |

JUVENILE INFORMATION

| 70. Parent/Guardian/Probation—Contacted By | 71. Date Contacted | 72. Time Contacted | 73. Released to/Detained At |

| 74. Full Address—Number—Street—Municipality—State—Zip Code | 75. Phone Number (Area) | 76. Date | 77. Time |

| 78. Parent/Guardian's Name (First) (Middle) (Last) | 79. Full Address—Number—Street—Municipality—State—Zip Code | 80. Phone No. (Area) |

| 81. Co-defendants | 82. | 83. | 84. | 85. | 86. | 87. UCR — A.S.R. Reporting Mon. _____ Yr. _____ |

88. Narrative/Additional Charges

| 89. Rank/Name (Type) | 91. Status ☐ Pending ☐ Completed | 92. Date of Report |
| Signature / Unit | | 93. Reviewed By |

EXHIBIT 2.3

SAMPLE COMPLAINT

Felony of Murder

COURT   THE STATE OF _____

vs.

County of _____, _____   _____

Court Docket Number(s)   _____

_____   _____

Prior Case Docket Number

_____

Complaint result of case returned by prosecutor _____ .

Complainant _____ of _____
           name of complainant   identify dept or agency

Residing at _____
            address of private citizen complainant

Upon oath says that, to the best of (his) (her) knowledge, information and belief, the named defendant on or about _____ day of _____ 19 ____ in the _____ of _____ County of _____ did:

within the jurisdiction of this court commit the murder of (name of victim)
by knowingly or purposely causing his death in violation of

Charge Number 1 _____

Charge Number 2 _____

Charge Number 3 _____

Subscribed and sworn to before me this _____ day of _____, 19 ____.

Signed _____   Signed _____
     (Name and title of person   Complainant
     administering oath)

---

passion. All people have their emotional thresholds, and a capacity to exhibit anger and frustration and hence, one could say, if the circumstances were right, the capacity to kill. Manslaughter might be defined as follows:

> **MANSLAUGHTER.** An act resulting in homicide, an act committed reck-
> lessly, or an act that results from the influence of extreme mental or emo-
> tional disturbance of which there is reasonable explanation.

Every jurisdiction has a statute similar in some way to this and may even further break down manslaughter into second and third degree, or further characterize it as behavior that is *voluntary*, or *involuntary*. The *voluntary* scenario usually arises in severe domestic disputes or other arguments, while the involuntary designation is usually applied in cases mitigated by drunkenness of the most severe nature, addiction, insanity, or other such factors. The *involuntary* designation is frequently applied to *criminally negligent* homicide or *auto manslaughter* cases in which a person dies as a result of a driving violation or DWI.

c. FELONY MURDER RULE

An interesting rule still utilized in many jurisdictions is the felony murder rule. All members of any conspiracy to commit any major criminal felony (remember LABREAKEM) will be responsible for the deaths of any parties, participants or victims, at least where those crimes are committed in furtherance of the conspiracy and the murder is a foreseeable result of it. Substantial criticism of the rule concerns the fact that the felony murder doctrine makes people guilty of murder with little or no requirement of proof on mens rea. That criticism has led a majority of American jurisdictions to adopt various defenses for the accused who hopes to show he never would have been a participant in murder.

d. MISCELLANEOUS ISSUES IN THE LAW OF HOMICIDE

1. Omission and Duty to Act. While affirmative actions that result in murder are clearly punishable, so too are omissions—failure to act. However, before any duty is imposed on a party there must be a legally binding relationship. Moral obligations are not necessarily legal ones.

2. Provocation in Manslaughter. Before any accused can effectively argue that emotion or passion controlled the tenor of events that resulted in a homicide, he or she must demonstrate that the provocation was sufficient or reasonable enough to excite one's passion beyond control.

3. Violation of Ordinance/Statute as Proof of Negligent Homicide. An owner of a building who refused to honor fire code or housing regulations even after repeated citations and warnings could easily be held to criminally negligent homicide or other form of involuntary manslaughter if anyone died as a result of a fire in that building. Statutes, codes, or regulations are often a great help in deciding criminal responsibility because the audience they are passed for, or directed to, is placed on notice about acceptable normative behavior.

4. Abortion. The legalization of abortion in the various stages of fetal development as guided by *Roe* vs. *Wade* decision of the Supreme Court has forced all states to reexamine and redefine their criminal proscriptions against abortion. The moral and ethical dilemma of describing legally a fetal life, a potential life, of deciding whether the fetus is a human being wracks legislators as well as philosophers. What is certain is that prenatal and neonatal science has become much more highly developed since the late 1970s. This emerging technology gives rise to even more troubling questions in discerning the origination of human life and accordingly affording that being's rights of existence. Some states are so troubled by these issues that they have been totally unable to adopt a statute clearly defining an illegal abortion.

2. Assault

A common-law assault was defined as the attempt to commit a battery. The battery was the physical result. Most states have merged the two offenses and created varying degrees of the offense.

a. SIMPLE ASSAULT

A small crime, generally a misdemeanor, which is an *attempt to cause bodily injury* or in fact *negligently causes injury, or places another party in fear of imminent serious bodily harm*. Nothing too complex here except the often contrary and nonuniform assessment of what is *fear of imminent harm*.

b. AGGRAVATED ASSAULT

A felony offense frequently coupled with other charges such as rape, robbery, and kidnapping. A solid statute might read:

AGGRAVATED ASSAULT. An attempt to cause serious bodily injury to another or to cause such injury purposely, knowingly, or recklessly or attempt to cause or purposely or knowingly cause bodily injury to another with a deadly weapon.

c. RECKLESS ENDANGERMENT

Many states have felt it prudent to adopt a less severe statute that covers behavior less intentional yet just as frightening to a reasonable person. This type of statute would cover a drunk or other less-than-cogent person who is waving a shotgun around at a party or other event obviously endangering others.

3. Kidnapping

In common law, kidnapping was the forcible abduction of any person from his or her own country and sending him or her to another. While a forcible removal is still critical in the analysis of kidnapping, the parameters of the crime have been greatly extended. The crime can now include the removal and confinement for any of the following purposes:

- As ransom or reward or as shield or hostage
- To facilitate commission of any felony
- To inflict bodily injury or terrorize the victim
- To interfere in the performance of any governmental function

This type of expanded, more elasticized definition has markedly improved the chances of prosecutors in securing convictions, but its content is also tragic evidence of how our world has so changed. Kidnapping has become a tool of the terrorist.

Most kidnapping statutes are well drafted at both the state and federal levels. However, some violent disagreement on what is true "removal" from one place to another still exists. Does a rapist who drags his victim a city block to a dark alley fall within the statute's definition? Some states say yes.

Lastly, less heinous versions of kidnapping have been uniformly adopted, for instance, when people restrain others in an argument or disagreement or deprive a party of his or her liberty for a period of time. That type of crime is *false imprisonment*.

4. Sexual offenses

Dramatic reforms have taken place in this area of the criminal law in the last twenty years. In a sizeable portion of states, the term *rape* is fading from the code books. Statutes are becoming sexually neutral owing to the finally recognized reality that both men and women, and boys and girls, can be the targets of sexual abuse. Other changes have been the questionable reductions in the age of consent, enlightened elimination of character evidence on sexual history, and the earnest-resistance requirement, as well as a redefinition of penetration to include the anus and mouth. The trend toward reform does not appear to be ending, with the states of Michigan and New Jersey still in the forefront.

a. RAPE/AGGRAVATED SEXUAL ASSAULT

Numerous variables exist in this crime but the primary elements are (1) sexual intercourse (penetration), (2) lack of consent (implying force or threat of harm), and (3) any female (not his wife).

The reform movement has been pervasive in all three elements. First, sexual intercourse has been broadly defined as sexual penetration, cunnilingus, fellatio, anal intercourse, or any other intrusion with a penis or any other foreign object. Second, earnest resistance or any resistance at all is no longer required, since all clinicians and law-enforcement practitioners in the sexual-offense area advise against it. Rape is not a sexual crime. It is a crime of violence. Third, since many states are now sexually neutral, element 3 is changed to any *person*. Equally significant is the remarkable increase of jurisdictions permitting a wife to charge her husband with rape. They include Pennsylvania, New Jersey, and Delaware.

b. OTHER SEXUAL OFFENSES

The majority of jurisdictions then further break down other less violent, though equally reprehensible, sexual offenses into categories including:

1. Sexual assault (first, second)

2. Sexual contact—This new designation takes in a good deal of the lewd and lascivious behavior and public-exposure type of codification.

3. Incest—A horrendous crime that has increased dramatically in the last twenty years.

4. Corruptions of minor seduction—In an age when youth is most valued as a social status and when children regularly are placed in adult situations, the justice system is witnessing an immeasurable proliferation in all forms of behavior relating to child abuse including obscene productions, child prostitution and slavery, statutory rape, and general sexual abuse of children.

V. CRIMES AGAINST PROPERTY

A. Larceny/Theft

1. General discussion

Larceny was the designation in common law for any misappropriation of property that was nonforcible. The crime was also further distinguished by evaluating the value of property taken. Hence the terms, *petty* vs. *grand larceny*. All states do the same today, though some prefer the term *theft* because it is more comprehensive.

The essential elements of any larceny theft are a taking of property of value, no lawful right to possession, and movement, transfer or asportation of the property.

Tangible property was the chief concern of old larceny code definitions, but the technological complexities of the modern age certainly require a new definition. In particular all new codes have greatly expanded the definition of property to mean "*anything of value including real estate, tangible and intangible property, contract rights, amusement tickets, animals, food, drink, utilities or their power.*"

B. Theft by Deception and Fraud

Statutes attempt also to codify the varieties of *theft by deception or fraud*. From scams and cancer cures to door to door rip-offs, consumer protection as well as activism have led legislatures to view theft by deception very seriously. In order to be considered deception, statements or misrepresentations must relate to material issues of fact, not peripheral matters or puffing. The tactics of some used-car salesmen may appear to fall within the description. The American Law Institute's Model Penal Code defines **deception** as

> Purposely creating or reinforcing an impression in the mind of the owner to
> induce his consent to the appropriation when the impression is false and the
> actor does not believe it to be true.

C. Theft of Services/Public Utilities

In the last twenty years, a rising tide of crime has occurred against the public-utility sector of our economy. Crime has been a natural way of venting frustration against utility companies for the dramatic rise in energy costs. A similar situation exists for restaurants where the check or tab is sometimes not picked up, and the restaurateur is left with no renumeration. All modern statutory codes have provisions relating to the misappropriation of utilities or services in general. The Model Penal Code defines **services** as

> Labor, professional service, telephone or other public service,
> accommodation in hotels, restaurants or elsewhere, admission to exhibitions,
> use of vehicles or other movable property.

D. Theft of Lost or Abandoned Property

A person who comes into control of property he or she knows to have been lost, mislaid, or delivered by mistake commits a theft if he or she doesn't take reasonable measures to return the property to the proper party. The law requires that each individual have an honest conscience about lost property. So if one finds fifty thousand dollars on the street in an unmarked package, with no hint or clue as to ownership, what reasonable steps are required?

E. Theft by Extortion

With the emphasis on crime consolidation, extortion is now found under most larceny/theft statutes. Extortion is a widely used mode of coercion for organized crime and as a rule quite effective! Theft by extortion occurs when a person obtains property by threat to

1. Inflict bodily injury or other offense
2. Falsely accuse anyone of an offense
3. Expose secrets
4. Take or withhold official action
5. Cause a strike or boycott
6. Withhold legal testimony
7. Threaten any harm

Your friendly loan shark can and does employ any of these techniques regularly as do individuals offering "protection" to businesses in exchange for a piece of the action.

F. Receiving Stolen Property

This offense generally rounds out the larceny/theft grouping in the code. One who pays a bargain price for certain goods that any individual would know is ridiculous relative to its normal value can be viewed as knowing the property was stolen. Assume a salesman attempts to sell you a brand new air conditioner for thirty-five dollars and insists payment be made now! What reasonable person won't realize there is something awry. That is the trick in the analysis of this offense—whether a person knew that the property was stolen. Actual knowledge can be inferred from the facts.

G. Robbery

The primary difference between robbery and larceny is the amount of force exerted by the actor. In robbery as the theft is being committed, the person (1) inflicts serious bodily injury; or (2) threatens another with, or purposely puts him in fear of, immediate serious bodily injury.

As such, robbery is an offense against the person as well as the property, and as a result is much more threatening and generally more physical than larceny.

The most common dilemmas emerge when courts consider whether or not the *force* utilized is sufficient. Is a push, grab, or shove violent or threatening enough? Does the victim truly have to be in fear? Can the threats relate to the destruction of the victim's property rather than injury to the person? In general, courts assess these and other questions within a reasonable-person framework.

VI. CRIMES AGAINST THE HABITATION

A. Burglary

The next two crimes for review are, in a sense, really hybrids. Burglary is always first considered a property offense by the majority of laypersons. While it can be a property offense, it doesn't have to be and quite frequently is not. First and foremost, burglary is a crime against the habitation, the place people call home. Since the offense invades the sanctity of our abode, it is viewed in the gravest terms. As such, a burglary is defined as (1) entry into a building or occupied structure, (2) with purpose to commit a crime therein, (3) with no license or privilege. Compared to common-law enunciations these three elements are downright elementary. Gone is the specification of a *residence*. An occupied structure or building includes just about anything—cars, boats, or a cardboard box, which sadly enough some people live in. Gone is the *nighttime* requirement, though in some jurisdictions such as New York the time of day is relevant to the gradation of the offense. Gone also is the requirement of some *breaking*. An entry, forcible or not, is all that is required. Remaining is that often misunderstood criterion—that the entry can be for the purpose of committing *any crime therein*. Any crime means rape, arson, assault, kidnapping, and so on. If the accused decides to steal property, that is a perfectly sound intent for the proof of burglary. If the accused wants to rape a victim and enters the house to do so, he will be just as guilty of burglary.

One final note in this area has been the legislative proliferation of *criminal trespass* laws, which cover a much less severe offense such as surreptitious entries into buildings with no clear or necessarily deliberate purpose.

B. Arson

Arson is a most serious offense, which frequently results in the death of innocent parties. Sometimes it is utilized as a cover-up for a party already killed, the perpetrator hoping to destroy the evidence. Arson is traditionally viewed as an economic crime for the purposes of business-insurance collection, but recent statistics show a marked increase in political or social fire bombings, vandalism, and general malicious mischief as motives.

Generally, the evaluation of arson law parallels that of burglary.

1. *What structures or buildings can be arsoned?* Just about any, including ships, trailers, cars, and airplanes.
2. *What are the methods of destruction?* Fire, of course, but also chemical burning, explosions, or other incendiaries.
3. *How much damage is required?* Arson does not require a successful destruction of the building or structure; *mere*

charring will suffice as well as partial damage, alligator char patterns, smoke damage, or other damage.

4. What intent must the accused have? So long as the accused has actual subjective intention to burn, destroy, and set fire to property and does so with an awareness that such conduct involves highly substantial risks, he or she will be held to have formulated the appropriate intent for arson.

VII. CRIMES CLASSIFIED AS *INCHOATE*

A. Introduction

For practical purposes, the amount of time and energy dedicated to the inchoate crimes is not justified, especially in the training of paralegals. What is certain is that paralegals who work for public defenders or district attorneys will find that these inchoate crimes are the subject of indictments as regularly as the sun comes up. In fact, the entire process of formulating an indictment has become a predictable routine since prosecutors immediately infer some form of conspiracy any time more than one participant is involved.

B. Conspiracy

When evaluating the American system of criminal law, this nation prides itself on its dedication to not punishing people for *what they think*. Conspiracy is an *exception* to that highly principled ideal, and it is the first of the inchoate crimes. The modern crime of conspiracy is predominantly mental in construction because it demands that the state prove that (1) two or more people have conspired, (2) to engage in conduct constituting a crime, (3) have agreed to aid in the planning or commission of the crime, and (4) have committed an overt act in furtherance thereof.

A cursory review of these elements leads a reasonable mind to some misgiving since these definitions appear to clamp down on adverse or contrary thoughts that have not been implemented. Proponents of the conspiracy doctrine quickly retort by noting the *overt act* requirement. The overt act need not be the substantive crime itself, but it must not be mere mental preparation. The vague delineations in this area are beyond codification, but common sense dictates that any step beyond the initial agreement of the conspirators adequately suffices the standard of an overt act.

The majority of conspiracy statutes are also unclear about the level of intent required to meet the mens rea standard. Which level of intent qualifies—an intent to commit a conspiracy or an intent to commit the object crime of the conspiracy? Or are both forms of intent required? Whatever one thinks of conspiracy, it is a frequently used weapon in the prosecutorial arsenal but one that is recurrently subject to substantial criticism.

C. Attempts

Readers are reminded that the topic of attempts was extensively covered in Section III B (4) infra, and no further treatment will be accorded here.

D. Solicitation

This final major inchoate crime seeks to punish individuals who promote, facilitate, command, incite, or encourage other parties to commit criminal offenses. A subversive cheerleader of sorts, the solicitor engages another to accomplish certain actions because he or she is too timid to attempt them or simply enjoys watching the eventual moral devastation of others. Nothing is really complex about this crime, for if the solicitor is successful in his or her encouragement, the solicitor and the actual perpetrators will be equally liable on the offense eventually committed.

The solicitor generally argues in his or her defense that he or she renounced the criminal purpose before a crime was committed, but that argument requires that the accused (1) notified the person he or she solicited and (2) gave timely warning to the appropriate law-enforcement authorities or made a reasonable effort to halt the criminal behavior.

VIII. DEFENSES TO CRIMINAL LIABILITY

A. Introduction

The reverse side of the criminal act is the defendant's explanation. Defendants are naturally never in short supply of stories, some obviously legitimate, other obviously not. This section will review all traditional defenses as well as some of the more avant-garde approaches to limiting criminal liability.

B. Particular Defenses

1. Necessity/justification

Remember the story of the men in the lifeboats with no food whatsoever? Instead of all the crew on the boat dying, they decided to kill the sickest man on board and eat his flesh to remain alive. Was this conduct absolutely necessary for survival? This is a short paraphrase of a most famous case, *Regina* v. *Dudley*, 14 Q.B.D. 273 (1884), in which the court explained:

> To preserve one's life is generally speaking a duty, but it may be the plainest and highest duty to sacrifice it. . . . It is not needful to point out the awful dangers of admitting the principle which has been contended for. Who is to be judge of this sort of necessity?

In some valid circumstances *necessity* can negate the mens rea of the criminal act. The necessity defense has deep moral overtones since its rationale rests in choosing the least painful alternative or in avoiding harm clearly greater than the harm of the statute's proscribed behavior.

2. Duress

The Model Penal Code of the American Law Institute poses eloquently the defense of duress in criminal conduct. In simplest terms, the defense of duress requires a reasonable person to show that the crime was the result of two factors: (1) coercion, threat of unlawful force; and (2) a person of reasonable firmness is unable to resist. Endless fact patterns have emerged in criminal defense tactics, from a threat to family members—children or a spouse—to a loss of position in the community or loss of employment. Again, that duress must be measured by a reasonable-person interpretation.

A place where this defense has been popular and arisen frequently is in the prison setting. How would you rule in a prosecution for escape from a federal prison if the accused stated that the escape was the product of duress, induced by fear of homosexual assaults and physical reprisal? Consider the practical consequences of your ruling.

3. Defense of property

Property is a tangible product that cannot be equated with the human life. As a result, the right to defend it is substantially tempered. In fact, the use of deadly force is never justified in the defense of property unless that property is one's domicile, and then in limited circumstances. The force utilized in the defense of property can only equal that being exerted against that property, and once the property has been effectively taken by another party no force may be exerted in its recapture unless the pursuit is fresh.

What may sound at first cowardly is really an intelligent approach, since our society does not hope for or promote vendettas over issues in property. Our systems of adjudication, no matter how imperfect, can eventually rectify these disagreements. In sum, force can be utilized in the protection of property only (1) to prevent unlawful entry on to land or the larceny of tangible property, (2) to retake property if in "fresh pursuit," or (3) to protect one's domicile if appropriate.

In the defense of the domicile, substantial disagreement comes forth from the various jurisdictions. The Model Penal Code poses a compromise stand by requiring the individual opting to defend with force to request the perpetrator to desist, unless logic dictates otherwise, and permits the use of deadly force if the trespasser is seeking to dispossess him of his dwelling or is engaging in a major felony within his domicile.

4. Defense of the person

The integrity of the individual calls for self-defense in the appropriate circumstances. Under what circumstances can deadly force be justified? Is there such a thing as proportionate force? When can an initiator of a conflict then reverse course and argue self-defense? These and many other questions are difficult to give quick, fixed answers to. Some clear delineations do come forth from across the nation, however.

 a. Self-defense should not be allowed against a peace officer.
 b. The use of deadly force can be utilized only if the defender believes that such force is necessary to protect himself or herself against death, serious bodily harm, kidnapping, or forced sexual intercourse.
 c. The use of deadly force is also justified in the protection of the person in one's own dwelling if there is no chance of retreat or no sense in a request to desist.

When compared to protection of property, the law provides far more latitude in the use of force in the protection of human life, but it demands that the defender objectively believe that he or she was in imminent peril of death or serious bodily harm and that the response was necessary to save oneself. Even more imperative in the understanding of these doctrines is the general notion of proportionality—that is, the force exerted by the defender must have a reasonable relationship or similarity to the force expended by the aggressor.

5. Entrapment

The notoriety of the John DeLorean trial as well as the Abscam convictions brought entrapment into the public eye recently. Historically, entrapment has been viewed as a sniveling governmental trap, viciously tempting and prodding innocent parties to dabble in illegality and perversion, something normally distasteful. The defense interpretation of entrapment would lead us to believe that the accused would *never*, and they mean *never*, have considered such conduct if the government had not made the proposition in the first place. Naive as it seems, these accused have neither seen nor heard of crime before that vengeful day the proposed illegality was offered. All kidding aside, actual defendants do exist who have never before in their lifetimes dreamt of criminality. When the government feeds on these innocents, it is clearly a perversion of justice.

On the whole, case law does not support the defense contention of entrapment, simply because the "naive" defendant is a rarity in the jungle of justice. In essence, entrapment only works for a defendant who has no *criminal predisposition*, or no *criminal plan*. In a world of 85 percent recidivism, it is pretty hard to claim, "Gee, I never thought of that before." Substantially even more unbelievable is this notion that government officials overwhelmed the innocent wills of defendants by their criminal inducements or representations. The art of persuasion has just not generally reached that level of sophistication. Did John DeLorean effectively argue the entrapment? Why? Why not?

6. Consent

Consent negates criminal liability in rape cases and, accordingly, does the same in most other felonies. A person who gives you a TV cannot later claim that you committed a larceny against him. In the absence of some public-policy arguments, consent is generally an effective defense.

7. Insanity

a. THE NATURE OF THE INSANITY REVIEW

Since the attempted assassination of President Reagan by John Hinckley, the insanity defense has come under rigorous review. A hallmark of American law is that no person is liable for acts in which he or she cannot cognitively design or formulate. Persons who are severely disturbed emotionally, mentally retarded, comatose, or totally unconscious can all fall into this exclusionary mold. While the consensus is strong on these issues of mental incapacity, when arguments turn on mental disease as a defense to criminal behavior, the consensus disintegrates. Psychiatric explanations of criminality are as varied as fish in the sea, and a natural skepticism exists in this whole arena. What is unquestioned is the controversial role the psychiatrist plays in the administration of justice. Why so?

First, psychiatry is an inexact science, not an exact discipline. Second, for every psychiatrist attesting to the validity of the defense case, one can find another who will counter with opposite conclusions. Third, in the general prison population all have some descriptive diagnosis that could be classified as a mental illness. Fourth, the imprecision of the designed tests for insanity in the criminal law makes the task of determining insanity absolutely mind boggling. Critics of the insanity arguments could fill reams with assorted diatribes, but that is not our purpose. Understanding the law of insanity requires an introduction into its turbulent past and extremely unstable future.

b SPECIFIC TESTS OF INSANITY

McNaughten Test.   A majority of American jurisdictions still utilize this test from the 1850s. McNaughten is fundamentally a test of cognitive capacity or reason. At its base, the test asks:

1. Does the individual have the ability to reason?
2. Does the individual know or understand the difference between right and wrong?
3. If not, is this the result of some mental defect?

Continually attacked for being a test rooted in moral values, McNaughten has had to mature slowly. Its cognitive dimension has been elasticized to consider the impact of emotional trauma and disease but only in respect to its corollary adoption of the irresistible-impulse test. As a general proposition, McNaughten remains a cognitive test, with thinking, reasoning, and values differentiation as its chief criteria.

Irresistible Impulse.   In those cases where a recognition of right and wrong still flourished, the irresistible-impulse test took root. Psychiatric reality called for a recognition of behaviors that are utterly uncontrollable, such as manias, phobias, and obsessional neuroses. Note well that these behaviors are irresistible, which suggests responses that are sudden, momentary, or spontaneous. Prodding, slowly emerging mental diseases do not fall under this category. The psychiatric lobby was clearly displeased with this insistence on cognitive impairments. But should the law excuse a person who knows his or her conduct is wrong but still proceeds to effect it? This inquiry led to the eventual passage of our next test.

American Law Institute's Test (ALI).   The liberal culmination of the psychiatric lobby was eventually molded in the ALI test, the test by which John Hinckley was adjudged, and surely much to his delight. The ALI test does much to liberalize the accused's position when arguing the defense of insanity. (1) It defines *Mental Disease or Defect* in much broader terms, to reflect cognitive and also emotional influences. (2) It relaxes the exacting "product" causal formulations of previous tests by asking simply that the accused *lack substantial capacity to* (3) *appreciate the criminality of his or her act.*

These standards are a far cry from the rigidity of right-wrong value judgments. The liberalization of the ALI rules has brought blistering criticism in the last three to four years, primarily because public perceptions about crime are so jaded and have reached their tolerance threshold. In the most humanitarian sense, no one disagrees that truly retarded people or those totally and blatantly psychotic or schizoid should not be liable for their deeds, if they are in fact mentally incapacitated. However, that is a far cry from the criminal theatrics regularly seen in the media of defendants who write books and movie scripts and then receive royalties for their production. The balance has been lost somewhere.

8. Miscellaneous defenses

a. INTRODUCTION

There will be no comprehensive review here but instead a cursory listing of new defenses currently being posed by defense counsel. While many defenses appear off the wall, that same perception existed historically about many defenses so readily accepted now. Various appellate cases have reported the following defenses:

☐ PMS syndrome (premenstrual syndrome)
☐ PTS (post-traumatic stress, the Vietnam syndrome)
☐ Astrology
☐ Genetic predetermination
☐ Sugar/food or diet
☐ Drug or alcohol addiction
☐ Biogenic disorders
☐ Environmental influences

IX. GENERAL SCHEME OF CRIMINAL PROCESS

A. Arraignment

This is the occasion when a defendant against whom an accusatory instrument has been filed (information or indictment) is informed of the charge against him or her and informed of his or her rights, especially to the aid of counsel. The right to counsel exists at this stage, since it is deemed a critical stage in the adversarial process.

B. Bail or ROR

The following factors are to be considered by the court on bail application:

1. The nature of the offense
2. The penalty that may be imposed
3. The probability of the voluntary appearance of the defendant or flight to avoid punishment
4. The pecuniary and social position of the defendant
5. The general reputation and character of the defendant
6. The apparent nature and strength of the proof as bearing on the probability of his or her conviction

Bail is without question the preferred method of pretrial disposition. ROR means a release on a person's own recognizance.

C. Disposition without Plea of Guilty

Upon or after arraignment in a local criminal court upon an information, a simplified information, a prosecutor's information or a misdemeanor complaint, and before entry of a plea of guilty or the commencement of a trial, the court may, on its motion or that of either the prosecution or the defendant and with the consent of both parties, order that the action be "adjourned in contemplation of dismissal" upon such conditions of conduct as the court may prescribe and release the defendant on his or her own recognizance. While this disposition is not common, it will occur when the prosecution has no witnesses and wishes to end the matter and believes that the nature of the state's case is so trivial that it will not endanger the community. This type of disposition also recognizes that a guilty party can sometimes be best served by simple dismissal.

D. Specialized Hearings or Dispositions

In most jurisdictions various specialized processes exist to adjudicate the following:

1. First-time or small-time drug offenders
2. Youthful offenders and violent juveniles
3. First time-offenders
4. Candidates whose crimes are so small that their disposition should be accelerated. (As an example, in Pennsylvania, a program called ARD [Accelerated Rehabilitative Disposition] exists.)

E. Preliminary Hearings

When a defendant is arraigned on a *felony* complaint, which is indictable by a grand jury and cannot be disposed of in the local criminal court, he or she is entitled to a hearing to determine whether there is sufficient evidence to warrant the matter's being transferred to the grand jury. The purpose of the hearing is to test the sufficiency of the evidence, and if it does not *establish prima facie evidence*, then the complaint may be dismissed. A defendant usually wants to learn as much as possible about the evidence against him or her at such a hearing. He or she may waive such a hearing. If there is sufficient evidence presented, the court will direct that the defendant be held to await grand jury action.

A defendant who has been held in custody for more than five days without a disposition or without having the hearing commence may petition the court for a release on his or her own recognizance, and the local criminal court must grant it.

F. Grand Jury

A grand jury is impaneled by some form of superior court and consists of between ten and twenty-three citizens. The grand jury hears testimony presented by the prosecution. It does not determine the guilt or innocence of the defendant but merely determines whether there is sufficient evidence to proceed in the prosecution. No judge presides over the grand jury. Witnesses are sworn and may be subject to perjury charges if untruthful. The defendant's case is usually not heard unless the defendant requests permission to attend and testify and can demonstrate with particularity why he or she should be there. A witness who testifies is entitled to immunity from prosecution of what he or she testifies to, if not perjurious, unless he or she signs a waiver of immunity. The grand jury may return indictments for felonies and indictable misdemeanors, recommend that the prosecutor file a prosecutor's information in a local criminal court, or dismiss the charge by returning a "no true bill." Grand juries have been soundly criticized for being prosecutorial rubber stamps.

G. Plea Bargaining

Plea bargaining is an integral part of the criminal-justice system. One of the chief purposes in recent years has been to assist in the disposition of heavy case loads in the criminal courts. Other reasons for its use are that witnesses occasionally are not available or are reluctant to testify, or certain of the prosecution's evidence is lacking or questionable. Plea bargaining enables the prosecution to dispose of an indictment on a reasonable basis and in the interest of the public. For a defendant, it eliminates a long trial where he or she runs the risk of conviction on a higher degree of crime. Primarily, the defendant is interested in what penalty will be imposed and "plea bargaining" becomes "sentence bargaining." By pleading to a lesser charge, even if no sentence promise is made, the defendant is surrendering the right to force the prosecution to prove his or her guilt. A sentence promise made in return for a plea generally must be honored. If the court cannot honor a sentence promised after investigation, the plea of guilty must be vacated and the case restored to its original status. However, a defendant who is not satisfied with the leniency of his or her eventual sentence cannot then complain.

H. Omnibus Motion

Previously, motions to dismiss informations and indictments to inspect grand jury minutes, for discovery for a pretrial lineup to suppress evidence, for bills of particulars, and so on, were separately made, resulting in the filing of many papers and consuming the time of the court and the parties. Many jurisdictions have adopted standardized forms, which list check-off sections for law and every motion requested. Other motions that are possible include:

1. Motion for severance
2. Motion for suppression of evidence (see exhibit 2.4)
3. Motion for psychiatric examination
4. Motion to quash the indictment or information
5. Motion for change of venue
6. Motion to recuse the trial judge
7. Motion to dismiss (see exhibit 2.5)
   –as to speedy trial
   –sufficiency of the evidence
8. Motion to continue (see exhibit 2.6)
9. Motion to supress identification testimony (see exhibit 2.7)

EXHIBIT 2.4

IN THE COURT OF _____ OF _____ COUNTY, _____

Criminal Division

State of _____)
)
vs.   )   No. 820079
)
John Q. Public   )

Omnibus Pretrial Motion:
Motion to Suppress Physical Evidence and
Admissions or Confessions

And now comes defendant by his attorney, R. C. Jones, Esq., and respectfully represents as follows:

1. At all times material, defendant was the lawful occupant of a motor vehicle owned and operated by co-defendant, John J. Brown.

2. Defendant was arrested without an arrest warrant and was taken into police custody without probable cause.

3. During the time defendant was in such unlawful custody, he made either admissions or confessions regarding the possession or use of marijuana without being adequately advised of his rights under the Fifth Amendment or without appreciating those rights under all the circumstances.

4. Officers searched defendant's pockets and the contents thereof without his consent, without probable cause and without a warrant and found contraband which is the subject of this proceeding.

Wherefore, defendant requests that a rule issue upon the State to show cause why the physical evidence and admissions or confessions should not be suppressed.

_____
R. C. Jones
Attorney for Defendant

EXHIBIT 2.5

NOTICE OF MOTION
MOTION TO DISMISS

STATE OF _____ : COUNTY OF _____
      COURT OF

- -

THE PEOPLE OF THE STATE OF _____

         Plaintiff,

     —against—

         Defendant

- -

SIRS:

PLEASE TAKE NOTICE, that upon the annexed affirmation of Larry Brown, Esq. duly affirmed to on the _____ day of _____ 19 ____, and upon all the papers and proceedings heretofore had herein, the undersigned will move this Court, held at _____, _____, on the _____ day of _____ 19 ____, at _____ o'clock in the _____ of that day, or as soon thereafter as counsel can be heard, for an order to dismiss in the furtherance of justice under Section 70.30 (1) (g) of the Criminal Procedure Law and for such other and further relief as to this Court may seem just and proper.

PLEASE TAKE FURTHER NOTICE, that in accordance with Rule 2214 (b) of the Civil Practice Law and Rules, answering papers must be filed at least five (5) days prior to the return date of this motion.

Dated: _____

_____
Larry Brown, Esq.

EXHIBIT 2.6

IN THE COURT OF _____ OF _____ COUNTY, _____

Criminal Division

State of _____)

vs.

John Doe

)
No.

)
MURDER

)

Omnibus Motion:
Motion to Continue

And now comes defendant, John Doe, by his attorney, Larry Smith, Esq., and respectfully represents as follows:

1. This matter is listed for trial _____, 19 _____.

2. Counsel herein was appointed by the Court and since his appointment has been making efforts to secure an expert witness vital to the defense of this case.

3. The Court has limited counsel to the sum of $500.00 for the purpose of securing an expert and the only qualified man who has expressed a desire to assist in this matter is Ace Jones, Ph.D., of California, but he is not willing to accept the position for the sum offered.

4. Dr. Jones referred counsel to _____, who, on _____ replied to counsel that he could not accept this commission although qualified in the field.

5. Co-defendant, Tom Brown, is represented by _____, Esq., private counsel, who is in a position to supplement the expenses in this case if the Court can provide more than $500.00 to Dr. Jones.

6. In any event, Dr. Jones is not available for the month of _____. Defendant Doe is presently confined at _____ Correctional Institution at _____, where he is serving an extended sentence for burglaries and will not be unduly prejudiced by the delay of this trial.

7. Because of the unavailability of an expert witness at this time defendant will be deprived of the effective assistance of counsel if compelled to proceed to trial on _____ or at any time prior to counsel's obtaining a qualified expert in the field of microscopy.

Wherefore, defendant respectfully moves that the trial of this case be continued generally.

_____
Attorney for Defendant

EXHIBIT 2.7

IN THE COURT OF _____ OF _____ COUNTY, _____

Criminal Division

State of _____)

)

vs.

O.J. Criminal

)

)

)

)

)

)

)

)

)

No. 8259 of 1979
ARMED ROBBERY
No. 8260 of 1979
ARMED ROBBERY
No. 8261 of 1979
ARMED ROBBERY
No. 8406 of 1979
THEFT

Omnibus Pretrial Motion:
Motion to Suppress Identification Testimony

And now comes defendant by his attorney, R. C. Smith, Esq., and respectfully represents as follows:

1. As to the Theft indictment, defendant does not know whether any personal identification of him has been made, but in the event that it was, defendant believes that any identification was the product of suggestion and therefore basically unfair and desires a hearing, prior to trial, to determine that issue.

2. As to the Robbery indictments, defendant unwittingly and without the benefit of counsel waived both his right to counsel at the line-up procedures and his preliminary hearings.

3. As to the Robbery indictments, defendant believes that because his car, which he reported stolen, was found near the scene of one of the robberies that all of the identification evidence followed from that and from improper suggestion to identification witness that defendant was the robber in each indictment.

Wherefore, defendant requests that a hearing be held prior to trial to determine the issues pertinent to pretrial identification.

_____
Counsel for Defendant

I. Discovery

The bill of particulars is a motion the purpose of which is to request specified items of factual information that are not recited in the indictment and that the defendant alleges he or she needs to adequately prepare and conduct his or her defense.

The purpose of discovery is to find out from the prosecutor:

1. Any statements the defendant or a codefendant made to a public servant
2. Any testimony the defendant or a codefendant gave before a grand jury
3. Reports or documents of physical and mental examination or scientific tests relating to the proceeding
4. Photographs or drawings made by a public servant relating to the action
5. Any property obtained from the defendant or codefendant
6. Any tapes or electronic recordings prosecutor intends to introduce at the trial
7. Any material the prosecutor has that exculpates the defendant

Discovery can also be done by the prosecutor toward the defense though in a less vigorous way owing to constitutional restrictions. Discovery and disclosure is an ongoing process during a trial, and is frequently based on constitutional principles. (See exhibits 2.8 and 2.9.)

EXHIBIT 2.8

**DEMAND FOR DISCOVERY
AND INSPECTION**

STATE OF _____ : COUNTY OF _____
COURT OF

_____

THE PEOPLE OF THE STATE OF _____

          Plaintiff,

    —against—

          Defendant

_____

SIRS:

    PLEASE TAKE NOTICE, that pursuant to Section 240.20 of the Criminal Procedure Law, defendant demands that the following be disclosed to the defendant and made available for his inspection, photographing, copying or testing:

    1. Any written, recorded or oral statement of the defendant, and of a co-defendant to be tried jointly, made other than in the course of the criminal transaction, to a public servant engaged in law enforcement activity or to a person then acting under his discretion or in cooperation with him.

    2. Any transcript of testimony relating to the criminal action or proceeding pending against the defendant, given by the defendant, or by a co-defendant to be tried jointly, before any grand jury.

    3. Any written report or document, or portion thereof concerning a physical or mental examination, or scientific test or experiment, relating to the criminal action or proceeding and made by, or at the request or direction of a public servant engaged in law enforcement activity.

    4. Any photograph or drawing relating to the criminal action or proceeding made or completed by a public servant engaged in law enforcement activity.

    5. Any other property obtained from the defendant, or a co-defendant to be tried jointly.

    6. Any tapes or other electronic recordings which the prosecutor intends to introduce at trial.

    7. Anything required to be disclosed, prior to trial, to the defendant by the prosecutor, pursuant to the constitution of this state or of the United States.

DATED: _____   _____

                                                           Larry Wilson, Esq.

EXHIBIT 2.9

OMNIBUS MOTION

MOTION FOR DISCOVERY AND INSPECTION

DEMAND FOR BILL OF PARTICULARS

MOTION TO PRECLUDE DISTRICT ATTORNEY FROM USING DEFENDANT'S PRIOR CONVICTIONS OR PRIOR BAD ACTS AT TRIAL

MOTION TO SUPPRESS

MOTION TO DISMISS

STATE OF _____ : COUNTY OF _____
         COURT OF

_____

THE PEOPLE OF THE STATE OF _____

          Plaintiff,

        —against—

          Defendant

_____

SIRS:

       PLEASE TAKE NOTICE, that upon the annexed affirmation of Larry Wilson, Esq., duly affirmed to on the _____ day of _____, 19 ____, motions will be made in this Court, held at _____ State of _____, on the _____ day of _____, 19 ____ at 9:30 in the morning of that day, or as soon thereafter as counsel can be heard for an

       ORDER pursuant to Article 240.90 of the Criminal Procedure Law for discovery, inspection and disclosure of the following matters:

       1. All written, recorded or oral statements of the defendant. If such statements were oral provide the substance of said oral statements.

       2. All police reports, records and memoranda concerning the arrest of the defendant.

       3. A copy of defendant's arrest record.

       4. Discovery and inspection of names, addresses and statements of witnesses.

       5. Discovery and inspection.

       6. Discovery and inspection of the items of defendant's Demand served pursuant to CPL Section 240.20; and for an

       ORDER pursuant to Article 200.90 of the Criminal Procedure Law (made applicable by Article 100.45 (4) of the Criminal Procedure Law) granting to the defendant a Bill of Particulars for the following items:

       1. State the exact time and date when, and place where the alleged incident occurred.

       2. State the exact time and date when, and place where the defendant was arrested for the crime for which defendant now stands charged.

       3. State whether there were any eyewitnesses to the alleged incident. If so, state the names and addresses of the witnesses.

       4. State the nature of the alleged physical injury.

       5. State where the alleged incident took place.

       6. State complainant's relationship to defendant; and for an

       7. Order, under Article 710 of the Criminal Procedure Law and a pretrial hearing to determine:

         a) the admissibility of evidence or testimony which consists of tangible property obtained by unlawful search and seizure under circumstances precluding admissibility; thereof; and

         b) the voluntariness of any statement or admission allegedly made by the defendant.

         c) whether probable cause existed for the arrest and detention of the defendant.

       8. ORDER to preclude the District Attorney from using defendant's prior convictions or prior bad acts at trial; and for such other and further relief as to this Court may deem just and proper.

J. Trial

The process of trial is as follows:

1. *Jury selection.* Each attorney is entitled to review the potential jurors and to exercise preemptory challenges. This process is called the *voir dire*.
2. *Opening statements.* A general recitation of strategy and tactics is possible here as well as counsel's interpretation of the law as applied to the particular facts.
3. *Direct examination.* Witnesses are directly examined by the side proposing them. (Both prosecution and defense cases.)
4. *Cross-examination.* Witnesses may be subsequently crossed.
5. *Redirect or rebuttal.*
6. *Summation or closing.* Counsel are entitled to summarize their positions.
7. *Jury instructions.* Judge instructs the jury in the law as it relates to the facts.
8. *Verdict.* Jury deliberates and returns a verdict.

K. Nonjury Trial

A defendant may elect to be tried by a judge alone, and because the valuable constitutional right to a jury trial is being abandoned, a waiver of that right must appear on the trial record. In proceeding nonjury, the trial judge determines all questions of law and fact and renders a verdict that has the same force and effect as a verdict by a jury.

EXHIBIT 2.10

GUILTY PLEA — STATEMENT OF DEFENDANT

COMMONWEALTH OF _____ VS. _____

T _____, INFORMATION NO(S). _____, _____ SESSION 19____

CHARGES:

I, _____, hereby state that I am ____ years old, that I have been advised by my Attorney, _____, Esquire, of all the following rights:

1. My right to have my case tried by a judge and a jury of 12 people from the community and of my right to challenge the jury and/or the jury panel for cause shown and of my right to participate in the selection of those 12 jurors, and that a verdict of guilty by said jury would have to be unanimous.

_____

2. My privilege to have my case heard by a judge without a jury by leave of court, wherein the judge would be the sole fact finder.

_____

3. My right to take an appeal, with the assistance of counsel provided free, without any cost to myself, from a verdict of the jury, or from a verdict of a court without a jury.

_____

4. My right to file motions for a new trial and to have an attorney provided free without any cost to myself, to file and argue such motions.

_____

5. My right to refuse to testify and to stand mute, and I have been further advised that if I refuse to testify, such refusal will not prejudice me in any way.

_____

6. My right to confront and hear any witness who will give evidence against me and through counsel to cross-examine all witnesses.

_____

7. My right to waive (i.e. not to have) a trial by a jury and/or by a judge, and to enter a plea of guilty. That I have limited appeal rights if the plea is accepted and sentence imposed. That is, I may only appeal the legality of sentence, jurisdiction of this Court and the involuntariness of the plea.

_____

8. My right to take the above limited appeal with the assistance of counsel free, without any cost to myself, from the judgment of sentence.

_____

I further state that I have been advised of the nature of the crime(s) of which I am charged, that

(a) _____ is a felony/misdemeanor and that the penalty as provided in 18 P.S. _____ is

_____

(b) _____ is a felony/misdemeanor and that the penalty as provided in 18 P.S. _____ is

_____

(c) _____ is a felony/misdemeanor and that the penalty as provided in 18 P.S. _____ is

_____

(d) _____ is a felony/misdemeanor and that the penalty as provided in 18 P.S. _____ is

_____

(e) _____ is a felony/misdemeanor and that the penalty as provided in 18 P.S. _____ is

_____

I understand that I could be sentenced to the maximum penalty set forth above for each charge to which I am pleading guilty and that the possible sentence resulting from consecutive sentences on the above charges is

_____

I state that in pleading guilty I am admitting that I committed the crimes charged and admitting my guilt of these charges, that the guilty plea will appear on my record as a conviction, that the above possible penalties and sentences have been explained to me, and I understand them, that I make this statement of my own free will, that it is voluntary, that I have not been threatened, forced or pressured to enter a plea of guilty nor received any promise of the sentence I will receive in return for entering a plea, that I have read this statement and discussed it with my attorney and I fully understand my constitutional rights.

I also understand that if I am on parole or probation that this guilty plea might well result in the revocation of that probation or parole.

I also state that I have fully discussed my case with my attorney, that we have discussed the possible defenses to the charges; that my attorney is fully familiar with the facts of my case. I acknowledge that I have reviewed the factual basis for these crimes with my attorney and that in pleaing guilty I admit committing the acts alleged. My attorney has advised me that the law presumes me to be innocent, and that the burden is upon the Commonwealth to prove me guilty beyond a reasonable doubt. I am satisfied that he is fully prepared to represent me and that he has advised me that he is ready to defend me to the above charges if I did not enter a guilty plea.

I further state that I am not now suffering from any mental illness or the effects of any narcotics or drugs or alcoholic beverages.

_____
Defendant

I, _____ , Esquire,   Attorney for _____

Hereby state that I have advised my client of the foregoing rights; that the client has discussed them with me and believe that he understands them; that I am prepared to try this case, and that defendant understands what he is doing in entering the above guilty plea.

_____
Attorney for Defendant

Note: To Assistant District Attorney—have this form filled in and signed by the defendant. If defendant signs it and understands what he is doing, have his attorney sign it before the guilty plea is taken, read this form into record, then enter this statement as an exhibit with record papers.

L. Guilty Pleas

Since the decision by a defendant to enter a plea of guilty involves the relinquishing of important constitutional safeguards, such as trial by jury, the right to confront and cross-examine witnesses, the right to present testimony, and the right to avoid self-incrimination, the trial judge must engage in a colloquy, that is a questioning of the defendant, to ascertain if the plea is voluntarily and understandingly tendered. Should the plea be a bargained one, this agreement must appear on the record. The plea cannot be accepted until the court is satisfied that it is knowingly, intelligently, and voluntarily entered.

The motive for plea bargaining may vary in each case. Consider why you as a prosecutor and as a defense lawyer would plea bargain. (See exhibit 2.10, pp. 62-63.)

M. Postverdict Motions

Following trial, jury or nonjury, within ten days after the finding of guilt, the defendant may file written motions requesting a new trial or asking that the charges be dismissed notwithstanding the verdict. In the former motion, the defendant essentially lists all the reasons why he or she believes a new trial should be granted. In the latter motion, sometimes called motion in arrest of judgment, the defendant seeks a discharge on the basis of insufficient evidence.

The significance of these motions is that only issues raised in these motions may be argued on appeal. If the issue was not presented at trial and not included in these motions, it is deemed waived so far as appellate review is concerned. (See exhibits 2.11 and 2.12.)

EXHIBIT 2.11

IN THE COURT OF _____ OF _____ COUNTY, _____

Criminal Division

State _____)
)
vs.   )   MISC. DOCKET 403 of 1982
)   CRIMINAL
John Green   )

Petition for Writ of Habeas Corpus

And now comes the defendant, John Green, by his attorney H. E. Jones, Esq., and respectfully represents as follows:

1. On Wednesday, March 3, 1982, at or about 2:30 a.m. police officers of Whiskey Borough, Elk County, forcibly entered Mr. Green's residence at 1414 Elm Drive.

2. The aforesaid officers entered Petitioner's bedroom and arrested him; Petitioner was handcuffed, removed from his house and taken to the borough jail where he was and still remains in a cell.

3. At the time of entry, police did not have nor have they ever produced search or arrest warrant.

4. Petitioner has not been informed of any charges against him despite his demands to be so informed.

5. Twenty-four days have elapsed since Petitioner was arrested and no formal charges have been lodged against him.

6. During the period of detention, Petitioner has not been permitted to contact a lawyer and the undersigned only became aware of Petitioner's plight as a result of a note Petitioner threw out of his cell window.

7. Petitioner's custody is unlawful and constitutes a violation of his right of due process of law guaranteed by the Fifth and Fourteenth Amendments and the Constitution of _____, and constitutes as well a violation of his right guaranteed by the Eight and Fourteenth Amendments and Article 1, section 13 of the _____ Constitution.

Wherefore, Petitioner prays that a Writ of Habeas Corpus issue and that an immediate hearing be set to determine the averments contained herein.

_____
H. E. Jones
Attorney for Petitioner

EXHIBIT 2.12

IN THE COURT OF _____ OF _____ COUNTY, _____

Criminal Division

State of _____)
)
vs.   )   No. 82578
)   MURDER AND ROBBERY
John Q. Johnson   )

Motion for a New Trial and In
Arrest of Judgment

And now comes John Q. Johnson by his attorney, R. C. Smith, Esq., and respectfully moves for a New Trial or Arrest of Judgment for the following reasons:

1. The verdict was contrary to the law and the evidence;
2. The verdict was against the weight of the evidence;
3. The Court erred in not suppressing the eyewitness testimony of witness Horace Jones;
4. The Court erred admitting the defendant's confession since it was obtained in the absence of counsel;
5. The Court erred in its instruction to the jury as to the elements of the offense of robbery.

Wherefore, the defendant moves for Arrest of Judgment in the conviction or a new trial.

_____
R. C. Smith
Attorney for Defendant

6. The defendant has been represented by the following lawyers since his/her arrest in this case: (Lawyers' names and stage of case at which each represented the defendant).

7. The defendant requests the following relief:
_____ Release from custody and discharge;
_____ New trial or withdrawal of plea;
_____ Modification of sentence;
_____ Post-trial motions or appeal *nunc pro tunc*;
_____ Other (specify): _____

8. The grounds for this relief are: (State each ground relied upon for the relief requested. Failure to state such a ground will preclude defendant from raising it.)

9. The facts that support each ground for relief and that appear in the record are: _____
These facts appear at the following places in the record: _____
_____

These facts are supported by the following affidavits, documents, and other evidence, which are attested to this motion: _____
_____

10. The grounds for the relief requested, as set forth in paragraph 8, _____ have _____ have not been raised before in this case, at the following stage: (Specify grounds raised before and stage of case at which raised).

11. (a) _____ The defendant is represented by: (name of lawyer and address).
    (b) _____ The defendant does not have a lawyer, is unable to afford or otherwise procure a lawyer, and hereby requests the appointment of a lawyer to represent the defendant in this proceeding. There are $ _____ in the defendant's prison account, and the defendant's other financial resources are: _____.
    (c) _____ The defendant does not want an attorney for the proceeding.

Respectfully submitted,

_____
Signature of Defendant

N. Sentencing

The imposition of sentence can be the most traumatic point in the trial, even greater than the return of the verdict. The legislature sets forth the maximum and minimum periods of imprisonment as well as the fine for each offense. Within these parameters, the trial judge has broad discretion in determining the sentence. Presently, the only limitation on the trial judge is that the reasons for the sentence must appear on the record.

The judgment of sentence is the final order entered in the case and permits the defendant to appeal. (See exhibit 2.13.)

EXHIBIT 2.13

IN THE COURT OF _____ OF _____ COUNTY, _____

Criminal Division

State of _____)
)   No. 812134

vs.   )
)

Sam Good   )

Application for Modification of Sentence

And now comes Defendant, Sam Good, by his attorney, R. C. Smith, and respectfully represents as follows:

1. Defendant was adjudged guilty, upon a two count indictment, of possession of marijuana and dealing in drugs.

2. On or about September 25, 1981, following receipt by the Court of a pre-sentence investigation, defendant appeared with counsel for sentencing and was sentenced by this Honorable Court to a term of imprisonment of not less than one year nor more than four years. In addition, defendant was fined $1,000.00.

3. Defendant immediately commenced serving that sentence.

4. As a matter of record, this defendant came before the Court as a first offender. It is respectfully submitted, the evidence in this case was insufficient to establish the offense of dealing in drugs but since the evidence of defendant's guilt on the charge of possession of marijuana was clear, an appeal did not appear warranted; it is respectfully submitted that as a first offender the sentence of imprisonment was not in accord with other sentences imposed in _____ County in similar instances. It is common for a first offender to receive probation.

5. It is respectfully submitted that the fine imposed was out of proportion to the severity of the offense, and the amount of the fine is beyond defendant's ability to pay, and it will create a severe financial hardship on defendant upon his release.

6. Defendant, since his trial in January of this year, has developed a novelty candle manufacturing business which he operated from his mother's home at _____; defendant was shipping his product to many parts of the country; after expenses, was realizing a net income of $150.00 to $175.00 per week. He was living a peaceful and law-abiding existence and he was well on the way to rehabilitating himself.

Defendant had registered his business as a fictitious name in _____ County under the name of Elvee Candle Co., as evidenced by a copy of his order form which is attached and made a part hereof and marked Exhibit "A". This business evidenced original ingenuity on the part of defendant because he was designing his own molds for candles and because he developed the process by his own initiative and experimentation. This business really evidenced defendant's ability to engage in productive and lawful activities. The sentence of imprisonment seriously interrupts these endeavors and only serves to discourage the defendant and his family who were satisfied that he was rehabilitating himself.

Wherefore, defendant respectfully requests that a Rule issue upon the State to show cause why the following relief should not be granted;

a) That a hearing be held to consider matters of rehabilitation as set forth herein;
b) That defendant be placed on probation;
c) That the fine be reduced in accord with defendant's ability to pay a fine.

                                                       R. C. Smith
                                                       Attorney for Defendant

O. Appellate Review

Within a specified period of days of the imposition of sentence, the defendant may appeal to the appellate court as of right. Briefs are filed by both parties, and oral argument may occur before a panel or other body of the superior court. Following argument, the court notifies the parties of its decision. The losing party may then seek review from the next highest court. Review is discretionary.

X. BASIC CRIMINAL PROCEDURE

A. Some Constitutional Considerations

A course in criminal procedure could take thirty weeks or more of any practitioner's time. The complexity of procedural law is due to its technical nature, its susceptibility to change, and its substantive depth. Critically important to note from the start is the influence of the federal Constitution on how the criminal process operates. An abridged list of constitutional amendments often cited in court cases follows.

- ☐ 1st: privacy, freedom of speech, religion, association
- ☐ 4th: search and seizure, warrants, probable cause
- ☐ 5th: federal due process, self-incrimination, double jeopardy
- ☐ 6th: confrontation, presence, jury trial, speedy trial, counsel
- ☐ 8th: cruel and unusual punishment, excessive bail and fines
- ☐ 14th: state due process, equal protection of the law

(See text of Constitution provided in appendix 2A.) The foregoing enumerates the essential standards or legal buzz words so frequently mentioned in the analysis of criminal procedure. How these amendments fit into the processing of criminal defendants is a recurring question. At best, the system endeavors to provide the most equitable justice affordable and approved by the society. At worst, the system defers the ideal standards of the Bill of Rights and hopes to improve shortly. Much can be criticized in our system of criminal process, but in a global, comparative sense, no nation holds a candle to the services provided.

1. Search and seizure

The fourth amendment prohibits *unreasonable* searches and seizures of the person, house, papers and effects, and no warrant shall issue but upon *probable cause*, supported by oath or affirmation and particularly describing the place to be searched and the things to be seized.

The right protects against *unreasonable* searches and seizures not only of tangible items but of the person as well. It applies *only* to searches and seizures made by public officials or those cooperating with them and not to searches by *private* citizens. It does not prohibit *reasonable* searches, and what is reasonable becomes a matter for judicial determination.

a. EXCLUSIONARY RULE

As guided by the fourth amendment, any search and seizure made in violation of a constitutional right is subject to being excluded from evidence, and additional evidence uncovered as a result of the initial violation of the right is subject to suppression under the theory that it is the "fruit of the poisonous tree."

b. LEGALITY OF ARREST

A police officer may arrest a person without a warrant for any offense when (1) the officer has reasonable cause to believe that such person has committed such offense in his or her *presence*; and (2) for a *crime* when the officer has reasonable cause to believe that such person has committed such crime, whether in his or her presence or otherwise.

The constitution does not use the word *arrest* but does use the word *seizure*. The seizure of a person occurs *whenever* his or her freedom to walk away is restricted.

There are three levels of justifiable police intrusion upon a citizen in a public place, short of an arrest, each in itself a form of seizure in which the person's liberty of movement is significantly interrupted. At the first level, a police officer may approach for the purpose of requesting information; at the second and more intense level, he has the common law right to inquire, which is activated by a founded suspicion that criminal activity is afoot; and at the third he has the statutory right to forcibly stop and detain a person when he entertains a reasonable suspicion that the person has committed, is committing, or is about to commit a felony or misdemeanor. [*Terry* v. *Ohio*, 392 U.S. 1.]

This last level of intrusion refers to what is known as stop and frisk.

A police officer may stop a person in a *public place* located within the geographical area of such officer's employment when he reasonably suspects that such person is committing, has committed or is about to commit either a felony, or a misdemeanor defined in the penal law, and may demand of him his name, address and an explanation of his conduct.

If he reasonably suspects that he is in danger of physical injury, he may search such person for a deadly weapon or any instrument, article, or substance readily capable of causing physical injury and of a sort not ordinarily carried in public places by law-abiding persons. If he finds such a weapon or instrument, or any other property possession of which he reasonably believes may constitute the commission of a crime, he may take it and keep it until the completion of the questioning, at which time he shall either return it, if lawfully possessed, or arrest the person.

Stop and frisk involves two different factual situations or suspicions. The intent of the officer in stopping to resolve an ambiguous situation is based upon reasonable suspicion, which is somewhat below "probable cause" required for an arrest. This does not justify an immediate frisk. A frisk is justified only when as a result of the stop, the officer believes he or she is in danger of physical injury from a weapon or instrument. The frisk consists only of a "pat down" of the outer clothing and cannot extend to the inner clothing unless such a "pat down" indicates the presence of a weapon or instrument that might endanger the officer.

c. Search Incident to Arrest, with or without a Warrant

A search incident to a lawful arrest is permissible. The search, however, must be only of the person and that immediate geographical area within his or her control, that is, the area from which the person might gain possession of a weapon or the ability to destroy evidence. The search must be substantially contemporaneous with the arrest. If the arrest is invalid, the results of the search must be suppressed.

d. Entry of Premises without a Warrant

Police may not make a warrantless and nonconsensual entry into a *suspect's home* in order to make a routine felony arrest. A "hot pursuit" of a felon who flees into a house is considered an "exigent circumstance" and is an exception to the rule.

The warrantless entry of a *third person's* premises to arrest a suspect *without a warrant to search* the third person's premises is invalid even though there is an outstanding arrest warrant for the suspect.

e. Motor Vehicles

One of the most difficult areas of the law of search and seizure deals with the stopping and searching of an automobile. Because of the transient nature of an automobile and the ability of its operator to move the vehicle and thus remove any evidence of wrongdoing before a search warrant can be obtained, special rules apply.

What was once called a general maintenance check of an auto and considered fully proper police function, has since been overturned by the Supreme Court in *Delaware* v. *Prouse*. A *roadblock* mechanism is now the only appropriate mode of checking a vehicle for maintenance of registration. Random selection is no longer permissible.

If the stopping results in a custodial arrest, the officer may search the occupants as incident to the arrest or necessary to protect the officer's safety. The extent to which the search may be extended into the interior of the automobile is another unclear question.

The U.S. Supreme Court has ruled that after the lawful arrest of the occupants of an automobile, the police may search the entire *interior* of the automobile. However, the trunk area of a car is still not clearly included, especially when one reviews various state rulings. (See exhibit 2.14.)

EXHIBIT 2.14

WAIVER OF SEARCH RIGHTS: AUTO

_____ 19 ____

STATE OF

COUNTY OF

I,_____ having been informed of my constitutional right not to have a search made of my automobile hereinafter mentioned without a search warrant and of my right to refuse to consent to such a search, hereby authorize _____ and _____ Officers of the _____ Police Department, _____, _____, to conduct a complete search of my automobile, a _____ registration _____.
These officers are authorized by me to take from my automobile any letters, papers, materials or other property which may have been involved in an unlawful act. I realize that anything found by said officers, that I cannot account for may be used as evidence against me in the event of a court trial.

This written permission is being given by me to the above named Police Officers voluntarily and without threats or promises of any kind.

Signed: _____

Witnesses:

_____

_____

_____

EXHIBIT 2.15

PERMISSION TO SEARCH

The undersigned, residing at _____ does hereby voluntarily authorize _____, and other officers he may designate to assist him, to search my residence (or other real property) located at _____ _____,
and my motor vehicle, namely my _____ bearing license plate number _____
 (year)   (make)
of the State of _____, presently parked or located at _____
_____
and I further authorize said officers to remove from my residence, real estate and/or motor vehicle, whatever documents, or items of property whatsoever which they deem pertinent to their investigation, with the understanding that said officers will give me a receipt for whatever is removed.

I am giving this written permission to these officers freely and voluntarily, without any threats or promises having been made, and after having been informed by said officer that I have a right to refuse this search and/or seizure.

_____
Signature

Witnesses:

_____

_____

Date: _____, 19 ____. Time _____ m.

f. Consent Searches

A person may consent to a warrantless search of his or her premises, vehicle, or possessions but the prosecution must show that the consent was voluntarily and freely given by the person. There is a presumption that a person who is in custody does not freely consent. A third person may consent to the search of premises provided that person has common or joint authority or control over the premises. (See exhibit 2.15.)

g. Search Warrants

To be valid, a search warrant must be issued by a neutral and detached magistrate. It must contain an adequate showing of probable cause to issue such warrant to search. Probable cause is defined as being where the facts and circumstances within the arresting officer's knowledge and of which they had reasonable trustworthy information are sufficient in themselves to warrant a man of reasonable caution in the belief that an offense has been committed or is being committed by the defendant. It must also satisfy the magistrate that the place to be searched contains the items connected with the criminal activity and must particularly describe the things to be seized and the persons to be searched. Thus, a warrant to search a building must describe the building, and the term does not include a vehicle found at the premises. A search warrant to search a bar does not allow for a search of unnamed persons or patrons at the establishment.

If a search warrant is based on an informant's statement, the affidavit must show his or her reliability. While the police do not have to reveal the name of the informant in the application, there must be a finding as by the magistrate to reliability. The name may have to be revealed if there is a suppression hearing granted as to the validity of the warrant to search.

The fact that the search may have resulted in finding evidence does not cure an invalid search warrant since probable cause must precede the arrest and/or search.

XI. SUPPRESSION OF "IN-COURT" IDENTIFICATION

The unreliability of eye-witness identification poses one of the serious problems in the administration of criminal justice. A majority of mistakes in identifying a suspect are attributable both to the inherent unreliability of human perception and memory of past events and the human susceptibility to unintended and often subtle suggestive influences. To insure "in-court" identification of a suspect by victims and witnesses to crime and to afford a defendant the constitutional right to due process and fair trial (fourteenth amendment) and to the aid of counsel (sixth amendment), a pretrial hearing, commonly called a Wade hearing from the Supreme Court case of that name, can be held when a defendant claims a suggestive identification has been made.

Lineup. A method of identification by which a number of persons are exhibited to a victim or witness and asked to pick out a suspect. Since the physical characteristics of the persons chosen to be in the lineup may be suggestive, the presence of counsel for the suspect *is required* as soon as a criminal proceeding is commenced or counsel has appeared for the suspect. The right to counsel *is not required* where:

1. criminal proceedings have not commenced or counsel appeared on behalf of the suspect,
2. photographic identification by display is made,
3. prompt on-the-scene one-to-one show ups take place, or
4. accidental or "unarranged" viewing of a suspect occurs.

However, all identification by means of viewing photographs or mug shots, lineups, or accidental show ups (chance viewing of a suspect) are subject to examination pretrial to determine whether they were in fact suggestive. This is under the due-process and fair-trial provisions of the fourteenth amendment. If found to be suggestive, an in-court identification by the victim or witness is suppressed. However, if prosecution can establish to the satisfaction of the pretrial judge, by clear and convincing evidence, that the in-court identification was by independent sources rather than stemming from an unfair pretrial confrontation, the court will allow the "in-court" identification by the witness.

An independent source exists when the court is able to find that the identifying witness, by drawing on his or her memory of the crime, has retained such a definite image of the suspect that the in-court identification can be made without dependence upon or assistance from a suggestive pretrial confrontation and unaffected by any observations, promptings, or suggestions that have taken place.

Of course, if the court cannot find any suggestiveness in the previous confrontation, it will allow in-court identification testimony.

XII. MOTION TO SUPPRESS STATEMENTS

Most state decisions have held that evidence of a written or oral "confession, admission or other statement made by a defendant, inculpatory or exculpatory, may not be admitted into evidence against him in a criminal proceeding if such statement was 'involuntarily made.'"

A *confession* is a direct admission of guilt. An *admission* is a declaration from which either alone or with other evidence, his guilty may be inferred. A *statement* is any declaration by a defendant that does not amount to a confession or admission or an exculpatory statement but which is sought to be used against a defendant in a criminal proceeding.

Since a statement "voluntarily made" is admissible and one "involuntarily made" is inadmissible, that preliminary issue must be determined before trial by a pretrial hearing often held on this very topic. In New York, as an example, it is a very specialized process.

A. Self-Incrimination

In the case of *Miranda* v. *Arizona*, 384 U.S. 436 (1966), the United States Supreme Court ruled that whenever questioning is initiated by law-enforcement officers after a person has been taken into *custody* or otherwise deprived of his or her freedom of action in any significant way, he or she must be given a four-fold warning:

1. The defendant must be warned, prior to any custodial interrogation, that he or she has a right to remain silent.
2. The defendant must be warned that anything he or she says to the police or prosecutor can be used against him or her in a court of law.
3. The defendant must be informed that he or she has a right to the presence of counsel of his or her own choosing prior to and during any interrogation.
4. The defendant must be informed that if he or she cannot afford to engage an attorney, one will be appointed for him or her prior to the questioning, and the defendant does not have to pay for such services.

The police officer or prosecutor is not required to recite *verbatim* the four warnings, but their full substance and meaning must be conveyed to the suspect in understandable terms so that he or she may decide whether or not to invoke that right, and as a practical matter, a verbatim reading is intelligent police behavior.

The Miranda warnings are required before any "custodial interrogation" may be validly made. Two issues arise. When is a person "in custody" and what is "interrogation"? The word *custody* is much broader than *arrest*. Even in the absence of a formal arrest, a person is in custody when the circumstances would lead a reasonable person to believe that he or she was not free to go. Statements made in the presence of the suspect, although not specifically directed to him or her, which invite an incriminating response have been held to be "interrogation" while in custody.

When the Miranda warnings have been given, the suspect may either waive his or her right to remain silent, usually in writing since the prosecution would have difficulty in proving an oral waiver, or the suspect may invoke his or her privilege, after which all questioning must cease until an attorney appears. Once an attorney appears or the suspect has invoked her or his right, no waiver is thereafter valid until counsel has appeared to advise the suspect. (See exhibit 2.16.)

B. Right to Counsel

All states must adhere to the sixth amendment's requirement that counsel be provided at custodial interrogation and other critical stages of the adversarial process. As a general rule, counsel should be provided at *arraignment, preliminary hearings, motion hearings on insanity or suppression, sentencing or transfer hearings, or competency hearings.*

Once an attorney obtained by or for a suspect has entered the proceeding, or the suspect has invoked his or her privilege, the suspect may not be questioned by the police or prosecutor except with the consent, and in the presence of, his or her attorney. If interrogation has already commenced, it must cease. It does not matter how or at whose request the attorney appears, or whether or not the defendant was even aware of such appearance. The attorney is not required to request the police not to interrogate and does not have to personally interrogate or personally inform the interrogating officers. Notice to the police station is considered notice to all officers. It is not important that the interrogation was noncustodial or that the client was a mere witness rather than a suspect.

EXHIBIT 2.16

CERTIFICATE OF
MIRANDA WARNING AND WAIVER

I hereby declare: That I am an officer of the _____ Department, and that on _____,
19___ at _____ m. I interviewed _____ at _____
         (time)   (location)
and that prior to that interview, and before any questioning, I advised the person named above the following:

"1. You have the right to remain silent.

2. Anything you say can and will be used against you in a court of law.

3. You have the right to talk to a lawyer and have him present with you while you are being questioned.

4. If you cannot afford to hire a lawyer, one will be appointed to represent you, before any questioning, if you wish one.

5. You can decide at any time to exercise these rights and not answer any questions or make any statements."

That after informing the person named above of the foregoing, I asked him if he understood the rights that I had stated, to which he replied: _____
_____
_____.

That I then asked him if, having in mind and understanding his rights, he was willing to talk to me, to which he replied: _____
_____

That the above answers were given freely and voluntarily, without the making of any threats or promises, and not under duress, pressure or coercion of any kind.

I declare under penalty of perjury that the foregoing is true and correct.

Executed at _____ on _____, 19 _____.

_____
Signature of Officer

DISCUSSION QUESTIONS AND PRACTICAL EXERCISES

1. Johnson and Smith are discussing Johnson's loss of $2,000 to Brown at poker the previous night. During the course of the conversation, Johnson says to Smith, "I hope someone gets him [Brown]." Johnson and Smith were best of friends. Johnson was surprised when Smith broke into Brown's house the next night while Brown was asleep and shot him. Brown survived the shooting. What types of criminal offenses could Johnson be charged with?

2. While Mr. and Mrs. Ryan are sleeping in their bedroom, O'Connell breaks into their house and shoots and kills Mr. Ryan. As O'Connell is making his escape, Mrs. Ryan, distraught at what she has just seen, takes her husband's rifle from his bedside table and shoots and kills O'Connell, who is in the driveway at the time. Mrs. Ryan could be charged with what possible offenses?

3. Washington walks into Sage Allen just before closing time. As he walks by the umbrella rack, he puts a collapsible umbrella under his coat and walks out without paying for it. What types of criminal offenses could Washington be charged with?

4. Rook is stopped by a police officer for a traffic violation. As the officer approaches Rook, the latter pulls a gun from his pocket, aims the gun at the police officer, and fires several shots in the officer's direction. The shots miss the police officer but strike D. Runk, killing him, and strike a store owner, injuring him. Briefly discuss what offenses C. Rook has committed.

5. Vinnie Jones and Mikey Smith were having drinks one afternoon in the Dead End Saloon when they were joined by Lefty Green. Smith, who had consumed seven beers and four highballs, said, "I need some dough—let's go rob a bank." Jones was reluctant at first but then said, "Sounds good to me." Green also agreed but insisted that he not go into the bank but remain behind the wheel of the getaway car. As they proceeded to leave the bar, the bartender hollered: "Hey, you guys didn't pay the bill!" Smith retorted, "So what, stick it in your ear!" All three then jumped into Lefty's car and left the bar.

   At the bank Jones and Smith walked up to the teller's counter while Green remained in the car. Jones, who was not armed, put his hand in his raincoat, causing it to protrude forward in the direction of a teller and said, "Hand over the dough or I'll blow you into next week." The frightened teller gave him several hundred dollars in cash. Jones and Smith then ran toward the door. As they neared the exit, they ran into Mrs. Feeble, who had just come in to cash her Social Security disability check. "Get out of the way, you old hag!" roared Smith and with a vicious shove pushed her to the pavement, causing her to bang her head. Smith and Jones then jumped into the waiting car and sped off.

Mrs. Feeble was rushed to the Little Hope Hospital where she died a few minutes later, the result of a severe concussion.

Jones, Smith, and Green have all been arrested as a result of this episode. What crimes may each be charged with, and what defenses, if any, might they use?

6. Chuck, a taxicab driver, one evening picked up as fares John, who was seventeen years old, and Mary, who was fifteen, but who looked two or three years older. John asked Chuck to drive them to some unfrequented place where he and Mary could have sexual relations without being bothered by the police. Chuck knew of an old deserted house outside the city limits and drove them there. He told them that he would wait for them. John broke open the front door, which was locked, and he and Mary went inside. About an hour later, Chuck saw flames inside the house and John and Mary came running out. Once inside the cab, Mary said that John had intentionally kicked over a lantern and started the fire, and that she was going to tell the police the whole story. John drew a revolver and threatened her. Chuck, with the idea of protecting Mary, tried to get the revolver away from John, and Mary at the same time struggled with John. While all three had their hands on the revolver, it went off, killing John.

Of what crime or crimes could each be convicted?

7. Review the facts, investigation, and evidence in the following case. Discuss the possible criminal charges that may be brought against the defendant. Discuss and decide what evidence the defendant may seek to have excluded and upon what legal grounds. Discuss what evidence may be admitted at trial.

Trooper Lane observes Blake swerving all over the highway for no apparent reason. Lane therefore pulls Blake over to the side of the road. As he approaches Blake's car, Lane notices in the back seat a package of what appears to be marijuana. When he reaches Blake, he is able to smell alcohol on Blake's breath. Lane then asks Blake to open the trunk of his car. When Blake refuses, Lane opens it with a crowbar. Inside is a gun. Thereupon, Blake confesses to having used the gun to kill Stevens.

ENRICHMENT ACTIVITY

Accompany a police officer to the scene of a crime and ask him or her to demonstrate and explain police investigative procedure. Periodically follow up on the investigation and chart the progression of the case until it has reached a final disposition, noting each stage of development.

SUGGESTED READING

CASPER, JONATHAN, D. *Criminal Courts: The Defendant's Perspective: Executive Summary*. Washington, D.C.: National Institute of Law Enforcement and Criminal Justice, Law Enforcement Assistance Administration, U.S. Dept. of Justice, Government Printing Office, 1978.

CLARK, E. C. *An Analysis of Criminal Liability*. Littleton, Colo.: F. B. ROTHMAN, 1983.

DEFOREST, PETER R., et al. *Forensic Science: An Introduction to Criminalistics*. New York: McGraw-Hill Book Co., 1983.

GILBERT, JAMES N. *Criminal Investigation*. Columbus, Ohio: Charles E. Merrill, 1980.

GRAY, CHARLES M., ed. *The Costs of Crime*. Beverly Hills, Calif.: Sage Publications, 1979.

GROSS, HYMAN. *A Theory of Criminal Justice*. New York: Oxford University Press, 1979.

HAGAN, FRANK E. *Research Methods in Criminal Justice and Criminology*. New York: Macmillan Co., 1982.

LEWIS, MERLIN, ET AL. *An Introduction to the Courts and Judicial Process*. Englewood Cliffs, N.J.: Prentice-Hall, 1978.

NEUBAUER, DAVID W. *America's Courts: The Criminal Justice System*. Monterey, Calif.: Brooks/Cole, 1984.

PONTELL, HENRY N. *A Capacity to Punish: The Ecology of Crime and Punishment*. Bloomington: Indiana University Press, 1984.

ARTICLES IN ADDITION TO, AND AMENDMENT OF, THE CONSTITUTION OF THE UNITED STATES OF AMERICA, PROPOSED BY CONGRESS, AND RATIFIED BY THE LEGISLATURES OF THE SEVERAL STATES PURSUANT TO THE FIFTH ARTICLE OF THE ORIGINAL CONSTITUTION

ARTICLE [I]*

Congress shall make no law respecting an establishment of religion, or prohibiting the free exercise thereof; or abridging the freedom of speech, or of the press; or the right of the people peaceably to assemble, and to petition the Government for a redress of grievances.

ARTICLE [II]

A well regulated Militia, being necessary to the security of a free State, the right of the people to keep and bear Arms, shall not be infringed.

ARTICLE [III]

No Soldier shall, in time of peace be quartered in any house, without the consent of the Owner, nor in time of war, but in a manner to be prescribed by law.

ARTICLE [IV]

The right of the people to be secure in their persons, houses, papers, and effects, against unreasonable searches and seizures, shall not be violated, and no Warrants shall issue, but upon probable cause, supported by Oath or affirmation, and particularly describing the place to be searched, and the persons or things to be seized.

ARTICLE [V]

No person shall be held to answer for a capital, or otherwise infamous crime, unless on a presentment or indictment of a Grand Jury, except in cases arising in the land or naval forces, or in the Militia, when in actual service in time of War or public danger; nor shall any person be subject for the same offence to be twice put in jeopardy of life or limb; nor shall be compelled in any criminal case to be a witness against himself, nor be deprived of life, liberty, or property, without due process of law; nor shall private property be taken for public use without just compensation.

ARTICLE [VI]

In all criminal prosecutions, the accused shall enjoy the right to a speedy and public trial, by an impartial jury of the State and district wherein the crime shall have been committed, which district shall have been previously ascertained by law, and to be informed of the nature and cause of the accusation; to be confronted with the witnesses against him; to have compulsory process for obtaining Witnesses in his favor, and to have the assistance of counsel for his defence.

ARTICLE [VII]

In Suits at common law, where the value in controversy shall exceed twenty dollars, the right of trial by jury shall be preserved, and no fact tried by a jury, shall be otherwise reexamined in any Court of the United States, than according to the rules of the common law.

---

*Only the 13th, 14th, 15th, and 16th articles of amendment had numbers assigned to them at the time of ratification.

ARTICLE [VIII]

Excessive bail shall not be required, nor excessive fines imposed, nor cruel and unusual punishments inflicted.

ARTICLE [IX]

The enumeration in the Constitution, of certain rights, shall not be construed to deny or disparage others retained by the people.

ARTICLE [X]

The powers not delegated to the United States by the Constitution, nor prohibited by it to the States, are reserved to the States respectively, or to the people.

The first 10 amendments to the Constitution, and 2 others that failed of ratification, were proposed by the Congress on September 25, 1789. They were ratified by the following States, and the notifications of the ratification by the Governors thereof were successively communicated by the President to the Congress: New Jersey, November 20, 1789; Maryland, December 19, 1789; North Carolina, December 22, 1789; South Carolina, January 19, 1790; New Hampshire, January 25, 1790; Delaware, January 28, 1790; New York, February 24, 1790; Pennsylvania, March 10, 1790; Rhode Island, June 7, 1790; Vermont, November 3, 1791; and Virginia, December 15, 1791.

Ratification was completed on December 15, 1791.

The amendments were subsequently ratified by Massachusetts, March 2, 1939; Georgia, March 18, 1939; and Connecticut, April 19, 1939.

ARTICLE [XI]

The Judicial power of the United States shall not be construed to extend to any suit in law or equity, commenced or prosecuted against one of the United States by Citizens of another State, or by Citizens or Subjects of any Foreign State.

The 11th amendment to the Constitution was proposed by the Congress on March 4, 1794. It was declared, in a message from the President to Congress, dated January 8, 1798 to have been ratified by the legislatures of 12 of the 15 States. The dates of ratification were: New York, March 27, 1794; Rhode Island, March 31, 1794; Connecticut, May 8, 1794; New Hampshire, June 16, 1794; Massachusetts, June 26, 1794; Vermont, between October 9, 1794 and November 9, 1794; Virginia, November 18, 1794; Georgia, November 29, 1794; Kentucky, December 7, 1794; Maryland, December 26, 1794; Delaware, January 23, 1795; North Carolina, February 7, 1795.

Ratification was completed on February 7, 1795.

The amendment was subsequently ratified by South Carolina on December 4, 1797. New Jersey and Pennsylvania did not take action on the amendment.

ARTICLE [XII]

The electors shall meet in their respective states and vote by ballot for President and Vice-President, one of whom, at least, shall not be an inhabitant of the same state with themselves; they shall name in their ballots the person voted for as President, and in distinct ballots the person voted for as Vice-President, and they shall make distinct lists of all persons voted for as President, and of all persons voted for as Vice-President, and of the number of votes for each, which lists they shall sign and certify, and transmit sealed to the seat of the government of the United States, directed to the President of the Senate;—The President of the Senate shall, in the presence of the Senate and House of Representatives, open all the certificates and the votes shall then be counted;—The person having the greatest number of votes for President, shall be the President, if such number be a majority of the whole number of Electors appointed; and if no person have such majority, then from the persons having the highest numbers not exceeding three on the list of those voted for as President, the House of Representatives shall choose immediately, by ballot, the President. But in choosing the President, the votes shall be taken by states, the representation from each state having one vote; a quorum for this purpose shall consist of a member or members from two-thirds of the states, and a majority of all the states shall be necessary to a choice. [And if the House of Representatives shall not choose a President whenever the right of choice shall devolve upon them, before the fourth day of March next following, then the Vice-President shall act as President, as in the case of the death or other constitutional disability of the President.]*   The person having the greatest number of votes as Vice-President, shall be the Vice-President, if such number be a majority of the whole number of Electors appointed, and if no person have a majority, then from the two highest numbers on the list, the Senate shall choose the Vice-President; a quorum for the purpose shall consist of two-thirds of the whole number of Senators, and a majority of the whole number shall be necessary to a choice.   But no person constitutionally ineligible to the office of President shall be eligible to that of Vice-President of the United States.

The 12th amendment to the Constitution was proposed by the Congress on December 9, 1803. It was declared, in a proclamation of the Secretary of State, dated September 25, 1804, to have been ratified by the legislatures of 13 of the 17 States. The dates of ratification were: North Carolina, December 21, 1803; Maryland, December 24, 1803; Kentucky, December 27, 1803; Ohio, December 30, 1803; Pennsylvania, January 5, 1804; Vermont, January 30, 1804; Virginia, February 3, 1804; New York, February 10, 1804; New Jersey, February 22, 1804; Rhode Island, March 12, 1804; South Carolina, May 15, 1804; Georgia, May 19, 1804; New Hampshire, June 15, 1804.

Ratification was completed on June 15, 1804.

The amendment was subsequently ratified by Tennessee, July 27, 1804.

The amendment was rejected by Delaware, January 18, 1804; Massachusetts, February 3, 1804; Connecticut, at its session begun May 10, 1804.

ARTICLE XIII

Section 1. Neither slavery nor involuntary servitude, except as a punishment for crime whereof the party shall have been duly convicted, shall exist within the United States, or any place subject to their jurisdiction.

Section 2. Congress shall have power to enforce this article by appropriate legislation.

The 13th amendment to the Constitution was proposed by the Congress on January 31, 1865.   It was declared, in a proclamation of the Secretary of State, dated December 18, 1865, to have been ratified by the legislatures of 27 of the 36 States.   The dates of ratification were: Illinois, February 1, 1865; Rhode Island, February 2, 1865; Michigan, February 2, 1865; Maryland, February 3, 1865; New York, February 3, 1865; Pennsylvania, February 3, 1865: West Virginia, February 3, 1865; Missouri, February 6, 1865; Maine, February 7, 1865; Kansas, February 7, 1865; Massachusetts, February 7, 1865; Virginia, February 9, 1865; Ohio, February 10, 1865; Indiana, February 13, 1865; Nevada, February 16, 1865; Louisiana, February 17, 1865; Minnesota, February 23, 1865; Wisconsin, February 24, 1865; Vermont, March 9, 1865; Tennessee, April 7, 1865; Arkansas, April 14, 1865; Connecticut, May 4, 1865; New Hampshire, July 1, 1865; South Carolina, November 13, 1865; Alabama, December 2, 1865; North Carolina, December 4, 1865; Georgia, December 6, 1865.

Ratification was completed on December 6, 1865.

The amendment was subsequently ratified by Oregon, December 8, 1865; California, December 19, 1865; Florida, December 28, 1865 (Florida again ratified on June 9, 1868, upon its adoption of a new constitution); Iowa, January 15, 1866; New Jersey, January 23, 1866 (after having rejected it on March 16, 1865); Texas, February 18, 1870; Delaware, February 12, 1901 (after having rejected it on February 8, 1865; Kentucky, March 18, 1976 (after having rejected it on February 24, 1865).

The amendment was rejected (and not subsequently ratified) by Mississippi, December 4, 1865.

ARTICLE XIV

Section 1. All persons born or naturalized in the United States, and subject to the jurisdiction thereof, are citizens of the United States and of the State wherein they reside.   No State shall make or enforce any law which shall abridge the privileges or immunities of citizens of the United States; nor shall any State deprive any person of life, liberty, or property, without due process of law; nor deny to any person within its jurisdiction the equal protection of the laws.

Section 2. Representatives shall be apportioned among the several States according to their respective numbers, counting the whole number of persons in each State, excluding Indians not taxed.   But when the right to vote at any election for the choice of electors for President and Vice President of the United States, Representatives in Congress,

---

*The part included in heavy brackets has been superseded by section 3 of the twentieth amendment.

the Executive and Judicial officers of a State, or the members of the Legislature thereof, is denied to any of the male inhabitants of such State, being twenty-one years of age,* and citizens of the United States, or in any way abridged, except for participation in rebellion, or other crime, the basis of representation therein shall be reduced in the proportion which the number of such male citizens shall bear to the whole number of male citizens twenty-one years of age in such State.

Section 3. No person shall be a Senator or Representative in Congress, or elector of President and Vice President, or hold any office, civil or military, under the United States, or under any State, who, having previously taken an oath, as a member of Congress, or as an officer of the United States, or as a member of any State legislature, or as an executive or judicial officer of any State, to support the Constitution of the United States, shall have engaged in insurrection or rebellion against the same, or given aid or comfort to the enemies thereof. But Congress may by a vote of two-thirds of each House, remove such disability.

Section 4. The validity of the public debt of the United States, authorized by law, including debts incurred for payment of pensions and bounties for services in suppressing insurrection or rebellion, shall not be questioned. But neither the United States nor any State shall assume or pay any debt or obligation incurred in aid of insurrection or rebellion against the United States, or any claim for the loss or emancipation of any slave; but all such debts, obligations and claims shall be held illegal and void.

Section 5. The Congress shall have power to enforce, by appropriate legislation, the provisions of this article.

The 14th amendment to the Constitution was proposed by the Congress on June 13, 1866. It was declared, in a certificate by the Secretary of State dated July 28, 1868, to have been ratified by the legislatures of 28 of the 37 States. The dates of ratification were: Connecticut, June 25, 1866; New Hampshire, July 6, 1866; Tennessee, July 19, 1866; New Jersey, September 11, 1866 (subsequently the legislature rescinded its ratification, and on March 5, 1868, readopted its resolution of rescission over the Governor's veto); Oregon, September 19, 1866 (and rescinded its ratification on October 15, 1868); Vermont, October 30, 1866; Ohio, January 4, 1867 (and rescinded its ratification on January 15, 1868); New York, January 10, 1867; Kansas, January 11, 1867; Illinois, January 15, 1867; West Virginia, January 16, 1867; Michigan, January 16, 1867; Minnesota, January 16, 1867; Maine, January 19, 1867; Nevada, January 22, 1867; Indiana, January 23, 1867; Missouri, January 25, 1867; Rhode Island, February 7, 1867; Wisconsin, February 7, 1867; Pennsylvania, February 12, 1867; Massachusetts, March 20, 1867; Nebraska, June 15, 1867; Iowa, March 16, 1868; Arkansas. April 6, 1868; Florida, June 9, 1868; North Carolina, July 4, 1868 (after having rejected it on December 14, 1866); Louisiana, July 9, 1868 (after having rejected it on February 6, 1867); South Carolina, July 9, 1868 (after having rejected it on December 20, 1866).

Ratification was completed on July 9, 1868.[1]

The amendment was subsequently ratified by Alabama, July 13 ,1868; Georgia, July 21, 1868 (after having rejected it on November 9, 1866); Virginia, October 8, 1869 (after having rejected it on January 9, 1867); Mississippi, January 17, 1870; Texas, February 18, 1870 (after having rejected it on October 27, 1866); Delaware, February 12, 1901 (after having rejected it on February 8, 1867); Maryland, April 4, 1959 (after having rejected it on March 23, 1867); California, May 6, 1959; Kentucky, March 18, 1976 (after having rejected it on January 8, 1867).

ARTICLE XV

Section 1. The right of citizens of the United States to vote shall not be denied or abridged by the United States or by any State on account of race, color, or previous condition of servitude.

Section 2. The Congress shall have power to enforce this article by appropriate legislation.

The 15th amendment to the Constitution was proposed by the Congress on February 26, 1869. It was declared, in a proclamation of the Secretary of State,

---

*See, the twenty-sixth amendment.

[1] The certificate of the Secretary of State, dated July 20, 1868 [15 Stat. 706, 707], was based on the assumption of invalidity of the rescission of ratification by Ohio and New Jersey. The following day, the Congress adopted a joint resolution declaring the amendment a part of the Constitution. On July 28, 1868, the Secretary of State issued a proclamation of ratification without reservation [15 Stat. 708–711]. In the interim, two other States, Alabama on July 13 and Georgia on July 21, 1868, had added their ratifications.

dated March 30, 1870, to have been ratified by the legislatures of 29 of the 37 States. The dates of ratification were: Nevada, March 1, 1869; West Virginia, March 3, 1869; Illinois, March 5, 1869; Louisiana, March 5, 1869; North Carolina, March 5, 1869; Michigan, March 8, 1869; Wisconsin, March 9, 1869; Maine, March 11, 1869; Massachusetts, March 12, 1869; Arkansas, March 15, 1869; South Carolina, March 15, 1869; Pennsylvania, March 25, 1869; New York, April 14, 1869 (and the legislature of the same State passed a resolution January 5, 1870, to withdraw its consent to it, which action it rescinded on March 30, 1970); Indiana, May 14, 1869; Connecticut, May 19, 1869; Florida, June 14, 1869; New Hampshire, July 1, 1869; Virginia, October 8, 1869; Vermont, October 20, 1869; Missouri, January 7, 1870; Minnesota, January 13, 1870; Mississippi, January 17, 1870; Rhode Island, January 18, 1870; Kansas, January 19, 1870; Ohio, January 27, 1870 (after having rejected it on April 30, 1869); Georgia, February 2, 1870; Iowa, February 3, 1870.

Ratification was completed on February 3, 1870, unless the withdrawal of ratification by New York was effective; in which event ratification was completed on February 17, 1870, when Nebraska ratified.

The amendment was subsequently ratified by Texas, February 18, 1870; New Jersey, February 15, 1871 (after having rejected it on February 7, 1870); Delaware, February 12, 1901 (after having rejected it on March 18, 1869); Oregon, February 24, 1959; California, April 3, 1962 (after having rejected it on January 28, 1870); Kentucky, March 18, 1976 (after having rejected it on March 12, 1869).

The amendment was approved by the Governor of Maryland, May 7, 1973; Maryland having previously rejected it on February 26, 1870.

The amendment was rejected (and not subsequently ratified) by Tennessee, November 16, 1869.

ARTICLE XVI

The Congress shall have power to lay and collect taxes on incomes, from whatever source derived, without apportionment among the several States, and without regard to any census or enumeration.

The 16th amendment to the Constitution was proposed by the Congress on July 12, 1909. It was declared, in a proclamation of the Secretary of State, dated February 25, 1913, to have been ratified by 36 of the 48 States. The dates of ratification were: Alabama, August 10, 1909; Kentucky, February 8, 1910; South Carolina, February 19, 1910; Illinois, March 1, 1910; Mississippi, March 7, 1910; Oklahoma, March 10, 1910; Maryland, April 8, 1910; Georgia, August 3, 1910; Texas, August 16, 1910; Ohio, January 19, 1911; Idaho, January 20, 1911; Oregon, January 23, 1911; Washington, January 26, 1911; Montana, January 30, 1911; Indiana, January 30, 1911; California, January 31, 1911; Nevada, January 31, 1911; South Dakota, February 3, 1911; Nebraska, February 9, 1911; North Carolina, February 11, 1911; Colorado, February 15, 1911; North Dakota, February 17, 1911; Kansas, February 18, 1911; Michigan, February 23, 1911; Iowa, February 24, 1911; Missouri, March 16, 1911; Maine, March 31, 1911; Tennessee, April 7, 1911; Arkansas, April 22, 1911 (after having rejected it earlier); Wisconsin, May 26, 1911; New York, July 12, 1911; Arizona, April 6, 1912; Minnesota, June 11, 1912; Louisiana, June 28, 1912; West Virginia, January 31, 1913; New Mexico, February 3, 1913.

Ratification was completed on February 3, 1913.

The amendment was subsequently ratified by Massachusetts, March 4, 1913; New Hampshire, March 7, 1913 (after having rejected it on March 2, 1911).

The amendment was rejected (and not subsequently ratified) by Connecticut, Rhode Island, and Utah.

ARTICLE [XVII]

The Senate of the United States shall be composed of two Senators from each State, elected by the people thereof, for six years; and each Senator shall have one vote. The electors in each State shall have the qualifications requisite for electors of the most numerous branch of the State legislatures.

When vacancies happen in the representation of any State in the Senate, the executive authority of such State shall issue writs of election to fill such vacancies: *Provided*, That the legislature of any State may empower the executive thereof to make temporary appointments until the people fill the vacancies by election as the legislature may direct.

This amendment shall not be so construed as to affect the election or term of any Senator chosen before it becomes valid as part of the Constitution.

The 17th amendment to the Constitution was proposed by the Congress on May 13, 1912. It was declared, in a proclamation by the Secretary of State, dated May 31, 1913, to have been ratified by the legislatures of 36 of the 48 States. The dates of ratification were: Massachusetts, May 22, 1912; Arizona, June 3, 1912; Minnesota, June 10, 1912; New York, January 15, 1913; Kansas,

January 17, 1913; Oregon, January 23, 1913; North Carolina, January 25, 1913; California, January 28, 1913; Michigan, January 28, 1913; Iowa, January 30, 1913; Montana, January 30, 1913; Idaho, January 31, 1913; West Virginia, February 4, 1913; Colorado, February 5, 1913; Nevada, February 6, 1913; Texas, February 7, 1913; Washington, February 7, 1913; Wyoming, February 8, 1913; Arkansas, February 11, 1913; Maine, February 11, 1913; Illinois, February 13, 1913; North Dakota, February 14, 1913; Wisconsin, February 18, 1913; Indiana, February 19, 1913; New Hampshire, February 19, 1913; Vermont, February 19, 1913; South Dakota, February 19, 1913; Oklahoma, February 24, 1913; Ohio, February 25, 1913; Missouri, March 7, 1913; New Mexico, March 13, 1913; Nebraska, March 14, 1913; New Jersey, March 17, 1913; Tennessee, April 1, 1913; Pennsylvania, April 2, 1913; Connecticut, April 8, 1913.

Ratification was completed on April 8, 1913.

The amendment was subsequently ratified by Louisiana, June 11, 1914.

The amendment was rejected (and not subsequently ratified) by Utah, February 26, 1913.

[ARTICLE [XVIII]

[SECTION 1. After one year from the ratification of this article the manufacture, sale, or transportation of intoxicating liquors within, the importation thereof into, or the exportation thereof from the United States and all territory subject to the jurisdiction thereof for beverage purposes is hereby prohibited.

[SECTION 2. The Congress and the several States shall have concurrent power to enforce this article by appropriate legislation.

[SECTION 3. This article shall be inoperative unless it shall have been ratified as an amendment to the Constitution by the legislatures of the several States, as provided in the Constitution, within seven years from the date of the submission hereof to the States by the Congress.]*

The 18th amendment to the Constitution was proposed by the Congress on December 18, 1917. It was declared, in a proclamation by the Acting Secretary of State, dated January 29, 1919, to have been ratified by the legislatures of 36 of the 48 States. The dates of ratification were: Mississippi, January 8, 1918; Virginia, January 11, 1918; Kentucky, January 14, 1918; North Dakota, January 25, 1918; South Carolina, January 29, 1918; Maryland, February 13, 1918; Montana, February 19, 1918; Texas, March 4, 1918; Delaware, March 18, 1918; South Dakota, March 20, 1918; Massachusetts, April 2, 1918; Arizona, May 24, 1918; Georgia, June 26, 1918; Louisiana, August 3, 1918; Florida, December 3, 1918; Michigan, January 2, 1919; Ohio, January 7, 1919; Oklahoma, January 7, 1919; Idaho, January 8, 1919; Maine, January 8, 1919; West Virginia, January 9, 1919; California, January 13, 1919; Tennessee, January 13, 1919; Washington, January 13, 1919; Arkansas, January 14, 1919; Kansas, January 14, 1919; Alabama, January 15, 1919; Colorado, January 15, 1919; Iowa, January 15, 1919; New Hampshire, January 15, 1919; Oregon, January 15, 1919; Nebraska, January 16, 1919; North Carolina, January 16, 1919; Utah, January 16, 1919; Missouri, January 16, 1919; Wyoming, January 16, 1919.

** Ratification was completed on January 16, 1919.

The amendment was subsequently ratified by Minnesota on January 17, 1917; Wisconsin, January 17, 1919; New Mexico, January 20, 1919; Nevada, January 21, 1919; New York, January 29, 1919; Vermont, January 29, 1919; Pennsylvania, February 25, 1919; Connecticut, May 6, 1919; and New Jersey, March 9, 1922.

The amendment was rejected (and not subsequently ratified) by Rhode Island.

ARTICLE [XIX]

The right of citizens of the United States to vote shall not be denied or abridged by the United States or by any State on account of sex.

Congress shall have power to enforce this article by appropriate legislation.

The 19th amendment to the Constitution was proposed by the Congress on June 4, 1919. It was declared, in a certificate by the Secretary of State, dated August 26, 1920, to have been ratified by the legislatures of 36 of the 48 States. The dates of ratification were: Illinois, June 10, 1919 (and that State readopted its resolution of ratification June 17, 1919); Michigan, June 10, 1919; Wisconsin, June 10, 1919; Kansas, June 16, 1919; New York, June 16, 1919; Ohio, June 16, 1919; Pennsylvania, June 24, 1919; Massachusetts, June 25, 1919; Texas, June 28, 1919; Iowa, July 2, 1919; Missouri, July 3, 1919; Arkansas, July 28, 1919; Montana, August 2, 1919; Nebraska, August 2, 1919; Minnesota, September 8, 1919; New Hampshire, September 10, 1919; Utah, October 2, 1919; California, Novem-

---

* Repealed by section 1 of the twenty-first amendment.
** See *Dillon* v. *Gloss*, 256 U.S. 368, 376 (1921).

ber 1, 1919; Maine, November 5, 1919; North Dakota, December 1, 1919; South Dakota, December 4, 1919; Colorado, December 15, 1919; Kentucky, January 6, 1920; Rhode Island, January 6, 1920; Oregon, January 13, 1920; Indiana, January 16, 1920; Wyoming, January 27, 1920; Nevada, February 7, 1920; New Jersey, February 9, 1920; Idaho, February 11, 1920; Arizona, February 12, 1920; New Mexico, February 21, 1920; Oklahoma, February 28, 1920; West Virginia, March 10, 1920; Washington, March 22, 1920; Tennessee, August 18, 1920.

Ratification was completed on August 18, 1920.

The amendment was subsequently ratified by Connecticut on September 14, 1920 (and that State reaffirmed on September 21, 1920); Vermont, February 8, 1921; Maryland, March 29, 1941 (after having rejected it on February 24, 1920; ratification certified on February 25, 1958); Virginia, February 21, 1952 (after rejecting it on February 12, 1920); Alabama, September 8, 1953 (after rejecting it on September 22, 1919); Florida, May 13, 1969; South Carolina, July 1, 1969 (after rejecting it on January 28, 1920; ratification certified on August 22, 1973); Georgia, February 20, 1970 (after rejecting it on July 24, 1919); Louisiana, June 11, 1970 (after rejecting it on July 1, 1920); North Carolina, May 6, 1971.

The amendment was rejected (and not subsequently ratified) by Mississippi, March 29, 1920; Delaware, June 2, 1920.

ARTICLE [XX]

SECTION 1. The terms of the President and Vice President shall end at noon on the 20th day of January, and the terms of Senators and Representatives at noon on the 3d day of January, of the years in which such terms would have ended if this article had not been ratified; and the terms of their successors shall then begin.

SECTION 2. The Congress shall assemble at least once in every year, and such meeting shall begin at noon on the 3d day of January, unless they shall by law appoint a different day.

SECTION 3.* If, at the time fixed for the beginning of the term of the President, the President elect shall have died, the Vice President elect shall become President. If a President shall not have been chosen before the time fixed for the beginning of his term, or if the President elect shall have failed to qualify, then the Vice President elect shall act as President until a President shall have qualified; and the Congress may by law provide for the case wherein neither a President elect nor a Vice President elect shall have qualified, declaring who shall then act as President, or the manner in which one who is to act shall be selected, and such person shall act accordingly until a President or Vice President shall have qualified.

SECTION 4. The Congress may by law provide for the case of the death of any of the persons from whom the House of Representatives may choose a President whenever the right of choice shall have devolved upon them, and for the case of the death of any of the persons from whom the Senate may choose a Vice President whenever the right of choice shall have devolved upon them.

SECTION 5. Sections 1 and 2 shall take effect on the 15th day of October following the ratification of this article.

SECTION 6. This article shall be inoperative unless it shall have been ratified as an amendment to the Constitution by the legislatures of three-fourths of the several States within seven years from the date of its submission.

The 20th amendment to the Constitution was proposed by the Congress on March 2, 1932. It was declared, in a certificate by the Secretary of State, dated February 6, 1933, to have been ratified by the legislatures of 36 of the 48 States. The dates of ratification were: Virginia, March 4, 1932; New York, March 11, 1932; Mississippi, March 16, 1932; Arkansas, March 17, 1932; Kentucky, March 17, 1932; New Jersey, March 21, 1932; South Carolina, March 25, 1932; Michigan, March 31, 1932; Maine, April 1, 1932; Rhode Island, April 14, 1932; Illinois, April 21, 1932; Louisiana, June 22, 1932; West Virginia, July 30, 1932; Pennsylvania, August 11, 1932; Indiana, August 15, 1932; Texas, September 7, 1932; Alabama, September 13, 1932; California, January 4, 1933; North Carolina, January 5, 1933; North Dakota, January 9, 1933; Minnesota, January 12, 1933; Arizona, January 13, 1933; Montana, January 13, 1933; Nebraska, January 13, 1933; Oklahoma, January 13, 1933; Kansas, January 16, 1933; Oregon, January 16, 1933; Delaware, January 19, 1933; Washington, January 19, 1933; Wyoming, January 19, 1933; Iowa, January 20, 1933; South Dakota, January 20, 1933; Tennessee, January 20, 1933; Idaho, January 21, 1933; New Mexico, January 21, 1933; Georgia, January 23, 1933; Missouri, January 23, 1933; Ohio, January 23, 1933; Utah, January 23, 1933.

Ratification was completed on January 23, 1933.

*See, the twenty-fifth amendment.

The amendment was subsequently ratified by Massachusetts on January 24, 1933; Wisconsin, January 24, 1933; Colorado, January 24, 1933; Nevada, January 26, 1933; Connecticut, January 27, 1933; New Hampshire, January 31, 1933; Vermont, February 2, 1933; Maryland, March 24, 1933; Florida, April 26, 1933.

ARTICLE [XXI]

SECTION 1. The eighteenth article of amendment to the Constitution of the United States is hereby repealed.

SECTION 2. The transportation or importation into any State, Territory, or possession of the United States for delivery or use therein of intoxicating liquors, in violation of the laws thereof, is hereby prohibited.

SECTION 3. This article shall be inoperative unless it shall have been ratified as an amendment to the Constitution by conventions in the several States, as provided in the Constitution, within seven years from the date of the submission hereof to the States by the Congress.

The 21st amendment to the Constitution was proposed by the Congress on February 20, 1933. It was declared, in a certificate of the Acting Secretary of State, dated December 5, 1933, to have been ratified by conventions in 36 of the 48 States. The dates of ratification were: Michigan, April 10, 1933; Wisconsin, April 25, 1933; Rhode Island, May 8, 1933; Wyoming, May 25, 1933; New Jersey, June 1, 1933; Delaware, June 24, 1933; Indiana, June 26, 1933; Massachusetts, June 26, 1933; New York, June 27, 1933; Illinois, July 10, 1933; Iowa, July 10, 1933; Connecticut, July 11, 1933; New Hampshire, July 11, 1933; California, July 24, 1933; West Virginia, July 25, 1933; Arkansas, August 1, 1933; Oregon, August 7, 1933; Alabama, August 8, 1933; Tennessee, August 11, 1933; Missouri, August 29, 1933; Arizona, September 5, 1933; Nevada, September 5, 1933; Vermont, September 23, 1933; Colorado, September 26, 1933; Washington, October 3, 1933; Minnesota, October 10, 1933; Idaho, October 17, 1933; Maryland, October 18, 1933; Virginia, October 25, 1933; New Mexico, November 2, 1933; Florida, November 14, 1933; Texas, November 24, 1933; Kentucky, November 27, 1933; Ohio, December 5, 1933; Pennsylvania, December 5, 1933; Utah, December 5, 1933.

Ratification was completed on December 5, 1933.

The amendment was subsequently ratified by Maine, December 6, 1933; Montana, August 6, 1934.

The amendment was rejected (and not subsequently ratified) by South Carolina, December 4, 1933.

ARTICLE [XXII]

SECTION 1. No person shall be elected to the office of the President more than twice, and no person who has held the office of President, or acted as President, for more than two years of a term to which some other person was elected President shall be elected to the office of the President more than once. But this Article shall not apply to any person holding the office of President when this Article was proposed by the Congress, and shall not prevent any person who may be holding the office of President, or acting as President, during the term within which this Article becomes operative from holding the office of President or acting as President during the remainder of such term.

SECTION 2. This article shall be inoperative unless it shall have been ratified as an amendment to the Constitution by the legislatures of three-fourths of the several States within seven years from the date of its submission to the States by the Congress.

The 22d amendment to the Constitution was proposed by the Congress on March 21, 1947. It was declared, in a certificate by the Administrator of General Services, dated March 1, 1951, to have been ratified by the legislatures of 36 of the 48 States. The dates of ratification were: Maine, March 31, 1947; Michigan, March 31, 1947; Iowa, April 1, 1947; Kansas, April 1, 1947; New Hampshire, April 1, 1947; Delaware, April 2, 1947; Illinois, April 3, 1947; Oregon, April 3, 1947; Colorado, April 12, 1947; California, April 15, 1947; New Jersey, April 15, 1947; Vermont, April 15, 1947; Ohio, April 16, 1947; Wisconsin, April 16, 1947; Pennsylvania, April 29, 1947; Connecticut, May 21, 1947; Missouri, May 22, 1947; Nebraska, May 23, 1947; Virginia, January 28, 1948; Mississippi, February 12, 1948; New York, March 9, 1948; South Dakota, January 21, 1949; North Dakota, February 25, 1949; Louisiana, May 17, 1950; Montana, January 25, 1951; Indiana, January 29, 1951; Idaho, January 30, 1951; New Mexico, February 12, 1951; Wyoming, February 12, 1951; Arkansas, February 15, 1951; Georgia, February 17, 1951; Tennessee, February 20, 1951; Texas, February 22, 1951; Nevada, February 26, 1951; Utah, February 26, 1951; Minnesota, February 27, 1951.

Ratification was completed on February 27, 1951.

The amendment was subsequently ratified by North Carolina on February 28,

1951; South Carolina, March 13, 1951; Maryland, March 14, 1951; Florida, April 16, 1951; Alabama, May 4, 1951.

The amendment was rejected (and not subsequently ratified) by Oklahoma in June 1947; Massachusetts, June 9, 1949.

ARTICLE [XXIII]

SECTION 1. The District constituting the seat of Government of the United States shall appoint in such manner as the Congress may direct:

A number of electors of President and Vice President equal to the whole number of Senators and Representatives in Congress to which the District would be entitled if it were a State, but in no event more than the least populous State; they shall be in addition to those appointed by the States, but they shall be considered, for the purposes of the election of President and Vice President, to be electors appointed by a State; and they shall meet in the District and perform such duties as provided by the twelfth article of amendment.

SECTION 2. The Congress shall have power to enforce this article by appropriate legislation.

The 23d amendment to the Constitution was proposed by the Congress on June 17, 1960. It was declared, in a certificate by the Administrator of General Services, to have been ratified by 38 of the 50 States. The dates of ratification were: Hawaii, June 23, 1960 (and that State made a technical correction to its resolution on June 30, 1960); Massachusetts, August 22, 1960; New Jersey, December 19, 1960; New York, January 17, 1961; California, January 19, 1961; Oregon, January 27, 1961; Maryland, January 30, 1961; Idaho, January 31, 1961; Maine, January 31, 1961; Minnesota, January 31, 1961; New Mexico, February 1, 1961; Nevada, February 2, 1961; Montana, February 6, 1961; South Dakota, February 6, 1961; Colorado, February 8, 1961; Washington, February 9, 1961; West Virginia, February 9, 1961; Alaska, February 10, 1961; Wyoming, February 13, 1961; Delaware, February 20, 1961; Utah, February 21, 1961; Wisconsin, February 21, 1961; Pennsylvania, February 28, 1961; Indiana, March 3, 1961; North Dakota, March 3, 1961; Tennessee, March 6, 1961; Michigan, March 8, 1961; Connecticut, March 9, 1961; Arizona, March 10, 1961; Illinois, March 14, 1961; Nebraska, March 15, 1961; Vermont, March 15, 1961; Iowa, March 16, 1961; Missouri, March 20, 1961; Oklahoma, March 21, 1961; Rhode Island, March 22, 1961; Kansas, March 29, 1961; Ohio, March 29, 1961.

Ratification was completed on March 29, 1961.

The amendment was subsequently ratified by New Hampshire on March 30, 1961 (when that State annulled and then repeated its ratification of March 29, 1961).

The amendment was rejected (and not subsequently ratified) by Arkansas on January 24, 1961.

ARTICLE [XXIV]

SECTION 1. The right of citizens of the United States to vote in any primary or other election for President or Vice President, for electors for President or Vice President, or for Senator or Representative in Congress, shall not be denied or abridged by the United States or any State by reason of failure to pay any poll tax or other tax.

SEC. 2. The Congress shall have power to enforce this article by appropriate legislation.

The 24th amendment to the Constitution was proposed by the Congress on August 27, 1962. It was declared, in a certificate of the Administrator of General Services, dated February 4, 1964, to have been ratified by the legislatures of 38 of the 50 States. The dates of ratification were: Illinois, November 14, 1962; New Jersey, December 3, 1962; Oregon, January 25, 1963; Montana, January 28, 1963; West Virginia, February 1, 1963; New York, February 4, 1963; Maryland, February 6, 1963; California, February 7, 1963; Alaska, February 11, 1963; Rhode Island, February 14, 1963; Indiana, February 19, 1963; Utah, February 20, 1963; Michigan, February 20, 1963; Colorado, February 21, 1963; Ohio, February 27, 1963; Minnesota, February 27, 1963; New Mexico, March 5, 1963; Hawaii, March 6, 1963; North Dakota, March 7, 1963; Idaho, March 8, 1963; Washington, March 14, 1963; Vermont, March 15, 1963; Nevada, March 19, 1963; Connecticut, March 20, 1963; Tennessee, March 21, 1963; Pennsylvania, March 25, 1963; Wisconsin, March 26, 1963; Kansas, March 28, 1963; Massachusetts, March 28, 1963; Nebraska, April 4, 1963; Florida, April 18, 1963; Iowa, April 24, 1963; Delaware, May 1, 1963; Missouri, May 13, 1963; New Hampshire, June 12, 1963; Kentucky, June 27, 1963; Maine, January 16, 1964; South Dakota, January 23, 1964.

Ratification was completed on January 23, 1964.

The amendment was rejected (and not subsequently ratified) by Mississippi on December 20, 1962.

ARTICLE [XXV]

SECTION 1. In case of the removal of the President from office or of his death or resignation, the Vice President shall become President.

SEC. 2. Whenever there is a vacancy in the office of the Vice President, the President shall nominate a Vice President who shall take office upon confirmation by a majority vote of both Houses of Congress.

SEC. 3. Whenever the President transmits to the President pro tempore of the Senate and the Speaker of the House of Representatives his written declaration that he is unable to discharge the powers and duties of his office, and until he transmits to them a written declaration to the contrary, such powers and duties shall be discharged by the Vice President as Acting President.

SEC. 4. Whenever the Vice President and a majority of either the principal officers of the executive departments or of such other body as Congress may by law provide, transmit to the President pro tempore of the Senate and the Speaker of the House of Representatives their written declaration that the President is unable to discharge the powers and duties of his office, the Vice President shall immediately assume the powers and duties of the office as Acting President.

Thereafter, when the President transmits to the President pro tempore of the Senate and the Speaker of the House of Representatives his written declaration that no inability exists, he shall resume the powers and duties of his office unless the Vice President and a majority of either the principal officers of the executive department or of such other body as Congress may by law provide, transmit within four days to the President pro tempore of the Senate and the Speaker of the House of Representatives their written declaration that the President is unable to discharge the powers and duties of his office. Thereupon Congress shall decide the issue, assembling within forty-eight hours for that purpose if not in session. If the Congress, within twenty-one days after receipt of the latter written declaration, or, if Congress is not in session, within twenty-one days after Congress is required to assemble, determines by two-thirds vote of both Houses that the President is unable to discharge the powers and duties of his office, the Vice President shall continue to discharge the same as Acting President; otherwise, the President shall resume the powers and duties of his office.

The 25th amendment to the Constitution was proposed by the Congress on July 6, 1965. It was declared, in a certificate of the Administrator of General Services, dated February 23, 1967, to have been ratified by the legislatures of 39 of the 50 States. The dates of ratification were: Nebraska, July 12, 1965; Wisconsin, July 13, 1965; Oklahoma, July 16, 1965; Massachusetts, August 9, 1965; Pennsylvania, August 18, 1965; Kentucky, September 15, 1965; Arizona, September 22, 1965; Michigan, October 5, 1965; Indiana, October 20, 1965; California, October 21, 1965; Arkansas, November 4, 1965; New Jersey, November 29, 1965; Delaware, December 7, 1965; Utah, January 17, 1966; West Virginia, January 20, 1966; Maine, January 24, 1966; Rhode Island, January 28, 1966; Colorado, February 3, 1966; New Mexico, February 3, 1966; Kansas, February 8, 1966; Vermont, February 10, 1966; Alaska, February 18, 1966; Idaho, March 2, 1966; Hawaii, March 3, 1966; Virginia, March 8, 1966; Mississippi, March 10, 1966; New York, March 14, 1966; Maryland, March 23, 1966; Missouri, March 30, 1966; New Hampshire, June 13, 1966; Louisiana, July 5, 1966; Tennessee, January 12, 1967; Wyoming, January 25, 1967; Washington, January 26, 1967; Iowa, January 26, 1967; Oregon, February 2, 1967; Minnesota, February 10, 1967; Nevada, February 10, 1967.

Ratification was completed on February 10, 1967.

The amendment was subsequently ratified by Connecticut, February 14, 1967; Montana, February 15, 1967; South Dakota, March 6, 1967; Ohio, March 7, 1967; Alabama, March 14, 1967; North Carolina, March 22, 1967; Illinois, March 22, 1967; Texas, April 25, 1967; Florida, May 25, 1967.

ARTICLE [XXVI]

SECTION 1. The right of citizens of the United States, who are eighteen years of age or older, to vote shall not be denied or abridged by the United States or by any State on account of age.

SEC. 2. The Congress shall have power to enforce this article by appropriate legislation.

The 26th amendment to the Constitution was proposed by the Congress on March 23, 1971. It was declared, in a certificate of the Administrator of General Services, dated July 5, 1971, to have been ratified by the legislatures of 39 of the 50 States. The dates of ratification were: Connecticut, March 23, 1971; Delaware, March 23, 1971; Minnesota, March 23, 1971; Tennessee, March 23, 1971; Washington, March 23, 1971; Hawaii, March 24, 1971; Massachusetts, March 24, 1971; Montana, March 29, 1971; Arkansas, March 30, 1971; Idaho, March 30, 1971; Iowa, March 30, 1971; Nebraska, April 2, 1971; New Jersey, April 3, 1971; Kansas, April 7, 1971; Michigan, April 7, 1971; Alaska, April 8, 1971; Maryland, April 8, 1971; Indiana, April 8, 1971; Maine, April 9, 1971; Vermont, April 16, 1971; Louisiana, April 17, 1971; California, April 19, 1971; Colorado, April 27, 1971; Pennsylvania, April 27, 1971; Texas, April 27, 1971; South Carolina, April 28, 1971; West Virginia, April 28, 1971; New Hampshire, May 13, 1971; Arizona, May 14, 1971; Rhode Island, May 27, 1971; New York, June 2, 1971; Oregon, June 4, 1971; Missouri, June 14, 1971; Wisconsin, June 22, 1971; Illinois, June 29, 1971; Alabama, June 30, 1971; Ohio, June 30, 1971; North Carolina, July 1, 1971; Oklahoma, July 1, 1971.

Ratification was completed on July 1, 1971.

The amendment was subsequently ratified by Virginia, July 8, 1971; Wyoming, July 8, 1971; Georgia, October 4, 1971.

[EDITORIAL NOTE: There is some conflict as to the exact dates of ratification of the amendments by the several States. In some cases, the resolutions of ratification were signed by the officers of the legislatures on dates subsequent to that on which the second house had acted. In other cases, the Governors of several of the States "approved" the resolutions (on a subsequent date), although action by the Governor is not contemplated by article V, which requires ratification by the legislatures (or conventions) only. In a number of cases, the journals of the State legislatures are not available. The dates set out in this document are based upon the best information available.]

CHAPTER THREE

LEGAL INVESTIGATIONS

CHAPTER DESCRIPTION

In this chapter, we discuss the various means of conducting criminal and civil investigations. Emphasis is on techniques for gathering information from various records and witnesses.

PARALEGAL FUNCTIONS

Investigate criminal and civil cases.

Prepare investigations and write reports.

Interview potential witnesses.

I. ROLE OF THE PARALEGAL IN LEGAL INVESTIGATIONS

Remember the TV series "Columbo"? Peter Falk did a splendid job of portraying a rumpled, raincoated, seemingly less-than-intelligent police detective. On closer inspection, Columbo was really a kind of detective genius. First, Columbo always religiously tried to recreate events as he thought they probably happened. Step by step, his mind sought reconstruction of the event much to the irritation of his suspected offenders. Second, Columbo gave unflagging attention to detail, minutiae that at first seemed trivial and irrelevant. That dedication to the smaller items in the larger picture of a crime scene usually solved his crime. Third, Columbo always saw his suspects in a human sense, for he always played on their faults, whether greed, lust, or power seeking. In sum, Columbo knew the foibles so common to all of us, and he was brilliant at tying them into his criminal investigation. Call it motive or inclination, but whatever case he was on, he always seemed to know from the very start who the perpetrator was. Lastly, Columbo was doggedly persistent in his drive to solve the crime, so much so that he drove everyone around him crazy. That persistence, no matter how tiring, was what made him the accomplished investigator he was. In the final analysis, these traits—*organizational ability, attention to detail, human perception, and unswerving persistence*—make a successful investigator.

As paralegals, you will find these very traits essential to success just as with Columbo. One of the major reasons for the growth of the paralegal profession has been the increased investigatory role paralegals play for their employers. Paralegals must become adept in the collection of information and in documentation and preparation of reports; they must be prepared to organize materials for both trials and appeals; they must enhance their human-relations skills and work effectively with numerous agencies, from the police to hospitals, and they must provide the firm or other employer with insightful, relevant evidence, witnesses, and other needed material.

More and more, then, firms are delegating investigation to their paralegals and the trend is likely to continue.

II. GENERAL PRINCIPLES OF INVESTIGATION

A. Characteristics of a Good Investigation

Regardless of whether a case is criminal or civil in content, investigative strategy is fundamentally the same. While the record keeping and other strategies may be slightly different in the two major actions, the investigator must keep the following points in mind:

   1. Each investigator is a unique individual and has his or her own methods. Do not assume that there is only one road to the answers.

   2. Experience is the greatest teacher in the field of investigation. Expect to make mistakes. Do not be surprised when what seemed to be an essential clue or theory turns out to be inadequate.

   3. Hustle, imagination, and mental and emotional flexibility are attributes every investigator should possess. Investigation is an offensive science, not a reactive or passive discipline.

   4. The investigator must be guided by goals and priorities. The investigator must be open-minded enough to be receptive to the unexpected and to come up with leads that may not be readily at his or her fingertips.

   5. Investigation is closely related to negotiation and trial. The investigator must always keep two questions in mind while conducting an investigation: How will this fact assist or hurt the firm in attempting to settle or negotiate the case without a trial? How will this fact assist or hurt the office in presenting the client's case at trial?

      An investigator's report will often be a valuable tool that can be used by an attorney at a settlement conference or as a basis for decisions relating to the actual trial of a case. Some of the ways a report can help the attorney are as follows:

□ Deciding whether or not to go to trial

□ Deciding which witness to call

□ Deciding what questions to ask of witnesses

□ Deciding how to attach the credibility of opposing witnesses

□ Deciding what physical evidence to produce

□ Deciding how to attack the physical evidence produced by the other side

6. The investigator must be able to distinguish between "absolute proof of fact" and "some evidence of a fact." (The following tests should be used by the investigator to determine whether or not a particular fact should be pursued).

□ Am I reasonable in assuming that a particular fact will help to establish the case of the client?

□ Am I reasonable in assuming that if I can gather evidence on such a fact a judge, jury, or hearing officer might accept it as true?

□ Am I reasonable in assuming that a particular fact will help to challenge or discredit the case of the opposing party?

□ Am I reasonable in assuming that I can gather enough evidence to challenge or discredit the case of the other side and that a judge, jury, or hearing officer might accept it as true?

7. The investigator must know the territory. The investigator's knowledge of the area should include:

□ *The political structure of the area.* Who are the political powerbrokers in the community? Who is the opposition? In what direction is the political structure headed?

□ *The social and cultural structure of the area.* Are there racial problems? Are there ethnic groupings that are diffuse or unified? Are there different value systems at play?

□ *Miscellaneous specific information.* If you want to get something done at City Hall, whom do you see? Does the director of a particular agency have control over his or her staff? What agencies offer services that might be helpful to an investigator? Which court clerk is most helpful?

B. Fundamental Steps in the Investigation Process

1. Preliminary investigation

All cases require a preliminary assessment and analysis. In order to facilitate this review, an investigator should begin the accumulation of data immediately.

A successful investigator must also be skilled at preliminary observation. As examples, if there is a crime, is it possible to visit the crime scene for observation? The same question can be asked in an auto accident or other mishap. Next, is the investigator keeping in close contact with the appropriate agencies responsible for the processing and custodial control of evidence? Once the investigator has preliminarily evaluated the scene and compiled a general list of evidentiary matter, he or she is in good stead. He or she has trapped the time and event as well as can be expected. From this stage on, the investigator must provide the answers to five fundamental investigative questions:

□ *WHAT* caused this event to happen?

□ *WHO* is responsible for this act?

□ *WHERE* did the event take place?

□ *WHEN* did the event take place?

□ *HOW* did the event take place?

Good investigative practice suggests that the paralegal draw a diagram of the scene. Use as a model the diagram in figure 3.1. That completed diagram will be a permanent reflection of the perceptions you had the day of the observation. Photography can serve the very same purpose and be even more objective. Review figure 3.2.

As paralegals, we must go one step further. To insure the best possible legal slant on the investigative process, cite legal issues or queries countered by a proposed resolution. Call the resolution a proposition. Use figure 3.3 as a format.

2. The gathering of information

Preliminary questions aside, the investigator now has more than enough issues to work with. These propositions, suppositions, deductions, and inferences are at best educated conjecture that now must be demonstrated by law and scientific evidence. Therefore, information gathering becomes integral to a successful case. What kinds of information are required?

FIGURE 3.1

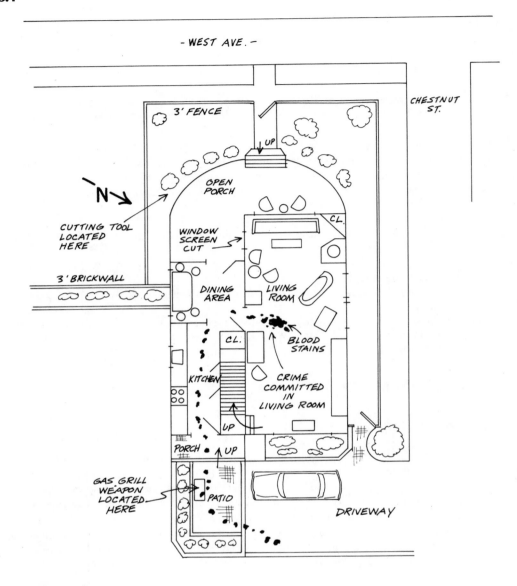

a. Reports and Documentation

Field Notes. In any regular criminal or civil case, law-enforcement authorities commonly take field notes in their daily investigative process. While such information is not freely discoverable, a paralegal with solid police contacts can frequently gain access to an officer's recollection. This source of information is merely one of many in which a paralegal's contacts, connections, and general approach are his or her most formidable allies. On the whole, a good investigator can really get any information he or she wants.

Crime or Accident Reports. Exhibits 3.1 and 3.2 are examples of crime and offense reports. Generally, these reports are the freshest accounts possible on the events under investigation since officers will respond quickly to the scene of a crime. While these reports are not public record, possibly they are discoverable in some jurisdictions. In other jurisdictions, they may be deemed work products and hence not discoverable.

Other Official Reports. Opportunities exist also to collect a wealth of other official documentation that may assist the investigative effort. A short summary follows.

Alcohol influence reports	(see exhibit 3.3)
Arrest reports	(see exhibit 3.4)
Forensic examination request	(see exhibit 3.5)

FIGURE 3.2

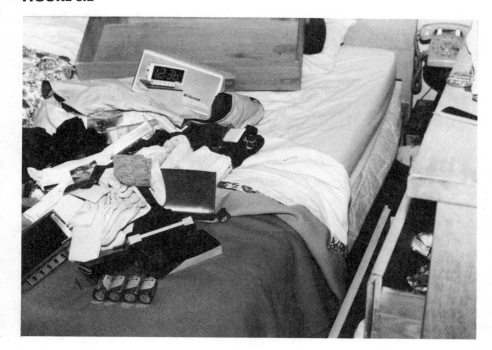

The area that was "burgled" must be photographed to prove the crime and for possible clues that might show reason for the crime. (Example: Was this the only room "hit" or did "time run out" for the burglar? Or did the burglar know what and where the specific item(s) were stored?) A thorough job of photography will assist the investigator(s) and the prosecutor at time of trial.

FIGURE 3.3

Client _____
Nature of Case _____
Date Prepared _____
Prepared by _____

TO: _____
RE: Issues and Relevant Law

Issues
1. _____
2. _____
3. _____
4. _____

PROPOSITION	CITATION
1.	
2.	
3.	
4.	
5.	

EXHIBIT 3.1

1. NATURE OF INCIDENT	2. DATE	3. TIME	4. CLASSIFICATION	5. COMPLAINT NUMBER			
6. VICTIM – COMPLAINANT – ACCUSED			RACE	SEX	D.O.B.	S.S.	
7. ADDRESS - NUMBER - STREET - MUNICIPALITY - ZIP			8. PHONE				
9. LOCATION OF INCIDENT							
10. REPORTED BY:			RADIO	PHONE	VIEW	OTHER	
11. ADDRESS - NUMBER - STREET - MUNICIPALITY - STATE - ZIP			12. PHONE				
13.							
14.							

15. ACTION TAKEN:

16. SIGNATURE _____	17. BADGE NO.	18. HOURS	19. DATE	20. REVIEWED	21. PENDING	22. COMPLETE

EXHIBIT 3.2

1. Complaint Number	21. Prosecutor's Case Number	22. Department Case Number

75. Name		76. Badge Number	77. Page	78. Date Report	79. Reviewed By
			80.	81.	82.
Signature _____					

EXHIBIT 3.3a

<table>
<tr><td colspan="2">

(Check)   (Check)
☐ Driver   ☐ Accident
☐ Pedestrian ☐ Violation
☐ Passenger ☐ Other

Date and time of
Accident or Violation _____ am/pm
</td>
<td>

ALCOHOLIC
INFLUENCE
REPORT FORM
</td>
<td>

Police Dept. _____
Arrest No. _____
Accident No. _____
Arresting Officer _____
Date and time in custody_____ am/pm
</td></tr>
</table>

Name_____ Address_____

Age_____ Sex_____ Approx. Wt._____ Operator Lic. No._____ State_____

OBSERVATIONS:

CLOTHES	Describe: (Type & Color)	Hat or Cap_____ Jacket or Coat_____ Shirt or Dress_____ Pants or Skirt_____
	Condition:	☐ Disorderly ☐ Disarranged ☐ Soiled ☐ Mussed ☐ Orderly (Describe)_____
BREATH	\multicolumn{2}{l}{Odor of Alcoholic Beverage: ☐ strong ☐ moderate ☐ faint ☐ none}
ATTITUDE	\multicolumn{2}{l}{☐ Excited ☐ Hilarious ☐ Talkative ☐ Carefree ☐ Sleepy ☐ Profanity ☐ Combative ☐ Indifferent ☐ Insulting ☐ Cocky ☐ Cooperative ☐ Polite}
UNUSUAL ACTIONS	\multicolumn{2}{l}{☐ Hiccoughing ☐ Belching ☐ Vomiting ☐ Fighting ☐ Crying ☐ Laughing}
SPEECH	\multicolumn{2}{l}{☐ Not Understandable ☐ Mumbled ☐ Slurred ☐ Mush Mouthed ☐ Confused ☐ Thick Tongued ☐ Stuttered ☐ Accent ☐ Fair ☐ Good}

Indicate other unusual actions or statements, including when first observed: _____
_____
_____

Signs or complaint of illness or injury: _____

PERFORMANCE TESTS: (Note—See departmental instructions for conducting these tests)

Check Squares If Not Made		Check appropriate square before word describing condition observed
☐	**BALANCE**	☐ Falling ☐ Needed Support ☐ Wobbling ☐ Swaying ☐ Unsure ☐ Sure
☐	**WALKING**	☐ Falling ☐ Staggering ☐ Stumbling ☐ Swaying ☐ Unsure ☐ Sure
☐	**TURNING**	☐ Falling ☐ Staggering ☐ Hesitant ☐ Swaying ☐ Unsure ☐ Sure
☐	**FINGER-TO-NOSE**	Right: ☐ Completely Missed ☐ Hesitant ☐ Sure Left: ☐ Completely Missed ☐ Hesitant ☐ Sure
☐	**COINS**	☐ Unable ☐ Fumbling ☐ Slow ☐ Sure ☐ (Other)_____ (Balance during coin test)_____

Ability to understand instructions: ☐ Poor ☐ Fair ☐ Good   Tests performed: Date_____ Time_____ am/pm

OBSERVER'S OPINION:

Effects of alcohol: ☐ extreme ☐ obvious ☐ slight ☐ none   **Ability to drive:** ☐ unfit ☐ fit

Indicate briefly what first led you to suspect alcoholic influence:_____
_____
_____

Observed by: _____ Assignment: _____
Witnessed by: _____ Date_____ Time_____ am/pm

CHEMICAL TEST DATA:

Specimen: ☐ Blood ☐ Breath ☐ Saliva ☐ Urine ☐ None ☐ Refused ☐ Unable	Analysis result:
	If Breath, what instrument?
If refused, why?_____	

Source: National Safety Council. Used with permission.

EXHIBIT 3.3b

INTERVIEW:

Were you operating a vehicle?_____Where were you going?_____

What street or highway were you on?_____Direction of travel?_____

Where did you start from?_____What time did you start?_____

What time is it now?_____What city (county) are you in now?_____

What is the date?_____What day of the week is it?_____

INTERVIEWER TO FILL IN ACTUAL: _____ _____am/pm _____ _____ _____

| Time | am/pm | Day | Date | Interviewer's Name |

When did you last eat?_____What did you eat?_____

What were you doing during the last three hours?_____

Have you been drinking?_____What?_____How much?_____

Where?_____Started?_____am/pm Stopped?_____am/pm

Are you under the influence of an alcoholic beverage now?_____

What is your occupation?_____When did you last work?_____

Do you have any physical defects?_____If so, what?_____

Are you ill?_____If so, what's wrong?_____

Do you limp?_____Have you been injured lately?_____If so, what's wrong?_____

Did you get a bump on the head?_____Were you involved in an accident today?_____

Have you had any alcoholic beverage since the accident?_____If so, what?_____

Where?_____How much?_____When?_____

Have you seen a doctor or dentist lately?_____If so, who?_____When?_____

What for?_____Are you taking tranquilizers, pills or medicines of any kind?_____

If so, what kind? (Get sample)_____Last dose?_____am/pm Do you have epilepsy?_____

Diabetes?_____Do you take insulin?_____If so, last dose?_____am/pm

Have you had any injections of any other drugs recently?_____If so, what for?_____

What kind of drug?_____Last dose?_____am/pm When did you last sleep?_____

How much sleep did you have?_____Are you wearing false teeth?_____Do you have a glass eye?_____

| **HANDWRITING SPECIMEN** Signature and/or anything he chooses. | |

REMARKS:_____

_____

_____

_____

SUPPLEMENTARY DATA: (Note—Get witnesses, including officers who observed, to prove driving)

WITNESSES			Was Suspect Driving or Operating	What Was His Condition	Where Observed
Name	Address	Tel. No.			
Passengers in Suspect's Vehicle Name		Address		Condition	

National Safety Council 444 North Michigan Avenue • Chicago, Illinois 60611

25M877   Printed in U.S.A.   Stock No. 321.99

EXHIBIT 3.4

6. Dept. File No. _____

ARREST REPORT

FBI Identification Number

SBI Identification Number

SPN Identification Number

1. Department	2. Mun. Code	3. Phone Number	4. UCR

Municipal B.C.I. Numbers

5. Prosecutor's Case Number

7. Name (First)	(Middle)	(Last)	8. Phone No. (Area)	9. Alias/Nickname

10. Full Address (No.) (Street)	10A. Municipality	10B. County	10C. State	10D. Zip	11. Place of Birth (City)	(State)

12. Date of Birth	13. Age	14. Sex	15. Race	16. Ht. (Ft./In.)	17. Weight	18. Hair	19. Eyes	20. Complexion	21. Marital Status

22. Other Descriptive Information—Marks—Scars—Tatoos	23. Driver's License Number

24. Employer/School	25. Occupation	26. Social Security Number

27. Employer's/School Address	28. Business Phone (Area) (Extension)

DETAILS OF ARREST

29. Arrest Date	30. Time	31. Loc of Arrest (No.-Street)	31A. Municipality	31B. County	31C. State	32. Mun. Code

33. Crime	33A. Total Crimes	34. NJ Statue	35. Warrant Docket Number

36. Complainant's Name and Address—Zip Code	37. Phone Number (Area)

38. Crime Date	39. Time	40. Loc. of Crime (No. Street)	40A. Municipality	40B. County	40C. State	41. Mun. Code

42. Arrest ☐ W/Warrant ☐ W/O Warrant ☐ On View ☐ Summ. ☐ Juv. ☐ P.R.A.	43. Juv. Code	44. Constitutional Rights ☐ Yes ☐ No	45. Constitutional Rights—By Whom	46. How Responded

47. Own	48. Multiple	49. Other	50. Fingerprinted/By ☐ Yes ☐ No	51. Photographed/By ☐ Yes ☐ No	52. NCIC ☐ Yes ☐ No ☐ Wanted ☐ No Record	53. Previous Record ☐ Yes ☐ No

54. Vehicle Information ☐ Owned ☐ Used	Year	Make	Body Type	Color	Reg. Number and State	Other Discription Information—VIN

BAIL HEARING

55. Date	56. Court	57. Judge Setting Bail

58. Amount Bail	59. Results of Hearing ☐ Released on Bail ☐ R.O.R. ☐ Committed in Default ☐ Committed W/O Bail	60. Code	61. Place Committed/Detained

FINAL DISPOSITION

62. Date	63. Court	64. Judge

65. Disposition ☐ Gulty ☐ Dismissed ☐ Lesser Offense ☐ Acquitted	66. Code	67. T.O.T.	68. Sentence	69. Code

JUVENILE INFORMATION

70. Parent/Guardian/Probation—Contacted By	71. Date Contacted	72. Time Contacted	73. Released to/Detained At

74. Full Address—Number—Street—Municipality—State—Zip Code	75. Phone Number (Area)	76. Date	77. Time

78. Parent/Guardian's Name (First) (Middle) (Last)	79. Full Address—Number—Street—Municipality—State—Zip Code	80. Phone No. (Area)

81. Co-defendents	82.	83.	84.	85.	86.	87. UCR — A.S.R. Reporting Mon. _____ Yr. _____

88. Narrative/Additional Charges

89. Rank/Name (Type) Signature	Unit	91. Status ☐ Pending ☐ Completed	92. Date of Report 93. Reviewed By

EXHIBIT 3.5

REQUEST FOR EXAMINATION OF EVIDENCE

Submitting Agency (Case Number)	Laboratory Number

STATE OF NEW JERSEY
DEPARTMENT OF LAW AND PUBLIC SAFETY
DIVISION OF STATE POLICE
SPECIAL AND TECHNICAL SERVICES SECTION
POST OFFICE BOX 7068
☐ WEST TRENTON, NEW JERSEY 08625
(609) 882 - 2000

☐ North Regional Lab.	☐ South Regional Lab.	☐ East Regional Lab.
State Highway 46	Post Office Box 126	Sea Girt Avenue
Little Falls, NJ 07424	Hammonton, NJ 08037	Sea Girt, NJ 08750
(201) 256-7790	(609) 561-2060	(201) 449-0303

(Laboratory Use Only)

CRIME: COUNTY OF:

VICTIM:	Age	Sex	Race	SUSPECT:	Age	Sex	Race

SUBMITTING AGENCY: (Address)

FORWARD REPLIES TO: (Name)   (Address)   Telephone Number:

INVESTIGATED BY: DELIVERED BY: (Signature of Person Delivering Evidence)

BRIEF HISTORY OF CASE: (Include Date and Location, If Applicable)

EXAMINATION REQUESTED ON SPECIMENS LISTED BELOW:

Item #	* Code	LIST OF SPECIMENS *SOURCE OF EVIDENCE CODE (V - Victim S - Suspect SC - Scene)

DRUG ☐
TRACE ☐
BIO / CHEM ☐
TOX ☐
ABC ☐
EQUINE ☐
(LABORATORY USE ONLY)

FOR ADDITIONAL INFORMATION USE FORM 631A AND ATTACH   Page _____ of _____ Pages

S.P. 631 (Rev. 4-83)

Fingerprint records   (see exhibits 3.6 and 3.7)
Voluntary statement of confession   (see exhibit 3.8)

Again, no attempt is made to be exhaustive here, only to provide illuminating documentation. With proper law-enforcement contacts this information is generally accessible.

Insurance Records.   In the realm of civil litigation, insurance companies can provide reams of documentation, particularly in accident or compensation cases.

Public Records.   Most people are unaware that all public records are in the public domain unless some security or military classification restricts their usage and accessibility. Do not forget that the following records are generally open to the public:

All land deeds and mortgages

All lien and security-interest filings

State records of vital statistics

State and federal administrative records if properly authorized

Auto records

Government publications

Tax records

All other public filings such as corporate charters, foreign certificates, and other related issues

EXHIBIT 3.6

EXHIBIT 3.7

A PLAIN ARCH is that type of pattern in which the ridges enter upon one side, make a rise or curve in the center, and flow or tend to flow out upon the opposite side, without forming an angle or upthrust, and lacking two of the basic characteristics of the loop.

A TENTED ARCH is that type of pattern which possesses either an angle, an upthrust, or two or the three basic characteristics of the loop.

A LOOP is that type of pattern in which one or more ridges enter upon either side, recurve, touch or pass an imaginary line between delta and core and pass out or tend to pass out upon the side from which such ridge or ridges entered.

A SUFFICIENT RECURVE consists of the space between the shoulders of a loop, free of any appendages which abut upon it at a right angle.

TYPE LINES are the two innermost ridges which start or go parallel, diverge, and surround or tend to surround that pattern area.

THE DELTA is that point on a ridge at or nearest to the point of divergence of two typelines, and located at or directly in front of the point of divergence.

DELTA RULES:

1. when there are two or more possible deltas which conform to the definition, the one nearest the core should be chosen.

2. the delta may not be located in the middle of a ridge running between the typelines toward the core, but at the nearer end only.

3. the delta may not be located at a bifurcation which does not open toward the core.

4. where there is a choice between a bifurcation and another type of delta, the bifurcation is selected.

A PLAIN WHORL consists of one or more ridges which make a complete circuit, with two deltas, between which, when an imaginary line is drawn, at least one recurving ridge is cut or touched.

A CENTRAL POCKET LOOP consists of at least one recurving ridge, or an obstruction at right angles to the line of flow, with two deltas, between which, when an imaginary line is drawn, no recurving ridge within the pattern area is cut or touched.

THE LINE OF FLOW of a central pocket loop is determined by drawing an imaginary line between the inner delta and the center of the innermost recurving ridge.

A DOUBLE LOOP consists of two separate loop formations, with two separate and distinct sets of shoulders and two deltas.

AN ACCIDENTAL consists of a combination of two different types of pattern with the exception of the plain arch, with two or more deltas, or a pattern which possesses some of the requirements for two or more different types of a pattern which conforms to none of the definitions.

All Other Potential Sources of Information. As comprehensive as our review is thus far, the capable investigator knows that information leads are even more prolific. To be an effective, professional investigator requires that no stone be left unturned. Our list of leads would include the following also:

Statement of the client
Documents the client brings along or can get

Use of alias
Court records

EXHIBIT 3.8

VOLUNTARY STATEMENT
(Not Under Arrest)

I, _____, am not under arrest for, nor am I being detained for any criminal offenses concerning the events I am about to make known to _____. Without being accused of or questioned about any criminal offenses regarding the facts I am about to state, I volunteer the following information of my own free will, for whatever purposes it may serve.

I am _____ years of age, and I live at _____ .

_____

_____

_____

_____

_____

_____

_____

_____

_____

_____

_____

_____

_____

_____

_____

_____

_____

_____

_____

_____

_____

_____

_____

_____

_____

_____

_____

_____

_____

_____

_____

I have read each page of this statement consisting of _____ page(s), each page of which bears my signature, and corrections, if any, bear my initials, and I certify that the facts contained herein are true and correct.

Dated at _____, this _____ day of _____ 19 _____.

WITNESS: _____

                                              _____
                                             Signature of person giving voluntary statement

WITNESS: _____

FIGURE 3.4

INVESTIGATION WORKSHEET: MAJOR CRIMINAL CASE

Attorney Assigned _____

Case Captioned and Number _____

Interviews/potential witnesses

NAME	ADDRESS	BUSINESS PHONE	HOME PHONE	DATE OBTAINED
1				
2				
3				
4				
5				
6				

Photographs

	DATE REQUESTED	DATE TAKEN	BY-OTHER INFO
Crime			
Victim			
Defendant/Suspect			
Victim's Injuries At time			
Victim's Injuries Now			
Other			

Records/exhibits/test results

	1st DATE REQUESTED	1st DATE RECEIVED	2nd DATE REQUESTED	2nd DATE RECEIVED
Medical Examiner				
Coroner				
Pathology				
Document Examiner				
Print Lab				
Microanalysis				
General Lab Results				
Psychiatric				
Federal Agencies				
Defendant's Discovery				
State's Discovery				
Employment				
School				
Experts				
Assets/Check-Def				

OTHER

_____
_____
_____
_____

The attorney for the other side (may be willing to provide information)

Attorneys involved with case in the past

Interrogatories, depositions, and letters requesting information from the opposition

Pleadings (e.g., Complaint) filed thus far in the case

Newspaper accounts and notices in the media requesting information

Business records (e.g., cancelled receipts)

Employment records

Photographs

Hospital records

Informers or the "town gossip"

Surveillance of the scene

School records

Office of politicians

Records of Better Business Bureaus and other consumer groups

Telephone book and directories of organizations

Accounts of eyewitnesses

Agencies of the federal government

Hearsay accounts

Telling your problems to a more experienced investigator and asking him if he or she can think of any leads

Credit bureaus

Reports of investigative agencies written in the past

Resources of public library

Associations, trade or otherwise

"Shots in the dark"

Military records

C. Strategies to Gain Access to Records

Finally, these suggestions presume accessibility and ease of inspection. At this juncture, it is imperative that the paralegal gain some insight into the clues that might unlock the door to that information, aside from the suggestions noted thus far. Establishing viable contacts with professionals in the field and the justice system is certainly the most substantive advice that can be posed. The ease with which you gain access to records will depend on where the records are. For example:

   1. Records already in the possession of the client or of an individual willing to turn them over to you on request

   2. Records in the possession of a governmental agency or of a private organization and available to anyone in the public

   3. Records in the possession of a governmental agency or of a private organization and available on request to the client only or to the individual who is the subject of the records

   4. Records in the possession of a governmental agency or of a private organization and claimed to be confidential for everyone except in-house staff

Obviously there should be no difficulty in gaining access to the first category of records unless they have been misplaced or lost. In that event ask other interested parties for a copy of those records. As to records in the latter three categories, the following checklist should provide some guidelines on gaining access to them:

   □ Write, phone, or visit the organization and ask for them directly.
   □ Have the client write, phone, or visit and ask for them directly.
   □ Draft a letter for the client to sign asking for them directly.
   □ Have the client sign a form stating that he or she gives you authority to see any records that pertain to the client and specifically waiving any right to confidentiality that he or she has with respect to such records.
   □ Find out if the opposing party has them, and if so, ask to have a copy sent to you.

D. Preparation for Trial or Other Settlement

The investigator's a priori duty is the preparation for any eventual litigation or criminal adjudication. At this stage of the investigation paralegals must call upon all their organizational skills. The wide expanse of information gathered and analyzed must be effectively organized and synthesized for trial activity.

First, the paralegal should compile and organize compactly all relevant data needed for trial.

Second, all documents should be indexed, labeled, and properly identified for possible admission. An example of a document index is reproduced in figure 3.5.

Use checklists and worksheets to effectively keep track of witnesses, real evidence, documents, records, and forensic applications.

Third, a list of exhibits is useful to the attorney handling the case. (See figure 3.6.) The paralegal should notice that the designation *limitations* keeps the attorney abreast of strategic weaknesses in an exhibit, and depending on the ebb and flow of the trial, such exhibits may be more or less persuasive.

FIGURE 3.5

DOCUMENT INDEX

DOCUMENT	PAGES	DATE	DESCRIPTION	LOCATION	CROSS-INDEX

FIGURE 3.6

		PLAINTIFF'S/DEFENDANT'S TRIAL EXHIBITS			
TRIAL NO.	DATE	DESCRIPTION	IDENTIFIED DATE/WITNESS	IN EVIDENCE DATE/WITNESS	LIMITATIONS

Fourth, a jury selection roster is a practical tool for the attorney. (See figure 3.7.) By identifying and noticing individual jurors, the attorney will recall whom to focus on when it comes to particular issues. Individual juror characteristics are certainly easy to forget.

A courtroom supplies list is provided below. An efficient paralegal will have a box or other depository available at all times with these basic items included. Each item plays an important role in the presentation of evidence and the demonstration of the proponent's case.

COURTROOM SUPPLIES LIST

---

three-by-five-inch note pads
legal pads
pleading paper
letterheads
plain bond
Mylar-reinforced paper
pens
pencils
stapler
staples
cellophane tape
tape dispenser
paper clips
liquid white-out
large envelopes, labels
manilla folders

accordion folders
extension cords (as required)
money for cab fare
coins for telephone and coin-operated copiers
mints, antacid tablets, and aspirin
pre-issued trial subpoenas in blank
Evidence Code or Federal Rules of Evidence
Local rule
perpetual calendar
chalk
tape recorder
scissors
markers
exhibit paper
ruler

FIGURE 3.7

JURY SELECTION ROSTER

Plaintiff: _____   Defendant: _____

Peremptory: _____   Peremptory: _____

Amount: _____   Amount: _____

Cause: _____

1	2	3	4	5	6		1	2

7	8	9	10	11	12

III. WITNESSES: USE AND PREPARATION

Witnesses are obviously crucial to a variety of cases because their direct evidentiary value is hard to overcome. Besides considering the weight of their testimony, the paralegal must be knowledgeable about the proposed witnesses before recommending their use in a trial. A good witness can do a world of good, but a bad one can ruin an entire case.

A. Types of Witnesses

In order to properly prepare witnesses for any litigation, it is essential to recognize their overall alignment or purpose. Consider these suggestions about the following five types of witnesses:

1. Hostile witnesses. The hostile witness wants your client to lose and will try to set up roadblocks in your way. If the hostile witness is the opposing party who has retained counsel, it is improper for the investigator to talk directly with this person without going through counsel. If the hostile witness is not the represented party, the investigator should check with his or her supervisor on how to attempt to approach such a witness or if the attempt should be made at all.

2. Skeptical witnesses. The skeptical witness is not sure who the investigator is or what he or she wants in spite of the investigator's explanation of his or her role. The witness is guarded and unsure of whether to get involved.

3. Friendly witnesses. The friendly witness wants your client to win and will cooperate fully.

4. Disinterested or neutral witnesses. The disinterested or neutral witness doesn't care who wins. He has information that he tells to whoever asks.

5. All of the above. Witnesses are seldom totally hostile, skeptical, friendly, or neutral. At different times during the investigator's interview, and at different times throughout the various stages of the case, they may shift from one attitude to another. While it may be helpful to determine what general category a witness fits into, it would be more realistic to view any witness as an individual in a state of flux in terms of what she wants to say and what she is capable of saying.

Recognition of these general characteristics should greatly assist the paralegal in planning.

B. Quality Witnesses

It's one thing to identify prospective witnesses and quite another to get cooperation from them. Of course, a subpoena can force testimony from any witness, but the hostility generated may backfire. Then again, many witnesses may look good on paper but have such an antagonistic or arrogant way about them that there is just no sense in using them. Even more relevant is the witnesses' capacity or general skill at testimony or in the general reconstruction of events. Some witnesses are just plain incompetent mentally and emotionally and can do more damage than good. Keep a running list of all prospective witnesses but also realize that their use is neither mandatory nor necessarily wise.

C. Procedure for Gaining a Cooperative Witness

If the paralegal decides that a given witness is essential to the overall case, then the following procedures should enhance the chances of gaining a cooperative witness:

1. Introduce yourself as the paralegal, not the investigator. No one trusts anyone who says he or she is investigating.

2. Say the following, "Hello, my name is _____, I work for the law office of _____, and we are trying to get some information on _____.

3. Since the witness is under no obligation to speak with the paralegal, consider the following strategies to insure a cooperative witness:

    a. Make the witness feel important.

    b. Congratulate the witness for knowing anything, however insignificant, about this case.

    c. Give assurances that the witness will not get in any trouble by talking to you.

    d. Insure the witness anonymity if possible and desirable.

    e. Allow the witness to have peer support.

    f. If the witness is a codefendant, cooperation may benefit the witness.

    g. If the witness does not desire to talk initially, allow him or her the opportunity to think about it for a day or two.

    h. Negotiate for the testimony of the witness. Can a favor be done?

    i. Assist the witness in recollection.

In short, the investigator must gain the trust of the individual by assessing her needs and by knowing when she is ready to tell you what she knows. The investigator who takes out his notebook immediately upon introducing himself is probably too insensitive to establish the communication that he needs.

Listen to the witness's story first in detail, and then write down her statement in the first person. As you write, recite your written statements. When completed, ask the witness to review the statement for its accuracy. Ask her if she wishes to make any corrections. If she says she would like to, then let her make the corrections herself and ask her to initial them. Ask the witness to sign and date the statement. If she refuses, ask her to include her full name, address, place of employment (with address), and home and work telephone numbers.

In criminal cases, witnesses are imperative for identification purposes. Assess the quality of your identification by utilizing forms and checklists, like those shown in exhibit 3.9. A witness who precisely defines a suspect by employing a wide array of descriptive terms has an excellent memory for testimonial purposes.

Other aids can also assist witnesses' identification process, including mug shots and the lineup process.

D. Expert Witnesses: Special Issues

While an expert witness can certainly be characterized as any of the kinds we have listed, their unique status in the courtroom requires added attention.

Any major law firm or busy practice will have extensive dealings with experts in a variety of fields. In criminal cases, an expert often is a pathologist, medical examiner, or ballistics engineer. In civil cases, accident reconstruction, medical evaluation and analysis rely heavily on the use of expert witnesses including casualty engineers, professional medical specialists, psychiatrists, and damage assessors. Whatever the field or problem, experts are uniquely part of our legal system's adjudication of various issues, and the system gives great weight to expert analysis.

E. Location of Expert Witnesses

Expert witnesses are available from either the public or private sector. Increasingly, the public sector has resisted continued requests owing to the costs and loss of manpower productivity in state or federal government. Hence, the private sector has stepped in. Examples of both are listed below.

1. Public-agency experts

Medical Examiners	FBI
State and local police	Military
Governmental units: DEA, FAA, and so on	Universities/colleges

2. Private experts

Companies specializing in the Location and Preparation of Experts	Referral
Local associations	Universities/colleges
Professional associations	Private companies

F. Preparation of Experts for Litigation

Since the majority of experts in the scientific community and related fields rarely see the inside of a courtroom, the paralegal must amply prepare the witness for all the eventualities. Experts should be instructed in these vital issues:

Never Talk Down to Your Audience.　　At times people with intellectual breadth think they are better than others, maybe not intentionally, but that tone or flavor comes forth. Juries are particularly sensitive to this kind of elitism.

Be Simple and Precise.　　No one is impressed with verbosity and contorted language, except maybe lawyers. Clarity of presentation will be appreciated by all interested parties.

If Ignorant of Certain Facts, Just Admit It.　　The sin of pride can be devastating to any expert witness. The trait of humility is far more endearing and realistic, since no expert can possibly know everything.

If Paid for Services, Admit That Too.　　Opposing counsel will also attempt to paint a picture of an expert who is

EXHIBIT 3.9

WITNESS QUESTIONNAIRE*
TYPE OF CASE: TRAFFIC, DUI: NEGLIGENT AUTO

Your name has been given as a witness to the following described accident. It is only through the friendly cooperation of witnesses such as yourself that disinterested information can be obtained for the purpose of justly determining the rights of the parties involved. Therefore, it will be appreciated if you will answer each of the following questions and promptly return the completed statement in the enclosed envelope.

The accident referred to occurred on or about _____ at or near _____
between "A," which was a _____ owned by _____
and a _____ "B," owned by _____.
Hereafter the respective vehicles will be called A and B as indicated above.

Please state the following:

1. Your name _____

2. Your address _____

3. Your telephone number _____

4. Your occupation and employer _____

_____

5. Location of accident _____

_____

6. Date and time of accident _____

7. Did you see the accident occur? _____. If not, how soon afterward did you arrive? _____

8. Where were you when you observed the accident or other events? _____

_____

9. Where was A when you first saw it? _____

_____

Going what direction? _____

10. Where was B when you first saw it? _____

_____

Going what direction? _____

11. When you first saw the vehicles, what was the speed of A? _____

The speed of B? _____

12. When the collision occurred, what was the speed of A? _____

The speed of B? _____

13. Describe what you observed (use back of form if necessary) _____

_____

_____

_____

_____

_____

_____

_____

_____

_____

_____

_____

---

* Excerpted from *Working with Legal Assistants: A Team Approach for Lawyers and Legal Assistants*, Paul G. Ulrich and Robert S. Mucklestone, eds. Reprinted with permission of the American Bar Association.

drooling for money. Few private experts are charitable enterprises, so no shame can be attached to payment of an expert's fee.

Expect Cross-Examination.   An expert not instructed in the theatrics of cross-examination will turn hostile or paranoid. Calm advice should be given to the experts informing them of cross-examination on possible contradictory testimony or viewpoint on the matter.

Expect Impeachment.   Prepare experts for the often abrasive tactics of impeachment. Experts are regularly impeached on their educational level, their record of research and scholarly work, and their character, habits, and customs.

In general, the better prepared the paralegal's expert is, the better the presentation will be.

IV. SOME FINAL THOUGHTS ON THE INVESTIGATIVE PROCESS

As each story unfolds, individualized strategies are needed in the investigation process. From sexual offenses to arson, a whole new set of issues and evidentiary matters become the crux of an inquiry. While the fundamental steps are always the same, the unique characteristics of individual crimes and civil actions cannot be forgotten. Some suggestions follow.

1. Create individualized checklists for each crime. Those checklists should focus on that crime's particular elements.

2. Prepare for the rigors of trial. If any doubts exist as to the quality of the evidence, at least as to its evidentiary competency or quality, then exclude it. Use only what is solid, unerringly admissible.

3. Be certain to support the case with real evidence, not opinion and conjecture. Success in the trial arena is often guided by the weight of testimony, documentation, expert analysis, and scientific reliability. A case supported by mere assertion is no case at all.

4. Acquire equipment to perform the tasks of investigation. At a minimum, a competent investigator should possess the following:

cameras and film	paper
chalk and chalk line	picks
compass	plaster of paris
containers	pliers
crayon or felt marker	rope
depressors	scissors
envelopes	screwdriver
fingerprint kit	scriber
first-aid kit	sketching supplies
flashlight and batteries	spatula
knife	steel measuring tape
labels	string
magnifier	tags
mirror	tweezers
money	tubes
notebook	wrecking bar

5. Develop stable, professional, and reciprocal relationships. Much of the success a paralegal has depends on others. While no man is an island, that phrase is particularly applicable to the investigator. At best, the paralegal/investigator should establish and foster endearing relationships with:

Police departments	Insurance adjusters
Public Defenders' offices	State officials at all levels
District Attorneys' offices	County and municipal officials at all levels
Private investigators	Keepers of all public records

6. Write everything—everything—down. Memories are not what they should be, so leave nothing to chance. Don't forget how old Detective Columbo used to carry around that crumpled pad though he never had a pencil. While he annoyed the daylights out of the person he borrowed a pen or pencil from, his persistence proved the necessity of writing things down. Normally no person can arrive at a consensus of anything until all data are collected, reviewed, and evaluated. Strict reliance on memory cannot provide any investigator, even the most meticulous and mentally photographic, with a solid evaluation worthy of trust. Let's stick with crumpled raincoats, pen and pads, and an unswerving dedication to the truth as it once was.

DISCUSSION QUESTIONS AND PRACTICAL EXERCISES

Practical Exercises

1. Chronological Order: The Importance of Sequence. Practice writing a set of notes in the proper order and form for an investigation. Information for your set of practice notes is given below. However, it is not in proper form and it is not in the order in which an investigator would have obtained the information in an investigation. Write the information as a proper set of notes: in chronological order, under appropriate headings, and correctly worded. When you have completed your notes, compare them with the original. What differences do you see? How can these differences be important to the investigator in writing a report?

INFORMATION FOR NOTES

The victim is John Doe, white male, age 45, who lives at 106 Burden Lane; telephone 001-7821. Business phone 002-1976.

The scene of the offense is the Z service station, located at 206 South Pine Street. John Doe was the attendant when the crime was committed.

The offense is armed robbery. It occurred at about 3:00 A.M., April 2, 1976.

The complaint was called in by John Doe, and the officer received it by police radio at about 3:30 A.M., same date.

Item Number is 4-7-76. The officer is Joseph Noname, Badge 001, Car 56.

Officer arrived at the scene at about 3:35 A.M. and talked with John Doe.

Subject is unknown white male, early 30s, about 6 feet, 180 to 190 pounds. He had blond hair, blue eyes, and fair complexion. He was wearing blue jeans and a T-shirt.

The Subject came in through the front door of the Z station and asked the attendant for directions to a restaurant that would be open at that hour. Then he pulled a pistol (no description) on the attendant and said, "Empty the cash register and give me the money—now." Attendant did as he was told. He gave the Subject about $350 in 20, 10, 5, and 1 dollar bills. Subject held pistol on attendant and ordered him to the men's room and locked him in. Attendant got out of men's room after about twenty or twenty-five minutes and called police.

No indication of direction in which Subject disappeared.

Description of Subject was broadcast.

Area canvassed for witnesses; none were found.

Area around front door and cash register was examined and dusted for prints. None lifted.

Supplementary report to follow.

2. Six Basic Questions: Who? What? When? Where? How? Why? Assume you have been requested by a public defender to do an investigation of the following case in preparation for an appeal. From the facts given and all available resources, how would you answer the six basic questions?

Teenager Convicted of First-Degree Murder

A Burgsville teenager was convicted of first-degree murder by a judge who said the youth showed no remorse for the crime.

Maystone County Circuit Judge Albert Singleton found Jack Smith, 16, guilty of first-degree murder, abduction, grand larceny, and use of a gun in the commission of a felony in the slaying May 5 of Joe Myers, 17.

"I've found no remorse whatever in this young man—a nice-looking young man." Singleton said. "Another young man now lies in his grave because of Smith's actions." The defense argued Smith was not responsible for his actions during the shooting or when he later confessed because he was under the influence of drugs and alcohol. In a confession to Maystone County authorities, Smith said he was running away with a companion when they pulled a gun on Myers and took his car. Myers was shot in the head by the side of the road. Smith said he told Myers to get out of the car, and then followed him to the opposite side of the road. Smith pushed Myers over the bank so passing cars would not see him. "Then he started to run up the hill or do something fast, so I shot him," the confession read. "When I get high, some fast movement or something bothers me. I just blanked out and started pulling the trigger." Smith and his companion were arrested the next day when they were found sleeping in Myer's car.

Smith, who was 15 at the time of the slaying and was living with a couple that planned to adopt him, will be sentenced later.

QUESTIONS:

1. *Who?*
   Victim(s) _____

   Suspect _____

   Witnesses _____
   _____
   _____

2. *What?*
   Description of event _____
   _____
   _____
   _____

3. *When?*
   Time of event _____

   Time of report _____

4. *Where?*
   Place of event _____

   Address of victim _____

   Address of suspect _____

5. *How?*
   Method of attack _____

   Use of weapons _____

   Type of mens rea _____

6. *Why?*
   Motive _____
   _____
   _____
   _____

Writing with Specificity in Police Reports. Once you have considered the six basic questions, you must direct your attention to the particulars of the investigation; for instance, descriptions of persons involved.

3. *Description of Suspect.* Take some time to find a picture from your family album or other source. Use exhibit 3.3, which provides you with the standard descriptive terms and words as to various parts of the body, and write an accurate description of the subject you have selected. Show the end result to another person along with the picture and ask if your description is a good one.

☐ Eyes _____
☐ Hair _____
☐ Race _____
☐ Sex _____
☐ Teeth _____
☐ Nose _____
☐ Complexion _____
☐ Face _____
☐ Scars _____
☐ Ears _____
☐ Lips _____
☐ Neck _____
☐ Deformity _____

□ Body build _____

□ Personal appearance _____

□ Clothing _____

4. Description of Place. The investigating officer must become skilled at describing not only events and people but also the location, place, or premises where the offense occurred. Keep the following in mind when describing the place:

1. Exact address, including room or apartment number.
2. Nearest other address if in front or back of.
3. Nearest block number whether odd or even.
4. Distance and direction from known point.
5. Type of residence, e.g., duplex, multiple dwelling, income type.
6. General structural characteristics.
7. If not residence, then is it a business?

In a clear writing style, describe the following:

1. Your residence _____

2. Your supermarket _____

3. Your school _____

4. Your place of worship _____

5. Your doctor's office _____

ENRICHMENT ACTIVITY

Observe an autopsy and ask the coroner to explain the procedures of forensic investigation work. Write to several major publishers of legal materials and request that they provide you with information on what resource tools are available to the legal investigator.

SUGGESTED READING

Cleary and Strong's Cases and Problems on Evidence, Minneapolis: West Publishing Co., 1975.
Criminal Investigation, Minneapolis: West Publishing Co., 1981.
Crime Scene Search and Physical Evidence Handbook, Washington, D.C.: Government Printing Office, 1974.
Federal Bureau of Investigation Law Enforcement Bulletin, Washington, D.C.: Government Printing Office, 1985.
Felony Investigation Decision Model: An Analysis of Investigative Elements of Information. Final Report, Stanford Research Institute, 1975.
Journal of American Forensic Association, The Assoc., Cur.
Law and Legal Information Directory, Gale Research, 1980.
Public Affairs Information Service, Carrollton Press, Cur.
The Scientific Investigator, Thomas, 1965.

CHAPTER FOUR

FAMILY LAW

CHAPTER DESCRIPTION

The legal formalities of family law and its impediments are discussed, including marriage, annulments, divorce, property rights and distribution, children and visitation, alimony, separation agreements, adoptions, and parent and child law. Students will learn to interview clients with family-law problems and to prepare complaints and agreements.

PARALEGAL FUNCTIONS

Conduct necessary interviews.

Draft retainer agreement.

Participate in obtaining necessary interim relief (i.e.; support, custody, or visitation) by investigating facts and preparing necessary pleadings.

Draft settlement agreements.

Assist clients in rearranging their affairs in light of breakup of marriage.

Prepare witnesses and gather evidence for trial.

Draft postjudgment enforcement pleadings.

I. THE ROLE OF THE PARALEGAL IN FAMILY LAW

Aside from adoption petitions and a few sundry actions, the law of domestic relations, or as it is more popularly called, family law, exists because of human discord, the inability of people to get along in a domestic setting. In a way, the whole foundation of family law fundamentally rests in human tragedy. That characterization is what makes this area so challenging for the paralegal and attorney and equally so emotionally draining. If paralegals view life realistically, that is, if they know that people are capable of the worst behavior in domestic or familial disputes, they will survive, and do so in a most positive way. The paralegal must simply accept that some men and women commit adultery, fail to provide any humane level of support for their spouses or children, marry without the capacity, and react spitefully and even viciously in domestic squabbles. Of course, lest this be forgotten, some men and women are very proper toward one another, most humane and thoughtful, and handle their familial disagreements with a minimum of legal assistance. Either way, much of a paralegal's time will be dedicated to resolving family disagreements by appropriate counseling, personal phone and written contact, filing of required documentations and records, and tabulation of property valuation. In the most general sense, paralegals serve the lawyer best in this field because the paralegal handles many of the mechanical steps necessary for a remedy in law, and thereby frees the lawyer to spend his or her time counseling clients.

While family law should not simply be viewed as a negative exercise, it is critically important that the paralegal not see life from an idealistic or naive perspective. The "burnout" phenomenon of domestic-law lawyers is well documented, and studies clearly demonstrate a cycle of disillusionment, cynicism, and eventual withdrawal in some of the most experienced practitioners in the field. Reality is often a bitter pill to swallow, and both the clients and their lawyers become deeply submerged in the emotional torrents of dispute. Those waves of argumentation are much easier to accept if the lawyers and paralegals refrain from putting their clients on a pedestal, in spite of the emotional framework from whence those clients come. Whatever the case, *always, always, always* remember that a client is not a saint, not a perfect, model spouse, not absolutely free from all error or wrongdoing. As simplistic as it sounds, there are two sides to every story, and while one party may be obviously more victimized than the other, temper all judgments before getting all the facts from both sides. In this way, the paralegal will serve more skillfully and objectively the needs of any person requesting family-law assistance.

II. THE SCOPE OF FAMILY LAW

So much of family law has social, religious, and moral overtones. Think of divorce; compare the role of the judicial system today in the dissolution of marriage with its role thirty years ago. Traditionally, the dissolution of a marriage was guided by religious doctrine and by the court's analysis of fault—that is, there had to be a solid, rational justification for a divorce. Courts in the 1950s were not readily willing to grant divorces unless the petitioner could meet his or her burden of proving why the marriage was no longer viable. Today, in an age of no-fault, a divorce is possible with little or no demand for proof as to why the marriage should be dissolved.

Yet while divorce law has been dramatically liberalized, that state or commonwealth obligation remains the same—to insure the tranquility of the family unit, or at least do all in the government's power to oversee the orderly separation of parties. As such the court and the state or commonwealth play a major role in those same social, moral, and religious undercurrents in the community. On either side of the fence, whether one is liberal or conservative on the issue of judicial remedies for the dissolution of marriage, one fact remains clear—our society is deeply influenced by the mode or manner in which family-law disputes can be resolved. Our society can be viewed as slowly decaying or as becoming more enlightened as the liberalization of family-law disputes becomes more obvious. And these are the fundamental dynamics in domestic relations law, with its influence so easily discerned, its policies so precisely piercing to the whole of the community. In this light, family law's scope can be defined as a highly influential body of law attempting to regulate basic human relationships. Specifically, it includes:

1. Capacities to marry
2. Remedies for illegal or unfounded marriages—Annulments
3. Rights of spouses and children to support
4. Rights of spouses to alimony
5. Factors in the determination of custody
6. Grounds in divorce
7. Defenses to the divorce action
8. Separations and agreements between the parties
9. Suits to establish paternity

10. Petitions to change name

11. Adoption of children

All of the above areas naturally affect the basic social foundation of the community and accordingly place a heavy burden and most challenging obligation on the legal system to resolve domestic disputes with integrity and respect for moral and legal dilemmas. Nothing is to be viewed lightly in this field, for each and every policy and decision promulgated eventually influences the quality of life in the society at large. (See exhibits 4.1 and 4.2 for excellent intake sheets.)

Exhibit 4.1

DOMESTIC RELATIONS TELEPHONE
INTAKE SHEET

Date _____

Client's full name _____

Spouse's first name _____

Source of referral to office _____

Client's town of residence _____

Spouse's town of residence _____

Ages of any children involved _____

Whether parties are living together or separated _____

Name of spouse's attorney _____

Whether client is currently represented by counsel _____

Reason for seeking alternative counsel _____

Current status of legal proceedings, hearings, trial dates _____

_____

_____

Any immediate matters to be attended to _____

_____

_____

Telephone numbers where client can be reached _____

_____

Address where literature/letter may be sent _____

_____

Other _____

_____

_____

IF APPOINTMENT MADE	IF CASE REFERRED
Date and time _____	To whom referred _____
Office conference fee _____	_____
Advice given _____	For what reason _____
_____	_____
_____	_____

Master Index run _____

Names added to Master Index _____

Exhibit 4.2

DOMESTIC RELATIONS QUESTIONNAIRE

Date of office conference:
Office conference fee:
To be credited:
Date to be billed:
Time spent: Asst. _____ Atty. _____
Mailing list: Yes/No
Retainer Requested:
Minimum fees quoted:
Off. conf. fee pd: Date _____ Amt. _____ Dep. _____ Initials _____

Client's name:
Preferred name:
Maiden name:
Maiden or former name to be resumed: Yes/No
Residence: Mailing address if different:
How long at present residence:
With whom residing:
Age at marriage:
Present age:
Date of birth:
Home telephone number:
Work telephone number:
Social Security number:

Spouse's name:
Maiden name:
Maiden or former name to be resumed: Yes/No
Residence: Mailing address if different:

How long at present residence:
With whom residing:
Age at marriage:
Present age:
Date of birth:
Social Security number:
Name of spouse's attorney:
Does spouse know client is here today: Yes/No
Date of marriage:
Where married:
Marriage certificate available: Yes/No

Date of present separation:
Address last lived together:
Cities or towns parties lived in Massachusetts:
Any previous separations: Yes/No
      When   For how long   Details

NAMES OF CHILDREN:	AGE	DATE OF BIRTH	LIVING WITH WHOM	NATURAL CHILDREN

If wife presently pregnant and by whom:
Pregnancies interrupted or issue who died after birth:
Does client anticipate custody dispute:
Client's relationship with children:
Spouse's relationship with children:
How children will react to separation:
Parties communicating about children:
Medical history/problems of children:

Number of prior marriages: Husband   Wife
How terminated:
When terminated:
Where terminated:
To whom married:
Former married name:
Age of any children:
With whom children residing:
Cash or other support received:
Cash or other support paid:

Does husband have a criminal record:
Does wife have a criminal record:
Nature of any previous court actions:
Parties represented by counsel:
How long ago action filed:
Results:

Are parties presently in good health: Yes/No
Either party on any medication of any kind: Yes/No
Any serious illnesses, operations, diseases for either:
Any history of mental illness in parties, children, family:
Ever any suicide attempts by the parties:
Are the parties covered by medical insurance:
What type of medical insurance:
Who pays the premiums:

What religion are the parties:
Detail original family—who, where living, occupation, financial status etc.:
   Husband   Wife

Is either party dependent upon original families:

Did the parties ever attend any marriage or other counseling:
Professional capacity of counselor:
Name of counselor:
How many sessions and for how long:
Who attended:
Who suggested:
Is either or both presently attending:
Reason/Nature of counseling:
Dates attended/period of time:

Husband's employer:
Business address:
Job security: Work hours:
Length of employment: Availability of overtime:
Nature of job: Previous annual income:
Gross wages: Net wages:
No. of exemptions: Pay stub available:
Promotions/Raises:
Loans: Educational:
Dues: Retirement:
Cost of living: Pension:
Bonuses: Disability:
Commissions: Credit union:
Expense account: Company car:
Medical insurance: Stocks:
Stock options: Bonds:
Profit sharing: Other:

Previous employer: Location:
Dates of employment: Annual income:
Nature of job: Why terminated:

High school education:
College education:
Other special skills or training:
Indicate whether veteran:

Graduate:
Graduate:

Benefits derived:

Wife's employer:
Business address:
Job security:
Length of employment:
Nature of job:
Gross wages:
No. of exemptions:
Promotions/Raises:

Work hours:
Availability of overtime:
Previous annual income:
Net wages:
Pay stub available:

Loans:
Dues:
Cost of living:
Bonuses:
Commissions:
Expense account:
Medical insurance:
Stock options:
Profit sharing:

Educational:
Retirement:
Pension:
Disability:
Credit union:
Company car:
Stocks:
Bonds:
Other:

Previous employer:
Dates of employment:
Nature of job:
High school education:
College education:
Other special skills or training:
Indicate whether veteran:

Location:
Annual income:
Why terminated:
Graduate:
Graduate:

Benefits derived:

Other income from any source: Yes/No
Jobs:
Interests:
Trust income:
Veterans:
Welfare:
Other:

Rental income:
Dividends:
Social security:
Unemployment:
Disability:

Joint tax returns filed for previous year: Yes/No
Can copy be obtained:
Amount of refund:
Distribution of refund:
Was all income claimed on returns: Yes/No

Name of accountant:
Amount of payment:
Source of payment:

Management of money while living together:
Management of money after separation:
Management of money presently:

Description of real estate:
In whose name:
Form of ownership:
Amount of down payment:
Trace down payment:
Fair market value:
Amount of equity:
First mortgagee:
Amount of mortgage payments:
Ever borrowed against:

Location:
Purchase price:

Source of down payment:

Balance of mortgage:
Whose name on mortgage:
Second mortgagee:
Occupied by whom:
For what purpose and whose benefit:

BANK ACCOUNTS NAME OF BANK	BRANCH LOCATION	TYPE ACCOUNT	WHOSE FUNDS IN ACCOUNT	BALANCE OF ACCOUNT	IN WHOSE NAME	WHO HOLDS PASSBOOK AND IF NEEDED TO WITHDRAW $
1.						
2.						
3.						
4.						
5.						
6.						
7.						
8.						
9.						
10.						

AUTOMOBILES	YEAR AND MAKE	IN WHOSE NAME	PURCHASE PRICE	F M V	EQUITY	WHO MAINTAINS
Driven by Husband						
Driven by Wife						

LIFE INSURANCE	I.	II.	III.	IV.
Company				
Face value				
Type insurance				
Insured				
Cash surrender value				
How long been paying				
Beneficiary				
Whether revocable				
Owner				
Who holds policy				
Ever borrowed against				
For what purpose				
Who pays premiums				

Does client have a Will: Yes/No
Type of Wills:
Trustees:
Terms of Will:
Location of original Wills:

Does spouse have a Will: Yes/No
Executors:
Guardians:

Stocks: _____	Boats: _____
Bonds: _____	Snowmobiles: _____
Stock options: _____	Trailers: _____
Safety deposit box: _____	Business interests: _____

III. ISSUES RELATED TO THE LAW OF MARRIAGE

A. Ante Nuptial Agreements

Romantics cringe at the thought of contractual negotiations taking place before the cutting of the wedding cake, but many parties feel more comfortable delineating all economic rights and issues before the marriage ceremony. While a majority of couples do not engage in this practice, in an age of divorce and generally unstable family conditions, individuals with substantial economic interests are quite wary of losing all those interests if any eventual dissolution is requested. Even more skeptical is a party who has already experienced a divorce, especially one in which he or she was raked over the coals. While love may conquer all for some, others do not desire a second burning, so to speak. These agreements are also popular when the parties differ substantially in age, or in socioeconomic level. Examples of such differences are often publicized as Hollywood-type marriages.

The legal requirements of the prenuptial agreement are guided by rudimentary contract principles. First, the agreement must be in *written form* as required by the Statute of Frauds. Second, as in fundamental contract law, there must be an *offer acceptance* and sufficient *consideration* to support the contract. Third, the contract must be *fair and accurate on its face* and not *violative of any local laws or general public policy*. As always, the contract must not be the result of duress, coercion, or ignorance.

B. Procedural Steps

Our legislatures impose more obstacles in the acquisition of a driver's license than they do in the procurement of a marriage license. One certainly hopes that the ease of becoming a married person is not evidence of a disregard for marriage's solemnity, but as baffling as it may seem, getting married is one of the simplest things to do! All states have licensing and solemnization requirements of one form or another. Those requirements generally fall into the categories described below.

1. Application for, and payment of, a state license to marry

This process usually requires a trip to the court clerk's office or the local justice of the peace. Fees usually range from $3 to $25, and the party requesting the license will generally take an oath and provide information to the agency on essential vital statistics.

2. Waiting period

The mandatory waiting period once was considered a very important requirement, since the state hoped to temper the passions of couples whose decision to marry was grounded in less than logic. The waiting period can run from twenty-four hours to three to four weeks, and in some jurisdictions, such as Maryland, no waiting period is required at all. Maryland's town of Elkton is well known for its "commerce" in marriage, with couples from all over the country regularly traveling to this quaint little town for their final vows.

3. Physical examination

In an effort to control all forms of communicable diseases, most states require the parties applying for the license to take some form of blood test. Parties to a potential marriage often appreciate this law, particularly when the test is positive for a disease, and medical steps can prevent transmission.

4. Solemnization of the marriage

a. AUTHORIZED OFFICIAL

While nautical lore indicates the right of a ship's captain to perform the marriage ceremony on the high seas, no existing legislation in the U.S. authorizes the practice. Instead, the law of all states requires either a civil officer—e.g., justice of the peace, magistrate—or an official of a religious body or group, e.g., minister, rabbi, priest.

b. FORM OF MARRIAGE CEREMONY

There is usually little guidance or restriction as to how the ceremony is to be performed, particularly as to its overall content. All that is required is an *affirmation, oath, or declaration* within that ceremony's content of an intention to marry the other party.

Every state also requires some witnesses to the marriage ceremony, who will attest to their signatures on the formal certificate of marriage.

c. CONSUMMATION

While not directly related to the ceremony itself, the common-law tradition of our country does require a sexual act of consummation between the couple before the marriage is deemed final and legally solemnized.

C. Common-Law Marriage

Common-law marriages have long been legally recognized in at least fifteen jurisdictions in the United States, and by tradition in many more. Comparing the formal marriage with a common-law marriage is an elementary task, since the common-law marriage lacks the formalities as just described in the above section. Common law marriage is no less valid and no less valued by its proponents since the parties to this relationship do intend, just as seriously, to be husband and wife. If anything, some parties to common-law relationships say that their committment of love and companionship is superior to the state-blessed relationship because their love need not be justified or approved by governmental authority. Be that as it may, states that do authorize the practice require:

1. An express agreement, presently to marry

Parties asserting the common-law relationship must evidence a present intention to be married, not a futuristic plan of companionship. Some states require a declaration of sorts, an affirmation to others that this companion of mine is my wife or husband. Such a declaration can be proven by direct or influential evidence.

2. Actual cohabitation

Since actions speak louder than words, states allowing the practice mandate a formal, physical period of cohabitation. Historically, many states attempted to formalize this cohabitation period by assessing a time frame of from *three to seven years*. These arbitrary figures have been generally knocked down and replaced with an assessment of all relevant factors, including the duration of that cohabitation.

3. A "holding out," or opennesss

The community's perception of the relationship is also critically important in the proof of the common-law marriage. To be credible marriage partners, they must hold themselves out to the community at large as husband and wife. The partners must not be secretive, reclusive, or wary of this fact's being publicly known.

While the law does not favor the common-law marriage, it must accept that in certain areas and communities in this country, it is a common and respected method of exchanging the vows of marriage.

D. Capacity to Marry

As seen thus far, the formalities of marriage are not difficult to meet, but never bypass the fundamental issues related to *capacity*, that is, the ability to get married. All the formalities in the world are irrelevant to a party who is legally incapable of entering into the marriage relationship.

1. Bigamy—preexisting marriage

Polygamy has not received any significant approval from the society at large, and while some splintered religious groups and unique individuals may praise its glories, all states have laws outlawing the practice. Rightfully, a man or woman who is already in an existing marriage cannot marry again until that previous relationship is dissolved. Imagine the social anarchy of a culture that tolerated the practice. Whose rights could be enforced? Whose children would be whose? The task of rectifying these situations would be unmanageable. Therefore, all states stipulate that a marriage cannot take place, that is, no capacity exists to marry, until a preexisting marriage is dissolved.

2. Incest/issues of consanguinity

Universally, all nations ban and prohibit incestuous relationships that are sexual in design. There are both religious and humanistic prohibitions. Genetic disorders resulting from inbreeding and sexual jealousies and rivalries are affronts to the integrity of the nuclear family and are reasons to support the restriction. The degrees of consanguinity give rise to some level of disagreement, especially in the drafting of legislation. Which of the following potential marriages would be declared incapable because they were considered incestuous?

Mother to son	Brother to sister
Mother to stepson	Uncle to niece
Grandfather to granddaughter	First to second cousin
Father to adopted daughter	First to fifth cousin

3. Nonage

The capacity to marry also depends on the age of the parties to a marriage. Since marriage can be viewed in a contractual context, a presumption has to exist as to the ability of the parties to understand the nature of the contract's language and resulting obligations. While at common law, men were formerly permitted to marry at fourteen and women at twelve, all states have increased the minimum age. Why? Are people less mature at twelve and fourteen today? Divorce rates from earlier times, when lower age requirements were in effect, tend to evidence a stable family life with less disruption than in modern times. Many interesting policy and legislative questions do emerge in the analysis of nonage, and the wide array of statuatory provisions further attests to these policy issues. In general the statutes specify (1) higher age for men than women; (2) lowest age of fourteen for women, sixteen for men; and (3) consent of parents or guardians in cases of legal minors.

4. Physical defects/infirmities

Two major infirmities can be impediments to one's capacity to marry, namely, *venereal disease* and *impotence*. In both cases, the heart of the consensual relationship is directly affected. As discussed previously, most states require a physical examination for communicable diseases, and the failure to adhere to the statutory mandate gives rise to a claim of incapacity. In terms of impotence, a natural inference can be drawn that the *consummation* requirement cannot be met, which in turn fails to solemnize the marriage. Impotence relates, of course, to the incurable inability to have sexual intercourse with a spouse.

5. Same-sex marriages

In an age of gay and lesbian advocacy, repeated requests have been made to legislatures for laws allowing same-sex marriages. To date, no person has the capacity to marry another person of the same sex.

How does a transsexual fit into this picture? What if you married someone of the opposite sex, and then your spouse underwent a surgical operation to modify gender? Is there any case law in your jurisdiction on this topic?

What would be the ramifications of a court's allowing same-sex marriages? Think of Social Security, veterans' benefits, and pension plans.

6. Mental incompetence

The gravity of the marriage contract requires parties who act by their own volition and who possess a basic intellect that makes them capable of making the decision to marry. Therefore, the capacity to marry inextricably defends the mental competence of the parties choosing to be married. No level of genius is sought in the marriage decision, only that the parties not be defined as mental defectives, legal lunatics, morons, or idiots, words not used in a chiding fashion, but instead descriptions used in clinical analysis of IQ quotients, psychomotor skills, and past history. Simply put, the parties to the marriage contract *must have the capacity to understand the nature of the contract and the duties and responsibilities it creates.*

7. Duress/coercion

The capacity to marry also depends on free choice, an exercise of behavior that is volitional rather than forced or coerced. A marriage that results from physical threat or abuse, economic or professional extortion, or other forms of unfair coercion should not be upheld since it is not reflective of the parties' intentions. Measurement of that duress or coercion must be by the "reasonable person" standard.

8. Fraud

Highly creative arguments have been developed in this area of marriage dissolution, and because the nature of fraud is so general, so flexible, that is to be expected. Fraud relates to a person's own perception of truth, or expectation of what the other party was supposed to deliver on the date of the contract. Fraud, in purely tort terms, is a *misrepresentation of a material fact, which results in a justifiable reliance to the injury* of a party. Can that happen from a marriage exchange? Consider these examples:

a. Sally tells Bob she is pregnant, when in fact she is not. He feels obligated to marry her and does.
b. Bob failed to tell Sally that he is sterile and will never be able to have children. During their courtship they often talked of children.
c. Bob claimed that Sally was his first and only sexual mate, and Sally later learns that Bob was a notorious gigolo.
d. Sally claimed that Bob was her first and only sexual mate, and Bob later learns that Sally was a former madam.

E. The Annulment Process

1. Void/voidable distinctions

Our discussion so far is most relevant to the law on *annulments.* In fact, one's capacity to marry directly relates to the legal remedy of an annulment, though an annulment may not be the only possible solution. Why? Annulments are concerned only with marriages that are *void* or *voidable,* that is, the law holds that those marriages never existed or should not exist. The marriages never existed because the parties proposing marriage had no capacity to effect the marriage.

Subtle distinctions in statutory analysis make annulments more complex than they really are, especially the *void/voidable* distinction. In order for a marriage to be typified as *void,* it did not, it could not, it has never existed; it had no chance of ever existing! For example:

a. Bob, with three wives he has never divorced, married Janey.
b. Janey, stepmother to her new husband's son, likes the son so much, she decides to marry him.

In the above two examples, those marriages are *void, ab initio* right from the start. At best, these meretricious relationships can be defined as bigamous and incestuous.

So what is a *voidable* marriage? Again the subtle differences in definition can be elusive, but the most cogent distinction rests in the state's original acceptance of the marriage state, an affirmation that it did exist at some point but that it must now be overturned, destroyed, or obliterated from the record and reality. In this sense, annulments are legal fantasies. *Voidable* marriages could be:

a. Fred, who is thirteen, and Betty, who is eleven, elope to Elkton, Maryland, for a weekend fling.
b. Mary marries Phil, who is permanently incurable when it comes to his impotence disability.
c. Bob tells Mary that if she doesn't marry him, he will "blow my brains out and kill all your friends."

In one final analysis, the policy of all annulments whether for *void* or *voidable* rationales, is to undo a relationship that never should have happened.

Annulment is also an available remedy in many religions, including Roman Catholicism and Lutheranism. Recent promulgations from the Vatican, under the leadership of Pope John Paul II, have expressed extreme dissatisfaction with the ease with which American Catholics have been awarded annulment decrees. Recent statistics show a tenfold increase in grants of annulment decrees in American dioceses. The paralegal must become attuned not only to the state remedy in annulment but also to the ecclesiastical approval, something frequently far more important to the client.

2. Consequences of the annulment

The paralegal will quickly determine that while annulments essentially deny the existence of a marriage, the eventual decree does not negate any primary spousal or parental responsibilities. Keep in mind the following issues:

a. Custody and support questions will be determined just as if a marriage had taken place.
b. Children of the nonexistent marriage will be characterized as *legitimate.*
c. Alimony is sometimes possible in a temporary or limited way.
d. Tax refunds for years of a nonexistent marriage generally must be *amended* to reflect a nonmarried status.
e. Benefits from *Social Security, veterans' and pension plans* are still payable in some jurisdictions. Check your local laws.

3. Procedural steps in the suit to annul

In general, the pleadings for the suit to annul are similar to those utilized in the processes of divorce. As in all litigation, a determination of domicile and subject-matter jurisdiction is essential. Next, file a petition or complaint for an annulment with the appropriate prothonotary. Await an answer to that petition or complaint or possible counterclaim, and then reply. Comply with all discovery requests and have an eventual adjudication, trial, or hearing on the annulment petition.

IV. THE LAW OF DIVORCE

Remember the "realism" aspect of domestic-relations law discussed in the introductory part of the chapter? Divorce is the arena, the battlefield, of human emotion, where that type of survival mechanism pays off. The paralegal must accept the fact that a majority of marriages in our society are ending in divorce and realize that some people will go to any limit to insure their needs in this emotional period of their life.

The law of divorce has gone through some revolutionary changes in the last two decades and is primarily divided into two camps: *grounds* and *defenses.* The grounds for divorce are further categorized by what are known as *fault* or *no-fault* grounds. An oversimplification would be to say that the no-fault grounds are now favored because they are less costly to litigate and less emotional for all parties concerned. But there has been a tradeoff for that reduction in emotional drain—that of a fast-increasing divorce rate along with a general trend to the nontraditional family as normative and generally changing values and social mores. These comments are not judgmental but reflective of the modern era of family relationships in our society. Barring no other, divorce laws, with their rules, and regulations, are probably the most influential factor in the altered structure of the American family.

A. Grounds for Divorce: Fault

1. Adultery

Aside from the general lurid appeal adultery has in the culture, on the merits it is a sound basis for a dissolution of a marriage. Since a marriage is based on fundamental trust and sexual integrity, most people take tremendous offense at a spouse who feels the field is his or hers to play. Adultery can be defined as *the voluntary sexual intercourse of a married person with a person other than the offender's husband or wife.* Simple enough upon a first reading, but consider these quandries:

☐ Can adultery be committed by homosexual contact?
☐ Does adultery require only traditional sexual intercourse, that is, vaginal-penile penetration?
☐ What if the offending spouse is mentally ill or incapable of consensual relationships?

□ Is a women who is artifically inseminated an adulterer?

□ Can a spouse consent to the other spouse's sexual activity and then later claim adultery?

2. Desertion

All states have some provision for the dissolution of a marriage state when one spouse deserts the other. That term, *desertion*, is also sometimes referred to as *abandonment*. Desertion is also not to be taken lightly or proven in a frivolous manner, since it connotes a permanent situation, not a temporary trifle or disagreement. As such, the first essential requirement in the proof of desertion is evidence manifesting a statutory period of absence. How much time suffices? The length of the period of desertion ranges from six months to five years. But time is not enough by and in itself, for the complainant must amply show that the period of desertion was "continuous" and "uninterrupted." Hence a complainant who is periodically visited by his or her spouse cannot assert desertion.

Assume Bob is gone for two years in a state whose desertion requirement is three years. Bob stops in one night and has a sexual encounter with his wife. Is the absence requirement ruined?

The proponent of the desertion argument must also show that the deserting spouse left with no justification or excuse. Hence, a spouse whose job or career forces a substantial separation cannot be penalized. Lastly, the complainant is obliged to show that the desertion is nonconsensual on his or her part. To be thrown out of the house and attempt to return is not an act of volitional desertion.

In summary, the defense of desertion requires:

a. Voluntary period of separation

b. Permanent, intentional act of desertion

c. With no spousal consent

d. With no legal justification

3. Cruelty/inhumane or barbarous treatment

Cruelty is a subjective word that gives rise to a multitude of divorce complaints. That subjectivity has been resoundingly criticized. Which of the following could be characterized as a sufficient justification for the grant of divorce on the grounds of cruelty?

a. Physical beatings

b. Threats of violence

c. Passing on a veneral disease to the spouse

d. Spouse boasting of sexual exploits

e. Spouse who had himself sterilized without consent of wife

f. Refusal of sexual relations

g. Having wild parties in the home

h. Fanatical attempts to convert spouse to another religion

All of the above situations have resulted in a favorable grant of divorce on the theory of cruelty. What do these applications say of cruelty? Without question, cruelty is an elastic ground, not rigidly applied in any domestic scenario. Potentially, cruelty can take many forms. Just ruminate on these varying statutory definitions:

□ The willful infliction of pain, bodily or mental

□ Treatment which is cruel and inhuman, whether practiced by personal violence or any other means

□ Cruel treatment causing great mental distress

□ Mental suffering sufficient to make complainant's life intolerable

No claim of legislative precision can be trumpeted here, but then again, precision may not be plausible. In *cruelty*, people are just plain mean to each other, maybe even vicious! What is paramount in the analysis of cruelty is a demonstration that certain behaviors are detrimental to:

□ The personal life or physical health of spouse

□ The mental stability and health of a spouse
□ The legitimate ends or purposes of a marriage
□ Objects or purposes of a relationship

On its face, cruelty should be easy to prove, almost a mere formality, since any marriage on shaky grounds can plausibly evidence the described levels of cruelty.

4. Indignities to the person

Not to be outdone in the vagueness category is the ground of *indignities*. There is little difference between it and *cruelty*, except in some jurisdictions. Some jurisdictions view *cruelty* as a more "physical" ground; that is, the intent of the ground is to protect innocent spouses from being physically hurt or threatened, or mentally abused to such an extent that their health suffers. An indignity, by its very implication, is an affront, a form of continual abuse that is not necessarily physical. Examples might include habitual drunkenness, chronic verbal exchanges, various sexual demands that are unreasonable, intrafamily harassment or verbal abuse. An excellent sample definition might be:

> Conduct to an innocent and injured spouse that renders his or her condition intolerable and makes life burdensome.

5. Conviction of a crime

In general, most states have provisions that will grant a divorce to the unfortunate spouse of a convicted felon. However, the paralegal must be sure that the following issues are resolved before pleading this ground:

□ Has the offending spouse been convicted of a felony or other infamous crime? (Generally very major capital offenses qualify.)
□ How much time will the defendant serve? (All states have a minimum time period, e.g., Pennsylvania requires a sentence of two years or more.)

6. Incompatibility

This ground has been popularized by the media, but its real influence on domestic law is rather minimal since so few jurisdictions have adopted it (Virgin Islands, New Mexico, and Alaska). Stated simply, incompatibility is when the spouses just don't get along. Incompatibility refers to conflicts in personalities and dispositions so deep as to be irreconcilable and which make it impossible for the parties to continue a marital relationship. Sound rigid in design? What could such a ground include? What if one party feels everything is just fine? If this a a "fault" ground, who is the spouse that is incompatible? Answers are hard to come by in this ground.

7. Miscellaneous fault grounds

The grounds listed below can really be labeled minority positions in a few states. The proliferation of these avant-garde defenses become more a mystery when one considers the elasticity of the traditional grounds. But these new avenues of marriage dissolution make paralegals and lawyers alike appear endlessly creative. Such grounds include:

a. Habitual drunkenness
b. Drug addiction
c. Nonsupport
d. Neglect of duty
e. Unchastity
f. Deviate sexual conduct
g. Obtaining an out-of-state divorce
h. Insanity resulting in a period of confinement

For sample fault complaint see exhibit 4.3.

Exhibit 4.3

COMPLAINT FOR DIVORCE

Phone:

SUPERIOR COURT OF
CHANCERY DIVISION
        COUNTY
DOCKET NO. M-_____

              Plaintiff,
   vs.
             Defendant.
    Plaintiff,

Civil Action
COMPLAINT FOR DIVORCE

who lives at

in the City

of   County of
and State of   says:

1.   Plaintiff was lawfully married to the defendant on   , by   at
2.   was a bona fide resident of the State of   when this cause of action arose and has
ever since and for at least one year next preceding the filing of this Complaint continued to be such a bona fide resident.
3.   Defendant resides at   , in the City of   , County of
    and the State of   .
4.   Plaintiff and defendant have lived separate and apart in different habitations since   , for a period in
excess of eighteen (18) consecutive months, and there is no reasonable possibility of a reconciliation; at the end of the said
eighteen (18) months,   , resided at   , in the City of   ,
    County of   , and the State of   .
OR
4.   The defendant has been guilty of extreme cruelty towards the plaintiff, commencing on or about   ,
and continuing from that day until   , at which time plaintiff was compelled to discontinue habitation with
the defendant on account of   extreme cruelty toward plaintiff. Particularly specifying the acts of extreme
cruelty committed by defendant, plaintiff says:
        a.   "On October 15, 1976, defendant kicked me in my stomach while I was six months pregnant with my second
child;
        b.   On November 5, 1976, defendant called me a 'slut, whore, pig,' and used other foul language to describe me in
front of our neighbors at a party and continued to humiliate me verbally in front of my parents and children and later that day
at my parents' home, causing me severe emotional anguish;
        c.   On December 2, 1976, defendant gave me a black eye and bruises all over my body, especially in and around the
head because 'his coffee wasn't ready on time. As a result, I sought medical attention at the Dover General Hospital.'"
        The above-named acts of extreme cruelty endangered the safety and health of plaintiff and made it improper and
unreasonable to expect the plaintiff to continue to cohabit with the defendant.
        More than three months have elapsed since the last act of extreme cruelty complained of as constituting plaintiff's
cause of action herein. The acts of extreme cruelty committed by defendant within a period of three months before the filing of
the complaint, as set forth above, are alleged not as constituting in whole or in part the cause of action set forth herein, but as
relating back to qualify and characterize the acts constituting said cause of action.
        At the time of the last act of extreme cruelty,   , resided at   ,
in the City of   , in the County of   , in the State of   and was resident
there at the time the cause of action for divorce on the ground of extreme cruelty arose.
5.   There were _____ children born of the marriage, to whit:
_____, who is _____ years of age;
_____, who is _____ years of age;
_____, who is _____ years of age;
_____, who is _____ years of age;
_____, who is _____ years of age;
_____, who is _____ years of age;

live with plaintiff; _____
_____ live with defendant.
6.   There have been no previous proceedings between plaintiff and defendant in any court respecting the marriage, divorce, or
support for the wife, except those in the following courts on the dates shown: _____

7.   During the course of the marriage, plaintiff and defendant acquired the following debts:

8.   During the course of the marriage, plaintiff and defendant acquired the following property

WHEREFORE, Plaintiff demands judgment
A. Dissolving the marriage between plaintiff and defendant;

_____
Date

_____
Counsel for Plaintiff
Attorney ID Number

B. Grounds for Divorce: No-Fault

Of increasing importance to the paralegal is a recognition that no-fault divorce is the preferred method of marriage dissolution. Spouses, caught in an already tangled web of emotional turmoil, often desire the easiest, least exhausting mode of divorce. Two major categories of no-fault come to the forefront.

1. Irreconcilable differences/irretrievable breakdown

This form of ground is consensual in nature because it requires both spouses to concur in the granting of the divorce. The agreement or consent is usually evidenced by the signing of a standard form. General authority rests with the court to grant a divorce where a complaint has been filed alleging that the marriage is irretrievably broken. The court does not concern itself with the proof thereof or the fault of either party, for it accepts the assertion on its face as backed by the consents of the parties. Most jurisdictions also require a waiting period of, say, 90–180 days before certain consents can be filed. This traditionally could be called a cooling-off, or waiting, period. Incredibly, a divorce can be granted by any of the following:

   a. Filing a complaint alleging irreconcilable differences
   b. Filing other documents including vital statistics
   c. Waiting out the statutory cooling-off period before submitting the consents of the parties
   d. Waiting for the decree signed by the court

Note also that some states require a hearing before a judge or a master before a final decree can be granted. However, the majority of states have made every effort to make this kind of divorce no more than a paper transaction. If any other issues are involved, such as equitable distribution, custody, or alimony, a special master or judge will hear evidence on those matters. (See exhibit 4.4 a and b.)

2. Living separate and apart for a statutory period

This type of divorce ground is referred to as unilateral since one party to the marriage is obviously not cooperating either by choice or from ignorance. While marriage should be upheld at all costs, the futility of a marriage where one spouse is absent is self-explanatory. Therefore, many states provide for the grant of divorce when the parties have lived separate and apart for a period of years, usually two to three, and the marriage is no longer salvageable.
Various issues have been argued at the state level on this manner of divorce, including the following:

   □ The effect of attempted reconciliation.
   □ From what point in time is the separation period computed?
   □ Is cohabitation defined in the same way as in the grounds of desertion?

C. Defenses to the Divorce Action

In an age of no-fault, technical defenses become even more poignant.

1. Technical issues

   a. Res judicata.   A previous decree on this same divorce petition or complaint has already been granted.
   b. Improper venue.   The complaint as filed is in the wrong state, county, or district.
   c. Improper jurisdiction.   The complaint as filed is not pertinent to the court's subject-matter jurisdiction.

Exhibit 4.4a

Name:
Address:
Phone:
Attorney for Plaintiff

IN THE COURT OF COMMON PLEAS OF   COUNTY,

          CIVIL ACTION—LAW

                  :   NO. _____ , TERM, _____

          PLAINTIFF,

V.   :   ATTORNEY ID NUMBER:

          DEFENDANT. :   IN DIVORCE, A.V.M.

NOTICE TO THE DEFENDANT

If you wish to deny any of the statements set forth in this affidavit, you must file a counteraffidavit within twenty days after this affidavit has been served on you or the statements will be admitted.

Plaintiff's Affidavit Under
Section 201(d) of the Divorce Code

1. The parties to this action separated on _____ and have continued to live separate and apart for a period of at least three years.

2. The marriage is irretrievably broken.

3. I understand that I may lose rights concerning alimony, division of property, lawyer's fees or expenses if I do not claim them before a divorce is granted.

I verify that the statements made in this affidavit are true and correct. I understand that false statements herein are made subject to the penalties of   relating to unsworn falsification to authorities.

Date: _____   _____
                                                            Plaintiff

Exhibit 4.4b

IN THE COURT OF COMMON PLEAS OF   COUNTY,

          CIVIL ACTION-LAW

_____   Plaintiff   :   No. _____

          vs.   :   Attorney ID No. _____

_____   Defendant   :   IN DIVORCE, A.V.M.

          Affidavit of Consent

1. A Complaint in divorce under Section _____ of the Divorce Code was filed on _____ .

2. The marriage of plaintiff and defendant is irretrievably broken and ninety days have elapsed from the date of filing the Complaint.

3. I consent to the entry of a final decree of divorce.

4. I understand that if a claim for alimony, alimony pendente lite, marital property or counsel fees or expenses has not been filed with the court before the entry of a final decree in divorce, the right to claim any of them will be lost.

I verify that the statements made in this affidavit are true and correct. I understand that false statements herein are made subject to the penalties of   relating to unsworn falsification to authorities.

Date: _____   _____

d. *Statute of limitations.* The complaint fails to assert the grounds within the proper time frame.

e. *Laches.* The complaint as filed is so delayed that to award relief would be unfair to the defendant.

f. *No marriage exists.* An excellent defense, which can be forgotten by the practitioner.

2. Connivance

A previous comment alluded to the fact that if one party consents to his or her spouse's extramarital sexual activity, he or she has no right then to assert adultery. The defense of connivance will bar the plaintiff's remedy here to this conduct. Hence active participation in adulterous conduct bars that ground if later asserted. The troublesome questions about connivance rest in defining consent. Is consent merely acquiescence? What if either spouse could easily halt the opportunity of adultery but fails to take any steps?

3. Collusion

Collusion is often mistaken for connivance because there is a certain level of corruption in the behavior of the parties. In connivance, one party is promoting the illegality or consenting to the corruption, and the other party does not realize this fact. In collusion, *both* parties know full well that their behavior is corrupt and know they want to perform it because the behaviors provide a basis for a divorce ground. Both parties then represent to the court that one party is innocent and injured. In essence, collusion is a form of marital conspiracy to effect the appropriate divorce grounds. The rampancy of collusions provided legislatures with a rationale to adopt no-fault, since collusion makes a hypocrisy of existing grounds.

4. Condonation

In condonation, the injured and innocent party forgives or pardons the sins of the transgressing party. This forgiveness usually takes the form of a brief period of renewed cohabitation, sexual intercourse, or other human exchange. Think specifically of desertion/abandonment in this context. All that is required is that the forgiveness be volitional. Amazingly, some people put up with a great deal and still are willing to forgive.

5. Provocation

When one spouse uses the ground of cruelty, the defense of provocation can usually be expected in response. The allegations of cruelty are negated by proof that the defendant was provoked into this behavior.

6. Recrimination

An old doctrine, recrimination has baffled many paralegals and legal scholars, but it is an equitable doctrine that bars a remedy in divorce if the complainant does not possess "clean hands." The law simply does not reward or grant a divorce to an unscrupulous, or less than innocent, complainant. This questionable lack of logic in this defense has led some jurisdictions to adopt *comparative rectitude* as a substitute, highly analagous to comparative negligence. Thus, in a case where both parties have some degree of fault, the more innocent of the two parties will be awarded the divorce.

V. SUPPORT/ALIMONY

A. General Principles

The obligation to support both children and spouse is both moral and legal. A myriad of legislative enactments in all jurisdictions mandate the payment of support, or as the mandate is sometimes called, separate-maintenance action. Support is another one of those multifaceted words, though primarily economic in design. While support is a general right, its eventual award is sometimes influenced by the "fault" of the parties, particularly as support law relates to traditional alimony.

Suffice it to say, while support must be paid, the amount must be determined by the court in a separate or joint hearing in the court. Support is also a sex-neutral issue in many states, with the primary criterion being need. In sum, each spouse owes a duty of support to the other.

Support orders and determinations come in all shapes and sizes, so to speak. They can be temporary, permanent, conditional, modifiable, or capable of termination due to a change of circumstances.

The court must also ponder a variety of issues in its eventual award of support. (See exhibit 4.5 for a sample complaint.)

Exhibit 4.5

The complaint in an action for support shall be substantially in the following form:

COURT OF COMMON PLEAS OF _____ COUNTY
DOMESTIC RELATIONS SECTION

PLAINTIFF   : CIVIL ACTION–SUPPORT

    v.   NO. _____ OF

DEFENDANT   : 19 ____

Complaint for Support

1. Plaintiff resides at _____ _____, _____ County.
                    (Street)   (City)   (Zip Code)

2. Defendant resides at _____ _____, _____ County.
                  (Street)   (City)   (Zip Code)

3. (a) Plaintiff and Defendant were married on _____, at _____.
                                  (Date)   (City and State)

   (b) Plaintiff and Defendant were separated on _____.
                                    (Date)

   (c) Plaintiff and Defendant were divorced on _____, at _____.
                               (Date)   (City and State)

4. Plaintiff and Defendant are the parents of the following children:
   (a) Born of Marriage:

NAME	BIRTH DATE	AGE	RESIDENCE
_____	_____	_____	_____
_____	_____	_____	_____

   (b) Born out of Wedlock:

NAME	BIRTH DATE	AGE	RESIDENCE
_____	_____	_____	_____
_____	_____	_____	_____

5. Defendant has neglected the duty to support or sufficiently support the aforementioned person(s).

6. (a) Plaintiff is (not) receiving public assistance in the amount of $_____ per _____ for the support of _____.
                   (Name(s))

   (b) Plaintiff is receiving additional income in the amount of $_____ from _____.

7. A previous support order was entered against the defendant on _____ in an action at _____
                                           (Date)   (Court, term)
   _____ in the amount of $_____ for the support of _____. There are (no) arrearages in the
   (and docket number)   (Name)
   amount of $_____. The order has (not) been terminated.

8. Plaintiff last received support from the Defendant in the amount of $_____ on _____.
                                                               (Date)

WHEREFORE, Plaintiff requests that an order be entered against Defendant and in favor of the Plaintiff and the aforementioned child(ren) for reasonable support.

I verify that the statements made in this Complaint and attached Income and Expense Statement are true and correct. I understand that false statements herein are made subject to the penalties relating to unsworn falsification to authorities.

                                                                      _____
                                                                       Plaintiff

---

B. Factors in the Award of Support

While each party would like as much as possible, the court's discretion in approving the grant is guided by many variables including:

> *1. A Spouse's Ability to Pay.* Some states have a rule of thumb that says support payments should never exceed one-third of a responsible party's income.
>
> *2. Actual Earnings.* A party's real income might not accurately reflect his or her actual earnings. A review of the tax records is usually a valuable lesson.
>
> *3. Capital Assets.* What is the amount of stocks, bonds, and other securities held by the responsible party?
>
> *4. Future Earnings.* The court should be well aware that a recent years' earnings or income is not necessarily indicative of future earnings.
>
> *5. Real Property.* Again, an individual who is cash short may have millions locked up in land.
>
> *6. Standard of Living.* If a responsible party's lifestyle is exorbitant and not within the realm of normal consumption, the court should not give sympathy to the extravagant lifestyle at the expense of spouse or children.
>
> *7. Other Interests/Partial Ownerships.* These might include corporations, closely held businesses, unearned income, depreciable tax benefits, or payment from a judgment or other suit.
>
> *8. Other Spouse's Earnings*
>
> *9. Children's Earnings or Net Worth*
>
> *10. A New Spouse's Income or Voluntary Contributions*
>
> *11. College Expenses*
>
> *12. Responsible Party's Second Spouse's Income*
>
> *13. Accumulated Wealth*

C. Questions Involving Support of Children

In fairness to all the parties, support has to attempt to divide as equitably as possible the available resources. While maintenance of the spouse is a crucial issue, the support of children is a time-honored duty. Both spouses are liable for the support of the child, though that spouse with the highest income must share a higher burden. Case law on the support of children manifests recurring, yet challenging, inquiries into this obligation.

> □ Does a parent owe an obligation of support to illegitimate children? *Generally yes.*
>
> □ Can the parent paying support demand that the other spouse get a job and contribute more money to the upbringing of the child? *Maybe, though if the best interests of the child are served by the parent's remaining home, no employment is required.*
>
> □ Is a parent obligated to continue support payments to a child over eighteen and attending college? *Generally yes.*
>
> □ Is a stepparent liable for the support of a spouse's child of a former marriage if stepparent assumed an active and controlling role as a parent? *Probably yes.*
>
> □ Can a parent still be obligated to support an adult child where that child is in a dire psychiatric condition and essentially unemployable? *Probably yes.*

There are as many potential questions on the issue of support as there are potential family situations. Support obligations do not cease with spouse and child. The law in many states also imposes a legal obligation on children to care for their indigent parents. An indigent parent is one who does not have sufficient means to pay for his or her own care and maintenance, and is not necessarily one who is completely destitute.

D. Modification and Enforcement of Support Rights

1. Modification factors

Generally, no order in the law of domestic relations is final. It can always be modified, depending on circumstances and events that are changed or altered. Some conditions include:

> *a.* Any significant or marked change in circumstances of the parties, including loss of job or remarriage
> *b.* Children growing past the age of majority
> *c.* The effect of inflation
> *d.* Retirement or other significant income changes

2. Enforcement

Just as there are diverse ways of securing support, so too are there many modes of order enforcement. While support is primarily a civil matter, the backlog of support payments, the public outcry over the lack of repercussions for failure to pay support, and the general judicial apathy in the sentencing or fining of those parties who deliberately thumb their noses at support orders have led to a legislative demand for sharper, more stringent criminal remedies. Federal legislation passed in 1984 supplements traditional remedies with more enforcement capability. The array of enforcement tools includes:

  a. Garnishment or attachment of wages
  b. Attachment of, or execution against, property
  c. Contempt proceedings: civil (in some jurisdictions, criminal)
  d. Entry of judgments
  e. Awarding of interests and costs of collection
  f. Security or escrow funds
  g. Criminal convictions for failure to pay support
  h. Injunctions
  i. Sequestration
  j. Receivership
  k. Doctrine of necessities

This plethora of remedies attests to the priority society gives to the support of children and of former spouses with few economic resources.

E. Alimony

The diversity of approaches adopted by the states in the field of alimony point to the need for a uniform law. Historically, alimony has been a husband's obligation to his wife in recognition of her traditional supportive role in the home. Since the wife sacrificed career goals and aspirations, and often bore children faithfully and raised them responsibly, she was obviously entitled to some measure of the couple's joint resources. Countering this in an age of feminism is the self-sufficient model modern women should be adopting, an argument that should be carefully balanced with the realism of change and reform. It is not enough to expound the rights of women, for the marketplace must be ready to accept them as workers and absorb them into the mainstream of economic life. Maybe that is all happening now. Maybe that is why alimony is becoming a taboo word and being replaced by the less sexist term, *support*. Regardless of one's politics, everyone agrees that some alimony (support) is necessary for the party who has no job and needs time to fend for himself or herself. It can't happen in seconds!

Alimony also attempts to keep some semblance of a once-assured standard of living. No court would tolerate a total disintegration of a spouse's standard of living, say from $100,000 a year to a minimum-wage position at K-Mart.

Alimony can be awarded temporarily if the financial conditions of the parties so warrant. Party must file a *petition for alimony pendente lite*. Equally possible is the award of permanent alimony. Permanent alimony can be paid out in a variety of ways, including periodic payments, lump-sum payments, and annuity trusts or contracts. The paralegal should be cognizant of the varying tax treatments in the payment of alimony.

The amount of alimony to the ex-wife granted depends on a variety of factors:

  a. Needs of wife
  b. Age and health of both spouses
  c. Husband's present income level
  d. Husband's future earnings
  e. Costs in caring for children
  f. Minimization of social and financial disruption
  g. Compensation for faithful service
  h. Degree of fault in husband (though not all states are concerned with this factor)
  i. Duration of marriage
  j. Standard of living
  k. Jointly owned property
  l. Assets and liabilities of both parties

The above factors reflect a humane concern that does not allow the automatic ditching of a spouse. One final note regards the fact of alimony being paid to husbands. A sizable group of jurisdictions have adopted this policy. (See exhibit 4.6.)

Exhibit 4.6

IN THE COURT OF COMMON PLEAS OF   COUNTY,
FAMILY DIVISION

,

     Plaintiff   )

vs.   )   No.   Term, 19

,

     Defendant   )

Petition for Alimony Pendente Lite, Child
Support, Counsel Fees and Expenses, and
Other Preliminary Relief

TO THE HONORABLE JUDGES OF THE SAID COURT:

AND NOW, comes Petitioner, _____, by her attorney, _____, ESQUIRE, and respectfully represents that:

1. On _____, Respondent filed a Complaint in Divorce herein.

2. Petitioner was served with a copy of the aforesaid Complaint in Divorce on _____.

3. Petitioner has filed an Answer and Counterclaim to the aforesaid Complaint.

4. The parties hereto are the parents of three children, who were born on _____, and who are in the care and custody of Petitioner.

5. Since the parties separated in _____, 19____, Respondent has unreasonably failed and refused to contribute to the financial support of Petitioner and the minor children of the parties.

6. Petitioner is unemployed, and is unable to support herself and her children and is unable to pay counsel fees and expenses in order to properly litigate this action in the absence of a reasonable contribution by Respondent.

7. Respondent is self-employed and earns in excess of $_____ per year.

8. The parties are the owners of substantial marital property, virtually all of which is under the exclusive control of Respondent who has acted to exclude Petitioner from the use and enjoyment thereof.

9. A substantial portion of Petitioner's separate property is in the possession and control of Respondent.

10. Respondent has unreasonably refused to permit Petitioner to obtain her sole and separate property and has excluded her from the use and enjoyment thereof.

11. Petitioner believes and therefore avers that it will be necessary for her to employ investigators and appraisers in order to determine the location and value of the marital assets.

WHEREFORE, Petitioner prays that the Court grant her the following preliminary relief:

A. That Respondent be ordered to pay a reasonable sum as child support;

B. That Respondent be ordered to pay a reasonable sum as alimony pendente lite, counsel fees and expenses;

C. That Respondent be enjoined from transfering, selling, removing, or otherwise disposing of marital property during the pendency of these proceedings;

D. That Respondent be directed to permit Petitioner to regain possession of her sole and separate property forthwith;

E. And for such other and further preliminary relief as the nature of her cause may require.

_____
, Esquire

Attorney for Petitioner

VI. PROPERTY RIGHTS AND DIVISION

A. Defining Marital Property

Numerous opportunities exist for both parties to mutually divide all their property interests without the assistance of a court, and of course most people do. Don't disregard the highly effective separation agreement, which has enormous influence over the parties' behavior since it generally enunciates the rights of the parties in their property. The term *property* should be further described as *marital property* and probably includes all property, every bit and piece except the following exclusions:

    a. Property acquired prior to marriage
    b. Property excluded by agreement
    c. Property acquired after separation until the date of divorce
    d. Property sold, granted, conveyed, or otherwise disposed of in good faith prior to the proceeding for divorce
    e. Certain veterans' benefits
    f. Other encumbered property prior to the proceeding in divorce

B. Criteria in the Distribution of Marital Property

As such, all property that is not excluded by statute, and is acquired during the period of marriage is characterized as "marital property." After the parties discern what exactly is marital property, the most grandiose question of all arises, *Who gets what?* A crude inquiry, but one that courts each and every day are required to face. How should this property be divided? What factors should be carefully pondered? How is it done fairly? Can it be done with equitable principles in mind? Can the process be referred to as *equitable distribution*, or *fair property distribution*? The questions posed are not strictly academic ones. The majority of jurisdictions have already resolved these issues because practitioners have insightfully viewed the divorce process as a dissolution of economic interests, of an economic partnership or venture. To divide property equitably does not imply equal distribution by any means—only fair, honorable, and ethical distribution in light of the following factors:

1. Length of the marriage

Obviously the more entrenched the parties become, the more accustomed they are to a set lifestyle, and the more attached they are to the property itself. As a simplistic rule, one could posit, "*The longer the marriage, the more equal the distribution.*" While hardly foolproof, the rule reflects an awareness of a lifelong or other dedicated, substantial commitment to the spouse, which should accordingly result in a more balanced distribution. The "short" marriage would imply an opposite conclusion.

2. Age and health of the parties

The eventual division of property must be guided by the health needs of the parties as well as their ages.

3. Standard of living

It is the court's desire and general intention to maintain, uphold, and insure, as far as possible, both parties' standards of living as experienced prior to the separation.

4. Income levels

This criterion is self-explanatory.

5. Occupational and vocational skills of the parties

An ability to earn income and to exist independently is highly relevant to the court's inquiry in property distribution.

6. Estate of the parties (net worth)

It makes little sense to award the bulk of marital property to a party whose net worth will shortly rival Howard Hughes's. The court must also consider separate property, though which statutorily excluded from calculation, affects the court's determination on what is a fair and equitable distribution. As such, it is peripherally required to assess all property each party acquires by bequest or devise or gift after separation. While not dominant factors in the court's eventual property distribution, it must be considered to make that distribution equitable. The court must look to the net worth of the parties at present but with an eye to potential assets, earnings and bequests.

7. Liabilities of the parties

To arrive at a party's net worth, a review of liabilities is mandatory.

8. Needs of the parties

Each distribution must uniquely reflect the individual needs of the parties. If either party has medical, educational, or legal expenses that could be characterized as greater than average, those expenses must be carefully scrutinized and weighed in the eventual distribution.

9. Past contribution of one party to another

Publicity on cases involving a woman who sacrificed her career so her husband could enter medical or law school and complete his term of studies, only to find once the diploma was awarded the husband "split" have hit the media regularly. Is there an obligation here?

10. Contribution of personal assets in the acquisition of marital property

Any major expenditure by the married couple entails some loss, or better said, investment, by both parties. If one party invested an inordinate amount of funds compared to the other, that disparity should be recognized. In order to arrive at that conclusion, the court must assess the following:

a. The extent of each party's premarital assets
b. Acquisitions made during the marriage
c. Appreciation and depreciation of marital property
d. Interspousal gifts
e. Capital contribution of each party during the marriage
f. One party assuming the debts of the marriage out of his or her own assets
g. History of each party's gainful employment
h. Either party's wasting of the marriage assets

11. Future capital assets

In deciding equitable distribution, the court must also look to potential trusts, contingencies, expectancies, and other future interests.

12. Value of services as a homemaker

While no quantified formula exists in this calculation, most courts concur that there is a substantial value inherent in the work of a homemaker, and it must be reflected in the eventual property distribution.

13. Other relevant factors

From this brief analysis, the paralegal should realize that the standards are highly flexible for the determination of an equitable or just property settlement. Instead of rigid and narrow rules, most legislatures have provided suggested guidelines as to how property should be equitably distributed. That is the undaunted intent in the law of equitable distribution. (See exhibits 4.7-4.9)

Exhibit 4.7

EQUITABLE DISTRIBUTION

Property Checklist

1. Separate and jointly owned real/personal property.
2. Out-of-state real/personal property.
3. Separate real/personal property which has increased in value since marriage.
4. Real/personal property jointly owned with other(s) prior to marriage but sole title acquired after marriage.
5. Real/personal property acquired through inheritance at time of marriage, increase in value thereof.
6. Property acquired in exchange for pre-marital property.
7. The marital home—purchase price, mortgage, fair market value.
8. Automobile (title, encumbrance).
9. Furniture (appraised value).
10. Stocks, bonds, securities (reserves or margins) and options, agreements of sale on real estate.
11. Certificates of deposits (title, maturity, amount).
12. Bank accounts (savings and checking).
13. Contents of safe deposit boxes (inventory).
14. Mortgages (notes or other instruments of indebtedness) owned by a spouse.
15. Trusts (expectancies).
16. Life insurance policies (term or whole life—cash value).
17. Annuities.
18. Endowment insurance policies.
19. Partnership interests (and capital account).
20. Spouse's professional practice (professional goodwill—valuation).
21. Art objects (check rider on insurance policies—sterling silver, camera, furs, coin/stamp collections).
22. Pre-divorce personal injury claim (workman's compensation claim, other litigation awards).
23. Money loaned to others during the marriage.
24. Other businesses owned by a spouse.
25. Separate assets of spouse.
26. Employment termination benefits—severance pay.
27. Profit-sharing plans (stock option).
28. Military retirement benefits (bearing in mind that a spouse in a civilian job may be a retired regular or reservist).
29. Military elective disability benefits.
30. Pension plans (contributory, non-contributory, pay status, maturity, valuation).
31. Railroad retirement pensions.
32. Federal disability payments.
33. Teachers' retirement plans (annuity).
34. Value of law or medical degree or license (e.g. architecture, accounting, psychology).

VII. CHILD CUSTODY

A. Introduction

The deepest tragedy of divorce is always seen in the eyes of children. No matter how civilized the separating parents are, an indelible mark of sorrow will be etched in children's faces. Divorced parents know this only too well, and that recognition gives them the greatest agony. Remarkably, that realization often inflames emotions rather than tempering them because most parents value their children beyond measure. Both hope to have dominant access and control. Neither parent can live with the "partial" child. Of course, in some cases, one or the other parent couldn't care less about the children he or she should take responsibility for. But such parents don't usually fight vigorous battles to insure their rights. At best, one can only hope that the parents will not fragment their own children for their (the parents') benefit.

In the broadest terms, custody has numerous connotations, but in the most graphic way it refers to that person

Exhibit 4.8

PROPERTY SETTLEMENT AGREEMENT CHECKLIST

Checking Needed

PREAMBLE

_____ A. Date of Marriage _____ Place of Marriage _____

_____ B. Names, birthdates of children _____ _____

_____ _____

_____ _____

_____ C. Prior Agreements with Statement of Intention (Date) _____

_____ D. What this Agreement intends to do _____

_____ E. Prior proceedings including present status of each.
Include docket numbers _____

I. SUPPORT OF SPOUSES

_____ A. Support of Wife
    1. Amount to be paid _____; frequency of payments _____
      a. In kind payments: Elec. _____ Other (specify) _____
          Heat _____ _____
          Car payments _____
      b. Contractual right to require payments through
      Probation Office of _____ County
_____   2. Waiver of Support
_____   3. Duration of Rehabilitative Alimony _____ How Long _____
_____ B. Support of Husband
_____   1. Amount to be Paid _____; frequency of payments _____
      a. In kind payments: Elec. _____ Other (specify) _____
          Heat _____ _____
          Car payments _____
      b. Contractual right to require payments through
      Probation Office of _____ County
_____   2. Waiver of Support
_____ C. Medical, Dental, Prescription Expenses
_____   1. Ordinary Medical, Dental, Prescription Expenses
      a. Whose responsibility? _____
      b. Cut off _____
      c. Definition of ordinary
         ($ limit) _____
_____   2. Extraordinary
      a. Prior approval if not emergency _____
      b. Selection of treating physician _____
    3. Blue Cross, Blue Shield (Rider J) or Equivalent _____
               Other (state name) _____
      a. Cut Off at Divorce (Yes or No) _____
_____   4. Major Medical Insurance _____
      a. Cut Off at Divorce (Yes or No) _____
_____   5. Dental Insurance _____
_____ D. Termination of Obligation
    1. Death of _Either_ Spouse _____
    2. Remarriage (Yes or No) _____
    3. Term Alimony _____
_____ E. Effects of Special Events
_____   1. Assumptions as to Income Levels: Husband _____
                        Wife _____

_____ 2. Termination if Wife works and earns _____ per annum
_____ 3. Disability of Husband _____
_____ 4. Unemployment of Husband _____
_____ 5. General Changed Circumstances Clause _____

II. CUSTODY AND SUPPORT OF CHILDREN

_____ A. Custody of children to _____ including general statement as to responsibilities of custodial parent
_____   1. If joint custody, set forth general living arrangements _____
_____   2. If split custody of more than one child, indicate who lives with whom _____

_____ B. Child Support
_____   1. To whom paid _____
_____   2. How much _____; How often _____; How paid
     (Probation Office or Direct) _____
     If Probation, _____ County
_____   3. Contractual right to require Probation Office payments at later time
_____   4. Partial abatement during extended visitation _____
     If so, how much _____

_____ C. Medical, Dental, Prescription Expenses
     1. Ordinary Medical, Dental, Prescription Expenses
       a. Whose responsibility? _____
       b. Definition of ordinary ($ limit) _____
_____   2. Extraordinary
       a. Prior approval if not emergency _____
       b. Selection of Treating Physician _____
     3. Blue Cross, Blue Shield (Rider J) _____
       or equivalent (state name) _____
_____   4. Major Medical Insurance _____
_____   5. Dental Insurance _____
_____   6. Orthodonture _____
_____   7. Agreements Concerning Special Illnesses
     State name of child _____
     Special illness _____
     Agreement concerning costs _____
_____ D. Termination of Obligation—Definition of Emancipation _____
                           Death of Payor _____
_____ E. College Education (various clauses—choose one)
_____   1. Mutual obligation _or_ _____
_____   2. Husband pays _or_
       a. Prior approval _____
       b. Dollar limit _____
       c. Definition of what is included _____
_____   3. Shared Expense
       a. Contribution of Husband _____
       b. Contribution of Wife _____
       c. Child required to get loan _____
       d. Definition of what is included _____
_____ F. Include agreements, if any, concerning Postgraduate or Professional Courses _____
_____ G. Effects of Special Events
_____   1. Assumptions as to income levels: Husband _____
                                   Wife _____
_____   2. Termination if Wife works and earns _____ per annum
_____   3. Disability of Husband _____
_____   4. Unemployment of Husband _____
_____   5. General Changed Circumstances Clause _____
_____ H. Change of Custody upon death of spouse _____
_____ I. Removal from State _____
_____ J. Agreements concerning religious upbringing of children _____

III. VISITATION

_____ A. Type of Visitation (select one)
_____   1. Structured visitation *or*
         a. Weekend—From _____ at _____ until _____ at _____
         b. Overnight—Which night _____ from _____ until _____
         c. Midweek dinner on _____ from _____ until _____
         d. Holidays from _____ until _____
             New Year's Day _____
             Presidents' Day _____
             Easter _____
             Memorial Day _____
             4th of July _____
             Labor Day _____
             Columbus Day _____
             Thanksgiving _____
             Christmas _____
         e. School vacations from _____ at _____ until _____ at _____
             Christmas _____
             Easter _____
         f. Summer vacation for ____ weeks to be selected prior to _____
         g. Birthdays from _____ until _____
_____   2. Unstructured visitation—"Liberal Rights of Visitation"
_____ B. Visitation to commence at _____
_____ C. Required Notice if not exercised _____ hours
_____ D. Parties to consult
_____ E. Prohibition of alienation of affections

IV. INSURANCE AS SECURITY

_____ A. Amount _____; Type _____; Beneficiary _____;
       New or Existing Policy _____; Duration _____
_____ B. Requirement that Proof of Insurance be furnished annually

V. EQUITABLE DISTRIBUTION OF PROPERTY

_____ A. Transfer of Former Marital Home _____
                                                                  (Address)
       from _____ to _____; when _____
       Subject to existing mortgage with approximate balance of _____
_____ B. Other Transfer of Real Property:
       Address _____ from _____ to _____
                   _____ from _____ to _____
                   _____ from _____ to _____
_____ C. Distribution of Securities:
       _____ shares of _____ from _____ to _____
       _____ shares of _____ from _____ to _____
       _____ shares of _____ from _____ to _____
       When: _____
_____ D. Distribution of Bonds:
       _____ units of _____ from _____ to _____
       _____ units of _____ from _____ to _____
       _____ units of _____ from _____ to _____
       When: _____
_____ E. Waiver by Wife of Interest in Business of Husband:
       Name of Business _____; Number of shares held by _____
_____ F. Cash Payment by Husband to Wife:
       Total Amount _____ payable in _____ installments _____ of _____ from _____
                                                  (when)   (how much)
       from _____ until _____; Security (if any) _____

_____ G. Distribution of Accounts:
    1. To be Retained by Husband
       a. Name of bank _____ Type of Account _____ Approximate balance _____
       b. Name of bank _____ Type of Account _____ Approximate balance _____
       c. Name of bank _____ Type of Account _____ Approximate balance _____
    2. To be Retained by Wife
       a. Name of bank _____ Type of Account _____ Approximate balance _____
       b. Name of bank _____ Type of Account _____ Approximate balance _____
       c. Name of bank _____ Type of Account _____ Approximate balance _____

_____ H. Distribution of Motor Vehicles
    1. Husband to Retain _____ _____
                (yr.)   (make)
       now titled in name of _____
    2. Wife to Retain _____ _____
             (yr.)   (make)
       now titled in name of _____
    3. Other _____

_____ I. Distribution of Tangible Personal Property
    1. Property Already Distributed _or_:
    2. Property Partially Distributed:
       _____ to be permitted to remove _____
       _____
       _____
       _____
       _____
       _____
    within _____ days

_____ J. Distribution of Pension Plan
    1. Waiver of Wife's interest in pension plan _____ name of employer _____
    type of plan _____ approximate value of plan _____; _OR_
    2. Wife to receive limited portion of pension plan as received by Husband:
       name of employer _____ type of plan _____
       extent and method of distribution _____

_____ K. Waiver by _____ of interest in insurance policies of _____
    1. Name of Company _____ Policy # _____
    Owner _____ Cash Surrender Value _____
    2. Name of Company _____ Policy # _____
    Owner _____ Cash Surrender Value _____
    3. Name of Company _____ Policy # _____
    Owner _____ Cash Surrender Value _____

_____ L. After Acquired Property

VI. RETURN OF CREDIT CARDS AND RESPONSIBILITY FOR PAST DEBTS

_____ A. Wife to Return Credit Cards to Husband:
_____   1. Company _____ Account # _____
_____   2. Company _____ Account # _____
_____   3. Company _____ Account # _____
_____   4. Company _____ Account # _____
_____   5. Company _____ Account # _____
_____   6. Company _____ Account # _____
_____   7. Company _____ Account # _____
     B. Husband to be responsible for all debts of Wife incurred prior to _____; Wife to be responsible for all debts incurred thereafter.
     C. Husband specifically responsible for the following debts: _____
       _____
       _____
       _____
_____ D. Wife specifically responsible for the following debts: _____
       _____
       _____
       _____
       _____

VII. TAXES

_____ A. Renegotiation upon shift of tax liability.
_____ B. Deficiencies and Refunds; Allocation agreed upon _____
              _____
              _____
_____ C. Agreement concerning income tax returns: Type of return(s) to be filed: _____
_____ D. Exemptions for Federal and State Income Tax Purposes. Allocation agreed upon _____

VIII. INDEPENDENT LEGAL ADVICE

_____ A. Name of Opposing Counsel _____

IX. DIVORCE

_____ A. No Bar to Divorce _____
              1. Designation of limitations contained _____
              _____
_____ B. No Merger; Incorporation within Judgment

X. COUNSEL FEES

_____ A. Each party to pay own counsel fees, _OR_:
_____ B. Husband to pay _____ to _____ for services rendered to Wife

XI. WAIVER OF CLAIMS

_____ A. General Release between the parties
_____ B. Indemnification as to claims of third parties.

Exhibit 4.9

Name:
Address:
Phone:
Attorney for (Plaintiff)(Defendant)

IN THE COURT OF COMMON PLEAS OF   COUNTY,
                        CIVIL ACTION — LAW

            PLAINTIFF,   :   NO. _____, TERM, _____

  v.   :   ATTORNEY ID NUMBER:

            DEFENDANT.   :   IN DIVORCE, A.V.M.

                        Inventory and Appraisement
                                    of

                        _____

(Plaintiff)(Defendant) files the following inventory and appraisement of all property owned or possessed by either party at the time this action was commenced and all property transferred within the preceding three years.

(Plaintiff)(Defendant) verifies that the statements made in this inventory and appraisment are true and correct. (Plaintiff)(Defendant) understands that false statements herein are made subject to the penalties of relating to unsworn falsification to authorities.

_____
(Plaintiff)(Defendant)

Assets of Parties

(Plaintiff)(Defendant) marks on the list below those items applicable to the case at bar and itemizes the assets on the following pages. If an item has been appraised, a copy of the appraisal report is attached.

( )   1.   Real property
( )   2.   Motor vehicles
( )   3.   Stocks, bonds, securities and options
( )   4.   Certificates of deposit
( )   5.   Checking accounts, cash
( )   6.   Saving accounts, money market and savings certificates
( )   7.   Contents of safe deposit boxes
( )   8.   Trusts
( )   9.   Life insurance policies (indicate face value, cash surrender value and current beneficiaries)
( ) 10.   Annuities
( ) 11.   Gifts
( ) 12.   Inheritances
( ) 13.   Patents, copyrights, inventions, royalties
( ) 14.   Personal property outside the home
( ) 15.   Businesses (list all owners, including percentage of ownership, and officer/director positions held by a party with company)
( ) 16.   Employment termination benefits–severance pay, workman's compensation claim/award
( ) 17.   Profit sharing plans
( ) 18.   Pension plans (indicate employee contribution and date plan vests)
( ) 19.   Retirement plans, Individual Retirement Accounts
( ) 20.   Disability payments
( ) 21.   Litigation claims (matured and unmatured)
( ) 22.   Military/V.A. benefits
( ) 23.   Education benefits
( ) 24.   Debts due, including loans, mortgages held
( ) 25.   Household furnishings and personalty (include as a total category and attach itemized list if distribution of such assests is in dispute)
( ) 26.   Other

Marital Property

(Plaintiff)(Defendant) lists all marital property in which either or both spouses have a legal or equitable interest individually or with any other person as of the date this action was commenced:

ITEM NUMBER	DESCRIPTION OF PROPERTY	NAMES OF ALL OWNERS	DATE OF ACQUISITION

ITEM NUMBER	COST OR VALUE AS OF DATE OF ACQUISITION	VALUE AS OF DATE ACTION COMMENCED	AMOUNT OF ANY LIEN

ITEM NUMBER	NATURE OF ANY LIEN	EFFECTIVE DATE OF LIEN	HOLDER OF LIEN

Nonmarital Property

(Plaintiff)(Defendant) lists all property in which a spouse has a legal or equitable interest which is claimed to be excluded from marital property:

ITEM NUMBER	DESCRIPTION OF PROPERTY	NAMES OF ALL OWNERS	DATE OF ACQUISITION

ITEM NUMBER	COST OR VALUE AS OF DATE OF ACQUISITION	VALUE AS OF DATE ACTION COMMENCED	AMOUNT OF ANY LIEN

ITEM NUMBER	NATURE OF ANY LIEN	EFFECTIVE DATE OF LIEN	HOLDER OF LIEN

ITEM NUMBER	BASIS FOR EXCLUSION FROM MARITAL PROPERTY

Property Transferred

ITEM NUMBER	DESCRIPTION OF PROPERTY	NAMES OF ALL OWNERS	DATE OF ACQUISITION	DATE OF TRANSFER

ITEM NUMBER	COST OR VALUE AS OF DATE OF ACQUISITION	VALUE AS OF DATE OF TRANSFER	AMOUNT OF ANY LIEN AT DATE OF TRANSFER

ITEM NUMBER	NATURE OF ANY LIEN AT DATE OF TRANSFER	EFFECTIVE DATE OF LIEN	HOLDER OF LIEN

Liabilities of Parties

(Plaintiff)(Defendant) marks on the list below those items applicable to the case at bar and itemizes the liabilities on the following pages:

SECURED

( ) 1. Mortgages
( ) 2. Judgments
( ) 3. Liens
( ) 4. Other secured liabilities

UNSECURED

( ) 5. Credit card balances
( ) 6. Purchases
( ) 7. Loan payments
( ) 8. Notes payable
( ) 9. Other unsecured liabilities

CONTINGENT OR DEFERRED

( ) 10. Contracts or agreements
( ) 11. Promissory notes
( ) 12. Lawsuits
( ) 13. Options
( ) 14. Taxes
( ) 15. Other contingent or deferred liabilities

Liabilities

(Plaintiff)(Defendant) lists all liabilities of either or both spouses alone or with any person as of the date this action was commenced:

ITEM NUMBER	DESCRIPTION OF LIABILITY	NAMES OF ALL CREDITORS	DEBTORS

ITEM NUMBER	DATE LIABILITY WAS INCURRED	AMOUNT OF LIABILITY ON DATE INCURRED & ACTION WAS COMMENCED

who performs the normal, dutiful functions of a parent in caring for a child. Visitation is not custody. A vacation with a child is not custody. Child support or payment of educational costs is not custody. Custody is a reflection of the bits and pieces of daily life; it is the daily grind of existence—the place the court decides the child will eat, sleep, and function the best. Custody is at a parent's house, the house that is the best environment for the child. Custody implies dependency and makes one responsible for neglect. Custody places grave responsibilities on the parent to raise the child properly but also provides ample authority to accomplish the task. So who should get custody of children in a divorce? How is custody decided? Is there anything like joint custody? Can an award of custody be modified? What factors are controlling in the eventual determination of custody? Maybe looking to the courts for these answers is misplaced allegiance, but paralegals quickly see the highly cooperative spirit between the courts, social services, clinical and marriage counseling centers, and other relevant agencies. To say the least, the court makes very few decisions in a vacuum. (See exhibits 4.10. and 4.11.)

B. Factors in the Award of Custody

The hallmark of every judicial determination concerning child custody is the "best interests of the child." Whatever is perceived as furthering the welfare of the individual child is valued as evidence. All criteria posed by either party are evaluated within this child-oriented framework. Consider some of the following factors:

1. Morals and values of the parents

While some subjectivists argue that morality is irrelevant to an award of custody, the argumentation is folly when realism demands an introspective look at either parent. Given the choice of a parent who believes that adultery is fine, that God is a loser, that incest is normative, and that work is meaningless and one who feels otherwise, the choice is fairly self-evident. Of course, lesbians and gay parents feel this objective moralism has been used harshly against them in their efforts to gain custody of their own or other children by adoption. Would you award custody of a child to a hard-working, responsible lesbian parent or to a hard-working, responsible heterosexual parent?

2. Ability to care for the child: material means

While money does not buy love or affection, or anything else intangible for that matter, it goes a long way in assuring some decent living conditions.

Assume one parent has a net worth of $400,000, and the other $40,000. If both are good people with no other real differences, whom will you award custody to? What if the richer of the two was once a draft dodger? What if the poorer of the two is more affectionate?

Exhibit 4.10

COURT OF COMMON PLEAS OF _____ COUNTY

PLAINTIFF   :   CIVIL ACTION—(CUSTODY)
                                                     (PARTIAL CUSTODY) (VISITATION)

        v.   :

DEFENDANT   :   NO. _____ OF 19____

COMPLAINT FOR (CUSTODY)(PARTIAL CUSTODY)(VISITATION)

1.   The plaintiff is _____,
residing at _____,
                    (Street)   (City)   (Zip Code)   (County)

2.   The defendant is _____,
residing at _____.
                    (Street)   (City)   (Zip Code)   (County)

3.   Plaintiff seeks (custody)(partial custody)(visitation) of the following child(ren):

NAME	PRESENT RESIDENCE	AGE

The child (was)(was not) born out of wedlock.
The child is presently in the custody of _____.
                                                          (Name)

who resides at _____,
                        (Street)   (City)   (State)

During the past five years, the child has resided with the following persons and at the following addresses:

(LIST ALL PERSONS)	(LIST ALL ADDRESSES)	(DATES)

The mother of the child is _____,
currently residing at _____.
She is (married)(divorced)(single).

The father of the child is _____,
currently residing at _____.
He is (married)(divorced)(single).

4.   The relationship of plaintiff to the child is that of _____. The plaintiff currently
resides with the following persons:

NAME	RELATIONSHIP

5.   The relationship of defendant to the child is that of _____. The defendant
currently resides with the following persons:

NAME	RELATIONSHIP

6.   Plaintiff (has)(has not) participated as a party or witness, or in another capacity, in other litigation concerning the custody of the child in this or another court. The court, term and number, and its relationship to this action is: _____

_____

    Plaintiff (has)(has no) information of a custody proceeding concerning the child pending in a court of this Commonwealth. The court, term and number, and its relationship to this action is: _____.

    Plaintiff (knows)(does not know) of a person not a party to the proceedings who has physical custody of the child or claims to have custody or visitation rights with respect to the child. The name and address of such person is:

_____.

7.   The best interest and permanent welfare of the child will be served by granting the relief requested because (set forth facts showing that the granting of the relief requested will be in the best interest and permanent welfare of the child): _____.

8.   Each parent whose parental rights to the child have not been terminated and the person who has physical custody of the child have been named as parties to this action. All other persons, named below, who are known to have or claim a right to custody or visitation of the child have been given notice of the pendency of this action and the right to intervene:

NAME	ADDRESS	BASIS OF CLAIM
_____	_____	_____
_____	_____	_____
_____	_____	_____

    Wherefore, plaintiff requests the court to grant (custody)(partial custody)(visitation) of the child.

_____
Attorney for Plaintiff

    I verify that the statements made in this Complaint are true and correct. I understand that false statement given are made subject to the penalties of   relating to unsworn falsification to authorities.

_____
Plaintiff

Other material factors considered are the nature of the domicile, cultural opportunities in home location, and household support.

3. Sibling placement

Overwhelmingly, courts are hesitant to fragment the family unit unless there are obvious advantages. If one parent has problems controlling a child, that may necessitate an award to the other parent. The bottom line is to uphold the family unit as much as possible.

4. The child's wishes

At one stage in history, little attention was given to a child's own desires. Today children's desires are valued in this context, especially if they are over twelve years old. Courts essentially give weight to a child's preference according to how much maturity and sense they feel the child exhibits.

5. Wishes of the parents/responsible parties

Since the court is the final arbiter of the custody decision, it should respectfully weigh the wishes of the more interested parent. It is not beyond the power of the court to totally disregard those wishes, if the evidence manifests a parental preference that is without logic or meaning. The court's own disposition often adheres to a previous separation agreement executed by the parties.

6. Religious orientation

This factor has been recently downplayed and may in time be declared unconstitutional. The fact remains, however, that cultural traits, heritage, or religious orientation sometimes make a custody decision a little easier on the child.

Exhibit 4.11

```
          IN THE COURT OF COMMON PLEAS OF _____ COUNTY,

_____              :

        vs.                          :    NO. _____

                                     :    _____, TERM, 1980

_____              :    ATTORNEY NO. _____

                    Petition to Confirm Custody
```

TO THE HONORABLE, THE JUDGES OF THE SAID COURT:

   1.   Petitioner is _____, who resides at _____.

   2.   Respondent is _____, who resides at _____.

   3.   Petitioner and Respondent were married on _____ in _____, and were separated (divorced) on _____.

   4.   _____ children were born of the marriage, said children being _____, born _____; _____, born _____; (etc.).

   5.   The said children are currently in the lawful custody of Petitioner.

   6.   The best interests and welfare of the said children would best be served by placing permanent custody in Petitioner.

   7.   The present address of the children is _____.

   8.   The children have resided at the following places during the past five years: _____, etc.

   9.   The names and present addresses of the persons with whom the children have lived during the past five years are: _____, _____, etc.

   10.   Petitioner *has/has not* participated as a party, witness, or otherwise in any other litigation concerning the custody of the said children in Pennsylvania or any other state. (If so, give details).

   11.   Petitioner *had/does not have* information of any custody proceeding concerning the said children in any court of Pennsylvania or any other state. (If so, give details).

   12.   Petitioner *does/does not* know of any person not a party to these proceedings who has physical custody of the said children or who claims to have custody or visitation rights with respect to them. (If so, give details).

   WHEREFORE, Petitioner respectfully prays that Your Honorable Court order that permanent custody of the children, _____, _____, etc. be placed in Petitioner.

```
                                            _____
                                            Attorney for Petitioner
```

7. Race

The U.S. Supreme Court in 1984 ruled rightfully and firmly that race has no place in the determination of custody in a modification hearing. Rest assured, race may be a subliminal factor in the decision-making process, but no state action or judicial decision can be justified if this criterion was used.

8. Sex of the parent

Under the "tender-years" doctrine, a presumption existed that a child under the age of six was best given over to the custody of his natural mother. The rationale was that the mother, both biologically and emotionally, could best care for that child and satisfy the "best interest" factor in the award of custody.

Recent national case law has shown some erosion in this presumption. In some jurisdictions, the male petitioner need not present compelling or utterly convincing evidence to overcome this presumption. As a result, in some jurisdictions both the man and woman are now on an even plane during the tender-years period. The constitutional dimensions of the tender-years doctrine have been frequently litigated.

Even past the tender-years rule, most states no longer assume, prefer, or presume that the female is better suited to child custody. In an age of joint careers, house husbands, and the equal rights amendments at the state level, opposition to male custody is plainly unfounded. Realistically, the bias against men will be around for a long time to come.

9. Emotional and mental state

A court can rightfully award custody to any party who has successfully conquered past mental strife, but no individual can automatically expect that award if problems persist and may be detrimental to the child.

10. History of neglect and cruelty

The court will look suspiciously on any petitioner whose history indicates abuse toward children.

11. Sexual orientation

A few recent cases have supported the proposition that homosexuality should not be a factor in the determination of custody unless there is some indication that the person seeking custody would promote certain sexual orientations. In a majority of jurisdictions homosexuals have an uphill battle.

12. Third-party support

Does the parent have a support team that can assist in the raising of the child, such as a cooperative grandparent or other relatives? In fact, courts are now considering and even granting visitation rights to certain grandparents. Partial custody has been awarded to grandparents in a few jurisdictions.

13. Age of the parent

While most people would not object if a very ill individual was not awarded custody, the opinion on age is split. How old is too old to be given custody? Should age be a factor at all?

C. Visitation Rights

As a general principle, the law hopes to promote all relationships between parents and their children, and will order, require, and enforce a system of visitation rights for the noncustodial parents.

Most problems arise not over the grant of visitation but in its parameters. The paralegal must clearly delineate to all clients the schedule of visitation. A typical visitation scheme might include:

1. Alternating weekends, from 7:00 P.M. Friday to 6:30 P.M. Sunday.
2. Major holidays in alternating years, like Easter, Memorial Day, and Christmas.
3. A block of time from two to eight weeks during the school break.
4. Alternating feast days, birthdays, and other agreed time frames.

The paralegal must also know that restrictions on visitation are legal and imposed at the court's discretion. Some restrictions include third-party supervision, board, payment of traveling expenses, and counseling. Be aware that restriction of visitation rights is frequently used as a weapon against the spouse's failure to pay support. Check local rules for these consequences.

D. Joint or Shared Custody

A recent legal phenomenon, particularly in the eastern U.S. is the joint, or shared, custody award. Joint custody can be legal as well as physical in scope with all major decisions being joint in nature. The child can be shared by both parents equally over the course of an entire year.

While not a panacea for the children of divorce, the grant appears to work successfully in certain cases. The child gains access to both parents, and that access is reciprocal to the parents. In the ideal sense, the joint-custody grant hopes to provide, at least on some appearances, the most unified, cohesive family setting possible in a divorced environment. Joint custody seeks to foster deeper, more firmly rooted relationships with both parents, rather than viewing one parent as a sporadic visitor. But again, the threshold issue is whether the child would be benefited. Initial reactions indicate that a joint arrangement certainly requires mature adults and a child willing to exhibit a cooperative spirit. Parents must be supportive of a child's wish to love *both* parents and should not exhibit needless jealousy.

VIII. ADOPTION

In most circumstances, this is a pleasant task for the paralegal and attorney. While much of domestic law is reactive or negative in focus, the decision to adopt is usually a positive, touching decision by a couple who want a child. The role of the attorney and paralegal can be pivotal in securing a child, particularly in these times when adoptive children are in short supply.

Adoption is a far-reaching process generally allowing a petitioner to adopt any child under eighteen years of age and any adult who is related to the adoptive parents and who has resided with them for a sufficient duration.

While no mold exists for who makes an appropriate adoptive parent, the general rule is that adoptive parents should be married with no legal disability, of good character, and of sufficient economic means to support the child.

Tremendous strides have been made in allowing single persons to adopt children, especially in large urban areas.

A. Procedure

1. Filing of a petition

A petition may be filed by an individual, agency, or other appropriate party. The petition contains all standard information, including names of petitioners, ages, marital status, and other pertinent data. (See exhibit 4.12.)

2. Notice

If the natural parents are not put on notice of a prospective adoption of their child by other parties, serious due-process problems may later arise. All legally significant parties to the adoption should be put on notice of the intention to adopt.

3. Interim hearing and order

After all notices have been served, the court will frequently hold an interim or initial hearing to make a temporary award to the prospective parents. That interim award usually runs six months and will be upheld if all agency reports and investigators assure the court of the quality of the petitioners, and if all consent problems have been resolved.

4. Acquisition of consent

Especially in the case of natural parents, the paralegal must insure that appropriate consent documentation has been secured. Unwillingness on the part of a natural parents should not deter a prospective adoptive parent because some natural parents refuse to cooperate even though they are clearly unfit to raise their own children. Be also mindful of the newly emerging rights of the father of an illegitimate child. Only a minority of jurisdictions give any credence to the father's wishes, but a movement is afoot concerning the natural father's rights in relation to adoption, visitation, and the decision of abortion.

Also, please note that the consent of an adoptive child over the age of twelve is considered a crucial factor in some jurisdictions.

5. Hearing on involuntary termination

In cases of desertion, child abuse of an extreme nature, conviction of crimes, and general disregard of a parent toward his or her child, that parent's rights can be terminated without his or her consent. This is accomplished by a termination hearing. A heavy burden rests upon the state or commonwealth asserting the justice of involuntary termination as the court carefully ruminates on the historical relationship between child and parent, the duration of abuse, the physical and mental state of the child, and the overall evidence of neglect and abject parental care.

6. Agency investigation/recommendation on placement

After a petition has been filed describing the prospective parents, courts frequently ask social agencies regularly dealing with adoptive services to investigate the petitioners or to make an appropriate recommendation on where this particular child should be placed. The agency does a thorough investigation into the petitioner's work background,

Exhibit 4.12

FORM 3050

FAMILY COURT DIVISION — ADOPTION SECTION

COUNTY
COURT OF COMMON PLEAS

In Re Adoption of

_____ Term, 19 ____

No. _____

PETITION FOR ADOPTION

The petition of

respectfully represents:

1. Facts as to the petitioner   are as follows:
    (a) The date and place of birth of petitioner:
    (b) Petitioner (do)es now reside at
         and for the past five years has (have) resided at the following addresses during the periods specified:

    (c) The marital status of petitioner   is (are):
         (If married, state date and place of marriage and whether living together. If parties were previously divorced, give particulars and identify proceedings.)

    (d) The names and ages of children of petitioner   , if any, and state whether adopted or otherwise.

    (e) The occupation of petitioner   is(are):

    (f) Religious affiliation and racial background:

    (g) Relationship of petitioner   to adoptee, if any:

2. The Report of Intention to Adopt has been filed on: *(If not required, state reason.)*

3. Name and address of intermediary, if any:

4. Facts as to the adoptee are as follows:
    (a) Date and place of birth:
    (b) The adoptee has resided with petitioner from the date of   . Prior to that date, the adoptee has resided with the following parties and at the following places, during the periods specified:

    (c) Religious affiliation and race:

5. If there is no intermediary or if the adoptee is over the age of 18, state the following:
    (a) Facts as to the natural parents of adoptee:
         (For each parent, state name, age, racial background, religious affiliation, marital status as of one year prior to birth of child, and marital status at time of birth.)
         (Information as to father is unnecessary if child is illegitimate.)

    (b) Identify proceedings in which any decree of termination of parental rights or parental rights and duties with respect to the adoptee was entered.

    (c) If no decree of termination has been entered, state residence of parent(s) of adoptee.

    (d) Describe fully and state the value of all property owned or possessed by adoptee:

    (e) No provision of any act regulating the importation of dependent, delinquent, defective children has been violated with respect to the placement of the adoptee.

6. The intermediary's report was filed with this court on _____ and written notice of same was given to petitioner on _____

7. If a change in name of the adoptee is desired, state the new name: _____

8. Exhibits attached to this petition are:
   (a) Consent of adoptee over twelve.

   (b) Consent of petitioner's spouse, unless both are petitioners.

   (c) An affidavit as to character of petitioner.

financial history, community reputation and relationships, and general personal and emotional stability as well as the age, mental abilities, and personality of the adoptive child in question.

7. Final hearing or decree

Once all available data are collected and analyzed, a hearing may be scheduled to hear testimony on the award or grant of the adoption petition. That final decree is usually rendered in a private hearing or by private action by the judge, who relates his findings to the appropriate parties. Within that final decree can also be a pleading space for a change of name or adoption of a new name as requested.

8. Problems in the adoption process

Recent headlines indicate a thriving industry in the marketing of children to prospective adoptive parents. Owing to the legalization of abortion and the decision of many unwed adolescent mothers to keep their offspring, there is a severe shortage of children for adoption, particularly white children. The paralegal would be wise to consider the ethical ramifications of his or her involvements in programs or enterprises that literally "sell" babies or provide surrogate-mother services. A thriving black-market business now exists in the sale and exchange of children. Many of these practices are in direct violation of existing state laws whose legislatures have placed primary and rightful authority for the placement of adoptive children in certain administrative agencies.

DISCUSSION QUESTIONS AND PRACTICAL EXERCISES

Discussion Questions

1. State whether each of the following propositions is TRUE or FALSE.
   a. A husband and wife, by means of a separation agreement may to the exclusion of the court legally bind themselves to pay (and receive) a particular sum of money as child support.
   b. A man and woman who openly cohabitate and hold themselves out to be husband and wife and plan to marry in the future are validly married by common law.
   c. The fact that a husband alone caused irreconcilable differences to exist is no defense to a divorce action based on that ground.
   d. No specific length of residence is necessary to enable a party to file for a divorce from bed and board.
   e. A court cannot inquire into the assets and income of a husband's second wife to determine the amount of child support payable to children by his first wife.
   f. The three-month "cooling-off" period is required only for divorces obtained on a fault ground.
   g. A woman may change her name after divorce whether or not it is included as part of the divorce action.
   h. A marriage ceremony performed before the town librarian, if valid in all other respects, is void nonetheless.
   i. Under the new irreconcilable-differences statute, the parties will not be allowed to testify as to fault.
   j. No divorce can be granted by default.
2. List and explain fully the differences between the following types of financial relief available to litigants in divorce actions: alimony, child support, assignment of property.

Practical Exercises

1. John and Juliet were high school and college sweethearts in New York. John had long promised to marry Juliet, and based on his promises, they began living together in New York, and as a result of this union, a child, Rocco, was born on February 8, 1973. Exactly two months following Rocco's birth, John and Juliet were married and subsequently had two other children—Marie, who was born on August 15, 1975, and Tina, who was born on December 24, 1976. In late 1978 they all moved to South Kingstown, where Juliet taught in the physics department at a local college. John at this time ran a small neighborhood tavern in the vicinity of the university.

   Fortunately, John's tavern prospered, but unfortunately he had to work long hours for this result, and these hours were much too long for Juliet. Juliet believed that her husband was seeing another woman based upon the fact that income from the tavern had begun to decrease, he had begun coming home much later than his normal closing hour with perfume on his shirts, and not the least, their love life had certainly grown stale.

   Another woman had been a problem earlier, but John and Juliet had discussed it, and Juliet was willing to live and let live and therefore attempted to forget about her husband's conduct. Not discussed or known was Juliet's affair with the graduate teaching assistant. John's conduct, however, continued, and finally last week, when Juliet raised the subject once and for all, her husband flew into a rage, screamed at her, and threatened that he would leave her high and dry if she attempted to take any action. He suggested to her that that was exactly what she wanted to occur anyway and that he was going to leave, and she could have the house but would have to pay all household expenses. He stated that he would not pay support since he did not want any of the children and wondered whether or not Rocco was even his. Additionally he said that he would not give her any of the insurance policies that he had taken out on his life, and that he had already emptied the bank account and had planned to move into the second floor of the bar with Ella, the barmaid. The bar, which is in a rented building, located at 1515 Annaquatucket Road in South Kingstown, is a cash business, and Juliet is not fully familiar with the details of how well the business is doing at this time.

   a. Prepare a complaint, summons, divorce-information sheet, and motion for temporary support, etc.

   b. What defenses might John raise to counter any fault ground brought up by Juliet?

2. Your boss presents you with the following information and tells you to prepare all documents necessary to start suit for divorce for your client and obtain the immediate relief she needs.

Facts.   Alice and Joe were married on January 21, 1969, by the Reverend Jones in Dallas, Texas. They have two children, Jack, born November 26, 1971, and Jill, born July 1, 1973. Alice had an excellent job and owned her own home before she met Joe. After their marriage both Alice and Joe lived in Alice's house, and they bought a condominium and later a cottage on the lake, which Alice paid for. Joe has had a series of jobs. He is very handsome and has always had plenty of free time while Alice works. In 1975, he began to stay away from home many nights. He spent a lot of money taking other women on weekend trips and buying them gifts. He was cruel to Alice and struck her on her birthday, last Christmas, and on several occasions when she complained of his behavior. He ignored their children.

Joe left their home on August 7, 1980.

Alice has realized that Joe may be handsome, but she doesn't need the problems of being married to him. She has contacted our office, and we will represent her in obtaining a divorce from Joe, gaining full custody of the two children of the marriage and retaining the property she provided in the marriage.

Additional Information

Client's Name:	Alice Smith	Maiden Name: Brown
Date of Birth:	7/2/47	Social Security No.: 111-11-111
Birthplace:	El Paso, Texas	Current Residence: Your home address for the last 5 years
Spouse's Name:	Joseph Smith	Date of Birth: 8/12/47
Birthplace:	Chicago, Illinois	Current Residence: Address where you are taking this course
Social Security No.:	222-22-222	Employed by: Joseph Smith is employed by the attorney teaching this course as of the first of this year.
Salary:	$1,500 per month	
Assets:	1978 Buick Stationwagon & 1981 Buick Regal Sedan, household furnishings, condominium, and cottage on the lake.	

Prepare the pleadings necessary to institute divorce proceedings, the papers necessary to obtain immediate support relief for your client and custody of the children, and the final judgment of divorce.

ENRICHMENT ACTIVITY

Interview a representative of a family-counseling or family-crisis-intervention agency. Detail what services are provided to families in hardship. What cooperative efforts exist between the agency and the courts? Have these efforts proved to be beneficial to the families? To the courts? Think of some recommendations that would enhance existing services to families in need of assistance.

SUGGESTED READING

FAMILY LAW REPORTER. *Desk Guide to the Uniform Marriage and Divorce Act*. Washington, D.C.: BNA Books, 1982.

FISHER, E. O. and M. S., EDS. *Therapists, Lawyers and Divorcing Spouses*. New York: Haworth Press, 1982.

GLENDON, MARY ANN. *The New Family and the New Property*. Toronto: Butterworths, 1981.

GOLDEN, LAWRENCE J. *Equitable Distribution of Property*. Colorado Springs: Shepard's/McGraw-Hill, 1983.

GREEN, SAMUEL. *Marriage and Family Law Agreements*. Colorado Springs: Shepard's/McGraw-Hill, 1984.

McCAHEY, JOHN P., ed. dir. *Valuation and Distribution of Marital Property*. New York: M. Bender, 1984.

MITNICK, HAROLD. *How to Handle Your Divorce Step by Step: A Marital Mediation Primer*. Bethesda, Md.: Lone Oak Books, 1981.

O'DONNELL, WILLIAM J. *The Law of Marriage and Marital Alternatives*. Lexington, Mass.: Lexington Books, 1982.

REDDEN, KENNETH R. *Federal Regulations of Family Law*. Charlottesville, Va.: Michie Co., 1982.

STATSKY, WILLIAM P. *Family Law*. St. Paul: West Publishing Co., 1984.

CHAPTER FIVE

TORT LAW

CHAPTER DESCRIPTION

This chapter involves a study of traditional tort law, including intentional torts, such as assault and battery and negligence. Also, no-fault laws, product liability, nuisance, misrepresentation, defamation, invasion of privacy, trespass, and workmen's compensation are covered.

PARALEGAL FUNCTIONS

Investigate facts relating to the various causes of actions.

Obtain copies of police, hospital, medical, or engineering reports.

Interview potential witnesses and take statements.

Take photographs of scene of accident and damages sustained.

Prepare witnesses for trial.

Assist in trial proceedings.

I. GENERAL NATURE OF TORT LAW

The law of torts fascinates most people, for it is the stuff crazy cases are made of. Think of the woman in New York City who claimed a plastic surgeon misplaced, or better said, mis-centered her belly button in a surgical process. Think of the elderly man who while shopping in a national supermarket chain trips on the errant banana or grape on the floor. If the elderly man falls to the ground, why is he suing the store for mental distress, nightmares, depression, and possibly a loss of sexual relations with his spouse? Such cases as these are played up by the press and TV because of their ability to attract our attention and provide a light touch to the news. Regardless of the public's impressions, the above described facts are the substance of tort law, actions *that are "civil" in nature and that cause harm, personal injury, or property damages.* Every tort is actually called a *cause of action*, a basis from which the injury arises. Every tort influences the person's right to be not interfered with, physically or mentally damaged, or to own, operate or exercise rights in real and personal property. In a sense, tort law primarily hopes to assure the most placid existence attainable in a complex world. Also, lest one believe that torts are generally frivolous or nonserious in nature, remember asbestos cases, airline tragedies, chemical and toxic contaminations, and other deeply serious injuries people have become victims of. Tort law, as a general policy dramatically affects all sectors of society, particularly the corporate and professional worlds. Enforcing the principles of tort law gives us some assurance that products sold on the marketplace are fundamentally safe; that doctors, lawyers and other professionals are basically competent; and that environmental regulations, union-wage scales, and civil rights for all in the workplace are all being upheld as best as possible. Hence, the policy influence of tort law is probably immeasurable yet felt very personally by the majority of the society.

What else distinguishes and makes the tort? What makes the tort different from the crime? As seen above, the seriousness of the action is not always an indicator. The obvious severity of environmental-waste dumping makes shoplifting pale by comparison. Shoplifting is a crime, while the dumping of most forms of environmental waste generally gives rise to a civil action, though in many jurisdictions both remedies are available. Of course, the popular notion is that all crimes are inherently serious deeds that must be accorded the gravest treatment. But what makes a tort less serious in terms of how society responds?

First, torts are very personalized actions, with the victim or injured party being required to show the unique effects on their person or property. A crime is an act that affronts the whole world, as when a criminal kills or a robber robs. The act of a criminal utterly disrupts the peace and tranquility of a community. The act of a criminal disrupts the normal ebb and flow of commercial, social, and political life. Again, while torts can certainly accomplish these same results, the impact is fundamentally more personalized. A crime is an act against the whole society, while a tort is an act against the individual. As a result, society generally evaluates a tort in a different light and poses different remedies. Consider the penalties for both actions. In crime, imprisonment, fines, or other restrictions on personal freedom are common responses. In torts, the cause of action prods *a lawsuit*, which if successful, eventually awards *damages*, in the form of money or other remedy.

Second, so much of the law of torts deals with less life-threatening situations. While no attempt is made here to view torts as a trivialized exercise, it is imperative to be rational and view the traditional cause of action as less than a threat of death. Trespass, infliction of mental distress, interference with contracts or employment, or fundamental negligence should not be lightly regarded, but at the same time our society cannot commit resources, enforcement personnel, and other human expenditure in the solving of these personalized disputes. Comparing acts of rape, murder, arson, incest, and other assorted atrocities makes these distinctions very sensible.

Lastly, tort law, while making every effort to distinguish itself from crimes, does cross over in many ways. Citizens

Exhibit 5.1

CASE SUMMARY REMINDER

( ) Client
    ( ) Obtain a fee contract from client
    ( ) Obtain signed medical authorizations from client
    ( ) Obtain financial statements to date to support special damages
    ( ) Obtain income tax returns for last two years
    ( ) Remind client to notify own insurance carrier and file accident reports required by law

( ) Investigation
    ( ) Obtain medical information from doctors, hospitals and other sources
    ( ) Take statements from all witnesses
    ( ) Obtain or take pictures and place newspaper clippings in evidence file of:
        ( ) Accident scene
        ( ) Vehicles
        ( ) Visible injuries to client
        ( ) Other _____
    ( ) Obtain appraisals of property, warranty deeds, plats and surveys
    ( ) Obtain engineer's drawing of accident scene
    ( ) Obtain copy of accident reports and reported testimony of traffic hearing
    ( ) Obtain copy of death certificate where applicable

( ) Notice preparatory to filing suit
    ( ) Write letter of notice to opposing party or party's insurance carrier if known

( ) Office Information
    ( ) File handled this office _____
    ( ) Associate attorney _____
    ( ) Address _____ Phone _____
    ( ) Referral by _____
    Address _____ Phone _____

( ) Obtain letter in file as to fee arrangement in associate and referral matters

always have a dual right to request the state or commonwealth to initiate criminal proceedings against an alleged defendant and to commence their own civil action or lawsuit against the same party. As an example, more and more sexual-offense counseling centers are advising their clientele not only to cooperate in the prosecution of offenders but also to sue for damages for possible assaults, mental distress, false imprisonment, and loss of consortium. That advice is even more enlightened when the dramatically different burdens of proof are evaluated. In crime, and if a sexual offense is considered, the prosecutor must demonstrate that this sexual offender performed the crime *beyond a reasonable doubt*. The reasonable doubt standard is the highest-level of evidentiary proof and the most difficult to substantiate. When compared to the requirement that the injured party make out or demonstrates a *prima facie* case, that is, proof of each and every element in the cause of action by *clear or convincing evidence* or by a *preponderance of the evidence*, the civil action or lawsuit is much easier to prove and thereby win something for the anguish of a sexual offense. This same reasoning can be applied to all torts.

All torts have *elements*, that is, required standards or definitions that must be met before satisfactory proof has been met. A tort can have three to seven elements, and a primary task of the paralegal is to master the elements of each cause of action. This "elemental" analysis is critical in case review, in initial client-counseling sessions, and in the investigation thereafter. So essential is this elemental inquiry that the paralegal's entire approach in the preparation of the civil action must be guided by it. All discovery should attempt to discern how the opponent's information can assist in the proof of these elements. All direct and cross-examination should again be guided by the proof of these elements. As a rule, the paralegal must adhere rigorously to the elements for the proposed cause of action for any expectation of success to be justified.

The chapter will review in detail the following three main types or categories of torts: intentional torts, negligence, and strict liability torts. Remember how imperative it is to conquer those elements of every tort and how analytically essential those elements are in the preparation and completion of a typical lawsuit. Use interview forms and checklists to assist in your analysis. (See exhibits 5.1–5.6.)

Exhibit 5.2

RETAINER AGREEMENT

I, , hereby retain the firm of , to represent me in connection with injuries sustained by my infant child, , as the result of an accident which occurred on or about

It is understood and agreed that for the services they render in connection with this retainer, , are to receive one-third (1/3) of any sum recovered, whether by suit, settlement or otherwise, or such other sum as a court may direct, together with all disbursements and expenses incurred by them.

Dated:

_____

II. INTENTIONAL TORTS

Designating a tort as intentional implies some level of mind set or mental process operating in the person who causes injury to another. As in the criminal law, injuries that are caused inadvertently, accidentally, or of course in justifiable self-defense, are sometimes excusable. In torts, that level of mind or intent does not have to be as sophisticated or developed. In torts, *intentional* means *wanted to injure, desired to injure, knew injury would come forth, or should have known injury was possible*. This elasticized description of *intentional* is really a far cry from a criminal mens rea of premeditation, purposeful conduct, or depraved indifference to human life. What is so necessary for the paralegal to fathom is that an intentional tort requires a less essential mental process. Simply wanting to perform the act is usually sufficient. Also note that most intentional torts require no proof of *damages*.

A. Assault

Our first tort is a classic example of the criminal law crossover discussed earlier. In order for an assault cause of action to be upheld, the injured party must prove:

(go to p. 164)

Exhibit 5.3

CHECKLIST FOR BACKGROUND INFORMATION

☐ Name of client
☐ Ever used other names (aliases)
☐ Ever been through a formal change of name procedure
☐ Maiden name (if applicable)
☐ Other married names
☐ Current address and phone (home)
☐ Prior residences
☐ Length of time lived at current residence
☐ Current address and phone (work)
☐ Nationality/citizenship/place of birth
☐ Addresses and phones where spouse and/or closest relative can be reached
☐ Age (date of birth)
☐ Religion, race
☐ How referred to this law office
☐ Ever hired another attorney on this case
☐ Ever spoken to another attorney about present case
☐ If a minor, is there a legal guardian
☐ Marital status
☐ Prior marriages (information on divorces)
☐ Date of present marriage
☐ Date of present divorce
☐ Current status of alimony/lump sum/child support payments
☐ Any children
☐ Ages/addresses
☐ Name of other parent of each child
☐ Current employer of self and spouse
☐ Job title/salary
☐ Length of employment there
☐ Prior employment history
☐ Self-employment/business ventures
☐ Tax data (filing status, gross income, availability of copies of returns, etc.)
☐ Real property in own name
☐ Real property in joint names
☐ Personal property
☐ Personal property (cash, bank accounts, furniture, motor vehicles)
☐ Education
☐ Prior litigation involvement (dates, courts, attorneys, outcomes)
☐ Present state of health
☐ Names and addresses of doctors currently treating client
☐ Nature of treatment
☐ Medical problems for which no medical treatment is being sought
☐ Prior medical history (for the last _____ years)
☐ List every hospital treatment (dates, addresses, doctors, treatment, outcomes)
☐ Name of every insurance company (past/present) that covered medical care
☐ List every insurance claim you ever filed for medical care
☐ Names of people who could verify your prior medical condition

Exhibit 5.4

INITIAL INTERVIEW CHECK LIST—PERSONAL INJURY ACTION

1. Personal Information:
    A. Client(s) name:
        1) _____
        2) _____

    B. Address:
        _____
        _____

    C. Telephone No.:
        h) _____
        b) _____

    D. Age and Date of Birth:
        Client 1: _____
        Client 2: _____

    E. Marital Status:
        Client 1: _____
        Client 2: _____

2. Facts of Accident   (automobile only; if not auto injury, go to #4):
    A. Date of Accident: _____
    B. Approximate Time: _____
    C. Place of Accident: _____
                                    _____
    D. Did police come to scene?   Yes _____ No _____
        If yes, department involved _____
                                    _____

3. Automobile Information:
    A. Client's car
        Owner and Address: _____
                                    _____
                                    _____

        Driver and Address: _____
                                    _____
                                    _____

        Make and Model: _____
        License # and/or V.I.D.   _____
                                    _____

        Owner's Insurance Carrier and Address: _____
                                    _____
                                    _____
                                    _____

    B. Defendant's (car #1):
        Owner and Address: _____
                                    _____
                                    _____

        Driver and Address: _____
                                    _____
                                    _____

        Make and Model: _____
        License # and/or V.I.D.   _____
                                    _____

        Owner's Insurance Carrier and Address: _____
                                    _____
                                    _____

    C. Defendant's (car #2, if applicable): _____
                                    _____
        Owner and Address: _____
        Driver and Address: _____
                                    _____
                                    _____

Make and Model   _____

License # and/or V.I.D.   _____

Owner's Insurance Carrier and Address: _____
_____
_____
_____

D. Other occupants of any vehicle involved: _____
_____
_____
_____
_____

4. Information on Defendant(s) (other than auto accident; if auto accident, proceed to #5):

   A. Defendant #1

      Name: _____

      Address: _____
_____

      Insurance Carrier and Address: _____
_____
_____
_____

   B. Defendant #2

      Name: _____

      Address: _____
_____
_____
_____

      Insurance Carrier and Address: _____
_____
_____

      Relationship to Case   _____

5. Witnesses

   Name: _____

   Address: _____
_____
_____

   Phone No.:   _____

   Name: _____

   Address: _____
_____

   Phone No: _____

   Name: _____

   Address: _____
_____

   Phone No: _____

6. Property Damage   (if no property damage, go to #7):

   Written estimate available: Yes _____ No _____

   Company effecting repairs:

   Name: _____

   Address: _____
_____

   Phone No.:   _____

   Description of damage: _____

_____
_____
_____
_____

Does client have photos?   Yes _____ No _____

7. Personal Injuries:
    A. Hospital: _____
       Address: _____
                                   _____
       Date Admitted: _____
       Date Discharged: _____
       Estimated Hospital Charges: $ _____
    B. Treating Physician #1:   _____
       Address: _____
                                   _____
       Phone No.:   _____
       Specialty: _____
       1st Treatment Date: _____
       Last Treatment Date: _____
       Est. Dr. Bill: _____
       Is this physician still treating you?   Yes _____ No _____
    C. Treating Physician #2   _____
       Address: _____
                                   _____
       First Treatment Date: _____
       Last Treatment Date: _____
       Est. Dr. Bill   _____
       Is this physician still treating you?   Yes _____ No _____
    D. If student,
    Name of School: _____
    Address: _____
                                   _____
    Dates Absent: _____
    E. Length of Time Confined to Bed After
       Discharge From Hospital: _____
    F. Length of Time Confined to House After
       Discharge From Hospital: _____
    G. Medical Expenses incurred other
       than those listed above: _____
    Physical Therapy (Appx.) $ _____
    Private Nurse (Appx.) $ _____
    Homemaker $ _____
    Medical Equipment $ _____
    Pharmaceutical $ _____
    H. Nature of Injuries:

_____
_____
_____
_____

    I. Was this injury an aggravation of a prior
       ailment or injury?   Yes _____ No _____
    J. Does client have photos?   Yes _____ No _____

8. Employer Information:
    A. Name: _____
       Address: _____
                                   _____
       Phone No.:   _____
       Person to Contact: _____

B. Type of Job: _____

C. Gross Weekly Income: $_____

D. Days per week normally worked: _____

Hours per day normally worked: _____

E. Last date worked prior to accident: _____

F. 1st date worked following accident: _____

G. Total days absent from work as result of accident: _____

NOTE: If client had second job or other part time income, obtain information for this as well.

9. Information Re: Dependents   (wrongful death only):

A. Husband/Wife: Name: _____

Address: _____
_____
_____
_____

Phone No.: _____

Person to Contact _____

Annual Salary: $_____

B. Dependent Child #1:

Name: _____

Address: _____
_____
_____

Age and Date of Birth: _____

Attending School: Yes _____ No _____

School Name: _____

Address: _____
_____
_____

Grade: _____

10. Client's Narrative Re: Accident:

11. Diagram of Accident

Exhibit 5.5

DIAGRAM OF INJURIES

Client _____

Indicate location and dimension of cuts, scars, bruises, burns, bumps, sutures, fractures, points of bleeding, missing teeth, etc. Show any radiations of pain by tracing pattern on areas of body involved.

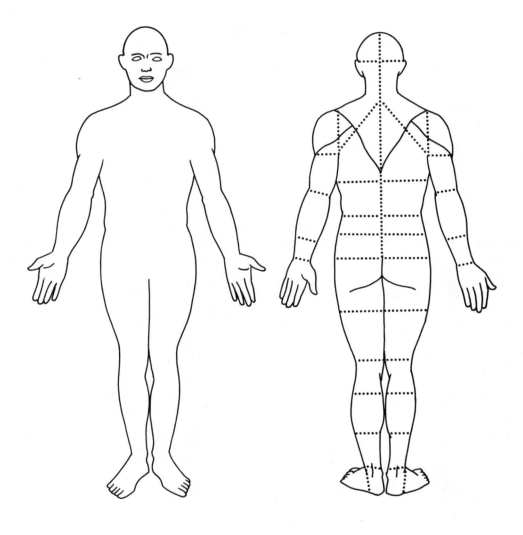

Source: Courtesy of ATLA.

Exhibit 5.6

CHECKLIST OF INJURIES

SUMMARY OF INJURIES: (indicate degree of disability, restriction of activities in work, recreation, etc.)

_____

_____

_____

_____

_____

_____

AREAS OF PAIN
_____

( )Symptoms

    ( )Headaches
    ( )Dizziness
    ( )Nausea
    ( )Nervousness
    ( )Insomnia
    ( )Appetite

( )Head

    ( )Brain
    ( )Forehead
    ( )Ears
    ( )Eyes
    ( )Nose
    ( )Mouth
    ( )Teeth

( )Neck

    ( )Muscles
    ( )Spine
    ( )Throat

( )Chest
    ( )Heart
    ( )Lungs
    ( )Ribs

( )Abdomen
( )Internal injuries
    ( ) _____
    ( ) _____

( )Arms (right or left)

    ( )Upper
    ( )Forearm
    ( )Elbows
    ( )Wrists
    ( )Hands
    ( )Fingers

( )Trunk

    ( )Shoulders
    ( )Spine
    ( )Thoracic
    ( )Scapula
    ( )Lumbar
    ( )Sacrum
    ( )Coccyx
    ( )Pelvis
    ( )Hips

( )Legs (right or left)

    ( )Thighs
    ( )Upper
    ( )Lower
    ( )Knees
    ( )Ankles
    ( )Feet
    ( )Toes

( )Circle: Cuts, bruises, burns, bumps, sutures, fractures swelling, contusions, missing teeth, points of bleeding, unconsciousness, other:

_____

Source: Courtesy of ATLA.

1. An act
2. With intention to cause _offensive contact_ or to cause an _apprehension_ of such offensive contact
3. Actual, resulting apprehension
4. Causation

    Other writers have described the assault as an incomplete battery simply because the contact really never takes place. In this respect, assault is more an act against one's mind than against one's body.

    The elements listed above are not subject to major intellectual disagreement as long as they are viewed in a _reasonable person_ context. This _reasonable person_ frequently assists in the interpretation of tort elements, and rightfully so, because the law of torts does not protect people from their eccentricities, oddities, or unreasonable phobias. The law of torts does not meddle in trifles or trivialities and gauges the majority of elemental interpretations by what a reasonable person, an average, ordinary Homo sapiens does in given situations. In assault cases, the reasonable person's questions are: What is offensive contact? What is true apprehension? If someone like Gary Coleman or Tiny Tim goes up to Mr. T and says, "Hey, you big dope, I'm going to punch all your teeth out," can we say that Mr. T will suffer the appropriate apprehension? He may very well, because fear is not required to prove apprehension. What if Tiny Tim says to Mr. T, "I'm going to get the spaghetti noodle and beat you over the head with it!" Could Mr. T argue that this demonstrates an intent to engage in offensive contact? In a reasonable person framework, it is doubtful that Mr. T was very worried.

B. Battery

Battery is sometimes described as the culmination of the assault whereby the actor causes the true physical contact. The elements of battery are:

1. An act
2. With intent to cause harmful or offensive contact
3. Actual harmful or offensive contact
4. Causation

Battery is similar to assault except for the actual contact, which again must be measured by reasonable person standards. As such, when is contact really offensive? What if a bum goes up to a pedestrian on a city street, taps him on the back, and says, "Hey, please spare me twenty cents." If the pedestrian is frightened by the tapping can he claim a battery?

Under most sensible jurisdictions the key to battery rests in a reasonable interpretation of what behaviors are offensive. Tapping, slight shoves, and pushes do not appear the least bit offensive or harmful. The ordinary person is not irrationally emotional or unduly sensitive and can buffer these physical intrusions of a minor nature without much of a struggle. The physical contact must, if it has any chance of qualifying, affront the dignity and sensitivities of the reasonable person. Riding a subway car in and of itself might be a physical hardship, but unless the injured party can prove more direct action, such as a mugging, or a passenger who throws another out of his seat, a case of true battery will be unsubstantiated.

C. False Imprisonment

Inherent in a free society is the right to free and unfettered travel and movement. Ideally, that is not possible in a world with toll booths, lights, and stop signs and where most people do expect a minimum of intrusion as daily life goes on. When a severe intrusion, or better said, restriction, of that freedom of movement take place, a variety of torts are available as potential remedies. False imprisonment is the most potent in the group. The required elements for a prima facie case of false imprisonment are:

1. An act of confinement
2. Intent to confine
3. Causation
4. Victim or injured party conscious of confinement or harmed by it

Numerous problems emerge in the analysis of these standards, especially as the elements relate to the essence of confinement. To confine another person does not require a solid mass of walls, doors, locks, or other physical barrier. Confinement can arise by verbal threat or other coercion, including the assertion of legal authority, shop owners' rights, or threats to third parties. Equally required in the parameters of confinement is the nonexistence of, or unawareness of, any safe or reasonable means of escape. Accordingly, an injured party can be the victim of false imprisonment by the aiming of a weapon at him or her.

As in all intentional torts, *damage*, that is, the proof of injury, including loss of income, emotional disorders, humiliation, discomfort, or illness, are not required. The courts view the confinement as inherently sufficient, unless the victim of the imprisonment was completely unaware of it. Other problems that emerge in this tort involve an interpretation of intent to confine. What of the store owner who believes an individual has shoplifted? Can that owner be liable for a lawsuit of wrongful confinement? Are there statutory exclusions protecting merchants? The *intent of confine* can be for legal means or nonevil rationales, but unless statutorily excepted or approved, the party confining the plaintiff, no matter how well intentioned, will be liable. How does an *accidental* confinement fit in this review?

D. False Arrest

Both public employees, such as "police" and other officials with police powers, and private citizens have the power to arrest. Although vigilantism and self-protection are gaining acceptability, the role of private citizens in the arrest process is relatively insignificant. Our society can and does expect its law-enforcement agencies to effect criminal and civil confinements. Can police officers falsely arrest people, or more precisely, can they improperly arrest people? An obvious yes applies to the latter part of the question, and realistically the justice system cannot expect law-enforcement practitioners to always make correct and perfect choices. So in any given day, there will be a small number of citizens improperly identified, arrested, then released for inconsistent evidence, and investigatively filtered out as potential suspects in a criminal investigation. To continue this inquiry, does it then follow that all citizens who are improperly arrested can file lawsuits against public officials for false arrest? An emphatic no is the only possible answer. A better question might be, "Can a citizen sue a police officer for a false arrest in some set of circumstances?" Clearly an affirmative response fits here. The elements of false arrest are:

1. Act of arrest
2. Intent to arrest
3. With no basis, probable cause, right or other legal authority
4. An absence of privilege

In the police sector, arrests can be justified with or without warrants, depending on the circumstances. Crucial to the paralegal's understanding is the fact that all arrests require *probable cause*, a term that does not intimate absolute perfection. *Probable cause* is a reasonably factual basis for believing that a crime (1) has been committed, (2) is being committed, (3) is about to be committed. Probable cause is an often argued and litigated defense question, but in its most rudimentary form, the standard relates to the "probabilities" of things rather than their quantified demonstration in science. Inherent in this type of legal definition is room for error, harmless and unintentional mistake, and technical difference. The paralegal must therefore discern what level or severity of mistake gives rise to false arrest that is not grounded in probable cause. The answer is exceedingly complex because just when the probable cause standard was or was not met has been the subject of numerous Supreme Court diatribes in the last twenty-five years.

Some specific suggestions can be posed. First, a police officer can be sued for false arrest if the officer had absolutely no factual basis for the arrest. Second, the police officer's arrest was legally groundless and generated by ill will, spite, or other emotional motivations. Third, the police officer's manner or mode of arrest was exceptionally forceful in light of the offense, or unmindful of appropriate procedural guarantees granted all defendants.

In sum, the justice system in order to operate with efficiency and to feel free to investigate, question, and diligently solve and prevent criminal activity must be granted some administrative leeway in the arrest process. The leeway is of course balanced with the individual's rights, and as a result, the *probable cause* standard can be viewed as a reflection of that concern.

E. Malicious Prosecution

Closely allied with false arrest is the intentional tort of malicious prosecution. At times the false arrest can lead to an eventual prosecution in which a defendant is exonerated. The lesson for the paralegal in this scenario is that *multiple* causes of action are not only plausible but likely. Normal complaints filed in a civil action almost always list multiple actions, not only because the practice is legally and conceptually proper but also because multiple theories of action provide a broader basis to negotiate from.

Just as the society values the right to be free from intrusive and unfair arrest processes, so too the society abhors cases that are prosecuted with *maliciousness*. Notice the very descriptive term in this tort, *malice*. That means that the authorities, or individuals responsible for the prosecution knew, understood, and realized the falsehood of their case yet proceeded anyway. The party responsible for the prosecution used the adjudicatory system as a form and means of punishment for the victim. The elements required for malicious prosecution are:

1. Initiation of legal proceedings
2. With no probable cause
3. With malice
4. Plaintiff's (accused's) proceedings are resolved in his or her favor

As in false arrest, the discretion granted to a prosecutor to charge an individual with an offense sometimes results in the wrong person's being chosen. Prosecutorial error or mistaken identity by a private citizen do not automatically result in this claim of action. *Malice* is the key. The tort serves the society well by reminding the initiators of legal proceedings that the decision to prosecute is not made lightly, and that the decision should never be mocked or sullied by personal vendettas, spite, or similar motivations.

F. Abuse of Process

Some jurisdictions also have the abuse of process tort, which is highly similar to our two previous examples because the tort seeks to protect the civil and criminal system from misuse. The elements of abuse of process are:

1. Initiation of legal proceedings
2. Improper ulterior motive
3. Actual damages

Unlike malicious prosecution and false arrest, the legal proceeding was properly commenced, but the adjudication was utilized to collect a bribe, or to protect loan sharks or extortionists.

G. Deceit

Consumerism has bolstered the use of the tort of deceit and as a result substantially influenced the practices of the marketplace. Deceit requires proof of the following:

1. Statement, or lack hereof, of a past or present tort
2. Statement is false and misleading
3. Intention to mislead (scienter)
4. Actual and justifiable reliance
5. Damages

Difficult queries emerge in this tort, but none are more compelling than, "What is a statement of fact?" The question is even more troubling when one views the modern practice of American advertising. Where are the facts? In a toilet bowl with a man in a boat? In a toy-covered wagon that a dog chases? In a pair of designer jeans that symbolize romantic interludes? Distinguishing fact from hype and Madison Avenue gimmick is probably an impossible task. All that is clear is that the "facts" should be important or *material*, inextricably tied to the product, like "the engine in this car is brand new," when in fact it is ten years old. If the fact is critical, essential, and utterly necessary to the product, scheme, or plan, then designate that fact as material. Exaggeration, braggadocio, and puffing are normative behavior in the marketplace. The law reasons people can see through all that. The law probably assumes too much.

Next, once the fact is determined to be material enough, the trier must ponder the mind of the proponent of that fact. Deceit can be supported by proof that the declarant of the fact knew, or had knowledge (scienter) that the fact being expounded was clearly a falsehood. Various levels of mental awareness are possible when this element is scrutinized. Simply put, does the declarant know only what he or she wants to know? Should the declarant be required to know what he or she is saying is false or have some ethical or professional obligation to know? The thrust of deceit mandates a treacherous, deceptive mind. While ignorance is not applauded, it sometimes provides a defense.

Intricately connected to scienter is the reliance factor that delves further into the mental trickery the tort tries to define. By the time the deceptive material fact is represented, the reliance rule in deceit also expects the declarant to hope to get a reaction, a suckering in, so to speak, for the final sale or deal. In this sense, deceit requires two levels of thought: (1) intent to state a falsehood, and (2) intent to generate a reliance on that falsehood.

Lastly, even if the plaintiff can evidence all of the above elements, this cause of action will have no viability unless the plaintiff justifiably relied on that misrepresentation and suffered actual damages. Again, reliance will be deemed justifiable when compared to the reasonable person standard. The law assumes some level of consumer awareness in the normal reasonable person and will expect not to protect the irrational or impulsive party whose own faults turn normal salesmanship into coerced buying.

H.   Trespass to Land

Thus far, we have focused on causes of action that relate more to personal injury or harm. What about the injuries inflicted on people's land? The value of land and all forms of real property does not have to extolled here, but worth mentioning is the tremendous importance our society places on the ability of its owner to live on it peacefully and to be free from interference of all forms. Western images are conjured up with desperadoes being ordered to "stay off my land, or else!" That peace and tranquility is probably the greatest value there is in land.

So what do you do when the neighbor decides to cut lumber and leave it on your lawn, or that same considerate neighbor creates conditions that cause mud slides, run-off, and avalanches in your living space? Every neighborhood always has a clown like this, whose absence when you attempt to resolve disagreements makes you glad courts exist, and as well, that the tort of trespass exists. A prima facie case of trespass requires:

1. An intrusion in land
2. Possessed of another
3. Intent to intrude
4. Causation

No enormous puzzles exist in the interpretation of these elements. Trespass does not mandate that the person intruding actually enter the property because the intrusion can be accomplished by direct or indirect means. Trespass can also occur against a person who has no title or legal ownership in the property. Instead, a possessory interest is all that is required to support an action.

I.   Trespass to Chattels

A chattel is pure personal property, such as a television set, clothing, and jewelry. Liability for trespass to one's personal property arises as the result of the wrongful detention of such property to the exclusion of, or inconsistent with, the rights of the party with the rights of possession. Possession may be actual or constructive. Therefore, a bailor or mortgagee entitled to possession upon demand may recover for injury to the chattel.

For one to be liable in trespass, the wrongful detention may be fleeting and temporary. Trespass actions often arise as the result of the wrongful attachment to property by a sheriff. For more permanent deprivations of property the law of torts provides a remedy in conversion, which will be reviewed.

Before a trespass action can be maintained, the victim must allege the existence of actual damages as a result of the tortfeasor's conduct. The elements are:

1. An act of the defendant that interferes with the plaintiff's right of possession. An entire taking of the personal property is not required. It is enough if the defendant damages the chattel.
2. Intent to perform the act resulting in interference with the plaintiff's right of possession. Intent to deprive is not required, only an intentional act leading to the deprivation of the property right.
3. Causation.
4. Damages—Nominal damages are not awarded in an action in trespass. There must be actual damage.

J.   Conversion

Conversion is the tort law's answer to larceny or theft. Any permanent deprivation of personal property by a tortfeasor can be described as a conversion, a literal explanation for taking what was once personal property of one person and then "converting" it to another's use. So if Bob's TV is taken by Mary and placed in Mary's house she—obviously in the absence of other facts—has no intention of returning it. Keep in mind this permanent deprivation requirement because the previous trespass to chattels covers the temporary possession cases. The required elements in a conversion case are:

1. Personal property (chattel)
2. Possessory right
3. Intent to control personal property
4. Substantial or serious interference with the possessory right

Conversion is not mere dispossession, impairment of use, or inconvenience. Conversion is a concerted, intentional effort to modify permanently ownership in the chattel. That *serious interference* can also result from partial or total destruction of the chattel, which makes useless and worthless the personal property. A variety of other factors are considered in defining serious interference including time of control or extent thereof, good or bad faith of the converter, and extent of inconvenience or expense suffered by victim.

Quite illuminating are the gradations of intent that are possible under a conversion action. An evil mind is not required, only a mind bent toward substantial dispossession or interference.

Hence, conversion may be committed by intentionally dispossessing the owner or rightful possessor of the chattel, destroying or substantially altering it, using it without authority or beyond the terms of the authorized use, misdelivering it contrary to instructions, or refusing to surrender it following demand by the rightful owner or possessor. As in cases of trespass, the tortfeasor need not have intended to commit the tort (e.g., good-faith purchaser who buys the chattel from a thief).

Where the possession of the chattel is wrongful from the start, an action for conversion can be maintained without awaiting the results of a demand for the return of the property. If, however, the converter's possession of the property is rightful in the first instance and subsequently becomes wrongful simply by reason of the wrongful detention, then demand and refusal are necessary prerequisites for bringing an action in conversion and must be alleged in the complaint. Thus one does not become a converter by purchasing property from a thief until the rightful owner or possessor has made demand for its return and such demand has been refused.

Generally the measure of damages for conversion is the market value of the chattel at the time of the conversion plus interest.

K. Intentional Infliction of Mental Distress

Until recent legal history, the tort of infliction of mental distress was strictly viewed as a parasitic action; that is, mental distress could not rise independently, for the distress resulted only if there were other actional damages such as an assault, battery, or other physical injury. In prepsychiatric times, the quantification or proof of mental distress was no more scientifically accepted than voodoo. Some critics still believe so! However, sizable intellectual support has emerged from the academic, professional and legal communities for the proposition that mental damages are in fact measurable and compensable. What exactly has to happen before an action wi'' arise under this tort?

1. An act of extreme or outrageous conduct
2. Intent to cause severe distress
3. Actual substantial mental anguish
4. Causation

Horror stories abound on how people feign and improvise nightmares, phobias, loss of sexual enjoyment, depression, and psychic injury. Generally, such stories are fodder for yellow journalists and wild-eyed reporters. Why is it that mental distress is so hard for some to accept? At its very root, mental distress is unseen, unheard, unprovable. Everyone likes a battery—you can see the lumps and other injuries. It is normal to distrust that which can't be seen.

What is clear about mental distress is that courts try to demand a quantum of proof in the proof of the complaint. A mere assertion of distress will not satisfy. Courts do not accept trifles and insults as bases for damages; the distress must be the direct result of *extreme or outrageous* conduct. If a person foul-mouths you, does the profanity qualify? If some kid throws a bug in your Coke, does that behavior appear outrageous? How about an order of french fries with a roach in the bag? Critics of mental distress argue that the tort suffers from unending relativism. The best response that can be mustered is that our old, reliable, *reasonable person* standard must be looked to when making a judgment about extreme or outrageous conduct.

In addition, the plaintiff must be able to provide solid evidence of that distress. That evidence can be in the form of expert testimony or direct testimony on the influence on job or career and family relationships. Critics and advocates of the tort whole-heartedly agree that mental illness, depression, and aberrations are actualities in daily living. The level of distress and its proof thereof is what separates the camps.

One final note, a minority of jurisdictions have also adopted negligent infliction of mental distress as a remedy for a defendant's lack of due cause or carelessness that results in mental injury to another.

L. Miscellaneous Intentional Torts

1. Intentional interference with a contract

A variety of torts could fall into a subheading involving businesses, negotiations, and the work place. If a contract is in existence and a defendant interferes with it that interference can be by inducing a party to breach, inducing a party to terminate, making performance an impossibility, or making performance more difficult.

The defendant must desire to interfere with the normal contract. Envision professional sports and the entertainment field, where such a scheme might emerge.

2. Disparagement

While defamation has not been covered thus far because the tort is not primarily intentional, disparagement is a form of business defamation that is thoroughly intentional. The elements are:

a. False statement of a material fact
b. Disparagement of a plaintiff and business
c. Publication
d. Intent
e. Damages

3. Injurious falsehood

While disparagement protects a business owner from misrepresentations or statements that are utterly false about the business, other fact patterns are covered by the tort of injurious falsehood. The tort protects an individual from any false statements of fact, material in scope, that result in severe economic loss. Examples might include statements by an employer to the IRS on incorrect tax amounts paid by an employee.

4. Invasion of privacy

As seen thus far, personal privacy is an important criterion in the elemental definitions of many torts. Privacy is so cherished that a band of four new torts under the invasion heading have come to the forefront in the last thirty years. Since privacy interests are multifaceted, the invasion of privacy tort has really four subsections:

a. Intrusion

Even Jackie Kennedy Onassis has successfully argued this theory against the photographers who pester her at every step. Essentially there are civil boundaries of privacy that everyone is entitled to.

b. Appropriation

Again, Jackie Kennedy Onassis comes to mind, with her recent case against a large distiller. Any pro athlete or other public figure whose name, likeness, or personality is used for the benefit of the defendant without any agreement or renumeration can fairly argue this tort.

c. Public Disclosure of Private Facts

Even the most public figures in our society can argue that certain very, very private facts are so personal that it is grotesque and offensive to release them.

d. False Light

To rearrange a photograph or effect conditions or events with the result that plaintiff is placed in a false light is impermissible. Read any issue of *The National Enquirer*.

M. Defamation

Defamation is defined as a false and malicious publication of statements made with the intent to injure a person's reputation or to cause him to be held in disrepute or to affect him adversely in his trade or profession. Before the tort becomes actionable, the statements must be published, i.e., disseminated to a third party. If the only person who hears or reads the statement is the subject of the defamatory remarks, the statements have not been published, and an action for defamation cannot be sustained. The two types of defamation are:

1. Libel—addressed to the eye.
    a. Libel per se—defamatory on its face. No need to plead or prove special damages. Jane Doe is a thief.
    b. Libel per quod—defamatory is coupled with extrinsic facts. No need to plead or prove special damages if within categories—a through d below; i.e., John Doe is Jane Doe's lover. Libel per quod—extrinsic fact: John Doe is married. No need to prove special damages.
2. Slander—addressed to the ear.
    a. Imputation of a crime involving moral turpitude or infamous punishment. Special damages need not be pleaded or proven.
    b. Imputation of loathsome disease—leprosy, VD.
    c. Imputation affecting plaintiff in his or her profession.
    d. Imputation of unchastity (of unmarried women). Special damages must be plead and must be proven.
    e. All others.

A private individual bringing a libel suit must prove actual injury and some degree of fault on the part of the publisher; such as either negligent failure to exercise due care or a greater degree of fault such as express or actual malice. General damages to the private individual may be presumed in a libel suit only upon a showing by the private individual that the publisher was guilty of actual malice. Punitive damages may be recovered in a libel suit only upon a showing that the publisher was guilty of actual malice.

III. NEGLIGENCE

In contrast to the intentional torts is the act of a person who is simply negligent—an act that is nonintentional, simply careless, accidental, or mistaken. A negligent person is the one who trips and falls, drives a car through lights and stop signs, sells a product that injures customers, or owns land with a variety of dangerous conditions. In the briefest form, *negligence is a tort that produces an injury to a person or property by unreasonable conduct*. As unreasonable as it might seem, that word reasonable comes into play again because the "reasonable person" standard is the measuring tool used to decide what is *reasonable conduct*. Who is this reasonable person? How does he or she act?

At best, the reasonable person is a homogenized, pasteurized human being with imperfections to be sure, but exhibiting what is known in the law as *due care* for everyone else. Due care can be defined as:

> Just, proper, and sufficient care, so far as the circumstances warrant it; the absence of negligence. That care which an ordinarily prudent person would have exercised under the circumstances. Due care is care proportioned to any given situation, its surroundings, peculiarities, and hazards.

The reasonable person is the man or woman who drives the appropriate speed and adjusts according to the weather conditions, who follows all signs, warnings, and edicts posted by governmental authorities, and who is generally conscious and aware of all potential and actual dangers, and endlessly vigilant so as not to injure other people. In all seriousness, the reasonable person is what all people try to be, and in a real sense, succeed at. When our vigilance falters and carelessness causes injury, the standard of conduct expected of the reasonable person has not been met, and the result may be a lawsuit for negligence. If the plaintiff can show a dereliction in the due care requirement, a case of negligence may be plausible. Precisely stated, the party who is at *fault* will be liable because of his or her negligence. (See exhibits 5.7–5.11.)

Negligence is a tort unto itself and while the tort's influence in civil practice is magnanimous, its elements are the same in every case.

    a. Duty of due care
    b. Breach of duty of due care
    c. Proximate causation
    d. Damages

Exhibit 5.7

LETTER AUTHORIZING RECORDS RELEASE

Date _____

TO: _____:

You are hereby authorized and directed to permit the examination of, and the copying or reproduction in any manner, whether mechanical, photographic, or otherwise, by my attorney or such other person as he may authorize, all or any portions desired by him of the following:

a. Hospital records, x-rays, x-ray readings and reports, laboratory records and reports, all tests of any type, character and reports thereof, statement of charges, and any and all of my records pertaining to hospitalization, history, condition, treatment, diagnosis, prognosis, etiology or expense;

b. Medical records, including patient's record cards, x-rays, x-ray readings and reports, laboratory records and reports, all tests of any type and character and reports thereof, statements of charges, and any and all of my records pertaining to medical care, history condition, treatment, diagnosis, prognosis, etiology or expense.

You are further authorized and directed to furnish oral and written reports to my attorney, or his delegate, as requested by him on any of the foregoing matters.

By reason of the fact that such information that you have acquired as my physician or surgeon is confidential to me, you are also requested to treat such information as confidential and requested not to furnish any of such information in any form to anyone, without written authorization from me.

I also authorize my attorneys or their delegates to photograph my person while I am present in any hospital.

I further authorize the sending of medical and hospital bills to my attorney, and in the event of recovery by trial or settlement to allow my attorney to withhold an amount sufficient to cover these bills and to make payment directly to you and to deduct the same from any recovery which may be due me.

Patient _____

Exhibit 5.8

REQUEST FOR HOSPITAL RECORDS

Client: _____
Address: _____
Date of Accident: _____

Gentlemen:

Our office represents the above named client for injuries received on the date indicated.

Please forward to us the items checked below:

_____ Complete photo copies of all hospital records including x-ray reports; summary of charges, operational log, if any; emergency log; medical photographs, if any; all doctors' orders, nurses' notes, etc.; tissue committee report, if any; employees day sheet showing names of nurses; physical therapy records; all out-patient records.

_____ Copies of all x-ray reports.

_____ Summary or abstract of hospital record.

_____ Emergency room record.

Also please send us duplicate copies of your bill for services rendered, and please keep us advised of future billing or future developments. Please bill us separately for your report or photocopy costs. On your bill for hospital services, please do not show any amount paid by insurance as we cannot use these in court. We will protect your bill out of any amounts received in trial or settlement of this case.

Enclosed please find Medical Authorization which authorizes us to receive this information. May we thank you for your cooperation.

Very truly yours,

Exhibit 5.9

PROFESSIONAL INVESTIGATION REPORT: A SAMPLE

Dear Mr. X:

We were assigned to do an investigation on the above-captioned accident by your office on May 24, 1979. The assignment involved: (1) Professional photographs of the motorcycle and the accident scene; (2) Measurements and diagram of the accident scene; (3) Photos of the defendant's car, if at home; (4) To pick up the police report and interview the officer; and (5) To itemize the damages to the motorcycle.

Date, Time And Place:

The accident occurred on May 20, 1979 at 8:57 p.m., a Sunday, at the intersection of Monroe Avenue and Boston Post Road.

The intersection has two streets, which almost face each other. To the West is Chatsworth Avenue and to the East is Monroe Avenue. The intersection has a traffic control of several traffic lights strung on a cable across the intersection. The traffic lights are red, amber and green and none of them show green arrow for a left turn across traffic.

A complete understanding of the intersection can be gained by studying the enclosed diagram, the photographs and the police report.

Description Of The Accident:

The accident involved the collision of two vehicles: a motorcycle, driven by Mr. Y and an automobile, driven by Mr. Z.

The police report states that the Z vehicle was apparently making a left turn, from Boston Post Road, onto Monroe Avenue.

Plaintiff's Injuries:

The Plaintiff, Mr. Y, of 16 Shea Place,   , State of   ; date of birth is February 1, 1953. He was also the owner of the motorcycle, a 1978 Kawasaki, and at the time of the accident there was a passenger, Ms. V, riding with the plaintiff, Mr. Y.

Mr. Y was admitted to New Rochelle Hospital with a compound fracture of the left femur.

Plaintiff's Vehicle:

I inspected the Plaintiff's vehicle at the garage of Mr. T, of 140 Locust Avenue. Mr. T is the Plaintiff's friend and is keeping the motorcycle for him while he is in the hospital.

We have photographs of the vehicle. The vehicle is identified by license plate number 690-775. The VIN number is KZT000AE054237. The model is the Kawasaki KZ1000; its color is red and the odometer indicates a mileage of 1,166 miles.

The following is a list of new parts that will be needed to restore the vehicle to a pre-damaged condition:

1. Handlebar
2. Left handgrip
3. Front brake lever
4. Instrument mounting cluster unit
5. Speedometer
6. Tachometer
7. Front light, complete
8. Front left and right signal lights, complete
9. Front fork
10. Front fender
11. New cylinder head and gasket set
12. Exhaust headers
13. Left crank cover
14. Left side electric cover box
15. Left rear shock absorber
16. Left and right rear signal lights
17. Highway peg

The above is a list of new parts that will be needed. The following repairs will also be needed: The seat will need to be recovered, as the trim is torn, and the front wheel will need to be straightened and aligned.

The cost for the above work would have to be ascertained by a Kawasaki dealer as there is no general book on motorcycle repairs.

DEFENDANT'S VEHICLE:

The defendant's vehicle is a 1979 Datsun, four-door sedan, registered in the State of _____ , plate number 852-WHY, owned by Mr. Z.

DEFENDANT OPERATOR:

The operator was Mr. Z, who was also the owner of the vehicle.

Exhibit 5.10

REQUEST FOR POLICE REPORT

Re: Accident Report

Dear Sir:

Enclosed please find a self-addressed, stamped envelope and our check for an Accident Report on the following accident:

Date of Accident _____

Location _____

_____

County _____ City _____

Names and Addresses of
Drivers of Vehicles _____

_____

_____

_____

Thank you for your cooperation in this and other matters.

Very truly yours,

Tomes have been written on each of these elements and for good cause. Essentially the law of negligence covers a diversity of situations, for each time a general principle or rule is established, some other party tests the principle with another factual variation. Think about how many ways there are to run a stop sign or produce a defective product.

A. Analysis of Duty

1. General obligations

In the most global terms, everyone owes a duty to everyone else. There are no exceptions to this, only increased obligations depending on the relationship. The fact that a legal relationship exists between the parties always implies a duty. Parents clearly have a duty to their own children—a very high one at that. Doctor-patient, lawyer-client, and psychiatrist-patient are equally illuminating examples. Natural duties emerge because of the legal responsibilities owed by the professional to his or her client and as a rule are very demanding duties. But the doctor and lawyer also owe to strangers or other noninterested parties due care, though much less than in the relationships cited, and of course they have to interface with them in some way. Depending on the circumstances, a person can owe very little or no duty at all. Daily life makes the nonexistence of duty unlikely. Every time people get in their cars they owe every other driver of an auto, every pedestrian, every public official a duty to drive safely and adhere to the law. Similarly, every person who walks down the hallways owes all other persons the freedom from pushing, shoving, or other personal injury as the person ambles by. While the normal human processes in daily life may not appear legally monumental, all have the potential and possibility of being acts characterized by negligence. That is why duty is ongoing and continuous.

Duty cannot be owed to someone totally out of range, or as the law prefers, utterly *unforseeable*. The question becomes, "When is an injury forseeable?"

Assume you are walking down the street with a new hammer you bought at the hardware store. What if you tripped in a pothole so graciously unrepaired by your state, and the hammer flew into a house and hit the owner in the head? Would you be responsible? What if the hammer bounced off the house and hit the driver of a truck going by?

Many other what ifs exist. The point to be made is that duty can be owed to many or only a few depending on the facts and circumstances. Think about these two legal tests:

a. Is a duty owed to only specific persons who were located in the *zone of danger* and thus were forseeable parties?
b. Is a duty owed to any person in the *world at large* if it was forseeable that person might be injured?

Both tests italicized above have been the subject of endless analysis, scholarly review, and litigation. What is certain is that both tests seek to enforce a responsibility for injuries caused by a negligent party, but how far that responsibility extends and to whom that duty is owed will probably never be uniformly settled.

B. Breach of Duty: Failure to Exercise Due Care

Due care, as seen from our previous definition, is highly flexible, and that characterization allows the trier of fact to assess unreasonable or reasonable conduct in a myriad of situations. That same versatility also provides frustrating imprecision across most jurisdictions. Whatever the vagaries of this area, a multitude of approaches can be utilized to discern the existence of a breach. Consider the following:

1. Under this entire factual situation alleging negligence, does it appear from the "totality of circumstances" that the defendant's conduct was unreasonable?
2. Must the person suspected of negligence have acted perfectly in order to be found not liable?

The law is very hesitant to impose perfection on any person, and as noted before, accepts the fact that the reasonable person can and does make mistakes. As long as the mistakes are not *careless*, the person may still be reasonable.

3. When the person suspected of failing to exercise reasonable care is compared to others in his or her age group, occupation, and condition, do they still appear unreasonable in their conduct?

Imposed on varied groups of persons are multiple standards of conduct. Particularly, higher standards of conduct are usually imposed on professional people, common carriers, experts in medical fields, and invitees and landowners. Since these four groups generally reap greater economic benefits and can be better educated than the average, the society imposes a higher standard of care. Again, to determine a breach of duty, compare the conduct of the suspected party with what others in a similar situation are doing. Please note that comparative analysis is also very beneficial in formulating a lower standard of care in such groups as children, mentally retarded people and the very old and physically maligned individuals. The law attempts to compare what similar people in similar situations do in order to arrive at a reasonable person standard.

4. Has there been a breach of the statute, rule, or ordinance in the defendant's conduct?

Sometimes the task of demonstrating negligence, and the required breach of due care is no more complex than proving the breach of a statute. Legislatures provide the appropriate standard to measure conduct by, such as traffic rules and housing requirements.

5. Is the injury caused by a condition, situation or event that speaks for itself and implies negligence?

This question delineates the doctrine of *res ipsa loquitor*, which means "the thing speaks for itself." Assume an elevator falls forty flights or a plane falls out of the sky. Is it not fair to give plaintiff a rebuttable presumption of negligence in cases like these? What other explanation is there? To overcome this presumption, the defendant must provide a rational explanation for why it is not his or her obligation or evidence of a breach of due care. Keep in mind also that the doctrine also requires the defendant charged with negligence have exclusive control over the event, condition, or instrumentality and that the plaintiff must not have contributed to this fate in any way.

Exhibit 5.11

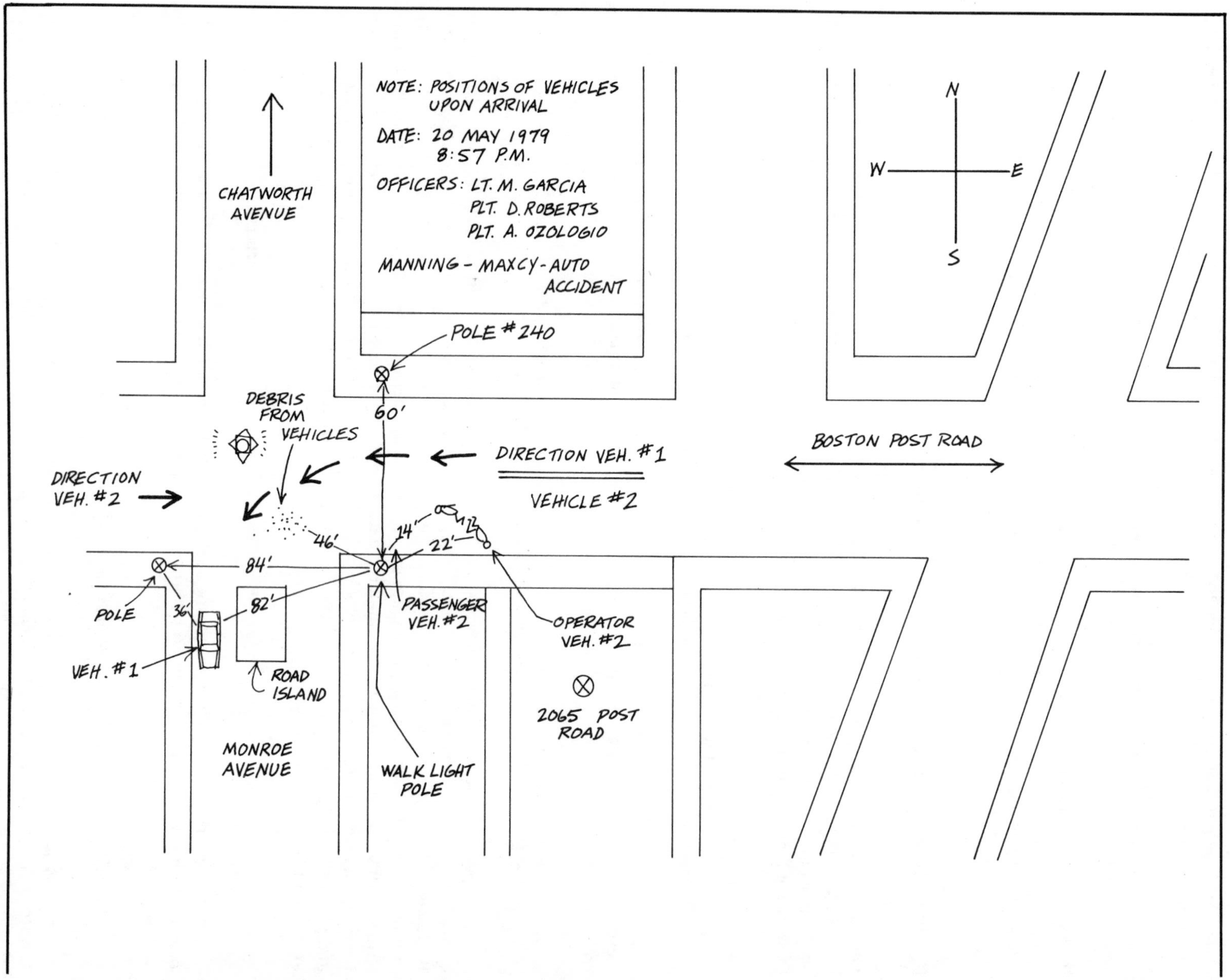
NOTE: POSITIONS OF VEHICLES UPON ARRIVAL
DATE: 20 MAY 1979 8:57 P.M.
OFFICERS: LT. M. GARCIA
PLT. D. ROBERTS
PLT. A. OZOLOGIO
MANNING - MAXCY - AUTO ACCIDENT
N
W
E
S
CHATWORTH AVENUE
POLE #240
60′
DEBRIS FROM VEHICLES
DIRECTION VEH. #1
VEHICLE #2
BOSTON POST ROAD
DIRECTION VEH. #2
14′
22′
46′
84′
82′
36′
POLE
VEH. #1
ROAD ISLAND
PASSENGER VEH. #2
OPERATOR VEH. #2
2065 POST ROAD
MONROE AVENUE
WALK LIGHT POLE

POLICE REPORT:

The police department, of the Village of Larchmont, was at the scene immediately after the accident and they indicated that they heard the noise of the crash at the time they were located at 2050 Boston Post Road. They went, immediately, to the area of the accident and they found vehicle #2, the motorcycle, and the plaintiff on the ground lying injured. They have a diagram with measurements locating the vehicle and the injured persons.

The police report states that the operator of vehicle #1 stated that he had been traveling West, on Boston Road, in the left lane and that he attempted to make a left turn onto Southbound Monroe Avenue. Operator of vehicle #1 stated that he did not see vehicle #2 when he attempted to make the turn.

The police report indicates that there was a witness, Mrs. W., of 9 Thompson Place. This witness stated that she saw vehicle #2 hit the pole, but did not see vehicle #1 and vehicle #2 collide. The coding on the police report indicates that this was an intersection accident, the time of day was dark, the road was lighted, the intersection has a traffic signal, the road was straight and level and that the pavement was dry and the weather was cloudy.

POLICE INTERVIEW:

I interviewed Patrolman P, Shield Number 210, of the Police Department of the Village of Larchmont at Police Headquarters.

Patrolman P stated that he and his partner were immediately on the scene of the accident and called the Volunteer Ambulance Corps, which came and administered First-Aid and transported the injured to the New Rochelle Hospital. He states that Patrolman R and he took the measurements at the scene.

LIABILITY:

This is one of two difficult intersections, on Boston Post Road, in Larchmont. The reason why this is a hazardous intersection is because Northbound, Northeastbound traffic attempting to make a left turn onto Chatsworth Avenue, line up in the left lane of Boston Post Road, and traffic going straight through must proceed down the right lane.

The Y motorcycle would have been blocked from the view of the Z car, by this lane of traffic, until it suddenly appeared in the intersection. It appears that Mr. Z could not have seen the motorcycle until the last minute.

It appears that the left fender, of the Z car, struck the Y motorcycle about even with the rear wheel. The impact, in all probability, caused the severe damage to the passenger's leg and then the motorcycle was knocked off course into the walk signal pole.

FURTHER INVESTIGATION RECOMMENDED:

1. A signed statement of the witness, Mrs. W.
2. An attempt to photograph the defendant's car.

Yours very truly,

C. Causation

On the whole, causation is never an overwhelming dilemma in the law of torts. It's only when inane scenarios crop up including multiple defendants, plaintiffs, autos, bystanders, and assorted other complications. Causal theory seeks to hold a person responsible for the actions generated by his or her deeds. In our analysis of negligence the questions are:

a. Does the defendant have a duty?
b. Has the defendant breached the duty?
c. Does that breach by the defendant *cause* the injury in fact to the plaintiff?

Just as in a link chain, until there is a break, the causal relationship can generally continue. How far can that general principle take us?

Assume Michael Jackson is going thirty-nine miles per hour in a twenty-five zone, and he runs right through a red light. He smashes a car and breaks the back of the driver. That driver goes out of control and his car runs into a house, trampling a garden and running over the leg of a sleeping dog. As Michael Jackson's car spins away from the collision, his white glove falls off and gets caught in a gust of wind. The glove flies two blocks over and lands on the face of a truck driver who can't see because it's stuck to his face. He crashes into a hot-dog stand. Then . . .

At what stage is Michael no longer the *cause* and therefore no longer liable? Anywhere? Or does this go on infinitely, almost in a teleological sense?

In tort law, all jurisdictions have adopted tests for what is known as *proximate causation*. By proximate causation, the tort finder looks for the "cause in fact" of the actual injuries. Two classic standards have become entrenched:

1. The but-for standard

But-for defendant's conduct there would be no injury is the standard test to prove causation. The test is highly personalized and has a difficult time handling multiple situations. Hence, the second test is adopted.

2. The substantial factor

Is the defendant a substantial factor in the cause of the plaintiff's injury? By substantial, courts infer chief, dominant, primary, and other appropriate qualifiers. The test allows easier insights into negligence with multiple parties. In the final analysis, at least in complex cases, the question is whether or not it is more than likely that the defendant's lack of due care resulted in plaintiff's injury.

As can be imagined, some liberal interpreters in the law would like causation to go on without limits. That is where the forseeability doctrine serves as a cut-off point. Most jurisdictions assess factual patterns, even one as crazy as Michael Jackson's, and search for a reasonable end to liability. Ponder these questions:

☐ How likely are these events and conditions?
☐ Could any reasonable person have ever predicted the eventual chain of events?
☐ Do normal reasonable people prepare for such eventualities?
☐ What does common sense tell me?
☐ Can any reasonable person be objectively required to think of such events?
☐ Are there any intervening, supervening, or superseding causes or factors in these facts?

At some moment, causation must end. Deciphering when is often a perplexing task.

D. Damages

Unlike intentional torts, damages are always required in the proof of negligence. The term *damages* includes but is not limited to the following:

1. Pecuniary losses
2. Earnings–projected

3. Value of life expectancy
4. Physical injury
5. Medical expenses; past, present and future
6. Value of all personal property lost
7. Investment losses
8. Services to household
9. All benefits
10. Emotional suffering
11. Taxes
12. Inflation
13. Loss of consortium
14. Pain and suffering
15. Inconvenience

Modern proof of damages is uncannily easy, with hundred of thousands of dollars being attributed to seemingly immeasurable categories such as suffering and distress. Expert witnesses now fairly dominate the courtroom in the presentation and computation of those damages. Varied forms of damages are also described below.

Damages.   A pecuniary compensation or indemnity, which may be recovered in the courts by any person who has suffered loss, detriment, or injury, whether to his or her person, property, or rights, through the unlawful act or omission of negligence of another.

Fee Damages.   Damages sustained by, and awarded to, an abutting owner of real property occasioned by the construction and operation of an elevated railroad in a city street, are so called because compensation is made to the owner for the injury to, or deprivation of, his easements of light, air, and access, and these are parts of the fee.

General Damages.   General damages are such as the law itself implies or presumes to have accrued from the wrong complained of, for the reason that they are its immediate, direct, and proximate result, or such as necessarily result from the injury, or such as did in fact result from the wrong, directly and proximately, and without reference to the special character, condition, or circumstances of the plaintiff.

Imaginary Damages.   This term is sometimes used as equivalent to *exemplary, vindictive,* or *punitive* damages.

Inadequate Damages.   Damages are called "inadequate," within the rule that an injunction will not be granted where adequate damages at law could be recovered for the injury sought to be prevented, when such a recovery at law would not compensate the parties and place them in the position in which they formerly stood.

Intervening Damages.   Such damages to an appellee as result from the delay caused by the appeal.

Irreparable Damages.   In the law pertaining to injunctions, damages for which no certain pecuniary standard exists for measurement.

Land Damages.   A term sometimes applied to the amount of compensation to be paid for land taken under the power of eminent domain or for injury to, or depreciation of, land adjoining that taken.

Liquidated Damages.   The term is applicable when the amount of the damages has been ascertained by the judgment in the action or when a specific sum of money has been expressly stipulated by the parties to a bond or other contract as the amount of damages to be recovered by either party for a breach of the agreement by the other.

Necessary Damages.   A term said to be of much wider scope in the law of damages than *pecuniary*. It embraces all those consequences of an injury usually denominated *general* damages, as distinguished from special damages.

Nominal Damages.   Nominal damages are a trifling sum awarded to a plaintiff in an action, where there is no substantial loss or injury to be compensated, but still the law recognizes a technical invasion of his rights or a breach of the defendant's duty, or in cases where, although there has been a real injury, the plaintiff's evidence entirely fails to show the amount of injury.

Pecuniary Damages.   Such as can be estimated in, and compensated by, money; not merely the loss of money or property or rights, but all such loss, deprivation, or injury as can be made the subject of calculation and of recompense in money.

Proximate Damages.   Proximate damages are the immediate and direct damages and natural results of the act complained of and such as are usual and might have been expected. Remote damages are those attributable immediately to an intervening cause, though it forms a link in an unbroken chain of causation, so that the remote damage would not have occurred if its elements had not been set in motion by the original act or event.

Remote Damages. The unusual and unexpected result, not reasonably to be anticipated from an accidental or unusual combination of circumstances—a result beyond which the negligent party has no control.

Compensatory Damages. Compensatory damages are such as will compensate the injured party for the injury sustained, and nothing more; such as will simply make good or replace the loss caused by the wrong or injury.

Contingent Damages. Where a demurrer has been filed to one or more counts in a declaration, and its consideration is postponed, and meanwhile other counts in the same declaration, not demurred to, are taken as issues, and tried, and damages awarded upon them, such damages are called contingent damages.

Continuing Damages. These are such as accrue from the same injury, or from the repetition of similar acts, between two specified periods of time.

Damages Ultra. Additional damages claimed by a plaintiff not satisfied with those paid into court by the defendant.

Direct Damages. Direct damages are such as follow immediately upon the act done.

Double Damages. Twice the amount of actual damages as found by the verdict of a jury allowed by statute in some cases of injuries by negligence, fraud, or trespass.

Excessive Damages. Damages awarded by a jury that are grossly in excess of the amount warranted by law on the facts and circumstances of the case; unreasonable or outrageous damages.

Exemplary Damages. Exemplary damages are damages on an increased scale, awarded to the plaintiff over and above what will barely compensate him for his property loss, where the wrong done to him was aggravated by circumstances of violence, oppression, malice, fraud, or wanton and wicked conduct on the part of the defendant and are intended to solace the plaintiff for mental anguish, laceration of his feelings, shame, degradation, or other aggravation.

Actual Damages. Real, substantial, and just damages, or the amount awarded to a complainant in compensation for his actual and real loss or injury, as opposed on the one hand to "nominal" damages, and on the other to "exemplary" or "punitive" damages.

IV. STRICT LIABILITY TORTS

Our third major category of torts is the oddball of the crowd, requiring no proof whatsoever of a mental state as discussed in intentional torts, and no demonstration of negligence or any form of carelessness or lack of due care. In short, the defendant in a case of strict liability has little or no room for excuses. The very conduct in which he or she engages makes him or her liable automatically. Did you ever wonder why all diving equipment is now made by only one major manufacturer in the United States? The liabilities incurred can be enormous and are what made diving companies almost extinct. While diving suits don't perfectly fit all state strict liability designs, explosives are always covered under the strict liability doctrine. Why should the seller of explosives be strictly liable for any injuries caused by their defective manufacture? Can't they provide a sound and rational explanation? Which brings us to the rationale for strict liability. Strict liability is fundamentally a social policy, a decision by our system to hold accountable certain types of activities that result in injury no matter what the excuse or justification. The duty to exercise reasonable and due care is absolute because the conduct engaged in has such potentially damaging ramifications. While some defenses can be asserted, it is important to learn this harsh policy and its rationale and basis. The two most traditional areas of strict liability include animals and ultrahazardous activities.

A. Animals

1. Nondomesticated beasts

Why some people persist in recreating the Tanzanian range of Africa in some neighborhoods has always been a mystery to many. Every neighborhood predictably has one zany who owns a boa, a cheetah, a tiger, a wild boar, or some other thoroughly inappropriate creature. All humor aside, these nondomesticated creatures pose substantial physical risks to the general community and also contribute to health and sanitation problems. In an effort to make people think twice before purchasing that cute little tiger cub, who of course grows up to be an adult tiger, the law in all jurisdictions imposes hard liability for any damages caused by these animals.

2. Domesticated animals

Probably in that same neighborhood exists another zany who owns 125 cats or 235 dogs and loves running this stray animal shelter. Touching to say the least, but the rest of the world must function in peace as well, and that is what is so often forgotten by people who impose their humane shelters on others. Not a day goes by across this country in which some action is filed in law or equity dealing with the nuisance of multiple animals. So true also for owners of animals that they know have a propensity for violence. In most jurisdictions, a domesticated animal is permitted and allowed one bite before its owner is strictly liable. This is appropriately called the one-bite rule. After that, strict liability attaches, and all the arguing in the world will not save you from the damages your pooch caused another!

B. Ultrahazardous Activities

An ultrahazardous activity involves any substantial risk of serious harm to person or property, no matter how much care is exercised. The prime example of this is the sale and manufacture of explosives. Any injury resulting from blasting certain chemical fumigations, toxic disposal, and nuclear storage could possibly fall under the umbrella of strict liability.

Other tests in the ultrahazardous category that must be reviewed are:

1. The activity cannot be performed with complete safety.
2. The activity is not commonly engaged in within the community.

V. DEFENSES

While the plaintiff's task is to prove the requisite elements to demonstrate a prima facie case, paralegals who work for the defendant will be searching long and hard for every available defense. Remember that many of the defenses enumerated below apply only to specific torts, as we indicate. Also be mindful that multiple defenses are just as attractive for the defense as multiple causes of actions. Never forget to consider diverse strategies in research, planning, and trial strategy. Utilize those same defenses in your counterdiscovery processes.

A. Particular Defenses of Negligence

1. Contributory negligence

Defense strategy should always entail a review of the plaintiff's behavior in the alleged negligent behavior. If by chance, the plaintiff was in some way careless or partially unreasonable in his or her behavior, that negligence may act as a total bar to plaintiff's recovery. Examples might include a thoroughly intoxicated driver who runs into an individual who is twenty mph over the speed limit. In that scenario the plaintiff's conduct partially caused the injury complained of. Therefore, always keep in mind the plaintiff's (1) own negligence and (2) resulting causation. As harsh as it may seem, most jurisdictions would bar any recovery if proof of contributory negligence was demonstrated.

2. Comparative negligence

In response to the stern result brought about the contributory negligence doctrine, many states have decided to apportion the damages between the parties. It simply becomes a question of who is more at fault than the other, at least in some jurisdictions, or in the final analysis, how much the plaintiff is really responsible for his own injury. Juries will subtract that determination from any potential award. Other states have restrictive formulas apportioning guilt and appropriate awards.

3. Last clear chance

Another adopted defense in reaction to contributory negligence was the doctrine of last clear chance. In this setting, a plaintiff has simply been negligent in getting into a predicament that injures him or her. Remember how Stan Hardy recites to Ollie every time there is trouble, "This is a fine mess you've gotten us into"? That recitation is symbolic of the careless person who gets into trouble but really doesn't realize it until it's too late. Where some relief is afforded to that plaintiff is if the defendant had one last clear chance to avoid injuring the plaintiff. If there was such a chance, he or she had an obligation to do so. Sounds nice doesn't it, but the doctrine is very rigid because the burden of proving last clear chance rests in the plaintiff who must amply demonstrate that: (a) plaintiff was in a *helpless peril*, and (b) defendant was knowledgeable of that peril and did not exercise due care in avoiding eventual damages and injury.

4. Assumption of risk

This defense is very closely allied with the contributory negligence theory. Significant differences do become lucid when one considers the level of consciousness this defense entails. The plaintiff must be shown as a person who (1) knew and understood the risks of the activity that produced the injury and (2) voluntarily chose to participate in that risk, regardless of the consequences.

Generally, a party who agrees to drag race heavy Chevies, or a boxer fighting another in the ring, or any professional athlete will have a troublesome time arguing personal injuries resulting from their activities.

A final problem in this defense is now becoming more common and raises many ethical dilemmas. How does the doctrine operate in the work place? Specifically, how can companies argue assumption when employees are subjected to toxic materials? Do they—that is, the employees—really understand the danger?

B. Defenses to Intentional Torts

1. Consent

With the exception of consenting to criminal behavior, a plaintiff who knowingly, intelligently, and understandably consents to any action can hardly sue to recover damages for injuries caused by that action. Certain people are also deemed incapable of giving their consent because of their age, mental state, or general physical condition. Nor can consent ever be justified when it is procured by mistake, fraud, duress or any other form of coercion, or when the activity performed exceeded the parameters of the consent given.

2. Self-defense/person/property

While the law does not favor the physical settling of disputes, it will honor and uphold the right of any individual who wishes to protect himself or herself from potential physical injury. In many jurisdictions a few caveats are in order:

☐ Deadly force can never be justified in the defense of or protection of property.
☐ The force used in self-defense can only be proportionate to the force exerted. The law would never justify the defensive use of a 357 Magnum when the assailant was using a rolled-up newspaper.
☐ In some jurisdictions a request to desist from the behavior may be required before self-defense tactics can be employed.
☐ In some jurisdictions a duty to retreat may exist, though that duty never exists in one's own dwelling.
☐ In the defense of property, if property is taken and not freshly pursued and retrieved, the right to personally retake ends. The courts then become the appropriate avenue for repossession.
☐ The same standards applicable to the defense of self can be applied to the defense of third parties.

3. Corporal punishment/loco parentis in the schools

Under the in loco parentis doctrine, some jurisdictions still provide teachers and school administrators with a license to use reasonable corporal punishment for purposes of disciplining their students. Recent legislative enactments have diminished this right substantially. Parents, however, are still generally afforded the right and privilege to discipline their own children as long as it is not abusive.

C. Other Major Defenses or Counterstrategies

1. Immunities

In the interest of governmental efficiency and taxpayer relief many state and local governments have set up barriers to suing them in tort. Other rationales for this barrier include allowing government to operate in an unfettered and uninhibited matter, not guided by, or frightened of, potential legal liabilities. All the immunities described below have strong, historical policy rationales for barring a cause of action.

SPECIFIC TYPES OF IMMUNITY

Charitable Immunity. Historically charitable groups, that is, entities of educational, religious, or other benevolent purpose have been immune to all lawsuits for personal injury. A majority of jurisdictions have amended this common-law principle to permit limited rights to parties injured by the legal entity. There is usually a cap, or ceiling, on amounts received.

Family Immunity. At common law an immunity existed between parent and child and between spouses so that a parent or a child could not recover damages against each other and a spouse could not recover damages against the other spouse for personal injury or property damage resulting from such other person's conduct. New challenges to this rule have recently arisen, owing to the rampant increase in child abuse, sexual molestation, and intrafamily violence.

D. Privileges

Privilege has been analyzed indirectly thus far, particularly concerning corporal punishment and the right of police officers to make arrests. Numerous other fact patterns give rise to the defense of privilege.

1. Defamation

There are two types of privilege that may be set up in defense to a civil action for defamation: absolute and conditional. Truth is an absolute defense to all such actions. There are few classes of absolute privilege, usually involving legislative or judicial proceedings. Judges, lawyers, witnesses, and jurors have an absolute privilege to publish defamatory matter relative to the judicial proceeding before them. Likewise, legislators may publish defamatory material concerning pending legislative or governmental questions. Finally, husbands and wives are entitled to publish to each other defamatory statements about others.

2. Occupational

Conditional privileges arise out of occasions. Whether the occasion allows for the invocation of a conditional privilege is a matter of law. In general, it arises when one acts in the bona fide discharge of a public or private duty. The news media have a conditional privilege to publish a true copy of matters that have taken place in legislative or judicial proceedings. A member of the clergy has a similar privilege when discussing spiritual and private matters with his or her parishioners. Similarly, physicians have such a privilege when discussing professional matters with patients. Members of the military have a conditional privilege to publish defamatory remarks about other military personnel. Statements made in the protection of a property interest have such privilege. Artistic and literary criticism also enjoy such privilege. If, however, the person possessing a qualified privilege makes his or her statements in bad faith or with malicious intent, the privilege has been abused and will not be a valid defense to a defamatory action.

3. Public officials

Statements about public officials also receive a qualified privilege. Such persons will succeed in libel or slander lawsuits only upon proof that the statements were made with malice, i.e., with knowledge of their falsity or with reckless disregard for their truth.

Public officials also have the right to enter land in an emergency and to take control of abandoned property, or to exercise rights by eminent domain.

4. Governmental and sovereign immunity

At common law no governmental entity would allow itself to be the target of a lawsuit, and for sound policy reason. Most states have watered down the immunity bar by allowing specific exceptions, such as (1) vehicle liability, (2) care and control of real and personal property, (3) traffic controls and street lighting, (4) utility service, and (5) road hazards and sidewalks. Some states and municipalities have totally done away with the doctrine, much to their treasury's chagrin. The federal government also consents to be sued in extremely limited circumstances under the Federal Tort Claim Act of 1946, and the various pieces of civil-rights legislation adopted since 1971 under Title 42 U.S.C. 1983.

E. Miscellaneous Defenses

1. Statute of Limitations. All states have established set lengths of time during which injured claimants must file their lawsuits or forfeit their claims. As a general proposition, tort claims must be filed within two years of the accident causing the injury or, in certain cases, the date on which the claimant learns of the injury.

2. Res Judicata. If a plaintiff has already had his or her day in court on the same matter, you simply cannot relitigate it. Defense must demonstrate that (a) a final disposition was reached, (b) on the substantive merits, (c) on the exact same cause of action.

3. Improper Venue

4. Lack of Subject Matter Jurisdiction

5. Release/Accord or Satisfaction

F. Special Situations in the Law of Torts: Vicarious Liability for Torts

In the analysis of torts, the defendant who actually committed the tort has been the one held responsible for the damages caused to the injured plaintiff. There are other categories of defendants who will also be held equally responsible with the defendant for damages caused by the defendant's negligence. These categories of defendants derive their liability for the tort based upon their special relationship with the defendant committing the tort.

1. Employer-employee relationship

The employer is held to be vicariously responsible for an employee's acts of negligence if the employee is engaged in his job for his employer at the time of the employee's negligence. For example, a bus company would be held liable to the plaintiff for its bus driver who negligently caused an accident with the plaintiff's automobile. As long as the injury results while the employee is operating within the scope of his employment, the employer will be liable.

2. Partners

Partners are held jointly responsible for the negligent acts of the other partners.

3. Joint enterprise

This occurs where two people share control in the performance of a single venture. For example, if two people are driving a car with each sharing the right of control over the car during the trip, then both would be held liable if one of them negligently caused an auto accident.

4. Independent contractors

An independent contractor is one who independently contracts to perform work according to his own methods, without being subject to control by his employer in the manner in which he carries out his work through the end results of the work are specified by the employer.

Generally, if an independent contractor commits an act of negligence, the one who contracted for his services will not be held liable.

G. Occupiers of Land: Differing Levels of Due Care

Possession rather than ownership of land carries with it the imposition of liability for injuries caused by the land. Accordingly, an allegation of control or possession is essential to all complaints for personal injuries arising out of an accident in connection with the land. The degree of care owed to the injured party is dependent upon the relationship of the injured party to the land.

Ordinarily the possessor of real estate owes no duty to trespassers to keep the property reasonably safe for their use. If the possessor has reason to know of the trespasser's presence on the land, she must exercise reasonable care to prevent her injury.

The possessor is subject to liability to a *licensee* (social guest) for injuries sustained from a natural or artificial condition if she knows of the condition, if she realizes it involves an unreasonable risk, if she has reason to believe the licensee will not discover the condition or realize the risk, and if she permits the licensee to enter or remain on the premises without exercising reasonable care to make the condition reasonably safe or to warn him of the condition or risk involved.

Invitees (business guests) are entitled to the highest level of care owed by an occupier of land. In addition, the possessor has a duty to inspect the premises and erect safeguards and, if necessary, to render the premises reasonably safe. Therefore, she is liable to the invitee for defects that are discoverable by reasonable inspection. She is charged with constructive notice of such defects. The invitee must show that the defect has been present for a sufficient period of time to give the possessor the opportunity to discover it. This policy insures safety in commercial establishments and a safe marketplace.

H. Parents' Liability for Their Children's Tortious Acts

Increasing pressures have come forth from the general public for a legislative enactment making parents more responsible for the behavior of their children, both in a criminal and civil context. The wave of juvenile crime, vehicle violations, accidents, and general malicious destruction of property more than justify this public fervor for parental liability. Most states now devise a dollar limit for parents, usually up to $1,000, for tortious acts committed by their children. These statutes do not negate the common-law liability imposed on parents for their direct negligence in controlling the behavior of their own children.

I. Good Samaritan Acts

At common law an individual was not liable in civil damages for injuries caused to another due to negligent acts committed while rendering emergency medical care of treatment. In the "sue-crazy" modern world, claims of negligence, assault, battery, and even false imprisonment have been brought against citizens who stopped to aid a person in need. No surprise to any rational person that the "hands-off" approach gained favor in the last thirty years, so much so that even doctors, nurses, and other trained personnel would not assist in an emergency unless they were paid to perform that function. Recent legislative enactments have brought some sanity back into this area and exempted or excluded all medical, and in some states firefighters and law-enforcement officers, from any potential liability or lawsuits.

J. An Action in Wrongful Death

The wrongful death statute generally provides for recovery of damages for an individual's death caused by a negligent, willful, wanton, or reckless act by another. The statutory scheme usually requires the executor or administrator of the decedent's estate to bring the wrongful death action even though the damages recovered do not pass to the estate but rather pass directly to specified statutory beneficiaries who have been harmed by the decedent's death.

The statute beneficiaries are (a) the spouse of the decedent if there are no children, (b) the spouse and children of the decedent if there are children, or (c) the next of kin of the decedent if there is no spouse or children.

The statute is principally compensatory in nature. Three types of damages are recoverable: (a) the fair value of the decedent's life to those statutory beneficiaries entitled to recover; (b) reasonable funeral and burial expenses of the decedent; and (c) punitive damages in a designated amount when the deceased's death was caused by malicious, willful, wanton, reckless or grossly negligent conduct. In determining the fair value of the decedent's life, the statute directs the courts to consider the reasonably expected net income, services, protection, care, assistance, society, companionship, comfort, guidance, counsel, and advice the decedent would have provided to those entitled to recover had he lived.

K. Workmen's Compensation

At common law an employee who was injured while working could only recover damages from his employer if he or she could prove that the employer was negligent or otherwise at fault. There were several defenses available to the employer, e.g., assumption of the risk, contributory negligence, etc. These defenses made an employee's recovery very difficult.

In response to the predicament of employees, the Workmen's Compensation system was adopted in the early 1900s. The system establishes compensation benefits for employees injured in the workplace if their injury arose out of an accident in the course of their employment. The benefits are awarded without regard to fault except in the case of serious and willful misconduct. If an employer's act is found to be serious and willful and leads to an employee's injury, then the employee is entitled to double compensation. On the other hand, if an employee contributes to his own injury by a serious and willful act, then he will not be entitled to benefits.

The benefits available to the employee include: (a) medical benefits; (b) wage benefits; and (c) compensation for permanent loss of specific bodily members or functions, or impairment in use of the body or senses. Additionally, the statute provides for widow's and children's dependency benefits if an employee dies as a result of an injury or disease arising out of and in the course of his employment.

The statute requires the employee to give notice of his injury to his employer as soon as practicable after his injury. If the employer does not voluntarily accept responsibility for payment of Workmen's Compensation benefits, the employee must file a written claim for compensation benefits with the appropriate state board or agency. The board is an administrative agency. It acts as a quasi-judicial tribunal to determine what benefits, if any, the employee is entitled to. An appellate court has the authority to review the orders and decisions of the administrative agency and to aid in the enforcement of agency orders.

Recovery under Workmen's Compensation bars recovery for the same injury in a tort action.

L. Medical Malpractice

A physician must exercise the degree of skill and diligence that other physicians in the same general branch of medicine and in the same specialty possess and practice. Failure to meet this standard is a form of negligence known as medical malpractice. The defendant physician is usually compared to other physicians in his or her specialty in order to establish a standard of care.

M. Product Liability Law: A Good Summary of Tort Theories

As you review this final section, it should serve as an excellent review of all tort remedies. A person who is injured by a product has three possible theories of law on which to base a lawsuit to recover damages for the person's injuries: *Strict liability in tort, negligence,* and *breach of warranty.* Liability may be imposed upon those who manufacture, sell or, lease products that are in a defective condition and unreasonably dangerous to the user or consumer at the time they leave their possession. This form of liability is generally known by the misleading term of *strict liability in tort.* It is misleading because the manufacturer or seller is not "strictly" liable but is only liable for those products a plaintiff proves are "defective." Liability may be imposed for negligence on the part of the individual defendant. Liability may also be imposed for breach of contract or warranty, express or implied. An action may be brought upon one or more of the foregoing theories.

1. Elements of strict liability in tort theory of products liability law

a. The manufacturer or seller of any product is liable regardless as to whether they have exercised reasonable care in the product's manufacture or sale; and

b. If the product is defective or inherently dangerous to the ultimate user; and

c. If the defect in the product existed at the time the product left the possession and control of the manufacturer or seller; and

d. If the defect in the product was a direct and proximate cause of the person's injury; and

e. If the product is used for a foreseeable or intended use; and

f. If the product has not been altered or substantially changed from the time of its manufacture or sale.

This products liability theory applies to any injured consumer or user of the product and to foreseeable bystanders.

2. Negligence theory of products liability law

The injured person must prove the manufacturer was negligent in producing the product either by faulty manufacture, faulty design, faulty warnings, or failure to test and inspect. This products liability theory also applies to any injured consumer, user, or foreseeable bystander.

3. Warranty express or implied theory of products liability law

a. In bringing suit against a seller of a product for breach of an *express warranty*, the purchaser would need to establish a breach of the seller's promise, description, claims or advertisements about the nature of the product.

b. In bringing suit against a seller of a product for breach of the *implied warranties*, the purchaser must establish that there was a breach of either the implied warranty or merchantability, which requires that the product be reasonably fit for the general purpose for which it is intended, or the implied warranty of fitness for a particular purpose; and

c. The purchaser must have relied on the express or implied warranty when making the purchase; and

d. A breach of the warranty proximately or directly caused the injuries; and

e. The purchaser notified the seller of the breach of warranty within a reasonable time after learning of the breach.

This products liability theory applies only to the purchaser and generally to the purchaser's immediate family and guests.

A product seller is not liable for harm that would have occurred but for the fact that his product was altered or modified by a third party unless the alteration or modification was in accordance with the instructions or specifications of the product seller or was made with his consent or should reasonably have been anticipated by him. In any investigation of a products liability claim, it is essential that the legal assistant trace the custody of the product from the product seller to the injured party to ascertain what, if any, changes have been made in it during its history.

Liability may arise in instances where the injury is attributable to the failure of the product seller to provide adequate warnings or instructions with or upon the product. Warnings will be considered inadequate unless they are devised to communicate with the person best able to take precautions against the potential harm.

VI. INSTRUCTIONS AND SUGGESTIONS FOR CLIENTS

TO CLIENTS

1. Talk to No One. Do not talk to anyone about your accident except one of the lawyers or investigators in our office. You should always require identification so that you are sure who you are talking to. Don't even talk to your own insurance company or to any lawyers hired by your own insurance company without notifying us so that we may be present if we desire. We will generally want these statements taken in our office.

2. Your Doctor. You should return to each of your doctors as often as necessary and should always tell them about all your complaints. If you see any additional doctors, be sure we are advised immediately of their names and addresses.

3. Records of Complaints. Please keep a daily or weekly record of your complaints and progress. This can be very helpful, when a year later, you are called upon to relate your pain and difficulties.

4. Wages and Earnings Lost. Please keep an accurate record of all days lost from work because of your injuries.

5. Medical Bills. Obtain and keep duplicate copies of all medical, hospital, and drug bills. You should periodically send these bills to us for our files. Also keep records of any other expenses you may have in connection with your accident, such as the hiring of extra help. All your bills should be paid by check, or you should obtain and keep receipts. You should keep a list of all your medical bills and the costs incurred in going to your doctor.

6. Car Repair. Do not have your automobile repaired until you are sure that we have obtained pictures of it. After pictures are taken by this office, have your collision insurance carrier repair your car.

7. Traffic Offenses. If you are arrested in connection with this accident, call one of the lawyers in the office immediately, and we will see that someone represents or advises you. In the event of a coroner's inquest or other type of hearing, be sure to notify this office so that we will be able to represent you in connection with this inquest.

8. Witnesses. Furnish to us immediately the correct names, addresses, and telephone numbers of any and all witnesses you may learn of.

9. Save Your Cast. If your injury requires a cast, brace, traction, or other appliance, save it. When the case is set for hearing you should bring these items with you.

10. Photographs. Send us the negatives and prints of any photographs pertaining to your case that you or any of your friends have taken. If you are required to be in the hospital and are receiving any type of treatment like traction or physical therapy, please notify our office.

11. Hospital and Doctor Bills. Have your own auto insurance carrier pay as many hospital and doctor bills under the medical payment provisions of your policy as possible. You should also have your hospitalization insurance, such as Blue Cross and Blue Shield, pay as much on your bills as possible.

12. Questions. We will probably not contact you until we have something definite to report. We will be contacting you for depositions and answers to interrogatories and when your case goes to trial, which may be in excess of one year from the time that suit is filed. If you have any specific questions in regard to these instructions or any other matters in regard to your case, please feel free to call or write us.

13. Your Address. Be sure to keep us advised of any change in your address or telephone number. Please do not come in expecting to see one of the attorneys without an appointment.

INSTRUCTIONS TO CLIENTS
"My Day"

1. "My Day". We have talked to you about "My Day" when you were in the office. We would like you to start keeping a diary at once. This record will be very valuable throughout your case. It will be kept strictly confidential.

2. How These Injuries Have Affected Your Life. We call it "My Day" because we want you to take a normal day, from the time you get up until the time you go to bed, and explain in detail how this occurrence has changed your life. For example, the way you put on your clothes, the way you get in and out of bed, the way you take a bath, etc. By your life, we mean your work, your playtime, your hobbies, your life as a husband or as a wife, etc. This includes your disposition, your personality, your nervousness, etc. We need to know how your injury has affected the marital relations between you and your spouse.

3. Your Pain and Suffering. We want a description of your pain, both at the scene of the occurrence and at all times thereafter. We want to know whether or not it is a shooting pain, throbbing pain, etc. We want your words and not anyone else's.

4. Start at Your Head When Recording Your Complaints and Injuries. A good rule to follow in order to remember all of your problems is to start at your head and, in detail, go down through all parts of your body, moving from your head, neck, shoulders, etc. Explain in detail any problem that you have with each part of the body. Also, give details with regard to the medications you are taking and what they are for, if you know.

5. Don't Use the Words "I Can't". Please do not use the words "I can't" because "can't" means physical impossibility. For example, you can't use your left hand, if you haven't got one. Don't say "I can't do it," "I never do it." We would prefer you would use such words as "I am not able to do it as well" or some other words meaning the same thing. You should always work towards the idea that "I am trying and I will continue to try to do more things." Everyone will admire you more if you try. In regard to your activities such as your housework, your yardwork, your work at the office or factory, you should detail what things you are not able to do as well as before.

6. "My Day" Witnesses. We would like for you to contact your friends, neighbors, associates at work, etc., and on a separate sheet of paper for each witness give us his name, address and telephone number. Have each describe, or you describe in detail, on a separate sheet of paper what he or she knows about how this injury has changed your life. For example, your neighbor might tell about how you are not able to work as much around the house, or your friends could tell how you don't bowl now, or you don't engage in some other type of hobby. It is better if these witnesses are not your relatives. It is all right if they are your friends, because they would be more likely to have observed you. It is impossible to be too detailed.

7. Loss of Wages or Loss of Potential Income. One of the major aspects of our case may be loss of income or potential income. We will need a copy of your union contract showing wage rates, copies of your W-2 forms and your income tax returns for at least the last five years. Please obtain from your employer the exact days you missed from work because of this accident and the amount of money you would have made if you would have been working these days. If this injury has prevented you from being advanced in your employment or has prevented you from obtaining employment, please give us the names, addresses and telephone numbers of witnesses who can prove this for you. We would also like to know in detail what services you have been prevented from performing around the house, such as supervision of the children.

8. Questions or Help in Answering Your "My Day". If you need any help in keeping your records, please call this office for an appointment. Do not come in without an appointment.

9. Use Your Imagination. You know your own life better than we do. Use your imagination and go into all aspects of your life. Explain to us, in the greatest detail possible, how this occurrence has affected your life.

VIII. DISCUSSION QUESTIONS AND PRACTICAL EXERCISES

Questions

1. John is an aspiring lion tamer and has been working at the zoo for about two years. On Monday, when the zoo was closed, he took the lion out of its cage and into the tent. He received an urgent phone call and went to answer the phone. On his way out he met his boss to whom he explained the situation. The boss, feeling that the tent was secure

enough to retain the beast, went to tend to some other business. Anthony, the six-year-old boy who lived across the street from the zoo, crawled under the tent and was mauled by the lion. Is John responsible?

2. There was a bad snowstorm. It had been snowing continually for twenty-four hours. Mrs. Mark had shoveled her driveway several times but finally gave up. Prior to the end of the storm, Lance, who was delivering the papers, slipped and fell on the driveway, causing severe injury to himself. Is Mrs. Mark liable?

3. It was winter and Anthony was walking along a main street in the business district. There had been a January thaw the day before, and now the temperature had dipped. Underneath the overhanging sign for the ABC Finance Company a puddle of water had accumulated and frozen over. Anthony slipped on the ice and was injured. What are his possible courses of action?

4. The Joneses own a summer cottage, where they keep a lot of antique glass. Their cottage was ransacked several times, and several pieces of glass are missing. They set up a spring gun and wired it so that it would discharge if the front door were opened. Some people came to the cottage and decided to enter it for a look around. Smith, one of the men, was struck by the gun in the stomach. He was severely injured. What possible courses of action can he take?

5. It was raining out, and a puddle of water had formed inside the front door of the Circus Supermarket and by the fruit and produce counter. Mary slipped on the puddle by the fruit stand. Is the store liable?

6. Mr. Jones asked Mary, his secretary, to purchase a gift for his wife while she was out to lunch. "Take a few extra minutes for lunch and buy my wife something nice." While Mary was at the department store, there was an accident in the parking lot. Mary had left her car in neutral and had not put on the emergency brake. Is Mr. Jones responsible?

7. Dr. Smith is a small-town doctor. When he operated on Bob, he thought he saw cancer of the pancreas. He told Bob that he had only 3 months to live. Bob, after 1½ months, went to Boston to a teaching hospital. An exploratory surgical method revealed that Bob did not have cancer of the pancreas but that bile had backed up into his pancreas. A simple procedure corrected this condition. What possible courses of action can Bob take?

8. Samson Elevator Company manufactures escalators. The only way this escalator can be shut down is by way of a special key. Laura, a three-year-old, fell while using the escalator and was cut as her leg was "sucked" into the teeth of the escalator. No one could turn the escalator off because the man with the key was at the other end of the store. Is this a products liability suit?

9. Peter had a bad back. As he was walking along the street, he fell into a small hole and wrenched his back. Had he not had that prior back injury he probably never would have hurt his back. Is the owner of the sidewalk responsible?

Practical Exercises

1. **Assault and battery.** A, while walking along a city sidewalk, sees his best friend B talking to A's three enemies, C, D, and E. A sneaks up behind his friend B, picks up a brick and throws it at C. The brick hits C in the head. C sees A throw the brick at him.

   The brick bounces off C and strikes A's friend B on the nose. B does not see the brick coming. D, who saw the brick when it was thrown, ducked out of the way. The brick just missed D. E was standing next to B, C, and D. E was looking down at the ground and never saw A throw the brick. E hears something fall behind him, turns, and sees the brick. After the brick falls to the ground, A reaches for another brick and says: "You're next, E!"

TRUE OR FALSE

   1. _____ A committed an assault on B.
   2. _____ A committed an assault on C.
   3. _____ A committed an assault on D.
   4. _____ A committed an assault on E.
   5. _____ A committed a battery on B.
   6. _____ A committed a battery on C.
   7. _____ A committed a battery on D.
   8. _____ A committed a battery on E.
   9. _____ A's words to E constitute an assault.
   10. _____ A's words to E, together with his act
        of reaching for another brick, constitute an assault on E.

2. **Livid Red.** Red is the proprietor of a local men's shop, which happens to be in a rough neighborhood. Red leaves his store late one evening and decides to take a shortcut through an alley to his car. After Red walks a few steps into the alley, he hears behind him, "Let's rob him!" Red turns and sees two thugs enter the alley. Red runs down the alley and the thugs chase him. Halfway down the alley, Red accidentally drops his briefcase, which happens to contain over $10,000 in cash, one month's earnings from his men's shop. The thugs pick up the briefcase, turn around, and run in the opposite direction from Red. Red yells, "Drop that briefcase!" When the thugs continue running, Red takes a gun out of his pocket, tries to point it over the heads of the thugs, and shoots twice. Red sees the thugs fall and then walks up to them, intending to retrieve his briefcase. With his gun poised in his hand, Red walks by thug #1, noting he is unconscious. As Red approaches thug #2, thug #1 wakes, takes a gun out of his jacket, and shoots Red in the leg. Red falls. Thug #2 then reaches for Red's wristwatch, whereupon Red bites the thug's hand.

Thug #2 jumps up and then tries to force himself through an apartment door fronting on the alley, until he sees a man standing behind a kitchen stove with a shotgun pointed at him.

Thug #2 then runs out of the alley and turns down the street where he encounters Bill and his friend, Carl. Bill heard the shots, sees the thug, notices the thug is carrying a briefcase, and sees that the thug's arm is bleeding and that he is looking frantically behind him.

As the thug nears Bill, Bill says, "You're under arrest." The thug retorts, "You've got to be kidding," and starts to chase Bill. Bill pushes Carl aside to avoid the thug, stops, turns and then tackles the thug. As the thug goes to hit Bill, Carl strikes the thug on the head with a stick, knocking him unconscious.

Identify and discuss the issues of self-defense, recovery of personal property, defense of personal property, defense of land and arrest.

3. **Neighborly love**. Jim and Bob were model next-door neighbors until the bicentennial picnic they held in Jim's backyard. Jim's family had supplied the food, and Bob brought several gallons of liquor, knowing only part of each bottle would be consumed that day. Late in the day Jim and Bob became involved in a heated argument about the possibility of peanut farming in Alaska. Becoming extremely angry, Bob says to Jim, "I'm going home." Bob leaves and goes back to his house by walking through the small gate in the fence separating the two yards. A few minutes later Bob comes out of his house. Jim sees him and yells from his backyard, "Since you don't agree with me, I'll just have to bring this liquor inside and make sure me and my buddies make good use of it at tomorrow night's poker game." Bob is furious. He charges into Jim's yard, knocking down the fence, breaking part of it.

Jim by this time is standing inside his doorway with Bob's liquor in his arms. Jim drops a bottle and it smashes on the floor. Bob demands the rest of the liquor. Jim sticks his tongue out at Bob. Bob then takes a step into the door opening, whereupon Jim slams the door on Bob's foot. Bob tries to get to Jim but falls because of his sore foot.

Bob decides to leave Jim's land. Seeing Jim's pet anteater in Bob's garden, eating Bob's peanut plants, Bob walks up to the anteater and begins to kick it. The anteater runs out of the garden. Jim then happens to look out of his window and sees his anteater is loose on Bob's property. Jim runs out of his house and retrieves his anteater from Bob's property.

Once inside, Jim proceeds to drink some of Bob's liquor. That night, when a friend stops by, Jim sells him two bottles of Bob's liquor.

Late that night a hurricane strikes the area. Bob's TV antenna flies off onto Jim's property, smashing one of Jim's windows. Bob sees that the antenna is about to blow away, so he races out of his house onto Jim's property to retrieve it, trampling through Jim's flower bed.

The storm gets worse. Jim wakes and sees that a tree on Bob's property is about to fall on his house and into his bedroom, where his goldfish are sleeping. Jim races out of his house with an ax and walks up to Bob's tree, whereupon he encounters Bob, who says, "Get away from my Mao Chinese tree with that ax!" Jim drops the ax and punches Bob, knocking him unconscious. Jim chops the tree down, but in pushing it away from his house, he accidentally strikes some electrical wires, which fall on the street, swishing and throwing sparks in all directions. Tim, driving down Jim's street, comes upon the wires just as a tree falls across the road behind him. Tim then drives his car over Jim's freshly seeded lawn and around the wires.

A gas company man then arrives on the scene and sees that a live wire is sparking near a gas main that cracked when the tree fell. He determines that he must enter Bob's house to shut off the gas. He asks Jim to help him carry his equipment into Bob's house. Receiving no answer to a pounding on Bob's door, Jim forces the door down and charges into the house. Bob comes in the back door to his house and sees Jim. Despite their explanation of the problem, Bob orders Jim and the gas man out of the house. The gas man and Jim then jump Bob, tie him up, and proceed to shut off the gas.

Identify and discuss the issues of defense and recovery of personal property, assault and battery, self-defense, trespass to land and chattels, public and private necessity and conversion.

4. **Good Samaritan.** John, a blind man, was walking on Elm Street, a public thoroughfare, when he came upon an excavation dug by Rush Job Construction Company, an independent contractor employed by State Sewer Company. Since the excavation was plainly visible, Rush Job had not erected any barriers around the excavation, and consequently John fell into the excavation, sustaining injuries. Bob, a passerby, heard John's cries for help and rushed to the pit, whereupon he leaned over to reach for John, lost his balance and fell into the pit, also sustaining injuries. Had Bob paused to think before leaning over the excavation, he would have seen a rope ladder nearby, which he could have used to climb down into the pit with complete safety.

Questions I–IV are based on the foregoing situation.

(I) In a negligence action by John against State Sewer Company, assuming for purposes of this question only that Rush Job was negligent and John was not negligent, John would
a. recover under the principle of strict liability for ultrahazardous activities
b. recover, because excavation requires special precautions for which liability is nondelegable
c. not recover, because there is no legal duty owed to John by State Sewer Company
d. not recover, because there is not vicarious liability of the employer for the torts of his independent contractor

(II) The minimum standard of care that John must exercise to be free of any contributory negligence is
a. the standard of care that would be exercised by a reasonable sighted man, because the "reasonable man" test is an objective one
b. a higher standard of care than that which would be exercised by a reasonable sighted man, because a blind man would make allowances for his handicap
c. a lower standard of care than that which would be exercised by a reasonable sighted person, because others should make allowances for his handicap
d. the same standard of care that would be exercised by a reasonable blind man, because this is the only method by which negligence can be measured

(III) In a negligence action by Bob against Rush Job, assuming for purposes of this question only that Rush Job was negligent, Bob would
a. recover, because Bob's rescue attempt and his consequent injuries were proximately caused by Rush Job's negligence
b. not recover, because a voluntary rescue attempt constitutes an intervening cause between Rush Job's negligence and Bob's injuries
c. recover, because under the "rescue doctrine" a person has a legal obligation to render assistance to another, and if he sustains injuries thereby, the original negligence is not superseded by the rescue attempt
d. not recover, because Bob was contributorily negligent

(IV) If Bob could recover compensatory damages from Rush Job, punitive damages may
a. be awarded at the discretion of the jury, subject to modification by the court
b. be awarded provided they bear a reasonable relationship to the compensatory damages
c. not be awarded because there was no malice or intent
d. not be awarded because Bob was not the primary victim of the negligence

5. **Undelivered pizzas.** John Doe was driving a new Ford van at sixty miles per hour along a quiet residential street to deliver pizzas for the OK Pizza Company.

Suddenly John Doe saw little Shirley Wilson dart out between parked cars to recover her frisbee. John Doe slammed on his brakes but because of defective brakes, was unable to stop the van, striking Shirley and subsequently striking one of the parked cars. Shirley sustained a fractured leg, and Doe sustained a fractured back for which both were taken to University Hospital by Ace Ambulance. On the way to University Hospital, Ace Ambulance, driven by Joe Brown, failed to sound its siren and use its flashing lights while racing through a red light at an intersection. Dave Harry, proceeding through the intersection on a green light, struck the Ace Ambulance. In the collision, Shirley fractured her arm, and Doe sustained serious internal injuries, which resulted in his death two months later. Dave Harry was not injured. Joe Brown sustained minor whiplash injuries.

Please identify and discuss the legal issues raised by the respective parties' claims and your reasoning for who you think should have won on each of the issues.

ENRICHMENT ACTIVITY

Accompany an insurance-claims adjuster on several investigations. Based upon your observations of gathered facts and evidence, prepare a memorandum of law for each case, which assesses the question of liability.

SUGGESTED READING

ABA TORT AND INSURANCE PRACTICE SECTION. *Extracontractual Damages.* Chicago: ABA, 1983.

DOOLEY, JAMES A. *Modern Tort Law: Liability and Litigation.* Willmette, Ill.: Callaghan, 1982.

EPSTEIN, RICHARD ALLEN. *A Theory of Strict Liability: Toward a Reformulation of Tort Law.* San Francisco: Cato Institute, 1980.

KEETON, W. PAGE, et al. *Prosser and Keeton on the Law of Torts.* St. Paul: West Publishing Co., 1984.

LAWSON, F. H., et al. *Tortious Liability for Unintentional Harm in the Common Law and the Civil Law.* New York: Cambridge University Press, 1982.

MINZER, MARILYN, ed. dir., et al. *Damages in Tort Actions.* New York: M. Bender, 1982.

MORRIS, CLARENCE. *Morris on Torts, 2d ed.* Mineola, New York: Foundation Press, 1980.

OLECK, HOWARD LEONER. *Oleck's Tort Law Practice Manual.* Englewood Cliffs, N.J.: Prentice-Hall, 1982.

SHEPARD'S/McGRAW-HILL, ed. staff. *Shepard's Causes of Action.* Colorado Springs: Shepard's/McGraw-Hill, 1983.

SOLYM, LASZLO. *The Decline of Civil Law Liability.* Rockville, Md.: Sijthoff and Noordhoff, 1980.

CHAPTER SIX

CIVIL PROCEDURE AND EVIDENCE

CHAPTER DESCRIPTION

In this chapter we analyze civil court procedures and court document preparation and filing requirements. The student is introduced to evidence law necessary to review depositions and other court-related materials to aid in preparing an attorney for trial.

PARALEGAL FUNCTIONS

Interview witnesses.

Take statements from witnesses.

Draft initial pleadings or responsive pleadings.

Draft interrogatories, bill of particulars, and the like.

Prepare witnesses for depositions and trial.

Digest depositions.

Prepare evidence for trial.

Index documents and exhibits

Draft necessary motions.

Maintain trial calendar and scheduling of cases.

Assist in litigation of case.

I. THE NATURE OF CIVIL LAW

A. General Characteristics of a Civil Action

Civil law encompasses a diverse area of litigation, legislation, and general human conduct. Aside from criminal law, this is the most publicized type of law in our society and an area that so directly influences a majority of citizens. What makes a law civil versus criminal? As discussed in the chapter on criminal law, civil law most markedly differs from criminal in its scope or effect on the society at large. Crimes are deeds against *all* of the society, an infraction of or affront to the peace and tranquility of the community. Civil actions are injuries, harms, losses to a given person, one individual whose mind has been distressed, whose finger was mutilated by a consumer product, or whose spouse fails to pay support or alimony. In the briefest of definitions, a civil action *is an individualized, personal harm, referred to as a lawsuit.*

How many forms of civil actions are there? Consider the following list as indicative of the diversity of civil-law topics:

1. Divorce
2. Annulment
3. Custody
4. Support
5. Mortgage foreclosure
6. Eviction/ejectment
7. Partition
8. Liens
9. Trespass
10. Attachment
11. All torts
12. Prevention of waste
13. Habeas corpus
14. Quiet title
15. Housing
16. Landlord-tenant
17. Environmental
18. Specific performance
19. Declaratory judgments
20. Injunctions

The list could easily be expanded, but the point remains that civil law is a very broad field covering a range of actions in law.

So how are the actions regulated or controlled? Is there some system of rules or regulations for procedure in civil cases? All states as well as the federal government have adopted rules of civil procedure in one form or another. These rules attempt to provide guidance on the appropriate pleadings, methods of discovery, and other relevant topics. This chapter will frequently refer, directly or indirectly, to the much emulated *Federal Rules of Civil Procedure for the United States District Courts*, which can be purchased from the government printing office for a nominal fee.

B. Some Specific Types of Civil Actions

Civil law also has an assortment of *actions*, which seek specific relief. Some of the terminology utilized borders on the absurd, but do not fear the "legalese." The majority of actions as cited in the previous section are plainly understood. The more foreign in nature are briefly described below.

1. Trespass

This action covers all torts against the person or property of all kinds. Under the trespass umbrella may be a negligence case or assault or wrongful death.

2. Assumpsit

This form of action lies for the recovery of damages for the nonperformance of a contract or other agreement.

3. Attachment

This is an action in which an injured plaintiff is enabled to acquire a lien upon property for satisfaction of a claim or judgment.

4. Class action

In order to simplify multiple lawsuits and litigation, all jurisdictions permit a class action, a lawsuit brought by a group or class. In order to be part of a class, there must be proof that:

a. The class is numerous.
b. Questions of law or fact are common to all.
c. Claims or defenses are typical.
d. Separate actions would cause inconsistency in legal application.

Who would be a good example of a class?

5. Replevin

A personal action brought to recover possession of goods unlawfully taken; arises in property disputes or title questions.

6. Protection from abuse

Broad-ranging action providing a remedy for adults and children who are abused physically or mentally by others; most commonly seen in domestic relations courts.

7. Ejectment

An action of ejectment may be brought to obtain possession of real property.

8. Quiet title

The quiet title right is usually due a covenant in a general warranty deed. That assurance of quiet title will be tested if there is any dispute as to liens, titles itself, possession, or other interest in land.

9. Mandamus

This is a writ forcing some governmental authority to act or simply do its job. It is usually directed at some governmental authority, such as an administrative head or mayor of a city, or any judicial officer.

10. Quo warranto

A civil proceeding utilized for the purposes of trying or testing rights to holding a public office.

11. Habeas corpus

This action is utilized at both the civil and criminal level and reviews the detention or custody of any party.

12. Prevention of waste

Used to halt damages or waste to jointly owned property.

II. THE PARALEGAL AND CIVIL PRACTICE: GENERAL CONSIDERATIONS IN EVERY ACTION

As mentioned previously, civil law is a diverse, multifaceted field, and predictably full of subtle, conceptual distinctions, personalities, and legal strategies. The paralegal must be prepared to deal with many competing interests and issues and to balance realism with exaggeration in his or her analysis of facts. The paralegal must be an accomplished investigator, an extremely capable counselor, an effective mediator, and, most critically, a technical purist able to keep track of time frames, dates, filings, and assorted other mind-boggling tasks! As mentally and emotionally demanding as the field may be, the paralegal will thrive within the emotional turbulence of divorce, the intricacies of contractual dispute, and the seemingly inane proof of negligence or mental distress. All of these actions are civil actions requiring the paralegal's services. All of these actions require the following bits of advice.

A. Relationship with Clients

Civil actions frequently produce actions that border on being laughable. Don't laugh! Bear with the idiosyncratic personalities and parties. Look through that foolishness and evaluate the *merits* only. Is the case based on a substantive issue with a legal remedy? Be objective. The best advice is to evaluate the case rather than the client, since the latter often ruins the interpretation of the former. Other thoughts for the paralegal include developing good human-relations skills with the client.

- ☐ Be attentive.
- ☐ Be supportive.
- ☐ Be a listener.
- ☐ Do not condescend.

B. Client Interview

Forms to assist the paralegal in the client interview are available. To insure efficiency and comprehensiveness, send such a form to the clients long before their appointment and ask them to fill it out before the scheduled appointment. That information along with an initial attorney/paralegal observation will go a long way in discerning the viability of a case in civil law. At some stage in the client interview, the parties to the process should reach some consensus on (1) whether the case has any merit, (2) whether the client is capable of withstanding any litigation, and (3) what the costs, fees, and expenses of the attorney will be.

Most essential to the success of this client interview is the open, uninterrupted opportunity a client has to relate the facts as he or she perceives them. No matter how boring those facts are, attorneys and paralegals have an obligation to let the client vent the issues. If the case is meritorious, eventual pleading preparation will depend upon that assimilation of facts.

In the same light, be forever aware that the client is not always truthful, perceptually cogent, or even sane. The most inexperienced advocate quickly learns that no person is exactly truthful and that his or her client's story always must be balanced with the opposition's perspective. In civil law, that balancing of stories is a mandatory practice.

C. Evaluation of Evidence

After the preliminary evaluation of the client's case and the acceptance by the attorney, the collection of evidence becomes a crucial function of the paralegal. Words, assertions, and verbal claims of the plaintiff are usually not enough to successfully litigate a civil action. To increase the likelihood of victory, the paralegal must professionally keep track of (1) documentary evidence, (2) real evidence, (3) expert witnesses, and (4) lay witnesses. This assimilation of evidence will be tremendously helpful to the attorney who is evaluating a case on the basis of its evidence.

D. Investigators

In areas such as domestic relations, environmental violations, and harassment, an investigator can serve the law firm in a most productive way. The private investigator is, of course, less restrained by constitutional restrictions on privacy and search-and-seizure requirements.

E. Check Lists

The paralegal should develop a system of check lists, including the following:

1. Contract for legal services (see exhibit 6.1)
2. Litigation file check list (see exhibit 6.2)
3. Investigative check list (see exhibit 6.3)

F. Discovery Processes

The discovery process will be comprehensively analyzed in section V. Suffice it to say, the paralegal must become an integral player in the collection of information and the discovery of facts, data, and evidence helpful to the client's case. At a minimum, the paralegal must discover the opposition's list of witnesses; records: medical or business; accident information; affidavits; and experts' results.

G. Possible Parties to Sue

The odds of successful litigation greatly depend on the number of potential defendants. Since not all defendants are economically capable of paying a judgment, the more parties to the action, the better the chances of collecting. Consider the following vicarious parties: employers, parents, agents, partners.

H. Appropriate Court

The choice of jurisdiction is not always an easy exercise. Volumes have been written on its strategic and technical nature. Why so? Well, jurisdiction can be based on a variety of theories, some multiple in approach and not necessarily exclusive of the others.

In the most basic context, jurisdiction rests (a) in the person (in personem); and (b) the thing (in rem or subject matter). Detailed analysis follows in section IV, but keep in mind that the integrity of the lawsuit can depend on any of the following factors:

Geographic location   Diversity of the parties
Subject matter of the lawsuit   Amount of damages
Federal or state questions   Age of the parties
                                    Legislative preemption

I. Rules of Civil Procedure

Absent an agreement to the contrary, the Rules of Civil Procedure for the jurisdiction control the lawsuit. Either follow them or pay the penalty! The rules were not promulgated for fun or whim. Malpractice cases abound for failure to adhere to them.

J. Requirements of Notice

The most credible cause of action imaginable will have no chance of success if proper notice is not given to the opposition. Every complaint filed by any plaintiff must attach a notice that substantially reviews the rights of the defendant in the lawsuit. Notice assumes knowledge. Failure to provide notice ruins a legitimate case.

Exhibit 6.1

CHARLES P. NEMETH
ATTORNEY AT LAW
366 CONCORD PIKE
ROUTE 202
P.O. BOX 255
CHADDS FORD, PENNSYLVANIA 19317

———

1-215-358-1689
1-302-798-4570

Dear

                         RE:

I am writing this letter to report that I have begun work on your behalf. My services at the outset have involved _____. I enclose copies of_____ _____. I will keep you informed as the matter progresses.

This letter will also confirm receipt of a retainer fee of $_____, which entitles you to _____ hours of professional time at the agreed rate of $_____ per hour. Travel time is billed at (_____ of the hourly rate)(the hourly rate). I indicated to you that I felt that the requested services could conceivably be completed within that time frame, given the most favorable circumstances. Thus, this retainer is my minimum fee for the time, preparation, and responsibility involved in this matter.

I am not certain of the extent of the legal services that will be necessary in your case. Thus, if it becomes clear that the time required to complete this matter will exceed the retainer, I will submit a statement for additional fees. I will expect prompt payment of the additional sum to enable me to continue my efforts on your behalf.

My normal practice is to bill on amounts due every 30 days, and I expect payment within 30 days, unless other arrangements are made in advance. My hourly rate is subject to possible upward adjustment after one year.

If you have any question, please do not hesitate to contact me. Thank you so much.

                         Respectfully,

                         Charles P. Nemeth
                         Attorney-at-Law

CPN:atc

Exhibit 6.2

ADVERSARIAL MODEL
Litigation File Checklist

TAB # **Pretrial** Pleadings, etc.	TITLE OF LEGAL DOCUMENT	FILED BY WHICH PARTY	DUE DATE	DATE FILED	DATE SERVED
_____	Praecipe for Summons	Plaintiff			
_____	Summons	Plaintiff			
_____	Rule to File Complaint	Defendant			
_____	COMPLAINT	Plaintiff			
_____	Notice of Appearance	Defendant			
_____	Preliminary Objections	Defendant			
_____	Answer to Prelim. Obj.	Plaintiff			
_____	Motion #1: _____				
_____	Reply to Motion #1				
_____	Motion #2: _____				
_____	Reply to Motion #2				
_____	Motion #3: _____				
_____	Reply to Motion #3				
_____	Motion #4: _____				
_____	Reply to Motion #4				
_____	Answer to Complaint	Defendant			
Discovery by Plaintiff					
_____	Interrogatories (1st Set)				
_____	Answer				
_____	Interrogatories (2d Set)				
_____	Answer				
_____	Document Request (1st Set)				
_____	Answer				
_____	Document Request (2nd Set)				
_____	Answer				
_____	Notice of Deposition of: _____				
_____	Notice of Deposition of: _____				
_____	Notice of Deposition of: _____				
_____	Request for Admissions				
_____	Answer				
Discovery by Defendant					
_____	Interrogatories (1st Set)				
_____	Answer				

_____	Interrogatories (2nd Set)				
_____	Answer				
_____	Document Request (1st Set)				
_____	Answer				
_____	Document Request (2nd Set)				
_____	Answer				
_____	Notice of Deposition of: _____				
_____	Notice of Deposition of: _____				
_____	Notice of Deposition of: _____				
_____	Request for Admissions				
_____	Answer				

TAB # **Pretrial** Pleadings, etc.	TITLE OF LEGAL DOCUMENT	FILED BY WHICH PARTY	DUE DATE	DATE FILED	DATE SERVED
After Close of Discovery					
_____	Plaintiff's Pretrial Statement				
_____	Defendant's Pretrial Statement				
_____	Discontinuance				
Trial					
_____	Plaintiff's Trial Brief				
_____	Defendant's Trial Brief				
_____	Discontinuance				
Post-trial By Plaintiff					
_____	Post-Trial Brief				
_____	Post-Trial Motion				
_____	Exceptions				
_____	Brief in Support of Posttrial Motion/Exceptions				
_____	Appeal				
By Defendant					
_____	Post-Trial Brief				
_____	Post-Trial Motion				
_____	Brief in Support of Posttrial Motion/Exceptions				
_____	Appeal				
Miscellaneous					

Exhibit 6.3

INVESTIGATIVE CHECKLIST: GENERAL BACKGROUND INVESTIGATION

Date Assigned	*Attorney's Initials*	*Case Name and Number*

Name of Subject	*Last Employment or Other Identifying Date*

SOURCES

☐ Telephone directory, directory assistance
☐ City directory check
☐ Motor Vehicle Department
☐ Post Office Check
   U.S. Main Post Office
   (Last Known Address)
☐ Registrar of Voters
☐ County Assessor's Office
☐ County Recorder's Office
☐ Docket Search: Plaintiff and Defendant
   (a) Superior Court
   (b) U.S. District Court
   (c) Marriage License Dept.
   (d) Child Support Payment Division
   (e) Municipal and Justice Courts
☐ Parole/Probation
☐ ARD
☐ Social and Family Services
☐ District Attorney
☐ Dept. of Corrections

☐ Local Police Departments
   (evidence of summary convictions)
☐ Bail Offices
☐ Mental Health Services
☐ Community Services
☐ Credit Bureau
☐ Social Security Administration, Bureau of Data Processing
   and Accounts, Baltimore, Maryland, 21235
☐ Secretary of State, UCC
☐ Registrar of Contractors
☐ Corporation Commission
☐ Better Business Bureau
☐ Previous address visit, former neighbors, friends, relatives
☐ Previous employment check
☐ Newspaper articles
☐ Various licensing depts., Real Estate Dept., etc.
☐ Other sources unique to subject, i.e., police departments,
   licensing agencies, city, county and state offices
☐ Asset check

K. Service

No jurisdiction waives the requirement that all pertinent documentation to a lawsuit must be "served" on the opposition. Failure to properly serve is destructive to the plaintiff's case. Adherence to local rules is mandatory. A review of the service process is provided in section IV.

L. Settlements in Writing

Since a majority of civil litigation ends in pretrial settlement, it is essential that the attorney and paralegal regularly apprise the client of the status of any negotiations on the claim. Neither the paralegal nor attorney can settle in a vacuum, and they must therefore have:

   ☐ A true belief in the merits of the case
   ☐ A complete and comprehensive knowledge of the case
   ☐ A thorough understanding of the nature of any injuries
   ☐ A quantified assessment of plaintiff's damages
   ☐ Thorough awareness of the opposition's counsel and the nature of his or her authority

Do not shy away from settled cases. Recent statistics of the ABA clearly demonstrate that an overwhelming majority of all civil actions are settled out of court. Some estimates are as high as 90 percent. That figure represents a success of sorts—justice is being served without endless bickering and adversarial carping in the courtroom. At least, that is one possible interpretation. What is inevitably true, in civil law at least, is that preparation is the key to success, that human endeavor beyond the average will be rewarded, and that a knowledgeable paralegal will outdistance the dim-witted and ill-prepared one.

III. PLEADINGS: PREPARATION AND DESIGN

A. Definition

Pleadings are the formal documents of civil litigation. The major functions of pleadings are to inform the court, parties to the dispute, and respective counsel of the issues to be decided and the questions or controversies in dispute. Pleadings not only assert the problem but also request an applicable *remedy*. A *remedy* is the relief sought, the solution hoped, and the enforcement empowered by statute. In a divorce action, the obvious remedy sought is a dissolution of the marriage. In a contract action, a party may be seeking damages, specific performance, and so on.

B. Types of Pleadings

1. The complaint

The complaint cites all the allegations that form the basis, the foundation, of the plaintiff's cause of action. As can be gleaned from our model complaint, the allegation must precisely provide facts that constitute a *cause of action*. (See exhibit 6.4, as well as the affidavit in 6.5.)

Exhibit 6.4

IN THE COURT OF COMMON PLEAS OF   COUNTY,
CIVIL ACTION—LAW

:

:

:   IN ASSUMPSIT

Complaint.

1. Plaintiff is   , a   Corporation doing business at

2. Defendant is   , a   Corporation doing business at

3. Plaintiff at the request of defendant sold and delivered to said defendant certain lumber and building supplies at the time set forth in the true and correct copy of plaintiff's books of original entry hereto attached, marked Exhibit "A," and made a part hereof.

4. The prices charged for the said lumber and building supplies were the fair, reasonable and market prices of the same at the time they were sold to the defendant and further are what the defendant agreed to pay therefore.

5. Defendant also agreed to pay a finance charge of one and one-half percent (1½%) per month on any outstanding balance over thirty days old. The finance charge assessed against defendant pursuant to such agreement is set forth in Exhibit "A" on those lines of said Exhibit which have the notations "SC."

6. All credits to which defendant is entitled are set forth in Exhibit "A."

7. Although plaintiff has demanded payment of $4,958.95 representing the balance due for the items sold to defendant and the finance charge, defendant has refused to pay the same.

WHEREFORE, plaintiff demands that this Honorable Court enter judgment against defendant in an amount of Four Thousand Nine Hundred Fifty Eight Dollars and 95/100 ($4,958.95) plus interest plus the costs of this suit.

                                   _____

                                          Esquire

                                Attorney for Plaintiff
                                  W. Front Street
                                  I.D. #

Exhibit 6.5

```
                    IN THE COURT OF COMMON PLEAS OF                      COUNTY,


                                          :

                                          :

                                          :

                                          :

                                     Affidavit

COMMONWEALTH OF
                                                   §
COUNTY OF                   :

                                            , being duly sworn according to law, depose and say
that                       the                in the above entitled matter; and that the facts set forth
in the foregoing
are true and correct to the best of      personal knowledge, information and belief.


                                                   _____


SWORN TO AND SUBSCRIBED
BEFORE ME THIS            DAY
OF               , 19 _____
```

Sample Allegation:

On July 19, 1984, Dr. Thomas James did hereby operate on plaintiff, Sally Lolly, for an appendectomy. Subsequent testing by the clinical lab showed the appendix had already been removed.

Within these facts is the complaint of the plaintiff—that Dr. James performed a totally unnecessary operation, at risk and expense to Ms. Lolly. What type of civil action might fit here? Negligence? Assault? Malpractice? Many possibilities exist. Again, please inspect the sample complaint in exhibit 6.4 for the multiple allegations asserted:

Aside from the allegations, the complaint requires a *prayer*, or *request for relief*, to follow the allegation.

Example:

WHEREFORE, the Plaintiff, Sally Lolly, prays judgment against Dr. James, in the sum of $950,000 plus costs of the lawsuit.

Note that numerous allegations can be posed by the plaintiff as well as requests for relief or remedy.

Other formalities to the complaint are the *jury demand clause* and *signature and verification clauses*. In the final analysis, the complaint, if drafted properly, has to recite all essential facts that allege a cause of action in law. The complaint should be precisely drawn and is not a forum for argumentation or creative exposition.

2. The response

The formal response to a complaint is called an answer. Responding to the complaint in a lawsuit is not as easy as it may seem, for a variety of options are available to a defendant. All those options will be covered, but to label them all "answers" would not be legally precise. For now, consider these options as possible *responses*.

a. FILE NO RESPONSE TO THE COMPLAINT

A defendant who fails to respond in any fashion is plainly stupid, unless he or she is positive that final vindication is assured. No sound advice could ever tolerate a failure to respond, since the end result may be liability imposed by *default judgment*. Failure to respond usually means a failure to appear at the eventual hearing on the complaint. Since the plaintiff's only obligation is to present evidence that is clear and convincing, or even less in some jurisdictions, the defendant's failure to rebut the presentation of the plaintiff's case does not bode well.

b. Motions Pleading

Numerous motions can be filed attacking the validity of the complaint, and these motions will be thoroughly discussed in section VII. For now, be aware that these options exist that attack the validity of the complaint's allegations:

1. Motion for a more definite statement
2. Motion on defenses
    (a) *Lack of jurisdiction over person*
    (b) *Lack of jurisdiction over subject matter*
    (c) *Improper venue*
    (d) *Insufficiency of process*
    (e) *Insufficiency of service*
    (f) *Failure to state a claim*
    (g) *Failure to join a party*
3. Motions to Dismiss (see exhibits 6.6 and 6.7)

Detailed discussion of these motions will be presented later in this chapter.

c. Summary Judgment

A defendant against whom a complaint has been filed may at any time move for a *summary judgment* in his or her favor. Essentially, defendant asserts that a judgment on the merits should come forth immediately since plaintiff's

Exhibit 6.6

**NOTICE OF MOTION TO
DISMISS COMPLAINT**

SUPREME COURT OF THE STATE OF
COUNTY OF _____

A.B., Plaintiff,	:	Notice of Motion to
	:	Dismiss Complaint
— against —		
	:	Index No.
X.Y.Z., Inc., Defendant.		
	:	_____

Upon the affidavit of C.D., sworn to December 1, 1966, and the complaint, the defendant will move this court at Special Term, Part I, in Room 130, County Court House, 60 Centre Street, New York, New York, on December 15, 1966, at 9:30 A.M., for an order pursuant to CPLR 3211:

1. Dismissing the complaint on the ground that the court does not have jurisdiction of the person of the defendant.

2. Dismissing the first cause of action on the ground that it fails to state a cause of action.

3. Dismissing the second cause of action on the ground that it may not be maintained because of the statute of limitations.

4. Dismissing the third cause of action on the ground that there is another action pending between the same parties for the same cause of action in the Superior Court of New Jersey.

5. Granting such other and further relief as to the court may seem just and proper, plus the costs of this motion.

Demand is made that answering affidavits be served at least five days before the hearing date.

Dated: _____

       _____[Print name]_____
       Attorney for Defendant
       Address:
       Telepone Number:

Exhibit 6.7

Motion To Dismiss, Presenting Defenses of Failure To State a Claim of
Lack of Service of Process, of Improper Venue, and of Lack of
Jurisdiction Under Rule 12(b)

The defendant moves the court as follows:

1. To dismiss the action because the complaint fails to state a claim against defendant upon which relief can be granted.

2. To dismiss the action or in lieu thereof to quash the return of service of summons on the grounds (a) that the defendant is a corporation organized under the laws and was not and is not subject to service of process within the Southern District of _____, and (b) that the defendant has not been properly served with process in this action, all of which more clearly appears in the affidavits of M. N. and X. Y. hereto annexed as Exhibit A and Exhibit B respectively.

3. To dismiss the action on the ground that it is in the wrong district because (a) the jurisdiction of this court is invoked solely on the ground that the action arises under the Constitution and laws of the United States and (b) the defendant is a corporation incorporated under the laws of the State and is not licensed to do or doing business in the Southern District, all of which more clearly appears in the affidavits of K. L. and V. W. hereto annexed as Exhibits C and D respectively.

4. To dismiss the action on the ground that the court lacks jurisdiction because the amount actually in controversy is less than ten thousand dollars exclusive of interest and costs.

Signed: _____
Attorney for Defendant
Address: _____

Notice of Motion

To: _____
  Attorney for Plaintiff.

_____

Please take notice, that the undersigned will bring the above motion on for hearing before this Court at Room _____, United States Court House, _____, City of _____, on the _____ day of _____, 19 _____, at 10 o'clock in the forenoon of that day or as soon thereafter as counsel can be heard.

Signed: _____
Attorney for Defendant
Address: _____

---

complaint provides no genuine controversy on any material fact. Simply, no dispute can be inferred or deduced from the allegations.

d. Demurrer

Recently abolished by the federal rules, the demurrer is an outdated response mechanism. In brief, the filing of a demurrer is an objection by the defendant that the complaint fails to state any factual cause of action. Reading the complaint does not provide a reasonable person with any sense of, or feeling for, the factual cause of action the plaintiff alleges. Since the amendment process is liberal, and other motions serve the defendant more efficiently, the demurrer strategy has lost some luster. Demurrer is better utilized as a technical response to the complaint such as when the plaintiff has no legal capacity to sue, a similar cause of action between the same parties is pending, or causes of action are improperly joined. Realistically, the paralegal will seldom come in contact with this response.

e. The Formal Answer

Once these preliminary motions and other pleadings are deciphered and decided, an *answer* may be necessary. Remember that in the complaint, while precision is applauded, factual elaboration is permissible. Drafting an answer requires even more conciseness and attention to detail, primarily because a failure to deny those factual allegations will result in admissions.

Denials. Accordingly, most answers provide a blanket denial for each and every allegation,

Count I

"This defendant denies each and all of the allegations in Paragraph I."

The answer to the complaint substantially mirrors the complaint and should correspond paragraph by paragraph. (See exhibit 6.8.) Each allegation can be:

1. Generally denied (though some jurisdictions require specific facts to the contrary)
2. Specifically denied (with contrary facts)

Exhibit 6.8

FORM 17

Answer to Complaint, Counterclaim
and Cross-Claim

SUPREME COURT OF THE STATE OF
COUNTY OF _____

A.B., Plaintiff,   :

    — against —   :   Answer

C.D. and E.F., Defendants.   :   Index No.

                                                                              :   _____

---

     1. Defendant C.D. admits the allegations in paragraphs 1 and 4 of the complaint; states that he lacks knowledge or information sufficient to form a belief as to the truth of the allegations in paragraph 2 of the complaint; and denies each and every other allegation in the complaint.

First Affirmative Defense

     2. The cause of action set forth in the complaint did not accrue within six years next before the commencement of this action.

Second Affirmative Defense

     3. Defendant C.D. entered into the contract annexed to the complaint as Exhibit A in reliance upon the truth of the oral statements made by plaintiff to defendant C.D. on or about July 1, 1966, that [specify alleged misrepresentation].

     4. Plaintiff made those statements in order to induce defendant C.D. to enter into the contract and with the intention that defendant C.D. rely upon plaintiff's statements.

     5. In fact and to the knowledge of plaintiff at the time he made those statements they were false in that [state facts].

Counterclaim

[Here set forth any cause of action as a counterclaim in the manner in which a claim is pleaded in a complaint].

Cross-Claim Against Defendant E.F.

[Here set forth any cause of action as a cross-claim against defendant E.F. in the manner in which a claim is pleaded in a complaint].

     Wherefore defendant C.D. demands judgment (1) against plaintiff dismissing the complaint, (2) against plaintiff on the counterclaim in the sum of _____ dollars, plus interest, (3) against defendant E.F. on the cross-claim in the sum of _____ dollars, plus interest, and (4) against plaintiff and defendant E.F. for costs and disbursements.

                                                              _____
                                                                [Print name]

                                                               Attorney for Defendant C.D.
                                                               Address:
                                                               Telephone Number:

---

3. Specifically denied with a demand for plaintiff's proof of the allegation
4. Not responded to because of insufficient knowledge
5. Not responded to because the knowledge or information needed to answer the allegation is not available

Affirmitive Defenses.   The answer can be further divided in a "new matter" section wherein all potential defenses are listed. Defenses are justifications, rationales, or plainly legitimate excuses that the defendant claims negates the allegation. Each affirmative defense must be specifically alleged, paragraph by paragraph, under a visible reading. Traditional affirmitive defenses include *release, satisfaction, arbitration, award, discharge in bankruptcy, justification, self-defense, consent, duress, estoppel, laches, illegality, impossibility, res judicata* and *waiver*. See the chapters on torts and criminal law for analysis of these defenses.

Counterclaims.   Within the same answer, after an enunciation of all denials and defenses, can be the defendant's cause of action against the plaintiff. A counterclaim is a cross-action arising out of the same issue or transaction. The counterclaim cannot be an independent issue or dispute.

> Assume Molly sues Billy for $2,000 in cash as compensation for a car crash. Billy counterclaims with a suit seeking to collect $2,000 for a mink stole he lent her ten years ago. Is this an appropriate counterclaim?

Stringent federal rules exist on the mandatory or compulsory nature of these counterclaims, whereby a defendant who fails to allege them loses all rights pertaining to them. See rule 13(a) of the Federal Rules for a description of the *compulsory/permissive* counterclaim. The key query is always: Does the defendant's claim or cause of action arise out of the same transaction or occurrence?

Cross-Claim.   This form of response is appropriate as a formal response when the defendant feels his or her co-party is responsible for the injury asserted in the complaint's allegations. The Federal Rules additionally state:

> Such cross-claim may include a claim that the party against whom it is asserted is or may be liable to the cross-claimant in the action against the cross claimant.

C.   Reply

Any responsive pleading that alleges new matter, such as a counterclaim or cross-claim, may require formal replies. Jurisdictional differences make this topic difficult to be specific about, but fundamentally a reply must conform to the elements of an answer. All the same objectives and strategic pleadings can be utilized as discussed thus far for other pleadings.

D.   Miscellaneous Issues Related to Pleadings

The following topics provide a brief inspection into many unrelated issues in the pleading process. For additional information, be most attentive to local rules, custom, and legislation.

1. Amendment/supplementation of the pleadings

Amendments are fully allowed in all systems of civil process. Federal Rule (15a) is quite characteristic of this liberal approach.

> A party may amend his pleading once as a matter of course at any time before a responsive pleading is served or, if the pleading is one to which no responsive pleading is permitted and the action has not been placed upon the trial calendar, he may so amend it at any time within 20 days after it is served. Otherwise a party may amend his pleading only by leave of court or by written consent of the adverse party, and leave shall be freely given when justice so requires.

That same adaptive philosophy is application to the supplementation of pleadings in most jurisdictions.

2. Additional parties to the pleadings

The plaintiff is generally permitted to add defendants to an original complaint by the filing of a *complaint to join* or a *praecipe or a writ*. Check time applications here carefully.

3. Rights of parties not named in the pleadings

Any person who stands to suffer severe adverse consequences as a result of the lawsuit may be permitted to *intervene*. A petition of intervention is filed and if an order of intervention is granted, that person has the same rights and liabilities as a party to the action.

4. Pleading special matters

When drafting pleadings at the federal level, the paralegal must be mindful that certain issues must be specifically averred in the complaint. In particular, rule 9 of the Federal Rules requires specific language describing any fraud, mistake, or issues as to the condition of the mind when claimed as part of plaintiff's case. Other matters that should be specifically averred include denial of performance or a contract, special damages, and admiralty or maritime claims.

Exhibit 6.9

THIRD-PARTY COMPLAINT

SUPREME COURT OF THE STATE OF _____
COUNTY OF _____

R.S.T., Inc., Plaintiff, :	
— against — :	Third-Party Complaint
U.V.W., Inc., Defendant. :	Index No.
U.V.W., Inc., Defendant and Third- :	
Party Plaintiff, :	_____
— against— :	
X.Y.Z., Inc., Third-Party Defendant. :	

1. [For form of allegation of parties' incorporation, see Form 4].

2. At all times herein mentioned, third-party defendant was in the business of manufacturing and selling building supplies to wholesalers and others, and third-party plaintiff was a wholesaler engaged in the business of selling building supplies to building contractors and others.

3. On or about June 1, 1966, third party plaintiff purchased from third-party defendant certain building supplies warranted by third-party defendant to be merchantable and fit for their ordinary use as building supplies.

4. On or about June 8, 1968, third party plaintiff sold these building supplies to plaintiff, a building contractor.

5. On or about December 1, 1966, plaintiff commenced an action against third-party plaintiff to recover damages for breach of warranty with respect to these building supplies. A copy of the complaint is attached hereto.

6. On or about December 5, 1966, third-party plaintiff gave written notice to third-party defendant of the claimed breach of warranty.

7. If plaintiff recovers judgment against third-party plaintiff, third-party plaintiff will be entitled to recover from third-party defendant the amount of such judgment.

Wherefore third-party plaintiff demands judgment against third-party defendant for all sums that may be adjudged against third-party plaintiff in favor of the plaintiff, plus costs and disbursements.

_____ [Print name]
Attorney for Third-Party Plaintiff
Address:
Telephone Number:

IV. SERVICE OF PROCESS: A MAJOR PARALEGAL RESPONSIBILITY

Paralegals serve lawyers in a useful way by accomplishing the procedural requirements of the lawsuit. No effort is made to denigrate the importance of these matters, but their time-consuming, harrying, and often insane guidelines and rules make the paralegal a welcome sight to the attorney trying to deal with legal theory.

A. Technical Matters

1. Filing of the complaint

An action in civil law is commenced the day the papers, particularly the complaint, are filed with the proper court. Those filings are usually with the prothonotary's office or other clerk of the court and should be evidenced by proper time stamps and copies.

2. Service of process

a. ISSUANCE OF SUMMONS

Upon the filing of the complaint, the court of proper jurisdiction will issue a summons to the plaintiff, who is held responsible for its service on the defendant. (See exhibit 6.10.)

b. SERVICE

No effort is made to uniformly apply the multitude of service methods across this country, so the paralegal must be cognizant of the local habit and rules in this technical framework. The service process is extraordinarily important since the tolling of the notice statute generally takes effect upon successful service. Stories abound of defendants successfully hiding from the sheriff seeking service, further substantiating the need for service knowledge and service alternatives.

Exhibit 6.10

SUMMONS AND COMPLAINT AGAINST THIRD-PARTY DEFENDANT

United States District Court for the

District of

Civil Action, File Number _____

A. B., Plaintiff

v.

C.D., Defendant and
Third-Party Plaintiff

v.

E.F., Third-Party
Defendant

} Summons

To the above-named Third-Party Defendant:

You are hereby summoned and required to serve upon _____, plaintiff's attorney whose address is _____, and upon _____, who is attorney for C.D., defendant and third-party plaintiff, and whose address is _____, an answer to the third-party complaint which is herewith served upon you within 20 days after the service of this summons upon you exclusive of the day of service. If you fail to do so, judgment by default will be taken against you for the relief demanded in the third-party complaint. There is also served upon you herewith a copy of the complaint of the plaintiff which you may but are not required to answer.

_____,

Clerk of Court.

[Seal of District Court]
Dated _____

Most states provide a variety of approaches in the service of process steps including:

1. Service can be by a U.S. marshall or deputy or other appointed person.
2. Service can be effected by any person who is not a party and is not less than eighteen years of age.
3. Service may also be effected by registered mail, or even first-class mailing, depending on the circumstances. Acknowledgment or receipt is generally required.
4. Service may also be accomplished by publishing copies of the summons and complaint in the local newspapers.
5. Service can also be accomplished by delivery of the proper documents to an agent.
6. Service can possibly be effected if the summons and complaint are mailed to the defendant's last known address.

Other unique situations arise involving service to corporations whose registered agents should be served the documents and state or municipal governments whose chief executive officer or other designated official would be properly served.

Service process reaches the heights of complexity when dealing with foreign countries. Federal Rule 5(i) states:

It is also sufficient if service of the summons and complaint is made: (A) in the manner prescribed by the law of the foreign country . . . (B) as directed by the foreign authority in response to a letter rogatory; or (C) upon an individual by delivery to him personally; and upon a corporation or partnership or association, by delivery to an officer . . . or (D) by any form of mail . . . or (E) as directed by the court.

Does this statute cover all the possibilities?

The complexities of time computation defy memory and mandate codification. Federal Rule 6 is a classic example:

In computing any period of time prescribed or allowed by these rules, by the local rules of any district court, by order of court, or by any applicable statute, the day of the act, event, or default from which the designated period of time begins to run shall not be included. The last day of the period so computed shall be included, unless it is a Saturday, a Sunday, or a legal holiday, in which even the period runs until the end of the next day which is not a Saturday, a Sunday, or a legal holiday. When the period of time prescribed or allowed is less than 7 days, intermediate Saturdays, Sundays, and legal holidays shall be excluded in the computation. As used in this rule and in Rule 77(c), "legal holiday" includes New Year's Day, Washington's Birthday, Memorial Day, Independence Day, Labor Day, Columbus Day, Veterans' Day, Thanksgiving Day, Christmas Day, and any other day appointed as a holiday by the President or the Congress of the United States, or by the state in which the district court is held.

V. GENERAL PRINCIPLES OF DISCOVERY

A. Introduction

Few actions in law can be supported without ample pretrial preparation, particularly the processes of *discovery*. The term *discovery* really means exactly that, since both parties to the action are seeking information that will assist them in the trial or in simply deciding whether their case has substantial merit. Discovery processes allow either party to ask questions, review documents, and interview prospective witnesses, long before the trial begins. Discovery is fully supported by our judicial and legislative systems since all elements of surprise or dramatic theatrics are removed from the courtroom. Believe it or not, there is rarely a surprise witness from the Himalayas appearing out of nowhere or a piece of evidence that is suddenly discovered, to the detriment of one party. Hollywood's standard portrayal of lawyers and litigation has always made the processes of discovery hard for most students to accept. To be sure, discovery affords fairness, removes unwarranted surprises, and crystallizes the issues long before trial but is equally capable of insuring some dullness. What follows is a review of the permissible scope of discovery—crudely put: What can be asked of the other side?—and the different discovery devices and tools available to the paralegal assigned to a civil case.

B. Scope of Discovery

By discovery's very purposes, that is, the assurance of fairness to the parties and as an evaluative tool to measure the relative merits of a case, any rules governing its use must be elastic. Liberal discovery is the rule rather than rigid restriction. The Federal Rules (26) hold:

Parties may obtain discovery regarding any matter not privileged which is relevant to the subject matter involved in the pending action, whether it relates to the claim or defense of the party seeking discovery or to the claim or defense of any other party, including the existence, description, nature, custody, condition and location of any documents, or other tangible things and the identity and location of persons having knowledge of any discoverable matter.

Sound rigid in approach? A better approach to scope may be to discern what is not discoverable, since almost everything is. Discoverable material can even be evidence that would never be admissible in a court of law. In this liberal setting, what objections could be made to a discovery request?

1. Relevancy

No systematic discovery process can tolerate requests for irrelevant information. Assume a car accident victim has become a client. The opposing party sends written questions, called *interrogatories*, which attempt to assess the sexual potency of the victim. How can this be a relevant issue? Can any plausible argument be made supporting its relevancy? If one can be posited—if, for instance, the victim in his or her complaint asserts damages for a loss of consortium or mental distress due to sexual dysfunction—then the discovery overcomes the relevancy objection. Relevancy is truly a chameleon in the law of evidence, with no set definition until the underlying facts of the case are assessed. Be mindful that many questions on their face may at first appear irrelevant, but if the proposing party can show any relevancy to the pending litigation, the discovery is appropriate.

2. Particularity in discovery requests

The process of discovery should not support questions that are so vague, so specious in design that no one can discern their intent. A question that cannot be understood cannot be answered. Hence some degree of specificity or particularity is required in the discovery system. Exactly what is it that the opposing party wants? Be clear. Be factual. Do not allow an opposing party to go on a "fishing expedition," that is, a junket with one general request. "Send over everything, please!" That type of overly generalized inquiry can never be properly responded to.

3. Trial-preparation, or work-product, material

While liberal discovery processes are promoted nationwide, that tradition must be balanced with the rights of the attorney to prepare his or her case for trial. That tradition must also accept the fact that one attorney cannot feed off the opposing attorney, cannot use the discovery process as a substitute means for his or her own work or trial preparation. To be certain, discovery must foster a liberal exchange of information, but not at the human and professional expense of an opposing attorney, an individual who may have spent countless hours in the library researching the case or compiling information for an appellate brief. In short, sweat equity or labor must be respected on either side.

Within this equitable framework emerges the *work-product* or *trial-preparation* rule. To understand this rule, the paralegal has to value both her own and her employer's time and energy. If both of them work cooperatively on an abestosis case, are they obliged to send over to the opposing side, upon request, their rough notes, interoffice correspondence, copies of researched cases, and general mental impressions, conclusions, and legal theories? Is this not their personal work? Are not these things the "product" of their sweat, unique to their pre–trial-preparation needs? Easy answers to these questions are not found in any set of federal or state rules. It appears that strong arguments favoring disclosure can be made if the opposing party shows a specialized rationale. Example of specialized reason might be that a witness has had a total memory lapse, or the party is completely and totally unable to obtain the substantial equivalent of the materials without undue hardship. Each case should be individually assessed.

In a sense, both federal and state rules are utterly perplexing on this work-product analysis. With the noblest of intentions, they have attempted to balance the needs of justice with the equity of an attorney's hard work. Clearly, work product that is *creative* in design or form should be protected from discovery. Creativity in legal theory, argument, and strategy is so personalized that invading this mental domain would be a travesty. Much of the pretrial work is not creative and accordingly is usually discoverable. Examples might be:

a. Pleadings and other documents
b. Hire expert to administer tests
c. Hire consultants to evaluate and testify at trial
d. List of experts

e. All witnesses

f. List of exhibits or evidence

While the paralegal is not expected to master the intricacies of an area presently boggling the minds of learned legal scholars, it is imperative that some defensive reaction or attitude emerge when the *work* of the firm is being discovered.

C. Tools and Devices of Discovery

Skilled utilization of the varied discovery techniques will insure excellent trial preparation and more artful settlement negotiation. What is helpful for the paralegal to understand is that all adjudicatory activities are forms of discovery. The preliminary hearing in the criminal case has long been thought of as a stage of discovery where the state and the defendant preliminarily assess each other's positions. As such, view each pretrial phase or activity as a form of discovery, including any conferences, meetings, or other settings.

The major tools of discovery can be either oral or written and are reviewed hereafter.

1. Written interrogatories

An interrogatory is a question asked. A set of *written interrogatories*, as provided in the Rules of Civil Procedure, is a series of questions posed to the opposing side in written form. This series of questions attempts to "discover" particular issues and types of information, to which the opposing party must respond unless the previously discussed objections can be raised.

As a rule, interrogatories are the least expensive way of securing information. All that is required is a typed document listing the questions and the postage to mail it. For this reason alone, it is a favored method. However, numerous disadvantages exist, such as lack of personal contact, an inability to examine witnesses, an inability to personally assess witnesses.

Review thoroughly the set of interrogatories provided in Exhibit 6.11 and utilize them as a model to the assignments. Notice that these interrogatories are admirably drafted and have all the hallmarks of a good discovery request. Keep in mind these rules:

- ☐ Rule 1:   Interrogatories must be precise
- ☐ Rule 2:   Interrogatories narrow the issues
- ☐ Rule 3:   Interrogatories should not be standardized
- ☐ Rule 4:   Interrogatories must be relevant

If these suggestions are kept close to the drafter's heart, no viable objection can be made to the discovery requests.

2. Depositions and oral examination

a. GENERAL DESCRIPTION

Prior to trial, any party may take the testimony of any person by a deposition upon oral examination. Depositions differ from interrogatories in many ways. First, an oral deposition is highly personalized since witnesses are physically present to be examined and crossed. Second, the deposition atmosphere gives the opposing counsels an opportunity to assess the demeanor of the witnesses and to participate in a minitrial of sorts before the real trial ever begins. Third, depositions also afford opposing counsel the time to assess each other's relative strengths and weaknesses. Fourth, depositions afford substantial inquiry into lines of thought developed by the attorney and regularly allows follow-up and enhancement of the testimony. Lastly, oral depositions can serve the attorney in a most formidable way later at trial if the deponent's testimony at trial is contradictory. Deposition transcripts are excellent tools of impeachment.

b. PRACTICAL STEPS IN THE DEPOSITION PROCESS

Notice.   The Federal Rules make clear that a party desiring to take the deposition of any person upon oral examination shall give *reasonable notice in writing* to every other party to the action. That notice shall state: (1) time

Exhibit 6.11

(Caption)

1. Full name, present address and date of birth.
2. Date, approximate time and condition of weather at time of accident.
3. Detailed description of nature, extent and duration of any and all injuries.
4. Detailed description of injury or condition claimed to be permanent together with all present complaints.
5. If confined to hospital, state name and address of same, date of admission and discharge therefrom.
6. If X-rays were taken, state the name and address of the place where they were taken, the name and address of the person who took them, the date each was taken and what it disclosed.
7. If treated by doctors, state the name and present address of each doctor, the dates and places where treatments were received and the date of last treatment. Annex true copies of all written reports rendered to you by any such doctors whom you propose to have testify in your behalf.
8. If still being treated, the name and address of each doctor rendering treatment, where and how often treatment is received and the nature thereof.
9. If a previous injury, disease, illness or condition is claimed to have been aggravated, accelerated or exacerbated, specify in detail the nature of each and the name and present address of each doctor, if any, who rendered treatment for said condition.
10. If employed at the time of accident, state:
    (a) The name and address of the employer.
    (b) Position held and nature of work performed.
    (c) Average weekly wages for past year.
    (d) Period of time lost from employment, giving dates.
    (e) Amount of wages lost, if any.
11. If other loss of income, profit or earnings is claimed:
    (a) State total amount of said loss.
    (b) Give a complete detailed computation of said loss.
    (c) State nature and source of loss of such income, profit and earnings and date of deprivation thereof.
12. If there has been a return to employment or occupation, state:
    (a) Name and address of present employer.
    (b) Position held and nature of work being performed.
    (c) Present weekly wages, earnings, income, or profit.
13. Itemize in complete detail any and all moneys expended or expenses incurred for hospitals, doctors, nurses, X-rays, medicines, care and appliances and state the name and address of each payee and the amount paid or owed each payee.
14. Itemize any and all other losses or expenses incurred not otherwise set forth.
15. State and names and addresses of all persons who have knowledge of any relevant facts relating to the case.
16. State the names and addresses of any and all proposed expert witnesses and annex true copies of all written reports rendered to you by any such proposed expert witnesses.

With respect to all expert witnesses, including treating physicians, who are expected to testify at trial, and with respect to any person who has conducted an examination pursuant to R. 4:19, who may testify, state such witness's name, address, and area of expertise, and annex a true copy of all written reports rendered to you. If a report is not written, supply a summary of any oral report rendered to you.

Note: Amended July 17, 1975 to be effective September 8, 1975.

CERTIFICATION

I hereby certify that the copies of the reports annexed hereto rendered by either treating physicians or proposed expert witnesses are exact copies of the entire report or reports rendered by them; that the existence of other reports of said doctors or experts, written or oral, are unknown to me, and if such become later known or available, I shall serve them promptly on the propounding party.

FORM B. UNIFORM INTERROGATORIES: PROPERTY DAMAGE TO MOTOR VEHICLE: SUPERIOR AND COUNTY COURT

(Caption)

1. Was the claimant the sole owner of the motor vehicle involved in the alleged accident?

2. State the name and address of the person, firm or corporation, from whom the claimant purchased said motor vehicle and the date of purchase.

3. Was the said motor vehicle new or used at the time of purchase?

4. State make, model and year of motor vehicle.

5. State amount paid by claimant for the said motor vehicle.

6. State whether said motor vehicle has been repaired since the accident.

7. If so, give name and address of person, firm, or corporation making said repairs.

8. If so, state specifically the part or parts of said motor vehicle alleged to have been damaged in the said accident and furnish a copy of the repair bill.

9. State date upon which claimant authorized the repair of said motor vehicle.

10. State date on which repairs were completed.

11. State the market value of this motor vehicle immediately before the said accident.

12. State the market value of this said motor vehicle in its damaged condition immediately after the said accident.

13. State the market value of motor vehicle in its repaired condition.

14. Was said motor vehicle used in connection with claimant's business and, if so, state whether claimant was obliged to hire another motor vehicle for use in connection with said business, giving the name and address of person, firm or corporation from whom claimant hired said motor vehicle, the dates during which it was hired and the amount paid for said hiring?

15. If no repairs have been made, but an estimate of the said repairs has been obtained, attach a copy of such estimate to the answers to these Interrogatories, stating further the name and address of the person, firm or corporation who made such estimate.

16. Has the claimant sold or otherwise disposed of the said motor vehicle?

17. If so, give the name and address of the person, firm or corporation to whom the said motor vehicle was transferred, and the date of such transfer, and the amount of consideration paid to the claimant therefor.

18. If it is alleged that the claimant incurred any other expenses or losses as a result of the alleged damage to the said motor vehicle, set forth such additional alleged losses in detail, giving an itemized statement of same.

19. State the names and addresses of all persons who have knowledge of any relevant facts relating to the case.

20. State the names and addresses of any and all proposed expert witnesses and annex true copies of all written reports rendered to you by any such proposed expert witnesses.

CERTIFICATION

I hereby certify that the copies of the reports annexed hereto rendered by proposed expert witnesses are exact copies of the entire report or reports rendered by them; that the existence of other reports of said experts, either written or oral, are unknown to me, and if such become later known or available, I shall serve them promptly on the propounding party.

* Note: If Form A is not used, questions 1 and 2 of Form A should be added to Form B
Note: Amended July 7, 1971 to be effective September 13, 1971.

FORM C. UNIFORM INTERROGATORIES BY DEFENDANT IN MOTOR VEHICLE COLLISION CASE INVOLVING PERSONAL INJURIES: COUNTY DISTRICT COURT

(Caption)

1. State:
   (a) Full name
   (b) Present address
   (c) Date of birth
   (d) Marital status at time of accident

2. State the following facts with respect to the collision:
   (a) Date
   (b) Time
   (c) Condition of weather
   (d) Condition of visibility
   (e) Condition of roadway

3. Give a detailed description of the nature, extent and duration of any and all injuries.

4. Give a detailed description of the injury or condition claimed to be permanent, together with all present complaints.

5. If confined to hospital, state name and address of same, and the date of admission and discharge therefrom.

6. If X-rays were taken, state the name and address of the place where they were taken, the name and address of the person who took them, the date each was taken and what it disclosed.

7. If treated by doctors, state the name and present address of each doctor, the dates and places where treatments were received and the date of last treatment. Annex true copies of all written reports rendered to you by any such doctors whom you propose to have testify in your behalf.

8. If still being treated, state the name and address of each doctor rendering treatment, where and how often treatment is received and the nature thereof.

9. If a previous injury, disease, illness or condition is claimed to have been aggravated, accelerated, or exacerbated, specify in detail the nature of each and the name and present address of each doctor, if any, who rendered treatment.

10. If employed at time of accident, state:
    (a) The name and address of the employer.
    (b) Position held and nature of work performed.
    (c) Average weekly wages for past year.
    (d) Period of time lost from employment, giving dates.
    (e) Amount of wages lost, if any.

11. If other loss of income; profit or earnings is claimed:
    (a) State total amount of the loss.
    (b) Give a complete detailed computation of the loss.
    (c) State nature and source of loss of income, profit and earnings and date of deprivation thereof.

12. If there has been a return to employment or occupation, state:
    (a) Name and address of present employer.
    (b) Position held and nature of work being performed.
    (c) Present weekly wages, earnings, income or profit.

13. Itemize in complete detail any and all moneys expended or expenses incurred for hospitals, doctors, nurses, X-rays, medicines, care and appliances and state the name and address of each payee and the amount paid or owed each payee.

14. Itemize any and all other losses or expenses incurred not otherwise set forth.

15. State the names and addresses of all persons who have knowledge of any relevant facts relating to the case.

16. State the names and addresses of any and all proposed expert witnesses and annex true copies of all written reports rendered to you by any such proposed expert witnesses.

With respect to all expert witnesses, including treating physicians, who are expected to testify at trial, and with respect to any person who has conducted an examination pursuant to R. 4:19, who may testify, state such witness's name, address, and area of expertise, and annex a true copy of all written reports rendered to you. If a report is not written, supply a summary of any oral report rendered to you.

Note: Amended July 17, 1975 to be effective September 8, 1975.

17. State the name and address of:
    (a) The operator of your vehicle.
    (b) The owner of your vehicle.
    (c) Each of the other occupants of your vehicle.
       (Note: The term "your vehicle" in this and other questions herein has reference to the vehicle in which you were an occupant at the time of the collision.)

18. State in what municipality, county and state the collision occurred.

19. State on what street, highway, road or other place (designate which) and in what general direction (north, south, east or west) your vehicle was proceeding immediately prior to the collision. (You may include a sketch for greater clarity.)

20. With respect to fixed objects at the location of the collision, state as nearly as possible the point of impact. If you included a sketch, place an X thereon to denote the point of impact.
       (Note: The term "point of impact" as used in this and other questions has reference to the exact point on the street, highway, road or other place where the vehicles collided.)

21. Describe in detail your version of how the collision occurred.

22. If you allege a violation of statute as a factor to be considered in establishing negligence, state the title, section and paragraph of the statute.

23. State whether there were any traffic control devices, signs or police officers at or near the place of the collison. If there were, describe them (i. e., traffic lights, stop sign, police officers, etc.) and state the exact location of each.

24. If the collision occurred at an uncontrolled intersection state:
    (a) Which vehicle entered the intersection first.
    (b) Whether your vehicle came to a full stop before entering the intersection.
    (c) If your vehicle did not come to a full stop before entering the intersection, the speed of your vehicle when it entered the intersection.

25. State in terms of feet the distance between:
    (a) The front of your vehicle and the point of impact at the time you first observed the other vehicle or vehicles collided with, and state the speed of your vehicle at that time.
    (b) The front of the other vehicle or vehicles collided with and the point of contact at the time you first observed it or them, and state its or their speed at that time.
    (c) Your vehicle and the vehicle or vehicles collided with at the time you first saw it or them.

26. State where each vehicle came to rest after the impact. Include the distance in terms of feet from the point of impact to the point where each vehicle came to rest.

27. State what part of your vehicle came into contact with what part of the other vehicle or vehicles involved.

CERTIFICATION

I hereby certify that the copies of the reports annexed hereto rendered by either treating physicians or proposed expert witnesses are exact copies of the entire report or reports rendered by them; that the existence of other reports of said doctors or experts, either written or oral, are unknown to me, and if such become later known or available, I shall serve them promptly on the propounding party.

FORM D. UNIFORM INTERROGATORIES BY DEFENDANT IN MOTOR VEHICLE COLLISION CASE INVOLVING PROPERTY DAMAGE: COUNTY DISTRICT Court

(Caption)

1. State whether the claimant was the sole owner of the motor vehicle involved in the alleged accident.

2. State the name and address of the person, firm or corporation, from whom the claimant purchased the motor vehicle and the date of purchase.

3. State whether the motor vehicle was new or used at the time of purchase.

4. State make, model and year of the motor vehicle.

5. State amount paid by claimant for the motor vehicle.

6. State whether the motor vehicle has been repaired since the accident.

7. If repaired, state the name and address of person, firm or corporation making the repairs.

8. If repaired, state specifically the part or parts of the motor vehicle alleged to have been damaged in the accident and furnish a copy of the repair bill.

9. State date upon which claimant authorized the repair of the motor vehicle.

10. State date on which repairs were completed.

11. State the market value of the motor vehicle immediately before the accident.

12. State the market value of the motor vehicle in its damaged condition immediately after the accident.

13. State the market value of the motor vehicle in its repaired condition.

14. State whether the motor vehicle was used in connection with claimant's business and, if so, state whether claimant was obliged to hire another motor vehicle for use in connection with his business. State the name and address of the person, firm or corporation from whom claimant hired another motor vehicle, the dates during which it was hired and the amount paid for its hire.

15. If no repairs have been made but an estimate of the said repairs has been obtained, attach a copy of the estimate to the answers to these interrogatories, and state the name and address of the person, firm or corporation who made the estimate.

16. State whether the claimant has sold or otherwise disposed of the motor vehicle.

17. If sold or otherwise disposed of, state the name and address of the person, firm or corporation to whom the motor vehicle was transferred and the date of the transfer; and the amount of consideration paid to the claimant therefor.

18. If it is alleged that the claimant incurred any other expenses or losses as a result of the alleged damage to the motor vehicle, set forth the additional alleged losses in detail, giving an itemized statement of them.

19. State the names and addresses of all persons who have knowledge of any relevant facts relating to the case.

20. State the names and addresses of any and all proposed expert witnesses and annex true copies of all written reports rendered to you by any such proposed expert witnesses.

21. State the following facts with respect to the collision:
    (a) Date
    (b) Time.
    (c) Condition of weather.
    (d) Condition of visibility.
    (e) Condition of roadway.

22. State the name and address of:
    (a) The operator of your vehicle.
    (b) Each of the other occupants in your vehicle.
    (Note: The term "your vehicle" in this and other questions herein has reference to the vehicle in which you were an occupant at the time of the collision.)

23. State in what municipality, county and state the collision occurred.

24. State on what street, highway, road or other place (designate which) and in what general direction (north, south, east or west) your vehicle was proceeding immediately prior to the collision. (You may include a sketch for greater clarity.)

25. With respect to fixed objects at the location of the collision, state as nearly as possible the point of impact. If you included a sketch, place an X thereon to denote the point of impact.
    (Note: The term "point of impact" as used in this and other questions has reference to the exact point on the street, highway, road or other place where the vehicles collided.)

26. Describe in detail your version of how the collision occurred.

27. If you allege a violation of statute as a factor to be considered in establishing negligence, state the title, section and paragraph of the statute.

28. State whether there were any traffic control devices, signs, or police officers at or near the place of the collision. If there were, describe them (i. e., traffic lights, stop sign, police officers, etc.) and state the exact location of each.

29. If the collision occurred at an uncontrolled intersection state:
   (a) Which vehicle entered the intersection first.
   (b) Whether your vehicle came to a full stop before entering the intersection.
   (c) If your vehicle did not come to a full stop before entering the intersection, state the speed of your vehicle when it entered the intersection.

30. State in terms of feet the distance between:
   (a) The front of your vehicle and the point of impact at the time you first observed the other vehicle or vehicles collided with, and state the speed of your vehicle at that time.
   (b) The front of the other vehicle or vehicles collided with and the point of contact at the time you first observed it or them, and state its or their speed at that time.
   (c) Your vehicle and the vehicle or vehicles collided with at the time you first saw it or them.

31. State where each vehicle came to rest after the impact. Include the distance in terms of feet from the point of impact to the point where each vehicle came to rest.

32. State what part of your vehicle came into contact with what part of the other vehicle or vehicles involved.

CERTIFICATION

I hereby certify that the copies of the reports annexed hereto rendered by proposed expert witnesses are exact copies of the entire report or reports rendered by them; that the existence of other reports of said experts, either written or oral, are unknown to me, and if such become later known or available, I shall serve them promptly on the propounding party.

Note: Amended July 7, 1971 to be effective September 13, 1971.

FORM E. UNIFORM INTERROGATORIES BY PLAINTIFF IN MOTOR VEHICLE COLLISION CASE: COUNTY DISTRICT COURT

(Caption)

1. With respect to the collision referred to in the complaint filed herein:

	UNDERLINE ANSWERS	
(a) Do you admit ownership?	Yes	No
(b) Do you admit operation?	Yes	No
(c) Do you admit agency?	Yes	No
(d) Do you admit control?	Yes	No
(e) Do you admit the date and place?	Yes	No

2. If you do not admit ownership:
   (a) State the name and address of the owner.
   (b) State the registration number, year, make, model and color of each motor vehicle owned by you on the date of the collision as alleged in the complaint.

3. If you do not admit operation, state the name and address of the operator.

4. If you do not admit agency and the owner was not also the operator, explain the circumstances under which the vehicle came into the possession of the operator, the purpose for which the vehicle was being used and its destination.

5. If you do not admit control:
   (a) State the name and address of the one in control.
   (b) If control was in another by agreement, state the names and addresses of the parties to the agreement, whether the agreement was oral or written and, briefly, the terms of the agreement.

6. If you do not admit the date and place of the collision as alleged in the complaint, state the date and place of the collision as you recall it.

7. State whether your vehicle was licensed under an Interstate Commerce Commission permit. If so licensed, state the number of such permit, the name and address of the permittee, and the name and address of the lessee or other party in control, if any.

8. State on what street, highway, road or other place (designate which) and in what general direction (north, south, east or west) your vehicle was proceeding immediately prior to the collision. (You may include a sketch for greater clarity.)

(Note: The term "your vehicle" in this and other questions herein has reference to the vehicle in which you were an occupant at the time of the collision.)

9. With respect to fixed objects at the location of the collision, state as nearly as possible the point of impact. If you included a sketch, place an X thereon to denote the point of impact.

(Note: The term "point of impact" as used in this and other questions has reference to the exact point on the street, highway, road or other place where the vehicles collided.)

10. State whether there were any traffic control devices, signs, or police officers at or near the place of the collision. If there were, describe them (i.e., traffic lights, stop sign, police officers, etc.) and state the exact location of each.

11. Describe in detail your version of how the collision occurred.

12. If the collision occurred at an uncontrolled intersection state:
    (a) Which vehicle entered the intersection first.
    (b) Whether your vehicle came to a full stop before entering the intersection.
    (c) If your vehicle did not come to a full stop before entering the intersection, state the speed of your vehicle when it entered the intersection.

13. State in terms of feet the distance between:
    (a) The front of your vehicle and the point of impact at the time you first observed the other vehicle or vehicles collided with, and state your speed at that time.
    (b) The front of the other vehicle or vehicles collided with and the point of contact at the time you first observed it or them and state its or their speed at that time.
    (c) Your vehicle and the vehicle or vehicles collided with at the time you first saw it or them.

14. State where each vehicle came to rest after the impact. Include the distance in terms of feet from the point of impact to the point where each vehicle came to rest.

15. State what part of your vehicle came into contact with what part of the other vehicle or vehicles involved.

16. State the names and addresses of all persons who have knowledge of any relevant facts relating to the case.

17. State the names and addresses of any and all proposed expert witnesses and annex the true copies of all written reports rendered to you by any such proposed expert witnesses.

18. State whether the defendant has insurance under which the insurance company may be liable to satisfy part or all of a judgment which may be entered in the action or to indemnify or reimburse for payments made to satisfy the judgment.

CERTIFICATION

I hereby certify that the copies of the reports annexed hereto rendered by proposed expert witnesses are exact copies of the entire report or reports rendered by them; that the existence of other reports of said experts, either written or oral, are unknown to me, and if such become later known or available, I shall serve them promptly on the propounding party.

Note: Amended July 7, 1971 to be effective September 13, 1971.

*Uniform Interrogatories Forms A–E from the New Jersey Rules of Court, published by West Publishing Co. Used with permission.

(generally thirty days thereafter), (2) place, (3) parties to be examined, and (4) statement of facts supporting the allegation.

Deposition Officer.   When compared to other discovery modes, the deposition process is somewhat formal, since the deposition is taken under oath and given before an officer authorized to administer oaths by the laws of the United States, or of the jurisdiction where the deposition occurs, or appointed by the court. The parties to the deposition can also "stipulate" or agree to any individual, including counsel or other third party, as the required officer for the deposition. This level of formality is intended to insure more accurate responses.

Method of Recording Depositions.   A thriving business exists in stenographic and court-reporting services for the recording of depositions. While a court reporter's presence adds to the solemnity of the occasion, and the transcription of the testimony will be an invaluable tool at trial, the paralegal can utilize other methods of recordation. The trend in most states is to permit the use of tape recorders, videotapes, film, and any other mechanical, electronic, or photographic means.

Conduct of the Deposition Hearing.   In some ways, the deposition hearing should simulate a trial setting, but the process cannot be identical since each serves a unique purpose. Remember that a deposition is a means of *discovery*. The following suggestions will facilitate a deposition hearing:

☐ Provide a relaxed, casual atmosphere for the hearing.
☐ Allow testimony to be liberal in scope.

□ Don't prepare questions that are overly harsh in design and too adversarial.
□ Limit all possible objections to the testimony.
□ Select a comfortable setting for the hearing.

As mentioned previously, the deposition is a discovery process, not the final adversarial event. To stimulate testimony is the better strategy.

3. Deposition upon written questions

This form of discovery is a hybrid—written questions are drafted and oral answers given. This form of discovery serves the attorney when distance is a factor. Assume the party to be examined is three hundred miles away, and the attorney who wishes to examine the party does not have a sufficient budget to travel for this deposition. Instead, the attorney drafts written questions and sends them to an agreed-upon deposition officer, who then poses the questions. The party examined responds orally, and the content is recorded.

This form of discovery also requires appropriate notice, a specific witness to examine, and the opportunity of the opposing side to respond with cross-questions.

In what setting would this form of discovery work very well?

4. Production of documents

Written correspondence, business records, data, test results, and all written documents are highly sought after forms of evidence and hence the frequent subject of discovery. Guided by the same principles of relevancy, specificity, particularity, and non-work product, it is generally held that documents are discoverable items. The Federal Rules (34) hold:

> Any party may serve on any other party a request (1) to produce and permit the party making the request, or someone acting on his behalf, to inspect and copy, any designated documents (including writings, drawings, graphs, charts, photographs, phonorecords, and other data compilations from which information can be obtained, translated, if necessary by the respondent through detection devices into reasonably usable form) or to inspect and copy, test, or sample any tangible things. . . .

Which of the following would be discoverable?

□ An insurance contract or agreement
□ Photographs of an accident case
□ Medical records
□ Trade secrets

5. Petition or motion for physical or mental examination

Authority exists nationally to order a party to submit to a physical or mental examination if the results of such an examination would be relevant to the controversy. Various tactical considerations must be assessed by opposing counsel before an examination is requested or objected to. Counsel who desires the examination should take great pains in the selection of an expert physician or psychiatrist, in regard to both their fees and their expertise. Counsel who objects to the examination should be prepared to file *protective orders* with the court or request another expert his client is more comfortable with to perform the examination. Counsel for the examined party obviously can discover the results.

6. Requests for admission

The last major form of discovery utilized in civil practice is the *request for admissions*. An admission is an agreement to a certain set of facts, or put another way, a nondenial of those facts. Opposing counsels often hope to get agreements in certain issues long before trial, so they attempt to get the other side to admit to an essential fact. This is done by filing a request for admission, a document that specifically highlights various facts the opposing side hopes to reach agreement on. Common examples of "admitted" facts are name, address, age, or sex of the parties; a specific injury, and the genuineness or authenticity of a document. Less common admissions are usually agreed-upon liability or legal responsibility of the opposing party. Of course, a party who admits the responsibility for injury or harm is in a weak position to negotiate. The effect of admission is to conclusively establish those facts in the record unless upon proper motion the court permits withdrawal.

7. *Practical suggestions*

a. SETTING UP THE HEARING

Procedural requirements in setting up a deposition are as follows:

1. Contact the other attorney's office for a date and time.
2. Send out a notice of deposition and/or a subpoena of those individuals in the control of the other party, such as, his client and his expert witness. If necessary, request production of documents.
3. Arrange for a court reporter.
4. Arrange for a place to hold the depositions. Note, the place usually will be at the opposing party's office unless otherwise arranged.
5. You must usually provide sufficient notice.

VI. PREPARING WITNESSES

A. Instructions to Witnesses

If clients or witnesses are nervous or fearful about testifying at a deposition or a trial, it is usually because they do not know what to expect. They may feel that they have forgotten some of the facts. Whether a case is to be heard by a judge, commissioner, auditor, master, or a judge and jury, they want to know only one thing, "What happened?" They do not desire to embarrass or harm you in any way.

A deposition is the taking of testimony before trial. Your testimony will be under oath. It will be recorded by a court stenographer. Other persons present will be the stenographer, your attorney, and an attorney for each defendant. A transcript of your testimony will be filed with the court. You will most likely be called again as a witness during the court hearing, if you are still available and able to testify.

We will review all of the facts of the case with you before you testify at the deposition. PLEASE STUDY THE FOLLOWING INSTRUCTIONS VERY CAREFULLY. DO NOT MERELY READ THEM ONCE.

1. You Must Have Complete Knowledge of All Facts. You must study the police report, all statements of witnesses, all hospital and doctor reports and bills, letters from your employers stating your job description, earnings, and absences from work following the accident, all photographs, all your answers signed under oath to questions sent to you by the opposition, and the questions asked. All this information is contained in our file of your case. Please telephone our office and make an appointment to study these documents in our file.

2. Go to Scene of Accident. Please go to the place where the accident occurred. Please take a large piece of paper with you and prepare a diagram. Draw on the diagram all significant objects, such as buildings, traffic lights, traffic signs, road markings, obstructions to vision, and angles of intersections. Please estimate the width of the streets by measuring or pacing. Please also measure or pace off the distances from significant objects to the spot where the impact occurred.

3. General Rules for Testifying

a. Courtesy. Be just as polite to the opposing lawyer as you are to your own. Never show any anger or raise your voice. Never give a fresh answer or answer a question with a question. Don't argue with the opposing lawyer.
b. If You Do Not Understand a Question. Never answer a question until you are certain that you understand it completely. If you do not understand it, tell the attorney and he will either ask the question again or will reword it. Never take a chance by answering a question that you do not fully understand. The jury or judge will not realize that you misunderstood the question. Your wrong answer may do great damage to your case.
c. Talk Loudly Enough. It is necessary for the stenographer to hear you clearly. It is annoying when witnesses speak inaudibly.
d. Never Exaggerate. It is always necessary to tell the truth. An exaggeration is not the truth. The jury or judge will probably conclude that if you exaggerated one thing, you probably exaggerated everything. One exaggeration, therefore, may cause the loss of your case.

e. Keep Your Answers Short.   Answer only the question asked. Do not continue on to something else. Don't make any speeches or try to prove your case. It is our job to bring out all the important facts by a series of questions, one at a time. If we overlook anything that you feel is important, please notify us later before the deposition ends.

f. Assistance from Your Attorneys.   When you are asked a question by the opposition, do not look at your attorneys for help in answering the question. If the question is improper, we will object to it. If we do not object, you must answer the question without any help from us.

g. Jokes and Wisecracks.   Don't make any while testifying.

h. The Truth.   You will take an oath before you testify. In this oath you will swear to tell the truth. If the jury or judge believes that you failed to tell the truth about some aspect of your case, they will probably conclude that your entire testimony is unreliable.

i. Clothes.   Men should wear a dress shirt, tie, and suit. Women should select conservative clothes.

j. Slouching.   Don't slouch forward, but rather sit up straight while testifying.

k. Discussion of Case.   Don't talk about the case with anyone but us. Strangers may speak to you about the case. These people may be connected with the opposition and may relate everything you say to the opposing attorney. They may even distort what you say. Be very careful when discussing the case with your other witnesses that you are not overheard by strangers.

4. *Choosing between Yes and No.*   The opposing attorney may try to make you answer a question with a yes or no. Sometimes, neither yes or no is the correct answer. In such cases, explain to the attorney that neither yes or no is the true answer.

5. *Swearing to the Truth of Your Answers.*   If your answer is truthful, don't hesitate to swear that it is true. Sometimes the opposing attorney may ask you a question like this: "Do you mean to tell the court and jury that such and such happened?" If you are telling what actually did happen, be forceful and positive in answering, "Yes sir, that is exactly how it happened," or something such as, "That is the absolute truth."

6. *How Many Feet and How Many Seconds.*   Attorneys know that a car traveling thirty miles per hour goes approximately forty-five feet per second. The formula they use is that a car travels one and a half times as many feet per second as it travels miles per hour. This is approximately correct, mathematically. Therefore, it is very unwise to guess how many feet or how many seconds. If you are asked a question concerning feet or seconds and you don't really know, the only truthful answer is, "I don't know." Sometimes the opposing attorney may ask you to give your best judgment. If you do not have any reliable judgment, you should decline to give one. You can explain that you would only be guessing.

7. *Photographs.*   Often the opposing attorney will show you photographs and ask you if they are fair and true representations of how the objects looked at a certain time. Before you answer such a question, examine the photographs very carefully. You may discover that certain appearances in the photographs are not in accord with your testimony. If so, tell the opposing attorney that the photographs are NOT fair and true representations of the objects shown.

8. *Your Examination by Defense Doctor.*   You should be able to tell approximately how long the examination lasted; how much of this time the defense doctor spent in asking you questions; how much time he or she spent actually examining you; what tests he or she performed on you. You should also be able to tell anything he or she said about your condition.

9. *Your Preparation for the Hearing.*   Both the judge and the opposing lawyer know that it is our duty to review the facts with you and all your witnesses. Very often, the opposing attorney will ask whether you have discussed the case with your attorneys. He knows that you have, but he wants to find out if you will tell the truth about it. Tell the truth, of course. But if he asks you if your attorneys told you what to say, you will know that is not true. You should answer that your attorneys told you not to say anything but the truth.

10. *Your Written or Recorded Statements to the Opposition.*   If you have made written or recorded statements to the opposition, be sure to tell us about this. We have the right to obtain copies of such statements. It is very important that we review together everything you said in such statements.

11. *Court Record.*   If you have ever pleaded guilty or been found guilty of an offense in any court, it is extremely important that you tell us about this. All convictions of persons over seventeen years of age are public records and are open to inspection by the opposition. If you do not tell us about your convictions, the opposition will surprise us with proof of them at the hearing.

12. *Hearsay Testimony and Conclusions.*   Usually, you may not tell what other people said. The courts require these people to testify themselves. Usually, you are not allowed to give your opinions and your conclusions. The general rule is that you may tell only what you saw and heard and felt.

13. When There Is an Objection. When one of the attorneys objects to a question asked of you, the stenographer will note the objection. *You should answer the question.* (If your attorney directs you to.)

14. Evasiveness. Be positive and definite whenever possible. Don't weaken your answers by saying, "As far as I remember," or "I believe," or "As far as I know," or "I think." If you really don't know the answer to the question, admit it by saying, "I don't know."

15. Some Questions You Will Most Likely Be Asked. Please read the following questions very carefully and think over your answers. Please have your answers ready when you come to our office for preparation:

    1. Where were you coming from at the time of the accident?
    2. Where were you going at the time of the accident?
    3. What time did you leave?
    4. Exactly what time did the accident happen?
    5. What was the date of the accident, and what day of the week was it?
    6. What was the weather at the time of the accident? Was visibility good? Do you wear glasses? Were you wearing them?
    7. What was the condition of the surface of the road at the time of the accident? Was it wet or dry? Was there snow, slush, or ice on the road?
    8. Did the police come to the scene?
    9. Who telephoned the police?
    10. Did the police make a written report?
    11. Did you make a written report after the accident?
    12. What type of neighborhood was it where the accident occurred? Was it commercial or thickly settled or thinly settled?
    13. Was the roadway divided by lines?
    14. Were the lines solid or broken lines?
    15. How many lanes were there in the road?
    16. Were there any speed-control signs or other traffic-control signs in the vicinity of the collision?
    17. Exactly what did you do, and what did you say right after the collision?
    18. Where is the first place you went after you left the scene of the accident?

VII. MOTIONS: PRACTICE AND PLEADING

A. The Nature of Pretrial Motions

To paraphrase Chief Justice Burger's recent comments about lawyers, the best lawyers in our society are those who never go to trial. Their inherent and developed skills of negotiation, mediation, and client counseling are evidenced by their absence from the adversarial courtroom. Our distinguished justice may be right, especially when one considers the array of legal strategies, remedies and pretrial pleadings that can effectively make a trial a slim possibility. Justice Burger's comments implied that the truly skilled legal practitioner has a better grip on his or her case than the lawyer who simply waits for his or her day of oral advocacy. Hence, a filer of motions can often reach justice more quickly and efficiently than one who does not file.

    What do motions do anyway? Well, regrettably, some lawyers use them to delay proceedings and harass the opposition. The proper use of motions essentially attempts to resolve generally critical issues pertinent to the case. In-depth analysis follows.

B. Types of Motions

All of the motions described below significantly affect the nature and direction of the civil action by exposing important technical defects in the nature of the law or by providing the court with insight on the baselessness of the claim in question.

1. Motion to dismiss for lack of jurisdiction over the subject matter

Federal and state courts have been specifically empowered to handle certain types of cases consisting of designated subject matters. Broadly stated, federal courts are designated the triers of all matters related to the U.S.

Constitution and federal law and legislation. The elasticized definition of a federal case' or controversy is now firmly embedded in legal folklore, but the fact remains that subject-matter jurisdiction is a technical consideration often overlooked.

More specifically, at least at the federal level, are the guidelines for the establishment of a real case or controversy on a federal question. Be attentive to the court's own hesitation to become involved in cases when:

□ The problem is *moot*, that is the disagreement between the parties has long been over.
□ There are no real, adverse parties, only friendly parties seeking a federal precedent.
□ The parties truly have a personal stake in what is known as legal "standing."

Hence, if these as well as other problems are resolved, the court can at least say a "controversy" exists. That controversy must be federal in scope and be termed a *federal question*. As noted, the liberal application of the *federal question* doctrine is much renowned. As long as some conceptual nexus can be discerned between the plaintiff's injury and a federal law or policy, a federal question is satisfied.

Another way of securing subject-matter jurisdiction is for the plaintiff to demonstrate that the parties to this dispute are from diverse statehoods. At the heart of the federal court systems is this notion that federal courts can serve as neutral arbitrators for interstate litigation. Hence, the *diversity* of citizenship rule allows jurisdiction to U.S. district courts in actions between:

a. Citizens of different states
b. Citizens of a state and foreign states or citizens or subjects thereof
c. Citizens of different states in which foreign states or citizens or subjects thereof are additional parties

The mental gymnastics required in this often litigated area are not worth our continued assessment.

Lastly, in order to meet the subject-matter requirement of federal jurisdiction, the plaintiff's damages or losses in the controversy must exceed $10,000. In certain select cases, the jurisdictional amount may be waived.

To sum up, the requirements of federal subject-matter jurisdiction are (1) a case or controversy in which there is a federal question or diversity of citizenship and (2) damage exceeding $10,000.

2. Motion for a more definite statement

When a complaint pleading is so vague on its fact or so ambiguous in design and construction, all jurisdictions provide some mechanism for clarification. If clarification is not forthcoming, a motion to dismiss can be well supported. This motion points out all defects in the complaint and at the same time requests required information. Experienced litigants uniformly say this motion is rarely filed and even more rarely granted.

3. Motion for judgment on the pleadings

A rather restrictive motion that simply asks the court to evaluate the content of the pleadings themselves. The court's decision must rest entirely on the allegations, or lack thereof, provided in the pleadings. If the court fails to see any merits or substantive data on which an action or law may be based, it may make a judgment favorable to the defendant.

4. Motion for a summary judgment

This motion is closely aligned to the judgment on the pleadings, and in fact is probably identical as long as only the pleadings are considered by the court. Even rule 12(c) of the Federal Rules recognizes the incredible similarity. However, this motion is strategically more sound because the court is asked to evaluate much more than our pleadings in its determination. As a result, courts are more substantively supplied with information to make a credible decision. That additional information might include affidavits, depositions, admissions, stipulated records, or other evidence readily agreed upon between the parties. Of course, this level of documentary sophistication may cloud the court's judgment in a fundamentally simple issue.

5. Motion to change venue

Geographic considerations are often cited as critical in the *due process* assurance to a defendant in a criminal case. In the civil realm, those constitutional factors are not as important, but media influences, community prejudice, and other factors may make another geographic area more preferable. Venue considerations are commonly described as "forum" shopping, and the paralegal must be attuned to the needs of the client and advise the attorney of any potential venue problems.

6. Motion to dismiss for lack of jurisdiction over the person

This form of motion is readily comprehended since all a court must determine is whether the party to the suit is a "resident" of the area within the court's jurisdiction. Is the party within the proper district, county, or region? When compared to subject-matter jurisdiction some similarities emerge, but in the motion's most rudimentary form, the court must assess its ability to hear the case and its parties based on the parties' domain.

7. Technical motions

a. INSUFFICIENT SERVICE OF PROCESS

As was seen in section IV, service is a highly technical process, often rigidly adhered to. Failure to file appropriate papers within the prescribed guidelines can result in a technical dismissal.

b. FAILURE TO STATE A CLAIM

If the court is not empowered to grant the relief requested in the complaint or is not capable of finding a basis for any claim stated in the allegations, it may upon motion dismiss for the lack of substance.

c. FAILURE TO JOIN A PARTY

A complaint that fails to join the proper parties to the cause of action is another technical ground and defense.

8. Motion to strike

While most motions filed address themselves to plaintiff's issues or allegations, the plaintiff will file the motion to strike if he or she wishes the court to strike a defense enumerated by a defendant in his or her answer. Courts manifest a natural reluctance to strike defenses because of insufficiency, since they prefer these questions of law to be determined in the factual contest at trial.

9. Motion for a directed verdict

A court can entertain a motion for a directed verdict upon the conclusion of the opponent's case on the ground that the evidence clearly does not, nor could it ever, support the necessary quantum of proof in a civil cause of action. This motion requires that the judge direct a verdict in favor of the defendant because the plaintiff's cause failed to meet the burden of proof or persuasion required in this type of case. If the motion is denied, the defendant proceeds with his or her case.

10. Motion for a judgment notwithstanding the verdict

At the close of all evidence by both plaintiff and defendant and after a verdict has been rendered by the judge or jury, a party who has moved for a directed verdict may move to have the verdict and any judgment set aside and a judgment entered in his or her favor. If no new judgment comes forth, either party may file a motion for a new trial.

VIII. BASIC CONCEPTS IN EVIDENCE

A. Nature of Evidence

The law of evidence generally deals with two issues: (1) admissibility of any matter and (2) proof of a factual proposition. The evidentiary arena is highly theoretical in scope and not of much real utility to the practicing paralegal. However, a basic knowledge of the field provides insight into the levels of proof required in a civil action. An analysis of evidence helps the paralegal to perform investigative functions more intelligently, converse with witnesses more effectively as well as prepare them for examination, and to see flaws in an opponent's case. If anything, evidence apprises the paralegal of the pitfalls, shortcomings, and weaknesses in his or her own case as it proceeds to the adjudicatory phase. What follows is a schematic review of the most relevant topics in the law of evidence.

B. Classifications of Evidence

1. Real and demonstrative

Real evidence is any direct or circumstantial evidence offered to the trier of fact in the form of physical things, animate or inanimate. The term generally includes physical evidence (e.g., photographs, x rays, guns, or blood) and other actual objects from the crime scene or place of action. In contrast, demonstrative evidence encompasses items not directly involved in the litigation (e.g., maps, diagrams, models, and the like), which make the factual situation easier to grasp as a whole.

2. Direct and circumstantial

Circumstantial evidence proves a fact as a basis for an inference of some other fact. Direct evidence proves a fact as an end in itself. Both types may be real evidence, and either type may be admissible. Circumstantial evidence by itself may be sufficient to warrant a decision in favor of a party who builds a solid case of circumstance. The difference between these two types of evidence is that direct evidence requires the trier of fact to reach the ultimate fact at issue, while circumstantial evidence proves the ultimate facts by a process of inference. Direct evidence is a witness's testimony, "I saw the defendant shoot a man." Circumstantial evidence is a witness's testimony, "I heard a shot and saw the defendant rush from the room, a smoking revolver in hand; I went into the room, and there was the victim sprawled in a pool of gore!"

3. Fact and opinion

Usually a person is allowed to testify only as to matters he or she has personally experienced or perceived. Opinion evidence is excluded because it is often undependable. Of course, the difference between fact and opinion is only a matter of degree. An *opinion* in this context is an inference, deduction, judgment, or supposition drawn by a witness. However, opinions and facts are often almost indistinguishable. Furthermore, some opinions are quite useful. Therefore, under appropriate circumstance, opinion evidence may be admissible.

> *1. Expert opinions* are desirable and even indispensable in actions where complex technical matters are at issue. Who qualifies as an expert is a determination to be made by the trial judge, based upon the training, education, or experience of the proposed witness.
>
> 2. Some opinions by lay witnesses, which do not require special skill or knowledge, are also admissible within the sound discretion of the trial judge. The rationale is that the observation could not be more precisely described and that with a low probability of error or prejudice, the testimony would help determine some fact at issue. Lay opinions routinely admitted are:
>
>> *a.* Any competent witness may state his or her opinion as to the approximate age of another person of his or her acquaintance.
>>
>> *b.* Similarly, any competent witness may offer his or her opinion as to the identity or ownership of persons, animals, or objects presented for his or her scrutiny.
>>
>> *c.* A person familiar with the handwriting of another may state his or her opinion confirming or denying the authorship of a writing at issue.
>>
>> *d.* Any competent witness may offer his or her opinion as to the degree of intoxication of another person.
>>
>> *c.* In nontechnical fashion, a competent witness may testify to the apparent degree of discomfort, pain, or illness in another person observed by the witness. However, a lay witness may not attempt to diagnose the cause, condition, or severity of an ailment he or she has observed.
>>
>> *f.* A competent witness may also offer his or her opinion as to the mental state of another person observed by the witness.
>>
>> *g.* Any competent witness may offer an opinion as to the approximate speed of a vehicle or other moving object.

4. Judicial or administrative notice

The acceptance of a fact as true without requiring a party to make an offer of proof is called *judicial or administrative notice*. To avoid delay and the possibility of a senseless legal position, public policy allows judicial notice of proper matters.

Judicial or administrative notice is possible under the following circumstances:

1. Notorious facts.   Facts of common knowledge among normal persons within a community are susceptible to judicial notice. It is not the judge's personal knowledge but the standard of the community that prevails.

2. Manifest facts.   Facts that are not readily known to most persons but are readily obtained by reference to incontrovertible sources are also subject to judicial notice. The exact time of sunrise in a given locale on a given date is an example of this type of judicial notice.

3. Scientific tests of principles.   If the scientific community generally accepts a test method or belief, the judicial community should permit judicial notice of the fact.

4. Law.   Judicial notice of laws may be either mandatory or permissive.

    a. Mandatory judicial notice is taken of:
        i. The state constitution, enactments of the state legislature, common law of states, and formal adoptions of substantive administrative regulations of state agencies
        ii. The United States Constitution, international treaties, enactments of Congress, federal case law, and formal federal administrative regulations.

    b. Because foreign laws and local rule making are less readily available, the courts are given the discretion of permissive judicial notice of such laws. A judge may require formal proof of the existence and content of laws under the following circumstances:
        i. The laws of sister states
        ii. The laws of foreign nations
        iii. Municipal ordinances, private acts, in formal actions by Congress, the state legislature, and unpublished rules of administrative agencies

C. Rules of Evidence

1. The best evidence rule

The best evidence rule is a rule of quality in evidence, requiring the proponent of any written document to put in evidence the best version of that writing, whether an original or other form. In other words, the rule requires the highest degree of proof to which a case is susceptible. The rule does not apply to matters of minor importance to the litigation. However, if the original copy of the evidence is unavailable, a suitable copy may be substituted as evidence if these criteria are met:

    a. Prove the existence of the original writing.
    b. Show its present unavailability after diligent attempts to produce the original writing.
    c. Establish that the copy truly and accurately reflects the original writing.

In some instances, it may be permissible to show that the original writing is impractical to produce in court. A frequently cited example of this situation is an original writing contained on a tombstone. Also, this rule would not be invoked where a fact has an independent existence apart from the writing. For example, a bill of sale or receipt would not be necessary where a witness wishes to testify that she has bought and paid for certain goods.

Certain documents may qualify in many jurisdictions as original writings despite their seeming character as copies. Example include:

    a. Carbon copies that are duly executed as multiple original writings.
    b. Unsigned copies of duplicate originals.
    c. Excerpts from records of public documents, if accompanied by a certification from an appropriate governmental official.
    d. If the sender selects the telegraph as a means of communication, a duly received telegram is deemed an original writing.
    e. Microfilmed materials and other public records that have been approved by the State Records Commission or made in the regular course of business are also considered original writings.

2. The hearsay rule

a. DEFINITION

Hearsay is an out-of-court declaration (oral, written, or by conduct) offered to prove the truth of a matter asserted at trial. Generally, hearsay is not admitted in evidence because it is impossible to confront or challenge the evidence, which may be inaccurate. The key to the hearsay rule—and its greatest difficulty for students—is the determination of what issue is sought to be proved by the proposed evidence.

At trial the most important consideration of hearsay is its reliability as evidence. The various exceptions to the hearsay rule have developed because such evidence is often quite dependable. These long-settled exceptions are believed to be trustworthy enough to outweigh the consideration that no opportunity to cross-examine exists.

The key question to ask in the assessment of hearsay is; What issue is this evidence offered to prove? The same quote may be admissible in support of one issue but inadmissible in support of another.

Some out-of-court statements simply do not constitute hearsay:

1. Words of independent legal significance are not deemed to be hearsay. For example, words of slander or words spoken in the formation of an oral contract have obvious legal consequences. One is allowed to testify on his hearing of such words because the issue is not the truth of the words but the legal operation arising from words that were spoken.

2. A statement that is offered to show the effect on a person who has heard the statement is not regarded as hearsay. Again, the truth of the statement is secondary to its impact on the listener. For example, a person may testify that he heard a third person tell the defendant in a criminal trial, "Someone raped your wife!" if the issue is the state of mind of the defendant when he killed the assailant. However, if the issue was simply, Did the rape occur? the statement would be inadmissible because its truth would then be at issue.

3. Similarly, a statement that is offered to show the declarant's state of mind is not considered hearsay. For example, the football player who overhears a teammate sighing, "I'm queen of the May prom!" may testify on the issue of his teammate's mental condition, but not if the issue is the identity of this year's queen of the May prom.

b. EXCEPTIONS TO THE HEARSAY RULE

Admission by a party opponent. Under our adversarial system of justice, it is believed that remarks, writings, or conduct by one party to another should be allowed in evidence. The other party cannot claim he has no opportunity to cross examine himself, and the evidence is typically quite probative. An issue that frequently arises concerning party admissions is whether the admission is too unambiguous as to be useful as evidence; thus, disputes over admissions generally go to the weight and not the admissibility of such evidence. Under the general rules of evidence, admissions are not even considered as hearsay. To be deemed a party admission, the following elements must be met:

1. Personal knowledge of the subject of the admission is not required.

2. Unlike a declaration against interest by a nonparty, it is not necessary that a party know at the time of the statement she is making a statement against her own interest.

3. An admission may be either expressed or inferred from conduct.

4. An admission may proceed from oral or written statements or be inferred from conduct.

Declarations Against Interest. Remarks made by a person other than a party to the legal action may be admissible as exceptions to the hearsay rule under appropriate circumstances. Ordinarily, people do not say things against their own interest unless such things are true. Therefore, a remark may be admissible as a declaration against interest if the following elements are met.

1. The remark must be against a penal, monetary, or proprietary interest of the declarant. To be sure, there are individuals who do like to denigrate themselves, but they are not the norm.

2. The declarant should have known the remark was against his interest at the time the remark was made. The Federal Rules apply the reasonable person standard, but the trial judge is free to inquire into the actual knowledge of the declarant.

3. The declarant is not presently available to testify.

Excited Utterances (Spontaneous Declarations). A remark made immediately after and in relation to a startling occurrence is likely to be true because most persons could not invent a lie so fast. An excited utterance is admissible if the following elements exist:

1. A startling occurrence sufficient to produce stress or excitement in persons of ordinary sensibilities.

2. The declarant was present at the occurrence, and his remark came very soon thereafter.

3. The startling occurrence is the subject of the remark.

4. The declarant need not be unavailable to testify.

Dying Declarations. The rationale for admitting dying declarations as an exception to the hearsay rule is that no person would die with a lie on his or her lips. Regardless of a person's past, religious inclinations, or general belief in God or lack thereof, very few people will end their lives with a falsehood. However, inveterate liars may choose to lie compulsively even at the very end of their lives.

Present Sense Impressions. In situations less shocking than those that provoke excited utterances, a statement may still be reliable by virtue of its immediate response, which leaves no time for fabrication of an untruthful response. Of recent origin, this exception is defined as a statement that responds to an event immediately after the perception of the event. The rationale for the exception is that no time exists for fabrication or lies or faulty memory.

Impeachment. Impeachment evidence is possible to show conduct or statements made out of court that contradict or undermine testimony made in court. Also it is impossible to put in evidence a witness's poor reputation for veracity to impeach his testimony. Often impeachment takes the form of a *prior inconsistent statement* to present testimony by a witness. The witness is allowed to explain the prior remark to rebut the impeachment if he has made a prior inconsistent statement indicating that his present testimony is untruthful or incorrect. If a party is surprised by testimony of his own witness, he may have the witness declared an *adverse witness* by the judge. Impeachment by prior convictions or infamous crimes may also be possible in limited circumstances.

Business or Public Records. Any record made systematically in the regular course of the operation of a business, or any other writing that serves as a memorandum of a business transaction is admissible.

Under this rule, only the proper custodian of business records, and not the author of an entry in question, is necessary to authenticate the evidence. Under the *public records* exception to the hearsay rule, however, a properly certified copy of a public document may be admitted into evidence without the testimony of its proper custodian. The reasoning behind this exception is that the public expense is eased as public records are called into litigation quite frequently. Also public officials usually have less personal stake in the contents of such documents than would business people in a comparable position.

Ancient Documents. Ancient documents were defined at common law as property-disposing documents that were properly authenticated and at least thirty years old. The reason for accepting these documents as an exception to the rule against written hearsay is that such documents have a very low possibility of fraud and because superior sources of evidence are usually very difficult to locate.

Matters of Pedigree. Personal and family history—including births, deaths, baptisms, marriages, divorces, and distant relationships—are admissible as an exception to the rule against hearsay by virtue of their necessity and high degree of reliability.

Declaration of Physical or Mental Condition. A statement of a declarant as to his current mental, emotional, or physical condition is admissible as an exception to the hearsay rule. Such statements need not be made to medical personnel; however, all but a minority of jurisdictions require a present and not a past condition.

H. Privileges

Public policy favors the need for candor in some human relations above the value that testimony at trial might have as a consequence of those relations. Accordingly, the law recognizes a number of privileges against testimony. Privileged information is neither discoverable nor admissible at trial.

1. Marital

Traditionally, the courts have recognized in both civil and criminal proceedings a privilege between spouses to suppress testimony of either spouse against the other concerning any private communication between them that did not directly pertain to the marriage or children of the marriage (e.g., child abuse, divorce, criminal battery, intrafamily tort). The privilege even survived the marriage. However, the privilege does not seem to have survived recent United States Supreme Court rulings. The court modified the traditional privilege to say that only the witness spouse can decide whether or not he or she wishes to testify. The spouse declarant cannot prevent the testimony.

2. Physician-Patient

Candor between a physician and his or her patient holds obvious importance. Generally, any information a patient discloses to his or her doctor or surgeon that is relevant to medical treatment is privileged against disclosure.

3. Attorney-Client

To encourage full communication between an attorney and his or her client, the law promises that any remarks made in a professional context concerning pending litigation are privileged. Under the canons of ethics, the legal assistant, the secretary, or other law-firm employee is also covered by the privilege.

I. Burdens of Proof and Presumptions

In civil litigation the burden of proof must be met by preponderance of the evidence. In criminal litigation the state, commonwealth, or other governmental authority has a burden of proof beyond a reasonable doubt. Who has the burden of proof often determines who prevails in a legal action. But there are other types of burdens.

1. Persuasion

The burden of persuasion is generally the meaning ascribed to the term *burden of proof*. This burden never shifts from party to party but is established as a matter of law from the outset of the trial. An example in the criminal realm is that the state has the burden of proof of establishing a defendant's guilt beyond a reasonable doubt.

2. Going Forward

The burden of going forward with the evidence, on the other hand, may shift several times during a trial. This burden shifts to the other party when one has introduced enough evidence to merit a judgment as a matter of law.

3. Quantum of Proof

The amount of proof necessary to meet either of these burdens varies with the type of lawsuit.

a. Proof beyond a Reasonable Doubt. This is the standard that applies in criminal cases. Although it is a heavy standard of proof, it does not require that no doubt at all remain in the minds of the trier of fact. Although mathematical standards are never suggested in court, it may be useful to consider this standard as requiring a high level of certainty before a conviction should be allowed. The quantum is set so high to minimize the risk of conviction of an innocent person.

b. Clear and convincing proof. In a few civil cases—such as fraud or an oral contract to make mutual wills—a higher standard of proof than usual may be invoked. Within an artificial mathematical formula, the standard of proof in this instance may be considered as high as 75 percent.

c. Proof on a preponderance of the evidence. This is the usual standard in civil actions. If the weight of the evidence on the scales of justice tilts ever so slightly in favor of one of the litigants, then that litigant should prevail.

d. Proof required for a directed verdict. The standard required for a directed verdict is clearly not that a mere scintilla of evidence will send the case to the jury.

4. Presumptions

A *presumption* is an evidentiary "short cut." It requires that upon the proof of a basic fact, another presumed fact must be inferred as a matter of law. Public policy favors presumptions because they balance the parties' knowledge of the facts in some instances. Also, presumptions may save time and money in avoiding unnecessary exercises in proof.

Presumptions may be *rebuttable* or *conclusive*. A conclusive presumption amounts to a rule of substantive law.

Closely related to presumptions are *permissible inferences*. Permissible inferences allow a litigant to meet a burden of proof without shifting the burden to an opponent. Presumptions in criminal cases are really permissible inferences. An example of a permissible inference is the principle of *res ipsa loquitur* ("the thing speaks for itself") in tort law. Under that principle, the inference of negligence is permitted when an injury has occurred caused by a thing entirely controlled by the defendant, and it was the type of injury that would not normally occur in the absence of negligence. Some examples of presumptions and inferences are as follows:

a. A rebuttable presumption exists that any death has not been a suicide. This presumption has its roots in an ancient equitable doctrine favoring church burial.

b. In both criminal and civil proceedings, every person is rebuttably presumed to be sane.

c. By law, a child less than thirteen years of age is conclusively presumed to be incapable of committing a crime (although the child may be a minor in need of supervision.)

CIVIL PROCEDURE GLOSSARY

☐ *Authentication*—identification of an item of evidence by means of preliminary proof of its genuineness as being something that in fact relates to the lawsuit.

☐ *"Best evidence" rule*—in order to prove the contents of a writing, the original writing must be the one produced, unless it is unavailable for a reason beyond the control of the proponent.

☐ *Complaint*—brief statement of facts alleging a cause of action against a defendant.

☐ *Contingent fee*—where the attorney's fee depends upon the amount of money recovered.

☐ *Counterclaim*—assertion of claim by defendant against the plaintiff who sued the defendant or a codefendant.

☐ *Cross-claim*—in Illinois, known as a counterclaim against a codefendant.

☐ *Cross-examination*—questions asked by the attorney opposing the attorney who called the witness. Leading questions are permitted and scope of CE is limited to the subject matter of DE and matters affecting the credibility of the witness.

☐ *Default*—failure on the part of the defendant to answer or otherwise appear in response to the complaint.

☐ *Deposition*—oral or written testimony of a witness or party.

☐ *Direct examination*—the process of eliciting facts from a witness called by a party. Leading questions (i.e., questions suggesting an answer) are generally not permitted.

☐ *Impeachment*—means ascertaining the truthfulness and/or accuracy of the testimony of a witness through cross-examination or extrinsic evidence, such as another witness.

☐ *Instructions*—In both civil and criminal cases, the court is required to give the applicable *Illinois Pattern Instructions*, in writing, if the court determines that the jury should be instructed on the subject, unless the court finds that the instructions misstate the law. The attorneys for the parties have the primary burden of preparing the jury instructions.

☐ *Interrogatories*—written questions directed to the other party concerning his claim or defense.

☐ *Judicial Notice*—where the facts are so universally known that they cannot possibly be the subject of dispute, the judge or jury may consider them without further proof.

☐ *Motion*—an application made to the court for an order permitting you to do something, requiring your adversary to do something, for sanctions, or other relief.

☐ *Privilege*—the right of a person to refrain from testifying to certain confidential communications and to prevent others from so testifying.

☐ *Prove-up or default trial*—proof of unliquidated damages sustained by plaintiff after default on question of liability by defendant.

EVIDENCE GLOSSARY

☐ *Admission*—a statement by a party offered at trial by his or her opponent.

☐ *Business records*—records made in the regular course of business, at or about the time of the act or event recorded, whose method and circumstance of preparation is not irregular.

☐ *Character evidence*—evidence of good/bad character.

☐ *Compromise*—offers of settlement.

☐ *Custom or habit*—that which is performed with great regularity.

☐ *Declaration against interest*—a statement against the declarant's own interest is admissible.

☐ *Declaration of co-conspirator*—a statement made by one party to a conspiracy in furtherance of that conspiracy is admissible against all members of the conspiracy.

☐ *Dying declaration*—a homicide victim's statement about the way he met his death, made with the expectation of death, which indeed came.

☐ *Former testimony*—testimony of a witness at a trial is admissible at another trial between the parties if the witness is dead, insane, or unavailable.

☐ *Hearsay*—an out-of-court statement offered to prove the truth of the matter asserted in the statement.

☐ *Past recollection recorded*—where a witness has no independent memory of a specific event and is unable to recall the event without the aid of a memo, but can testify as to what the memo was and that it was made by him at a time when events were fresh in his mind, the memo may be admitted to evidence as an exhibit or read to the jury.

☐ *Public records*—records kept by a public officer dealing with her or his official activities and reasonably necessary for the proper performance of the duties of the office are admissible to prove the matters recorded.

☐ *Relevance*—any evidence that tends to prove or disprove any matter at issue in the lawsuit.

☐ *Res gestae*—a declaration by a party to the transaction in suit, uttered at the time of the occurrence, and tending to explain the facts thererof may be admissible. The rule applies equally to actual participants in the event and observers.

☐ *Subsequent repairs*—evidence of subsequent remedial action taken by a party after an accident.

□ *Real evidence*—the production of some object that had a direct part in the incident, such as the murder weapon, as well as the display of personal injuries.

□ *Request for admission of fact or genuineness of documents*—as to fact not seriously in dispute, a request that your adversary admit such fact; as to document, a request that your adversary admit the genuineness of the document.

□ *Subject-matter jurisdiction*—the authority of a particular court to make a binding determination in a particular kind of controversy.

□ *Summary Judgment*—where the facts are not in dispute and the issues to be resolved are only a matter of law, a motion for summary judgment in your favor may be in order, if the law is in your favor.

□ *Summons*—a formal statement annexed to the complaint that gives defendant notice that an action has been filed against her or him and advising the defendant to file an answer or appear in court by a certain date.

□ *Third-party complaint*—complaint by a defendant to bring a person or entity into a case who may be liable to pay the defendant for all or part of the loss claimed by plaintiff, who also may be liable to plaintiff directly.

□ *Venue*—the place (usually the county) where the action is to be commenced.

□ *Voir dire*—an examination by the judge, in both civil and criminal cases, of prospective jurors to determine their qualifications to serve as jurors in the case on trial. The court may permit additional or supplemental questions by the attorneys for the parties if appropriate or necessary.

DISCUSSION QUESTIONS AND PRACTICAL EXERCISES

Discussion Questions

1. What makes federal jurisdiction so common in our society? Why is it generally so easy to claim a "federal question"?
2. Write up two short fact patterns that demonstrate the concept of diversity of citizenship.
3. When are counterclaims an appropriate form of pleading?
4. Name at least four types of motions that are available in responding to a complaint.
5. Why is hearsay not favored in the law of evidence?
6. If you had to argue for a new kind of evidentiary *privilege*, what would it be? What kind of new relationship deserves the doctrine of privilege?
7. What type of pleadings should be filed to get more information, or at least clearer information, from the opposition?
8. Why do we excuse civil wrongdoers from imprisonment? Would it not be an effective means of controlling civil wrongs?
9. When should a motion to change venue be filed?
10. What rationale could support a cross-claim?

Practical Exercises

1. Draft a model complaint with appropriate secondary forms. No set fact pattern is suggested except that your case must revolve around an auto crash and injury.
2. Draft and compile a complete set of interrogatories for an auto negligence case. A minimum of twenty-five questions is acceptable. Use again the model provided in the exhibits.

ENRICHMENT ACTIVITY

Visit the court houses of at least three counties and gather information on filing procedures and required forms for a selected topic. Develop a reference chart that reflects the variation found in county-to-county procedures.

Write to a variety of county offices and administrative agencies to obtain sample documents most frequently used by them.

Compile your own "sets" of forms by subject for your future reference.

SUGGESTED READING

BATES, FRANK. *Principles of Evidence*. Sydney: Law Book Co., 1980.

BLANCHARD, RODERICK D. *Litigation and Trial Practice for the Legal Professional*. St. Paul: West Publishing Co., 1982.

CASAD, ROBERT C. *Jurisdiction in Civil Actions: Territorial Basis and Process Limitations on Jurisdiction of State and Federal Courts*. Boston: Warren, Gorham & Lamont, 1983.

COUND, JOHN J., et al. *Civil Procedure, Cases and Materials*. St. Paul: West Publishing Co., 1980.

Civil Practice and Litigation in Federal and State Courts: Resource Materials. Philadelphia: American Law Institute, 1981.

Civil Trial Manual 2. Philadelphia: American Law Institute, 1980.

COYNE, THOMAS A. *Rules of Civil Procedure for the United States District Courts: Practice Comments*. New York: Clark Boardman Co., 1982

Current Problems in Federal Civil Practice. New York: Practicing Law Institute, 1984.

DANNER, DOUGLAS. *Expert Witness Checklists*. San Francisco: Bancroft-Whitney Co., 1983.

DOMBROFF, MARK A. *Dombroff on Demonstrative Evidence*. New York: John Wiley and Sons, 1983.

GRAHAM, MICHAEL H. *Evidence—Texts, Rules, Illustrations and Problems: The Commentary Method*. St Paul: National Institute for Trial Advocacy, 1983.

GREEN, R. KEITH. *Forensic Psychology: A Primer for Legal and Mental Health Professionals*. Springfield, Ill.: Charles C. Thomas, 1984.

KARLEN, SELMAR. *Civil Litigation*. Indianapolis: Bobbs-Merrill Co., 1978.

LILLY, GRAHAM C. *An Introduction to the Law of Evidence*. St Paul: West Publishing Co., 1980

MILLER, LARRY, et. al. *Human Evidence in Criminal Justice*. Cincinnati: Pilgrimage, 1983.

ROTHSTEIN, PAUL F. *Evidence in a Nutshell: State and Federal Rules*. St Paul: West Publishing Co., 1981.

SINCLAIR, KENT. *Federal Civil Practice*. New York: Practising Law Institute, 1980.

SOBEL, NATHAN R. *Eyewitness Identification: Legal and Practical Problems*. New York: Clark Boardman Co., 1981.

Using Experts in Civil Cases. New York: Practising Law Institute, 1982.

Video Techniques in Trial and Pretrial. New York: Practising Law Institute, 1983.

CHAPTER SEVEN

CORPORATIONS, PARTNERSHIPS, AND AGENCY

CHAPTER DESCRIPTION

In this chapter we survey the basic principles of corporation law, including the creation, formulation, and operation of the varied types of corporations, partnerships, and proprietorships. Substantial attention is given to document preparation, formalities mandated by law for legal operation, articles of incorporation, bylaws, shareholder's, officer's and director's rights and liabilities, and taxation issues. How to set up a business form as well as dissolve it is also described.

PARALEGAL FUNCTIONS

Collect client information for the purpose of choice of business form.

Prepare drafts of documents necessary to form a business, including: articles of incorporation, bylaws, stock subscriptions, minutes, certificates and appropriate regulatory forms, corporate reports and tax forms, and dissolution.

Research the selection of an appropriate corporate name.

Prepare all governmental applications.

Prepare stock or shareholders' agreements.

Draft and file documents for all forms of partnerships.

Analyze minutes from shareholders' and directors' meetings.

Review new legislation affecting corporate clients.

Prepare checklists, forms, and materials to assist the firm in efficient handling of business organization.

Draft stock certificates.

I. INTRODUCTION

A. General Forms of Business Organizations

A major component of business law is the content of corporate forms or entities. Since this country is capitalistic, great emphasis is placed on the formulation, regulation, and operation of all business forms. Essentially, business can be operated in the following diverse ways:

   1. Sole proprietorship
   2. Partnership: general and limited
   3. Corporation: (including close and subchapter S and professional)
   4. Joint stock company
   5. Joint venture
   6. Business trusts

B. General Attributes or Characteristics of Business Forms

All have unique requirements and legal slants, though all exist to make a profit in a competitive world. All business forms have certain attributes or characteristics, which include:

1. A method of business organization
2. The expense of formulation and operation
3. Tax treatment or liability
4. Liability of owners, operators, directors, or proprietors
5. Procedural steps in the creation of the business form
6. Continuity and duration of corporate existence
7. Transferability, divisibility, merger, dissolution, liquidation of the business form
8. Management and control of the enterprise
9. Capital, cash, and credit requirements of the enterprise

The choice of business form largely depends on how the client addresses these general factors. The lawyer and paralegal must elicit information from the client that will clearly indicate that one form of business will be most favorable to the particular situation. Each client is unique, as are their business requirements. The following questions, with commentary indicating their significance, are illustrative:

1. How many people will be active in the management of the business?
2. What are their ages?
3. How is management responsibility to be divided among them?

If more than one individual is to manage the business, the sole proprietorship is, by definition, unavailable. A wide disparity in the ages of the individuals may favor the corporate form because of the transferability of interest advantages.

The extent to which responsibility is to be shared equally or to which there is to be an allocation of specific responsibilities will be significant in a choice between a partnership or a corporation (or a statutory close corporation).

4. What is the nature of the business?
5. What capital contributions are to be made by the participants?

Some businesses are more capital intensive than others and accordingly have greater capital requirements. If the amount to be contributed by the participants is far less than the capital requirements of the business, funds will have to be obtained through loans or investments of others. Depending on the availability of loan funds (including interest rates), the capital needs may dictate the need to use either the limited partnership form or the corporate form.

6. Is there any existing business?
7. What is the business experience of the participants?
8. Will this business be the main occupation for the participants, or will they have other occupations?

An existing business with a proven record of performance and/or individuals who are experienced in the particular line of business will have an easier time raising capital both through loans and through investments. Where there is no such proven track record, the participants may initially have to rely on their own capital investments, investment by relatives and associates, and secured bank loans until there is sufficient evidence of viability to prompt others to invest. If the participants will have other business activities, aside from the one being contemplated, those activities may provide additional sources of capital. The extent to which some participants will be more active in the management of the business than others will bear on the choice of form, although it is generally possible to allocate authority and division of profits through agreement among the participants.

9. What are the likely profit prospects for the business in the foreseeable future?
10. Will the business be acquiring assets eligible for investment tax credit?
11. What are the tax brackets of the participants?

If the business will be incurring losses, it may be desirable to choose a form that will enable the principlals to use the potential losses in the business; it may be desirable to utilize the corporate form. The interplay between the taxes of the individuals and the business must be considered in concrete rather than abstract terms and actual computations should be made on projected profits of the business and alternate choices of business form.

12. What is the net worth of the participants?

13. Are their assets held in their own names or in joint tenancies with a spouse?

If the participants have little net worth or if their respective assets are held largely in joint tenancies with a spouse, such that they cannot be reached by their individual creditors, the risk of using the partnership form is diminished. On the other hand, the larger the net worth which one can pledge, the greater will be the ability to obtain a loan financing the business.

14. Is the business one that is likely to produce tort claims, e.g., a construction business?

Where there is great exposure to liability, the corporate form will probably be preferable.

15. Will all of the participants be active in the business, or will some be merely investors?

If some of the participants are merely investors, seeking a return on a specific investment, they will not want to incur liability as general partners. In that situation, the limited partnership or corporate form would be more appropriate.

16. What form of business do the participants have in mind?

17. What are their objectives?

The participants may have decided that they wish to form a partnership. In this situation, it is necessary to explore the reasons why they have chosen that form and to explain the different consequences that flow from that choice. In some situations, the advantages they seek from the partnership form can be obtained through the use of the statutory close corporation and the benefits of corporate form can simultaneously be obtained.

Whatever the eventual choice of form, both the paralegal and lawyer must recognize that choosing a business form is in large part an art rather than a science. In the final analysis, each situation is unique and requires an evaluation based upon an open mind with no preconceived notions. The proper choice also depends on one's experience and sense of history—something that legal practitioners acquire with the passage of time. (See exhibits 7.1 and 7.2.)

II. SOLE PROPRIETORSHIPS

A. General Description

A proprietorship is often said to be the mainstay of the American economic system, the bulwark of the rugged individualist who sets out to be an independent owner and operator. The simplicity of a proprietorship does not reflect negatively on its importance and value, for the majority of American businesses are of this type, from gas stations to law practices. The simplicity of starting up as well as other factors does account for some of its overwhelming popularity.

A paralegal working for an attorney often has to do the initial assessment of a client's situation and readily discern which form of business organization is most appropriate. The proprietorship will be a common choice of form, and for good reasons.

B. Advantages of a Sole Proprietorship

1. The proprietorship is easy to establish. Few, if any, formal filing requirements exist.

2. There is little statutory regulation or governmental oversight.

3. Costs for the initiation and organization of the business are minimal.

4. Management is totally centralized with no possibility of internal management struggles.

Exhibit 7.1

Features To Consider In Choosing A Business Form

Before one decides whether or not to incorporate, it is wise to review other alternatives.

There are two other fundamental ways to operate a business: individual proprietorship and partnership. Both have similar advantages and disadvantages. The main advantage is that they are slightly less expensive to start, since there are no incorporating fees. They are also a bit less formal.

In a corporation, periodic meetings and minutes of the meetings should be kept. This is a simple routine task.

Advantages of Partnerships and Proprietorships

1. Somewhat lower cost to organize since there are no incorporating fees.

2. Less formality in record keeping.

3. The owners file one tax return.

4. Owners can deduct losses that might be incurred during the early life of a business from other personal income.

5. The limit of tax-deductible contributions to "Keogh" type pension and profit-sharing plans has been increased to $15,000. This has reduced the tax advantage of benefit plans previously available to a corporation.

6. Profits of a partnership, unlike dividends paid by a corporation are not subject to a second Federal income tax when distributed to the owners. However, whether this is an advantage, taxwise, depends on certain other factors, namely:

    a. The individual tax brackets of the owners as compared with that of the corporation.

    b. The extent to which double taxation of earnings of the corporation is eliminated by deductible salaries paid to the owners and, by retention of earnings in surplus.

Some Of The Main Disadvantages Of Proprietorships And Partnerships

1. Unlimited personal liability. The owners are personally liable for all debts and judgments against the business, including liability in case of failure or other disaster.

2. In a partnership, each member can bind the other so that one partner can cause the other to be personally liable.

3. All profits are personally taxable to the owners at rates which are higher than corporate rates.

4. If the owner(s) dies or becomes incapacitated, the business often comes to a standstill.

5. The owner(s) do not have the full tax benefits of the tax-deductible plans including pension and profit sharing that are available to a corporation.

The Advantages of Incorporating

1. The personal liability of the founders is limited to the amount of money put into the corporation (with the exception of unpaid taxes).

2. If a business owner wishes to raise capital, a corporation is more attractive to investors who can purchase shares of stock in it for purposes of raising capital.

3. A corporation does not pay tax on monies it receives in exchange for its stock.

4. There are many more tax options available to corporations than to proprietorships or partnerships. One can set up pension, profit-sharing, stock-option plans that are favorable to the owners of the corporation.

5. A corporation can be continued more easily in the event of the death of its owners or principals.

6. Shares of a corporation can easily be distributed to family members.

7. The owners (stockholders) of a corporation that is discontinued due to its being unsuccessful can have all the advantages of being incorporated, yet be able to deduct up to $50,000 on an individual tax return or $100,000 on a joint return of money invested in the corporation from personal income.

8. The owner(s), stockholders, of a corporation, can operate with all the advantages of a corporation, yet be taxed on personal income-tax rates if this option provides a tax advantage.

9. Owners can quickly transfer their ownership interest represented by shares of stock, without the corporation dissolving.

10. The corporation's capital can be expanded by issuing and selling additional shares of stock.

11. Shares of stock can be used for estate and family planning.

12. The corporation can ease the tax burden of its stockholders by accumulating its earnings. This is possible provided the accumulation is not unreasonable and is for a business purpose.

13. It is a separate legal "being" separate and apart from its owner(s) (stockholders). It can sue and be sued and can enter into contracts.

14. A corporation may own shares in another corporation and receive dividends, 85% of which are tax free.

15. A corporation's federal income-tax rates may be lower than the owner's individual tax rates, especially for a smaller company. As of January 1, 1984, the income-tax rates on companies are as follows:

TAXABLE INCOME	RATE OF TAX
Up to 25,000	15%
25,000–50,000	18
50,000–75,000	30
75,000–100,000	40
Over 100,000	46

Disadvantages of Incorporating

1. The owners of a corporation file two (2) tax returns, individual and corporate. This may require added time and accounting expense. The owner of a proprietorship files one (1) return; a member of a partnership files two (2).

2. Unless the net taxable income of a business is a substantial, i.e., $25,000 or more, there may not be tax advantages. (However, in businesses where there is personal liability on the part of the owners, it may be desirable to incorporate even if the income is modest.)

3. Maintaining the corporate records may require added time.

4. If debt financing is obtained by a corporation, i.e., loan from a bank, the fund source may require the personal guarantee by the owner(s) thereby eliminating the limited advantage of a corporation at least to the extent of the loan.

Exhibit 7.2

TAX ASPECTS OF BUSINESS FORMS

The following table presents various other tax and compensation issues where differences based on choice of business form may be significant:

ISSUE	SOLE PROPRIETORSHIP	PARTNERSHIP	CORPORATION*
Investment Credit Benefit	Accrues to sole proprietor as credit against tax liability	Passes through to partners as individuals to be credited against their individual tax liability	For corporation use only as credit against corporation's tax liability
Dividend Exclusion	Maximum of $200 exclusion on joint return ($100 on single return)	Dividends pass through to partners as individuals, who have same exclusion as sole proprietor	85% of dividends from domestic corporations deductible from corporate income
Group Term Life Insurance	Non-deductible for owner	Non-deductible for partners	All premiums deductible by corporation and premium for up to $50,000 of insurance not taxable as income to employee
Medical Reimbursement Plans	Not applicable	Not available for partners	Available, but limited
Deferred Compensation Plans	Not available	Not available	Available
Pension and Profit Sharing Plans	Generally the maximum deduction is the lesser of $15,000 or 15% of net income	Partners may make contribution as individuals similar to sole proprietor	Greater deductions possible than for sole proprietor and greater flexibility for plans

* See Sections 1371-1379 of the Internal Revenue Code for the differences in treatment accorded in the case of a Subchapter S corporation.

In short, the proprietorship is the "common" man and woman's pipe dream, a chance at a slice of the American success story. Effective operation requires good sense but mostly luck and unending drive and endurance.

C. Disadvantages of a Sole Proprietorship

While the advantages are numerous, in selecting a proprietorship, beware of the pitfalls in this choice, including:

1. Higher tax rates than corporate schedules
2. Unlimited legal liability for the owner and operator
3. No business continuity in case of death or disability
4. No capital contributions by outside parties

D. Procedural Steps in Formation

1. Nature of the business must be evaluated for purpose and legality.
2. File appropriate fictitious name certificates, if required (see exhibit 7.3).
3. File appropriate tax forms as required by the IRS (see exhibit 7.4).

III. PARTNERSHIPS

A. General Description

Proprietorships often transform into partnerships, and for inevitable reasons. While simple and autonomous in nature, the proprietorship is constricting and narrow in the long run. Capital and human resources, leadership change, innovation, and large-scale improvements are difficult in the proprietorship, since the business can draw only from a single "well." That single well can run dry, or it can provide only its capacity. Hence, a business looks to others to participate in the endeavor and asks for their participation in both economic and human terms. The partnership admits by its form that being alone, or an island to itself, is not always the best course. The partnership admits by its form that the pooling of resources and the collaboration of many minds can be far more productive for any business. Thus, a partnership is defined as an *association of two or more persons to carry on as co-owners of a business for a profit*.

That drive for profit is the basis for most partnerships, and as a result, the interest in partnerships increases markedly at the governmental and judicial levels.

B. Advantages/Characteristics of the Partnership

Interest in business partnerships runs high since the advantages are many. First, the economic costs of formation are minimal, with the major initiation expense being the legal expenses for a partnership agreement. An expansive, though fairly typical, agreement is shown in exhibit 7.5. Second, few states require much paperwork to be filed, though the future trend in law indicates much more regulation in this area, especially when one considers tax-shelter issues. (See exhibit 7.6.) Third, the influx of potential cash and capital resources is most appealing to individuals who find themselves restricted in a proprietorship. The obvious pooling of economic resources makes a partnership enticing. Fourth, while tax rates are not at the corporate level, the ability to shelter income from the high proprietorship's rates is evident. Examples of preferential tax treatment includes the use of Keogh plans, up to and including $15,000 per year for the general partners; deductibility of losses, and deductibility of salaries paid to the partners of the enterprise. All in all, the advantages are quite strong in the appropriate set of circumstances.

C. Disadvantages/Characteristics of the Partnership

On the negative side of the coin, the paralegal must evaluate the client's individual situation and discern whether or not the client can fathom the dimensions of unlimited personal legal liability. While the business entrepreneur in a

Exhibit 7.3

SAMPLE APPLICATION FOR CONDUCTING BUSINESS UNDER AN ASSUMED OR FICTITIOUS NAME BY AN INDIVIDUAL OR INDIVIDUALS

Filed this __________ day of __________
19 ____
Commonwealth of
Department of State

Secretary of the Commonwealth

(Box for Certification)

COMMONWEALTH OF
DEPARTMENT OF STATE
CORPORATION BUREAU

In compliance with the requirements of section 1 of the act of May 24, 1945 (P.L. 967) (54 P.S. §28.1), the undersigned individual(s), desiring to carry on or conduct a business in this Commonwealth under an assumed or fictitious name, style or designation, does (do) hereby certify that:

1. The real name(s) and address(es), of all persons owning or interested in the business are:

NAMES	RESIDENCES

2. The name, style or designation under which the business is being, or will be, carried on or conducted is:

____

3. A brief statement of the character or nature of the business is:

____

4. The location of the principal office or place of business of the business in this Commonwealth is:

____

5. (Strike out this paragraph if at least one of the addresses set forth in Paragraph 1 is located in this Commonwealth). The name and residence address of the resident agent through which the business is being, or will be, carried on or conducted in this Commonwealth is:

____
(name)

____
(number) *(street)* *(city)* *(Pennsylvania)* *(zip code)*

IN TESTIMONY WHEREOF, the undersigned has(have) caused this application to be signed this __________ day of __________, 19 ____.

(Signature)	*(Signature)*
(Signature)	*(Signature)*
(Signature)	*(Signature)*
(Signature)	*(Signature)*

COMMONWEALTH OF

SS:

COUNTY OF __________

Personally appeared before me this __________ day of __________, 19 ____, __________

____

who, being duly sworn according to law, deposes and says that the statements contained in the foregoing application are true.

(SEAL) ______________________________ *(Notary Public)*

______________________________ *(Signature of Affiant)*

My Commission expires __________

Exhibit 7.4

| SCHEDULE C (Form 1040)
Department of the Treasury
Internal Revenue Service | **Profit or (Loss) From Business or Profession**
(Sole Proprietorship)
Partnerships, Joint Ventures, etc., Must File Form 1065.
▶ Attach to Form 1040 or Form 1041. ▶ See Instructions for Schedule C (Form 1040). | OMB No. 1545-0074
1984
09 |

Name of proprietor | Social security number

A Main business activity (see Instructions) ▶ | Product or Service ▶

B Business name and address ▶ .... | **C** Employer ID number

D Method(s) used to value closing inventory:
(1) ☐ Cost   **(2)** ☐ Lower of cost or market   **(3)** ☐ Other (attach explanation)

	Yes	**No**

E Accounting method: **(1)** ☐ Cash   **(2)** ☐ Accrual   **(3)** ☐ Other (specify) ▶ ....

F Was there any change in determining quantities, costs, or valuations between opening and closing inventory?. . . . . . .
If "Yes," attach explanation.

G Did you deduct expenses for an office in your home?. . . . .

Part I Income

1 a Gross receipts or sales	1a	
b Less: Returns and allowances	1b	
c Subtract line 1b from line 1a and enter the balance here	1c	
2 Cost of goods sold and/or operations (from Part III, line 8)	2	
3 Subtract line 2 from line 1c and enter the **gross profit** here	3	
4 a Windfall Profit Tax Credit or Refund received in 1984 (see Instructions) . . .	4a	
b Other income	4b	
5 Add lines 3, 4a, and 4b. This is the **gross income** . . . . ▶	5	

Part II Deductions

6 Advertising			**23** Repairs		
7 Bad debts from sales or services (Cash method taxpayers, see Instructions)			**24** Supplies (not included in Part III below)		
8 Bank service charges.			**25** Taxes (Do not include Windfall Profit Tax here. See line 29.)		
9 Car and truck expenses			**26** Travel and entertainment		
10 Commissions			**27** Utilities and telephone		
11 Depletion			**28 a** Wages . . .		
12 Depreciation and Section 179 deduction from Form 4562 (not included in Part III below).			**b** Jobs credit		
			c Subtract line 28b from 28a . .		
13 Dues and publications			**29** Windfall Profit Tax withheld in 1984		
14 Employee benefit programs			**30** Other expenses (specify):		
15 Freight (not included in Part III below) .			**a**		
16 Insurance			**b**		
17 Interest on business indebtedness . .			**c**		
18 Laundry and cleaning			**d**		
19 Legal and professional services . .			**e**		
20 Office expense.			**f**		
21 Pension and profit-sharing plans . .			**g**		
22 Rent on business property . . .			**h**		
			i		

31 Add amounts in columns for lines 6 through 30i. These are the **total deductions** . . . . ▶	31	
32 **Net profit or (loss).** Subtract line 31 from line 5 and enter the result. If a profit, enter on Form 1040, line 12, and on Schedule SE, Part I, line 2 (or Form 1041, line 6). If a loss, you **MUST** go on to line 33 .	32	

33 If you have a loss, you **MUST** answer this question: "Do you have amounts for which you are not at risk in this business (see Instructions)?" ☐ Yes ☐ No
If "Yes," you **MUST** attach **Form 6198.** If "No," enter the loss on Form 1040, line 12, and on Schedule SE, Part I, line 2 (or Form 1041, line 6).

Part III Cost of Goods Sold and/or Operations (See Schedule C Instructions for Part III)

1 Inventory at beginning of year (if different from last year's closing inventory, attach explanation)	1	
2 Purchases less cost of items withdrawn for personal use	2	
3 Cost of labor (do not include salary paid to yourself)	3	
4 Materials and supplies	4	
5 Other costs	5	
6 Add lines 1 through 5	6	
7 Less: Inventory at end of year	7	
8 **Cost of goods sold and/or operations.** Subtract line 7 from line 6. Enter here and in Part I, line 2, above. .	8	

For Paperwork Reduction Act Notice, see Form 1040 Instructions. | Schedule C (Form 1040) 1984

Exhibit 7.5

PARTNERSHIP AGREEMENT

This agreement made and entered into this   , day of   , 19   , between   of   , City of   , County of   , State of   , and   of   , City of   , County of   , State of   , hereinafter referred to as "Partners."

WITNESSETH:

WHEREAS, the partners desire to form a business association to pursue common business goals, and

WHEREAS, the partners desire to enter into a partnership agreement as the most advantageous business form for their mutual purposes.

NOW, THEREFORE, IT IS MUTUALLY AGREED AS FOLLOWS:

1. That a partnership shall be formed for the purpose of producing musical acts, consultation, production, tour coordination and publishing.

2. That the name of the partnership shall be   and its offices will be located at   , City of   , County of   , State of

3. That each partner shall apply all of his experience, training, and ability in discharging his assigned functions in the partnership and in the performance of all work that may be necessary or advantageous to further business interest of the partnership.

4. That each partner shall contribute five thousand and no/100 ($5,000.00) dollars before or at the execution of this agreement to be used by the partnership to establish its capital position. Any additional contribution required by the partners shall be determined and established only in accordance with the terms of this agreement. All initial capital contributions shall be made to the partnership capital account. The failure by one partner to contribute the specified capital shall result in an immediate return to the contributing partner of any capital contributed to date.

5. If any partner shall furnish to the partnership capital, an amount in excess of his required share, he shall receive interest at the rate of six (6%) percent yearly on the excess contribution, payable at the end of each fiscal year before any profits are distributed. Any interest earned on the partner's capital accounts shall not be paid by the partnership or be subject to withdrawal by the partner, but shall be retained as property of the partnership and shall be added to the capital of the partnership.

6. Partnership money received from all sources shall be deposited in the name of the partnership and all money withdrawn from the partnership account shall be by a check drawn and signed by   and counter-signed by

7. Separate money or funds of any partner or of a client or customer of the partnership that shall come under the separate control of a partner, shall be deposited in separate trust accounts for the benefit of the party owning the funds, with the partnership or an individual partner serving as trustee. Comingling of funds controlled by a party with that party's private funds shall be prohibited under all circumstances, and this prohibition shall be strictly construed against the party acting in a fiduciary capacity in holding any other party's funds.

8. The rental of the buildings where the partnership business shall be maintained, and the cost of repairs and alterations, all rates, taxes, payments for insurance, and other expenses in respect to the buildings used by the partnership, and the wages for all persons employed by the partnership are all to become payable on the account of the partnership. All losses incurred shall be paid out of the capital of the partnership or the profits arising from the partnership business, or, if both shall be deficient, by the partners on a pro rata basis, in proportion to their original contributions, as provided in this agreement.

9. The partners shall not enter into any bond or become surety, security, bail or cosigner for any person, partnership or corporation, or knowingly condone anything whereby the partnership property may be attached or taken in execution, without the written consent of the other partners.

10. Each partner shall punctually pay his separate debts and indemnify the other partners and the capital and property of the partnership against his separate debts and all expenses relating to the partnership.

11. Books of account shall be maintained by the partners, and proper entries shall be made of all sales, purchases, receipts, payments, transactions, and property of the partnership, and the books of accounts and all records of the partnership shall be retained at the principal place of business as specified in this agreement. Each partner shall have free access at all times to all books and records maintained relative to the partnership business.

12. The fiscal year of the partnership shall be from January 1 to December 31 of each year. On the 1st day of January, commencing in 19   , and on the 1st day of January in each succeeding year, a general accounting shall be made and taken by the partners of all sales, purchases, receipts, payments and transactions of the partnership during the preceding fiscal year, and of all the capital property and current liabilities of the partnership. The general accounting shall be written in the partnership account books and signed in each book by each partner immediately after it is completed. After the signature of each partner is entered, each partner shall keep one of the books and shall be bound by every account, except that if any manifest error is found by any partner and shown to the other partners within six (6) months after the error shall have been noted by all of them, the error shall be rectified.

13. The partners shall be liable for and shall discharge equally among them all expenses required for the maintenance and operation of the partnership business at all times. All profits that shall arise from the partnership business shall be divided equally among the partners, and all losses that the partnership shall incur by bad debts or otherwise shall be borne and paid equally by all partners.

The net profits or losses shall be determined within thirty (30) days thereafter. Losses of the partnership caused by the willful neglect or default, the gross negligent conduct, including acts and failures to act, or the intentional negligent conduct, of any partner which are not mere mistake or error shall be borne solely and made good by the partner causing the loss.

14. Each partner shall be at liberty to draw out of the business in anticipation of the expected profits any sums that may be mutually agreed and the sums are to be drawn only after there has been entered in the books of the partnership the terms of agreement, giving the date, the amount to be drawn by the respective partners, the times at which the sums shall be drawn, and any other conditions or matters mutually agreed on. The signatures of each partner shall be affixed on each consent form. The total sum of the advanced draw for each partner shall be deducted from the sum that partner is entitled to under the distribution of profits as provided in this agreement.

15. No partner shall receive any salary from the partnership, and the only compensation to be paid shall be as provided in this agreement.

16. In the event any partner shall desire to retire from the partnership, he shall give thirty (30) days' notice in writing to the other partner and the continuing partner shall pay to the retiring partner at the termination of the thirty (30) days' notice the value of the interest of the retiring partner in the partnership. The value shall be determined by a closing of the books and a rendition of the appropriate profit and loss, trial balance, and balance sheet statements.

17. On the retirement of any partner, the continuing partner shall be at liberty if he so desires, to retain all trade names designating the firm name used, and each partner shall be reasonably required for effectuating an amicable retirement.

18. In the event of the death of one partner, the legal representative of the deceased partner shall remain as a partner in the firm, except that the exercising of the right of the part of the representative of the deceased partner shall not continue for a period in excess of twelve (12) months, even though under the terms hereof, a greater period of time is provided before the termination of this agreement. The original rights of the partners herein shall accrue to their heirs, executors or assigns.

19. No partner shall hire or dismiss any person in the employment of the partnership without the consent of the other partners, except in cases of gross misconduct by the employee.

20. No partner shall compound, release or discharge any debt that shall be due or owing to the partnership, without receiving the full amount thereof, unless that partner obtains the prior written consent of the other partners to the discharge of the indebtedness.

21. No partner shall, during the continuance of the partnership or for five (5) years after its designation by any means, divulge to any person not a member of the firm any trade secrets or special information employed in or conducive to the partnership business and, which may come to his knowledge in the course of this partnership, without the consent in writing of the other partners, or of the other partners' heirs, administrators or assigns.

22. The partnership shall commence on the date of this agreement and shall continue thereafter for an indefinite period, to expire only by operation of law, by the giving of thirty (30) days written notice by a partner desiring to terminate this agreement or by mutual written consent of the parties or by the operation of the provisions of this agreement.

23. All partners are engaged in other business ventures, and no partner shall be required to devote all of his business time to the affairs of the partnership but each partner shall devote as much time to the business as he shall deem necessary for the proper and efficient conduct of the partnership business.

24. Each partner shall disclose to the other partners all business activities in which he has any interest whatever, and he shall conduct all transactions with the partnership in good faith and in a fiduciary capacity.

25. The partners shall not have to contribute any additional capital to the partnership to that required under this agreement, except as follows:

A. Each partner shall be required to contribute a proportionate share in additional contributions if the fiscal year closes with an insufficiency in the capital account or profits of the partnership to meet current expenses, or

B. The capital account falls below five hundred and no/100 ($500.00) dollars for a period of three (3) months.

26. If any difference shall arise between or among the partners as to their rights or liabilities under this agreement, or under any instrument made in furtherance of the partnership business, the difference shall be determined and the instrument shall be settled by the American Arbitration Association acting as arbitrator, and its decision shall be final as to the contents and interpretations of the instrument and as to the proper mode of carrying the provision into effect.

27. Where it shall appear to the partners that this agreement, or any terms and conditions contained herein, are in anyway ineffective or deficient, or not expressed as originally intended, and any alteration or addition shall be deemed necessary, the partners will enter into, execute, and perform all further deeds and instruments as their counsel shall advise. Any addition, alteration, or modification shall be in writing, and any oral agreement shall be ineffective.

28. If any of the parties violate any of the foregoing agreements, the other party may at his option dissolve this partnership by giving notice of election to the other party within thirty (30) days after acquiring the knowledge of such violation.

29. This agreement shall be construed and enforced in accordance with the laws of the State of   and be binding upon the parties, their heirs, executions, successors and assigns.

IN WITNESS WHEREOF, the parties have executed this agreement at   , the day and year first above written.

WITNESSES:

_____   _____

_____   _____

Exhibit 7.6

SCHEDULE K-1 (Form 1065) Department of the Treasury Internal Revenue Service	**Partner's Share of Income, Credits, Deductions, etc.** For calendar year 1984 or fiscal year beginning _____, 1984, and ending _____, 19____	OMB No. 1545-0099 **1984**

Partner's identifying number ▶ | **Partnership's identifying number ▶**

Partner's name, address, and ZIP code | Partnership's name, address, and ZIP code

A Is partner a general partner (see page 3 of Instructions for Form 1065)? . . . . ☐ Yes ☐ No

B Partner's share of liabilities (see page 10 of Instructions for Form 1065):
Nonrecourse . . . . $_____
Other . . . . $_____

C What type of entity is this partner? ▶ _____

D Enter partner's percentage of:

	(i) Before decrease or termination	**(ii)** End of year
Profit sharing	_____%	_____%
Loss sharing	_____%	_____%
Ownership of capital	_____%	_____%

E IRS Center where partnership filed return ▶ _____

F Reconciliation of partner's capital account:

(a) Capital account at beginning of year	(b) Capital contributed during year	(c) Ordinary income (loss) from line 1 below	(d) Income not included in column (c), plus nontaxable income	(e) Losses not included in column (c), plus unallowable deductions	(f) Withdrawals and distributions	(g) Capital account at end of year

(a) Distributive share item	(b) Amount	(c) 1040 filers enter the amount in column (b) on:

Income (Loss)

1	Ordinary income (loss)		Sch. E, Part II, col. (d) or (e)
2	Guaranteed payments		Sch. E, Part II, column (e)
3	Dividends qualifying for exclusion		Sch. B, Part II, line 4
4	Net short-term capital gain (loss)		Sch. D, line 4, col. f. or g.
5	Net long-term capital gain (loss)		Sch. D, line 12, col. f. or g. (See Partner's Instructions for Schedule K-1 (Form 1065))
6	Net gain (loss) from involuntary conversions due to casualty or theft .		
7	Other net gain (loss) under section 1231		Form 4797, line 1
8	Other (attach schedule)		(Enter on applicable lines of your return)

Deductions

9	Charitable contributions: 50% _____, 30% _____, 20% _____		See Form 1040 instructions (See Partner's Instructions for Schedule K-1 (Form 1065))
10	Expense deduction for recovery property (section 179)		
11a	Payments for partner to an IRA		See Form 1040 instructions
b	Payments for partner to a Keogh Plan (Type of plan ▶ _____) . .		Form 1040, line 27
c	Payments for partner to Simplified Employee Pension (SEP)		Form 1040, line 27
12	Other (attach schedule)		(Enter on applicable lines of your return)

Credits

13	Jobs credit		Form 5884
14	Credit for alcohol used as fuel		Form 6478
15	Credit for income tax withheld		See Form 1040 instructions
16	Other (attach schedule)		(Enter on applicable lines of your return)

Self-employment

17a	Net earnings (loss) from self-employment		Sch. SE, Part I
b	Gross farming or fishing income		(See Partner's Instructions for Schedule K-1 (Form 1065))
c	Gross nonfarm income		(See Partner's Instructions for Schedule K-1 (Form 1065))

Tax Preference Items

18a	Accelerated depreciation on nonrecovery real property or 15-year or 18-year real property.		Form 6251, line 4c
b	Accelerated depreciation on leased personal property or leased recovery property other than 15-year or 18-year real property		Form 6251, line 4d
c	Depletion (other than oil and gas)		Form 6251, line 4i
d (1)	Gross income from oil, gas, and geothermal properties		See Form 6251 instructions
(2)	Deductions allocable to oil, gas, and geothermal properties . . .		See Form 6251 instructions
e (1)	Qualified investment income included in line 1 above		(See Partner's Instructions for Schedule K-1 (Form 1065))
(2)	Qualified investment expenses included in line 1 above		(See Partner's Instructions for Schedule K-1 (Form 1065))
f	Other (attach schedule)		(See Partner's Instructions for Schedule K-1 (Form 1065))

For Paperwork Reduction Act Notice, see Form 1065 Instructions. | **Schedule K-1 (Form 1065) 1984**

	(a) Distributive share item	(b) Amount	(c) 1040 filers enter the amount in column (b) on:
Investment Interest	**19 a** Interest expense on:		
	(1) Investment debts incurred before 12/17/69		Form 4952, line 1
	(2) Investment debts incurred before 9/11/75, but after 12/16/69		Form 4952, line 15
	(3) Investment debts incurred after 9/10/75		Form 4952, line 5
	b (1) Investment income included in line 1 (not (1) above) . .		(See Partner's Instructions for Schedule K-1 (Form 1065))
	(2) Investment expenses included in line 1 (not (1) above). . . .		(See Partner's Instructions for Schedule K-1 (Form 1065))
	c (1) Income from "net lease property" included in line 1 (not (1) above). . .		(See Partner's Instructions for Schedule K-1 (Form 1065))
	(2) Expenses from "net lease property" included in line 1 (not (1) above) . . .		(See Partner's Instructions for Schedule K-1 (Form 1065))
Foreign Taxes	**20 a** Type of income		Form 1116, Check boxes
	b Name of foreign country or U.S. possession		Form 1116, Part I
	c Total gross income from sources outside the U.S. (attach schedule) .		Form 1116, Part I
	d Total applicable deductions and losses (attach schedule)		Form 1116, Part I
	e Total foreign taxes (check one): ► ☐ Paid ☐ Accrued		Form 1116, Part II
	f Reduction in taxes available for credit (attach schedule).		Form 1116, Part III
	g Other (attach schedule)		Form 1116 Instructions
Other	**21** Other items and amounts not included in lines 1 through 20g and 22 and 23 that are required to be reported separately to you.		(See Partner's Instructions for Schedule K-1 (Form 1065))
Property Eligible for Investment Credit	**22** Regular Percentage — Unadjusted basis of new recovery property	**a** 3-Year . . .	Form 3468, line 1(a)
		b Other . . .	Form 3468, line 1(b)
	Unadjusted basis of used recovery property	**c** 3-Year . . .	Form 3468, line 1(c)
		d Other . . .	Form 3468, line 1(d)
	Section 48(q) Election to Reduce Credit (Instead of Adjusting Basis) — Unadjusted basis of new recovery property	**e** 3-year . . .	Form 3468, line 1(e)
		f Other . . .	Form 3468, line 1(f)
	Unadjusted basis of used recovery property	**g** 3-year . . .	Form 3468, line 1(g)
		h Other . . .	Form 3468, line 1(h)
	i Other (see instructions for Schedule K-1 (Form 1065) in the Instructions for Form 1065)		(See Partner's Instructions for Schedule K-1 (Form 1065))

	23 Properties:	A	B	C	
Property Subject to Recapture of Investment Credit	**a** Description of property (State whether recovery or nonrecovery property. If recovery property, state whether regular percentage method or section 48(q) election used.)				Form 4255, top
	b Date placed in service				Form 4255, line 2
	c Cost or other basis				Form 4255, line 3
	d Class of recovery property or original estimated useful life				Form 4255, line 4
	e Date item ceased to be investment credit property				Form 4255, line 8

proprietorship is individually and personally liable, the gravity of potential liability increases in the partnership since partners can bind other partners by their behavior. The intent of the individual partner is irrelevant, and as a result, a completely honorable man or woman, with never a thought of evil, criminality, or fraud, can be held accountable jointly and singularly for the act of a less-than-scrupulous partner. From this scenario, an obvious suggestion emerges: *Before relying on another, know who your partner really is!* A partnership can be a risky venture in both economic and human terms.

In addition, with diverse backgrounds and personalities, disagreements in a management context are far more frequent. Other less favorable aspects of the partnership consist of a lack of business continuity in the event of a partner's death and sometimes stern tax treatment by Internal Revenue.

D. Theoretical and Practical Issues in Formation and Agreement

The greatest area of regulation and contractual argument really deals with the powers, duties, and authority of the overall partnership and those who claim to be partners. A clearly elucidated agreement at the origination of the partnership should cover the following queries:

1. What is the purpose of the partnership?
2. How long should this partnership last?
3. What are the duties, powers, and rights of the various partners?
4. How much will each partner contribute economically to the partnership?
5. How much, and in what specific manner, will the profits be divided and distributed?
6. What impact or effect will the sale or transfer of an individual partner's interest have upon the partnership's operation?

7. How are new partners admitted?
8. How is the partnership dissolved?
9. What method of accounting does the partnership desire?

E. The General Partner: Rights and Liabilities

Prevention of disagreements is most likely if all parties are clearly apprised of their rights and liabilities. Clients considering the partnership as a business entity must be resolutely instructed in the nature of a "fiduciary" relationship that each partner owes to each other. A fiduciary relationship demands honesty, integrity, and loyalty in all partnership dealings, including the reporting of accrued income, tax liabilities, record keeping, and profit distribution. The opportunities for fraudulent behavior are many, but a new sentencing harshness toward white-collar crimes may "instill" more ethics and values in business practice. Partners must be made fully aware of their solemn duties to one another. Partners also must be apprised of their "powers" as agents to bind all other partners by their acts or deeds. A partner may bind another partner by his or her tortious conduct (e.g., assaults, malpractice, negligence); undertakings; acquisition of capital or promissory notes; or conveyances of real property.

The critical importance of understanding this interrelationship or dependence of partners cannot be emphasized enough. Since partners invest money in the business and manage the business operation, they all have authority to act for the partnership. Each partner will be liable for partnership obligations arising from the acts of other partners.

F. Procedural Steps in Formation: Partnership

1. Evaluate the nature of the business for purpose and legality.
2. Formulate a legal agreement, outlining rights and liabilities of general partners and delineating powers, purposes, and administrative structure of the partnership.
3. File appropriate partnership certificates and filing fees, if required by law.
4. File appropriate tax forms on required dates.

G. Special Situation: Limited Partnership

1. General description

In seeking partners for a business enterprise, one continual drawback in the sale of the proposition is the nature of the fiduciary liability of all *general* partners to each other for each other's wrongdoing or errors in judgment. Individuals with capital and an idea that they might like to participate are hesitant to put their lives on the line, to gamble so much when they have neither the time nor the interest in the eventual management of the partnership. Hence, these questions arise: Can an individual participate in a limited fashion in the operation of a business partnership and in that way limit his or her eventual liability? Can a person just give money and hope to reap profits, while not being liable for any misdeeds of the general partners? State legislatures have answered both queries affirmatively and created a statutory hybrid: *the limited partnership.*

2. Nature of limited liability

While a variety of issues emerge under this form of business choice, the magic of this legislative invention is in its practicality—that is, it alleviates the fear in an investor's mind of general unlimited legal liability for the partnership. The hesitancy to join in is vanquished since limited partners are not liable as general partners, and their liability to the limited partnership is limited to the amount stated in the certificate of limited partnership. In sum, the limited partner has limited his or her eventual or potential risks!

H. Procedural Steps in Formation of a Limited Partnership

1. Evaluate the nature of the limited partnership for purpose and legality.
2. Formulate a legal agreement outlining rights, liabilities, and duties of partners, both general and limited, and delineating powers, purposes, and administrative structure of the limited partnership. (See exhibit 7.7.)

Exhibit 7.7

AGREEMENT OF LIMITED PARTNERSHIP
OF

_____

THIS AGREEMENT, dated as of November 1, 1977, among
("General Partner")
and
("Limited Partner")

W I T N E S S E T H:

WHEREAS, the parties hereto desire to form a Limited Partnership pursuant to the Uniform Limited Partnership Act for the purpose of holding, managing and retaining or disposing of any real property and other assests

and

WHEREAS, _____ is willing to act as General Partner of such Limited Partnership;

NOW, THEREFORE, it is agreed as follows:

1. The parties hereby associate themselves as partners in a Limited Partnership, under the partnership name of _____
_____.

2. The business of the partnership will be to hold, lease, manage and retain or dispose of real estate, to hold, manage and dispose of personal property, and to do such other acts and engage in such other business as the general partner in his sole discretion deems beneficial to the partnership.

3. The principal office of the partnership shall be maintained at such place within or without the State of _____ as the General Partner may determine from time to time.

4. The term of the partnership shall commence as of the date of this Agreement, and shall terminate on such date as the General Partner shall determine.

5. _____ shall be the General Partner of the partnership. A surety bond shall not be required. The management, operation and policy of the partnership shall be vested in the General Partner. The General Partner shall have the power by himself, on behalf and in the name of the partnership, to carry out and implement the purposes of the partnership and act on its behalf.

6. All of the partners will herewith convey to the partnership by way of capital contribution thereto, (their respective interests in)

7. The net proceeds realized on the liquidation of the assets of the partnership and the net profits therefrom shall be divided among the partners in proportion to their capital contributions.

8. The General Partner and the Limited Partners shall not be required to make any additional contribution to the capital of the partnership. An individual capital account shall be maintained for each partner which shall consist of his capital contribution, decreased by any capital distribution to him.

9. The term "net profits" of the partnership, as used herein, shall mean the net profit derived from the property owned by the partnership as ascertained through standard accounting practices, except that if the General Partner shall so determine, a reasonable reserve for real estate taxes and any other contingencies of the partnership shall be deducted.

10. The General Partner shall devote such time to the partnership as shall be required for its success. No Limited Partner shall participate in the management of the partnership business.

11. The partnership shall have the power to manage, maintain, develop, repair, improve and subdivide its property, to grant options for the sale of the property, for a period not exceeding one year; to foreclose mortgages and bid on property under foreclosure or take title to property by conveyance in lieu of foreclosure; to continue mortgage investments after maturity, either with or without renewal or extension upon such terms as the General Partner shall deem advisable; to consent to the modification, renewal or extension of any note, bond or mortgage owned by the partnership; to borrow money for the purposes of paying expenses of the partnership or otherwise, and to give security therefor, all upon such terms and for such periods as the General Partner shall deem advisable; to join with any Limited Partner or other person for the development of the property of the partnership; and to perform any other act which may be determined by the General Partner to be in the interests of the partnership in order to effect a prompt liquidation of the assests of the partnership and result in a distribution of the proceeds among the partners as promptly as practicable.

12. All of the partners hereby consent to the employment, when and if required, of such brokers, managing and other agents, accountants, and attorneys as the General Partner may determine from time to time.

13. All funds of the partnership shall be deposited in such bank account or accounts as shall be designated by the General Partner. Withdrawals from any such bank accounts or accounts shall be made upon such signature or signatures as the General Partner may designate.

14. Any deed, bill of sale, mortgage, assignment of mortgage, security agreement, lease, contract of sale, or other commitment purporting to convey or encumber the interest of the partnership as to all or any portion of any real or personal property at any time held in its name shall be signed by the General Partner and such other person or persons, if any, as the

General Partner may designate. No person dealing with the partnership shall be required to inquire in to the authority of the General Partner to sign any document pursuant to the provisions of this paragraph.

15. The partnership shall maintain full and accurate books in such place either within or without the State of_____ as shall be designated for such purposes by the General Partner, and all partners shall have the right to inspect, copy and examine such books at reasonable times. The books shall be closed and balanced at the end of each calendar year. Annual statements showing the partnership profits and expenses for the calendar year and indicating each partner's share in the same shall be prepared by the partnership and distributed to all the partners within a reasonable time after the close of each calendar year.

16. The death of a General or Limited Partner shall not dissolve or terminate the partnership. In the event of death, the deceased partner's personal representatives shall have all the rights of a Limited Partner in the partnership to the extent of the deceased partner's interest therein, subject to the terms and conditions of this Agreement.

17. In the event of the dissolution and termination of the partnership, the General Partner shall proceed with the liquidation of the partnership; and the proceeds of such liquidation shall be applied and distributed in the following order of priority:

(a) To the payment of the debts and liabilities of the partnership and the expenses of liquidation.

(b) To the setting up of any reserves which the General Partner may deem reasonably necessary for any contingent or unforseen liabilities or obligations of the partnership or the General Partner arising out of or in connection with the partnership.

(c) Any balance remaining shall be distributed among all Partners, General and Limited, in proportion to their respective capital accounts.

18. Additional _____ may be admitted as Limited Partners upon the approval of all other partners, signing the Limited Partnership Agreement, and making a capital contribution.

19. The Limited Partners may continue the business on the death, retirement or insanity of the General Partner, provided a suitable substitute General Partner acceptable to all remaining partners is willing to act as such General Partner.

20. This Agreement shall be binding upon the parties hereto and their heirs, legatees, successors or assigns.

21. This Agreement and the rights hereunder of the parties hereto shall be interpreted in accordance with the laws of the State of _____.

IN WITNESS WHEREOF, the parties hereto have executed this Agreement as of the day and year first above written.

GENERAL PARTNER:

_____   _____ L.S.)

LIMITED PARTNERS:

_____   _____ L.S.)

_____   _____ L.S.)

3. File appropriate limited partnership certificate and pay required fees.
4. File necessary tax forms on required dates.

IV. CORPORATIONS

A. General Description

Corporations are human inventions, with far less human responsibility than individuals have both in their design and in their eventual liability. Corporations are unique entities that exist apart from the individuals who own them. The corporation is probably the most familiar business organization to the general population, since corporations are America's largest source of employment opportunities. Consider the Du Pont Corporation. Could the state of Delaware exist without it? As the state's largest employer, the Du Pont Corporation is a major cog in the economic wheel of Delaware and, as well, a huge contributor to the state treasury. Regardless of how much citizens respect the Du Pont Corporation, or become enraged at the environmental damage this industrial corporation may cause. Delaware could not continue on without it! While this example is grandiose in scale, it is perfect testimony to the dramatic effect of the "corporate entity" on the general welfare of any community, even though the corporation does not live, breathe, or think. Even more critically, why does Du Pont choose to be a corporation? Why did the company change from a family enterprise, very similar to a proprietorship in its earlier days, to a corporation? What benefits or advantages exist in choosing the corporate form?

B. Positive Aspects of the Corporate Form

1. Perpetual duration

Corporations have a perpetual life, unlike other business organizations.

2. Transferability of interests

Corporate interests, as evidenced by stock shares, are fully transferable without destroying the underlying corporate entity.

3. Limited liability

Corporate shareholders and, in most circumstances, officers, directors, and other management parties are not personally responsible for the criminal acts or civil wrongs of a corporation. Compared to other business forms, limited liability exists.

4. Powers in articles and bylaws

Corporate powers are clearly enunciated in the articles of incorporation, which are approved by the appropriate jurisdiction. In addition, internal policy of the corporation is also well established in the bylaws of the corporation.

5. Management and control

The basic hallmark of all corporations is centralized thinking and policy. Power is not readily diffused to the lower echelons. The desire for consistency, continuity, and regularity of corporate policy and production is enhanced by centralized management, typically corporate officers and a board of directors.

6. Tax Treatment

Of all the business forms, the corporation can be taxed at the lowest rates. As of January 1, 1985, the income-tax rates on companies were as follows:

TAXABLE INCOME (DOLLARS)	RATE OF TAX
Up to 25,000	15%
25,000–50,000	18
50,000–75,000	30
75,000–100,000	40
Over 100,000	46

When compared to individual tax rates, the smaller business truly does receive preferred tax liability.

Other tax advantages include the corporation's ability to raise capital through the sale or exchange of its own stock without owing tax on that exchange. A variety of tax techniques exist that effectively shelter income within the corporation from taxation, such as intrafamily transfers, salaries, investment credits, benefit and wage packages, and incentives to invest in other corporations and receive limited tax liability on dividend disbursements.

7. Investment potential and business growth

Corporations are attractive to investors for good reasons. A simple purchase of stock that results in a short- or long-term gain receives favorable tax rates. Corporations can also pay dividends that still receive some tax advantage. The possibilities of striking gains on the investment, as well as losses, exist on corporate investments.

8. Social and political powers

Depending on size, economic base, and general business intentions, a corporation can be held in high regard and effectively move and shift the world in which it exists. Corporate entities have a strong record of legislative lobbying on both the national and federal level. In this age of economic competition, corporations are being ardently sought out by states, municipalities, and counties, which view the corporation as the hub of any plans for economic development.

C. Negative Aspects of the Corporate Form

1. Extent of regulation

As evidenced by the exhibits in this chapter, the corporate form is besieged by mounds of paperwork. Aside from the legal formalities of creation, the corporation is a regular contributor to the waves of statistics and data collected by the U.S. government. Frequent reports are required, on a monthly, semiannual, and annual basis on matters such as inventory, purchase orders of durable goods, investment capital, profits and losses, hiring practices, and environmental discharge. The governmental burden of regulations is not well liked by corporate America, but that burden must be balanced against the need for the society to know about such topics as equal-opportunity hiring and the nature of industrial discharges into our streams and rivers.

2. Legal formalities in daily operations

The corporation is not only answerable to its officers and its directors but also must give deference to every shareholder no matter how small his or her percentage of ownership. In the purest sense, anyone who owns a share of a corporation is a part owner. This basic relationship fosters the capitalistic system. This basic relationship is also similar to a "consumer" transaction, and as a result, a massive amount of regulations exist to protect that consumer. The corporation naturally wants to respond to its investors, but in case it forgets, the government mandates that it does. Those formalities of operations include:

Annual meetings	Corporate records
Corporate accounting practices	Corporate bylaws
Employer identification numbers	Annual reports and financial statements
Tax returns	Securities statements/prospectives
Corporate seals, stationery, and bills	Proxy documentation

The preceding examples, while not comprehensive, are intended to demonstrate that the corporate form does require expenditures of time, money, and personnel on meeting the demands of regulation and oversight.

3. Tax treatment

While the smaller business receives a highly favorable tax rate, as outlined in the previous section, corporations of a substantial size may not fare as well. The importance of tax planning, strategies, and shelters increase in the corporate form. Equally important is the fact that owners of a corporation must file two tax returns, both individual and corporate. The tax counsel costs in this form of business choice can be quite substantial.

4. Social and political powers

The influence a corporation has on the surrounding environment can be extremely negative. Consider the image problems suffered by Hooker Chemical Company of New York, which had the unpleasant fate of being almost synonymous with the name Love Canal. While no argument on merits is warranted here, it is plain that Hooker's prestige was thoroughly devastated in that situation, its political impact was severely diminished, and its image reduced to no better than that of a corporate criminal. Hooker has demonstrated that with the power to affect both people and the environment around them comes also the very harsh, and in the minds of management sometimes unfair, demand for total corporate responsibility.

D. Preincorporation Problems

1. Promoters: duty owed to the corporation

All things in life begin as ideas. Hence, the idea to have a company begins with a product or a service. Someone has to sell that product or service in order to acquire investment capital and funds to effect the formation of the corporation. *Promoters* are those persons who undertake to form the corporation and procure for it the rights, instrumentalities, and capital. Promoters are generally the incorporators of the eventual corporation. As a result of their relationship to themselves and other interested parties in the business form, they are bound to the following:

- ☐ To act as a fiduciary and agent
- ☐ To not profit by fraud or breach of trust between others in the promotion of the corporation, i.e., investors and potential officers or directors
- ☐ To disclose all material facts and issues about the corporation to potential investors
- ☐ To bind the corporation to only fair and reasonable practices between the corporation and other parties
- ☐ To not hold themselves out as agents for the corporation

A brief inspection of promoter's rights and liabilities in all jurisdictions indicate that a promoter must deal ethically and fairly with all. Common sense should alert the average person to potential frauds or swindles. But every day someone is suckered into another deal "made in heaven."

E. Formation of the Business Corporation

As noted thus far, the extent of regulations and formality is most extensive in the corporate form. As a result, paralegals will spend sizable time in their careers working in these procedural and mechanical steps. In particular, close attention should be given to the construction of a form file, which expedites the procedures of incorporation. An overview with substantive explanations and appropriate references to forms and exhibits follows.

1. Selection of a registered agent

A corporation should decide initially who its registered agent will be, whose main function is to receive service of process and other official communications from state agencies. The name and office address of that agent must be eventually included in the articles of incorporation. Also included for future reference and use is a check list for change of registered agent (exhibit 7.8).

2. Drafting articles of incorporation

The articles of incorporation must provide the state with information on various topics.

a. CHOICE OF CORPORATE NAME

In a world where there are only so many names to go around, a choice of a name that is not "confusingly similar" to another corporation's name is not an easy task. Consider the pending lawsuit in the Delaware Court of Chancery by the Bank of Delaware against The First National Bank of Delaware. Confusingly similar?

b. PURPOSES OF THE CORPORATION

The articles are required to lucidly outline all real and potential powers the corporation desires to exercise. Another word for *powers* is *objectives*. Generally powers can be to exercise any "lawful business," including manufacturing, research, development, processing, professional growth, and charitable or nonprofit purposes.

c. REGISTERED AGENT

As discussed, include name and office address.

Exhibit 7.8*

Billing No. _____   Attorney _____

CHECKLIST FOR CHANGE OF REGISTERED OFFICE
AND REGISTERED AGENT OF

_____

Review Bylaws to see if amendment of registered or principal office, is required; use Checklist for Amendment of Bylaws _____

Prepare documents:
       Board action: Minutes _____ Waiver _____ Notice _____ Consent _____
       Statement of Change of Registered Office and Registered
       Agent ("Statement") [or Article of Amendment] _____

Prepare letters and memo:
       Memo to lawyer _____
       Client forwarding documents for signature _____
       Secretary of State filing Statement _____
       Client forwarding "Filed" Statement _____

Review documents and letters _____

Forward drafts to lawyer for approval _____

Forward documents to client for adoption and signature _____

Receive documents from client _____

Review and complete documents _____

Photocopy minutes (and notice or waiver of notice) or consent for file _____

File minutes or consent in file and in original or duplicate minute book _____

File 2 executed copies of Statement with Secretary of State _____

Receive 1 copy of Statement from Secretary of State stamped "Filed" _____

Photocopy Statement for file and duplicate minute book _____

File Statement in file and in original or duplicate minute book _____

Forward original or copies of Statement to client _____

Update Corporation Data Sheet _____

Update list of corporations to receive reminder letters re annual reports _____

Update annual meeting tickler if address of principal office is changed _____

---

* Excerpted from *Working with Legal Assistants: A Team Approach for Lawyers and Legal Assistants*, Paul G. Ulrich and Robert S. Mucklestone, eds. Reprinted with permission of the American Bar Association.

d. DURATION

While a corporation is inherently perpetual, its duration can be designated and limited.

e. CAPITAL STOCK STRUCTURE

The articles also require a statement on the aggregate number of shares authorized to be issued and their par or no-par value. Further information is also required on the "classes" of stock, whether common, preferred, or other and any other preferences, qualifications, limitations, restrictions, or rights concerning those shares. More specifically, the articles should delineate voting rights in stock, dividend/liquidation preferences, and the general rules on preemption.

f. DIRECTORS

The articles must divulge the number, name, and address of each director.

g. Miscellaneous Provisions

Most states also allow the incorporators to include provisions that relate to the internal affairs of the corporation.

3. Filing articles of incorporation

File the required forms and all necessary fees with the department of state. An example of an articles of incorporation form is in exhibit 7.9. Exhibit 7.10 shows the check list for amendment of articles of incorporation. Future use of this form is likely since the corporation frequently changes the essential contents of its original articles. Examples of change entail new addresses for agents and incorporators and possibly a change in business purpose or powers, which often occurs in a diversified industry. Also to be submitted to the secretary of state is the application to conduct business as a corporation.

Exhibit 7.9

Filed this _____ day of _____
_____, 19 ____.

Commonwealth of
Department of State

_____ (Line for numbering)

Articles of
Incorporation—
Domestic Business Corporation

**COMMONWEALTH OF
DEPARTMENT OF STATE
CORPORATION BUREAU**

Secretary of the Commonwealth

(Box for Certification)

In compliance with the requirements of section 204 of the Business Corporation Law, act of May 5, 1933 (P.L. 364) (15 P.S. §1204) the undersigned, desiring to be incorporated as a business corporation, hereby certifies (certify) that:

1. The name of the corporation is:

_____

2. The location and post office address of the initial registered office of the corporation in this Commonwealth is:

_____
(NUMBER)   (STREET)

_____
(CITY)   (ZIP CODE)

3. The corporation is incorporated under the Business Corporation Law of the Commonwealth of _____ for the following purpose or purposes:

4. The term for which the corporation is to exist is: _____

5. The aggregate number of shares which the corporation shall have authority to issue is:

6. The name(s) and post office address(es) of each incorporation(s) and the number and class of shares subscribed by such incorporation(s) is (are):

NAME	ADDRESS (including street and number if any)	NUMBER AND CLASS OF SHARES

IN TESTIMONY WHEREOF, the incorporator(s) has (have) signed and sealed these Articles of Incorporation this _____ day of _____ , 19 _____ .

_____ (SEAL)   _____ (SEAL)

_____ (SEAL)

Instructions for Completion of Form

A. For general instructions relating to the incorporation of business corporations see   Code Ch.   (relating to business corporations generally). These instructions relate to such matters as corporate name, stated purposes, term of existence, authorized share structure and related authority of the board of directors, inclusion of names of first directors in the Articles of Incorporation, optional provisions on cumulative voting for election of directors, etc.

B. One or more corporations or natural persons of full age may incorporate a business corporation.

C. Optional provisions required or authorized by law may be added as Paragraphs 7, 8, 9 . . . etc.

D. The following shall accompany this form:

   (1) Three copies of Form DSCB:BCL—206 (Registry Statement Domestic or Foreign Business Corporation).

   (2) Any necessary copies of Form DSCB:17.2 (Consent to Appropriation of Name) or Form DSCB:17.3 (Consent to Use of Similar Name).

   (3) Any necessary governmental approvals.

E. BCL §205 requires that the incorporators shall advertise their intention to file or the corporation shall advertise the filing of articles of incorporation. Proofs of publication of such advertising should not be delivered to the Department, but should be filed with the minutes of the corporation.

4. Advertisement of the articles of incorporation

Some jurisdictions require that notice of an intention to formulate the corporation be advertised in local newspapers or legal publications, in the county in which the registered office is located.

5. Issuance of a certificate of incorporation

If the submission of all necessary documents is complete and correct in content, a certificate from the proper state agency comes forth, which indicates the existence and the validity of the corporation. The certificate should be maintained in the corporate record book.

6. Organizational meeting

At this stage, assuming directors have been named, initial issues are resolved, such as:

a. Ratification of incorporate acts

b. Election of officers

c. Approval of bank accounts and supply requisitions

d. Accept the subscription of shares

e. Draft and formulate bylaws

The last task listed above is a critical step in the operation of a corporation and will be treated at length in the next section. An example of the minutes from such an organizational meeting is provided in exhibit 7.11.

7. Draft, formulation, and adoption of bylaws

The bylaws are the organizational blueprint for the daily operation of the corporation. Attention to their contents

Exhibit 7.10*

Billing No. _____   Attorney

CHECKLIST FOR AMENDMENT OF ARTICLES OF INCORPORATION OF

_____

Confirm that corporation is in good standing _____

If changing name:
    Check name availability in List of Active Corporations _____
    Call Secretary of State re name availability _____
    Reserve corporate name _____

Review Articles of Incorporation for other amendments _____

Prepare documents:
    Board action: Minutes _____ Waiver _____ Notice _____ Consent _____
    Shareholder action: Minutes _____ Waiver _____ Notice* _____ Consent _____
        *Notice must include proposed amendment or summary thereof
    Articles of Amendment ("Articles") _____
    Amended Affidavit of Value, if required _____

Compute filing fee _____

Prepare letters and memo:
    Memo to lawyer _____
    Client forwarding documents _____
    Sec. of State filing Articles _____ Order cert. copy _____
    Other state(s) where qualified, filing certified copy of Articles _____
    Client forwarding "Filed" Articles _____

Review documents and letters _____

Forward drafts to lawyer for approval _____

Forward documents to client for adoption and signature _____

Receive documents from client _____

Review and complete documents _____

Photocopy minutes (and notices or waivers of notice) or consent for file _____

File minutes or consents in file and in original or duplicate minute book _____

File 2 executed copies of Articles with Secretary of State; check filing fee

Receive Certificate and Articles from Secretary of State _____

File certified copy of Articles with other state(s) _____

Photocopy Certificate & Articles for file and duplicate minute book _____

File Certificate & Articles in file and original or duplicate minute book _____

Forward original or photocopy of Certificate & Articles to client _____

Update Corporation Data Sheet _____

If name of corporation is changed:
    Change name on minute book(s) _____
    Order new corporate seal (using original date of incorporation) _____
    Change name on: data sheet _____ annual meeting tickler _____ year-end tickler _____
                    ledgers _____ file labels _____ annual report list _____ master list _____
    Change name on Corporation Data Sheet of related corporations _____
    Change name on Bylaws (adding effective date of change) _____
    Issue new stock certificates using new name (optional) _____
    Add new name and effective date of change to stock book and stock records _____
    Remind client to change name (see procedures) _____
    Change name on employee benefit plans _____
    File Certificate of Amendment of Trade Name (if applicable) _____

If additional class of stock is authorized:
    Prepare legends for certificates of each class and add to all outstanding certificates of each class _____
    Make notation on stock register _____

If amendment requires legend on stock certificates:
    Amend Bylaws to include legend, if appropriate (use checklist for amend. of Bylaws) _____
    Recall stock certificates and add legend (optional) _____
    Make notation on stock register _____

If par value or number of authorized shares is changed:
   Make appropriate notations on stock register _____
   Consider issuing new certificates for outstanding shares _____
   File Affidavit of Value, if applicable _____
If cumulative voting is granted or denied, make appropriate changes to Bylaws and Corporation Data Sheet _____
If preemptive rights are granted or denied, change Corporation Data Sheet _____
If amendment provides that the number of directors shall be set by the Bylaws, amend Bylaws accordingly
   (use checklist for amendment of Bylaws). _____

* Excerpted from *Working with Legal Assistants: A Team Approach for Lawyers and Legal Assistants,* Paul G. Ulrich and Robert S. Mucklestone, eds. Reprinted with permission of the American Bar Association.

Exhibit 7.11

_____, INC.

Minutes of First Meeting of the Board of Directors

The first meeting of the Board of Directors of _____, a _____ corporation, was held at _____ , at _____ a.m. on _____ , 19 . Both of the directors _____ were present. _____ , acted as Chairman of the meeting and _____ , as Secretary.

The Chairman stated that oral notice of the meeting had been given.

The minutes of the organization meeting of the corporation were then presented to the meeting by the Secretary, together with a copy of the bylaws which had been adopted at that meeting. Thereupon, on motion duly made, seconded and unanimously adopted, it was:

RESOLVED: That the minutes of the organization meeting of the corporation held on _____ , 19 , which have been presented to this meeting, be and they hereby are in all respects approved, and all actions of every nature thereby shown to have been taken or authorized by and the same hereby are and in all respects approved, ratified and confirmed; and

FURTHER RESOLVED: That the bylaws in the form adopted by the incorporator at the organization meeting by and they hereby are in all respects approved and adopted as the bylaws of the corporation and shall be entered into the minute book of the corporation.

The Chairman then stated that _____ , had been appointed by the incorporator as the corporation's statutory agent for service. Thereupon, on motion duly made, seconded and unanimously adopted, it was

RESOLVED: That the appointment of _____ , as the corporation's statutory agent for service is hereby approved, ratified and confirmed.

The Chairman then stated the next order of business is the election of the officers specified in the bylaws. Nominations having been made, the following persons were successively duly elected to the following offices:

_____   President

_____   Secretary

The Secretary submitted to the meeting a seal proposed for use as the corporate seal of the corporation. Thereupon, the motion was duly made, seconded and unanimously adopted, and it was:

RESOLVED: That the form of seal submitted to this meeting bearing the words and figures _____ Inc., Corporate Seal, be, and it hereby is, approved and adopted as and for the corporate seal for the corporation, and that an impression of said seal be made in the margin of these minutes.

The Chairman then stated that the corporation should be authorized to pay all expenses and reimburse all persons for expenditures made in connection with the organization of the corporation. After motion being duly made, seconded and unanimously adopted, it was

RESOLVED: That the corporation be and hereby is authorized to pay all charges and expenses incident to and arising out of the organization of the corporation and to reimburse persons who have made any disbursements therefore.

The Secretary then presented to the meeting the proposed form of certificate for the common shares of this corporation, and the Chairman directed that a copy of such form of certificate be annexed to the minutes of the meeting.

Upon motion being duly made, seconded and unanimously adopted, it was

RESOLVED: That the form of certificate submitted to this meeting for the common shares of the corporation be and it hereby is adopted as the certificate to represent fully paid and non-assessable shares and that a specimen of such certificate be annexed to the minutes of this meeting.

The Chairman then stated that the next order of business was the designation of a principal office of the corporation.
On motion duly made, seconded and unanimously adopted, it was

RESOLVED: That the principal office of the corporation be at

The Chairman then stated that the next order of business was the designation of a depository for the funds of the corporation.
On motion duly made, seconded, and unanimously adopted, it was

RESOLVED: That the _____ Bank be, and it hereby is designated as the depository or the funds of the corporation.

The Chairman then pointed out that it would be necessary to file certain reports with the State of _____ , incident to the formation of the corporation.
On motion duly made, seconded and unanimously adopted, it was

RESOLVED: That the Secretary be and hereby is authorized and directed to complete and file any and all reports with the Secreatary of the State of _____ relating to the formation and organization of the corporation.

The Chairman stated that the corporation should consider a plan for the issuance of its stock. After discussion, upon motion duly made, seconded and unanimously carried, the following resolution was adopted:

RESOLVED: That the corporation shall offer to _____ and _____ , and upon their acceptance, sell and issue to them an aggregate of not more than 2,000 shares of said stock in exchange for and in consideration of the transfer by each of _____ and _____ of Five Hundred Dollars, said total of 2,000 shares to be distributed as follows:
_____ 1,000 shares
_____ 1,000 shares

FURTHER RESOLVED: That the corporation intends hereby to offer Section 1244 stock pursuant to Section 1244 of the Internal Revenue Code of 1954, as amended.

There being no further business to come before the meeting, upon motion duly made, seconded and unanimously adopted, the meeting was adjourned.
Dated at _____ , _____ this _____ day of _____ , 19 _____ .

_____
Secretary

is imperative if one wants to be apprised of what a corporation's powers and limitations are, especially in relation to the officers, directors, and shareholders. Topics specifically covered in the bylaws include:

    a. Place, time, notices of shareholders' meetings
    b. Voting rights of shareholders and directors
    c. Quorum standards adopted by the corporation for both shareholders and directors
    d. Place, time, notices of board of directors meetings
    e. Powers of the board of directors:
        1. General: "as necessary"
        2. Specific: e.g., voting, committees, personnel
    f. Removal/replacement of directors
    g. Officers: president to secretary
        1. Election
        2. Duration
        3. Powers/duties of individual officers
    h. Stock rights
    i. Identification of rights of directors/officers
    j. Miscellaneous issues: e.g., benefits, insurance, rights to amend

As can be imagined, many battles are fought in the corporate trenches over the rights, duties, and liabilities of directors and officers. Think of the human power struggles, the locked votes, and the economic interests at stake. Precision of language and comprehensive coverage of all possible eventualities is demanded in the drafting of bylaws. An excellent sample of bylaws is provided in exhibit 7.12.

Exhibit 7.12

BY-LAWS OF

_____

ARTICLE 1—OFFICES

Section 1-1   Registered Office: The registered office of the Corporation shall be located within the Commonwealth of _____, at such place as the Board of Directors shall, from time to time, determine.

Section 1-2   Other Offices: The Corporation may also have offices at such other places within or without the Commonwealth of _____, as the Board of Directors may, from time to time, determine.

ARTICLE II—SHAREHOLDERS' MEETINGS

Section 2-1   Place of Shareholders' Meetings: Meetings of shareholders shall be held at such places within or without the Commonwealth of _____ as may be fixed by the Board of Directors, from time to time. If no such place is fixed by the Board of Directors, meetings of the shareholders shall be held at the registered office of the Corporation.

Section 2-2   Annual Meeting: A meeting of the shareholders of the Corporation shall be held in each calendar year, commencing with the year 19 _____, on such date and at such time as the Board of Directors may determine, or if the Board of Directors fails to set a date and time on the _____ day of _____ at _____ o'clock _____. M., if not a legal holiday, and if such day is a legal holiday, then such meeting shall be held on the next business day.

At such annual meeting, there shall be held an election of Directors.

Unless the Board of Directors shall deem it advisable, financial reports of the Corporation's business need not be sent to the shareholders and need not be presented at the annual meeting. If any report is deemed advisable by the Board of Directors, such report may contain such information as the Board of Directors shall determine and need not be certified by a Certified Public Accountant unless the Board of Directors shall so direct.

Section 2-3   Special Meetings: Special meetings of the shareholders may be called at any time:

(a) By the President of the Corporation; or

(b) By a majority of the Board of Directors; or

(c) By shareholders entitled to cast at least one-fifth of the votes, which all shareholders are entitled to cast at the meeting.

Upon the written request of any person or persons entitled to call a special meeting, which request shall set forth the purpose for which the meeting is desired, it shall be the duty of the Secretary to fix the date of such meeting, to be held at such time, not less than five nor more than sixty days after the receipt of such request, as the Secretary may determine, and to give due notice thereof. If the Secretary shall neglect or refuse to fix the date of such meeting, and to give notice thereof within five days after receipt of such request, the person or persons calling the meeting may do so.

Section 2-4   Notices of Shareholders' Meetings: Written notice stating the date, place and hour and, if required by law or these Bylaws, the purpose, of any meeting of the shareholders, shall be given to each shareholder of record entitled to vote at the meeting, at least five days prior to the day named for the meeting, unless otherwise required by law. Such notices may be given at the discretion of, or in the name of, the Board of Directors, President, Vice President, Secretary or Assistant Secretary. When a meeting is adjourned, it shall not be necessary to give any notice of the adjourned meeting or of the business to be transacted at an adjourned meeting, other than by announcement at the meeting at which such adjournment is taken.

Section 2-5   Quorum of and Action by Shareholders: Unless otherwise provided in the Articles of Incorporation or in a Bylaw adopted by the Board of Directors (or the Incorporators if no first Directors were named in the Articles of Incorporation) at its organization meeting following the filing of the Articles of Incorporation or by the shareholders, the presence, in person or by proxy, of shareholders entitled to cast at least a majority of the votes which all shareholders are entitled to cast on the particular matter shall constitute a quorum for the purpose of considering such matter, and, unless otherwise specifically provided by law, the acts, at a duly organized meeting, of the shareholders present, in person or by proxy, entitled to cast at least a majority of the votes which all shareholders present are entitled to cast, shall be the acts of the shareholders. The shareholders present at a duly organized meeting can continue to do business until adjournment, notwithstanding the withdrawal of enough shareholders to leave less than a quorum. If a meeting cannot be organized because a quorum has not attended, those present may, except as otherwise provided by law, adjourn the meeting to such time and place as they may determine, but in the case of any meeting called for the election of Directors, those shareholders who attend the second of such adjourned meetings, although less than a quorum as fixed in this Section, or in the Articles of Incorporation, shall nevertheless constitute a quorum for the purpose of electing Directors.

Section 2-6　　Voting: At least five days before any meeting of shareholders, the officer or agent having charge of the transfer books of the Corporation shall make a complete list of the shareholders entitled to vote at such meeting, arranged in alphabetical order with the address of and the number of shares held by each, which list shall be kept on file at the registered office of the Corporation and shall be subject to inspection by any shareholder at any time during usual business hours. Such list shall also be produced and kept open at the time and place of the meeting and shall be subject to the inspection of any shareholder during the whole time of the meeting.

At all shareholders' meetings, shareholders entitled to vote may attend and vote either in person or by proxy. All proxies shall be in writing, executed by the shareholder or by his duly authorized attorney in fact, and shall be filed with the Secretary of the Corporation. A proxy, unless coupled with an interest, shall be revocable at will, notwithstanding any other agreement of any provision in the proxy to be contrary, but the revocation of a proxy shall not be effective until the notice thereof has been given to the Secretary of the Corporation. No unrevoked proxy shall be valid after eleven months from the date of execution, unless a longer time is expressly provided therein; but in no event shall a proxy, unless coupled with an interest, be voted on after three years from the date of its execution.

Except as otherwise specifically provided by law, all matters, coming before the meeting shall be determined by a vote of shares. Such vote shall be taken by voice unless a shareholder demands, before the election begins, that it be taken by ballot, in which the vote shall be taken by written ballot, and the Judge or Judges of Election or, if none, the Secretary of the Meeting, shall tabulate and certify the results of such vote.

Section 2-7　　Participation in Meetings by Conference Telephone: Any shareholder, who is otherwise entitled to participate in any meeting the shareholders may attend, may be counted for the purposes of determining a quorum and exercise all rights and privileges to which he might be entitled were he personally in attendance, including the right to vote, by means of a conference telephone or similar communications equipment, by means of which all persons, participating in the meeting, can hear each other.

Section 2-8　　Action by Unanimous Consent of Shareholders: Any action, which may be taken at a meeting of the shareholders, or a class of shareholders, may be taken without a meeting if a consent or consents, in writing, setting forth the action so taken, shall be signed by all of the shareholders, who would be entitled to vote at a meeting for such purposes, and shall be filed with the Secretary of the Corporation. Insertion in the minute book of the Corporation shall be deemed filing with the Secretary regardless of whether the Secretary or some other authorized person has actual possession of the minute book. Written consents by all of the shareholders executed pursuant to this Section 2-8, may be executed in any number of counterparts and shall be deemed effective as of the date set forth therein.

Section 2-9　　Action by Less than Unanimous Consent of Shareholders: Only if the Articles of Incorporation so provide, any action, which may be taken at a meeting of the shareholders, or of a class of shareholders, may be taken without a meeting, if a consent or consents, in writing, to such action, setting forth the action so taken, shall be (1) signed by shareholders entitled to cast not less than the larger of (a) two-thirds of the total number of votes which all shareholders, of the corporation, or of a class of shareholders, would be entitled by the Articles of Incorporation to cast upon such action or (b) the minimum percentage of the vote, required by law, if any, for the proposed action and (2) shall be filed with the Secretary of the Corporation. Insertion in the minute book, of the Corporation, shall be deemed filing with the Secretary regardless of whether the Secretary or some other authorized person has actual possession of the minute book. Written consents executed, pursuant to this Section 2-9, may be executed in any number of counterparts. Such action shall not become effective until after at least ten days written notice of such action shall have been given to each shareholder, of record, entitled to vote thereon. This paragraph shall not be applicable to any action, with respect to any plan or amendment of the Articles of Incorporation, to which Section _____, of the _____, concerning dissenters rights, is applicable.

ARTICLE III—BOARD OF DIRECTORS

Section 3-1　　Number: The Board of Directors shall consist of _____ members. Once elected, Directors shall serve until the next annual meeting of shareholders and until their successors are duly elected and qualified or until their earlier resignation or removal.

Section 3-2　　Place of Meeting: Meetings of the Board of Directors may be held at such place within the Commonwealth of Pennsylvania or elsewhere as a majority of the Directors may, from time to time, appoint or as may be designated in the notice calling the meeting.

Section 3-3　　Regular Meetings: A regular meeting of the Board of Directors shall be held annually, immediately following the annual meeting of shareholders at the place where such meeting of the shareholders is held or at such other place, date and hour as a majority of the newly elected Directors may designate. At such meeting, the Board of Directors shall elect officers of the Corporation. In addition to such regular meeting, the Board of Directors shall have the power to fix, by resolution, the place, date and hour of other regular meetings of the Board.

Section 3–4   Special Meetings: Special meetings of the Board of Directors shall be held whenever ordered by the President, by a majority of the executive committee, if any, or by a majority of the Directors in office.

Section 3–5   Participation in Meetings by Conference Telephone: Any Directors may participate in any meeting of the board of Directors or of any committee (provided he is otherwise entitled to participate), be counted for the purpose of determining a quorum thereof and exercise all rights and privileges to which he might be entitled were he personally in attendance, including the right to vote, by means of conference telephone or other similar communications equipment by means of which all persons at the meeting can hear each other.

Section 3–6   Notices of Meeting of Board of Directors:

(a) Regular Meetings: No notice shall be required to be given of any regular meeting, unless the same is held at other than the time or place for holding such meetings, as fixed in accordance with Section 3–3 of these Bylaws, in which event one day's notice shall be given of the time and place of such meeting.

(b) Special Meetings: Written notice, stating the date, place and hour, of any special meeting of the Board of Directors, shall be given at least one day prior to the date named for the meeting.

Section 3–7   Quorum: A majority of the Directors in office shall be necessary to constitute a quorum for the transaction of business and the acts of a majority of the Directors present at a meeting at which a quorum is present, shall be considered as the acts of the Board of Directors. If there is no quorum present, at a duly convened meeting of the Board of Directors, the majority of those present may adjourn the meeting from time to time and place to place.

Section 3–8   Informal Action by the Board of Directors: Any action, which may be taken at a meeting of the Directors, or of the members of any committee of the Board of Directors, may be taken without a meeting if a consent or consents in writing, setting forth the action so taken, shall be signed by all of the Directors, or members of the committee, as the case may be, and shall be filed with the Secretary of the Corporation. Insertion in the minute book of the Corporation shall be deemed filing with the Secretary regardless of whether the Secretary or some other authorized person has actual possession of the minute book. Written consents by all of the Directors or the members of any committee of the Board of Directors executed pursuant to this Section 3–8 may be executed in any number of counterparts and shall be deemed effective as of the date set forth therein.

Section 3–9   Powers:

(a) General Powers: The Board of Directors shall have all the power and authority granted by law to the Board, including all powers necessary or appropriate to the management of the business and affairs of the Corporation.

(b) *Specific Powers* Without limiting the general powers, conferred by the last preceding clause and the powers conferred by the Articles and these By-Laws of the Corporation, it is hereby expressly declared that the Board of Directors shall have the following powers:

1. To confer upon any officer or officers of the Corporation the power to choose, remove or suspend assistant officers, agents or servants.

2. To appoint any person, Firm or Corporation, to accept and hold in trust for the Corporation any property belonging to the Corporation, or in which it is interested, and to authorize any such person, firm or corporation to execute any documents and perform any duties that may be requisite in relation to any such trust.

3. To appoint a person, or persons, to vote shares of another corporation held and owned by the Corporation.

4. By resolution adopted by a majority of the whole Board of Directors, to designate one or more committees, each committee to consist of two or more of the Directors of the Corporation. To the extent provided in any such resolution, and to the extent permitted by law, a committee, so designated, shall have and may exercise the authority of the Board of Directors in the management of the business and affairs of the Corporation. The Board of Directors may designate one or more Directors as alternate members of any committee, who may replace any absent or disqualified member at any meeting of the committee. If specifically granted this power by the Board in its resolution establishing the committee, in the absence or disqualification of any member and all designated alternates of such committee or committees or if the whole Board of Directors has failed to designate alternate members, the member or members thereof present at any meeting, and not disqualified from voting, may designate another Director to act at the meeting in the place of any such absent or disqualified member.

5. To fix the place, time and purpose of meetings of shareholders.

6. To fix the compensation of Directors and officers for their services.

Section 3–10   Removal of Directors by Shareholders: The entire Board of Directors, or a class of the Board of Directors, where the Board of Directors is classified with respect to the power to elect Directors, or any individual Director may be removed from office without assigning any cause by the vote of shareholders entitled to cast at least a majority of the votes, which all shareholders would be entitled to cast at any annual election of Directors or such class of Directors. In case the Board of Directors, or such class of the Board of Directors, or any one or more Directors is so removed, new Directors may be elected at the same time. If the shareholders are entitled to vote cumulatively for the Board of Directors or a class of the Board of Directors, no individual Director shall be removed unless the entire Board of Directors or class of the Board of Directors is removed in case the votes of a sufficient number of shares are cast against the resolution for his removal, which if cumulatively voted at an annual election of Directors would be sufficient to elect one or more Directors to the Board of Directors or to the class.

Section 3-11 Vacancies: Vacancies in the Board of Directors including vacancies resulting from an increase in the number of Directors, may be filled by a majority of the remaining members of the Board of Directors though less than a quorum, and each person so elected shall be a Director until his successor is duly elected by the shareholders, who may make such election at the next annual meeting of the shareholders or at any special meeting duly called for that purpose and held prior thereto, or until his earlier resignation or removal.

ARTICLE IV—OFFICERS

Section 4-1 Election and Office: The Corporation shall have a President, a Secretary and a Treasurer who shall be elected by the Board of Directors. The Board of Directors may elect as additional officers, a Chairman of the Board of Directors, one or more Vice-Presidents and one or more other officers or assistant officers. Any number of offices may be held by the same person.

Section 4-2 Term: The officers and assistant officers shall each serve at the pleasure of the Board of Directors and until the annual meeting of the Board of Directors, following the next annual meeting of shareholders, unless removed from office by the Board of Directors during their respective tenures.

Section 4-3 Powers and Duties of the President: Unless otherwise determined by the Board of Directors, the President shall have the usual duties of an executive officer with general supervision over and direction of the affairs of the Corporation. In the exercise of these duties, and subject to the limitations of the laws of the Commonwealth of _____, these Bylaws and the actions of the Board of Directors, he may appoint, suspend and discharge employees agents and assistant officers, fix the compensation of all officers and assistant officers, shall preside at all meetings of the shareholders, at which he shall be present, and, unless there is a Chairman of the Board of Directors, shall preside at all meetings of the Board of Directors. He shall also do and perform such other duties as from time to time may be assigned to him by the Board of Directors.

Unless otherwise determined by the Board of Directors, the President shall have full power and authority on behalf of the Corporation, to attend, act and vote at any meeting of the shareholders of any corporation, in which the Corporation may hold stock, and, at any such meeting, shall possess and may exercise any and all the rights and powers incident to the ownership of such stock and which, as the owner thereof, the Corporation might have possessed and exercised.

Section 4-4 Powers and Duties of the Secretary: Unless otherwise determined, by the Board of Directors, the Secretary shall be responsible for the keeping of the minutes of all meetings of the Board of Directors, shareholders and all committees, in books provided for that purpose, and for the giving and serving of all notices for the Corporation. He shall have charge of the corporate seal, the certificate books, transfer books, stock ledgers and such other books and papers as the Board of Directors may direct. He shall perform all other duties ordinarily incident to the office of Secretary and shall have such other powers and perform such other duties as may be assigned to him by the Board of Directors.

Section 4-5 Powers and Duties of the Treasurer: Unless otherwise determined, by the Board of Directors, the Treasurer shall have charge of all the funds and securities of the Corporation which may come into his hands. When necessary or proper, unless otherwise determined by the Board of Directors, he shall endorse for collection on behalf of the Corporation, checks, notes and other obligations, and shall deposit the same to the credit of the Corporation in such banks or depositories as the Board of Directors may designate and shall sign all receipts and vouchers for payments made to the Corporation. He shall sign all checks made by the Corporation, except when the Board of Directors shall otherwise direct. He shall be responsible for the regular entry in books of the Corporation to be kept for such purpose, full and accurate account of all funds and securities received and paid by him on account of the Corporation. Whenever required by the Board of Directors, he shall render a statement of the financial condition of the Corporation. He shall have such other powers and shall perform such other duties, as may be assigned to him, from time to time, by the Board of Directors. He shall give such bond, if any, for the faithful performance of his duties, as shall be required by the Board of Directors, and any such bond shall remain in the custody of the President.

Section 4-6 Powers and Duties of the Chairman of the Board of Directors: Unless otherwise determined by the Board of Directors, the Chairman of the Board of Directors, if any, shall preside at all meetings of Directors. He shall have such other powers and perform such further duties as may be assigned to him by the Board of Directors.

Section 4-7 Powers and Duties of Vice Presidents and Assistant Officers: Unless otherwise determined by the Board of Directors, each Vice-President and each Assistant Officer shall have the powers and perform the duties of his respective superior officer. Vice-Presidents and Assistant Officers shall have such rank as may be designated by the Board of Directors.

Vice-Presidents may be designated as having responsibility for a specific area of the Corporation's affairs, in which event such Vice-President shall be superior to the other Vice-Presidents in relation to matters within his area. The President shall be the superior officer of the Vice-Presidents. The Treasurer and Secretary shall be the superior officers of the Assistant Treasurers and Assistant Secretaries, respectively.

Section 4-8   Delegation of Office: The Board of Directors may delegate the powers or duties of any officer, of the Corporation, to any other person, from time to time.

Section 4-9   Vacancies: The Board of Directors shall have the power to fill any vacancies, in any office, occurring from whatever reason.

ARTICLE V — CAPITAL STOCK

Section 5-1   Share Certificates: Every share certificate shall be signed by the Chairman of the Board or the President or Vice-President and by the Treasurer, Assistant Treasurer, Secretary or Assistant Secretary and sealed with the Corporate seal, which may be a facsimile, engraved or printed, but where such certificate is signed by a Transfer Agent or a Registrar, the signature of any corporate officer upon such certificate may be a facsimile, engraved or printed.

Section 5-2   Transfer of Shares: Transfer of shares shall be made on the books of the Corporation only upon surrender of the share certificate duly endorsed or with duly executed stock powers attached and otherwise in proper form for transfer, which certificate shall be cancelled at the time of the transfer.

Section 5-3   Determination of Shareholders of Record and Closing Transfer Books: The Board of Directors may fix a time, not more than fifty days prior to the date of any meeting of shareholders, or the date fixed for the payment of any dividend or distribution, or the date for the allotment of rights, or the date when any change or conversion or exchange of shares will be made or go into effect, as a record for the determination of the shareholders entitled to notice of, or to vote at, any such meeting, or entitled to receive payment of any such dividend or distribution, or to receive any such allotment of rights, or to exercise the rights in respect to any such change, conversion or exchange of shares or otherwise. In such case, only such shareholders, as shall be shareholders of record, on the date so fixed, shall be entitled to notice or, of to vote at, such meeting, or to receive payment of such dividend, or to receive such allotment of rights, or to exercise such rights, as the case may be, notwithstanding any transfer of any shares on the books of the Corporation after any record date fixed as aforesaid. The Board of Directors may close the books, of the Corporation, against transfers of shares, during the whole or any part of such period, and in such case, written or printed notice thereof shall be mailed at least ten days before the closing thereof to each shareholder, of record, at the address appearing on the records of the Corporation or supplied by him to the Corporation for the purpose of notice. While the stock transfer books of the Corporation are closed, no transfer of shares shall be made thereon. Unless a record date is fixed by the Board of Directors for the determination of shareholders entitled to receive notice of, or vote at, a shareholders meeting, transferees of shares, which are transferred on the books of the Corporation within ten days next preceding the date of such meeting shall not be entitled to notice of or to vote at such meeting. The Corporation may treat the registered owner of each share of stock as the person exclusively entitled to vote, to receive notifications and otherwise to exercise all the rights and powers of the owner thereof.

Section 5-4   Lost Share Certificates: Unless waived in whole or in part by the Board of Directors, any person requesting the issuance of a new certificate, in lieu of an alleged lost, destroyed, mislaid or wrongfully taken certificate, shall (1) give to the Corporation his bond of indemnity with an acceptable surety and (2) satisfy such other reasonable requirements as may be imposed by the Corporation. Thereupon, a new share certificate shall be issued to the registered owner, or his assigns, in lieu of the alleged lost, destroyed, mislaid or wrongfully taken certificate, provided that the request, therefore, and issuance thereof, have been made before the Corporation has notice that such shares have been acquired by a bona fide purchaser.

ARTICLE VI—NOTICES; COMPUTING TIME PERIODS

Section 6-1   Contents of Notice: Whenever any notice of a meeting is required to be given pursuant to these Bylaws or the Articles of Incorporation, or otherwise, the notice shall specify the place, day and hour of the meeting and, in the case of a special meeting of shareholders or where otherwise required by law, the general nature of the business to be transacted at such meeting.

Section 6-2   Method of Notice: All notices shall be given to each person entitled thereto, either personally or by sending a copy thereof, through the mail or by telegraph, charges prepaid, to his address appearing on the books of the Corporation, or supplied by him to the Corporation for the purpose of notice. If notice is sent by mail or telegraph, it shall be deemed to have been given to the person entitled thereto when deposited in the United States mail or with the telegraph office for transmission.

Section 6-3   Computing Time Periods: In computing the number of days for purposes of these Bylaws, all days shall be counted, including Saturdays, Sundays or holidays; provided, however, that if the final day of any time period falls on a Saturday, Sunday or holiday, then the final day shall be deemed to be the next day, which is not a Saturday, Sunday or holiday.

In computing the number of days for the purpose of giving notice of any meeting, the date upon which the notice is given shall be counted, but the day set for the meeting shall not be counted. Notice given twenty-four hours before the time set for a meeting shall be deemed one day's notice.

ARTICLE VII—INDEMNIFICATION OF DIRECTORS AND OFFICERS AND OTHER PERSONS

Section 7-1 Indemnification: The Corporation shall indemnify any Director or officer of the Corporation against expense (including legal fees), judgments, fines and amounts paid in settlement, actually and reasonably incurred by him, to the fullest extent now or hereafter permitted by law in connection with any threatened, pending or completed action, suit or proceeding, whether civil, criminal, administrative or investigative, brought or threatened to be brought against him, including actions or suits by or in the right of the Corporation, by reason of the fact that he is or was a Director or Officer of the Corporation, its parent or any of its subsidiaries, or acted as a Director or Officer, or in any other capacity on behalf of the Corporation, its parent or any of its subsidiaries, or is or was serving at the request of the Corporation as a Director, Officer, Employee or Agent of another corporation, partnership, joint venture, trust or other enterprise.

The Board of Director by resolution may similarly indemnify any person, other than a Director or officer of the Corporation, to the fullest extent now or hereafter permitted by law for liabilities incurred by him, in connection with services rendered by him, for at the request of the Corporation, its parent or any of its subsidiaries.

The provisions of this section shall be applicable to all actions, suits or proceedings, commenced after its adoption, whether such arise out of acts or omissions, which occurred prior or subsequent to such adoption and shall continue as to a person who has ceased to be a Director or Officer or to render services for or at the request of the Corporation and shall inure to the benefit of the heirs, executors and administrators of such a person. The rights of indemnification, provided for herein, shall not be deemed the exclusive rights to which any Director, Officer, Employee or Agent of the Corporation may be entitled.

Section 7-2 Advances: The Corporation may pay the expenses incurred by any person entitled to be indemnified by the Corporation in defending a civil or criminal action, suit or proceeding in advance of the final disposition of such action, suit or proceeding upon receipt of an undertaking, by or on behalf of such person, to repay such amount, unless it shall ultimately be determined that he is entitled to be indemnified by the Corporation as authorized by law.

Section 7-3 Insurance: The Corporation may purchase and maintain insurance on behalf of any person who is or was a Director, Officer, Employee or Agent of the Corporation, or who is or was serving in any capacity in any other corporation or organization, at the request of the Corporation, against any liability asserted against him or incurred by him, in any such capacity or arising out of his status as such, whether or not the Corporation would have the power to indemnify him against such liability under law.

ARTICLE VIII—FISCAL YEAR

Section 8-1 The Board of Directors shall have the power by resolution to fix the fiscal year of the Corporation. If the Board of Directors shall fail to do so, the President shall fix the fiscal year.

ARTICLE IX—AMENDMENTS

Section 9-1 The shareholders entitled to vote thereon shall have the power to alter, amend or repeal these Bylaws, by the vote of shareholders entitled to cast at least a majority of the votes, which all shareholders are entitled to cast thereon, at any regular or special meeting, duly convened after notice to the shareholders of such purpose. The Board of Directors, by a majority vote of those voting, shall have the power to alter, amend and repeal these Bylaws, at any regular or special meeting, duly convened after notice of such purpose, subject always to the power of the shareholders to further alter, amend or repeal these Bylaws.

ARTICLE X—INTERPRETATION OF BYLAWS

Section 10-1 All words, terms and provisions of these Bylaws shall be interpreted and defined by and in accordance with the _____ Business Corporation Law, as amended, and as amended from time to time hereafter.

8. Organization and first annual report

Now that all required documentation has been filed, all necessary fees have been paid, directors and officers elected, bylaws adopted, and a certificate of incorporation issued, the corporation formally exists. As with all other legal creations, the paralegal must keep track of its growth and changes. As such, the corporation is now obliged to file yearly reports to the state of its incorporation as well as to its shareholders and owners. That annual report highlights corporate policies and events, fiscal condition, and other relevant data.

9. Filing appropriate tax forms

Corporations, like individuals, must file tax returns at both the state and federal levels. A major burden to most companies is being certain that tax deposits and filings are on time. (See exhibits 7.13 and 7.14.)

F. Rights and Liabilities of Corporate Shareholders

1. General powers in the organization

Shareholders, depending on percentage of ownership and their own self-esteem, often view themselves as more powerful than they are. Without a doubt, a shareholder is a part owner in the enterprise and, as such, does have some powers, which this outline will analyze, though they are limited in scope.

One certainty is that shareholders have no direct control over the management and operation of the corporation's day-to-day affairs. That function is strictly within the officers' and directors' responsibilities. Shareholders make no daily decisions of policy and control. Instead, shareholders' participation in the operation of a corporation can be viewed only in the broadest sense, through their rights to vote on certain important corporate matters. Those matters are

    a. Election of directors
    b. Removal of directors
    c. Adoption of bylaws
    d. Modification of bylaws
    e. Approval of fundamental corporate changes: merger, consolidation, and dissolution

In another sense, shareholders have the right to participate in a variety of corporate functions, and indeed the corporation has to provide the opportunity to participate. One of the most important communications is the annual meeting reminder to shareholders, which serves to notify the law office and the shareholders of an upcoming meeting (see exhibit 7.15).

2. Shareholder voting rights

A critically important function and right of a shareholder is voting rights. The mechanics and complexities of voting rights involve the following factors:

- □ What class of stock does the shareholder possess? (preferred always votes)
- □ When was that stock purchased? (Eligibility to vote often rests on the record date of purchase.)
- □ Who is in fact the record holder, the person who can exercise voting rights?
- □ How can a shareholder vote by a proxy (mail-in vote)?
- □ How will my vote be counted? Is it a *weighted* vote or a *contingent* vote?
- □ Can the shareholder vote, based on his or her percentage of stock control and ownership, for a board of directors?
- □ Can agreements such as voting trusts or pooling agreements, in which a mass of shareholders agree to vote as a block, be legal?

3. Shareholder right to inspection

Another area of rights of a shareholder that is worth considering is the *inspection of corporate books and records.* By statute, inspection demand requires that the inspecting shareholder must have held his or her share for six months immediately preceding the demand, or he or she must hold at least 5 percent of all outstanding shares. In addition, the

Exhibit 7.13

Form **1120**	**U.S. Corporation Income Tax Return**	OMB No. 1545-0123

Form **1120**
Department of the Treasury
Internal Revenue Service

U.S. Corporation Income Tax Return
For calendar 1984 or tax year beginning _____, 1984, ending _____, 19 _____
▶ For Paperwork Reduction Act Notice, see page 1 of the instructions.

OMB No. 1545-0123

1984

Check if a—

A. Consolidated return ☐

B. Personal Holding Co. ☐

C. Business Code No. (See the list in the Instructions)

Use IRS label. Otherwise please print or type.

Name	D. Employer identification number
Number and street	E. Date incorporated
City or town, State, and ZIP code	F. Total assets (see Specific Instructions) $

G. Check box if there has been a change in address from the previous year . . . . ▶ ☐

Gross Income

1 **(a)** Gross receipts or sales _____ **(b)** Less returns and allowances _____ Balance ▶	1(c)
2 Cost of goods sold and/or operations (Schedule A)	2
3 Gross profit (line 1(c) less line 2)	3
4 Dividends (Schedule C)	4
5 Interest	5
6 Gross rents	6
7 Gross royalties	7
8 Capital gain net income (attach separate Schedule D)	8
9 Net gain or (loss) from Form 4797, line 14(a), Part II (attach Form 4797)	9
10 Other income (see instructions—attach schedule)	10
11 TOTAL income—Add lines 3 through 10 and enter here . . . . ▶	11

Deductions

12 Compensation of officers (Schedule E)	12
13 **(a)** Salaries and wages _____ **(b)** Less jobs credit _____ Balance ▶	13(c)
14 Repairs	14
15 Bad debts (Schedule F if reserve method is used)	15
16 Rents	16
17 Taxes	17
18 Interest	18
19 Contributions (**see instructions for 10% limitation**)	19
20 Depreciation (attach Form 4562) 20	
21 Less depreciation claimed in Schedule A and elsewhere on return . 21(a)	21(b)
22 Depletion	22
23 Advertising	23
24 Pension, profit-sharing, etc. plans	24
25 Employee benefit programs	25
26 Other deductions (attach schedule)	26
27 TOTAL deductions—Add lines 12 through 26 and enter here . . . . . . ▶	27
28 Taxable income before net operating loss deduction and special deductions (line 11 less line 27) .	28
29 **Less: (a)** Net operating loss deduction (see instructions) . . . . 29(a)	
(b) Special deductions (Schedule C) . . . . . . 29(b)	29(c)
30 Taxable income (line 28 less line 29(c))	30

Tax

31 TOTAL TAX (Schedule J)	31
32 **Payments:**	
(a) 1983 overpayment allowed as a credit . .	
(b) 1984 estimated tax payments	
(c) Less 1984 refund applied for on Form 4466 . ( )	
(d) Tax deposited with Form 7004	
(e) Credit from regulated investment companies (attach Form 2439). .	
(f) Credit for Federal tax on gasoline and special fuels (attach Form 4136)	32
33 Enter any **PENALTY** for underpayment of estimated tax—check ▶☐ if Form 2220 is attached .	33
34 **TAX DUE**—If the total of lines 31 and 33 is larger than line 32, enter AMOUNT OWED	34
35 **OVERPAYMENT**—If line 32 is larger than the total of lines 31 and 33, enter AMOUNT OVERPAID	35
36 Enter amount of line 35 you want: **Credited to 1985 estimated tax** ▶ Refunded ▶	36

Please Sign Here

Under penalties of perjury, I declare that I have examined this return, including accompanying schedules and statements, and to the best of my knowledge and belief, it is true, correct, and complete. Declaration of preparer (other than taxpayer) is based on all information of which preparer has any knowledge.

▶ _____   ▶ _____
   Signature of officer   Date   Title

Paid Preparer's Use Only

Preparer's signature ▶	Date	Check if self-employed ▶ ☐	Preparer's social security number
Firm's name (or yours, if self-employed) and address ▶		E.I. No. ▶	
		ZIP code ▶	

Schedule A Cost of Goods Sold and/or Operations
(See instructions for line 2, page 1)

1 Inventory at beginning of year.	**1**	
2 Purchases	**2**	
3 Cost of labor	**3**	
4 Other costs (attach schedule).	**4**	
5 Total—Add lines 1 through 4	**5**	
6 Inventory at end of year.	**6**	
7 Cost of goods sold and/or operations—Line 5 less line 6. Enter here and on line 2, page 1 . . .	**7**	

8 (a) Check all methods used for valuing closing inventory:

    (i) ☐ Cost

    (ii) ☐ Lower of cost or market as described in Regulations section 1.471–4 (see instructions)

    (iii) ☐ Writedown of "subnormal" goods as described in Regulations section 1.471–2(c) (see instructions)

    (iv) ☐ Other (Specify method used and attach explanation) ▶ --

  (b) Check if the LIFO inventory method was adopted this tax year for any goods (if checked, attach Form 970) . . . . . . ☐

  (c) If the LIFO inventory method was used for this tax year, enter percentage (or amounts) of
     closing inventory computed under LIFO . . . . **8(c)**

  (d) If you are engaged in manufacturing, did you value your inventory using the full absorption method (Regulations section 1.471–11)? . . . . ☐ Yes ☐ No

  (e) Was there any change in determining quantities, cost, or valuations between opening and closing inventory? . . . ☐ Yes ☐ No
    If "Yes," attach explanation.

Schedule C Dividends and Special Deductions
(See instructions for Schedule C)

	(A) Dividends received	(B) %	(C) Special deductions: multiply (A) X (B)
1 Domestic corporations subject to 85% deduction (other than debt-financed stock) .		85	
2 Debt-financed stock of domestic corporations (section 246A)		see instructions	
3 Certain preferred stock of public utilities		59.13	
4 Foreign corporations subject to 85% deduction		85	
5 Wholly-owned foreign subsidiaries subject to 100% deduction (section 245(b)) . .		100	
6 Total—Add lines 1 through 5. See instructions for limitation	/////		
7 Affiliated groups subject to the 100% deduction (section 243(a)(3))		100	/////
8 Other dividends from foreign corporations not included in lines 4 and 5 . . .			
9 Income from controlled foreign corporations under subpart F (attach Forms 5471) .			
10 Foreign dividend gross-up (section 78)			
11 DISC or former DISC dividends not included in line 1 and/or 2 (section 246(d)) . .			
12 Other dividends			
13 Deduction for dividends paid on certain preferred stock of public utilities (see instructions)	/////		/////
14 Total dividends—Add lines 1 through 12. Enter here and on line 4, page 1 . . ▶			/////
15 Total deductions—Add lines 6, 7 and 13. Enter here and on line 29(b), page 1 . . . . ▶			

Schedule E Compensation of Officers (See instructions for line 12, page 1)
Complete Schedule E only if total receipts (line 1(a), plus lines 4 through 10, of page 1, Form 1120) are $150,000 or more.

1. Name of officer	2. Social security number	3. Percent of time devoted to business	Percent of corporation stock owned		6. Amount of compensation
			4. Common	5. Preferred	
		%	%	%	
		%	%	%	
		%	%	%	
		%	%	%	
		%	%	%	
		%	%	%	
		%	%	%	

Total compensation of officers—Enter here and on line 12, page 1 . . . .

Schedule F Bad Debts—Reserve Method (See instructions for line 15, page 1)

1. Year	2. Trade notes and accounts receivable outstanding at end of year	3. Sales on account	Amount added to reserve		6. Amount charged against reserve	7. Reserve for bad debts at end of year
			4. Current year's provision	5. Recoveries		
1979						
1980						
1981						
1982						
1983						
1984						

Schedule J   **Tax Computation**
                    (See instructions)

1 Check if you are a member of a controlled group (see sections 1561 and 1563) . . . . ▶ ☐

2 If line 1 is checked, see instructions and enter your portion of the $25,000 amount in each taxable income
    bracket:

    (i) $ _ _ _ _ _ _ _ _ _ _   *(ii)* $ _ _ _ _ _ _ _ _ _ _   *(iii)* $ _ _ _ _ _ _ _ _ _ _   *(iv)* $ _ _ _ _ _ _ _ _ _ _

3 Income tax (see instructions to figure the tax; enter this tax or alternative tax from Schedule D, whichever is
    less). Check if from Schedule D ▶ ☐ . . . . **| 3 |**

4 **(a)** Foreign tax credit (attach Form 1118). . . . . **4(a)**
    (b) Possessions tax credit (attach Form 5735) . . . .   **(b)**
    (c) Orphan drug credit (attach Form 6765) . . . .   **(c)**
    (d) Credit for fuel produced from a nonconventional source (see instructions) . . .   **(d)**
    (e) Research credit (attach Form 6765) . . . .   **(e)**
    (f) General business credit. Enter here and check which forms are
        attached ☐ Form 3800 ☐ Form 3468 ☐ Form 5884
                ☐ Form 6478 ☐ Form 8007 . . . . **(f)**

5 Total—Add lines 4(a) through 4(f) . . . . **| 5 |**
6 Line 3 less line 5 . . . . **| 6 |**
7 Personal holding company tax (attach Schedule PH (Form 1120)) . . . . . . **| 7 |**
8 Tax from recomputing prior-year investment credit (attach Form 4255) . . . . **| 8 |**
9 Minimum tax on tax preference items (see instructions—attach Form 4626) . . . **| 9 |**
10 Total tax—Add lines 6 through 9. Enter here and on line 31, page 1 . . . . . . **| 10 |**

Additional Information (See instruction F) | **Yes | No**

H Did the corporation claim a deduction for expenses connected with:
    (1) Entertainment facility (boat, resort, ranch, etc.)? . . . .
    (2) Living accommodations (except employees on business)? . .
    (3) Employees attending conventions or meetings outside the
        North American area? (See section 274(h).)
    (4) Employees' families at conventions or meetings? . . . .
        If "Yes," were any of these conventions or meetings outside
        the North American area? (See section 274(h).). . . . .
    (5) Employee or family vacations not reported on Form W-2? . .

I **(1)** Did the corporation at the end of the tax year own, directly or
        indirectly, 50% or more of the voting stock of a domestic
        corporation? (For rules of attribution, see section 267(c).) . .
        If "Yes," attach a schedule showing: (a) name, address, and
        identifying number; (b) percentage owned; (c) taxable income or
        (loss) before NOL and special deductions (e.g., If a Form 1120:
        from Form 1120, line 28, page 1) of such corporation for the tax
        year ending with or within your tax year; (d) highest amount owed
        by the corporation to such corporation during the year; and (e)
        highest amount owed to the corporation by such corporation
        during the year.
    (2) Did any individual, partnership, corporation, estate or trust at
        the end of the tax year own, directly or indirectly, 50% or more
        of the corporation's voting stock? (For rules of attribution, see
        section 267(c).) If "Yes," complete (a) through (e) . . . .
        (a) Attach a schedule showing name, address, and identifying
            number.
        (b) Enter percentage owned ▶ _ _ _ _ _ _ _ _ _ _ _ _
        (c) Was the owner of such voting stock a person other than a
            U.S. person? (See instructions) (Note: If "Yes," the
            corporation may have to file Form 5472.) . . . . .
            If "Yes," enter owner's country ▶ _ _ _ _ _ _ _
        (d) Enter highest amount owed by the corporation to such
            owner during the year ▶ _ _ _ _ _ _ _ _ _ _ _
        (e) Enter highest amount owed to the corporation by such
            owner during the year ▶ _ _ _ _ _ _ _ _ _ _ _

(Note: For purposes of I(1) and I(2), "highest amount owed" includes
    loans and accounts receivable/payable.) | **Yes | No**

J Refer to the list in the instructions and state the principal:
    Business activity ▶ _ _ _ _ _ _ _ _ _ _ _ _ _ _ _
    Product or service ▶ _ _ _ _ _ _ _ _ _ _ _ _ _ _

K Was the corporation a U.S. shareholder of any controlled foreign
    corporation? (See sections 951 and 957.) . . . .
    If "Yes," attach Form 5471 for each such corporation.

L At any time during the tax year, did the corporation have an interest
    in or a signature or other authority over a bank account, securities
    account, or other financial account in a foreign country? . . . .
    (See instruction F for exceptions and filing requirements for
    form TD F 90-22.1.)
    If "Yes," write the name of the foreign country ▶ _ _ _ _ _ _ _
    _

M Was the corporation the grantor of, or transferor to, a foreign trust
    which existed during the current tax year, whether or not the
    corporation has any beneficial interest in it? . . . . . .
    If "Yes," the corporation may have to file Forms 3520, 3520-A or 926.

N During this tax year, did the corporation pay dividends (other than
    stock dividends and distributions in exchange for stock) in excess of the
    corporation's current and accumulated earnings and profits? (See
    sections 301 and 316.). . . . .
    If "Yes," file Form 5452. If this is a consolidated return, answer
    here for parent corporation and on Form 851, Affiliations Schedule,
    for each subsidiary.

O During this tax year did the corporation maintain any part of its
    accounting/ tax records on a computerized system? . . . . .

P Check method of accounting:
    (1) ☐ Cash
    (2) ☐ Accrual
    (3) ☐ Other (specify) ▶ _ _ _ _ _ _ _ _ _ _ _ _ _ _

Schedule L — Balance Sheets

Assets	Beginning of tax year (A)	(B)	End of tax year (C)	(D)
1 Cash				
2 Trade notes and accounts receivable				
(a) Less allowance for bad debts				
3 Inventories				
4 Federal and State government obligations				
5 Other current assets (attach schedule)				
6 Loans to stockholders				
7 Mortgage and real estate loans				
8 Other investments (attach schedule)				
9 Buildings and other depreciable assets				
(a) Less accumulated depreciation				
10 Depletable assets				
(a) Less accumulated depletion				
11 Land (net of any amortization)				
12 Intangible assets (amortizable only)				
(a) Less accumulated amortization				
13 Other assets (attach schedule)				
14 Total assets				
Liabilities and Stockholders' Equity				
15 Accounts payable				
16 Mortgages, notes, bonds payable in less than 1 year				
17 Other current liabilities (attach schedule)				
18 Loans from stockholders				
19 Mortgages, notes, bonds payable in 1 year or more				
20 Other liabilities (attach schedule)				
21 Capital stock: (a) Preferred stock				
(b) Common stock				
22 Paid-in or capital surplus				
23 Retained earnings—Appropriated (attach schedule)				
24 Retained earnings—Unappropriated				
25 Less cost of treasury stock		( )		( )
26 Total liabilities and stockholders' equity				

Schedule M–1 — Reconciliation of Income Per Books With Income Per Return

Do not complete this schedule if the total assets on line 14, column (D), of Schedule L are less than $25,000.

1 Net income per books		7 Income recorded on books this year not included in this return (itemize)	
2 Federal income tax		(a) Tax-exempt interest $ _____	
3 Excess of capital losses over capital gains			
4 Income subject to tax not recorded on books this year (itemize) _____		8 Deductions in this tax return not charged against book income this year (itemize)	
5 Expenses recorded on books this year not deducted in this return (itemize)		(a) Depreciation . . $ _____	
(a) Depreciation . . $ _____		(b) Contributions carryover $ _____	
(b) Contributions carryover $ _____			
		9 Total of lines 7 and 8	
6 Total of lines 1 through 5		10 Income (line 28, page 1)—line 6 less line 9	

Schedule M–2 — Analysis of Unappropriated Retained Earnings Per Books (line 24, Schedule L)

Do not complete this schedule if the total assets on line 14, column (D), of Schedule L are less than $25,000.

1 Balance at beginning of year		5 Distributions: (a) Cash	
2 Net income per books		(b) Stock	
3 Other increases (itemize) _____		(c) Property	
		6 Other decreases (itemize) _____	
		7 Total of lines 5 and 6	
4 Total of lines 1, 2, and 3		8 Balance at end of year (line 4 less line 7)	

Exhibit 7.14

Form **1120S** — U.S. Income Tax Return for an S Corporation

Form **1120S**
Department of the Treasury
Internal Revenue Service

U.S. Income Tax Return for an S Corporation

For calendar 1984 or tax year beginning _____, 1984, ending _____, 19 _____

▶ **For Paperwork Reduction Act Notice, see page 1 of the instructions.**

OMB No. 1545-0130

1984

A Date of election as an S corporation

B Business Code No. (see Specific Instructions)

Use IRS label. Otherwise, please print or type.

Name

Number and street

City or town, State, and ZIP code

C Employer identification number

D Date incorporated

E Total assets (see Specific Instructions)
$

F. Check box if there has been a change in address from the previous year . . . . ▶ ☐

Income

1 a Gross receipts or sales _____ **b** Less returns and allowances _____ Balance ▶	**1c**	
2 Cost of goods sold and/or operations (Schedule A, line 7)	**2**	
3 Gross profit (subtract line 2 from line 1c)	**3**	
4 Nonqualifying interest and nonqualifying dividends	**4**	
5 Gross rents	**5**	
6 Gross royalties	**6**	
7 Net gain or (loss) from Form 4797, line 14(a), Part II . . .	**7**	
8 Other income (see instructions—attach schedule)	**8**	
9 TOTAL income (loss)—Combine lines 3 through 8 and enter here . . . . . . ▶	**9**	

Deductions

10 Compensation of officers	**10**	
11 a Salaries and wages _____ **b** Less jobs credit _____ Balance ▶	**11c**	
12 Repairs	**12**	
13 Bad debts (see instructions)	**13**	
14 Rents	**14**	
15 Taxes	**15**	
16 a Total deductible interest expense not claimed elsewhere on return (see instructions) **16a**		
b Interest expense required to be passed through to shareholders on Schedules K and K-1, lines 15a(2) and 15a(3) **16b**		
c Subtract line 16b from line 16a	**16c**	
17 a Depreciation from Form 4562 (attach Form 4562) **17a**		
b Depreciation claimed on Schedule A and elsewhere on return . . **17b**		
c Subtract line 17b from line 17a	**17c**	
18 Depletion (**Do not deduct oil and gas depletion.** See instructions).	**18**	
19 Advertising	**19**	
20 Pension, profit-sharing, etc. plans	**20**	
21 Employee benefit programs	**21**	
22 Other deductions (attach schedule)	**22**	
23 TOTAL deductions—Add lines 10 through 22 and enter here . . . . . . ▶	**23**	
24 Ordinary income (loss)—Subtract line 23 from line 9	**24**	

Tax

25 a Excess net passive income tax (attach schedule) **25a**		
b Tax from Schedule D (Form 1120S), Part IV. **25b**		
c Add lines 25a and 25b	**25c**	
26 Payments:		
a Tax deposited with Form 7004 . . . . **26a**		
b Credit for Federal tax on gasoline and special fuels (attach Form 4136) **26b**		
c Add lines 26a and 26b	**26c**	
27 TAX DUE (subtract line 26c from line 25c). See instructions for Paying the Tax. . . ▶	**27**	
28 OVERPAYMENT (subtract line 25c from line 26c) . . . . ▶	**28**	

Please Sign Here

Under penalties of perjury, I declare that I have examined this return, including accompanying schedules and statements, and to the best of my knowledge and belief, it is true, correct, and complete. Declaration of preparer (other than taxpayer) is based on all information of which preparer has any knowledge.

▶ _____ Signature of officer | Date | ▶ _____ Title

Paid Preparer's Use Only

Preparer's signature ▶	Date	Check if self-employed ▶ ☐	Preparer's social security number
Firm's name (or yours, if self-employed) and address ▶		E.I. No. ▶	
		ZIP code ▶	

Form **1120S** (1984)

Schedule A   Cost of Goods Sold and/or Operations (See instructions for Schedule A)

1 Inventory at beginning of year	**1**	
2 Purchases	**2**	
3 Cost of labor	**3**	
4 Other costs (attach schedule)	**4**	
5 Total—Add lines 1 through 4	**5**	
6 Inventory at end of year	**6**	
7 Cost of goods sold and/or operations—Subtract line 6 from line 5. Enter here and on line 2, page 1	**7**	

8 **(a)** Check all methods used for valuing closing inventory:

    (i) ☐ Cost

    (ii) ☐ Lower of cost or market as described in Regulations section 1.471–4 (see instructions)

    (iii) ☐ Writedown of "subnormal" goods as described in Regulations section 1.471–2(c) (see instructions)

    (iv) ☐ Other (Specify method used and attach explanation) ▶ ---

  (b) Check if the LIFO inventory method was adopted this tax year for any goods (if checked, attach Form 970) . . . . . . ☐

  (c) If the LIFO inventory method was used for this tax year, enter percentage (or amounts) of closing inventory

    computed under LIFO . . . . |**8(c)**|

  (d) If you are engaged in manufacturing, did you value your inventory using the full absorption method (Regulations section 1.471–11)? . . . . ☐ Yes   ☐ No

  (e) Was there any change in determining quantities, cost, or valuations between opening and closing inventory? . . . ☐ Yes   ☐ No

    If "Yes," attach explanation.

Additional Information Required

	Yes	No
G Did you at the end of the tax year own, directly or indirectly, 50% or more of the voting stock of a domestic corporation? (For rules of attribution, see section 267(c).).		
If "Yes," attach a schedule showing:		
(1) Name, address, and employer identification number;		
(2) Percentage owned;		
(3) Highest amount owed by you to such corporation during the year; and		
(4) Highest amount owed to you by such corporation during the year.		
(Note: *For purposes of G(3) and G(4), "highest amount owed" includes loans and accounts receivable/payable.)*		
H Refer to the listing of Business Activity Codes and state your principal:		
Business activity ▶ -----------------------------; Product or service ▶ ----------------------		
I Were you a member of a controlled group subject to the provisions of section 1561?		
J Did you claim a deduction for expenses connected with:		
(1) Entertainment facilities (boat, resort, ranch, etc.)?		
(2) Living accommodations (except for employees on business)?		
(3) Employees attending conventions or meetings outside the North American area? (See section 274(h).) . . .		
(4) Employees' families at conventions or meetings?		
If "Yes," were any of these conventions or meetings outside the North American area? (See section 274(h).) .		
(5) Employee or family vacations not reported on Form W-2?		
K At any time during the tax year, did you have an interest in or a signature or other authority over a bank account, securities account, or other financial account in a foreign country? (See instructions for exceptions and filing requirements for form TD F 90-22.1.)		
If "Yes," write the name of the foreign country ▶ --------------------------------		
L Were you the grantor of, or transferor to, a foreign trust which existed during the current tax year, whether or not you have any beneficial interest in it? If "Yes," you may have to file Forms 3520, 3520-A, or 926		
M During this tax year did you maintain any part of your accounting/tax records on a computerized system?		
N Check method of accounting: **(1)** ☐ Cash **(2)** ☐ Accrual **(3)** ☐ Other (specify) ▶ ------------------		
O Check this box if the S corporation has filed or is required to file Form 8264, Application for Registration of a Tax Shelter . . . . ☐		

Schedule K	**Shareholders' Share of Income, Credits, Deductions, etc. (See Instructions.)**		
a. Distributive share items		**b. Total amount**	

Income (Losses) and Deductions

1	Ordinary income (loss) (page 1, line 24) *	1	
2	Dividends qualifying for the exclusion	2	
3	Net short-term capital gain (loss) (Schedule D (Form 1120S))	3	
4	Net long-term capital gain (loss) (Schedule D (Form 1120S))	4	
5	Net gain (loss) from involuntary conversions due to casualty or theft	5	
6	Other net gain (loss) under section 1231	6	
7	Other income (loss) (attach schedule)	7	
8	Charitable contributions: 50%_____, 30%_____*_____, 20%_____	8	
9	Expense deduction for recovery property (section 179 expense) *	9	
10	Other (attach schedule)	10	

Credits

11	Jobs credit *	11	
12	Credit for alcohol used as fuel *	12	
13	Other (see instructions) *	13	

Tax Preference Items

14 a	Accelerated depreciation on nonrecovery real property or 15 (or 18)-year real property	14a	
b	Accelerated depreciation on leased personal property or leased recovery property other than 15 (or 18)-year real property	14b	
c	Depletion (other than oil and gas)	14c	
d (1)	Gross income from oil, gas, or geothermal properties	14d(1)	
(2)	Gross deductions allocable to oil, gas, or geothermal properties	14d(2)	
e (1)	Qualified Investment income included in line 1	14e(1)	
(2)	Qualified Investment expenses included in line 1	14e(2)	
f	Other (attach schedule)	14f	

Investment Interest

15 a (1)	Investment debts incurred before 12-17-69	15a(1)	
(2)	Investment debts incurred before 9-11-75 but after 12-16-69	15a(2)	
(3)	Investment debts incurred after 9-10-75	15a(3)	
b (1)	Investment income included in line 1	15b(1)	
(2)	Investment expenses included in line 1.	15b(2)	
c (1)	Income from "net lease property"	15c(1)	
(2)	Expenses from ''net lease property''	15c(2)	
d	Excess of net long-term capital gain over net short-term capital loss from investment property . .	15d	

Foreign Taxes

16 a	Type of income _____		
b	Name of foreign country or U.S. possession _____		
c	Total gross income from sources outside the U.S. (attach schedule)	16c	
d	Total applicable deductions and losses (attach schedule)	16d	
e	Total foreign taxes (check one): ▶ ☐ Paid ☐ Accrued	16e	
f	Reduction in taxes available for credit (attach schedule)	16f	
g	Other (attach schedule)	16g	

Other Items

17	Total dividend distributions paid from accumulated earnings and profits contained in retained earnings (lines 23 and 24 of Schedule L)	17	
18	Total property distributions (including cash) other than dividend distributions reported on line 17 . .	18	
19	Other items and amounts not included in lines 1 through 18 that are required to be reported separately to shareholders (attached schedule).		

* You are not required to complete lines 1, 9, 11, 12 and 13. Completion of these lines is optional because the amounts which would appear in column b appear elsewhere on Form 1120S or on other IRS forms or schedules which are attached to Form 1120S.

Schedule L	Balance Sheets	Beginning of tax year		End of tax year	
	Assets	(A)	(B)	(C)	(D)
1	Cash				
2	Trade notes and accounts receivable . . .				
	(a) Less allowance for bad debts				
3	Inventories				
4	Federal and State government obligations . .				
5	Other current assets (attach schedule) . . .				
6	Loans to shareholders				
7	Mortgage and real estate loans				
8	Other investments (attach schedule) . . .				
9	Buildings and other depreciable assets . . .				
	(a) Less accumulated depreciation				
10	Depletable assets				
	(a) Less accumulated depletion				
11	Land (net of any amortization)				
12	Intangible assets (amortizable only)				
	(a) Less accumulated amortization				
13	Other assets (attach schedule)				
14	Total assets				
	Liabilities and Shareholders' Equity				
15	Accounts payable				
16	Mortgages, notes, bonds payable in less than 1 year				
17	Other current liabilities (attach schedule) . .				
18	Loans from shareholders				
19	Mortgages, notes, bonds payable in 1 year or more				
20	Other liabilities (attach schedule)				
21	Capital stock				
22	Paid-in or capital surplus				
23	Retained earnings—Appropriated (attach schedule)				
24	Retained earnings—Unappropriated (see instructions)				
25	Shareholders' undistributed taxable income previously taxed				
26	Accumulated adjustments account				
27	Other adjustments account				
28	Less cost of treasury stock		( )		( )
29	Total liabilities and shareholders' equity . .				

Schedule M	Reconciliation of Shareholders' Undistributed Taxable Income Previously Taxed, Accumulated Adjustments Account, and Other Adjustments Account, lines 25, 26, and 27 above (see instructions).

		Shareholders' undistributed taxable income previously taxed	Accumulated adjustments account	Other adjustments account
1	Balance at beginning of year			
2	Ordinary income from page 1, line 24 . . .			
3	Other additions			
4	Total of lines 1, 2, and 3			
5	Distributions other than dividend distributions			
6	Loss from page 1, line 24			
7	Other reductions			
8	Add lines 5, 6, and 7			
9	Balance at end of tax year—Line 4 less line 8			

Exhibit 7.15

ANNUAL MEETING REMINDER AND QUESTIONNAIRE
Memorandum

(Date)

TO: (Lawyer)

FROM: (Legal Assistant)

RE: (Name of Corporation)

This is to remind you that the annual meetings of the shareholders and directors of (Name of Corporation) should be held on _____.

Attached for your review is a draft of a reminder letter to (Name of President of Corporation) and an annual meeting questionnaire.

Transmittal Letter

RE: Annual Meetings of _____

Dear _____:

This is to remind you that the Bylaws of _____ provide that the annual meetings of the Shareholders and Directors should be held on _____.

Because of the increasing emphasis on liability of Directors, with respect to their duties and obligations to shareholders, creditors and others, we urge all corporations to pay attention to the formalities of their corporate existence. This includes the holding of annual meetings for the purpose of electing Officers and Directors, making adjustments to salaries, declaring bonuses or dividends, reviewing the operations of the Company for the previous year and planning for the coming year.

Please review and complete the enclosed questionnaire and give me a call so we can plan for the annual meetings.

Sincerely,

---

shareholder must designate the types of records to be inspected and received; the purpose of the inspection—the purpose must be "proper;" and in some jurisdictions a written demand of inspection.

4. Shareholder actions

Shareholders have both the power and right to sue the corporation under two theories: direct and derivative.

a. If the shareholder can demonstrate that an officer and/or director of the corporation has breached his fiduciary duty to that shareholder, *not* to the corporation itself, a direct action will be possible against that officer and/or director.

b. If the shareholders can demonstrate that they are suing simply to enforce the rights of the corporation as an entity from being further victimized by director fraud, mismanagement, or other wrong, they then can sue in a derivative sense. A derivative suit requires:

1. Shareholder capacity to bring forth the suit.
2. Shareholder must have "contemporaneous ownership," that is, at the time of wrong, shareholder owned the stock.
3. Demand upon board of directors to enforce the corporation's rights.
4. In some jurisdictions, *security for expenses.*

G. Authority, Duties, and Liabilities of Corporate Directors

1. Directors' relationship to the corporation

The board of directors has the general task of managing the business and daily affairs of the corporation and to act in a fiduciary capacity. They are expected to use good sound business judgment. A director's failure to be smart all the time is not a basis for a breach of fiduciary duties. Directors are human beings prone to common error. Thus, the law can expect no more than diligence, loyalty, and obedience from any director, not infallibility and perpetual profit generation.

While no effort is being made to simplify the complexities in the area of law, directors are given broad powers and rights and, as a result, cannot be controlled as most shareholders might prefer. In the absence of fraud, self-dealing, proof of personal profit, or wanton acts of omissions and commission, directors of a business corporation are not personally liable.

2. Directors' liability in particular situations

As a fiduciary, a director owes undivided loyalty to the corporation. Consider the following inquiries:

☐ Is the director already working with a competing corporation?
☐ Is the director in any situation where a conflict of interest may take place?
☐ Is the director going to benefit personally from *insider trading* information?
☐ Has the director repressed or oppressed the rights of shareholders?
☐ Has the director usurped an opportunity that should have inured to the corporation?
☐ Has the director exceeded by his or her behavior the powers of the corporation? This is commonly known as an *ultra vires* question.

All of these queries give rise to fiduciary dilemmas and ethical concerns that are not always easily resolved.

H. Special Corporate Situations

Recent legislative inventions or agency formulations have provided the corporate planner with a few more slants to consider in the choice of business form. Review briefly the following, but know that expert tax advice is needed in this complex area.

1. Subchapter S corporation

The Subchapter S corporation is purely a product of the Internal Revenue Code, sections 1371-1379. The basic requirements for a Subchapter S corporation are the following. The corporation:

☐ Is a domestic corporation in form
☐ Is invested in by no more than twenty-five shareholders
☐ Has no nonresident alien as a shareholder
☐ Has only one class of stock
☐ Has no substantial amount of foreign income (80–20 percent ratios)

The tactical reasons for choosing this form are related to the beneficial tax treatment that shareholders receive as to distributions and losses. The tax savings can be substantial.

2. The closely held corporation

This is a subclass of corporation whereby the shareholders may have agreements under state law governing the operation of the affairs of the corporation. Shareholders essentially operate the corporation as if it were a partnership. Shareholders become the management team. There are rigid restrictions on the ability to be a closely held corporation: (1) no more than thirty shareholders, (2) no public offering of shares, and (3) restrictions on transferability.

3. The professional corporation

Another recent legislative invention allowing once clearly outlawed occupations to incorporate, namely, lawyers and doctors. Exhibit 7.16 shows a certificate of incorporation of a professional corporation.

4. The franchise

In an age of fast-food and other franchised businesses, the law office is frequently asked to prepare a franchise agreement.

Exhibit 7.16

CERTIFICATE OF INCORPORATION
OF PROFESSIONAL CORPORATION

THE UNDERSIGNED, being natural persons at least twenty-one years old and acting as incorporators of the corporation being formed under Article _____ of the _____ Law of the State of _____ certify as follows:

1. *Name*:   The name of the corporation is _____, P.C.

2. *Purpose*:   The corporation is formed for the following purposes:

   (a) To engage in the specific business of the practice of the profession of [Law or any other profession whose practitioners can incorporate] through individuals licensed under the laws of the State of _____ to practice [law] in that State.

   (b) To purchase or otherwise acquire, hold, own, maintain, improve, operate, mortgage, sell, convey, lease, sublease or otherwise deal in and dispose of personal and real property of every kind, character and description in furtherance of the corporation's professional business.

   (c) To enter into contracts of all kinds in furtherance of the corporation's professional business.

   (d) To borrow money with or without security in furtherance of the corporation's professional business, and to make, endorse, execute and issue those instruments for the payment of money that are necessary to evidence the corporation's borrowings.

   (e) To invest the corporation's funds in real properties, mortgages, stocks, bonds, or any other types of investments, and while the owner or holder of any real properties, mortgages, stocks, bonds, or other type of investments, to receive, collect, reinvest and dispose of the interest, dividends, and income arising from such property, and to possess and exercise all the rights, powers and privileges of ownership, including all voting powers of any stocks owned.

   (f) To establish and carry out pension, profit-sharing, share-bonus, share-purchase, incentive and benefit plans, trusts, and provisions for any or all of the corporation's directors, officers and employees.

   (g) Paragraphs 2(a) through 2(f) shall be construed as enumerating both objects and purposes of the corporation, and the enumeration of specific purposes shall not be held to limit or restrict in any manner the purposes of the corporation otherwise permitted by law.

   (h) To exercise all of the powers now or hereafter conferred by the _____ Law upon corporations formed thereunder, subject to any limitations contained in the _____ Law or in accordance with the provisions of any other statute of the State of _____.

3. *Address*:   The office, of the corporation, is to be located in the City of _____, County of _____, State of _____.

4. *Capital Stock*:   The aggregate number of common shares, which the corporation shall have authority to issue is _____ Common Shares, which shares are to have a par value of $ _____ per share. The aggregate number of preferred shares, which the corporation shall have authority to issue is _____ Preferred Shares, which shares are to have a par value of $ _____ per share.

5. *Ownership Only by Qualified Persons*:   The shares of capital stock of the corporation shall be issued and transferred (other than by operation of law or court decree) only to individuals who are authorized to practice [law] in the State of _____ No transferee of shares of capital stock of the corporation by operation of law or court decree may vote such shares for any purpose whatsoever except as permitted by the Laws of the State of _____.

6. *Names and Qualifications of Shareholders*:   The names, residences and licenses or certificate numbers of the individuals who are to be the original Shareholders, Directors and Officers of the corporation are:

NAME	RESIDENCE	LICENSE OR CERTIFICATE NO.
_____	_____	_____
_____	_____	_____

All of these persons are licensed by the State of _____ to practice the profession of [law].

7. *Secretary of State as Agent*:   The Secretary of State, of the State of _____, is designated as the agent of the corporation upon whom process against it may be served. The post office address to which the Secretary of State is to mail a copy of any process against it may be served upon him is _____.

   IN WITNESS WHEREOF, we have made, subscribed and acknowledged this certificate this _____ day of _____, 19 _____.

_____
(Signatures)

I. Dissolution: An End to the Enterprise

All things eventually end their existence, including business forms. There does exist a civil way for all these business forms to expire.

1. Proprietorship: grounds for termination

A proprietorship ends upon the death of the proprietor, voluntary withdrawal, or involuntary withdrawal.

2. Partnership: grounds for termination

There are a variety of grounds that permit the dissolution of this enterprise. Consider, first, the ramifications of a breach of a contract that was originally hammered out between the parties in the origination of this entity. Contract law can and will provide appropriate remedies for breaches to that agreement. Consider, second, the fundamental wills or desires of the parties to the enterprise. The partners may simply wish to end the venture honorably and amicably. Equally possible is the dissolution by specific agreement or by contractual termination, according to the original duration dates. Such grounds for dissolution are not troublesome or hard to prove. Third, consider those grounds for dissolution that are filled with problems, such as a request from a partner for a hearing on involuntary dissolution. Why would a partner desire to end the relationship and force a judicial remedy? A basic lesson in life is that all that begins well does not necessarily end in the same way. Imagine a partner who becomes so utterly deranged or senile that his decisions are deleterious to all. Envision a partner who has become so physically incapacitated that her judgment for management is questionable. All these rationales are logical bases for a dissolution. Consider, finally, the other reasons a dissolution may be granted or should be sought: bankruptcy, death of partners, illegal purpose, and total losses versus profits. Any of the above grounds can justify a dissolution of a partnership.

3. Dissolution of the corporate form

Even though a corporation is perpetual by nature, its duration can be fixed in the articles, or other factual patterns may emerge that will lead to eventual dissolution.

a. Voluntary Dissolution

This procedure is quite common and can be initiated by the incorporators, by the shareholders, or by the corporation's own resolution or act. As with all business enterprises, the rationales for their demise can be personal, economic, or political. The process of dissolution must be made known to shareholders, creditors, and all interested parties. A summary of the process follows. It can be streamlined by utilizing the check list for dissolution and liquidation provided in exhibit 7.17.

Steps in Dissolution/Liquidation:

1. File statement of intent to dissolve with secretary of state or other appropriate agency.
2. Notify all creditors and collect and liquidate all assets (winding-up process).
3. File articles of dissolution (if required).
4. State issues of certificate of dissolution.

b. Involuntary Dissolution: Grounds

As noted in the discussion on proprietorships and partnerships, a business entity may be dissolved without its consent. The most common scenarios in which this type of dissolution would occur include:

1. Action by the state attorney general for fraudulent procurement of the original articles of incorporation.
2. Action by the state attorney general for corporate behavior that exceeds its own powers or charter.
3. Action by the state attorney general for failure to appoint a registered agent or report a change of address during a prescribed period.
4. Action by the attorney general for failure to pay taxes.
5. Shareholder may apply for a judicial dissolution, if he or she can demonstrate that:
   a. The directors of the corporation are deadlocked in a management dispute.
   b. The directors are wasting the corporate assets.

Exhibit 7.17

Billing No. _____   Attorney _____

CHECKLIST FOR DISSOLUTION AND LIQUIDATION OF

_____

Determine whether dissolution by act of corporation _____ consent of shareholders _____ (see separate checklist for dissolution by act of incorporators)

Determine applicable IRC Provisions: # 331 ____ # 332 ____ # 333 ____ # 337 ____

Call Secretary of State to confirm no unpaid license fees _____

Prepare documents:

Board action: Minutes _____ Waiver _____ Notice _____ Consent _____
Shareholder action: Minutes _____ Waiver _____ Notice _____ Consent _____
Statement of Intent to Dissolve ("Statement") _____
Exhibit A to Statement (copy of shareholders' resolution authorizing dissolution) _____
Notice to Creditors _____
Articles of Dissolution ("Articles") _____
Document transferring property _____

Prepare forms:

IRS 966 and cert. copy of res. of shareholders _____ 964 _____ 1096 _____ 1099L _____ 1120
Application for excise tax status ("Application") _____ Guaranty _____

Prepare letters:

2 memos to lawyer: minutes or consents, Statement and IRS forms _____
                   Articles and misc. forms _____
Client forwarding minutes or consents, Statement, IRS forms for signature, and requesting endorsed stock cert. for cancellation _____
Secretary of State filing Statement _____
IRS filing 966 _____ IRS filing 964 _____ IRS filing 1096 and 1099L(1120) _____
Client forwarding dissolution section for minute book Statement and receipt _____
Client forwarding Articles and miscellaneous forms for signature _____
Department of Revenue filing Application (and Guaranty) _____
Client forwarding Department of Revenue clearance _____
Secretary of State filing Articles _____
Client reminding it to file Form 964 with income tax return _____
Withdraw from other states where qualified to do business _____
Review documents forms and letters _____
Forward drafts of minutes or consents, Statement and IRS forms to lawyer for approval _____
Forward minutes or consents, Statement and IRS forms to client for adoption and signature _____
Receive minutes or consents, Statement, IRS forms and stock certificates from client _____
Review and complete documents received from client _____
Photocopy and file minutes (and notices or waivers of notice) or consents, IRS forms and notice to creditors in file and duplicate minute book _____
Cancel stock certificate(s), make photocopies for file and duplicate minute book _____
File form 966 [and 964] with IRS (within 30 days of adoption of plan of liquidation) _____
File two executed copies of Statement with the Secretary of State _____
Forward Notice to Creditors to client for service, or directly to creditors
Receive Statement from Secretary of State _____
Photocopy and file Certificate & Statement in file and duplicate minute book _____
Prepare dissolution section for original and duplicate minute books _____
Forward dissolution section for minute book, Certificate & Statement to client _____
Confirm that debts have been paid or provided for _____
Forward drafts of Articles, Appl., Guaranty, IRS forms and transfer docs. to lawyer for approval _____
Forward Articles, Appl., IRS forms and transfer docs. to client for adoption & signature _____

Receive Articles, Application, Guaranty, IRS forms and transfer documents from client _____

Review and complete documents received from client _____

Photocopy and file affidavit, Guaranty and transfer documents in file and duplicate minute book _____

File Application (and Guaranty) with Department of Revenue _____

Receive Department of Revenue clearance _____

Forward Department of Revenue clearance to client _____

File two executed copies of Articles with Secretary of State _____

Receive Articles and Certificate of Dissolution from Secretary of State _____

File 1096 and 1099L (1122) with the IRS _____

Photocopy and file Certificate & Articles in file and duplicate minute book

Forward original of Certificate, Articles, minute book, stock book & seal to client _____

Remove corporation from system _____

*Excerpted from *Working with Legal Assistants: A Team Approach for Lawyers and Legal Assistants*, Paul G. Ulrich and Robert S. Mucklestone, eds. Reprinted with permission of the American Bar Association.

    c. The directors are illegally oppressing shareholders and their interests.

    d. The shareholders are deadlocked in their choices for successor directors.

  6. A creditor may request a judicial dissolution if it has a judgment against the corporation.

V. BASIC AGENCY

A. General Description of the Agency Relationship

So much of the practice of business organizations seems inevitably to deal, either directly or peripherally, with the law of agency. Agency is essentially the law of relationships and the resulting duties, rights, and liabilities that come forth from those relationships. In the broader sense, the outline will review three basic relationships: master/servant, principal/agent, and employer/independent contractor.

1. Master/servant relationship

At common law, it was a *master*, who employed, and a *servant*, who worked for the master. Out of this uneven relationship arose some responsibilities. Think about these questions:

    a. If a master hires a servant, is the master responsible for what the servant does? What if the servant does something tortious in nature?

    b. Is not the servant merely doing the work of the master and thereby making the master always responsible for the servant's errors in work? What if there is a breach in contract?

The old master/servant relationship was basically one grounded in servile or manual labor. Liability was extended to the master by the acts of a servant. The very existence of that relationship makes two people responsible when only one "did" it. That is the power of agency.

2. Principal/agent relationship

By the nineteenth century, the law became concerned with not only manual-labor relationships but also paper transactions. Consider the vast field this outline has just reviewed. Do you see the myriad opportunities for an agency relationship to exist in business organizations? While master/servant is proper in some situations, in our modern world of paper, contracts, and advertising, the term *principal/agent* is more frequently utilized. In every employer/employee relationship there is the potential of a principal/agent relationship. Some examples follow.

    □ Promoters who are agents of the incorporators or directors of a corporation

□ A partner's contractual negotiations on behalf of the partnership
□ Corporate vice-president who sells the product line on behalf of her own company
□ A real estate agent selling on behalf of a landowner
□ Attorneys acting on behalf of a trust fund

Examples of the principal/agent relationship are innumerable. The fundamental question that emerges continually is, is the principal liable for the acts of the agent? The answer depends on a variety of factors, including the agent's job description and resulting scope of employment, unauthorized acts of the agent, and whether or not a clear agency relationship even existed. If proof comes forth in the existence of this relationship, then the agent can bind the principal for (1) all promises made in contract, (2) all damages from tortious conduct, and (3) all restitution for unjust enrichment. The policy of the law in this area is based on the notion that the principal is, in fact, in control of the agent and that this agency relationship emerged by mutual choice.

3. Employer/independent contractor

The last relationship in the law of agency is that of employer/independent contractor. The whole purpose of this legal relationship is to deny the consequences of the principal/agent relationship. Hence, an employer who designates his or her employees as independent contractors will not be responsible for their contractual promises or their tortious behavior.

B. Termination of the Agency Relationship

As easily as the relationship can be created, so can it be dissolved. Termination of the agency relationship can occur by:

1. Mutual agreement
2. Death
3. Insanity
4. Bankruptcy
5. Expiration of contract

DISCUSSION QUESTIONS AND PRACTICAL EXERCISES

Office Memorandum #1

TO: Paralegal Administrator

FROM: John Stevens, Senior Associate
Wilson, Jacobs and Stevens

RE: Choice of Business Form in the Roberts Case, File No. 83–162

A long-standing and extremely wealthy client of ours, David Roberts, has come to me with a business proposition that he would like our firm to advise him on. Basically, Mr. Roberts wants to build a financial empire in the design, production, and marketing of solid steel drinking cups. Mr. Roberts feels very strongly that a solid steel drinking cup is a viable alternative to the standard drinking cup made of plastic, glass, or ceramic, since the latter materials are so easily broken or destroyed in the dishwashing cycle or by human error. Mr. Roberts firmly believes that solid steel drinking cups will be readily accepted.

Aside from the relative merits of his arguments, which frankly some members of the firm believe are not credible, it is our task to recommend to Mr. Roberts the most appropriate business choice. In light of these general questions, please compose a substantial review of the pros and cons of a particular business form, and make a final recommendation with these factual issues in mind:

1. The firm hopes to protect Mr. Roberts from as many personal losses as possible, in the event they occur.
2. How can Mr. Roberts receive the most favorable tax rates, assuming that the overall profit generated will exceed $1,000,000 a year?
3. How can Mr. Roberts obtain total creative, financial and management control? Mr. Roberts has expressed a strong distaste for working with any other parties.

4. How could Mr. Roberts receive substantial capital investment and yet still exercise management control?

5. Mr. Roberts has expressed a definite concern over the cost of business formation. If the cost is too high, he will not continue to organize the venture.

6. Mr. Roberts feels that with the invention of a solid steel drinking glass, the normal civil liabilities common to glass makers for injuries to their customers will disappear. Hence, could he risk unlimited personal liability?

7. Mr. Roberts has no desire to diversify into other products, except maybe the stainless steel toothbrush. Assuming he makes a profit on the drinking cup, would it pay to have a stock offering opportunity?

While I realize this problem is complex, the firm needs your assessment on each of these questions, and a final recommendation on what would be the most favorable business organization.

Thank you.

Office Memorandum #2

TO: Paralegal Administrator

FROM: Mary Jacobs, Senior Partner
                 Wilson, Jacobs and Stevens

RE: Revisions in the Corporate File No. 83–179
                 Armot and Company

A long overdue review of our corporate file on Armont and Company is necessary. A substantial amount of revisions, updates, and amendments are needed, and I would appreciate your advice on the following matters:

1. As of 1979, Armot and Company changed its registered agent from Stanley Williams of New York to Charles Donzak of Pittsburgh, PA, at 312 Van Buren Street, 15421.

2. Armot and Company wishes to change its policy on what constitutes a quorum. What documents would have to be changed?

3. Armot and Company, a maker of industrial ashtrays, desires now to diversify into the field of landscaping. Do we have to notify anyone about this change?

4. Johnny Armot, son of the founder of the company and on the board of directors, is being sued for the conversion of a minority stockholder's dividends. Is it possible that he could be liable?

5. Armot and Company wishes to raise investment capital. What possibilities exist to do so?

6. Armot and Company has yet to file for an employer identification number. How do we correct this?

7. Armot and Company wishes to schedule an annual meeting. Who must be contacted, and how can it be done?

8. Armot and Company wishes to end its corporate existence by the year 2014. What procedure must be followed?

9. Armot and Company does not wish its shareholders to have too much say in important corporate questions, and want to dilute shareholders' voting powers. What could it do to insure that desire?

10. Freddy Armot, a member of the board, has been negotiating a contract for the company, but instead of following through for the benefit of the company, he negotiated the contract for his own personal business gain. Can the shareholders vote his removal?

Office Memorandum #3

TO: Paralegal Administrator

FROM: Sally Wilson, Senior Associate
                 Wilson, Jacobs and Stevens

RE: Dissolution of Monco, Inc., File No. 83–122

As you are well aware, Monco, Inc., has fallen on hard times in the last three years. A declining economy, pending lawsuits, and bad corporate image have all contributed to the poor earnings of the company. On top of all these factors is the general disinterest the public is exhibiting toward Monco's newest product, the "computerized cake timer." Faults in design and marketing have resulted in major losses.

As a result, certain board members feel that some members of the board, as well as the management team, are not doing things in the best interest of Monco. In particular, a director, Phil Popal, feels the only legitimate course of action is dissolution. Could you respond to the following issues:

1. If Popal can prove that Monco's money and assets are being drained, can the corporation be dissolved?
2. Could this corporation be dissolved simply by looking to its bylaws?
3. Can a court order the dissolution?
4. What are all the potential grounds that exist for dissolution in a judicial framework?
5. What paper work must be filed in order to effect a dissolution?
6. Who has to be given notice?
7. Can the state, by its prosecutorial power, effect a dissolution? On what grounds?
8. Can any other parties possibly force a dissolution of the corporation?

ENRICHMENT ACTIVITY

Visit the legal department of a major corporation. What are the primary duties of counsel in serving the corporation? What legal questions are most often confronted, due to the nature of the corporation's business?

SUGGESTED READING

ABA Young Lawyers Section, Corporate Law Dept. *Model for a Corporate Law Department*. Chicago: ABA, 1971.

ANDERSON, JOSEPH C. *Chapter II Reorganizations*. New York: McGraw-Hill Book Co., 1983.

BLOOMENTHAL, HAROLD S. *Securities and Federal Corporate Law*. New York: Clark Boardman Co., 1972.

BORDEN, ARTHUR M. *Going Private*. New York: Law Journal Seminars Press, 1982.

CONARD, ALFRED FLETCHER, et al. *Corporations: Cases, Statutes and Analysis*. Mineola, N.Y.: Foundation Press, 1982.

Corporate Governance. New York: Practising Law Institute, c. 1979.

FITZGIBBON, SCOTT THOMAS. *Professional Ethics, Organizing Corporations, and the Ideology of Corporate Articles and By-Laws*. Chicago: ABA National Center for Professional Responsibility, 1982.

HENN, HARRY G. *Laws of Corporations and Other Business Enterprises*. St Paul: West Publishing Co., 1983.

HOWELL, JOHN COTTON. *Corporate Executive's Legal Handbook: Affidavits, Bills of Sale, Deeds, Guarantees, Partnership Agreements, Releases, Sample Contracts with Extra Clauses You May Need*. Englewood Cliffs, N.J.: Prentice-Hall, 1980.

KOLVENBACH, WALTER. *The Company Legal Department: Its Role, Function and Organization*. Hingham, Mass.: Kulwer Academic Publishers, 1979.

CHAPTER EIGHT

COMMERCIAL LAW

CHAPTER DESCRIPTION

In this chapter, we review the formation of contracts, consideration, the Statute of Frauds, the capacity to contract, third-party beneficiaries, parol evidence, breach of contract, remedies, and the Uniform Commercial Code provisions governing sales of goods and secured interests.

PARALEGAL FUNCTIONS

Interview client.

Draft contract phrases or contract documents.

Analyze contractual disputes.

Create check lists for contractual drafting.

Provide suggestions to the firm for contractual remedies or defense.

Filing and perfection of secured interests.

I. THE NATURE OF CONTRACTUAL RELATIONS

The complexities of modern life seem ever to increase the need for contracts. Contracts are agreements between individuals and businesses or governmental entities. Contracts are the civilized society's method of formalizing promises between individuals. Consider the world without contracts. What would ever get done? Would people simply do things because they felt like it? Or, as a specific example, would bridges across rivers be built by the community because they were needed or because it would be attractive to have one? Can we trust people? Can we possibly misunderstand them? Do people have different expectations? In a funny kind of way, contracts reflect the human condition better than any other legal subject. Contracts are the stuff of common everyday life, like purchasing a house, a car, or a television set. Equally so, contracts deal with that which is esoteric in life, from contracts for space shuttle expeditions to DNA research expenditures. No matter what the world requires, it cannot exist or function without contractual relationships. Unless the nature of the project is clearly defined, the natural differences of opinions and levels of expectations from person to person will emerge.

That is the subject matter of this chapter—a fundamental discussion about what a contract is; its requirements and prerequisites; and how those contracts can be enforced, remedied, and altered in some fashion or form.

A. Sources of Contract Law

The origins of contract law are similar to other types of law; they include:

1. Case law

Contracts rely heavily on traditional common-law interpretations, from medieval England to modern America. Contracts derive the bulk of their interpretive capacity from case law.

2. Statutory law

Most state legislatures have readily adopted statutory schemes that seek to outline and regulate contractual relations. An example is New York's General Obligations Law.

3. Uniform commercial code

No other statutory model is dreaded by students of law as much as the UCC, but its overall content governing a variety of settings is critical to the operation of contracts. We will refer to appropriate sections of the UCC as necessary and generally highlight some portions of article 2—Sales of Goods and article 9—Secured Transactions.

B. The Analytical Approach to Understanding Contracts

On any given day, the law office is besieged with questions about contracts. Keep in mind the following fundamental questions:

1. Is there a contract? Is there a basis for its existence? Look for evidence of an acceptance and evidence of consideration.

2. If there is a contract, is there some way out of it? Are there no defenses to its formation? Look for (1) illegality in the contract, (2) incapacity by the parties, (3) lack of a proper writing, and (4) unconscionable provisions.

3. If there is a contract, are there any other parties who may have a say in the terms or operation of the contract? Can anyone else enforce that contract? Look for (1) third parties, (2) creditors-donees, (3) persons with liens, (4) and assigned or delegated provisions.

4. If there is a contract, and it can be determined that one of the parties is not fulfilling the provisions (a situation that is called a breach), what remedies can the injured party exercise? Look for (1) injunctions or other equitable remedies, (2) damages provision, (3) discharge possibilities, (4) and restitution rights.

II. FORMATION OF CONTRACTS

A. The Agreement Process

Logic dictates that a student of contracts be informed that two parties are necessary to make a contract. No matter how diligent an individual might be, he or she simply cannot contract alone. Hence, two minds are needed to formulate this contractual exchange, and that is why the term *meeting of the minds* is so critical to basic contract formation. Whether by objective or subjective standards, contract enforceability depends upon proof that both sides agree to something, that both sides had mental states fundamentally on the same wavelength, and that their intentions were fundamentally similar. Thus, an agreement must be reached by an *offer* being made and an *acceptance* of the offer. (See exhibits 8.1 and 8.2.)

1. The offer

An offer is an act or possibly other conduct, by which one party confers upon the other party the power, by means of acceptance, to create a contract. An offer can be a statement like, "I hereby offer" or "This typewriter is on sale for $25," or it can be in the form of advertisements and circulars, or it can be in the form of a bid at auction. There are so many ways offers can be made and so many variables on human conduct that cannot be overlooked. Basically, however, all offers must exhibit:

a. Outward Intent to Contract Presently

The law hesitates to formulate contracts out of offers to discuss a possible contract, or from simple preliminary

Exhibit 8.1

EMPLOYMENT AGREEMENT

This is an agreement by and between   , with executive offices at   , is a corporation duly organized and existing under the laws of   , as referred to in this agreement as of   , is a psychiatrist, duly licensed as a physician under the laws of   , and is referred to in this agreement as "the psychiatrist."

   1. *Employment*.   Hereby employs the psychiatrist and the psychiatrist hereby accepts such employment on the terms and conditions set forth as follows:

   2. *Duties*.   The psychiatrist is employed to perform the following duties in the   clinic located at

    1. Medication evaluation

    2. Psychotherapy

    3. Emergency coverage

    4. Signing of commitment papers

    5. From time to time the psychiatrist may also be required to perform other duties, which are considered to be customary and usual in the practice of psychiatry in

   3. *Hours of Employment*.   The psychiatrist shall work ten hours each week at   clinic on the days of the week designated by the clinic manager. The psychiatrist is permitted to hold other employment and to teach and engage in other professional activities as long as he is able to perform the services required to be rendered to the employer pursuant to this agreement.

   4. *Salary*.   For all services rendered by the psychiatrist under this agreement (and in addition to other monetary and other benefits referred to herein),   , Department of Mental Health shall pay the psychiatrist at the rate of $ .00 per hour. For any week in which the psychiatrist works the agreed upon ten hours, he shall receive compensation (subject to the customary withholding tax and other employment tax) of $ .00. If the psychiatrist works fewer than ten hours in any week, he will receive compensation at the rate of $ .00 per hour.

   5. *Vacation*.   During the term of this agreement, the psychiatrist shall be entitled to two weeks paid vacation time per year or pro rata for any portion of a year. The psychiatrist shall take his vacation at such time or times as shall be approved by the clinic manager.

   6. *Other Fringe Benefits*.   The psychiatrist shall be entitled to one fourth the number of days allowed for sick leave and personal time which is allowed under the contract currently in force between the Nursing Association and the State of   . If the psychiatrist is employed under this agreement for a period of less than one year, the number of days of sick leave and personal time shall be adjusted proportionately.

   7. *Malpractice Insurance*.   The psychiatrist shall retain medical malpractice insurance which is adequate to cover him with respect to his employment at   by January   , 19   ; the psychiatrist shall submit a written statement to   indicating the name of the insurance carrier, the insurance policy number, the type and amount of coverage afforded, and a brief statement of his reasons for believing that the coverage is adequate for his employment at

   8. *Expenses*.   During the period of his employment under this agreement, the State of   , Department of Mental Health will reimburse the psychiatrist for those expenses which are indicated as reimbursable in Appendix B.

   9. *Supervision*.   The psychiatrist shall work under the supervision of the Clinic Manager of the   Clinic.   and the psychiatrist recognize that the Board of Directors of the corporation shall manage the business affairs of the corporation and that the psychiatrist shall have no authority or power to enter into or execute contracts on behalf of

   10. *Term*.   The effective date of this agreement shall be January   , 19 . This agreement shall be terminated when the psychiatrist III position at the   Clinic is converted from a so-called 01 permanent state employee to a so-called 07-contract for psychiatric services with the State of   . Upon such conversion the psychiatrist shall resign from his employment with the Commonwealth and waive all rights as a state employee. This agreement may also be terminated in any of the following ways:

    (a) Whenever the psychiatrist shall be disqualified as a duly licensed physician under the laws of the State of.

    (b) By mutual written agreement of the parties.

    (c) By demonstrable non-performance or improper performance of his duties by the psychiatrist.

    (d) At   option, if the psychiatrist shall suffer a permanent disability. For purposes of this agreement, "permanent disability" shall be defined as the psychiatrist's inability, through physical or mental illness or other cause, to perform the majority of his usual duties for a period of   months or more.   option shall be exercised in writing delivered to the psychiatrist and shall be effective on delivery.

    (e) Absence of the psychiatrist from his duties continuing for a period of more than   if   mails to the psychiatrist by certified mail, notice thereof, whether such notice is effectively delivered or not.

    (f) The death of the psychiatrist.

(g) Notwithstanding any of the above provisions, upon _____ days prior written notice by either _____ or the psychiatrist to the other.

11. *Records.* Upon the termination of this agreement, the psychiatrist shall not be entitled to keep or preserve records or charts of _____ as to any patient unless said patient shall specifically request a different disposition of his record, and in no event shall the psychiatrist be entitled to the records or files of patients not treated by him.

12. *Notices.* All notices required or permitted to be given under this agreement shall be sufficient, if in writing, sent by mail to his residence, in the case of the psychiatrist, or to its principal office, in the case of _____

13. *Miscellaneous.* This agreement is drawn to be effective in and shall be construed in accordance with the laws of the State of _____ . No amendment or variation of the terms of this agreement shall be valid unless made in writing and signed by the psychiatrist and a duly authorized representative of _____ . A waiver of any of the terms and conditions of this agreement shall not be construed as a general waiver by _____ and _____ shall be free to reinstate any such term or condition with or without notice to the psychiatrist.

BY: _____
President

Board of Directors

Dated: _____

_____
M.D.

---

negotiations. Hence, an exchange such as,"Let's talk about this some more" or "I hope we can come to some agreement on this" are not statements evidencing present contractual intent.

b. CERTAINTY AND SPECIFICITY IN TERMS

Common contractual misinterpretations and conflicts emerge when a contract is in its "formative" stages because the details have not been smoothed out. Again, the law will not create an offer where the language of the contract is utterly lacking in precision. The terms of the offer must be sufficiently clear and comprehensive so that the parties' real intent can be scrutinized. Certainty of the offer is measured by very essential terms, which include:

1. Parties to the contract
2. Subject matter of the contract
3. Time for performance
4. Cost or price

An offer that contains those four terms can easily be construed as definite and certain and will always be upheld as such. Unfortunately, human beings forget a thing or two on the road to contractual formation. Accordingly, the courts are not going to hold defective every offer lacking in an essential term. In fact, courts regularly accept reasonable substitutes for the essential terms. As an example, if the price is left out, the offer can be saved by substituting the fair market value of the goods or services. The same thing is true with time for performance; the court can easily substitute a reasonable time period for payment or completion of a duty. Whatever the case, it is often thought that courts generally try to save contracts and offers rather than destroy them, and of course that makes perfect sense in a capitalist country. Under the Uniform Commercial Code, at UCC 2-204, 305, 308, 309, and 310, particular provisions can be added to offers that are silent on these essential terms.

c. COMMUNICATION TO ANOTHER PARTY

An offer is not really an offer unless someone can respond to the content of the proposition. Clearly, an individual who desires to sell her car and thinks about selling it and about all the money she will make on its sale, yet fails to tell anyone of those desires, has made no offer. An offer must be communicated to at least one person or an entity, or even to the whole world. The proposal must be told to the offeree, who then can ruminate on, discuss, counter, or reject the contents of the offer. Since an offer is a promise to do something, it can have no meaning or substance unless the offer is communicated to another.

Exhibit 8.2

BUILDING AGREEMENT

THIS AGREEMENT, made the   day of   , 198   . by and between   ,
hereinafter called "Builder,"   AND   and   , husband
and wife, of   , hereinafter called "Owners,"
WITNESSETH:

That the parties hereto, intending to be legally bound, do hereby declare, promise and agree as follows:

1. Builder has caused to be conveyed simultaneously herewith, at a consideration of   Dollars ($ .00),
receipt of which is hereby acknowledged, to the Owners, Lot No.   , Plan of   , Susquehanna
Township, Dauphin County,

2. Builder is to construct on said premises a   . Builder shall furnish all of the materials and perform all of
the work for the construction thereof, and builder shall pay for all building permits required for the construction.

3. Builder agrees to construct the dwelling house in a good and workmanlike manner and in substantial accordance
with the plans and specifications which are attached hereto and become a part hereof.

4. Builder agrees to start construction on the dwelling on or before   , 198   , and shall complete
all work on the construction of the dwelling on or before   , 198   unless Builder is delayed by
reason of labor strikes, fire, unavoidable casualty or other causes beyond the control of the Builder.

5. Owners shall pay to Builder for the performance of this Agreement, the sum of   Dollars ($ .00),
to be payable as follows:

6. The said contract price of   Dollars ($ .00) shall be secured by a demand judgment note, without
interest, executed by Owners and delivered to Builder simultaneous with the execution of this Agreement. Builder
agrees not to enter of record the demand judgment note unless Owners default under this Agreement.

7. Possession of the dwelling shall be delivered to Owners upon payment of the last advance hereunder. Prior to said
time, any losses caused to the dwelling by fire or other hazard shall be the responsibility of and be borne by Builder.

8. Builder agrees that no Mechanic's Lien shall be filed against the premises and agrees to execute and file a
stipulation against liens in favor of Owners prior to commencement of construction and shall furnish to Owners a
complete release of all liens at the time of final payment of the contract price aforementioned. In the event the Title
Insurance Company insuring Owners' title requires an additional premium to insure against mechanics liens, said
additional premium shall be paid by Builder.

9. Any changes or additions in the plans or specifications desired by Owners or Builder during construction of the
dwelling which would either lower or raise the contract price in the amount of $100.00 or more shall be reduced to
writing, signed by the parties hereto and any change in the contract price shall be noted therein.

10. This agreement contains the final and entire agreement between the Owners and Builder and no prior written or
verbal representations shall be binding on either party, and any subsequent modifications to this Agreement must be
reduced to writing and signed by the parties hereto.

IN WITNESS WHEREOF, the parties have hereto executed this Agreement the day and year first above written.

ATTEST: BUILDER:

By _____   By _____

WITNESS: OWNERS:

_____   _____

_____   _____

---

2. The acceptance

The second stage in contractual formation is the acceptance. An acceptance is the culmination of the mental
processes, the *meeting of minds* between the two parties to the contract. The acceptance says simply, "I accept the offer
you have made to me." The acceptance is a legally binding act by the offeree, the person to whom the offer is made. What
are the legal mandates for a binding acceptance?

a. THE ACCEPTANCE MUST ADHERE TO THE TERMS OF THE OFFER

If the offer requires performance of the contract to constitute an acceptance, then so it must be. Simply a promise to perform will not suffice. Neither will an acceptance adhere to the terms of the offer if acceptance is manifested by a return promise, unless the offeree performs the terms of the offer.

b. The Acceptance Must be Consciously Chosen

The offeree must know of the offer and must understand that he or she is the person to whom this offer is being directed. Consider this problem:

Phil, the offeror, says to Mary, the offeree, that he will sell her two hundred smokeless coffee cups for $200. Phil is under the impression that Mary is a wholesale buyer for Morop Enterprises, a wholesale buyer of products. Mary, in fact, is a delicatessen operator. Mary likes this deal since she is sick and tired of smoky coffee cups in her delicatessen. Could Phil argue out of her acceptance by noting that there was no meeting of the minds and that the mistake in identity destroys Mary's ability to accept?

c. The Acceptance Must be Unconditional

An offer comes forth with terms and provisions. In order for an acceptance to evidence mental agreement between the parties, proof must be seen that demonstrates that the offeree likes and agrees to the contents of the offer. An acceptance should provide a "mirror image" of the offer. If the reflection is too foggy or fragmented, a contract is generally not possible. In short, an acceptance that so fundamentally changes the content of the offer is going to be viewed either as a counteroffer or a rejection.

Changes in the content of the offer are possible, provided those changes or alterations are minimal in scope and not major in construction. Most courts hold that an acceptance will be upheld even though its language provides:

- ☐ A nonmaterial, additional term to the offer.
- ☐ A suggestion for improvements in the contract.
- ☐ A request for warranty or merchantability.
- ☐ Additional proposals between merchants as permitted by UCC 2-207. The UCC provides liberal rules on the commercial negotiations of merchants and tends to uphold additional proposals on the offer, unless they "materially" alter the offer.

d. Other Legal Issues in the Acceptance

Silence as a Method of Acceptance. If the terms of the offer include the wording, "Your silence will be an acceptance," it is possible for silent conduct to be a valid form of acceptance. In particular, if the parties are regular business merchants or dealers, if the offeree solicited an offer, or if the offeree takes advantage of the benefits or services, as when books are sent on "approval" and are never returned by the offeree—all constitute situations that may be acceptance by silence.

Unsolicited Goods. Most consumers have been the target of mail-order companies or other merchants who send goods through the mail for purchase or eventual return. Under most state consumer laws and the UCC, unsolicited merchandise sent to a consumer cannot give rise to an acceptance, since a law to that effect really would promote mail-order fraud and duress. Instead, these goods are viewed legally as "unconditional gifts."

Termination of Offers: Effect on Acceptance. An offer is terminated by revocation by the person who makes the offer at any time before that offer is accepted. So an offer has legal life until it is stopped, withdrawn, or accepted. Of course, there are various ways an offer can terminate:

1. An offer may end by a lapse of time in its original language, like "good for thirty days," or within a reasonable period of time. An offer from 1910 is certainly a stale offer!

2. An offer is terminated by the death of the party making it. If someone accepts the deceased's offer, who can fulfill the contractual obligation?

3. An offer is terminated by the insanity of the party making it.

4. An offer is terminated by illegality of the proposed contract. Consider contracts that promote gambling in Virginia or set interest rates in violation of state usury laws or banking laws.

5. An offer, if directed at a particular individual, can be terminated by a simple rejection of the terms of the offer.

Of critical importance in this area as well is to understand that revocation by the offeror is not always easy in unilateral contracts, that is, contracts that are accepted by performance. Depending on the jurisdiction, an offer cannot be revoked if the offeree has already begun performance and, as a result, relied on it, so that revocation would be detrimental to her or him, or expended time, energy, and financial resources to honor the terms of the offer. Ponder this factual situation:

Sally says to Steve, "I'll pay you three thousand dollars if you paint my entire house." The offer is clear, and acceptance is possible only by performance. What if Steve paints 75 percent of the house and Sally says, "I changed my mind and I'm revoking my offer"? Is Sally legally in the clear if she does not pay Steve a dime?

B. The Consideration Requirement

Now that the manifestations of mutual assent in the law of offer and acceptance have been covered, the contract must next demonstrate, in order to be enforceable and legal, that the agreement was based upon true *consideration*. Mutual assent is simply not sufficient; the contract must be a reflection of some agreed-upon exchange, which the law feels is substantive enough to support, enforce, or modify contractual rights and obligations. Consideration is the bargained for, legal value of the contract. Consideration can be:

> 1. *Noneconomic detriment.*—e.g., changing one's personal habits, exchanging sentimental property of nonsignificant value, or going to a college at the request of an offeror.
> 2. *Economic detriment*—e.g., payment of money, contribution of services, conveyance of real property, or the sale of personal property.
> 3. *Promise not to exercise a legal right*—e.g., right to sue or promote other adjudication, discharge of a debt, or modification of a debt.

These three categories are very broad in scope and represent classes of situations in which parties to the agreement have invested sufficient time, money, or other loss to constitute a detriment. To make the analysis of consideration easy, just think of those things that are generally deemed nonsufficient consideration, and as a result will not allow the parties to enforce their contract. Consideration has been held insufficient when:

> □ The contract is fundamentally fraudulent and goes to the heart of the consideration.
> □ The detriment is simply a *preexisting duty,* already owed by the offeree to the offeror, such as payment for goods or services or a reward payment to a police officer who arrests a criminal.
> □ Forebearance to bring forth a lawsuit on a claim the litigant knows has no substance.
> □ Gifts of cash to individuals in return for nothing.

Whatever the example, the analysis must be able to see a *bargained-for* exchange, something that is a detriment—monetarily, socially, or emotionally—and that detriment forms the basis of the contract. In order to be held legal, it must be sufficient. (See exhibits 8.3–8.6.)

III. DEFENSES TO THE FORMATION OF CONTRACTS

Assuming the essential requirements of offer, acceptance, and sufficient consideration have been met, that does not insure contractual viability. Numerous defenses can be asserted that seek to overturn the basis of the contract. They are quite common and often successful.

A. Capacity to Contract

While "caveat emptor" traditions are going by the wayside in commercial practice, seller, merchandisers, and retailers have to be increasingly on their toes as to whom they are contracting with.

1. Can a minor create a contract?

Depending on jurisdiction, the answer is either yes or no, but all states have similar issues that must be addressed.

□ What is the age of the minor?
□ Has the minor reached the age of majority since contractual formation?

Exhibit 8.3

FEE AGREEMENT

CLAIMANT: _____

RE: Social Security Disability Appeal—Termination

This letter will confirm our office discussion of _____ . As I explained to you, if you wish my office to represent you on your appeal in this matter, my fee will be (A) $200.00 or (B) 25% of any past-due benefits, to which you and your family are entitled, whichever (A) or (B) is greater, plus expenses. This means that even if you do not win the appeal, you will be charged the fee of $200.00, plus expenses. Of course, any fee I may charge you is subject to the approval of the proper department of government.

The above fee, of $200.00, does not include any out-of-pocket costs, which may be incurred, such as filing fees, service fees, medical examinations and reports, photocopy expense, toll telephone expense, expert testimony, et cetera. If any such costs are incurred, you understand you are solely responsible for those costs whether or not you win. And as explained, these costs are not included in any fee I may be awarded and must be paid even if you lose the appeal. You will not be obligated for any large expense without your prior approval. You understand the $200.00 retainer will not be used to pay costs, unless a fee of less than $200.00 is awarded.

You understand also, there is no guarantee that you will be successful on your appeal. It is my opinion, however, that whether you proceed with my counsel or with another lawyer, or even on your own behalf, you should proceed with your appeal in this matter. Please do not delay. If you delay the filing of your appeal, you may, at some point, be barred from bringing it. You understand my offer to represent you is limited to proceedings through the decision of the Administrative Law Judge (ALJ). This agreement does not require my office to appeal the decision by the ALJ. Whether an appeal, of the ALJ's decision, will be made by my office is to be determined exclusively by my office.

If the above properly sets forth our agreement, please enter date and signature below and return the signed copy of this agreement together with the $200.00 retainer check, as aforesaid, to my office. A return envelope is enclosed for your convenience. The copy of the agreement, enclosed, is for your records. I look forward to working with you on your appeal, however, if I do not receive, in my office, the signed copy of the agreement, together with your retainer check of $200.00, by _____ , I shall assume that you have obtained other counsel or that you have decided to proceed without the assistance of counsel, and shall mark my file "closed", and do nothing further. If any of the above is not clear, or if you have any questions, please do not hesitate to call.

DATED: _____   _____

The above is understood and agreed to and the retainer check, in the amount of $200.00, is enclosed.

DATED: _____   _____

Exhibit 8.4

INSTALLMENT SALES AGREEMENT

THIS AGREEMENT, made this _____ day of _____ , 198 _____ , by and between _____ and _____ , his wife, of Harrisburg, Dauphin County, _____ hereinafter referred to as "Sellers", AND _____ and _____ , his wife, of Harrisburg, Dauphin County, hereinafter referred to as "Buyers."

THE PARTIES HERETO, with intent to be legally bound, do hereby agree, covenant and represent as follows:

1. *SALE AND PURCHASE.* The Sellers shall sell and convey to Buyers who shall purchase all that certain lot or piece of ground with improvements thereon erected, commonly known as _____ Street, Harrisburg, Dauphin County, _____ , as more fully described on Exhibit "A" hereto, hereinafter referred to as the "Premises," upon the following terms and conditions.

2. *PURCHASE PRICE.* The price or consideration shall be _____ Thousand Dollars ($ _____ ,000.00), which shall be paid to the Sellers by the Buyers as follows:

   a. The sum of Two Thousand Dollars ($2,000.00) on the signing of this Agreement, receipt of which is hereby acknowledged; and

   b. The sum of Three Thousand Dollars ($3,000.00) at the time of delivery of possessions of the Premises to Buyers; and

   c. The Balance of the purchase money ($ _____ ,000.00 in equal monthly installments of Three Hundred Dollars ($300.00) each, beginning _____ 1, 198 _____ , and ending January 31, 198 _____ , the same to be paid not later than the first day of each of said months, except that the final payment, on January 31, 198 _____ shall include a sum necessary to satisfy the outstanding principal, interest and other sums, if any, owing under this Agreement. Each of said payments shall be applied first to interest, the balance to principal, and shall be deemed to include a factor for interest at the rate of eight and one-half percent (8-½%) from the date possession is given.

3. *PREPAYMENT.* Buyers shall have the right to prepay principal balance in whole or in part at any time without fee, fine or penalty.

4. *EXISTING AND FUTURE ENCUMBRANCES.* The Premises are to be conveyed at time of final settlement by general warranty deed, free and clear of all liens, reservations, restrictions, encumbrances and easements except, however, those, if any, which are of record immediately prior to execution of this Agreement or which a physical inspection or competent survey of the Premises would disclose (other than the $ mortgage, described below, which shall be satisfied prior to final settlement). As of the date of this Agreement, the Sellers covenant that the Premises are subject to, among other matters, a mortgage given by Sellers held by the   dated   198   in the principal amount of $

5. *POSSESSION.* Possession of the Premises shall be given to Buyers on February 1, 198

6. *REAL ESTATE TAXES AND BENEFIT ASSESSMENTS.* Real estate taxes, water and sewer rents shall be apportioned as of February 1, 198   (the date of possession) and shall thereafter be borne and paid by Buyers prior to any penalty period, including the payment of any benefit assessments imposed against the Premises. Sellers agree to promptly forward to Buyers any tax statements issued by the taxing authorities, which it may hereafter receive. Buyers shall provide Sellers with proof of payment of said real estate taxes, charges, rents, etc., as soon as payment is made. At Sellers option, Sellers may pay any said real estate taxes, charges, rents, etc., provide Buyers with a receipt evidencing payment thereof, and require Buyers to reimburse Sellers at the next monthly payment date after request for reimbursement is made to Buyers.

7. *UTILITIES.* Buyers shall be responsible for and shall pay for all utilities used in connection with the Premises.

8. *INSURANCE.* Buyers agree to maintain, at their own expense, fire, extended coverage and flood insurance on the Premises in an amount not less than $ .00 with the designated payee being the mortgagee, referenced in paragraph 4, and Sellers, as their interests may appear. Buyers shall acquire and keep in full force and effect, during the term of this Agreement, liability insurance in an amount of at least One Hundred Thousand Dollars ($100,000.00) for accident, injury or death to any one person or to property, and Three Hundred Thousand Dollars ($300,000.00) for accident, injury or death to persons or property arising out of any one occurrence, with Seller's being named as additional insureds.

9. *DESTRUCTION.* Destruction of or damage to any building or other improvement now or hereafter placed on the Premises, whether from fire or any other cause, shall not release the Buyers from any of their obligations under this Agreement; it being expressly understood that the Buyers bear all risk of loss to, or damage of the Premises.

10. *SELLERS' MORTGAGE.* Sellers agree that they will make all payments, which are required to be made under the provisions of the mortgage, referenced in paragraph four (4), of this Agreement, and shall furnish such proof of payment of same as may, from time to time, be reasonably requested by Buyers, including statements from the holder of said mortgage. If Sellers are in default under said mortgage, for a period of at least thirty (30) days, Buyers shall have the right to pay in full such arrearages and thereafter make the periodic payments if Sellers fail to so do and shall receive an equivalent credit against the then outstanding purchase price hereunder, (and which shall also be credited against the monthly payments required of Buyers hereunder).

Sellers shall not further lien the Premises during the term of this Agreement, but in the event any lien should attach to the Premises, subsequent to the date of this Agreement, Buyers shall have the right to make such advances toward the retirement of such lien as they deem advisable to protect their interest in the Premises and shall be given an equivalent credit against the purchase price hereunder (and which shall also be credited against the monthly payments required of Buyers hereunder). Notwithstanding the foregoing sentence, prior to making any such advances, Buyers must give prior written notice to Sellers of their intent to make such advances, so that Sellers can object to the making of such payments in the event the lien was improperly or erroneously entered against the Sellers or the Property. If the lien was improperly or erroneously entered, the parties shall adopt a course of action that shall reasonably and equitably protect their respective interests.

11. *SELLERS' DEFAULT.* In the event that Sellers are unable to give title to Buyers, as set forth above, Buyers shall have the option of taking such title as the Sellers can give without abatement of price or of being repaid all monies paid on account by Buyers to Sellers (minus the fair market rental value of the Premises during such period), and in the latter event, there shall be no further liability or obligation by either of the parties, one to the other, and this Agreement shall become null and void and of no effect.

12. *BUYERS' DEFAULT.* Payment of all monies becoming due hereunder by the Buyers and the performance of all covenants and conditions of this Agreement to be kept and performed by the Buyers are conditions precedent to the performance by the Sellers of the covenants and conditions of the Agreement be kept and performed by the Sellers. In the event the Buyers shall fail, for a period of ten (10) days after they become due, to make any of the payments required by this Agreement, or should the Buyers fail to comply with any other covenant or condition of this Agreement on their part to be performed, the Sellers shall give written notice to the Buyers of such default and upon failure of the Buyers to cure said default within a period of ten (10) days after the giving of said written notice, the Sellers may, at their option, declare that the whole of the unpaid principal sum shall become forthwith due and payable; or the Sellers may at their option, declare the Agreement terminated, and all rights and obligations under this Agreement shall cease and terminate, and all payments made by Buyers shall be retained by Sellers as liquidated damages for the use of the Premises and not as a penalty.

13. *CONFESSION OF JUDGMENT.* In the case of such default by Buyers, the Buyers hereby authorize and empower any attorney, of any court of record, to appear for them and confess judgment for the principal sum and interest remaining unpaid thereon with five percent (5%) attorney's commission, hereby waiving the right of exemption and inquisition so far as the Premises is concerned. Or the Sellers may, at their option, in addition to any and all other remedies available to Sellers at law or

equity, proceed by action of ejectment on this Agreement after default is made as aforesaid for the recovery of the Premises and in such case the Buyers authorize and empower any attorney, of any court of record, to appear for them in an amicable action in ejectment for the Premises, to be entered by the Prothonotary, in which the Sellers shall be the plaintiffs and the Buyers the defendants, and confess judgment for the Premises and authorize the immediate issuing of a writ of possession (without asking leave of court) with cause for costs and five percent (5%) attorney's commission, waiving all stay and exemption laws.

14. *FINAL SETTLEMENT.* If Buyers discharge all of their obligations hereunder, Sellers shall convey good and marketable fee simple title to the Buyers, as required by paragraph four (4) of this Agreement, on or before January 31, 198   . All realty transfer taxes shall be divided equally between the parties.

15. *TENDER WAIVED.* Tender of an executed deed and purchase money is hereby waived.

16. *MAINTENANCE.* Buyers agree to keep the Premises (including landscaping and all shrubs) in as good repair and condition as exist at the time of execution of this Agreement, reasonable wear and tear alone excepted. Any notice, ordinance or other matter filed subsequent to the date of this Agreement, by any governing authority, for which a lien could be asserted against the Premises, is to be timely complied with at the expense of the Buyers.

17. *NON-REAL ESTATE EXTRAS.* This sale includes the following extras: central air conditioning, wall-to-wall carpeting, range, storm units, all shades, drapes, curtains and rods, refrigerator, dishwasher, disposal, washer and dryer. All such items are sold "as-is" and for no additional consideration.

18. *ENTIRE AGREEMENT.* This Agreement contains the entire agreement between the Sellers and Buyers and there are no other terms, obligations, covenants, representations, statements or conditions, oral or otherwise, of any kind whatsoever concerning this sale. The provisions of this Agreement supersede any and all prior writings be between the parties, including an Agreement of Sale, dated   , on the form of XYZ Real Estate. Any changes or additions, to this Agreement, must be made in writing and executed by the parties hereto.

19. *ASSIGNABILITY.* Buyers shall not assign all or any part of their interest under this Agreement without the express written consent of the Sellers.

20. *HEIRS AND ASSIGNS.* The said parties hereby bind themselves, their heirs, executors, administrators and assigns for the faithful performance of this Agreement as set forth above.

21. *TIME OF THE ESSENCE.* Time is hereby declared to be of the essence of this Agreement.

22. *NONRECORDABILITY.* Neither this agreement (nor any copy or any memorandum hereof) shall be filed or recorded by Buyers (or any of them, or their assignee or nominee) in any public office in the Commonwealth _____. Any unauthorized filing or recording shall be deemed a default by Buyers in the essence of this Agreement, whereupon Sellers may exercise its remedies herein provided, and further, Sellers may freely transfer, convey and deal with the Premises without liability by the Sellers or by any purchasers thereof to the Buyers, and in such case, Buyers expressly quit-claim and release unto Sellers any and all right, title and interest which Buyers may have in the Premises. Such unauthorized filing or recording shall, in no event, constitute a cloud on the title of Sellers to the Premises or any part thereof or any other lands of Sellers, and shall not constitute constructive or other notice to anyone whomsoever. (This non-recordability clause favors the Seller. A Buyer's attorney should probably seek to have an Installment Sale Agreement recorded.)

IN WITNESS WHEREOF, the parties hereto with intent to be bound hereby have hereunto set their hands and seals the day first above written.

WITNESS: SELLERS:

_____   _____

_____

                                                     BUYERS:

_____   _____

□ What was the contract for? Necessities? Luxuries?
□ Can a minor affirm or disaffirm the contract?

2. Can a person who is mentally incompetent create or avoid a contract?

Since so much of contract law and negotiation depends on agreement by the parties—a meeting of the minds—the law tends not to favor a contract of parties without mental capacity. Most of these contracts are voidable, if the party lacks understanding of the nature, purpose, and effect of the transaction. Courts have also extended this protection to persons who are temporarily incapacitated.

Exhibit 8.5

BUY—SELL AGREEMENT OF A BUSINESS

THIS AGREEMENT made this _____ day of May, 1984, by and between _____ hereinafter referred to as Buyer and _____ , hereinafter referred to as Seller; both of the parties are residents of _____ , presently the owners of _____ , hereinafter called the Corporation.

1. _____ a corporation of the _____ , has heretofore issued 50 shares of its capital stock to the Seller and said 50 shares are presently owned by Seller.

2. Seller desires to sell all of her shares of stock in Corporation and Buyer desires to purchase the same upon the terms hereinafter set forth.

NOW, THEREFORE, with the foregoing hereinafter incorporated by reference and deemed part of this Agreement, the parties hereto, intending to legally bind themselves, their heirs, personal representatives, successors, and assigns, hereby agree as follows:

1. (a) The Seller agrees to sell and the Buyer agrees to purchase 50 shares of the Corporation, being all the issued and outstanding stock, free of all liens and encumbrances, together with all rights and dividends, for the consideration hereinafter provided.

   (b) The purchase price shall be computed and paid as follows: $14,600.00 (Fourteen Thousand and Six Hundred Dollars).

2. At final settlement, Seller shall deliver the 50 shares each of the stock in the Corporation to Buyer, and Buyer, as set forth in Paragraph above, shall pledge said stock to Seller as security for the payment of the note provided for herein. Seller herewith agrees that Buyer may transfer the pledged stock provided the transferee or new owners of all or any portion of the stock transferred, agree to pledge the transferred stock as security for any unpaid balance due on Buyer's note, and Seller shall not release the certificates delivered and pledged as collateral for the note until the newly issued certificates on transfer of the stock are delivered and properly pledged. Buyer, as holder of 100 percent of the outstanding stock of the Corporation shall issue no further stock from its authorized shares unless such newly issued stock is further pledged for the payment of the Buyer's note by the holder thereof, until such time as the note is paid in full.

3. The Seller shall, at the time of final settlement, submit their resignations as officers and directors of the Corporation, and as a condition of this Agreement of Sale, Seller agree to deliver the resignation of all officers and directors. The aforesaid resignations shall take effect at settlement.

4. In the event Buyer defaults in complying with the terms of this Agreement, all sums paid by the Buyer on account of the purchase price may be retained by the Seller either on account of the purchase price or as liquidated damages for such breach as the Seller shall elect, and in the latter event Seller shall be released from all liability or obligation and this Agreement shall become null and void.

5. Settlement shall be held on _____ , 1984, at the office of _____ , Esquire.

6. This Agreement may not be modified or terminated orally, and no modifications, termination or attempted waiver shall be valid or enforceable unless in writing signed by the person against whom the same is sought to be enforced.

7. This Agreement shall be binding upon and inure to the benefit of the respective parties hereto, their legal representatives, heirs, executors, administrators, and assigns.

8. As an inducement to the Buyer to purchase their stock, the Seller warrants to the Buyer as follows:

(a) The Corporation is a Business Corporation organized pursuant to the Business Corporation Law of the State of _____ , is validly existing pursuant to said statutes, and is duly authorized to engage in the book business.

(b) The Corporation is now in good standing; there are no proceedings or actions pending to limit or impair any of the Corporation's powers, rights, and privileges or to dissolve the Corporation; and that the Corporation is duly licensed and authorized to do business as a _____ in the State of _____

(c) The Corporation has no subsidiaries.

(d) The Seller is the lawful owner and holder of 50 of the issued shares of the capital stock of the Corporation which is fully paid and nonassessable.

(e) The Seller has full power and right to enter into this Agreement and to sell the shares free of any liens, encumbrances, or agreements, and that the shares are in fact free of such restrictions or conditions.

(f) There are no suits or proceedings in equity, or liens, judgments, attachments, or other execution process pending against the Corporation, its properties, or business except as otherwise shown herein of which the Seller is aware of or has knowledge about.

(g) There are no actions or proceedings pending or proposed in which the Corporation is the plaintiff or petitioner of which the Seller is aware of or has knowledge about.

(h) No law suits or proceedings have been threatened by anyone of which the Seller is aware of or has knowledge about.

(i) The Corporation has good and marketable title to all of its assets and property, subject to no mortgage, pledge, lien, or conditional sale.

(j) The Corporation's assets are in good order and repair.

9. Seller further covenants, warrants, and represents that until settlement:

(a) The Corporation will not enter into any contract or agreement except in the ordinary course of its business.

(b) No dividends will be declared or paid on the capital stock of the Corporation, nor will there be any increase in the salary or compensation paid or to become payable to any employee, nor will any additional employees be hired.

10. At the time of settlement, seller shall deliver the following:

(a) Certificates of stock representing all the shares of the issued and outstanding capital stock of the Corporation, endorsed in blank with all transfer stamps required by governmental authorities attached thereto.

(b) Minute book, stock transfer book, stock certificate book, and corporate seal of the Corporation.

(c) Resignations of the present officers and directors, as aforesaid.

(d) All agreements and leases to which the Corporation is a party. Sellers covenant that there are no employment contracts of any kind.

11. Ancillary to the sale of the Seller's stock of the Corporation, and as an essential condition of this Agreement, Seller hereby covenants, promises and agrees with Buyer that they will not, directly or indirectly, individually or jointly, engage in a _____ business, either as agent, owner, partner, shareholder, employer, employee, manager, investor, or solicitor within a radius of 5 miles from _____, State of _____ for a period of 3 years. Seller acknowledges that the remedy at law for her, or her breach shall be inadequate, and the Buyer shall be entitled to injunctive relief as well as a claim for damages.

12. Buyer shall have full access to the Corporation's books, records, and properties.

13. (a) Sellers covenant that the Corporation has heretofore complied, and until settlement will continue to comply, with all state, federal, and local laws.

(b) No representation or warranties by the Seller, nor any statement or certificate furnished or to be furnished Buyer pursuant hereto, contains or will contain any untrue statement of a material fact, or will omit to state a material fact necessary to make the statements therein not misleading.

IN WITNESS WHEREOF, the parties hereto have executed these presents the day and year first above written.

Witnesses: Seller:

_____   _____ (Seal)

_____   Buyer

_____   _____ (Seal)

Exhibit 8.6

PURCHASE MONEY MORTGAGE

THIS INDENTURE MADE THIS _____ day of December 1983, between _____, hereinafter called the "Mortgagor," and _____, hereinafter called the "Mortgagee."

WHEREAS, the Mortgagor under the Note bearing even date herewith is indebted to the Mortgagee in the principal sum of Seventy-Thousand Dollars ($70,000.00), lawful money of the United States, which sum, with interest at nine percent (9%) per annum, is payable as follows:

1. The principal sum of the mortgage, Seventy-thousand dollars ($70,000.00) will be paid back by Mortgagor at a fixed rate of 9% per annum with a 30 year amortization, with the remaining unpaid balance of the principal portion of the mortgage due and payable *in full* at the end of the 180th payment. The terms of the agreement require a minimum of sixty (60) monthly payments, and allow a maximum of one hundred and eighty (180) payments.

2. The monthly payments of principal and interest shall be payable on the 1st day of each month with the first payment commencing _____ 1984, and the last required payment being on _____ 199____.

3. Prepayment of the principal balance in whole or in part is not permitted at anytime before the sixtieth (60th) payment.

NOW, THIS INDENTURE WITNESSETH that the Mortgagor, in consideration of the principal indebtedness, and to secure the payment there of and all other sums due or to become due under said Note and this Mortgage and the performance of all of the other provisions hereof and of said Note on the part of the Mortgagor to be performed, does hereby grant, bargain, sell, alien, release, convey, and confirm unto the Mortgagee:

All that certain land and residence at   . ALL THAT CERTAIN lot or piece of land, SITUATE IN THE TOWNSHIP OF   and   , County of   and State of   , more particularly bounded and described as follows, to wit:

BEGINNING at a point at the Southerly intersection of the present course of the West Chester to Wilmington Road, with the former course of the said road that leads past lands now or late of Nicolas Damico, the said point being a corner of lands now or late of J.R. Johnson, and measured Northward along the course of the said road being distance 130 Feet from a corner of lands now or late of L.T. Hanaway, extending from the said point of beginning by the said lands of J.R. Johnson (passing 8 Feet East of the North wall of a concrete block garage) South 65 degrees, 0 minutes East 134 Feet to a stake; thence by the said lands of L.T. Hanaway South 65 degrees, 0 minutes West 625.50 Feet to a stone; thence by lands now or late of T. Buckley North 24 degrees, 20 minutes West 1190.90 Feet to a stake, thence by lands now or late of Bertha Gill North 80 degrees, 13 minutes East 1165.17 Feet to the present center line of the aforesaid West Chester to Wilmington Road; thence along the present center line of the said road South 14 degrees, 29 minutes East 772.02 Feet to the first mentioned point, and place of beginning.

CONTAINING 24.335 Acres, more or less.

EXCEPTING THEREFROM AND THEREOUT ALL THAT CERTAIN lot or piece of parcel of land SITUATE IN THE TOWNSHIPS OF   AND   , County of Delaware and Commonwealth of   , more particularly bounded and described according to a survey by James R.   , Registered Engineer and Surveyor, dated May 26, 1959, as follows, to wit:

BEGINNING at a point in the course of the West Chester to Wilmington Road, on or near its center line of its South bound section as the said road is now being constructed, the said point measured along the center of the said road being 130.00 Feet from the corner of lands now or late of L.T. Hanaway, the said beginning point being a corner of lands late of J.R. Johnson, extending thence by the last named lands, passing parallel to and 8 Feet from the North wall of a cement block garage; South 65 degrees, 0 minutes West 325.93 Feet to a stake; thence continuing by the said lands, South 5 degrees, 0 minutes East 134.00 Feet to a stake, thence by the said lands of L.T. Hanaway South 65 degrees, 0 minutes West 625.50 Feet to a stone; thence by lands of Mary A. Glynn, et al., North 24 degrees, 20 minutes West 281.00 Feet to a stake; thence by other lands of the Grantors, passing over a stake on the Westerly side of the said Wilmington Road, North 70 degrees, 41 minutes East 1010.00 Feet to the point on or near the center line of the said road; thence along the course of the said road on or near the center line South 14 degrees, 29 minutes East 60.00 Feet to the first mentioned point, the place of beginning.

CONTAINING 4.383 Acres, more or less.

TOGETHER with all and singular the buildings, streets, alleys, passages, ways, waters, watercourses, rights, liberties, privileges, improvements, hereditaments, and appurtenances whatsoever, thereunto belonging or in any wise appertaining, and the revisions and remainders and rents, issues, and profits thereof. AND ALSO TOGETHER with all and singular the fixtures, appliances, property, and equipment appurtenant thereto or used in connection therewith, whether attached or detached, including, but not limited to, all heating, plumbing, cooking, lighting, laundry, ventilating, air conditioning, and refrigerating equipment, all awnings, blinds, dishwashers, screens, storm sash, kitchen cabinets, mirrors, mantels, and all fixtures, appliances, property and equipment of every kind and description now or hereafter installed in or used in connection with the aforesaid premises, or the operation of the plant, business, or dwelling situate thereon.

TO HAVE AND TO HOLD the aforesaid premises, property, and Hereditaments hereby granted, or mentioned and intended so to be, with the appurtenances, unto the Mortgagee, to and for the only proper use and behoof of the Mortgagee, forever.

PROVIDED ALWAYS, that if the Mortgagor shall promptly pay all sums becoming due under said note and this Mortgage and shall perform all the other provisions herein and in said note contained, then the estate hereby granted shall cease, terminate, and become void, but otherwise shall remain in full force and effect.

AND THE MORTGAGOR HEREBY FURTHER COVENANTS AND AGREES AS FOLLOWS:

1. In the event that any of the aforesaid payments of principal and interest shall become overdue for a period in excess of 15 days, the Mortgagor shall pay to the Mortgagee a "late charge" of 4% on interest and principal payable.

2. The Mortgagor shall pay annual taxes and water rents and sewer rents assessed or to be assessed against the mortgaged premises and the premiums on all policies of insurance held by the Mortgagee pursuant to the provisions of Paragraph 4 hereof.

3. The Mortgagor shall pay before they shall become delinquent, or shall procure the discharge or release of, all taxes (including corporate taxes) water and sewer rents, charges, claims, assessments, liens, and encumbrances now or hereafter assessed which with respect to the mortgaged premises shall or might have priority in lien or payment to the indebtedness secured by this Mortgage.

Proof of payment of property taxes or any other municipal charges to be provided each year by purchasers to sellers. Failure of mortgagors (purchasers) to pay taxes within (30) days of due date shall be a default.

4. The Mortgagor shall keep all buildings and improvements now or hereafter erected upon the mortgaged premises insured for the benefit of the Mortgagee against loss by fire and other casualities and hazards required by the Mortgagee, upon terms and in companies and amounts satisfactory to the Mortgagee, and shall assign and deliver such policies of insurance to

the Mortgagee as additional security. The Mortgagee may settle all claims under all such policies and may demand, receive, and receipt for all moneys becoming payable thereunder. The proceeds under any policy shall be paid by the insurer to the Mortgagee, and the Mortgagee in its sole discretion may apply the amount so collected, or any part thereof, toward the payment of the principal indebtedness and other sums covenanted by the Mortgagor to be paid thereunder, whether or not then due and payable, together with interest thereon, or toward the alteration, reconstruction, repair, or restoration of the damaged portion of the mortgaged premises or any portion thereof. Should Mortgagee, by reason of any insurance against loss by fire and/or other hazard as aforesaid, receive any sum or sum of money for any damage by fire and/or other hazard to the said building or buildings, such amount may be retained and applied by it toward payment of the amount hereby secured; or the same may be used, either wholly or in part to repair said buildings, or to erect new buildings in their place, or for any other purpose or object satisfactory to Mortgagee without affecting the alien of this mortgage, for the full amount secured thereby, before such damage by fire and/or other hazard or such payment over, took place.

5. The Mortgagor shall keep the mortgaged premises and improvements thereon in good condition and repair, but shall not remove, demolish, or materially alter the buildings or improvements on the mortgaged premises, nor commit or suffer waste with respect thereto. The Mortgagor shall comply with all laws, rules regulations, and ordinances made or promulgated by lawful authority which may now or hereafter become applicable to the mortgaged premises. The Mortgagor shall not take or permit any action with respect to the mortgaged premises which will in any manner impair the security of this Mortgage.

6. In the event of the failure of the Mortgagor to pay the taxes, water and sewer rents, charges, claims, assessments, liens, or encumbrances described in Paragraph 3 hereof, or to furnish and pay for the insurance as set forth in Paragraph 4 hereof, or to keep the mortgaged premises in good condition and repair as provided in Paragraph 5 hereof, the Mortgagee may, at its option, pay any or all such items, together with penalties and interest thereon, and procure and pay for such insurance and repairs; and the Mortgagee may at any time and from time to time advance such additional sum or sums as the Mortgagee in its sole discretion may deem necessary to protect the security of this Mortgage. All such sums so paid or advanced by the Mortgagee shall immediately and without demand be repaid by the mortgagor to the Mortgagee, together with interest thereon at the rate of six percent (6%) per annum, and shall be added to the principal indebtedness secured by this mortgage. The production of a receipt by the Mortgagee shall be conclusive proof of a payment or advance authorized hereby, and the amount and validity thereof.

7. The Mortgagor shall, if requested by the Mortgagee, and whether or not there shall be any default under this Mortgage or said note, assign to the Mortgagee, as additional security, any and all leases, now existing or hereafter created, covering any part of the mortgaged premises; and the Mortgagor hereby assigns and transfers to the Mortgagee any and all rents now or hereafter issuing from the mortgaged premises, and agrees that the Mortgagee may collect and apply the same to the payment of any sum required to be paid by the Mortgagor under said note or this Mortgagee, in such order of priority as Mortgagee in its sole discretion may determine.

8. The security of this mortgage shall extend to and cover any additional loans made by the Mortgagee to the Mortgagor at any time or times thereafter, provided that no such loans shall exceed in the aggregate the sum of all the amounts which the Mortgagor has heretofore paid on account of the principal of the original indebtedness and of any prior additional loans.

9. If the Mortgagee retains the services of counsel in order to cure any default under this Mortgage or said note, an attorney's commission amounting to 5% of the principal indebtedness, but in no event less than the sum of $200.00, shall be payable by the Mortgagor to the Mortgagee and shall be secured hereby. The Mortgagor shall pay the cost of the title search and all other costs incurred by the Mortgagee in connection with the proceedings to recover any sums secured hereby. The Mortgagor shall also pay any reasonable charge of the Mortgagee in connection with the satisfaction of this Mortgage of record.

10. If the Mortgagor shall fail to pay any sum required to be paid by the Mortgagor under said note or this Mortgage within 30 days after the same becomes due and payable, or if the Mortgagor shall fail to perform any other provision hereof or said note on the part of the Mortgagor to be performed, or shall transfer title to the mortgaged premises without the prior written approval of the Mortgagee, then in any such event, at the option of the Mortgagee: (a) the Mortgagee may apply on account of the indebtedness hereby secured the balance of accumulated installment payments made by the Mortgagor for taxes, water rents, sewer rents, and insurance premiums under Paragraph 2 hereof; (b) the whole unpaid balance of the principal indebtedness, together with all interest thereon and all other sums hereby secured, shall become due and payable immediately, without notice to the Mortgagor, and shall be recoverable by the Mortgagee forthwith or at any time or times thereafter, without say of execution or other process; (c) the Mortgagee may take possession of the mortgaged premises and (d) the Mortgagee may forthwith exercise all other rights and remedies provided in this Mortgage and in said note, or which may be available to the Mortgagee by law, and all such rights and remedies shall be cumulative and concurrent and may be pursued singly, successively, or together at the Mortgagee's sole discretion, and may be exercised as often as occasion therefor shall occur.

11. If the Mortgagee shall take possession of the mortgaged premises as provided in Paragraph 10 hereof, the Mortgagee may: (a) hold, manage, operate and lease the same, to the Mortgagor or any other person or persons, on such terms and for such periods of time as he the Mortgagee may deem proper, and the provisions of any lease made by the Mortgagee pursuant hereto shall be valid and binding upon the Mortgagor notwithstanding the fact that the Mortgagee's right of possession may terminate or this Mortgage may be satisfied of record prior to the expiration of the term of such lease; (b) make such alterations, additions, improvements, renovations, repairs and replacements thereto as the Mortgagee may deem proper; (c) demolish any part or all of the improvements situate upon the mortgaged premises which in the judgment of the Mortgagee may be in unsafe condition and dangerous to life and property; (d) remodel such improvements so as to make the same available in whole or in part for business purposes or multiple dwelling purposes; and (e) collect the rents, issues, and profits arising from the mortgaged premises, past due and thereafter becoming due, and apply the same, in such order of priority as the Mortgagee

may determine, to the payment of all charges and commissions incidental to the collection of rents and the management of the mortgaged premises and all other sums or charges required to be paid by the Mortgagor hereunder. In addition to the payment of such charges and commissions, the Mortgagee shall be entitled to retain 10% of such rents, issues, and profits in payment for the services of the Mortgagee in relation to the premises. All moneys advanced by the Mortgagee for the purpose aforesaid and not repaid out of the rents collected shall immediately and without demand be repaid by the Mortgagor to the Mortgagee, together with interest there on at the rate of six percent (6%) per annum, and shall be added to the principal indebtedness hereby secured. The taking of possession and collection of rents by the Mortgagee as aforesaid shall not be construed to be an affirmation of any lease of the mortgaged premises or any part thereof, and the Mortgagee or any other purchaser at any foreclosure sale may (if otherwise entitled to do so) exercise the right to terminate any such lease as though such taking of possession and collection of rents had not occurred.

12. For the purpose of procuring possession of the mortgaged premises in the event of any default hereunder or under said note, the Mortgagor hereby authorizes and empowers any attorney of any court of record in the Commonwealth of _____ or elsewhere, as attorney for the Mortgagor and all persons claiming under or through the Mortgagor, to sign an agreement for entering in any competent court an amicable action in ejection for possession of the mortgaged premises and to appear for and confess judgment against the Mortgagor, and against all persons claiming under or through the Mortgagor, for the recovery by the Mortgagee of possession of the same, without any stay of execution, for which this mortgage, or a copy thereof verified by affidavit, shall be a sufficient warrant, and thereupon a writ of possession may be issued forthwith, without any prior writ or proceeding whatsoever. The Mortgagor hereby releases the Mortgagee from all errors and defects whatsoever in entering such action and judgment and in causing such writ or error, appeal, petition to open, or strike off judgment, or other objection shall be filed or made with respect thereto. If for any reason after such action has been commenced the same shall be discontinued or possession of the mortgaged premises shall remain in or be restored to the Mortgagor, the Mortgagee shall have the right for the same default or any subsequent default to bring one or more further amicable actions as above provided to recover possession of the mortgaged premises. The Mortgagee may bring such amicable action in ejectment before or after the institution of foreclosure proceedings upon this Mortgage, or after judgment thereon or on said note, or after a sale of the mortgaged premises by the Sheriff.

13. The granting of an extension or extensions of time by the Mortgagee with respect to the performance of any provision of this Mortgage or said note on the part of the Mortgagor to be performed, or the taking of any additional security, or the waiver by the Mortgagee or failure by the Mortgagee to enforce any provision of the Mortgage or said note or to declare a default with respect thereto, shall not operate as a waiver of any subsequent default or defaults or affect the right of the Mortgagee to exercise all rights or remedies stipulated herein and therein.

14. The Mortgagor waives the right of inquisition on all property levied upon to collect the indebtedness hereby secured and does voluntarily condemn the same, and authorizes the prothonotary to enter such condemnation; and the Mortgagor also waives and releases all laws, now in force or hereafter enacted, relating to exemption, appraisement or stay of execution.

15. In the event that there is more than one party named herein as Mortgagor, the word "Mortgagor" whenever occurring herein shall mean the plural. The obligation of each and every party hereto, and also the authority and powers conferred herein, shall be joint and several and shall inure to the benefit of and bind each and every party hereto and its, his, her, and their, and each of their, respective heirs, executors, administrators, successors, and assigns.

16. This mortgage shall not be assignable. Any transfer of an interest in the property subject to the mortgage without written permission of the mortgagee (seller) above be a default.

17. This is intended to be a purchase-money mortgage and have lien priorities as permitted by statute.

IN WITNESS WHEREOF, the Mortgagor has executed these presents the day and year first above written.

Sealed and Delivered
In the Presence of:

_____ (Seal)
                    Borrower

_____ (Seal)
                    Borrower

_____ (Seal)
                    Witness

_____ (Seal)
                    Witness

_____ (Seal)
                    Witness

B. Mistake

If a party to the contract has proceeded under an assumption about the contract that was clearly wrong and did not realize it was wrong, and the other party knew full well of that error, a contract may be avoided or defended against.

Since contracts are supposed to be a reflection of mutual assent, facts that are blatantly opposite or dissimilar in the parties' own minds are examples of how there is no mutual assent. Hence, a party may assert that he entered into the contract under a mistaken impression. But that mistake must be fundamental to the contract, and no rescission of the contract is possible unless the party can prove that:

☐ The mistake is material.
☐ Enforcement would be unfair or unconscionable.
☐ The mistake was not the product of culpable negligence.
☐ The nonmistaken party would suffer no more than the loss of his or her bargain if the contract was rescinded.
☐ Prompt notice of mistake was given.
☐ The mistake was not judgmental in nature.

C. Fraud

A contract may also be avoided if the injured party can prove that the basis of its formation was fundamentally fraudulent. To prove fraud, the victim must demonstrate that the contractual negotiations were marked by *intentional misrepresentations,* or *intentional nondisclosures,* of material facts to the agreement. Note the word *intentional* rather than mistaken or negligent misrepresentation. The law requires knowledge of the error. The growing awareness of consumer fraud in the marketplace is evidence of the power this area of law has. Contracts for "cancer cures," breast enlargers, and hair restorers are continually struck down on the basis of fraud.

D. Duress or Undue Influence

A true meeting of the minds requires volitional capacity, and duress negates free will. If someone puts a gun to your head and says, "Buy it!," he can hardly assert that you have an "agreement." Fortunately, the law recognizes that tactics of high-pressure sales persons often border on duress. Ponder a contract negotiated with organized crime. Can it be the product of free will? Any threats, extortion, or blackmail certainly affects the validity and enforceability of a contract. Equally important is the state of mind, the mental acumen of the contracting party, or the relationship that exists between the parties. If it can be shown that a fiduciary relationship exists, the potential for duress increases. Other situations exist in which the submitting party may be too emotionally unstable or too weak to agree rationally to anything, for instance, bereaved widows or widowers.

E. Unconscionability

Equitable and statutory remedies exist that will deny the existence of a contract that is truly unconscionable. Under UCC 2-302, an unconscionable contract is defined as, and effectively holds in contempt, any contract so utterly unfair or grotesque in design that enforcement of it would be highly unjust. Would it be fair for a court to uphold a contract for a refrigerator priced at $6000 if its wholesale price was $225? What about an automobile starter priced at $159 that was purchased by the dealer for $30? When is unconscionability simply excessive profits? Courts have a hard time answering these questions, but do try to view some objective factors:

1. Is the contract governed by the "small print" or some obscure provisions?
2. Is the contract utterly unclear and imprecise in language?
3. Does the contract disclaim all warranties and seller responsibility?
4. Is the contract grossly unfair to a reasonable person?
5. If the contract is enforced, will it not violate public and social policy?

F. Impossibility or Impracticability of Contractual Performance

Another major defense to contractual formation or eventual enforcement is legal or factual impossibility. In brief, three situations emerge that render the fruition or maturation of contractual obligation impossible.

1. Supervening illegality

If the state or federal government or municipality passes a new law or regulation, which makes a contractual understanding a crime, contractual liability ceases. An interesting historical example was the adoption and repeal of prohibition. Just think of all the contracts for corn meal, hops, bottles, caps, and labels that had to be rescinded. This is a good example of the power of law.

2. Destruction or loss of the contractual subject matter

If a contract exists that provides for the sale of artwork, a car, or other goods, destruction of those things makes performance impossible and thereby generally discharges the offeror. This is, by and large, a well-accepted principle in law, though the UCC has addressed the many "risk of loss" issues that often emerge between merchants in the sale of goods. (See UCC 2-510.) In addition, various localities regulate the "risk of loss" between parties in the sale of land or houses.

3. Supervening death or physical illness

Contractual enforcement is not possible if a party to the contract dies, unless the contract provides guidelines in this event. If the deceased party has already received appropriate consideration, his or her estate will have to delegate those duties to another party, assuming the contractual obligation is not too personal in form.

4. Contractual frustration as a form of impossibility

Much has been written on the complexities and nuances of impossibility and frustration. This outline will not attempt to simplify this area of law in a few paragraphs but will provide a general framework in which a *frustration* case may arise.

If a contract was entered into on a given day and time, it was hoped, by both parties, that the world would stay basically the same. "Frustration" cases arise when the world becomes radically altered. Consider the following:

1. Can a lettuce grower in California provide the twenty-one thousand heads of lettuce when his field is under water?
2. Can a car manufacturer provide cars when the auto workers have been on strike for three years?
3. Can a contract for candy be honored when the price of sugar has gone from thirty-nine cents a pound to seven dollars a pound?

In all these scenarios, the promisor is in trouble and without question frustrated in efforts to perform his or her obligation. In some circumstances, total frustration can lead to a discharge of the obligation if the events were not foreseeable; the contract had become worthless. Originally, both parties had mutually agreed on what they expected.

G. Contractual Illegality and Unenforceability

This area of defenses to the enforcement of contractual obligations has been referred to quite regularly throughout this book. For the sake of clarity, we will list all possible claims that can be asserted by persons hoping to discharge contractual obligations or simply hoping not to jeopardize their personal integrity. The following are void or voidable contracts:

1. Any agreement that violates the criminal law of the jurisdiction.
2. Agreements in violation of state usury laws.
3. Agreements that promote the commission of a tort or civil wrong.
4. Agreements clearly in violation of public or social policy: e.g., a separation agreement that the father will never pay child support.
5. Agreements that unfairly restrict an individual's right to compete in a profession. (Is it reasonable in time and place?)
6. Agreements that illegally disclaim all warranty liability, negligence liability, or other responsibilities. (Why can swimming pools regularly have no lifeguard in some jurisdictions?)
7. Agreements that require the parties to be licensed when, in fact, the parties are not.
8. Agreements that are truly "unconscionable," under the UCC, at 2-719 (3) in the sale of goods. Exculpatory clauses are valid as long as not unconscionable. Consider a contract that limits liability for any personal injuries between a patient and doctor.

H. Statute of Frauds: Written Contracts

The Statute of Frauds has been generally enacted and followed in all jurisdictions. The statute concerns itself with those contractual undertakings that must be in writing; otherwise they are unenforceable contracts. This statute never attempts to mandate that all contracts must be evidenced by a writing but instead outlines the very few contracts that are required in writing. In our world of red tape and legalese, it's hard to believe that oral contracts are still common and valid. Obviously the problems of proof and the ethics of the marketplace dictate a modern-day preference for writings.

The Statute of Frauds will provide a defense in the following contractual situations:

1. *Guaranty, or surety, contracts.* If a party promises to pay off your credit obligation, and that party is not responsible, that promise must be in writing.

2. *Contracts for the Sale of Land.* This includes not only the land itself but also the house, fixtures, liens, future interest, timber, and crops.

3. *Contracts for the Sale of Goods.* Under UCC 2-201, a contract for the sale of goods of five hundred dollars or more must be in writing.

4. *Contracts for Securities.* Under UCC 8-319, a contract concerning securities must be in writing.

5. *Contracts in consideration of marriage.* Contracts of this nature must be in writing.

6. *Contracts that are incapable of being performed within one year.* This is an oft-litigated section of the Statute of Frauds. If there is *any possibility* of performance of the contract within one year from the date the contract is made, then it does not have to be in writing. Consider these examples and decide if a writing is needed: a contract to loan money to be repaid when a will is thoroughly administered; or a contract to work for a year, performance to begin in a week

7. *Contracts evidencing loans or the sale of a business.* Contracts of this nature must be in writing in some jurisdictions.

8. *Contracts promising the establishment of a trust.* Contracts of this nature must be in writing in some jurisdictions.

In order to meet the formalities of the Statute of Frauds, particular attention also has to be given to the writing's formalities. All writings must be a sufficient memorandum of essential terms outlining (1) identity of the parties; (2) description of the subject matter; (3) terms and conditions of the agreement; (4) consideration; and (5) signature of the party sought to be charged.

IV. INTERPRETATION OF CONTRACTS

A. Parol Evidence Rule

Even the best intentions and the most rigorous attention to detail and contractual obligations do not always produce perfect contracts. At times that process of "meeting of the minds" is still not realized even though the offer and acceptance is complete, the consideration sufficient, and the defenses countered. The parties to a contract often claim that extrinsic evidence, both oral and written, of prior or contemporaneous agreements or negotiations should be admitted for various purposes. Since the courts do not by nature like "policing" or modifying bargains, such extrinsic evidence is usually not admissible under the parol evidence rules unless a party wishes to offer evidence to demonstrate:

1. Fraud and misrepresentation
2. Mistake as to contractual intent
3. Performance of the contract
4. Trade custom
5. The agreement is only "partially" integrated
6. Proof of additional consistent terms

The parol evidence rule is a product of both case and common law and is UCC 2-202.

V. PERFORMANCE OF THE CONTRACT

Parties to the contract have basically two paths to follow—either perform the obligations of the contract or breach the provisions of the contract. Naturally, the legal analysis must rest with the negative side since that is what people will come to the law office for. While disagreements and trivial arguments are quite common in the performance of contractual obligations, the law will remedy only those breaches that are *material* in scope.

A. Definition of Breach

A material breach occurs when:

1. The injured party suffers or will suffer serious economic losses.
2. The injured party is greatly inconvenienced early on in the performance.
3. The injured party has to literally suspend performance.
4. The injured party has not received assurances about good-faith performances.
5. The injured party has substantially performed the obligation of the contract, and the other party will not honor the contract.
6. The breaching party repudiates the contract.
7. Under the UCC 2-702 (1), a seller of goods who discovers a buyer is insolvent. (See also UCC 2-609.)

The effect of breach gives rise to remedies for the other party who must seek to uphold the contract in the best way he or she can.

B. Remedies for Breach of Contract

1. Rescission. As noted under the *Illegality* analysis, rescission or discharge may happen by operation of law. As common, that is, if the parties so agree, their agreement may be rescinded. However, this rescission does not destroy all other remedies available under the U.C.C., such as at 2-106 (4).

2. Novation. The parties may agree to the reformulation of their contract. A valid novation requires:
   a. A previous valid obligation
   b. Mutual agreement
   c. Intent to extinguish old obligations
   d. A new contract that is valid

3. Release. The parties may agree to legally release each other from further obligations.

4. Specific Performance. At times the "personal" nature of the services rendered, such as artwork or design, cannot be delegated or assigned or substituted by other means. Hence the equitable remedy of specific performance is available.

5. Injunction. A party can apply for an order of the court to demand that a party cease from performing the obligations of the contract in a particular way.

6. Performance. Eventual performance by the obliged party will discharge the contract.

7. Accord and Satisfaction. The parties can reach an accord by substituting the method of performance (e.g., instead of money, a painting given in its place). Once the provisions of the accord are followed through, a *satisfaction* has occurred.

8. Discharge by Operation of Law. (See illegality analysis.)

9. Statute of Limitations. Depending on jurisdiction, the statute's tolling will end liability under the contract.

10. Quantum Meruit. The philosophy behind this remedy is basically favorable to the person who breaches the contract. That person argues that he or she should be paid at least what he or she is worth in the overall performance of the contract. The injured party should not be enriched by the defaulting party.

C. Damages Available for Contractual Breach

The first step in determining relief is to determine your client's needs. If you represent the plaintiff, you should interview the plaintiff carefully to determine what the client desires from the result of a breach of a contract from the other party. In the event that you represent the defendant, your work is usually spelled out in the pleadings.

There are various forms of damages available in contract cases. Generally, law seeks to place the nonbreaching party in the status quo had the breach not occurred.

1. Money damages

The most common type of damage is money damage. There are two types of money damages, direct and consequential.

Direct damages are those directly attributable to the breach of the other party. For instance, in the event that the seller breaches in supplying the buyer with certain materials, the buyer's remedy would be in money damages the difference between the amount he would have paid the seller and the amount he now has to pay to obtain the goods.

Consequential damages are those additional damages to direct damages that are needed to put the nonbreaching party in the position of status quo. The test for consequential damages generally is whether or not they were foreseeable by the breaching party. For instance, if the supplier of a certain set of goods was to deliver the goods on a specific date and knew that the buyer would be greatly harmed if the goods were not delivered at a specific time, the seller would be responsible not only for the difference in the amount that the buyer would have to pay to obtain the goods elsewhere but for the damages that the buyer incurred by the delay. This type of damage is often termed lost profits. Lost profits are not the total amount of sales that the buyer would have lost but the difference between the sales and the expenses incurred had the goods been delivered on time.

On all money damages and other equitable damages the question arises as to whether the plaintiff mitigated damages. Thus, in any damage analysis, inquire as to how the nonbreaching party could have acted to correct any of the defective goods, failure to supply goods, or other performance. In other words, the nonbreaching party is under a duty to mitigate his or her losses by attempting to purchase the goods elsewhere in the event that the seller has failed to supply them. Thus, if the nonbreaching party can purchase the goods at the same price, he or she cannot go out and seek to purchase goods of a different and higher quality and charge the breaching party with the difference in cost. Another type of mitigation of damages is called *betterment*. Betterment occurs when the nonbreaching party attempts to correct a defect by, for instance, dealing with the defects in a newly built house by building a different and more grandiose type of house. Or stated another way, when the nonbreaching party repairs the defective item that she bought and makes it much better than before, such as repairing an old home and making it like a new one, that is betterment. The idea is that the nonbreaching party is not entitled to place himself or herself in a better position than status quo. Betterment is often a defense used by the contractor in construction contracts.

2. Proof of money damages and defenses

Often the proof of money damages, such as consequential or lost profits, involves the use of an expert. Thus, your job is to recognize when you need an expert to compute the damages that you are seeking. In the specialty areas of law, these types of damages have been specifically defined and require a great deal of factual and expert testimony for proof. For instance, in the construction field, the failure of a subcontractor to perform will have a ripple effect on the entire project. These ripple-effect damages have to be proved by claim experts, accountants, and other factual witnesses, such as bookkeepers. Your job is to recognize this and to assist the lawyer in obtaining the correct expert. You should always look to the professions, universities, and trade associations to which your client belongs.

The same type of analysis is needed when you are defending, and you are asserting mitigation of damages or a betterment theory. Under either of these two defense theories, you may need an expert witness. The expert may need to testify that there were other goods available at the same price or that the repairs undertaken by the plaintiff really placed him in a better position than status quo. You may thus need a construction expert or someone in the service industry for the specific type of goods involved.

Note: When you represent the nonbreaching party and are about to repair the item the breaching party defaulted upon, it is a good idea to give the breaching party notice of your repairs so that he or she can view the scene and see what you are going to do. This will cut down on a factual argument at the time of trial concerning what your client did and why.

3. Damages under the Uniform Commercial Code

a. SELLER'S REMEDIES

In general, the seller's remedies are governed by section 2-703 of the UCC as follows:

1. Withhold the delivery of goods.

2. Stop the delivery of goods by any bailee.

3. Proceed to salvage the goods unidentified under the contract.

4. Resell the goods and recover the damages, which are the difference between the resale price and the contract price together with incidental damages.

5. Recover damages for nonacceptance of the goods, which are the difference between the market price at the time and place of tender and the unpaid contract price together with incidental damages, or if said measure of damages is inadequate to put the seller in as good a position as performance would have done, the measure of damages is then the profit the seller would have made from the full performance by the buyer. Or the seller may have an action for the price if the seller is unable to resell the items after a reasonable effort.

6. Cancel the contract.

The seller's incidental damages have been defined to be any commercially reasonable charges, expenses, or commissions incurred in stopping delivery, in transportation, and in care and custody of the goods after the buyer's breach in connection with the return or resale of the goods or otherwise resulting from the breach.

b. Buyer's Remedies

Generally the buyer's remedies are governed by section 2-711 of the UCC as follows:

1. Recover part of the purchase price wrongfully paid.

2. Recover damages for cost of cover, which is determined after a good-faith effort without unreasonable delay has been made to purchase goods in substitution of those due from the seller. The damages would be the difference in the purchase price.

3. Recover damages for nondelivery. These are determined by calculating the difference between the market price at the time when the buyer learned of the breach and the contract price together with any incidental and consequential damages. However, they must be reduced by any expenses saved as a consequence of the seller's breach.

4. In addition, the buyer may be able to identify the goods and have them delivered under specific performance.

5. Finally, the buyer, where he has rightfully rejected or justifiably revoked goods and has paid part of the purchase price, has a security interest in the rejected or revoked goods. Not only are his payments taken into account but any expenses reasonably incurred in the inspection, receipt, transportation, and case and custody of the goods he holds for resale as an aggrieved buyer.

6. In most instances, the buyer has the same rights as the seller in that he may add to his damages such incidental and consequential damages as may be recovered. Incidental damages are defined as including expenses reasonably incurred in the inspection, receipt, transportation, and care and custody of the goods. Consequential damages are generally defined as any loss resulting from the general or particular requirements and needs that the seller at the time of contracting had reason to know about and that could not reasonably be prevented by cover or otherwise.

4. Liquidated damages

In both common law and under the UCC, liquidated damages are permitted. Liquidated damages are specific damages stated in a contract for the purpose of placing a nonbreaching party in a position of status quo, where the actual amount of damages is difficult to prove as a result of breach and it would be inconvenient or not feasible to make use of them in obtaining an adequate remedy. The rule on liquidated damages is that they must be reasonable and not operate as a penalty.

Note: Never use the word *penalty* in any contract where you are seeking liquidated damages, and always make sure that the amount of liquidated damages is reasonable.

VI. THIRD-PARTY RIGHTS IN CONTRACTS

The complexity of contract law reaches new heights in the consideration of the invasion of third-party interests in simple contracts. Third-party beneficiaries are generally of two basic types.

A. Creditor Beneficiary

In this situation, A owes B money. A makes a contract with C, who therefore promises to pay A's debt to B. Therefore, A and C are the initial contractual parties, but the nature of the contract is purely for the benefit of B, who is in fact a creditor of A. As a creditor beneficiary under the contract between A and C, B can exercise some rights.

B. Donee Beneficiary

In this situation, the father has a son whom he wishes well cared for. The father contracts with a bank to run a trust on behalf of his son. The bank is not satisfying the very basic needs for the son. The son is a donee beneficiary of the contract between the father and the bank and as a result can enforce his rights under that contract.

These are common situations in which third parties can exercise their rights, but upon close inspection, it is clear that there is a "direct" relationship between the beneficiaries and the contracts from which they benefit. As such, the law does not favor *incidental* beneficiaries. Incidental beneficiaries are those individuals who stand to gain from the contractual undertakings of others, for instance, a construction company that hopes for a hotel chain and private developer to agree on the building of a new hotel. But their gain is incidental, and not legal as in a creditor or donee sense.

VII. ASSIGNMENTS OF CONTRACTUAL RIGHTS

A. Assignments

In general, once a contract is formulated and legally enforceable, its rights, obligations, and duties are fully assignable or delegable. Under the UCC in both 2-210 and 9-318, express provisions declaring assignments "void" are generally not effective. In short, the law favors the assignment of rights under contracts and the delegation of duties. The law favors the alienability of interests whether they be goods, services, or monetary reward. As with all law, there are exceptions to assignablity:

Claims for wages

Claims for worker's compensation

Delegation of "personal" or specialized services
  (see UCC 2-210 (1-5); 2-609)

Any assignment or delegation in violation of public policy

Requirements or "outputs" contracts

Insurance

Credit

Future rights

B. Delegation of Duties

All duties under contract, from painting a house to fixing a swimming pool, can be delegated. (See exhibit 8.7.) Keep in mind the following rules:

1. The original party to the contract, the delegor, remains liable as surety for the performance of the delegatee.
2. A duty to buy all one's requirements from a seller is nondelegable.
3. Contracts may expressly prohibit delegation.
4. Delegation of a duty in violation of the contractual provisions can amount to a repudiation.

VIII. SECURED TRANSACTIONS: UCC ARTICLE 9

A. Introduction: Definitions

This is a field in which a nightmare of terminology exists. At best, expect to master only the rudiments of secured filings, since those filings are the general foundation upon which our banking and credit system operates. In secured transactions, three principal definitions emerge:

PLEDGOR. A debtor who transfers his or her interest in property to a lender.

PLEDGEE. A lender who retains the first interest in the property until the debtor pays off the debt.

SECURED INTEREST. Any interest in personal property or fixtures that secures payment or performance of an obligation (see UCC 1-201 [37]).

Say that you are buying a car. As with most people, your cash is short and reliance on a bank inevitable. The bank wants to "secure its interest" and will do so by demanding a lien to be marked on the title to the vehicle—they will retain title until the car is paid off. This is a simple transaction that clearly elucidates the secured-interest phenomenon. Cars are not the only form of property on which secured interests are exercised, as can be gleaned by the very broad definition of security interest in the UCC.

Exhibit 8.7

POWER OF ATTORNEY

I, _____, of _____ County, State of

_____, do hereby designate _____, of _____

County, State of _____, my true and lawful attorney in fact, or agent, to have
the following powers:

(Select or add appropriate provision)

to make, draw and indorse promissory notes, checks or bills of exchange and to waive demand,
presentment, protest, notice of protest, and notice of non-payment of all such instruments;

to make and execute any and all contracts;

to purchase, sell, dispose of, assign and pledge notes, stocks, bonds and securities and to exercise such
voting rights as my ownership of any notes, stocks, bonds and securities may entitle me, either in person or
by proxy;

to represent me in all matters pertaining to the business of any corporation in which I may have any
interest;

to receive and to demand all sums of money, debts, dues, accounts, bequests, interest, dividends, and
demands whatsoever which are now or shall hereafter become due or payable to me and to compromise or
discharge the same;

to bargain for, contract concerning, buy, sell, mortgage and in any and every way and manner deal
with personal property of any kind or nature;

to execute instruments to effect the transfer of title to any motor vehicle owned by me;

to execute and file tax returns;

to purchase, sell, mortgage, convey and lease any interest in real estate, wherever located, of which I
may be owner now or hereafter;

_____

_____

_____

_____

and I hereby ratify and confirm all that my said attorney in fact or agent shall do by virtue hereof.

I hereby reserve the right of revocation; however, this Power of Attorney shall continue in full force and
effect until:

(Select or add appropriate provisions)

(A)   I have executed and recorded in the Recorder's Office of the county of my domicile a written
revocation hereof.

(B)   The_____ day of _____, 19 _____.

(C)   _____

I further state that:

(Select appropriate provision)

(1)   This Power of Attorney shall not be affected by my incompetence.

(2)   This Power of Attorney shall become effective upon my incompetence.

IN WITNESS WHEREOF, I have hereunto set my hand and seal, this _____ day of

_____, 19 _____.

Signature   _____

STATE OF INDIANA   Printed   _____

                    } SS:

COUNTY OF

Before me, a Notary Public in and for said County and State personally appeared _____

_____

_____, who acknowledged the execution of the foregoing Power of Attorney.

WITNESS my hand and Notarial Seal, this _____ day of _____, 19 _____.

My commission expires   Signature   _____

_____   Printed   _____

                    Residing in _____ County

This Instrument was prepared by _____, Attorney at Law

© Copyright, 1980, by Indianapolis Bar Association

B. Types of Security Interests

1. Leases
2. Consignments (see UCC 2-326)
3. Fixtures in real estate (see UCC 9-313)
4. Sales of accounts, contract rights, and chattel paper (see UCC 9-102, 105, 106)

In the end, any interest in any personal property, whether it be the actual property itself, the right to sell it, or the right to receive payment for it, can be the subject of a secured interest.

C. Property Not under Article 9

It is important to note also the types of property not covered by article 9 of the UCC.

1. Mortgages
2. Land sale contracts
3. Landlord's lien
4. Insurance policy
5. Employee compensation

These exclusions are critical to know since they form a large part of a law office practice, and article 9 requirements are generally irrelevant.

D. Perfection of the Security Interest

The article lays down the special steps that must be taken to insure that a security interest is enforceable. The process is known as filing and "perfection" of the security interest. Fundamentally, it is a paper-pushing exercise. The steps require:

1. Entry into a security agreement
2. Writing that satisfies UCC 9-203-204. The writing must contain at least the debtor's signature, a description of the collateral, and enough additional matters to make the document an agreement.
3. The debtor must acquire "rights" in the collateral (e.g., the name of the owner of an automobile is included on the title).
4. The secured party, pledgee, must give value—that, is a loan or other negotiable instrument.
5. Once steps 3 and 4 are accomplished, the security interest is "attached," and the secured interest *exists*.
6. Perfection can then be accomplished by:
   a. Filing a financing statement to give notice to all potential creditors that this interest is secured
   b. Automatic perfection—as in consumer transactions at a department store
   c. Creditor possession of the collateral

The most complex process in perfection is in filing. The priority of rights in this area can be so complicated that a paralegal will rarely be asked to delve into this area. What a paralegal will be asked to do is to determine what is required to effect an appropriate filing in order to perfect a security interest. Keep in mind:

1. Where you are supposed to file the appropriate documentation—with the secretary of state, the Department of Motor Vehicles, or the county where the business is located.
2. How you classify the property inevitably affects the process of perfection. Be certain you have classified the property properly.
3. Which document must be filed to perfect the security interest—a financing statement.
4. The information needed on the financing statement—signatures, addresses, description of collateral.
5. The effect or impact that interstate operations will have upon filing.
6. Who it is that has priority in the same secured interest—e.g., first in time, first in right.

While the UCC greatly assists the filer in deciphering the perfection process, there are still many ways in which a secured creditor can be totally unprotected. The paralegal must cover every possible angle in this complex area of law, to protect all interests.

IX. SOME SUGGESTIONS ON DRAFTING CONTRACTUAL AGREEMENTS

As a paralegal in any law office, you may be called upon to draft certain written documents, including contracts for the purchase of real estate, buying and selling equipment, and agreements for any other commercial transaction. You may also be called upon to draft letter agreements or letter opinions for an attorney to execute. Thus, when you are preparing such documents, keep these few thoughts in mind as a guideline.

A. General Guidelines

The process usually begins by identifying the goal—your overall intent for the agreement. After you have the goal written down, then organize your agreement into topics. After you have the organization, then fill in the paragraphs as they fit under each particular topic. Revise this draft if it does not flow in a logical sequence. The final step is to proofread.

In drafting the actual document, use short sentences with one thought. Leave your headings in the document so that it is easily understandable and can be identified at a glance. Finally, when you have your rough draft completed, review it to make sure it is complete and answers all the questions in relation to your general topic and goal.

B. Special Considerations

1. It is a good idea in the agreement itself to spell out in "whereas" clauses what the intent of the agreement is. Simply state the intent of the parties.

2. Additionally, at some point, either before or after the rough draft, make a checklist and make sure that your checklist of items is completed in the document.

3. When a document is being proofread, it should be checked for grammatical construction and to make sure it is internally consistent.

4. Use certain phrases in agreements such as:
   a. The document is to be interpreted under the laws of (name of state).
   b. The agreement inures to the benefit of the parties' heirs, successors, and assigns
   c. In the event any portion of the document is constructed to be unenforceable, the remaining provisions of the document shall be construed to be enforceable.

C. Legal Requirements

Any time you are drafting a document you must be aware of the legal requirements for the transaction at hand. You should know the basic elements of contract law. One element that is most often overlooked concerns consideration.

When a document is a preliminary document that is a promise for a promise, that means that both parties are going to perform at some time in the future. Where the performance concerns a transaction for conveyance of personal property and real estate, the question needs to be answered, by what means is the conveyance to be represented—land contract, deed, bill of sale, or whatever? Thus, in drafting the original document, you can attach copies of the forms that will be used even though the terms cannot be filled in at the time the initial buy-sell agreement is prepared.

Obviously, the contract should be reviewed for any violations of statutes, such as usury laws for interest and board of directors' resolutions when a corporation is buying real estate.

In summary, drafting is an art, but it can be reduced in part to a science by planning and organizing. In your work as a paralegal, your ability to write concisely is of utmost importance.

X. AN OVERVIEW OF RELEVANT UCC PROVISIONS

A. Uniform Commercial Code

1. Goods (Sec. 2-105)
   a. Movable things
   b. Cf. real property
2. Sale—transfer of title for a price (Sec. 2-106)

B. Formation of a Contract of Sale

1. Contract—intent and reasonable certain terms (Sec. 2-204)
2. Offer—"firm" offer (Sec. 2-205). Acceptance—offer to perform for (Sec. 2-206)
   a. Performance
   b. Additional terms in acceptance (2-207)
3. Consideration
4. Writing—Statute of Frauds (2-201)
   a. Goods worth $500 or more
5. Check list of items to be included in contracts for the sale of goods

Each contract must be tailored to suit the particular transaction, but the following check list sets forth items that may be necessary or useful.

1. Description of the parties (Sec. 2-103, 2-104)
2. Description of the goods
   a. Quantity (Sec. 2-201)
   b. Quality (Sec. 2-313, 2-314, 2-315)
   c. Manner of selection (Sec. 2-311, 2-501)
3. Warranties
   a. Title (Sec. 2-312)
   b. Quality (Sec. 2-313, 2-314, 2-315)
      Disclaimer of warranties (Sec. 2-316)
   c. Limitation of liability for breach of warranty (Sec. 2-719)
4. Title to the goods (Sec. 2-401)
5. Seller's obligation to tender delivery of the goods
   a. Time of delivery (Sec. 2-309, 2-503)
      Place of delivery (Sec. 2-308, 2-319, 2-324, 2-503, 2-504)
   b. Manner of delivery (Sec. 2-311, 2-503)
      (1) Delivery in single or several lots (Sec. 2-307)
      (2) Shipment under reservation (Sec. 2-310 (b), 2-505)
      (3) Delivery on condition (Sec. 2-507 (2))
   c. Seller's right to cure improper tender (Sec. 2-508)
6. Buyer's obligation to accept goods (Sec. 2-507)
   a. Buyer's right to inspect the goods before acceptance (Sec. 2-513, 2-606)
   b. Buyer's right to reject goods (Sec. 2-601)
      (1) Manner of rejection (Sec. 2-602)
      (2) Obligation to state reasons for rejection (Sec. 2-605)
      (3) Obligation to care for rejected goods (Sec. 2-603, 2-604)
   c. Buyer's obligation to notify seller of breach discovered after acceptance (Sec. 2-607)
   d. Buyer's right to revoke his acceptance (Sec. 2-608)
7. Buyer's obligation to pay for goods (Sec. 2-507, 2-606)
   a. Price (Sec. 2-305)
   b. Medium of payment (Sec. 2-304, 2-511)
   c. Time of payment (Sec. 2-310)
   d. Obligation to pay before inspection of the goods (Sec. 2-512)

C. Performance, Breach, Repudiation and Excuse

1. Seller must deliver conforming goods (Sec. 2-503)
2. Buyer's obligation to accept and pay for goods (Sec. 2-507, 2-512)
3. Buyer's right of inspection and rejection (Sec. 2-513, 2-601, 2-602, 2-612)
4. Seller's right to "cure" (Sec. 2-508)
5. Excuse of performance (Sec. 2-615, 2-616)
   a. Failure of presupposed condition
   b. Commercial impracticability
   c. Release

D. Breach of Contract—Remedies

1. SELLER'S REMEDIES (Sec. 2-703)
Where the buyer wrongfully rejects or revokes acceptance of goods or fails to make a payment due on or before delivery or repudiates with respect to a part of the whole, then with respect to any goods directly affected and, if the breach is of the whole contract (Sec. 2-612), then also with respect to the whole undelivered balance, the aggrieved seller may

    a. withhold delivery of such goods;
    b. stop delivery by any bailee as hereafter provided (Sec. 2-705);
    c. proceed under the next section respecting goods still unidentified to the contracts
    d. resell and recover damages as hereafter provided (Sec. 2-706);
    e. recover damages for non-acceptance (Sec. 2-708) or in a proper case the price(2-709);
    f. cancel.

2. BUYER'S REMEDIES (Sec. 2-711)
    a. Where the seller fails to make delivery or repudiates or the buyer rightfully rejects or justifiably revokes acceptance then with respect to any goods involved, and with respect to the whole if the breach goes to the whole contract (Sec. 2-612), the buyer may cancel and whether or not he has done so may in addition to recovering so much of the price as has been paid

       (1) "cover" and have damages under the next section as to all the goods affected whether or not they have been identified to the contract; or
       (2) recover damages for nondelivery as provided in this article (Sec. 2-713).
    b. Where the seller fails to deliver or repudiates the buyer may also
       (1) if the goods have been identified recover them as provided in this article (Sec.-502); or
       (2) In a proper case obtain specific performance or replevy or recover the goods as provided in this article (Sec. 2-716).
    c. On rightful rejection or justifiable revocation of acceptance a buyer has a security interest in goods in his possession or control for any payments made on their price and any expenses reasonably incurred in their inspection, receipt, transportation, care, and custody and may hold such goods and resell them in like manner as an aggrieved seller (Sec. 2-706).

DISCUSSION QUESTIONS AND PRACTICAL EXERCISES

Discussion Questions

1. A tells B he'll sell his used 1970 Ford for $500. B says, "I'll give you $325 for the car." A says, "That's too low." B says, "I'll give you $400 for the car immediately." A says, "$425 is the lowest I can go." B says, "I accept." Has a contract been formed?

2. A sees a dress advertised in X store's catalog for $35. A has shopped at X store many times before. A sends X store the $35 with necessary COD charges. X store returns the check and refuses to send the dress. Was a contract formed?

3. X sees an ad on 7/9/77 in the classified section of the *Bergen Twilight Record,* which says: "$25.00 reward for finding Persian cat with collar and nameplate Rudolph. Lost at the intersection of Rt. 4 and Rt. 17 on 7/4/77." X finds the cat and returns it. Y, who placed the ad, refuses to pay X the $25. (a) Was a contract formed? (b) Suppose the cat was dead when X found it. Could X still collect the reward? (c) What if X returned the cat alive, never having read the ad? Contract?

4. A offers to repair B's front steps. B accepts. No price is mentioned. Has a contract been formed?

5. Two parties contract for a load of cotton to be shipped on the *Peerless* from Bombay. It turns out there are two such ships, and each party was thinking of a different ship. Neither party was aware of the ambiguity. Contract formed?

6. A is shopping for a refrigerator. B shows her a model that has an automatic ice maker as an additional feature. B tells A the price of the model is $350. A says the price sounds good. Thereafter B asks A to sign a contract, which is for a refrigerator without an automatic ice maker at a price of $1800. The contract is clear and unambiguous. The refrigerator without the ice maker is delivered to A's home. Must she pay for the refrigerator?

7. X calls to price goods sold by Y. When Y gives X the price, X says, "Send the goods on, but I sure wish you could give me a better price." Was a contract made?

8. A, Inc., sends records to X in the mail, offering the records for sale. Attached to the records is a notice, in very large letters, "YOUR SILENCE WILL BE CONSIDERED AN ACCEPTANCE OF THIS OFFER." If X does nothing, will X's silence be an acceptance?

9. A offers a reward for the return of his lost dog. B promises to find it and return it. C finds the dog. A refuses to pay the reward, saying he had a contract with B. If C sues A for the reward, will he win?

10. A is attending an auction without reserve on B's premises. B is auctioning off office equipment he owns. Halfway through the auction, B displays a beautiful typewriter and asks for bids. A is the highest bidder, but B has a heart attack after A's bid, and the hammer never falls. Who is entitled to the typewriter, A or B? What if the auction was with reserve?

11. Uncle says to nephew, "If you shave off your beard, I will pay your last year of college." Nephew shaves off beard. Was a contract made, and is it enforceable by the nephew since he shaved off his beard?

12. Elderly woman says to her young niece, "If you come live with me, I'll give my property to you." Niece goes to live with elderly aunt, but aunt refuses to give her the property. Is aunt's promise enforceable?

13. X owes Y $100 and had promised to pay him by January 1. X loses his job, and Y extends the time for payment to March 1. Y then needs the cash on February 1. Would X be legally correct in saying it is not due until March 1?

14. X owes Y bank $100. Payment is due on January 1. On January 1, X pays Y $95. Y bank promises to forgive the remaining $5 due it. One month later, Y bank changes its mind and demands the $5. Is Y bank's promise to forgive the $5 a binding contract? What if the amount owed was in dispute and Y bank had said this?

15. A promises to buy from B "such coal as I wish to order from B." Is A's promise enforceable by B?

16. A makes an offer of reward for stolen property. B, a police officer, while on duty recovers the property and demands the reward. Must A pay?

17. X promises to sell Y "all the bolts I produce this year." Is X's promise enforceable?

18. X promises to grow a crop of marijuana for Y, and Y promises to pay X $1,000 for the marijuana. If X grows this marijuana, must Y pay the $1,000?

19. X owes Y $1,000. Z tells Y he'll pay the $1,000 if X can't. If X can't pay the $1,000, is Z obligated to pay Y the money?

20. X and Y agree to pay each other's funeral expenses. Have they made an enforceable contract?

Practical Exercise

Office Memorandum

TO: Paralegal Staff

FROM: John Kranoski, Senior Partner
Kranoski, Johnson and Philips

RE: Recommendation on Contractual Dispute
Client File: #03-1945
Client Name: RONDO ENTERPRISES

As of June 1, 1983, our long-time client, Rondo Enterprises, appears to be in a serious contractual dispute with the city of Newark, New Jersey. Rondo has come to us with the following queries on this dispute. Please address all possible issues.

1. Rondo entered into the bidding process with the city of Newark for completion of a sidewalk around the new municipal building. Rondo contends that the city of Newark must award the contract to them because the bidding process is a personal offer directed at only one party. Can this be correct?

2. Rondo, in preparation for the sidewalk job with the city of Newark called Cemento Incorporated and said, "What's the price of your cement now?" Cemento is suing Rondo for breach of a contract, asserting that the question constituted a legally binding acceptance. Can this be correct?

3. Rondo, in further preparation for the sidewalk job, seeks to by-pass the use of union workers and bribes union officials to overlook the hiring of illegal aliens for the job. When the U.S. Labor Department seeks to force Rondo to use union labor, Rondo balks and says it has a contract with the union. Who is right?

4. Rondo eventually decides that it would like to subcontract its electrical work to Sparko Brothers. Can the city of Newark demand that only Rondo do the work?

5. Rondo buys four cement trucks for the upcoming job but has to borrow extensively from Marine Midland Bank. Rondo doesn't like the idea of the bank's having a secured interest in the trucks. Is there any way around it?

ENRICHMENT ACTIVITY

Obtain copies of blank sales agreements from a variety of businesses that provide goods or services. Compare and contrast the agreements you have gathered. Which contracts provide the consumer the best protection from "rip-offs"? Which provide the least protection? As an informed consumer, what elements would you look for before you signed your name to any contract?

SUGGESTED READING

CALAMARI, JOHN D., et al. *The Law of Contracts.* St Paul: West Publishing Co., 1977.

Doing Business with Troubled Companies. New York: Practising Law Institute, 1983.

Drafting Documents in Plain Language. New York: Practising Law Institute, 1979.

FARNSWORTH, EDWARD ALLEN. *Contracts.* Boston: Little, Brown & Co., 1982.

FELSENFELD, CARL, et al. *Writing Contracts in Plain English.* St Paul: West Publishing Co., 1981.

HJELMFELT, DAVID C. *Understanding Franchise Contracts.* Babylon, N.Y.: Pilot Industries, 1984.

MACNEIL, IAN R. *The New Social Contract: An Inquiry into Modern Contractual Relations.* New Haven, Conn.: Yale University Press, 1980.

MCGOVERN, WILLIAM M. *Cases, Statutes and Readings on the Law of Contracts: Cases and Materials.* Indianapolis: Bobbs-Merrill Co., 1980.

PEDEN, JOHN R. *The Law of Unjust Contracts: Including the Contracts Review Act 1980 (NSW), with Detailed Annotations, Procedure and Pleadings.* Sydney: Butterworth, 1982.

Restatement of the Law, Second: Contracts. St. Paul: American Law Institute, 1981.

CHAPTER NINE

REAL ESTATE TRANSFER AND OWNERSHIP

CHAPTER DESCRIPTION

In this chapter, we survey the law of real property and examine types of real-property ownership. Students will learn about the various interests in property and how they are created, including liens, mortgages, and the methods for transferring real estate. Real estate closings, landlord-tenant law, and eviction procedures are discussed.

PARALEGAL FUNCTIONS

Draft contracts, leases, deeds, and mortgages.

Prepare closing documents.

Assist buyer or seller with transfer of property.

Assist in title searching or securing of title insurance.

Assist in closing of title.

Record instruments affecting title.

I. THE ROLE OF THE PARALEGAL IN REAL ESTATE PRACTICE

The complexities of modern real estate practice insures a very bright future for paralegalism. In the usual law-firm setting, most attorneys have neither the time nor desire to be tackling the many mechanical tasks associated with real estate transactions. Settlement sheets, title abstractions and searches, and closing procedures are by their nature most mechanical and require a regular, consistent practice to insure expertise. Paralegals have become most adept at handling these and other tasks, allowing the attorney to counsel, negotiate, and interpret the parties' intents and documentation relevant to the real estate exchange.

In order to master the mechanical steps of real estate, some theoretical review is mandatory. Initial topics for analysis include a basic survey of the law of real property with attention being given to types of estates and singular and concurrent forms of ownership. While real property is not the most exciting topic, it is essential that the paralegal know the varied ways property can be owned and exchanged. That issue is always relevant to deed interpretation, capacity to contract, and enforcement of property rights.

Once the theory of real property is covered, the paralegal must become acquainted with the more technical and practical side. Some of the applied skills to be scrutinized include:

1. Deeds: basic elements and preparation
2. Agreements of sale: draftsmanship and interpretation
3. Mortgage: form and types
4. Real estate financing in the modern market
5. Surveys and boundary description
6. Settlement and closing procedures
7. Preparation of a settlement sheet
8. Landlord/tenant law: leases.

Substantial forms, checklists, and other aids are provided in the exhibits in this chapter and should serve as a reminder that real estate practice must be streamlined and methodical.

II. BASIC CONCEPTS OF REAL PROPERTY

A. Definitions

Understanding real property requires a comparison with *personal property*.

☐ What is *personal property*?
  cars, jewels, stocks, cash, and all other personal goods
☐ What is *real property*?
  land, fixtures, and those things permanently attached or inherently part of the land

In the most basic sense, real property is ownership in land, of varying sorts and degrees, from an incorporeal right in an easement exercised by a public utility to an estate deemed *fee simple*. The common thread in all of real property is its relationship to, or interest in, land, and that is the primary focus of this introductory review.

B. Degrees of Ownership in Land

1. General review of interests in land

For purposes of clarity and illumination, the scale below simply lists most interests in land. A thorough review will follow.

2. Scale of interests

TYPE OF INTERESTS IN LAND

FREEHOLD	NON-FREEHOLD/LEASEHOLD	INCORPOREAL RIGHTS
Fee Simple Absolute	Estate for Years	Easements
Fee Simple Conditional	Estate Year to Year	Profits
Life Estate	Tenancy at Will	Licenses
	Tenancy at Sufferance	

3. Specific interests in land

a. FREEHOLD ESTATES

A "freehold" estate is just what it says it is—the owner holds it *freely,* with no restrictions or limitations. Obviously this is the most favored form of land ownership.

Fee Simple Absolute. This is the least restrictive of all forms of land ownership. Possessors and owners of fee simple estates can do what they please to the property in question, subject to any public or privately adopted regulation. Inherent in the fee simple estate is its perpetuality, since the language of fee simple always accounts for the grantee and his or her *heirs.* That grim day when no more heirs exist is the day when the fee simple estate is extinguished and escheats to the state, a scenario that rarely ever occurs. By the way, this estate designation is the one most commonly applied to all normal residential interests.

Fee Simple Conditional. In this context, the grantor of land has decided that his or her transfer must be conditional upon some type of restriction. In other words, the land is transferred to you as long as, for example:

☐ It is used for religious purposes.
☐ It is turned into a boarding school for delinquent children.
☐ It is not sold to anyone outside the family.

Although the above conditions may seem reasonable to everyone, the wish of the grantor—the transferor of land—is what matters. Failure to follow the conditions elaborated in the deed or exchange results in what is known as a *reversion,* a right of the original grantor to retake, so to speak, the real property.

Surprisingly, these conditional estates are fairly common in some sections of the United States.

Life Estate. This freehold form is really a fee simple absolute with no heirs whatsoever allowed in the grant of property. Compare:

☐ *Fee simple:* I grant, convey, and sell my house at 212 Elm Street and its five acres to Jean Marie and her heirs and assigns forever.
☐ *Life estate:* I grant, convey, and sell my house at 212 Elm Street and its five acres to Jean Marie.

Clearly, this freehold estate has a limited life span, though while in existence its owners have unlimited rights and exclusive usage. That usage is tempered, however, by any interested parties—those designated as successors to the property who observe destructive or abusive use of the property.

So how does a life estate end? Who has to die?

b. NON-FREEHOLD/LEASEHOLD INTERESTS IN LAND

Less control in the owner or possessor of land exists at this level of real property interests. As each interest is reviewed, compare it with the freehold interest. At this level, a marked erosion of land control or rights in the possessor begins to take place.

Estate for Years. This designation is naturally misleading since the estate's duration is thought of in "years" only. Don't be fooled or tricked by the term since an estate for years can be for months or years. In essence, the estate for years is a determinable estate, bestowing on its owner or possessor full rights to a leaseholder, but within a restricted timetable. Common language might be:

I hereby grant and convey my property at St. Charles Street to Stephen for 6 years commencing June 10, 1984.

Estate from Year to Year.   The estate from year to year is also known as a *periodic tenancy.* While this tenancy has a particular origination date, it is not always clear when termination takes place. *Month-to-month* leases often fall under this category. Generally, some form of notice is required to terminate this form of interest, otherwise this tenancy is self-renewing.

Tenancy at Will.   Again, less control, power, or interest in land is in the tenancy at will since the leaseholder is not even entitled to notice of the termination. In most cases, there is not even an agreement as to rent, with a leaseholder simply entering the property under a void lease.

Tenancy at Sufferance.   This limited interest in land is best understood by comparing the tenant to a trespasser, or more precisely, "a cut above a trespasser." The only difference between a tenant by sufferance and a trespasser is that a tenant had a right to be on the premises in the first place, though that right might be extinguished, while the trespasser never had any rights.

Within this category fall tenants whose landlords fail to compel them to leave the premises. As such, the tenant is a holdover with no lease. Under these circumstances the best resolution is an extension on the previous lease.

c. INCORPOREAL RIGHTS IN LAND

From a practicing lawyer's point of view, this material borders, at least at times, on absolute nonsense. Paralegals will be gratified to know that they will share the burden of deciphering this field, the ultimate in "legalese"! Actually, *incorporeal,* nontangible rights in land have tremendous practical consequence, and almost everyone has been touched by this domain of property interests. Let's review this type of rights in the broadest of ways.

Easements.   Remembering the nontangible nature of incorporeal rights makes this easy, since easements are rights to use land in a certain way. Easements are not rights to extract from land—to live on its resources or utilize its bounty in any form or fashion. *Easements are rights to use land for particular purposes.* Common examples are

- ☐ to run electrical wires above the land for public-utility purposes
- ☐ for ingress and egress to a public roadway
- ☐ for sidewalks
- ☐ for parking facilities
- ☐ for highway crosswalks

Just imagine any average American home, and the influence of easements is obvious. These easements are generally cited in the deeds to those properties. Inherently, these interests in land are quite dull, but their importance emerges when owners of adjoining land are in severe disagreement over rights to use land. Why do easements and the law of trespass have much in common?

Licenses.   A license is a temporary right to utilize another person's interest in land for a particular purpose. It is highly limited in scope, easy to revoke, and generally of short duration, and a licensee has a very low level of rights in our scale of property or land interests.

Profits.   A profit is a hybrid between an easement owner and quasi-freeholder since a holder of the profit is not only entitled to enter another's land but is also permitted to take or extract certain goods from the land. Compared to a fee simple estate, the rights to profits is a rather timid form of rights in land but a mode that serves many parties very well. What economic interests would be served by such an arrangement? Minerals? Oil or gas? What other industries might prefer this type of legal relationship?

d. HYBRID FORMS OF INTERESTS IN LAND

Future Estates.   No effort will be made to cover the complexities of future estates in land since they will probably not come up frequently in the paralegal's career. Familiarity with terminology is the intent of this discussion.

Two fundamental forms of future estates are most common and are reviewed here in a cursory fashion.

Reversions/Reverter. Remember the fee simple estate that was conditional? What happens if the conditions of the grant of property are not met. Consider this example:

Eleanor, holding an estate in fee simple, conveys: "To Chuck and all his heirs as long as Chuck and his heirs use the land as a farm."

What happens if Chuck turns the farm into a taco stand? It should *revert.* Therefore, Eleanor has a possible future interest in the land.

How about this problem? Don't forget your life estate material here:

Phil, who owns a fee simple estate, conveys to Bob for *life.*

What does Phil have left? It is called a *reversion,* because when Bob dies, his life estate terminates, and the property reverts back to Phil. Let's use a good, common-sense example here:

Phil has a three-acre plot of land with a nice house on it that he wishes to convey to his brother John, who has been down and out lately. Phil does not wish to let him have it permanently, only for John's remaining years. Then, he wants the house and land to go to his own children.

Would a life estate to John and a reversion to Phil be plausible?

Remainders. Taking reversions one step further can sometimes lead to a future interest called *a remainder.* What about these illustrations?

Mary Anne grants a property to her son, Ryan, and his heirs and assigns, and then to Pat and his heirs.
Mary Anne grants to her brother Thomas the same property, but only for life, then to Pat and his heirs.

In both these examples Pat has the remainder interest, that is, the possible leftover of the estate if all of Ryan's heirs and assigns pass away, or upon the death of Thomas, who had a limited life estate. Do you see why these are called *future* interests?

e. FORMS OF OWNERSHIP IN LAND

Introduction. Our legal system recognizes a variety of approaches in the ownership and possession of land. Certain magic words encapsulate the entire field of ownership:

Single woman or single man   Tenants in common
Joint owners   Tenancy by the entireties

Ownership is either singular or concurrent in design, and all forms mandate legal requirements. What makes these forms different? Are there advantages either way? Which type of interest is more alienable? These and other issues will be tackled next.

Specific Types of Ownership

Singular. All persons have the right, both civilly and constitutionally, to own and possess land. What appears self-evident in 1984 was hardly so in 1960. Congress has legislated extensively to insure this fundamental right. Passage of bills under the Equal Opportunity Lending Act, the Fair Housing Act, and a variety of civil-rights provisions under 42 USCA have lent support to the proposition that all citizens have an inherent right in this country to own and alienate property.

Tenancy in Common. This is the most flexible form of co-ownership. It arises naturally when the conveyance does not clearly indicate the form of ownership and the property is conveyed to two or more persons. A tenant in common has equal rights as all others in the property and can use the property equally, with no greater rights to profits nor any greater responsibility for the debts of the property. In a tenancy in common, there is no right of *survivorship,* which means that the property does not pass to the surviving tenant in common, but instead passes to the decedent's heirs. As a result of this rule on survivorship, the tenancy in common is at times a favored method of ownership for tax-reduction purposes. A tenancy in common would arise in any of the following conveyancing patterns:

I give, grant, sell, and convey my land in Europe
   To Sally and Sudsy Davis, as tenants in common.
   To Bill and Bud Davis, to have equally.

Joint Ownership. Most jurisdictions accept the joint-tenancy form but only if the language of the grant unequivocally and clearly states that this interest in property is *jointly* owned. The classic language is:

I give, grant, devise, and sell my land in Ohio to Jim and Josie Reagan, as joint tenants, with rights of survivorship, and not as tenants in common.

It is a reasonable assumption that co-owners of property who are not related by blood or other familial ties generally will not want their share of that property to pass to their co-owners upon the death of any other co-owner, but instead want it to pass to their own heirs. Courts are rigid in the application and interpretation of a *joint tenancy,* so nonrelated co-owners of real property must make absolutely clear that they are in fact *joint tenants.* As a policy, the language outlined above cogently removes any vestige of doubt concerning the intentions of the parties.

Joint tenants therefore do have this distinctive right of survivorship, which passes the decedent's interest on to the remaining owner(s) equally. Joint owners share equally in all liabilities and, other interests just as in the tenancy in common. Its the survivorship characteristic that so emphatically distinguishes it.

Tenancy by the Entireties.   Language that conveys property in the following manner always creates a *tenancy by the entireties:*

To Helen Stevens and Billy Stevens, Husband and Wife.

Of course, husband and wife can opt to rephrase the language to exclude this possible tag of ownership, and as noted thus far, a lack of clear language in the drafting of the grant will not automatically imply a tenancy by the entireties or joint tenancy. As a general principle, precision in draftsmanship is the only assurance of effecting the proper type of concurrent ownership.

As in the joint tenancy, tenants by the entireties are equal owners of the property, and both parties have survivorship right.

III. AGREEMENTS OR CONTRACTS OF SALE

A. Introduction

When the magnitude of a real estate transaction is considered, it is little wonder that a written contract or agreement is advisable, and in most jurisdictions the Statute of Frauds, which mandates a writing, is vigorously upheld. Real estate practitioners cringe at the thought of unenforceable oral contracts and predictably support a writing's binding effect in the transaction. Since the sale and exchange of real property is highly emotional, the agreement of sale is the best pacifier available for all the parties; it comprehensively outlines the rights and liabilities of all parties to that contract.

B. Elements/Clauses in the Typical Agreement of Sale

Exhibit 9.1 is a standardized agreement of sale, which will be thoroughly reviewed in this section. Many paralegals, particularly those with real estate positions and assignments, are called upon to insure that the requisites of the agreement are met.

1. Parties to the agreement

Be careful to list the appropriate legal names of both buyers and sellers and to state their respective statuses to each other or to other signatories. Examples might be *guardian, trustee, agent,* and *corporate official,* all parties who are empowered to give legal effect to the agreement but may not assert legal ownership. Signatures are required under all circumstances.

2. Date

The importance of the date to this agreement cannot be overlooked, particularly in jurisdictions where the buyer of the property assumes equitable ownership of the property as of the date of the agreement. In the eventuality of damages, fire, or governmental intrusion by eminent domain, the "equitable" owner of the property, that is, the buyer, may be able to assert rights and remedies in the real estate.

3. Legal description

Ideally, the agreement of sale should contain an exacting description of the real property, to preclude potential disputes. Realistically, most contracts contain street number and a reference to a deed, and that will suffice. In the

Exhibit 9.1

AGREEMENT FOR THE SALE OF REAL ESTATE

This form recommended and approved for, but not restricted to, use by members of the Pennsylvania Association of REALTORS®

COPYRIGHT PENNSYLVANIA ASSOCIATION OF REALTORS® 1973

—— AGENT FOR THE SELLER ——

S 1969 B
(Rev. 1-81)

This Agreement, made this........................day of ...........................A.D. 19...........

1. **PRINCIPALS** *(1-78)* Between ....
.... (residing at
.... Zip.....................) hereinafter called Seller, and
....
.... (residing at
....Zip.....................) hereinafter called Buyer.

2. **PROPERTY** *(1-78)* Witnesseth: Seller hereby agrees to sell and convey to Buyer, who hereby agrees to purchase:
ALL THAT CERTAIN lot or piece of ground with buildings and improvements thereon erected, if any, known as: ..
....
.... in the .... of ....
County of .... State of ...., Zip ....

3. **TERMS** *(1-78)* (a) Purchase Price ....
.... Dollars

   which shall be paid to the Seller by the Buyer as follows:

   (b) Cash or check at signing this agreement: $ ....

   (c) Cash or check to be paid on or before:...................... 19 .... $ ....

   (d) .... $ ....

   (e) Cash or certified check at time of settlement: $ ....

                                                      TOTAL $ ....

   (f) Written approval of Seller to be on or before: ....19..................

   (g) Settlement to be made on or before: ....19..................

   (h) Conveyance from Seller will be by fee simple deed of special warranty.

   (i) Payment of Transfer taxes will be divided equally between Buyer and Seller.

   (j) The following shall be apportioned pro-rata as of and at time of settlement: Taxes as levied and assessed, rents, interest on mortgage assumptions if any, water and or sewer rents if any, together with any other lienable municipal services..

4. **MORTGAGE CONTINGENCY** *(1-79)* This sale and settlement hereunder are NOT conditional or contingent in any manner upon the sale or settlement of any other real estate NOR subject to any mortgaging or financing except as hereinafter provided.

5. **SPECIAL CLAUSES**

6. **ASSESSMENTS** *(3-70)* Seller covenants and represents as of the approval date of this agreement of sale, that no assessments for public improvements have been made against the premises which remain unpaid and that no notice by any governmental or other public authority has been served upon the Seller or anyone on the Seller's behalf, including notices relating to violations of housing, building, safety or fire ordinances which remain uncorrected unless otherwise specified herein. Buyer will be responsible for any notices served upon the Seller after the approval date of this agreement and for the payment of any assessments and charges hereafter made for any public improvements, if work in connection therewith is hereafter begun in or about said premises and adjacent thereto. Seller will be responsible for any such improvements, assessments or notices received prior to the date of this agreement, unless the improvements consist of sewer or water lines not in use on or prior to the date of approval hereof.

7. **TITLE & COSTS** *(1-78)*
   (a) The premises are to be conveyed free and clear of all liens, encumbrances, and easements, EXCEPTING HOWEVER, the following: Mortgage encumbrances, as aforementioned, if any; existing building restrictions, ordinances, easements of roads, privileges or rights of public service companies, if any; agreements or like matters of record or easements or restrictions visible upon the ground, otherwise the title to the above described real estate shall be good and marketable or such as will be insured by a reputable Title Insurance Company at the regular rates.
   (b) The Buyer will pay for the following:
   (1) The premium for mechanics lien insurance and/or title search, or fee for cancellation of same, if any.
   (2) The premiums for flood insurance and/or fire insurance with extended coverage, insurance binder charges or cancellation fee, if any.
   (3) Appraisal fees and charges paid in advance to mortgagee if any.
   (4) Buyer's normal settlement costs and accruals.
   (c) Any survey or surveys which may be required by the Title Insurance Company or the abstracting attorney, for the preparation of an adequate legal description of the premises (or the correction thereof), shall be secured and paid for by the Seller. However, any survey or surveys desired by the Buyer or required by his mortgagee shall be secured and paid for by the Buyer.
   (d) In the event the Seller is unable to give a good and marketable title or such as will be insured by a reputable Title Company, subject to aforesaid, Buyer shall have the option of taking such title as the Seller can give without abatement of price or of being repaid all monies paid by Buyer to the Seller on account of the purchase price and the Seller will reimburse the Buyer for any costs incurred by the Buyer for those items specified in paragraph 7(b) items (1), (2), (3), and in paragraph 7(c); and in the latter event there shall be no further liability or obligation on either of the parties hereto and this agreement shall become NULL AND VOID and all copies will be returned to Seller's agent for cancellation.

8. **FIXTURES, TREES, SHRUBBERY, ETC.** (1-81) All existing plumbing, heating and lighting fixtures (including chandeliers) and systems appurtenant thereto and forming a part thereof, and other permanent fixtures, as well as all ranges, laundry tubs, T.V. antennas, masts and rotor systems, together with wall to wall carpeting, screens, storm sash and/or doors, shades, awnings, venetian blinds, couplings for automatic washers and dryers, etc., radiator covers, cornices, kitchen cabinets, drapery rods, drapery rod hardware, curtain rods, curtain rod hardware, all trees, shrubbery, plantings now in or on property, if any, unless specifically excepted in this agreement, are included in the sale and purchase price. None of the above mentioned items shall be removed by the Seller from premises after date of this agreement. Any remaining heating and/or cooking fuels stored on the premises at time of settlement are also included under this agreement. Seller hereby warrants that he will deliver good title to all of the articles described in this paragraph, and any other fixtures or items of personalty specifically scheduled and to be included in this sale.

9. **PAYMENT OF DEPOSIT** (1-81) Deposits or hand monies shall be paid to agent for Seller, who shall retain the same until consummation or termination of this agreement in conformity with all applicable laws and regulations. Agent for the Seller may, at his sole option, hold any uncashed check tendered as deposit or hand monies, pending the acceptance of this offer.

10. **POSSESSION AND TENDER** *(1-77)*
    (a) Possession is to be delivered by deed, keys and physical possession to a vacant building (if any) at day and time of settlement, or by deed and assignment of existing lease(s) at time of settlement if premises is tenant occupied at the signing of this agreement, unless otherwise specified herein. Buyer will acknowledge existing lease(s) by initialing said lease(s) at time of signing this agreement of sale if tenant occupied.
    (b) Seller will not enter into any new leases, written extension of existing leases, if any, or additional leases for the premises without expressed written consent of the Buyer.
    (c) Formal tender of an executed deed and purchase money is hereby waived.
    (d) Buyer reserves the right to make a pre-settlement inspection of the subject premises.

11. **RISK OF LOSS** *(5-73)* Any loss or damage to the property caused by fire, or loss commonly covered by the extended coverage endorsements of reputable insurance companies between the date of this Agreement and the time of settlement, shall not, in any way, void or impair any of the conditions or obligations hereof unless the required mortgaging or financing, as specified herein, cannot be obtained because of such loss or damage. Seller shall maintain existing fire and extended coverage or homeowners' type insurance policies, if any, until the time of final settlement. Buyer is hereby notified that it is his responsibility to insure his interest in the said premises at his own cost and expense. Seller shall maintain the property (including all items mentioned in paragraph #8 herein) and any personal property specifically scheduled herein in its present condition, normal wear and tear excepted.

12. **REPRESENTATIONS** *(2-69)* It is understood that Buyer has inspected the property, or hereby waives the right to do so and he has agreed to purchase it as a result of such inspection and not because of or in reliance upon any representation made by the Seller or any other officer, partner or employee of Seller, or by the agent of the Seller or any of the latter's salesmen and employees, or by a cooperating Broker, if any, or any of his salesmen and employees and that he has agreed to purchase it in its present condition unless otherwise specified herein. It is further understood that this agreement contains the whole agreement between the Seller and the Buyer and there are no other terms, obligations, covenants, representations, statements or conditions, oral or otherwise of any kind whatsoever concerning this sale. Furthermore, this agreement shall not be altered, amended, changed or modified except in writing executed by the parties hereto.

13. **RECORDING** This agreement shall not be recorded in the Office for the Recording of Deeds or in any other office or place of public record and if Buyer shall record this agreement or cause or permit the same to be recorded, Seller may, at his option, elect to treat such act as a breach of this agreement.

14. **ASSIGNMENT** This agreement shall be binding upon the respective heirs, executors, administrators, successors and, to the extent assignable, on the assigns of the parties hereto, it being expressly understood, however, that the Buyer shall not transfer or assign this agreement without the written consent of the Seller being first had and obtained.

15. **AGENT** It is expressly understood and agreed between the parties hereto that the herein named agent, his salesmen and employees or any officer or partner of agent and any cooperating broker and his salesmen and employees and any officer or partner of the cooperating broker are acting as agent only and will in no case whatsoever be held liable either jointly or severally to either party for the performance of any term or covenant of this agreement or for damages for the nonperformance thereof.

16. **DEFAULT** *(1-79)* The said time for settlement and all other times referred to for the performance of any of the obligations of this agreement are hereby agreed to be of the essence of this agreement. Should the Buyer:
    (a) Fail to make any additional payments as specified in paragraph #3,
    (b) Furnish false or incomplete information to the Seller, the Seller's agent, or the mortgage lender, concerning the Buyer's legal or financial status, or fail to cooperate in the processing of the mortgage loan application, which acts would result in the failure to obtain the approval of a mortgage loan commitment, or
    (c) Violate or fail to fulfill and perform any of the terms or conditions of this agreement,

    then in such case, all deposit money and other sums paid by the Buyer on account of the purchase price, whether required by this agreement or not, may be (1) Retained by the Seller on account of the purchase, or
    (2) As moneys to be applied to the Seller's damages, or
    (3) As liquidated damages for such breach,

    as the Seller may elect, and in the event that the Seller elects to retain the moneys as liquidated damages in accordance with paragraph #16 (3), the Seller shall be released from all liability or obligations and this agreement shall be NULL AND VOID and all copies will be returned to the Seller's agent for cancellattion.

APPROVAL BY BUYER

IN WITNESS WHEREOF, the parties hereto, intending to be legally bound hereby, have hereunder set their hands and seals the day and year first above written.

	BUYER .... (SEAL)
WITNESS AS TO BUYER	BUYER .... (SEAL)
WITNESS AS TO BUYER	BUYER .... (SEAL)

APPROVAL BY SELLER

Seller hereby approves the above contract this .... day of .... A.D. 19........... and in consideration of the services rendered in procuring the Buyer, Seller agrees to pay to the named Agent a commission of .... of the herein specified sale price. In the event Buyer defaults hereunder, any monies paid on account shall be equally divided between Seller and Agent, but in no event will the sum paid to the agent be in excess of the above specified commission.

WITNESS AS TO SELLER	SELLER .... (SEAL)
WITNESS AS TO SELLER	SELLER .... (SEAL)
AGENT BY:	SELLER .... (SEAL)

TO: ....(Agent) Date..19...............

In conjunction with the purchase of the premises described in the agreement of sale attached hereto, I/We hereby authorize your firm to perform the services as indicated below by my/our initials.

A. Order Title insurance in any reputable title insurance company.. ____________ **(INITIALS)**

B. Order insurance in the amount of $.................... ☐ **Homeowners** ☐ **Fire & Extended Coverage** ☐ **Flood** ____________ **(INITIALS)**

C. .... ____________ **(INITIALS)**

interests of perfectionism and professionalism, an agreement should include a more comprehensive description, which cites a legal description from a deed, plat or plan numbers in a subdivision, acreage, or other points of reference.

4. Fixtures

While general principles of real property law adequately cover fixture disputes, caution dictates in the preparation of an agreement of sale that all items in a home that are not easily movable be accounted for. Make sure that washers, dryers, ceiling fans, fireplaces, woodstoves, and energy systems are accounted for in the language. What other household items could be subject to a dispute?

5. Purchase price and terms of payment

Since most contracts do not rest on simple good will, the law requires clear consideration. The agreement should list:

a. Gross selling price
b. Initial down payment or earnest-money deposit
c. Secondary down payment (usually 30–60 days later)
d. Balance due on settlement date
e. Method of payment (e.g., cash, certified check)

Many states have adopted legislation requiring real estate companies to pay interest when they put deposit monies into *escrow* accounts until the date of settlement.

6. Condition of title

Crucial to the buyer is an assurance by the seller that he or she possesses good and marketable title. *Title* really means "ownership," and while a seller may have an impressive legal description of property and may satisfy you that the street number, tax folio number, and subdivision designation are correct, those legal niceties are no reflection on his or her "quality" of title or right to possession. The right to own and possess property is directly affected by liens, encumbrances, mortgages, easements, zoning, riparian rights, title objections, leases, and other restrictions. Accordingly, the agreement of sale needs a clause clarifying these issues and giving assurances to the buyer that title is *good* and *marketable* or subject to a variety of restrictions. Rightfully, buyers desire the good-and-marketable title, which assures them of:

a. Rightful, legal ownership of the property
b. Freedom from liens and other encumbrances
c. Rightful possession
d. Insurability of title

The last aspect of *insurability* plays a keen role in the acquisition of financing for the purchase as well as insuring the buyer from any future claims or disputes on the property. More on title insurance later.

7. Settlement date

Selection of a settlement date is not as easy as throwing a dart at a calendar. Consider the financial needs of both buyers and sellers. Frequently, buyers desire a few months to meet down payments or mortgage amounts. On the other hand, sellers are often extremely desirous of quick and immediate settlement, since the possibility of contractual default or dispute is lessened. Settlement dates also must reflect the wishes of the parties as to moving schedules, former leases, potential loss of security deposits, and interest-rate volatility (a change of one or more points in the interest rate can be most upsetting).

Lastly, selection of a settlement date should be guided by the prepaid interest required at settlement. Buyers are just not intrigued by second day of the month dates, since they are obliged to pay twenty-nine days of interest of settlement. Cash-short buyers prefer a later date.

Custom also controls who gives notice of the settlement—attorneys, agents, or brokers.

8. Possession

For the sake of all concerned, possession—that is, the actual physical possession of the premises—should commence at the time of settlement date. Parties who wish possession before settlement should have a written lease. If a seller wishes to retain possession after settlement, a written lease should be drafted and an escrow fund established at settlement for coverage of damages.

9. Apportionment of taxes/rents/interest

In a perfect world, all settlements would be on the first day of the month, when rents were due, and at the end of all local and state tax years. Since this is hardly a perfect world, care must be given to the apportionment, the sharing of these fixed expenses, as of the date of settlement. Both buyer and seller must equitably divide the tax obligations, rents received, and interest accrued, and the amounts are determined by the times of ownership. As an example, if settlement is on March 30, 1984, and the tax year ends on June 30, 1984, the seller, who has already paid his real property taxes is entitled to a proportionate refund from March 30 to June 30, 1984. Buyer must pay it because buyer now owns the house from that date forth.

10. Transfer tax

Most jurisdictions impose a tax on the transfer of real property. Local custom dictates the responsibility for the payment of those taxes, with the majority of American jurisdictions requiring both seller and buyer to split the obligation.

11. Default clauses/appropriate remedies

Buyers and sellers are more than likely to let a default on contract simply pass. The costs of enforcement are generally prohibitive, and the earnest-money deposit usually covers the damages. However, the agreement of sale recognizes every eventuality and should provide adequate remedies for both parties if the default cannot be borne or tolerated.

As a rule, both buyer and seller may file *suits for damages,* or an *action for specific performance.*

12. Contingencies to the agreement

At this point, the agreement of sale is rather long winded, but do not deter from in-depth analysis concerning potential contingencies. Contingencies are conditional issues to the agreement, which must be resolved before the contract can ever be formal. Until the contingencies are clarified and legally removed, that closing, or settlement, will not take place. The astute paralegal must account for numerous contingencies:

a. Subdivision approval
b. Zoning clarification/usages
c. Septic capacity/sewage rights
d. Building permits
e. Certificates of occupancy
f. Percolation
g. Public utilities
h. Environmental factors
i. Mortgage financing

Mortgage financing is a frequently forgotten contingency by real estate professionals, for they assume their clients have been properly prequalified and should have little difficulty securing financing. Don't ever assume that fact.

13. Warranty clauses

No seller of real property wants to stick his or her neck out and guarantee anything associated with the property. No buyer wants property with no guarantees. Remember good-and-marketable title? That is a form of warranty, though warranties are more relevant to other factors such as:

□ Condition of major systems in a residence like a roof, electrical design, plumbing and structural foundation
□ Termite damage
□ Service contracts
□ Investment income

All the above warranties are regularly included in the agreement. New-home construction now may include structural protection under the implied warranty of habitibility theory or through commercial warranties like *HOW*, Home Ownership Warranty, Inc.

14. Miscellaneous provisions

Standard agreements of sale may also include clauses dealing with:

□ Purchaser's right to final inspection (This usually occurs a day before settlement.)
□ Requirement of recordation
□ Rule on assignment
□ Captions or headings
□ Integration clause
□ Termite-inspection rights

15. Signatures

As noted, the agreement of sale has no legal effect unless signed by the legally responsible parties and attested by witnesses.

IV. DEEDS/INDENTURES

A. Introductory Thoughts

Thus far, a variety of terms relating to land have been used, from *title* to *possession*. We have also covered various contingencies and conditions that affect the legality of the agreement of sale. But what document really evidences that ownership? Is there some formal, recorded legal document that speaks to the true and just owner of the property? Fortunately, *deeds* serve these functions. Deeds are not title but merely evidence that a property's title rests in the individual who really owns the property. In a civilized society a deed verifies ownership and attempts to formalize a chain of ownership from the original date of grant. Owing to the deed's convenience and simplicity, all American jurisdictions have adopted its use and rely on its content to resolve conflicts in claim of ownership. Review the deed in exhibit 9.2 as its provisions are analyzed below.

B. Elements of a Deed

1. Date

The date of the deed's execution is not evidence of a passage of title, since delivery of the deed is required. If no other evidence is espoused by a party seeking to prove passage of title, a presumption exists that delivery occurred as of the deed's date of execution.

2. Parties

a. GRANTOR

The present person who holds title and who desires to transfer it is known as the grantor. Be aware that full names and appropriate status should follow in the spaces provided.

b. GRANTEE

The person to whom the title is transferred to is referred to as the grantee.

Exhibit 9.2

This Deed, Made this

day of   *in the year of*
our LORD one thousand nine hundred and
        BETWEEN,

Witnesseth,

That the said part   of the first part, for and in consideration of the sum of

lawful money of the United States of America,

the receipt whereof is hereby acknowledged, hereby grant   and convey   unto the said

part   of the second part,

ALL

In Witness Whereof, the said part   of the first part ha   hereunto set
hand   and seal   , the day and year aforesaid.

Sealed and Delivered in the Presence of

.... | .... (SEAL)

.... | .... (SEAL)

State of Delaware,

County, } **ss.**

Be It Remembered, that on this

                    day of   in the year of our LORD, one thousand
nine hundred and   personally came before me,

part   to this Indenture known to me personally to be such, and
acknowledged this Indenture to be   Deed.

GIVEN under my Hand and Seal of office, the day and year aforesaid.

....
Notary Public

DEED

Received for Record

A. D. 19

Recorder.

Fee for Recording, &c., $

State of Delaware,

County, } ss.

Recorded in the office for the Recording of Deeds, &c., at .... in and for the said County of .... in Deed Record ....Vol. .... Page .... &c., the .... day of .... A. D., 19......... WITNESS my Hand and the Seal of said office.

....
Recorder.

3. Consideration

Fundamental contract law requires sufficient consideration before a transaction of this sort has a binding effect. In most jurisdictions, the value of the transfer tax is computed on the basis of the consideration listed. As a result, exchanges between relatives, friends, or other parties that are not for economic gain can be treated as tax-free gifts or exchanges. In cases such as these, the consideration is usually $10 and requires the filing of a state or county affidavit attesting to the purposes of the exchange and the market value of the property.

4. Granting or conveyancing clause

Standardized deeds like the one in exhibit 9.2 contain language such as:

> Grantors do grant, bargain, sell and convey unto the said Grantees, their heirs and assigns, the following described premises.

Local custom must be adhered to when drafting these granting clauses, but every jurisdiction attempts to make unequivocally clear that title will pass from one person to another after execution and delivery of this deed.

The import of the granting or conveyancing clause can also be appreciated by an elementary review of court interpretations of this language. Ponder these queries:

☐ Does the clause warrant anything, at least in an implied way?
☐ To whom does this estate pass upon the death of the named grantee? To heirs and assigns? Yes, all heirs, since this is a fee simple transaction, not a life estate.
☐ Can the words of grant be changed or modified? Yes, especially if a different deed is utilized, like a quit-claim deed.

5. Legal description

Since a deed is the final recorded document of the final real estate transaction, great pains should be taken to draft a completely accurate property description. The legal description should adequately define the boundaries of real property whether by subplot, rectangular survey, or metes and bounds.

6. Recital, or "being," clause

Not all jurisdictions call for a recital clause, but in a practical sense, conveyances and paralegals alike appreciate its utility. The "being" clause helps trace that chain of title by providing a legal explanation of how the present grantor secured his or her present interest in the property about to be conveyed. An example might be:

> Being the same premises which Robert and Sally Lolly, husband and wife, by Indenture dates January 8, 1982, and recorded in the Recorder of Deeds of Delaware County, New York, in Deed Book 26 No. 19000, page 18, granted and conveyed into the said Mary Burns and Stephen her husband, in fee.

7. Encumbrances or restrictions

Increasing numbers of jurisdictions are requiring a recitation of any existing encumbrances, covenants, easements, or other restrictions. Recordation of the deed, with this recitation, puts prospective owners on notice of them.

8. Habendum clause

Popularly known as the "to have and to hold" clause, the habendum clause is more a relic from the Middle Ages than a significant legal clause. The words, as included in the sample deed usually are:

> To have and to hold the said lot or piece of ground above described with the buildings and improvements thereon erected, hereditaments and premises granted unto the said grantee, his heirs and assigns forever.

If you think this is a mere repetition from the front page of the deed, you are perfectly correct. At best, the habendum clause is a reaffirmation of the parties' intentions and also tactically limits the use of the estate.

9. Covenant, or warranty, clauses

A full warranty, or general warranty deed includes explicitly a variety of *covenants* or promises by the grantor about the state and condition of the property. That information will be covered infra at Section C below. While some covenants are implied in the transfer, grantees should insist on their inclusion in the deed.

10. Execution clause

No precise formula is required to formally devise the execution section, but the drafter is advised to cite the proper party for a corporate or fiduciary transfer.

11. Signatures

See exhibit 9.2 for an acceptable method.

12. Acknowledgment or notarization

Every jurisdiction requires notorial seals on the deed, or other witness acknowledgment.

C. Types of Deeds

1. General warranty

In this favored form of deed, the grantor promises that he or she will *warrant, defend, and guarantee* the grantee complete and total right to utilize the transferred property free from all encumbrances, liens, and other matters. Are grantees favored here? Wouldn't the buyer of a $300,000 house prefer this form of deed?

Specifically, the general warranty deeds provide all standard covenants.

a. COVENANTS IN GENERAL WARRANTY DEED

1. Covenant of Seisin. In this covenant, the grantor assures the grantee that he or she has possession of the premises.

2. Covenant of Good Right to Convey. Grantor further warrants that he has rightful, lawful possession to the property and can convey.

3. Covenant Against Encumbrances. Another easily accepted provision by the grantee, since it assures the grantee that no outstanding tax or mechanic's liens, assessments, leases, mortgages, or other restrictions exist.

4. Covenant of Quiet Enjoyment. This clause protects the grantee from any attempts at eviction or other forced removal from the conveyed property.

5. Covenant of Warranty. Here the grantor asserts that he or she will defend any and all lawful claims and demands of all persons on the right to enjoy the land.

6. Covenant of Further Assurances. Grantor further promises to execute or cause to be executed or done all such further acts, deeds or things for the better, more perfectly and absolutely conveying and assuring the premises conveyed to the grantee as the grantee may reasonably request.

Since these covenants are so encompassing and so protective of grantees, the preference for their use is overwhelming in residential real estate.

2. Limited warranty (special)

When compared to the general warranty form, one major distinction emerges. In the general warranty format, the grantor assures, covenants, and guarantees the quality of his title and possession for not only himself, but also all those who previously owned the property. In the limited warranty deed, the grantor simply warrants that during his ownership no encumbrances or other violations of standard covenants occurred. Distinguishing the two deeds is a subtle task, requiring close inspection of the language of the deed. To make certain the grantor's liability ends with the grantor only, certain words of limitation must be added. Check local rules for specific language schemes.

3. Quit-claim deed

The antithesis of the general warranty deed is the quit-claim, where the grantor sells his or her empire, "as is." No warranties, assurances, or promises are made in this type of transfer. Why so? What types of situations lend themselves to the drafting of a quit-claim?

Some possible explanations may be in the domestic relations sector of law. Parties to a divorce have no concern about giving each other assurances on the property, and realistically they really shouldn't. Simply put, a divorcing couple wants to transfer quickly that property, whether it is worth a lot, a little, or absolutely nothing. Other examples might include quick transfer to block creditor execution or foreclosure, tax strategies, and gifts. As a general principle, the intrafamily exchange of real property is a very appropriate place for the quit-claim deed, since the parties are reasonably certain that assurances, covenants, and guarantees are thoroughly unnecessary legal exercises.

4. Fiduciary's deed

Before this type of deed can be understood, the designation *fiduciary* must be mastered. A fiduciary is really a party serving the needs of another and includes: *guardians, trustees, administrators, receivers,* and *executors.* In all these capacities, a person is performing a task, possessing certain property or otherwise engaging in duties for the benefit of another.

If a testator hoped to leave a premises to a specific person after the first owner died, a will could be drafted that named an executor who was ordered to transfer that property. In order for the executor to transfer the property, a deed, fiduciary in nature, would be drawn up for the executor's required signature when the circumstances warranted.

5. Sheriff's deed

In an age of rampant mortgage foreclosures resulting in sheriff's sales at public auctions, prospective buyers should beware of what they are getting. While the sheriff provides a deed on purchase, no warranties or covenants are made. The buyer gets the entire estate just as it presently is.

V. SURVEYS AND BOUNDARY DESCRIPTIONS

A. Definitions

Of certain importance to both sellers and buyers of real property is an accurate, dependable, and legally sufficient property description, which can be relied on in the transfer of real property. A *survey* is a graphic description of real property that attempts to show boundary lines, location of buildings, easements, and encroachments to the property. While the graphic design can never be relied on as an infallible tool, if the survey is performed by a competent surveying engineer, one can be assured of a solid, reliable description. (See Figure 9.1.)

B. The Paralegal's Role in Survey Analysis

Paralegals, of course, are not capable of performing surveys, but they are expected to order the survey for the potential real estate transaction and to develop a dependable network of skilled surveyors. Do not be averse to shopping around for surveyors for comparative pricing. Enormous differences in cost are not uncommon in some regions.

The paralegal can also expect to be asked to compare the results of the survey with the written legal description of the property as noted on the deed, tax folios, or other documents. The task of comparing written descriptions with graphic depictions is sometimes formidable, especially when property has been subdivided and subject to multiple easements. Review the following example. Do they fit? What makes you think so?

Written Description

> All that certain lot, piece or parcel of land, with the buildings thereon erected, situate in Graylyn Crest, Brandywine Hundred, New Castle County and State of Delaware, now known as 1113 Piper Road, and being Lot No. 100, Block H, as shown on the Plan of GRAYLYN CREST, as prepared by Howard L. Robertson, Civil Engineer and Surveyor, and now remaining of record in the Office for the Recording of Deeds, at Wilmington, in

FIGURE 9.1

Rectangular Survey

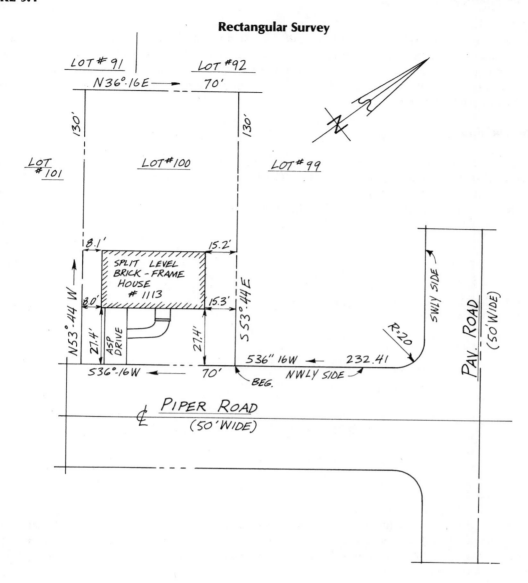

and for New Castle County and State of Delaware, in Plat Book Volume 3, Page 49, and being more particularly bounded and described as follows, to wit:

Beginning at a point on the northwesterly side of Piper Road, at fifty feet wide, as marked out on said Plan, said point being located South thirty-six degrees, sixteen minutes West two hundred thirty-two feet and forty-one hundredths of a foot from a point in the southwesterly end of a twenty-foot radius intersection curve joining the said side of Piper Road with the southwesterly side of Pan Road, at fifty feet wide, as marked out on said Plan, said point of Beginning being also in the division line between Lots Nos. 99 and 100; thence by said side of Piper Road South thirty-six degrees, sixteen minutes West seventy feet to a point in the division line between Lots Nos. 100 and 101; and thence by the same North fifty-three degrees, forty-four minutes West one hundred thirty feet to a point in the division line between Lots Nos. 91 and 100; and thence by the same and also along the division line between Lots Nos. 92 and 100 North thirty-six degrees, sixteen minutes East seventy feet to a point in the division line between Lots Nos. 100 and 99; and thence by the same South fifty-three degrees, forty-four minutes East one hundred thirty feet to a point in the aforesaid northwesterly side of Piper Road, the first mentioned point and place of BEGINNING. Be the contents thereof what they may.

Being the same lands and premises which Graylyn Construction Co., a corporation of the State of Delaware, by its indenture dated the Thirteenth Day of June, 1955, and recorded in the Office for the Recording of Deeds, &c., in and for New Castle County, at Wilmington.

C. General Mechanical Steps in Surveys

Unfortunately, no uniform system of describing or depicting land exists. Many of the accepted survey steps are so antiquated that one can only assume tradition dies hard in this field. (See exhibit 9.3.) No matter what, a survey requires a *point of reference,* a point of origination, usually some permanently affixed stone, monument, or street path. At this point of reference, a survey can naturally be reproduced over time, and thereby regularly verified. All survey processes fall into one of the following categories:

1. Metes and bounds

Assuming a solid point of reference, the surveyor will select a starting point at the property boundary and then draw several lines from various points to that property line. The direction of the line selected by the surveyor is known as the *bound,* and its overall length, that is, from point of reference to boundary line is called a *mete.* Imagine a compass that seeks to define property directions and angles. Review the graphic in Figure 9.2.

FIGURE 9.2

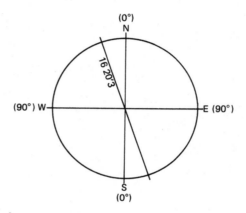

2. Rectangular surveys

While metes and bounds is not difficult in urban areas, where there are settled property lines and numerous points of reference, it does not lend itself well to undeveloped areas. As a result, the rectangular-survey system came into favor and still is utilized in a majority of American jurisdictions. The complexities of this boundary system are not a major issue in the career of a paralegal, but a review of Figure 9.3 gives a sense of the method:

D. Verification of the Legal Description

No assignment is more essential than the verification of the legal description with the survey. Ultimate responsibility rests with the attorney and with those who provide assistance, to insure that the real estate transaction is not subject to any dispute, inaccuracy, or potential lawsuit on the legal description of the property. Check that description by verifying the *proper street name and its number.* Look also for *monuments* in the survey that are cited in the survey. Compare all *reference numbers, lot designations, subdivisions, or parcel numbers,* or any other category of information that accurately verifies the validity of the survey with the property's written or legal description.

Exhibit 9.3

BERKS TITLE INSURANCE COMPANY
READING, PENNSYLVANIA

No. ....

Instructions for Land Title Surveys

All surveys must be based on sufficient title abstracts and searches to prove ownership of premises and to determine effect of adverse conveyances, agreements and miscellaneous recorded instruments.

Field surveys, whether city, town or farm properties, must be made by an accurate, transit, balanced traverse of the property. Compass surveys are not acceptable. References to true meridian are preferred, but bearings may refer to magnetic meridian.

The map drawn from the survey must show all details graphically which bear witness to boundary lines and corners. Buildings and improvements must be located and shown on the plan. Boundary line distances and intersecting angles, as well as bearings, must be shown. Encroachments of all kinds and descriptions or evidences of adverse users must be located, shown and reported. The surveyor reports and certifies as to the following:

1. Rights of way, old highways, or abandoned roads, lanes or driveways, drains, sewer, water, gas or oil pipe lines across said premises:

   _____

2. Springs, streams, rivers, ponds, or lakes located, bordering on or running through said premises:

   _____

3. Cemeteries or family burying grounds located on said premises:

   _____

4. Telephone, telegraph or electric power poles, wires or lines overhanging or crossing said premises and serving other properties:

   _____

5. Joint driveways or walkways; party walls or rights of support; porches, steps or roofs used in common or joint garages:

   _____

6. Encroachments, or overhanging projections. (If the buildings, projections or cornices thereof, or signs affixed thereto, fences or other indications of occupancy encroach upon or overhang adjoining properties, or the like encroach upon or overhang surveyed premises, specify all such):

   _____

7. Fences, walls, shrubbery or other evidences of physical boundary lines:

   _____

8. Evidences of recent building construction, repairs or alterations:

   _____

9. Changes in grade or street alignment completed or proposed:

   _____

10. Are there indications of recent street or sidewalk construction or repairs?:

    _____

11. If the surveyed premises are subject to restrictive covenants, do the improvements, use and occupancy comply with such? (If the premises are subject to restrictive covenants, have the examining attorney or Title Company furnish you verbatim copy of them):

_____

12. Remarks: _____

_____

_____

I, _____, hereby certify that I have made

a survey of premises situated at _____,

City/Township of _____, County of _____,

State of _____, title to which appears of record in the name of

_____

_____, and that I have prepared a plan from the survey

dated _____, and entitled _____

_____

and at the time the survey was made I found the premises in possession of _____

_____

_____

_____

I further certify to the accuracy of my report under the foregoing items, one to twelve inclusive.

Date: _____   _____
                                                                    Engineer, Surveyor

FIGURE 9.3

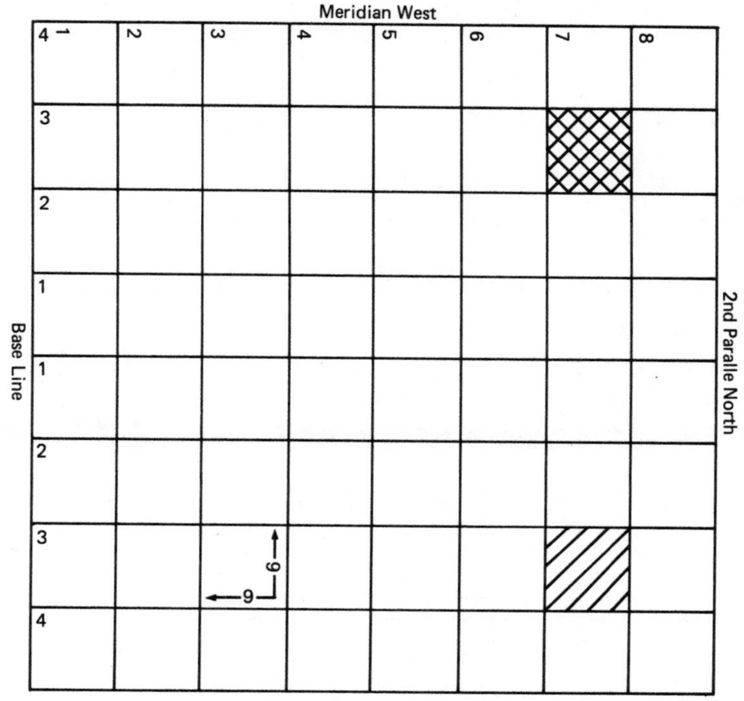

Meridian West

Base Line

2nd Paralle North

VI.   MORTGAGES AND FINANCING

A.   Introduction

In today's volatile interest markets, the task of securing a favorable mortgage in the purchase of any real property has become a formidable one. Less than fifteen years ago, mortgages could still be obtained in the 5–6 percent range, and that low rate translates into much, much lower home-ownership costs, thereby insuring a pool of qualified buyers and a strong housing industry. Modern market conditions can no longer justify, much to everyone's dismay, these low rates of interest on home or commercial mortgages. The reality of money affected by inflation, unchecked federal deficits, and poor governmental control on the credit markets as well as the demand for money, both real and speculative, have all contributed to the changing reality of mortgage financing. In better times, money stayed the same, so to speak, for longer periods of time, and financial institutions felt secure in granting twenty-to-thirty-year mortgages at fixed rates. At best, previous financing practices could be described as very staid and almost boring. At present, a variety of alternative financing techniques have emerged. The paralegal's duty is to master the differing strategies of mortgage financing so that buyers, potential clients, can be qualified rather than rejected. (See exhibits 9.4–9.7.)

B.   Definition of a Mortgage

A *mortgage* as a "debt" instrument can be generally defined as "any form of instrument whereby a lien is created upon real estate or whereby title to real estate is reserved or converged as security for the payment of a debt or fulfillment of their obligations." A *mortgagor* is the person(s) who seeks the funds and promises to repay under agreed conditions. A *mortgagee* is the party who lends or provides the source of funds for purchase. In common terms, the *mortgage* is the tangible written evidence of the money exchange between the parties, which outlines their obligations, duties, and rights.

Exhibit 9.4

RESIDENTIAL LOAN APPLICATION

MORTGAGE APPLIED FOR	☐ Conventional ☐ FHA ☐ VA ☐	Amount $	Interest Rate %	No. of Months	Monthly Payment Principal & Interest $	Escrow/Impounds (to be collected monthly) ☐ Taxes ☐ Hazard Ins. ☐ Mtg. Ins. ☐

Prepayment Option

SUBJECT PROPERTY

Property Street Address	City	County	State	Zip	No. Units

Legal Description (Attach description if necessary)		Year Built

Purpose of Loan: ☐ Purchase ☐ Construction-Permanent ☐ Construction ☐ Refinance ☐ Other (Explain)

Complete this line if Construction-Permanent or Construction Loan	Lot Value Data Year Acquired _____ $_____	Original Cost $_____	Present Value (a)	Cost of Imps. (b) $_____	Total (a + b) $_____	ENTER TOTAL AS PURCHASE PRICE IN DETAILS OF PURCHASE.

Complete this line if a Refinance Loan		Purpose of Refinance	Describe Improvements [ ] made [ ] to be made
Year Acquired	Original Cost $	Amt. Existing Liens $	Cost: $

Title Will Be Held In What Name(s)	Manner In Which Title Will Be Held

Source of Down Payment and Settlement Charges

This application is designed to be completed by the borrower(s) with the lender's assistance. The Co-Borrower Section and all other Co-Borrower questions must be completed and the appropriate box(es) checked if ☐ another person will be jointly obligated with the Borrower on the loan, or ☐ the Borrower is relying on income from alimony, child support or separate maintenance or on the income or assets of another person as a basis for repayment of the loan, or ☐ the Borrower is married and resides, or the property is located, in a community property state.

BORROWER			CO-BORROWER		
Name	Age	School Yrs. _____	Name	Age	School Yrs. _____
Present Address No. Years _____ ☐ Own ☐ Rent			Present Address No. Years _____ ☐ Own ☐ Rent		
Street			Street		
City/State/Zip			City/State/Zip		
Former address if less than 2 years at present address			Former address if less than 2 years at present address		
Street			Street		
City/State/Zip			City/State/Zip		
Years at former address ☐ Own ☐ Rent			Years at former address ☐ Own ☐ Rent		
Marital Status ☐ Married ☐ Separated ☐ Unmarried (incl. single, divorced, widowed)	Dependents other than listed by Co-Borrower No. Ages		Marital Status ☐ Married ☐ Separated ☐ Unmarried (incl. single, divorced, widowed)	Dependents other than listed by Borrower No. Ages	
Name and Address of Employer	Years employed in this line of work or profession? _____ years Years on this job _____ ☐ Self Employed*		Name and Address of Employer	Years employed in this line of work or profession? _____ years Years on this job _____ ☐ Self Employed*	
Position/Title	Type of Business		Position/Title	Type of Business	
Social Security Number ***	Home Phone	Business Phone	Social Security Number ***	Home Phone	Business Phone

GROSS MONTHLY INCOME				MONTHLY HOUSING EXPENSE**			DETAILS OF PURCHASE	
Item	Borrower	Co-Borrower	Total	Rent	Present	Proposed	Do Not Complete If Refinance	
Base Empl. Income	$	$	$	First Mortgage (P&I)	$	$	a. Purchase Price	$
Overtime				Other Financing (P&I)			b. Total Closing Costs (Est.)	
Bonuses				Hazard Insurance			c. Prepaid Escrows (Est.)	
Commissions				Real Estate Taxes			d. Total (a + b + c)	$
Dividends/Interest				Mortgage Insurance			e. Amount This Mortgage	( )
Net Rental Income				Homeowner Assn. Dues			f. Other Financing	( )
Other† (Before completing, see notice under Describe Other Income below.)				Other			g. Other Equity	( )
				Total Monthly Pmt.	$	$	h. Amount of Cash Deposit	( )
				Utilities			i. Closing Costs Paid by Seller	( )
Total	$	$	$	Total	$	$	j. Cash Reqd. for Closing (Est.)	$

DESCRIBE OTHER INCOME

◇ B—Borrower   C—Co-Borrower   NOTICE:† Alimony, child support, or separate maintenance income need not be revealed if the Borrower or Co-Borrower does not choose to have it considered as a basis for repaying this loan.   Monthly Amount $

IF EMPLOYED IN CURRENT POSITION FOR LESS THAN TWO YEARS COMPLETE THE FOLLOWING

B/C	Previous Employer/School	City/State	Type of Business	Position/Title	Dates From/To	Monthly Income
						$

THESE QUESTIONS APPLY TO BOTH BORROWER AND CO-BORROWER

If a "yes" answer is given to a question in this column, explain on an attached sheet.	Borrower Yes or No	Co-Borrower Yes or No	If applicable, explain Other Financing or Other Equity (provide addendum if more space is needed).
Have you any outstanding judgments? In the last 7 years, have you been declared bankrupt?			
Have you had property foreclosed upon or given title or deed in lieu thereof?			
Are you a co-maker or endorser on a note?			
Are you a party in a law suit?			
Are you obligated to pay alimony, child support, or separate maintenance?			
Is any part of the down payment borrowed?			

*FHLMC/FNMA require business credit report, signed Federal Income Tax returns for last two years, and, if available, audited Profit and Loss Statements plus balance sheet for same period.

**All Present Monthly Housing Expenses of Borrower and Co-Borrower should be listed on a combined basis.

***Neither FHLMC nor FNMA requires this information.

FHLMC 65 Rev. 9-30-80   MM P-4 9/83 jtr   FNMA 1003 Rev. 9-30-80

This Statement and any applicable supporting schedules may be completed jointly by both married and unmarried co-borrowers if their assets and liabilities are sufficiently joined so that the Statement can be meaningfull and fairly presented on a combined basis; otherwise separate Statements and Schedules are required (FHLMC 65A/FNMA 1003A). If the co-borrower section was completed about a spouse, this statement and supporting schedules must be completed about that spouse also. ☐ Completed Jointly ☐ Not Completed Jointly

STATEMENT OF ASSETS AND LIABILITIES

ASSETS		LIABILITIES AND PLEDGED ASSETS

Indicate by (*) those liabilities or pledged assets which will be satisfied upon sale of real estate owned or upon refinancing of subject property.

Description	Cash or Market Value	Creditors' Name, Address and Account Number	Acct. Name If Not Borrower's	Mo. Pmt. and Mos. left to pay	Unpaid Balance
Cash Deposit Toward Purchase Held By	$	Installment Debts (include "revolving" charge accts)		$ Pmt./Mos. /	$
Checking and Savings Accounts (Show Names of Institutions/Acct. Nos.)				/	
				/	
				/	
Stocks and Bonds (No./Description)				/	
				/	
Life Insurance Net Cash Value Face Amount ($)		Other Debts Including Stock Pledges		/	
SUBTOTAL LIQUID ASSETS	$				
Real Estate Owned (Enter Market Value from Schedule of Real Estate Owned)		Real Estate Loans			
Vested Interest in Retirement Fund				/	
Net Worth of Business Owned (ATTACH FINANCIAL STATEMENT)					
Automobiles (Make and Year)		Automobile Loans			
				/	
Furniture and Personal Property		Alimony, Child Support and Separate Maintenance Payments Owed To			
Other Assets (Itemize)				/	
		TOTAL MONTHLY PAYMENTS		$	
TOTAL ASSETS	A $	NET WORTH (A minus B) $		TOTAL LIABILITIES	B $

SCHEDULE OF REAL ESTATE OWNED (If Additional Properties Owned Attach Separate Schedule)

Address of Property (Indicate S if Sold, PS if Pending Sale or R if Rental being held for income)		Type of Property	Present Market Value	Amount of Mortgages Liens	Gross Rental Income	Mortgage Payments	Taxes, Ins. Maintenance and Misc.	Net Rental Income
			$	$	$	$	$	$
TOTALS →			$	$	$	$	$	$

LIST PREVIOUS CREDIT REFERENCES

	B-Borrower C—Co-Borrower	Creditor's Name and Address	Account Number	Purpose	Highest Balance	Date Paid
					$	

List any additional names under which credit has previously been received _____

AGREEMENT. The undersigned applies for the loan indicated in this application to be secured by a first mortgage or deed of trust on the property described herein, and represents that the property will not be used for any illegal or restricted purpose, and that all statements made in this application are true and are made for the purpose of obtaining the loan. Verification may be obtained from any source named in this application. The original or a copy of this application will be retained by the lender, even if the loan is not granted. The undersigned ☐ intend or ☐ do not intend to occupy the property as their primary residence.

I/we fully understand that it is a federal crime punishable by fine or imprisonment, or both, to knowlingly make any false statements concerning any of the above facts as applicable under the provisions of Title 18, United States Code, Section 1014.

_____ Date _____ _____ Date _____
Borrower's Signature   Co-Borrower's Signature

VOLUNTARY INFORMATION FOR GOVERNMENT MONITORING PURPOSES

The following information is requested by the Federal Government if this loan is related to a dwelling, in order to monitor the lender's compliance with equal credit opportunity and fair housing laws. You are not required to furnish this information, but are encouraged to do so. The law provides that a lender may neither discriminate on the basis of this information, nor on whether you choose to furnish it. However, if you choose not to furnish it, under Federal regulations this lender is required to note race and sex on the basis of visual observation or surname. If you do not wish to furnish the above information, please initial below.

BORROWER: I do not wish to furnish this information (initials)_____

RACE/NATIONAL ORIGIN ☐ American Indian, Alaskan Native ☐ Asian, Pacific Islander ☐ Black ☐ Hispanic ☐ White ☐ Other (specify)
SEX ☐ Female ☐ Male

CO-BORROWER: I do not wish to furnish this information (initials)_____

RACE/NATIONAL ORIGIN ☐ American Indian, Alaskan Native ☐ Asian, Pacific Islander ☐ Black ☐ Hispanic ☐ White ☐ Other (specify)
SEX ☐ Female ☐ Male

FOR LENDERS USE ONLY

(FNMA REQUIREMENT ONLY) This application was taken by ☐ face to face interview ☐ by mail ☐ by telephone

_____   _____
(Interviewer)   Name of Employer of Interviewer

Exhibit 9.5

NOTICE OF LOAN APPROVAL AND OFFER OF COMMITMENT

DATED: December 10, 1981
EXPIRES: December 31, 1981

APPLICANT:
SECURED PROPERTY:

PURCHASE PRICE	AMOUNT OF LOAN	INTEREST RATE	TERM		INTEREST	
$ 59,900.00	$ 25,000.00	18 %	12	MONTHS	$ 375.00	per month

This Association hereby offers to grant to the captioned applicant only, a first mortgage loan to be secured by a fully completed dwelling on the above noted secured property upon compliance with terms and conditions contained herein:

SUBJECT TO: 1½% of the origination fee due at final settlement.

Anything to the contrary contained herein notwithstanding, Borrower shall pay all taxes, assessments, and other charges, which would attain priority over said Mortgage, when due, and shall promptly furnish to Lender receipts evidencing such payments.

Anything to the contrary notwithstanding interest only to be paid monthly. Balance of the principal due to be paid in full on or before twelve months from the date of settlement.

1. This offer becomes an obligation of the Association only upon receipt of a non-refundable commitment fee of $125.00 within (15) fifteen days of the date hereof together with a signed acceptance of this offer from the applicant. If final settlement occurs on or before the expiration date stated above and within the terms of this approval and offer, this fee will be credited on account of our 1½% Loan Origination Fee, Leaving a balance of $275.00 due at the time of final settlement.

2. Receipt of all enclosed truth in lending disclosure forms must be acknowledged. Signed copy of each form to be returned to this Association within (15) fifteen days of the date hereof, together with approved copy of this letter and check, not cash, noted in No. 1 above.

3. Final settlement hereunder must be in strict accordance with the Real Estate Settlement Procedures Act of 1974, (RESPA), as amended.

4. The mortgage is to be insured as a first lien by a title insurance company acceptable to this Association, with settlement certificate and mortgage title policy containing no exceptions other than those approved by this Association. Secondary financing is not permitted.

5. This Association is to be given at least fifteen (15) days written notice of settlement together with a copy of the required title report. Notice of settlement as herein required shall not extend the expiration date stated above.

6. Applicant to contact his Real Estate or Insurance Broker in order to furnish a prepaid fire insurance policy with extended coverage, including malicious mischief and vandalism, (not a binder) on the secured property in an amount at least equal to the mortgage naming this Association as first mortgagee, in a company satisfactory to this Association. Such insurance shall be maintained at buyers expense together with any other insurance this Association may require. In the event that at a future date it is determined that the subject property is in a flood hazard area, Applicant agrees to furnish this Association with a satisfactory flood insurance policy.

7. This Association does not collect water or sewer rents, however, in addition to the above noted principal and interest payment, arrangements will be made at the time of settlement, to collect escrow funds for the payment of taxes, and where required, fire insurance, private mortgage insurance and flood insurance, all of which will be held in an interest bearing account.

8. This Association does not warrant the value or condition of the property. The appraised valuation is arrived at to determine the maximum mortgage that will be considered. The Applicant should satisfy himself/herself that the price and condition of the property are acceptable.

9. Applicant to pay at or before settlement all normal closing costs and expenses. This loan when closed, must conform in all respects to Rules and Regulations of this Association and all Supervisory Authorities.

I/we hereby accept the terms and conditions of this offer.

_____ (SEAL)

_____ (SEAL)   By: _____
                                                          Vice President

DATED _____

Exhibit 9.6

NOTICE TO CUSTOMER REQUIRED BY FEDERAL LAW
FEDERAL RESERVE REGULATION Z
(To Be Executed in Duplicate)

The FINANCE CHARGE on this transaction will begin to accrue on _____ December 15, 1981 _____ LOAN NO. ___ To be assigned ___

The AMOUNT OF THE LOAN in this transaction is _____ $25,000,00

Less the PREPAID FINANCE CHARGE on this transaction which includes:

1. Service Charge	$ 375.00	6.		$
2. Initial Credit Ins. Premium	$	7.		$
3. Int. to	$	8.		$
4. Sellers Points	$	9.		$
5.	$	10.		$
			TOTAL	$ 375.00

Equals the AMOUNT FINANCED in this transaction _____ $4,625.00

This amount includes:

1. Title Fees	$	5. Settlement fee	$
2. Recording	$	6. Survey	$
3. Notary	$	7.	$
4. Mortgage papers	$	8.	$

The ANNUAL PERCENTAGE RATE on this transaction is _____ 19.5% _____ %

NET PROCEEDS _____ $ _____

Itemized CHARGES EXCLUDABLE from the FINANCE CHARGE in this transaction:

1. Title Fees	$ 545.50	6. Survey	$ 599.00
2. Recording	$ 23.00	7. Appraisal Fee	$ 100.00
3. Notary	$ 10.00	8. Credit Report Fee	$ 25.00
4. Mortgage papers	$ see above	9. Transfer Tax	$ 898.00
5. Settlement Spec. Inn. Yr.	$ 125.00	10. Conveyancing Deed	$ 150.00

Payments for interest only on this mortgage shall be _____ monthly installments of $ _____ estimated to begin on the _____ day of _____ 19_____, and due on the _____ day of each month thereafter. The total payments on this transaction will be $ _____, including the $25,000, principal amount which is due on or before

This institution's security interest in this transaction is a mortgage on property located at _____

also specifically described in the documents furnished for this loan. The documents executed in connection with this transaction cover all after-acquired property and also stand as security for future advances, the terms for which are described in the documents.

A late payment charge is made under which a penalty of _____ % of any payment is charged on any payment made over _____ days after the due date thereof.

A prepayment penalty is imposed which requires _____

Miscellaneous disclosures, or explanations. If title to mortgaged premises is transferred to anyone other than the survivor of borrowee without prior written consent of lender, then the entire principal balance remaining, with interest, may at option of lender be immediately due and payable.

INSURANCE

PROPERTY INSURANCE, if written in connection with the loan, may be obtained by borrower though any person of his choice provided creditor reserves the right to refuse, for reasonable cause, to accept an insurer offered by borrower.

CREDIT LIFE AND DISABILITY INSURANCE is not required to obtain this loan. No charge is made for credit insurance and no credit insurance is provided unless the borrower signs the appropriate statement below:

(a) The cost for Credit Life Insurance alone for the initial one month term is $ _____
(b) The cost for Credit Life and Disability Insurance for the initial one month term is $ _____
(c) The cost for Disability Insurance for the initial one month term is $ _____

All the above insurance coverage is subject to the requirements and approval of the insurance company.

I desire Credit Life and Disability Insurance	I desire Credit Life Insurance Only	I desire Disability Insurance Only	I DO NOT want Credit Life or Disability Insurance
NA	NA	NA	NA
Date Signature	Date Signature	Date Signature	Date Signature

INSTITUTION

FEDERAL SAVINGS AND LOAN ASSN.

I hereby acknowledge receipt of the disclosures made in this notice

BY _____   CUSTOMER _____
Vice President

Exhibit 9.7

MORTGAGE

THIS MORTGAGE is made this .... 31 .... day of ..... May ....,
19...., between the Mortgagor, ...
.... (herein "Borrower"), and the Mortgagee, ...
...., a corporation organized and
existing under the laws of ...., whose address is ....
..... One Custom House Square – Eighth and King Streets — Wilmington, Delaware 19801 .... (herein "Lender").

WHEREAS, Borrower is indebted to Lender in the principal sum of ..... (30,000). Thirty. Thousand .....
.. Dollars, ...Dollars, which indebtedness is evidenced by Borrower's
note dated ... May. 31,. 1983 .... (herein "Note"), providing for monthly installments of principal and
interest, with the balance of the indebtedness, if not sooner paid, due and payable on ... June .1, .2013 ....
.... ;

To SECURE to Lender (a) the repayment of the indebtedness evidenced by the Note, with interest thereon, the
payment of all other sums, with interest thereon, advanced in accordance herewith to protect the security of this
Mortgage, and the performance of the covenants and agreements of Borrower herein contained, and (b) the repayment
of any future advances, with interest thereon, made to Borrower by Lender pursuant to paragraph 21 hereof (herein
"Future Advances"), Borrower does hereby mortgage, grant and convey to Lender the following described property
located in the County of ... New. Castle ...., State of Delaware:

ALL that certain lot, piece or parcel of land, with the buildings
thereon erected, situate in parcel of land, with the buildings thereon erected, situate in Graylyn
Crest, Brandywine Hundred, New Castle County and State of Delaware, now known as 1113
Piper Road, and being Lot No. 100, Block H, as shown on the Plan of GRAYLYN CREST, as
prepared by Howard L. Robertson, Civil Engineer and Surveyor, and now remaining of record in
the Office for the Recording of Deeds, at Wilmington, in and for New Castle County and State
of Delaware, in Plat Book Volume 3, Page 49, and being more particularly bounded and
described as follows, to wit:
BEGINNING at a point on the northwesterly side of Piper Road, at fifty feet wide, as
marked out on said Plan, said point being located South thirty-six degrees, sixteen minutes West
two hundred thirty-two feet and forty-one one-hundredths of a foot from a point in the
Southwesterly end of a twenty feet radius intersection curve joining the said side of Piper Road
with the Southwesterly side of Pan Road, at fifty feet wide, as marked out on said Plan, said
point of Beginning being also in the division line between Lots Nos. 99 and 100; thence by said
side of Piper Road South thirty-six degrees, sixteen minutes West seventy feet to a point in the
division line between Lots Nos. 100 and 101; and thence by the same North fifty-three degrees,
forty-four minutes West one hundred thirty feet to a point in the division line between Lots Nos.
91 and 100; and thence by the same and also along the division line between Lots Nos. 92 and
100 North thirty-six degrees, sixteen minutes East seventy feet to a point in the division line
between Lots Nos. 100 and 99; and thence by the same South fifty-three degrees, forty-four
minutes East one hundred thirty feet to a point in the aforesaid northwesterly side of Piper
Road, the first mentioned point and place of BEGINNING. Be the contents thereof what they
may.
BEING the same lands and premises which Graylyn Construction Co., a corporation of the
State of Delaware, by its indenture dated the Thirteenth day of June, 1955, and recorded in the
Office for the Recording of Deeds, &c., in and for New Castle County, at Wilmington,
Delaware, in Deed Record L, Vol. 56, Page 362, did grant and convey unto Paul L. Gallagher and
Opal M. Gallagher, his wife, in fee.

which has the address of ... 1113 .Piper. Road ..... Graylyn. Crest., ... Wilmington ....,
....[Street]..[City]
.DE ... 19803 .... (herein "Property Address");
[State and Zip Code]

TOGETHER with all the improvements now or hereafter erected on the property, and all easements, rights,
appurtenances, rents, royalties, mineral, oil and gas rights and profits, water, water rights, and water stock, and all
fixtures now or hereafter attached to the property, all of which, including replacements and additions thereto, shall be
deemed to be and remain a part of the property covered by this Mortgage; and all of the foregoing, together with said
property (or the leasehold estate if this Mortgage is on a leasehold) are herein referred to as the "Property".

Borrower covenants that Borrower is lawfully seised of the estate hereby conveyed and has the right to mortgage,
grant and convey the Property, that the Property is unencumbered, and that Borrower will warrant and defend
generally the title to the Property against all claims and demands, subject to any declarations, easements or restrictions
listed in a schedule of exceptions to coverage in any title insurance policy insuring Lender's interest in the Property.

DELAWARE—1 to 4 Family—6/75—FNMA/FHLMC UNIFORM INSTRUMENT

SAF (2613-8)
American Savings & Accounting Supply, Inc.

UNIFORM COVENANTS. Borrower and Lender covenant and agree as follows:

1. Payment of Principal and Interest. Borrower shall promptly pay when due the principal of and interest on the indebtedness evidenced by the Note, prepayment and late charges as provided in the Note, and the principal of and interest on any Future Advances secured by this Mortgage.

2. Funds for Taxes and Insurance. Subject to applicable law or to a written waiver by Lender, Borrower shall pay to Lender on the day monthly installments of principal and interest are payable under the Note, until the Note is paid in full, a sum (herein "Funds") equal to one-twelfth of the yearly taxes and assessments which may attain priority over this Mortgage, and ground rents on the Property, if any, plus one-twelfth of yearly premium installments for hazard insurance, plus one-twelfth of yearly premium installments for mortgage insurance, if any, all as reasonably estimated initially and from time to time by Lender on the basis of assessments and bills and reasonable estimates thereof.

The Funds shall be held in an institution the deposits or accounts of which are insured or guaranteed by a Federal or state agency (including Lender if Lender is such an institution). Lender shall apply the Funds to pay said taxes, assessments, insurance premiums and ground rents. Lender may not charge for so holding and applying the Funds, analyzing said account, or verifying and compiling said assessments and bills, unless Lender pays Borrower interest on the Funds and applicable law permits Lender to make such a charge. Borrower and Lender may agree in writing at the time of execution of this Mortgage that interest on the Funds shall be paid to Borrower, and unless such agreement is made or applicable law requires such interest to be paid, Lender shall not be required to pay Borrower any interest or earnings on the Funds. Lender shall give to Borrower, without charge, an annual accounting of the Funds showing credits and debits to the Funds and the purpose for which each debit to the Funds was made. The Funds are pledged as additional security for the sums secured by this Mortgage.

If the amount of the Funds held by Lender, together with the future monthly installments of Funds payable prior to the due dates of taxes, assessments, insurance premiums and ground rents, shall exceed the amount required to pay said taxes, assessments, insurance premiums and ground rents as they fall due, such excess shall be, at Borrower's option, either promptly repaid to Borrower or credited to Borrower on monthly installments of Funds. If the amount of the Funds held by Lender shall not be sufficient to pay taxes, assessments, insurance premiums and ground rents as they fall due, Borrower shall pay to Lender any amount necessary to make up the deficiency within 30 days from the date notice is mailed by Lender to Borrower requesting payment thereof.

Upon payment in full of all sums secured by this Mortgage, Lender shall promptly refund to Borrower any Funds held by Lender. If under paragraph 18 hereof the Property is sold or the Property is otherwise acquired by Lender, Lender shall apply, no later than immediately prior to the sale of the Property or its acquisition by Lender, any Funds held by Lender at the time of application as a credit against the sums secured by this Mortgage.

3. Application of Payments. Unless applicable law provides otherwise, all payments received by Lender under the Note and paragraphs 1 and 2 hereof shall be applied by Lender first in payment of amounts payable to Lender by Borrower under paragraph 2 hereof, then to interest payable on the Note, then to the principal of the Note, and then to interest and principal on any Future Advances.

4. Charges; Liens. Borrower shall pay all taxes, assessments and other charges, fines and impositions attributable to the Property which may attain a priority over this Mortgage, and leasehold payments or ground rents, if any, in the manner provided under paragraph 2 hereof or, if not paid in such manner, by Borrower making payment, when due, directly to the payee thereof. Borrower shall promptly furnish to Lender all notices of amounts due under this paragraph, and in the event Borrower shall make payment directly, Borrower shall promptly furnish to Lender receipts evidencing such payments. Borrower shall promptly discharge any lien which has priority over this Mortgage; provided, that Borrower shall not be required to discharge any such lien so long as Borrower shall agree in writing to the payment of the obligation secured by such lien in a manner acceptable to Lender, or shall in good faith contest such lien by, or defend enforcement of such lien in, legal proceedings which operate to prevent the enforcement of the lien or forfeiture of the Property or any part thereof.

5. Hazard Insurance. Borrower shall keep the improvements now existing or hereafter erected on the Property insured against loss by fire, hazards included within the term "extended coverage", and such other hazards as Lender may require and in such amounts and for such periods as Lender may require; provided, that Lender shall not require that the amount of such coverage exceed that amount of coverage required to pay the sums secured by this Mortgage.

The insurance carrier providing the insurance shall be chosen by Borrower subject to approval by Lender; provided, that such approval shall not be unreasonably withheld. All premiums on insurance policies shall be paid in the manner provided under paragraph 2 hereof or, if not paid in such manner, by Borrower making payment, when due, directly to the insurance carrier.

All insurance policies and renewals thereof shall be in form acceptable to Lender and shall include a standard mortgage clause in favor of and in form acceptable to Lender. Lender shall have the right to hold the policies and renewals thereof, and Borrower shall promptly furnish to Lender all renewal notices and all receipts of paid premiums. In the event of loss, Borrower shall give prompt notice to the insurance carrier and Lender. Lender may make proof of loss if not made promptly by Borrower.

Unless Lender and Borrower otherwise agree in writing, insurance proceeds shall be applied to restoration or repair of the Property damaged, provided such restoration or repair is economically feasible and the security of this Mortgage is not thereby impaired. If such restoration or repair is not economically feasible or if the security of this Mortgage would be impaired, the insurance proceeds shall be applied to the sums secured by this Mortgage, with the excess, if any, paid to Borrower. If the Property is abandoned by Borrower, or if Borrower fails to respond to Lender within 30 days from the date notice is mailed by Lender to Borrower that the insurance carrier offers to settle a claim for insurance benefits, Lender is authorized to collect and apply the insurance proceeds at Lender's option either to restoration or repair of the Property or to the sums secured by this Mortgage.

Unless Lender and Borrower otherwise agree in writing, any such application of proceeds to principal shall not extend or postpone the due date of the monthly installments referred to in paragraphs 1 and 2 hereof or change the amount of such installments. If under paragraph 18 hereof the Property is acquired by Lender, all right, title and interest of Borrower in and to any insurance policies and in and to the proceeds thereof resulting from damage to the Property prior to the sale or acquisition shall pass to Lender to the extent of the sums secured by this Mortgage immediately prior to such sale or acquisition.

6. Preservation and Maintenance of Property; Leaseholds; Condominiums; Planned Unit Developments. Borrower shall keep the Property in good repair and shall not commit waste or permit impairment or deterioration of the Property and shall comply with the provisions of any lease if this Mortgage is on a leasehold. If this Mortgage is on a unit in a condominium or a planned unit development, Borrower shall perform all of Borrower's obligations under the declaration or covenants creating or governing the condominium or planned unit development, the by-laws and regulations of the condominium or planned unit development, and constituent documents. If a condominium or planned unit development rider is executed by Borrower and recorded together with this Mortgage, the covenants and agreements of such rider shall be incorporated into and shall amend and supplement the covenants and agreements of this Mortgage as if the rider were a part hereof.

7. Protection of Lender's Security. If Borrower fails to perform the covenants and agreements contained in this Mortgage, or if any action or proceeding is commenced which materially affects Lender's interest in the Property, including, but not limited to, eminent domain, insolvency, code enforcement, or arrangements or proceedings involving a bankrupt or decedent, then Lender at Lender's option, upon notice to Borrower, may make such appearances, disburse such sums and take such action as is necessary to protect Lender's interest, including, but not limited to, disbursement of reasonable attorney's fees and entry upon the Property to make repairs. If Lender required mortgage insurance as a condition of making the loan secured by this Mortgage, Borrower shall pay the premiums required to maintain such insurance in effect until such time as the requirement for such insurance terminates in accordance with Borrower's and

Lender's written agreement or applicable law. Borrower shall pay the amount of all mortgage insurance premiums in the manner provided under paragraph 2 hereof.

Any amounts disbursed by Lender pursuant to this paragraph 7, with interest thereon, shall become additional indebtedness of Borrower secured by this Mortgage. Unless Borrower and Lender agree to other terms of payment, such amounts shall be payable upon notice from Lender to Borrower requesting payment thereof, and shall bear interest from the date of disbursement at the rate payable from time to time on outstanding principal under the Note unless payment of interest at such rate would be contrary to applicable law, in which event such amounts shall bear interest at the highest rate permissible under applicable law. Nothing contained in this paragraph 7 shall require Lender to incur any expense or take any action hereunder.

8. Inspection. Lender may make or cause to be made reasonable entries upon and inspections of the Property, provided that Lender shall give Borrower notice prior to any such inspection specifying reasonable cause therefor related to Lender's interest in the Property.

9. Condemnation. The proceeds of any award or claim for damages, direct or consequential, in connection with any condemnation or other taking of the Property, or part thereof, or for conveyance in lieu of condemnation, are hereby assigned and shall be paid to Lender.

In the event of a total taking of the Property, the proceeds shall be applied to the sums secured by this Mortgage, with the excess, if any, paid to Borrower. In the event of a partial taking of the Property, unless Borrower and Lender otherwise agree in writing, there shall be applied to the sums secured by this Mortgage such proportion of the proceeds as is equal to that proportion which the amount of the sums secured by this Mortgage immediately prior to the date of taking bears to the fair market value of the Property immediately prior to the date of taking, with the balance of the proceeds paid to Borrower.

If the Property is abandoned by Borrower, or if, after notice by Lender to Borrower that the condemnor offers to make an award or settle a claim for damages, Borrower fails to respond to Lender within 30 days after the date such notice is mailed, Lender is authorized to collect and apply the proceeds, at Lender's option, either to restoration or repair of the Property or to the sums secured by this Mortgage.

Unless Lender and Borrower otherwise agree in writing, any such application of proceeds to principal shall not extend or postpone the due date of the monthly installments referred to in paragraphs 1 and 2 hereof or change the amount of such installments.

10. Borrower Not Released. Extension of the time for payment or modification of amortization of the sums secured by this Mortgage granted by Lender to any successor in interest of Borrower shall not operate to release, in any manner, the liability of the original Borrower and Borrower's successors in interest. Lender shall not be required to commence proceedings against such successor or refuse to extend time for payment or otherwise modify amortization of the sums secured by this Mortgage by reason of any demand made by the original Borrower and Borrower's successors in interest.

11. Forbearance by Lender Not a Waiver. Any forbearance by Lender in exercising any right or remedy hereunder, or otherwise afforded by applicable law, shall not be a waiver of or preclude the exercise of any such right or remedy. The procurement of insurance or the payment of taxes or other liens or charges by Lender shall not be a waiver of Lender's right to accelerate the maturity of the indebtedness secured by this Mortgage.

12. Remedies Cumulative. All remedies provided in this Mortgage are distinct and cumulative to any other right or remedy under this Mortgage or afforded by law or equity, and may be exercised concurrently, independently or successively.

13. Successors and Assigns Bound; Joint and Several Liability; Captions. The covenants and agreements herein contained shall bind, and the rights hereunder shall inure to, the respective successors and assigns of Lender and Borrower, subject to the provisions of paragraph 17 hereof. All covenants and agreements of Borrower shall be joint and several. The captions and headings of the paragraphs of this Mortgage are for convenience only and are not to be used to interpret or define the provisions hereof.

14. Notice. Except for any notice required under applicable law to be given in another manner, (a) any notice to Borrower provided for in this Mortgage shall be given by mailing such notice by certified mail addressed to Borrower at the Property Address or at such other address as Borrower may designate by notice to Lender as provided herein, and (b) any notice to Lender shall be given by certified mail, return receipt requested, to Lender's address stated herein or to such other address as Lender may designate by notice to Borrower as provided herein. Any notice provided for in this Mortgage shall be deemed to have been given to Borrower or Lender when given in the manner designated herein.

15. Uniform Mortgage; Governing Law; Severability. This form of mortgage combines uniform covenants for national use and non-uniform covenants with limited variations by jurisdiction to constitute a uniform security instrument covering real property. This Mortgage shall be governed by the law of the jurisdiction in which the Property is located. In the event that any provision or clause of this Mortgage or the Note conflicts with applicable law, such conflict shall not affect other provisions of this Mortgage or the Note which can be given effect without the conflicting provision, and to this end the provisions of the Mortgage and the Note are declared to be severable.

16. Borrower's Copy. Borrower shall be furnished a conformed copy of the Note and of this Mortgage at the time of execution or after recordation hereof.

17. Transfer of the Property; Assumption. If all or any part of the Property or an interest therein is sold or transferred by Borrower without Lender's prior written consent, excluding (a) the creation of a lien or encumbrance subordinate to this Mortgage, (b) the creation of a purchase money security interest for household appliances, (c) a transfer by devise, descent or by operation of law upon the death of a joint tenant or (d) the grant of any leasehold interest of three years or less not containing an option to purchase, Lender may, at Lender's option, declare all the sums secured by this Mortgage to be immediately due and payable. Lender shall have waived such option to accelerate if, prior to the sale or transfer, Lender and the person to whom the Property is to be sold or transferred reach agreement in writing that the credit of such person is satisfactory to Lender and that the interest payable on the sums secured by this Mortgage shall be at such rate as Lender shall request. If Lender has waived the option to accelerate provided in this paragraph 17, and if Borrower's successor in interest has executed a written assumption agreement accepted in writing by Lender, Lender shall release Borrower from all obligations under this Mortgage and the Note.

If Lender exercises such option to accelerate, Lender shall mail Borrower notice of acceleration in accordance with paragraph 14 hereof. Such notice shall provide a period of not less than 30 days from the date the notice is mailed within which Borrower may pay the sums declared due. If Borrower fails to pay such sums prior to the expiration of such period, Lender may, without further notice or demand on Borrower, invoke any remedies permitted by paragraph 18 hereof.

NON-UNIFORM COVENANTS. Borrower and Lender further covenant and agree as follows:

18. Acceleration; Remedies. Except as provided in paragraph 17 hereof, upon Borrower's breach of any covenant or agreement of Borrower in this Mortgage, including the covenants to pay when due any sums secured by this Mortgage, Lender prior to acceleration shall mail notice to Borrower as provided in paragraph 14 hereof specifying: (1) the breach; (2) the action required to cure such breach; (3) a date, not less than 30 days from the date the notice is mailed to Borrower, by which such breach must be cured; and (4) that failure to cure such breach on or before the date specified in the notice may result in acceleration of the sums secured by this Mortgage, foreclosure by judicial proceeding and sale of the Property. The notice shall further inform Borrower of the right to reinstate after acceleration and the right to assert in the foreclosure proceeding the non-existence of a default or any other defense of Borrower to acceleration and foreclosure. If the breach is not cured on or before the date specified in the notice, Lender at Lender's option may declare all of the sums secured by this Mortgage to be immediately due and payable without further demand and may foreclose this Mortgage by judicial proceeding. Lender shall be entitled to collect in such proceeding all expenses of foreclosure, including, but not limited to, reasonable attorney's fees of . . . . % of the amount decreed for principal and interest, which fee shall be allowed and paid as part of the decree of judgment in such proceeding, and costs of abstracts, title reports and documentary evidence.

19. Borrower's Right to Reinstate. Notwithstanding Lender's acceleration of the sums secured by this Mortgage,

Borrower shall have the right to have any proceedings begun by Lender to enforce this Mortgage discontinued at any time prior to entry of a judgment enforcing this Mortgage if: (a) Borrower pays Lender all sums which would be then due under this Mortgage, the Note and notes securing Future Advances, if any, had no acceleration occurred; (b) Borrower cures all breaches of any other covenants or agreements of Borrower contained in this Mortgage; (c) Borrower pays all reasonable expenses incurred by Lender in enforcing the covenants and agreements of Borrower contained in this Mortgage and in enforcing Lender's remedies as provided in paragraph 18 hereof, including, but not limited to, reasonable attorney's fees; and (d) Borrower takes such action as Lender may reasonably require to assure that the lien of this Mortgage, Lender's interest in the Property and Borrower's obligation to pay the sums secured by this Mortgage shall continue unimpaired. Upon such payment and cure by Borrower, this Mortgage and the obligations secured hereby shall remain in full force and effect as if no acceleration had occurred.

20. Assignment of Rents; Appointment of Receiver. As additional security hereunder, Borrower hereby assigns to Lender the rents of the Property, provided that Borrower shall, prior to acceleration under paragraph 18 hereof or abandonment of the Property, have the right to collect and retain such rents as they become due and payable.

Upon acceleration under paragraph 18 hereof or abandonment of the Property, Lender shall be entitled to have a receiver appointed by a court to enter upon, take possession of and manage the Property and to collect the rents of the Property, including those past due. All rents collected by the receiver shall be applied first to payment of the costs of management of the Property and collection of rents, including, but not limited to, receiver's fees, premiums on receiver's bonds and reasonable attorney's fees, and then to the sums secured by this Mortgage. The receiver shall be liable to account only for those rents actually received.

21. Future Advances. Upon request of Borrower, Lender, at Lender's option prior to release of this Mortgage, may make Future Advances to Borrower. Such Future Advances, with interest thereon, shall be secured by this Mortgage when evidenced by promissory notes stating that said notes are secured hereby. At no time shall the principal amount of the indebtedness secured by this Mortgage, not including sums advanced in accordance herewith to protect the security of this Mortgage, exceed the original amount of the Note.

22. Release. Upon payment of all sums secured by this Mortgage, Lender shall release this Mortgage without charge to Borrower. Borrower shall pay all costs of recordation, if any.

IN WITNESS WHEREOF, Borrower has executed this Mortgage.

Signed, sealed and delivered
in the presence of:

....(Seal)
                                                                                          —Borrower

....(Seal)
                                                                                          —Borrower

STATE OF DELAWARE, ...County ss:

BE IT REMEMBERED that on this.. 31........day of...May....................., 19..83, personally came before me.... ...., part.... to this Mortgage personally known to me to be such, and severally acknowledged this Mortgage to be ....act and deed.

Given under my Hand and Seal of Office, the day and year aforesaid.

....
                                          Notary Public

———————————— (Space Below This Line Reserved For Lender and Recorder) ————————————

C. Form and Content of the Mortgage

1. Writing

Aside from the Statute of Frauds, the lack of a writing as evidence of a mortgage cannot be justified. Most banks, thrift institutions, and governmental agencies have standard forms.

2. Parties

The names of *mortgagors,* the parties making or asking for the financing, must appear exactly on the mortgage. The names of *mortgagees,* the parties providing the financing, names must appear exactly on the mortgage.

3. Consideration

In order for the mortgage to have legal, contractual validity, there must be some reference to the purchase price.

4. Obligations

Borrowers' obligations must then be recited including: *terms of payment, interest rate, length of term, prepayment, rights and penalties,* and *charges for late payments or lawyer's fees.*

5. Conveyance clause

Legal description of the property subject to the mortgage must be included. Refer to the deed for an appropriate description.

6. Warranty of title

Purchase of the property generally requires purchase of title insurance, which will uphold the lender's interest in case of dispute.

7. Maintenance/repairs

Almost all mortgages place some duty and obligation upon the purchasers to keep up the premises or land as long as the lender has an interest.

8. Taxes and insurance

All lenders obviously require their borrowers to insure the premises and to pay all appropriate taxes, assessments, and changes.

9. Damage/waste

Purchase of the property generally requires purchase of title insurance, which will uphold the lender's interest in case of dispute.

10. Condemnation

In the event of condemnation, the rights of the parties should be enumerated.

11. Security agreement

The lender will desire the right to secure his or her debt by placing a lien against the personalty (property that is not permanently attached or affixed, generally not deemed a fixture). UCC provisions require a security-agreement clause.

12. Rights of conveyance/assumption

In-depth analysis of the document is critical here since assumption is out of favor with lenders. Check closely the parties' rights to convey the property as well as the rights of purchaser to assume the interest rate.

13. Default

Every mortgage must outline those conditions that create a default whether by failure to pay monthly payments or failure to pay the appropriate taxes. Clear indications of *notice* provisions must be included in the clause.

14. Enforcement rights

In the event of default, the lenders after giving all appropriate notices may then enforce their rights. This clause should contain some discussion of: *acceleration of debt, collection of interest, foreclosure, possession, counsel fees,* and *alternative remedies.*

15. Execution and acknowledgment

Consult local rules for appropriate notarization, certification, and acknowledgments.

It is also important to note that mortgages can be also utilized in interests other than real property, such as leaseholds, fixtures and chattel, and easements and appurtenances.

D. Mortgage Financing

1. Traditional fixed-rate mortgages

The traditional methods of home or commercial financing consisted of a set term, between twenty and thirty years, and at a set rate such as 11–15 percent. In the recent past, set rates of interest reached near 21 percent, which were obviously disastrous for the housing industry. Financial institutions were wary of making any long-term commitments due to volatile interest and money markets and considered any long-term fixed interest as unsound banking practice. Hence, the fixed rate mortgage may be a financial dinosaur in the near future. What is certain is that this form of financing can only be acquired by paying a premium, usually 2 to 3 points above other forms of financing. That premium, however, may be well worth the cost to an individual homeowner who does desire certitude in rates and does not wish to become a rider on the interest-rate rollercoaster. Any substantial increase in general credit rates does not affect the fixed rate mortgage.

2. Variable-rate mortgages

Since financial institutions are wary of long-term debt instruments, owing to market conditions, they have been most creative in designing and devising financial schemes that can vary and accordingly reflect realistic market conditions. All variable-rate mortgages give the lender the capacity to adjust the interest rate or its mortgages according to various means. Consider the following modes of variance:

a. RENEGOTIABLE-RATE MORTGAGES (RRM)

Subject to legislative and executive controls at both the state and federal level, RRMs permit the lender to renegotiate the rate of interest in a fixed period, say every three to four years in the life of a thirty-year mortgage. That renegotiation may be upward in rate, and that upward revision is discretionary, but RRMs also permit, and in some states mandate, downward revision of the rate based on the credit indexes of the federal government, such as treasury rates, or on the prime rate of lending institutions.

b. ADJUSTABLE-RATE MORTGAGE (ARM)

This form of financing is more unpredictable since institutions are allowed to revise the interest-rate provisions at six-month intervals. This type of lender activity makes this form of mortgage more oppressive and volitile, but ARMs generally cannot be increased more than 5 percent over the life of the loan and cannot be increased more than 1 percent in any given year. The borrower at least knows how bad it can get and is also afforded rights and prepayment and extended loan maturity dates.

c. Graduated-Payment Mortgages (GPM)

FHA 245 mortgages have allowed this form of financing for quite a while. Simply, a GPM defers a portion of interest owed on the mortgage in its earliest years, thereby allowing a new buyer an initial lower monthly payment. Logically, the buyer's income level will increase in time, making increased monthly payments possible. GPMs work quite effectively as long as the borrower appears financially secure in the long run and does appear capable of earning larger sums of money. Otherwise, the GPM can give false hope in the purchase of a house clearly beyond the means of the buyer. GPMs can only be adjusted for a fixed period, usually the first five years of the loan.

d. "Buy-Down" Mortgages

New-home construction frequently utilizes this form of financing. Critics of the buy-down label it a form of "bait and switch" advertising, since huge ads in real estate sections applaud strikingly lower rates of interest on new homes, sometimes as much as 5 percent lower. Much of that criticism is directed at the thirty-year mortgage with a five-year balloon item at a fixed rate far below previous rates, or at a similar mortgage term with the first few years discounted to entice the buyer. In these scenarios the borrower must be clearly attuned to how a balloon requires full payment of the balance at the end of its short term or how, in the second case, rates will revert to normal market reality after the initial period ends. In sum, rates that look too good to be true usually are, and the borrower must prepare for the long run, not the short period of economic benefit.

Buy-down mortgages should not be perceived as shady practices, since by analogy they operate from the same premise as a GPM, and as long as a borrower is thoroughly knowledgeable about its ramifications there are no problems. Buy-down mortgages can also be viewed another way; that is, actually buying the interest rate that you desire by paying a premium on the house. Developers frequently "mark up" the price of a house to reflect a lower interest rate. Banks permit a discounted rate of interest when a large down payment is made, since their long-term risk is alleviated.

3. Fannie-Mae mortgages (FNMA)

FNMA, the Federal National Mortgage Association, is also a provider of secondary mortgage financing on some existing properties. Check with the seller of the property to see if the primary mortgage was purchased by FNMA. If so, the FNMA offer provides the new purchaser with the opportunity to refinance at markedly lower rates.

4. Governmental mortgages

Governmental agencies are major sources of mortgage support. Those agencies include:

1. Federal Housing Administration (FHA)
2. Veterans' Administration (VA)
3. Farmers' Home Administration (FMHA)

These agencies do not lend mony but instead insure the investment of banks and other institutions who wish to lend money. This governmental assurance obviously minimizes the risks of lending and greatly increases borrower eligibility. The mechanics, costs, and bureaucracy of these types of mortgages are well known, but the low down payments required, market stability, and generally lower fixed rates make this an attractive form of financing. It's the sellers who usually dislike this form of financing, since they are usually required to pay "points." Contact any of the above agencies for literature on materials on their programs.

5. Emerging forms of mortgage financing

a. Pension Funds

Drastically high interest rates have led various pension funds, particularly union funds, to assist their members in the purchase of a home. Long-term pension and retirement funds are natural companions to long-term residential mortgages. This technique of financing generally provides lower rates and lower costs in acquiring the money. Private sources of funds are usually less inclined to charge points or other costs in lending money.

b. SHARED-APPRECIATION MORTGAGES (SAM)

Escalating values in the real estate market translate into potentially enormous capital gains and equity appreciation in a given home. A bank may decide to share in your property's increased value and make a claim for a portion of its value after a set period of years or on resale, in exchange for a lower rate of interest. Regulations vary in this form of financing, but generally the lender's share cannot exceed one-half of the appreciation; the interest rate cannot vary, and the borrower must pay all capital gains.

c. BALLOON MORTGAGES

Want to buy a house or property at a very low rate of interest and have very manageable monthly payments? Consider a balloon, which requires a borrower to pay the entire amount of the principal due in a fixed period, usually five years or less. This plan requires a buyer to refinance at current rates when the five years are up or come up with the cash. The risks are obvious.

d. PURCHASE MONEY MORTGAGE

While sellers dislike this mode, it is sometimes the only way they can sell the property. Generally, the sellers advance a portion of the purchase price of the property in mortgage form, just as a bank would, and collect in the same fashion, with principal and interest. This, of course, prevents the seller from receiving a lump-sum payment and really being rid of the property. PMMs are well received by buyers because there are few costs when compared to banks, and the interest rates are traditionally lower than market rates.

e. ASSUMPTIONS

Since the Supreme Court's "due on sale" ruling of 1982, it has become much more difficult for nongovernmental mortgage holders to automatically permit the purchaser of their property to assume their mortgages with their old fixed rates. However, all lenders as well as the FHA do have some method of assumption; whether at the same rate or a few points higher depends on the financial institution and governmental policy. Never overlook the possibility of assumption, since older rates are usually lower. Read most closely all assumption or due-on-sale clauses in the mortgage.

E. Conclusion

Securing financing requires sophisticated knowledge of both economic and legal issues. The main duty in all mortgage financing is to qualify a purchaser of property so that the deal may be closed. Diverse instruments and methods now exist, and it is imperative that the paralegal review all potential avenues of financing. The traditional fixed-rate mortgage is no longer the focal point of real estate practice and has been replaced with variable-rate mortgages, governmental assurances, owner financing, and graduated schemes. The American purchaser of real estate must now be reeducated in the changing world of mortgages, and the paralegal plays a major role in this instruction.

VII. SETTLEMENT/CLOSING PROCEDURES

A. The Role of the Paralegal

Settlements may be one of the most influential factors in the development of the paralegal profession. The settlement process, once a job for a country lawyer, has become a herculean task, with a multitude of forms to complete and procedures to follow, as well as an array of personalities and parties to keep track, all of whom are necessary to a successful settlement. Paralegals are the saviors to the beleaguered attorney in this quagmire of bureaucratic process.

The elements involved in the agreement of sale are a good starting point for the paralegal in real estate-closing processing.

B. Specific Steps in the Closing Process

1. Analysis of agreement of sale after execution

Be certain to verify the amounts listed on the agreement, which are relevant to eventual settlement-sheet tabulation. Those amounts usually encompass *earnest-money deposits, purchase price,* and *cash payments for appliances or other goods.*

Verify potential dates for settlement as it relates to the acquisition of mortgage financing. Is there enough time allotted? Use a worksheet similar to exhibit 9.8. Glean all relevant information from the agreement, and create a tickler file demonstrating the various dates for deposits, contingencies, and settlement. Emphasize to all interested parties the importance of adhering to the time frame set forth in the agreement.

2. Extension agreements

A frequent occurrence in real estate transactions is for one party to request an extension to the dates outlined in the agreements. Because of slow mortgage review by a financial institution, personal illness, or any other legitimate concern, extensions are needed. Be certain to formulate a written agreement to extend.

3. Title searches and title insurance

a. SOURCES OF TITLE INFORMATION

Much of what a paralegal attempts to accomplish in the finalization of a real estate settlement depends upon whether title is marketable or not. Good and marketable title has already been defined in a previous comment, and the issues revolving around the questions, such as elimination of judgments, other mortgages, and other encumbrances, have also been outlined. But where do you find out about all the obstructions or obstacles? Many elementary ways exist, when you consider that the buyers and sellers advance such information regularly and willingly. All parties to the transaction hope for a quick and expeditious settlement. Memory and intentions, however good, sometimes fail. That is why a title search is an imperative step in the settlement process, a step that takes place long before settlement occurs. This preparation assures a fluid settlement.

b. BASIC RECOMMENDATIONS ON TITLE SEARCHES

Depending on the jurisdiction, a title search can be performed by an attorney, a title company, a title abstractor, or a conveyancer. Paralegals frequently perform this duty and often yearn to be taught this skill from a textbook. While many an energetic author has attempted this feat, experience appears to be the only teacher in this arena. While the steps to title search are not conceptually overwhelming, the technical drudgery is impossible to describe.

What are easily mastered, however, are the general elements of the title examination.

Proof of Marketability. As the paralegal rummages through dusty deed books, lien files, and other exciting reading, careful attention must be given to any notations indicating:

- ☐ All adverse or secondary conveyances
- ☐ All other posted mortgages not yet satisfied
- ☐ Any restrictions markedly influencing the use of property
- ☐ Any outstanding judgments
- ☐ Any inconsistencies with legal descriptions in past surveys
- ☐ Any liens filed by municipalities for sewer charges, refuse collection, or other assessment
- ☐ Any state, local, or federal tax liens

As long as any of these encumbrances exist, marketability is in question.

Techniques of Title Examination. The wide disparity in statewide approaches in the process of title searches points to the dramatic need for a uniform law. Depending on your jurisdiction, you could fall into one of the following four categories.

> *1. Abstracts.* Some jurisdictions allow title abstractors to compile a current and complete list of all recorded documents related to the property in question. The buyer's attorney reviews the abstract and poses a legal opinion on its marketability.

Exhibit 9.8

LINE (ITEM) NO.	PAYEE AND EXPLANATION	AMOUNT TO BE TRANSFERRED TO PAGE 1 OR 2			
		BORROWER		SELLER	

Exhibit 9.9

Meridian Title Insurance Company

A **Meridian** Company

P.O. BOX 619, READING, PA. 19603

APPLICATION FOR TITLE INSURANCE

FOR OWNER INSURANCE

Name of Owner(s) to be Insured:

Address of Insured:

Consideration paid or to be paid for Property: $

(NOTE: Owner's Policy must be for full value of Property.)

FOR MORTGAGE OF DEED OF TRUST INSURANCE

Name of Insured:

Address of Insured:

Name of Proposed Mortgagors:

Amount of Mortgage or Deed of Trust to be Insured: $

GENERAL INFORMATION

Name of present Owner(s) of Property and Marital status

Address of present Owner(s):

Deed Book No.....................Page.....................from last deed

County parcel #

Lot# on recorded plan

Agreement of Sale and/or copy of plan attached

New Construction

Mobile Home

Date search required

(Applicant(s)   **Settlement to be held on**

Description of Property: (Complete description to be attached.)

Deliver Interim Binder (Settlement Certificate) to

_____

_____

_____

_____

_____

_____

Date:

FORM FL-11 (TC-1 Revised 6/80)

Exhibit 9.10

Meridian Title Insurance Company

A **◎ Meridian** Company

ATTORNEY'S REPORT of TITLE

No. _____

I have examined the record title to the real estate described in Schedule "A" to the date hereof for the protection of:

OWNER or LEASEHOLDER to be insured: _____ $_____

LENDER to be insured: _____ $_____

Type of Mortgage/Deed of Trust: Conv._____ VA_____ FHA_____ VRM_____ Const._____ Other_____ (Specify)

Title vested in: _____

Estate or Interest: _____ Type of Tenancy: _____

Being (the same) (part of the same) premises acquired by Deed from _____

_____ dated ___/___/___ and recorded ___/___/___ in Deed Book _____ page _____ .

Note: if acquired by more than one deed or through an estate set forth the additional information and attach hereto.

Schedule A
Attach complete description of Real Estate (including heading) to be insured.

Schedule B
ATTORNEY'S OBJECTIONS
NOTE: Please fill all spaces; "None" where applicable.

1. Property is occupied by: _____
    If tenant, give particulars of lease: Does tenant have renewal and/or purchase option? _____
2. Taxes are paid to and including the year 19_____. Tax Parcel No._____
3. Water Rent accruing from_____
4. Sewer Rent accruing from_____
        Note: if 3 and 4 are private sources, so state.
5. Any unpaid water and sewer connections, paving charges or other assessments_____
        (define)
6. Easements, servitudes, variation in dimensions or area content, improper location of buildings and improvements, conflict with lines of adjoining property, encroachments, projections or other matters which might be disclosed by an accurate survey of the premises.
7. Liability for claims for work done or materials furnished for which a lien might be filed.
    Construction (if applicable) is. (   ) contemplated   (   ) in progress   (   ) completed_____and statutory lien period has
    (   ) expired – (   ) has not expired.   (date)
8. Is property located in a coal area? Yes_____No_____. If so, Bituminous_____; Anthracite_____.

List all liens and other exceptions and conditions disclosed by the examination. (Furnish verbatim copies of easements, rights of way and restrictions INCLUDING REVERTER CLAUSE, IF ANY).

Certified at_____this_____day of_____, 19_____.
        (AM/PM)

        (Signature) _____ Attorney at Law

        (Note – Please type name under signature.)

No liability is assumed by Meridian Title Insurance Company under this Attorney's Report of Title until a commitment, title binder or title policy is issued pursuant to this report.

TF5 (Rev. 11/84)

2. Attorney Examination. In many eastern states, an attorney makes direct examination of records at the Recorder of Deeds Office in the county where the land is located. After extensive analysis, the attorney will set forth an opinion on the marketability of title.

3. Torrens System. Still utilized in a minority of jurisdictions, under this system of land registration, an applicant—buyer, that is—files a request for registration of land in the proper county. If the title is good and marketable, the county official issues a certificate of title to the buyer.

4. Title Insurance. Private enterprise's answer to the title-search issue was to develop companies that performed the searches and guaranteed the results. If the insurer is satisfied with the results of the search, it will issue a title-insurance policy to both the lender and owner, if the owner so desires. Title companies also submit title reports, which must be "marked up" by the buyer's attorney assuring that all stated objections have been removed. (See exhibits 9.9 and 9.10.)

4. Create a checklist system for documents

Settlements are paper blizzards! Devise an effective checklist that assures coordination of all documentation. Primarily, all documentation is broken into basic categories:

a. Bank

1. Loan closing statement
2. Assumption forms
3. Payoff forms
4. Title policy
5. Credit report
6. RESPA settlement sheet
7. Appraisal
8. Deed of trust
9. Mortgage notes
10. Releases
11. Attorney's title opinion
12. Survey

b. Buyer

1. Copies of most bank forms
2. Owner's title policy
3. Tax certificate
4. Survey
5. Warranty deed
6. Tax filings
7. Insurance policy
8. Settlement sheets
9. Water bills
10. Property inspection report
11. Escrow assignment
12. Amortization schedules
13. Bill of sale
14. Check disbursement sheet
15. Lien affidavit
16. Other affidavits
17. Judgment note
18. Financing statements

c. Seller

1. Settlement sheet
2. Release or satisfactions
3. Insurance credit
4. Bill of sale
5. Water/sewer bill
6. Tax prorations
7. Installment sales contract
8. Judgment note
9. PMM mortgages
10. Leases

Considering the myriad of complex documentation, is it any wonder paralegals are essential to all lawyers in the real estate field?

5. Investigation and collection of information for settlement

a. INSURANCE FOR THE BUYER

As previously noted, some jurisdictions impose an equitable form of ownership on the party executing an agreement of sale. Risk-of-loss provisions require that an insurance binder be secured immediately. Shop around for insurance, since rates vary dramatically. Better yet, seek coverage through the seller's present insurer, who will usually provide lower rates.

b. UTILITIES AND FUEL OIL

Contact the buyer and inform them that names must be changed on all utilities as of the date of settlement. Some paralegals take care of this function for the client, and it is a good generator of good will.

Fuel oil can be measured the day before settlement or pumped out for credit to the seller.

c. LEASES

As discussed, a seller who wishes to remain on the premises after settlement must be bound by the provision of a lease. If the dwelling to be purchased is multifamily, review all present leases to see the effects this transaction will have on those leases. Notify all tenants in writing of the change of ownership. Verify also the status of the previous owner's right to security deposits and personal property. In most cases, a written assignment of all leases should be drafted.

d. Amortization

The paralegal should also acquire the amortization schedule and enter its costs to both buyer and seller, if applicable, on the settlement sheet. Schedules can be obtained from many financial institutions and realty companies.

e. Taxes

1. Real estate. Contact the state and local tax assessors', or collectors', offices and determine the current state of taxes on the property. Provide the tax officials with an exact address, name, and any other information that will expedite their task. If delinquent taxes are reported, be sure to ascertain the amount of penalties and interest that will accrue up to the date of settlement.

2. Inheritance/estate taxes. Investigate possible estate taxes owed with the office of the register of wills or other designated authority.

3. Federal taxes. Visit your local district office of the Internal Revenue Service to see if the files contain a list of federal tax liens on the property. Written correspondence with the IRS is also advisable on a particular client who may have a problem.

f. Liens and Other Nontax Encumbrances

Mortgages. If the seller's property is subject to any initial or secondary mortgages, they must be satisfied before any settlement can occur. In order to compute the settlement-sheet, request from the mortgagee a statement regarding:

1. Mortgagor's account number
2. Name of mortgagor as it relates to satisfaction
3. An itemized payoff amount designating principal, interest, and other charges
4. All credits, like escrow balances
5. Interest fee per day for late payment

Mortgage-Assumption Barriers. Take great pains to verify that an assumable-mortgage plan is legally plausible. If a due-on-sale clause is present in the existing mortgage, it is imperative that a written modification come forth from the bank allowing the assumption.

Judgments. Seller of the property must satisfactorily demonstrate that all judgments lodged against the premises have been satisfied prior to settlement.

Miscellaneous Objections

1. Divorce Problems. Interestingly enough, any domestic breakdown may make a potential lender nervous about financing the transaction, especially in this age of equitable distribution and community property. Usually satisfactory is a separation agreement clarifying property rights in a prospective purchase.

2. Municipal Liens. Increasingly, fees for municipal water rent, refuse collection, and sewer assessments turn up as liens on real property. Check with the prothonotary's office or other authorized official to verify their status.

g. Warranty Assurance: Inspection of Systems

As we have pointed out, buyers can negotiate to assure certain warranties. At a minimum, in most residential real estate, sellers must warrant the *roof* and *septic system* as well as *plumbing, furnace,* and *electrical system.* Order all relevant inspections to insure that the systems are functioning.

h. Document Preparation

While the list of documents provided in this chapter covers all the necessary ones, the preparation of those documents rests with various parties, including the bank, seller's or buyer's attorney, and the title company. The paralegal's organization of all pertinent data and documentation is a critical function in the law office.

At a minimum, a paralegal can expect to be responsible for the coordination and collection of the following from his or her own law office:

1. Deed
2. Mortgage
3. Mortgage note
4. Judgment releases and notes
5. Satisfaction pieces
6. Purchase money mortgages

7. Installment sales contracts
8. Creative finance agreements
9. Assumption agreements
10. Leases
11. Corporate or partnership documentation
12. Assignment of leases
13. Title report
14. Attorney's certificate of title
15. Right-of-way agreements
16. Powers-of-attorneys
17. Stipulation against mechanic's liens
18. Other relevant documents

i. SECURITY CERTIFICATES AND OTHER DOCUMENTS

Check local rules and customs for presentation of the following documents at settlement:

1. Termite inspection and report
2. Percolation tests
3. Water potability
4. Certificate of occupancy
5. FHA or VA certificates
6. Licenses
7. Zoning certifications
8. Corporate certificate of authority
9. Copies of the survey

j. ROUGH DRAFT OF THE SETTLEMENT SHEET

At the rough-draft stage, the paralegal should strive for perfection. Since mathematical errors are possible, and new information may change the figures, it usually pays to wait until settlement before a final version is tabulated. Psychologically, it's better to prepare the sheet and then verify it against the data generated at the settlement table. More on the preparation of the sheet later.

6. The settlement process

a. BEING ORGANIZED AND COMFORTABLE

As the paralegal can readily envision, the bulk of the work for settlement takes place *long* before settlement, and if the paralegal is well organized and attentive to detail and cooperates with the assigned attorney, the entire settlement should take no more than one hour. Some very experienced people feel more than thirty minutes is evidence of a sloppy settlement. Well-intended as everyone may be, invariably things always crop up. Be prepared for such eventualities as a miscalculation, forgotten satisfaction, or insufficient tax payout. As sure as the sun rises, so too those little hitches. Emphasize the word *little,* because people have a tendency of making grandiose issues out of them. Settlement is not the end of the world, yet it must be in a slightly formal atmosphere. This assures the attention of all parties.

b. THE SETTLEMENT SHEET

RESPA, an act of Congress concerning settlements, has provided a uniform process and form to be adhered to in the tabulation of a settlement sheet. A sample settlement sheet is shown in Figure 9.5. What follows is a general review of the major features of the settlement sheet.

1. Summaries of borrower's and seller's transaction: page 1. One feature promoting ease of preparation is the columnar separation between figures for buyer and seller.

2. Settlement charges at page 2 L. One confusing feature of the settlement form is that page 2 must be completed before you do page 1. Do you know line 1400 on 2 is referred back over to 1 at lines 103 and 502 accordingly?

3. Gross amounts are listed at 101–401.

4. Personal property (washer, dryer, etc.) is also provided space at 102–402.

5. Prorations for taxes, sewer assessments due are provided for both buyer and seller at lines 106–108; 406–408. Note the *to*—fill in dates for purposes of proration.

6. Adjustments for these prorations are balanced out on either side of the sheet to reflect an advance payment by the seller,

FIGURE 9.4

BUYERS ESTIMATE OF CLOSING COSTS

Property: _____ Date: _____

Furnished by: _____ Consideration: _____

Listed below are the approximate settlement charges required to complete settlement on this property. These charges are estimates and are as accurate as could be determined at this date.

Settlement Items as of: _____

1. Title Insurance $ _____
2. Title Endorsement # 300 $ _____
3. Recording Deed & Mortgage $ _____
4. Notaries $ _____
5. Conveyancing & Realtor Services $ _____
6. Transfer Tax @ 1% of Sales Price $ _____
7. Mechanics Lien Insurance $ _____
8. Fire Insurance $ _____
9. Tax Adjustments: (Debit or Credit) $ _____

       School _____ $_____
       Township _____ $_____
       County _____ $_____
       Sewer _____ $_____
             Total:$_____ $ _____

10. _____ $ _____
11. _____ $ _____ $ _____

Mortgage Charges

1. Mortgage Company Fee $ _____
2. Appraisal & Credit Report $ _____
3. Mortgage Interest to: _____ $ _____
4. FHA Insurance Premium $ _____
5. _____ $ _____ $ _____

Prepaid Escrow Account

1. Taxes _____ $ _____
2. Fire Insurance $ _____
3. Sewer Rent $ _____
4. FHA-MIP $ _____ $ _____

            Grand Total: $ _____

Monthly Payment: _____

     Interest & Principle $ _____
     1/12 Annual Taxes $ _____
     1/12 Annual Sewer Rent $ _____
     Monthly Fire Insurance $ _____
     _____ $ _____
          Total: $ _____

Settlement will be held on _____ in the Offices of TITLE ABSTRACT COMPANY OF PENNSYLVANIA, located at _____. Please bring a certified check made payable to TITLE ABSTRACT COMPANY OF PA. in the amount of $ _____.

Buyers hereby acknowledge that they have read and received a copy of these estimated costs.

_____ (SEAL)

_____ (SEAL)

         For: _____
                              Broker

credit given for that payment, and a buyer's reimbursement to the seller for those payments. See lines 210–212 and 510–512.

    7. Blank lines on the front page at 213–219 and 513–519 are provided for any other adjustments between buyers and sellers.

    8. Spaces are provided at 203 and 504, 505 for pay offs of existing initial and secondary mortgages.

    9. On page 2 at lines 701–702, provision is made for real estate commission. Don't assume any rate of commission, since the rate is negotiable.

    10. At page 2 at lines 801–807, all fees related to the loan acquisition are highlighted. These are generally borrower's expenses.

    11. At line 901, prepaid interest computed at a daily rate as paid by borrower.

    12. Other borrower's expenses including hazard and mortgage insurance and escrow deposits are supplied at lines 902–1005. Always borrower's expense.

FIGURE 9.5

A. **MERIDIAN TITLE INSURANCE COMPANY** POLICY NO. _____ U. S. DEPARTMENT OF HOUSING AND URBAN DEVELOPMENT **SETTLEMENT STATEMENT**	B. TYPE OF LOAN
	1. ☐ FHA 2. ☐ FMHA 3. ☐ CONV. UNINS. 4. ☐ VA 5. ☐ CONV. INS.
	6. File Number: 7. Loan Number:
	8. Mortgage Insurance Case Number:

C. NOTE: This form is furnished to give you a statement of actual settlement costs. Amounts paid to and by the settlement agent are shown. Items marked "(p.o.c.)" were paid outside the closing; they are shown here for informational purposes and are not included in the totals.

D. NAME OF BORROWER:	E. NAME OF SELLER:	F. NAME OF LENDER:
G. PROPERTY LOCATION:	H. SETTLEMENT AGENT: PLACE OF SETTLEMENT:	L. SETTLEMENT DATE:

J. SUMMARY OF BORROWER'S TRANSACTION		K. SUMMARY OF SELLER'S TRANSACTION	
100. GROSS AMOUNT DUE FROM BORROWER:		**400. GROSS AMOUNT DUE TO SELLER:**	
101. Contract sales price		401. Contract sales price	
102. Personal property		402. Personal property	
103. Settlement charges to borrower (line 1400)		403.	
104.		404.	
105.		405.	
Adjustments for items paid by seller in advance		*Adjustments for items paid by seller in advance*	
106. City/town taxes to		406. City/town taxes to	
107. County taxes to		407. County taxes to	
108. Assessments to		408. Assessments to	
109. School tax		409. School tax	
110. Water rent		410. Water rent	
111. Sewer rent		411. Sewer rent	
112.		412.	
120. GROSS AMOUNT DUE FROM BORROWER		420. GROSS AMOUNT DUE TO SELLER	
200. AMOUNTS PAID BY OR IN BEHALF OF BORROWER:		**500. REDUCTIONS IN AMOUNT DUE TO SELLER:**	
201. Deposit or earnest money		501. Excess deposit (see instructions)	
202. Principal amount of new loan(s)		502. Settlement charges to seller (line 1400)	
203. Existing loan(s) taken subject to		503. Existing loan(s) taken subject to	
204.		504. Payoff of first mortgage loan	
205.		505. Payoff of second mortgage loan	
206.		506.	
207.		507.	
208.		508.	
209.		509.	
Adjustments for items unpaid by seller		*Adjustments for items unpaid by seller*	
210. City/Town taxes to		510. City/Town taxes to	
211. County Taxes to		511. County taxes to	
212. Assessments to		512. Assessments to	
213. School tax		513. School tax	
214. Water rent		514. Water rent	
215. Sewer rent		515. Sewer rent	
216.		516.	
217.		517.	
218.		518.	
219.		519.	
220. TOTAL PAID BY/FOR BORROWER		520. TOTAL REDUCTION AMOUNT DUE SELLER	
300. CASH AT SETTLEMENT FROM/TO BORROWER		**600. CASH AT SETTLEMENT TO/FROM SELLER**	
301. Gross amount due from borrower (line 120)		601. Gross amount due to seller (line 420)	
302. Less amounts paid by/for borrower (line 220)	( )	602. Less reductions in amount due seller (line 520)	( )
303. CASH ([ ] FROM) ([ ] TO) BORROWER		603. CASH ([ ] TO) ([ ] FROM) SELLER	

L. SETTLEMENT CHARGES	PAID FROM BORROWER'S FUNDS AT SETTLEMENT	PAID FROM SELLER'S FUNDS AT SETTLEMENT
700. TOTAL SALES/BROKER'S COMMISSION based on price $ @ % =		
Division of Commission (line 700) as follows:		
701. $ to		
702. $ to		
703. Commission paid at Settlement		
704.		
800. ITEMS PAYABLE IN CONNECTION WITH LOAN		
801. Loan Origination Fee %		
802. Loan Discount %		
803. Appraisal Fee to		
804. Credit Report to		
805. Lender's Inspection Fee		
806. Mortgage Insurance Application Fee to		
807. Assumption Fee		
808.		
809.		
810.		
811.		
900. ITEMS REQUIRED BY LENDER TO BE PAID IN ADVANCE		
901. Interest from to @ $ /day		
902. Mortgage Insurance Premium for months to		
903. Hazard Insurance Premium for years to		
904. years to		
905.		
1000. RESERVES DEPOSITED WITH LENDER		
1001. Hazard insurance months @ $ per month		
1002. Mortgage insurance months @ $ per month		
1003. City property taxes months @ $ per month		
1004. County property taxes months @ $ per month		
1005. Annual assessments months @ $ per month		
1006. months @ $ per month		
1007. months @ $ per month		
1008. months @ $ per month		
1100. TITLE CHARGES		
1101. Settlement or closing fee to		
1102. Abstract or title search to		
1103. Title examination to		
1104. Title insurance binder to		
1105. Document preparation to		
1106. Notary fees to		
1107. Attorney's fees to		
(includes above items numbers;)		
1108. Title insurance to		
(includes above items numbers;)		
1109. Lender's coverage $		
1110. Owner's coverage $		
1111. Endorsements		
1112.		
1113.		
1200. GOVERNMENT RECORDING AND TRANSFER CHARGES		
1201. Recording fees: Deed $; Mortgage $; Releases $		
1202. City/county tax/stamps: Deed $; Mortgage $		
1203. State tax/stamps; Deed $; Mortgage $		
1204.		
1205.		
1300. ADDITIONAL SETTLEMENT CHARGES		
1301. Survey to		
1302. Pest inspection to		
1303.		
1304.		
1305.		
1400. TOTAL SETTLEMENT CHARGES (enter on lines 103, Section J and 502, Section K)		

THE ABOVE SETTLEMENT EXAMINED, APPROVED AND COPY OF SAME RECEIVED, AUTHORIZATION IS GIVEN TO MAKE DISTRIBUTION AND PAYMENTS IN ACCORDANCE HEREWITH.

SELLER
ADDRESS

PURCHASER
ADDRESS

13. All title charges in insurance and title examination, as well as legal fees and notorial fees are included at lines 1101–1110.

14. Lines 1200–1302 include tax, recordation fees, and survey expenses.

Of course, the trick is to have all this information at your disposal. The actual tabulation is a snap! Getting to that point requires hard work. To ease anxieties, use check lists and disbursement-check ledgers. Be very liberal in the distribution of all relevant documentation. Bring enough copies for everyone!

7. Post-settlement

a. RECORDATION

To secure the safety of this transaction, all necessary documents including mortgage and deed must be recorded at the courthouse. Take along the required fees.

b. TITLE POLICY

Upon receipt of actual title-insurance policy, review and send to purchaser.

c. ESCROW ACCOUNTS

If any repairs were necessary or there were other contingencies, see that they were dealt with and then disburse funds.

The final tasks are to mail recorded documents to the buyer, send a letter of thanks to the client, and close the file.

VIII. LANDLORD/TENANT LAW: GENERAL PRINCIPLES

A. General Background of the Leasehold

This is a big area of law, so large that legal specializations are becoming more common in law firms, particularly in the commercial realm. Discussed thus far are some of the leasehold interests common between landlord and a tenant. They include:

1. Periodic tenancy (estates from year to year)
2. Tenancy at will
3. Tenancy at sufferance

See section II for a review of these leaseholds. A normal lease with durational requirement met is simply known as a *tenancy for a term*. Remember that these leasehold estates in land do not give tenants a formidable interest in the land, only a possessory interest in the land, to the exclusion of all others including the landlord for the duration of the lease.

B. Termination of the Leasehold

A variety of mechanisms exist to legally terminate the leasehold obligation. (See exhibit 9.11.)

1. *Expiration.* If the tenancy has a fixed durational period with no renewal provision, the lease expires automatically on the final day.
2. *Mutual Cancellation.* Both landlord and tenant have the right to cancel the lease.
3. *By Breach.* Depending on your jurisdiction, a material breach may justify termination of a lease without detriment to the party.
4. *Destruction.* A fire that destroys a rental unit usually destroys the underlying obligation.
5. *Constructive Eviction.* Landlord's absolute failure to repair premises gives rise to this remedy.
6. *Abandonment.*

EXHIBIT 9.11

SAMPLE FORM

IN THE COURT OF COMMON PLEAS OF DELAWARE COUNTY,

CIVIL ACTION-LAW

CHESTER HOUSING AUTHORITY   :   NO.
            VS.
            JOHN DOE   :   I.D.

Complaint

1. Plaintiff, Chester Housing Authority, is a political subdivision of the Commonwealth   , with its principal office at 250 Main Street, Chester, Delaware County,

2. The Defendant, John Doe, is an individual who resides at 3 Pine Terrace, Big Homes, Chester, Delaware County,

3. The Plaintiff is authorized to construct, own, maintain and operate Federally-Assisted low rent housing in the City of Chester and pursuant to such authorization, maintains and operates units known as the Big Homes which house low-income families.

4. By Lease Agreement dated, October 25, 1979, a copy of which is attached hereto and marked Exhibit "A", Plaintiff leased to Defendant the unit known and described as 3 Pine Terrace, Big Homes, Chester, Delaware County,

5. The initial monthly rent for the Defendant was $78.00 per month. However, on March 1, 1981, the rent was raised to $81.00 per month which is now the current rent.

6. In violation of the terms of said Lease the Defendant has failed to pay his rent and currently owes to the Plaintiff the sum of $1,072.50.

7. Notice to Remove was given to Defendant in accordance with Law.

8. The Defendant retains possession of the premises and refuses to give up possession of the premises to the Plaintiff and furthermore, refuses to pay the delinquent rent.

WHEREFORE, Plaintiff seeks possession of said premises and eviction of the Defendant therefrom in addition to Judgment for $1,072.50 plus costs and any rent due and owing at the time of the hearing of this matter.

                                         _____
                                    JACK LAWYER, ATTORNEY FOR THE
                                        HOUSING AUTHORITY

COMMONWEALTH OF

                    SS:

COUNTY OF   :

Bill Jones, being duly sworn according to law deposes and says that he is the Executive Director of the Chester Housing Authority, the Plaintiff in the within Complaint, and that the facts set forth herein are true and correct to the best of his knowledge, information and belief.

                                         _____
                                    BILL JONES

SWORN TO AND SUBSCRIBED
before me this   day
of   A.D., 1981

_____
NOTARY PUBLIC

C. Elements of a Lease

At a minimum, all leases should contain the following clauses and provisions:

1. Description of the leased premises
2. Description of the parties
3. Durational requirements
4. Consideration/rent
5. Purposes for which the leasehold may be used
6. Assignment or subletting clause
7. Security-deposit clause
8. Insurance provisions
9. Signatures
10. Attestation clauses

Please review the very comprehensive leases provided in exhibits 9.12 and 9.13a and b. A major portion of the paralegal's energy will be in the preliminary drafting and negotiation of leases.

EXHIBIT 9.12

COMMERCIAL LEASE AGREEMENT

THIS AGREEMENT, made the   day of   , 1981, by and between   and   , (hereinafter called Lessor), of the one part, and   and   , (hereinafter called Lessee), of the other part.

WITNESSETH THAT:

1. Lessor does hereby demise and let unto Lessee all that certain grocery store or food market, including all fixtures, equipment, furnishings, inventory and everything else now situate in premises E. Cedar Street, used in the operation of a grocery business, in the City of   , County of   State of   , to be used and occupied as a grocery store for the term of three (3) years with an option to continue an additional three (3) years, to commence on July   , 1981 for annual rent of Three Thousand ($3,000.00) Dollars, lawful money of the United States of America, payable in monthly installments in advance during the said term of this lease, or any renewal hereof, in the sum of Two Hundred Fifty ($250.00) Dollars per month for the first year and then with increases of Fifteen ($15.00) Dollars per month each year thereafter.

2. This lease is contingent upon the approval by the Commonwealth   and the City of   of various business privilege, merchandise, food, health and other licenses required for the lawful operation of the said grocery store.

3. If the Lessor is unable to give Lessee possession of the demised premises for any reason whatsoever then this lease shall become null and void and Lessee's security deposit shall be returned immediately to Lessee plus the return of any prepaid rents.

4. Lessor agrees to pay Seventy (70%) percent of any water rents arising by metered water connection or for any charges for water consumption upon the demised premises and Lessee agrees to pay Thirty (30%) percent of the said charges.

5. Lessee is to have fire, liability and theft insurance on the stock in trade, inventory and leased premises at Lessee's own expense.

6. Lessor agrees to pay for all charges with respect to the gas utility on the premises and covenants to make any repairs of the gas heater made necessary by wear and tear, accident of other causes.

7. All repairs of plumbing, heating and electrical connections and implements will be made by Lessor. Maintenance of the premises will also be the sole responsibility of the Lessor as made necessary by ordinary wear and tear, accident or other causes.

8. Lessor agrees to payment of Thirty (30%) percent of the electrical utility used in the demised premises and Lessee agrees to pay Seventy (70%) percent of the said utility.

9. All rent shall be payable without prior notice or demand at the office of _____, Esquire, 1534 Magee Avenue,   or at such other place as Lessor may from time to time designate by notice in writing.

10. Lessee covenants and agrees that he will:

    (a) Without demand pay the rent and all other charges herein reserved as rent at the times and at the place that the same are payable;

    (b) Keep the demised premises clean and free from all ashes, dirt and other refuse matter;

(c) Comply with any requirements of any of the constituted public authorities, and with the terms of any State or Federal statute or local ordinance or regulation applicable to Lessee for his use of the demised premises, and save Lessor harmless from penalties, fines, costs or damages resulting from failure so to do;

(d) Use every reasonable precaution against fire;

(e) Surrender possession of the demised premises at the expiration of this lease;

(f) Give to the Lessor prompt written notice of any accident, fire or damage occuring on or to the demised premises;

(g) Lessee shall be responsible for the condition of the pavement and curb in front of the leased premises, being the grocery store, and keep the pavement free from snow and ice.

11. Lessee shall be permitted to place any sign on or in any part of the premises to advertise its business so long as the sign is reasonably calculated to accomplish this purpose.

12. Lessee does herewith deposit with the Lessor the sum of Two Hundred Fifty ($250.00) Dollars as security for the full and faithful performance by the Lessee of its obligations under this said security deposit to be held by the Lessor in an escrow fund, pursuant to the terms and provision of the Assembly.

13. Lessor hereby agrees to assist Lessee in obtaining a food coupon and cigarette license from the Commonwealth of Pennsylvania, business privilege, merchandise, and health licenses from the City.

14. Lessor does hereby agree that Lessee is given the right of first refusal to purchase the property in the event that Lessor decides to sell said property. In the event that Lessor obtains a bona fide offer to purchase said property, Lessee shall be given the opportunity to match the price obtained by the Lessor and shall have sixty (60) days after receiving notice from the Lessor of the offer, a copy of which shall be submitted to determine whether or not Lessee will match the offer and purchase the property.

15. Should Lessee waive the purchase of the said property, Lessor covenants and warrants that the new owner takes the premises subject to this lease and is bound hereby.

16. Lessor further covenants and warrants that the leased premises includes shop, storage room, and sign.

17. In the event of the failure of Lessor promptly to make repairs, Lessee may perform such repairs, the cost thereof at the sole option of Lessee to be charged to Lessor against the monthly rent.

18. It is mutually agreed that either party hereto may terminate this lease at the end of said term by giving to the other party written notice thereof at least sixty (60) days prior thereto. All notices must be given by certified mail, return receipt requested.

19. All rights and liabilities herein given to, or imposed upon, the respective parties hereto shall extend to and bind the several and respective heirs, executors, administrators, successors and assigns of the said parties.

IN WITNESS WHEREOF, the parties hereto have executed these presents the day and year first above written, and intend to be legally bound thereby.

D. Tenants' Rights

A variety of rights made to the benefit of the tenant derive from both common-law and statutory principles. Some of the more commonly adopted rights are listed below.

1. Unconscionable lease clauses

As in other consumer contracts, unconscionable provisions in a lease will not be upheld or enforced. Such provisions are repugnant to general public policy, for example, a provision requiring an excessive lease period or exorbitant security deposit.

2. Right to visitors and guests

Use of the leasehold bestows certain possessory rights including the right to have social guests on your property.

3. Protection of escrow money

All damage deposits and security deposits are statutorily protected in most states.

4. Habitability

A few states have adopted an implied warranty of habitability as a right for tenants:

EXHIBIT 9.13a

There are 4 copies
of this agreement.
1
1. White ....Lessor
2. Yellow ...Agent
3. Pink ......Lessee
4. Blue ....

LEASE FOR REAL ESTATE
PART ONE OF A TWO PART AGREEMENT
This form recommended and approved for, but not restricted to
use by members of the Pennsylvania Association of Realtors when
used with an approved addendum attached hereto.
—— **Agent For The Lessor** ——

PRINCIPALS
(1-78)

𝕿𝖍𝖎𝖘 𝕬𝖌𝖗𝖊𝖊𝖒𝖊𝖓𝖙, made this..............................day of ..........................A.D. 19.........

Between ....

....hereinafter called Lessor, and

....hereinafter called Lessee,

1. (a) WITNESSETH: Lessor agrees to let unto the Lessee premises being known as........................

PROPERTY
(11-74)

.... in the

.... of .... , County of .... , State of Penna.

with improvements consisting of ....

....

upon the following terms and conditions to wit:

(b)	Total rental for entire term payable to Lessor	$........................
(c)	Payments in advance ☐ Monthly ☐ .... in the amount of:	$........................
(d)	Cash or check to be paid before possession by Lessee which is to be applied on account as follows:	

Advance rent..... .... 19.....to.............19..... Paid $ .... Due $ ....

On account of final payment of rent......................... Paid $ .... Due $ ....

Security deposit (see par. 1 (f)........................... Paid $ .... Due $ ....

Credit report... Paid $ .... Due $ ....

.... Paid $ _____ Due $ _____

Totals – Paid to date .... Paid $.................

Balance due before possession........................... Due $ ....

(e)	Adjusted payment of rent until regular due date, if any	$........................
(f)	Security deposit	$........................
(g)	Late charge if rent not paid within grace period	$........................
(h)	Due date for each payment..	
(i)	Term of this lease...	
(j)	Commencement date of lease................................ day of ...................A.D. 19.....	
(k)	Expiration date of lease.................................... day of ...................A.D. 19.....	
(l)	Required written notice to terminate this lease...	
(m)	Renewal term if not terminated by either party...	
(n)	Lessee will occupy premises ONLY as	
(o)	Maximum number of occupants under this lease..	
(p)	Payments to be made promptly when due in lawful money of the United States of America to: ☐ Lessor ☐ Agent	
(q)	Utilities & services to be supplied as follows:	

Lessor will supply: ☐ cold water, ☐ hot water , ☐ gas, ☐ heat, ☐ electric, ☐ lawn care,
☐ snow removal, ☐ janitor service, ☐ yearly oil burner cleaning, ☐ cesspool cleaning, ☐ ....
☐ Lawn & Shrubbery care. ☐ ....

Lessee will supply: ☐ cold water, ☐ hot water ☐ gas, ☐ heat, ☐ electric, ☐ lawn care,
☐ snow removal, ☐ water in excess of yearly minimum charge, ☐ yearly oil burner cleaning,
☐ cesspool cleaning, ☐ Lawn & Shrubbery care. ☐ ....

(r) Notwithstanding anything herein to the contrary, Lessee will pay cost of any or all repairs of any kind whatsoever,
occurring after commencement of this lease where the individual cost of each repair is less than $ ....

(s) No pets or animals of any kind whatsoever will be permitted on or within the herein described premises excepting

....

SPECIAL
CLAUSES

2.

ADDENDUM

3. The Lessor and Lessee agree for themselves, their respective heirs and successors and assigns to the herein described terms and
also to those set forth in the addendum attached hereto entitled "TERMS AND CONDITIONS," (PART TWO) all of which are to be
regarded as binding and as strict legal conditions.

LESSEE................ LESSEE................ LESSEE................ LESSOR................ LESSOR................ AGENT................

INITIALS

Exhibit 9.13b

FORM 7-8
FORM L-1G
(REV. 1-78)

PART TWO OF A TWO PART AGREEMENT
GENERAL LEASE
TERMS AND CONDITIONS

This form recommended and approved for, but not restricted to,
use by members of the Pennsylvania Association of REALTORS®
Copyright Pennsylvania Association of Realtors 1973

Special Clauses	
Taxes (5-72)	4. (a) Lessee agrees to pay as rent in addition to the minimum rental herein reserved, all taxes, sewer rent, garbage and/or trash collection charges assessed or imposed upon the demised premises and/or the building of which the demised premises is a part during the term of this lease, in excess of and over and above those assessed or imposed at the time of making this lease. The amount due hereunder on account of such taxes shall be apportioned for that part of the first tax year, as assessed, and each subsequent tax year, as assessed thereafter during the term of this lease including extensions or renewals hereof. The same shall be paid by the Lessee to the Lessor as additional rent on or before sixty days from the Agent's or the Lessor's notice to the Lessee having been delivered as notice of any such tax increase.
	(b) Unless specified herein to the contrary, the percentage of any such tax increases to be paid by the Lessee hereunder shall be apportioned in accordance with that percentage which the Lessee's rent represents to the total income that the building would yield if fully leased.
Fire Insurance Premiums	(c) Lessee further agrees to pay to Lessor as additional rent all increase or increases in fire insurance premiums upon the demised premises and/or the building of which the demised premises is a part, due to an increase in the rate of fire insurance in excess of the rate on the demised premises at the time of making this lease, if said increase is caused by any act or neglect of the Lessee or the nature of the Lessee's business.
Sewer Rent	(d) Lessee further agrees to pay as additional rent, if there is a metered water connection to said premises. all sewer rental or charges for use of sewers, sewage system, and sewage treatment works servicing the demised premises in excess of the yearly minimum of such sewer charges, immediately when the same become due.
Condition of Pavement	(e) Lessee shall be responsible for the condition of the pavement, curb, cellar doors, awnings and other erections in the pavement during the term of this lease; shall keep the pavement free from snow and ice, and shall be, and hereby agrees that Lessee is solely liable for any accidents, due or alleged to be due to their defective condition, or to any accumulations of snow and ice.
Security Deposit (9-75)	5. The "security deposit" specified in Par. #1. (f) shall be held by Agent as security for the performance of all the terms, covenants and conditions of this lease and for the cost of any trash removal, housecleaning and the cost of repairs and/or the correction of damage (which is, in the opinion of the Lessor and/or Agent, in excess of normal wear and tear); otherwise, the "security deposit" or any balance thereof shall be returned after the Lessee has vacated and left the premises in an acceptable condition (following a personal inspection by Lessor and/or Agent) and surrendered all keys to Agent. If the Lessor determines that any loss, damage or injury chargeable to the Lessee hereunder, exceeds the security deposit, the Lessor at his option, may retain the said sum as liquidated damages or may apply the sum against any actual loss, damage or injury and the balance thereof will be the responsibility of the Lessee. Lessor's determination of the amount, if any, to be returned to the Lessee shall be final. It is further understood and agreed that the said security deposit is not to be considered as the last payment under the lease, however the rights of the Lessor shall not be hindered to retain the security deposit, or a portion therefrom as payment on account of uncollected rents, if any.
	The aforementioned "security deposit" shall be paid to the Agent who will deposit same in a separate custodial type account. Agent shall keep records of all funds so deposited as required in accordance with the Act of July 9, 1957, P.L. 608, Section 4. Said account will be clearly identified as required indicating the date and from whom he received money, the date deposited, the date of withdrawals and other pertinent information concerning this transaction. It is understood and agreed that should the property herein mentioned be sold, exchanged, transferred or conveyed to a new owner, that at the time of settlement, any money held as a security deposit shall be transferred to the new owner or his agent, to be continued to be held as a security deposit.
Affirmative Covenants of Lessor	6. (a) If the terms in paragraph #1. (q) provide for the Lessor to supply heat to Lessee, the Lessor agrees to furnish a reasonable amount of heat commencing not before the first day of October, and continuing not later than the first day of May following, in each year. In consideration that no extra charge is made therefor, should Lessor fail to supply same for any reason, Lessor shall not be liable for any damage caused by any such failure not due to gross negligence on the part of the Lessor, not for any damage to property of Lessee caused in any manner by fire, water or stream, or the lack thereof.
	(b) If the Lessee so desires, Lessor, if possible, may make available to Lessee, without charge, a space in the building for the storage of goods and effects of Lessee. In consideration of the fact that no extra charge is made for the furnishing of such space by the Lessor, it is understood that Lessor shall not be liable for loss or damage to any stored goods through fire or theft or any cause whatever, and Lessee expressly releases Lessor as bailee or otherwise from all claims for any such loss or damage. It is further understood that the use of storage space by the Lessee shall be limited to the time of the Lessee's occupancy, and that goods left over thirty days after the expiration of Lessee's occupancy may be sold for storage charges at public or private sale without further notice to Lessee.
	(c) The Lessor may furnish additional service not herein provided for but any such service shall be gratuitous unless otherwise agreed and shall not be an obligation of the Lessor or part of the consideration for the rent.
Place of Payment	7. All rent shall be payable without prior notice or demand at the office of Lessor or Agent as specified in paragraph #1. (p).
Affirmative Covenants of Lessee (11-74)	8. Lessee covenants and agrees that he will without demand:
Payment of Rent	(a) Pay the rent and all other charges herein reserved as rent on the days and times and at the place that the same are made payable, without fail, and if Lessor shall at any time or times accept said rent or rent charges after the same have become due and payable, such acceptance shall not excuse delay upon subsequent occasions, or constitute or be construed as a waiver of any of Lessor's rights. Lessee agrees that any charge or payment herein reserved, included, or agreed to be treated or collected as rent and/or any charges, expenses, or costs herein agreed to be paid by the Lessee may be proceeded for and recovered by the Lessor by legal process in the same manner as rent due and in arrears.
Late Charges (11-74)	(b) All rental payments are due and payable on the due date as specified in paragraph #1. (h) of this agreement or within five days thereafter (grace period) without penalty. However, after 5:00 PM on the fifth day after due date as aforementioned, any rental payment not paid in full will be subject to a late charge. Payments not made on or before 5:00 PM on the tenth day after due date, together with late charge, may be referred to Magistrate or Justice of the Peace for the collection and/or ejectment.
Cleaning, Repairing, etc.	(c) Keep the demised premises clean and free from all ashes, dirt and other refuse matter; replace all broken glass windows, doors, etc.; keep all waste and drain pipes open; repair all damages to plumbing and to the demised premises; in general, keep the same in as good order and repair as they are at the beginning of the term of this lease, reasonable wear and tear and damage by accidental fire or other casualty not occurring through negligence of Lessee or those employed by or acting for Lessee alone excepted. The Lessee agrees to surrender the demised premises in the same condition in which Lessee has herein agreed to keep the same during the continuance of this lease.
Requirements of Public Authorities	(d) Comply with any requirements of any of the constituted public authorities, and with the terms of any State or Federal statute or local ordinance or regulation applicable to Lessee or his use of the demised premises, and save Lessor harmless from penalties, fines, costs or damages resulting from failure to do so.
Fire	(e) Use every reasonable precaution against fire.
Surrender of Possession (11-74)	(f) Peaceably deliver up and surrender possession of the demised premises to the Lessor at the expiration or sooner termination of this lease, promptly delivering to Lessor at his office, all keys for the demised premises, with all trash and personal belongings removed and building(s) broom-swept clean.
Notice of Fire, etc.	(g) Give to Lessor prompt written notice of any accident, fire or damage occurring on or to the demised premises.
Pay for Gas and Electricity	(h) Promptly pay for all gas and electricity, water, heat, lawn care and services consumed in the herein demised premises during the continuance of this lease if so specified in paragraph #1 (q); and should Lessee fail to make these payments when due, Lessor shall have the right to settle therefor, such sums to be considered additional rent and collectible from Lessee, as such, by distress or other process, and to have all the priorities given by law to claims for rent.
Indemnification	(i) Indemnify and save Lessor harmless from any and all loss occasioned by Lessee's breach of any of the covenants, terms and conditions of this lease, or caused by his family, guests, visitors, agents and employees.
Negative Covenants of Lessee	9. Lessee covenants and agrees that he will do none of the following things without the consent in writing of Lessor:
Use of Premises	(a) Occupy the demised premises in any other manner or for any other purpose than as above set forth in paragraph #1 (n).
Assignment and Subletting	(b) Assign, mortgage or pledge this lease or under-let or sub-lease the demised premises, or any part thereof, or permit any other person, firm or corporation to occupy the demised premises, or any part thereof; nor shall any assignee or sub-lessee assign, mortgage or pledge this lease or such sub-lease, without an additional written consent by the Lessor, and without such consent no such assignment, mortgage or pledge shall be valid. If the Lessee becomes embarrassed or insolvent, or makes an assignment for the benefit of creditors, or if a petition in

bankruptcy is filed by or against the Lessee or a bill in equity or other proceeding for the appointment of a receiver for the Lessee is filed, or if the real or personal property of the Lessee shall be sold or levied upon by any Sheriff, Marshal or Constable, the same shall be a violation of this covenant.

Signs

(c) Place or allow to be placed any stand, booth, sign or show case upon the doorsteps, vestibules or outside walls or pavements of said premises, or paint, place, erect or cause to be painted, placed or erected any sign, projection or device on or in any part of the premises. Lessee shall remove any sign, projection or device painted, placed or erected, if permission has been granted and restore the walls, etc., to their former conditions, at or prior to the expiration of this lease. In case of the breach of this covenant (in addition to all other remedies given to Lessor in case of the breach of any conditions or covenants of this lease) Lessor shall have the privilege of removing said stand, booth, sign, show case, projection or device, and restoring said walls, etc., to their former condition, and Lessee, at Lessor's option, shall be liable to Lessor for any and all expenses so incurred by Lessor.

Alterations Improvements

(d) Make any alterations, improvements, or additions to the demised premises. All alterations, improvements, additions or fixtures, whether installed before or after the execution of this lease, shall remain upon the premises at the expiration or sooner determination of this lease and become the property of Lessor, unless Lessor shall, prior to the determination of this lease, have given written notice to Lessee to remove the same, in which event Lessee will remove such alterations, improvements and additions and restore the premises to the same good order and condition in which they now are. Should Lessee fail to do so, Lessor may do so, collecting, at Lessor's option, the cost and expense thereof from Lessee as additional rent.

Machinery

(e) Use or operate any machinery that, in Lessor's opinion, is harmful to the building or disturbing to other tenants occupying other parts thereof.

Weights

(f) Place any weights in any portion of the demised premises beyond the safe carrying capacity of the structure.

Fire Insurance

(g) Do or suffer to be done, any act, matter or thing objectionable to the fire insurance companies, whereby the fire insurance or any other insurance now in force or hereafter to be placed on the demised premises, or any part thereof, or on the building of which the demised premises may be a part, shall become void or suspended, or whereby the same shall be rated as a more hazardous risk than at the date of execution of this lease, or employ any person or persons objectionable to the fire insurance companies or carry or have any benzine or explosive matter of any kind in and about the demised premises. In case of a breach of this covenant (in addition to all other remedies given to Lessor in case of the breach of any of the conditions of covenants of this lease) Lessee agrees to pay to Lessor as additional rent any and all increase or increases of premiums on insurance carried by Lessor on the demised premises, or any part thereof, or on the building of which the demised premises may be a part, caused in any way by the occupancy of Lessee.

Removal of Goods

(h) Remove, attempt to remove or manifest an intention to remove Lessee's goods or property from or out of the demised premises otherwise than in the ordinary and usual course of business, without having first paid and satisfied Lessor for all rent which may become due during the entire term of this lease.

Vacate Premises

(i) Vacate or desert said premises during the term of this lease, or permit the same to be empty and unoccupied.

Agency on Removal

10. The Lessee agrees that if, with the permission in writing of Lessor, Lessee shall vacate or decide at any time during the term of this lease, or any renewal thereof, to vacate the herein demised premises, prior to the expiration of this lease, or any renewal hereof, Lessee will not cause or allow any agent to represent Lessee in any sub-letting or reletting of the demised premises other than an agent approved by the Lessor, and that should Lessee do so, or attempt to do so, the Lessor may remove any signs that may be placed on or about the demised premises by such other agent without any liability to Lessee or to said agent, the Lessee assuming all responsibility for such action.

Lessor's Rights

11. Lessee covenants and agrees that Lessor shall have the right to do the following things and matters in and about the demised premises:

Inspection of Premises

(a) At all reasonable times by himself or his duly authorized agents to go upon and inspect the demised premises and every part thereof, and/or at his option to make repairs, alterations and additions to the demised premises or the building of which the demised premises is a part.

Rules and Regulations

(b) At any time or times and from time to time to make such rules and regulations as in his judgment may from time to time be necessary for the safety, care and cleanliness of the premises, and for the preservation of good order therein. Such rules and regulations shall, when notice thereof is given to Lessee, form a part of this lease.

Sale, Rent, Signs and Prospects (11-74)

(c) To display a "For Sale" sign at any time, and also, after notice from either party of intention to determine this lease, or at any time within six months prior to the expiration of his lease, a "For Rent" sign, or both "For Rent" and "For Sale" signs; and all of said signs shall be placed upon such part of the premises as Lessor may elect and may contain such matter as Lessor shall require. Prospective purchasers or tenants authorized by Lessor may inspect the premises Monday thru Saturday between the hours of 11:00 AM and 8:00 PM.

Discontinue Service, etc.

(d) The Lessor may discontinue all facilities furnished and services rendered by Lessor or any of them, not expressly covenanted for herein, it being understood that they constitute no part of the consideration for this lease.

12. (a) In the event that the demised premises is totally destroyed or so damaged by fire or other casualty not occurring through fault or negligence of the Lessee or those employed by or acting for him, that the same cannot be repaired or restored within a reasonable time, this lease shall absolutely cease and determine, and the rent shall abate for the balance of the term.

(b) If the damage caused as above be only partial and such that the premises can be restored to their former condition within a reasonable time, the Lessor may, at his option, restore the same with reasonable promptness, reserving the right to enter upon the demised premises for that purpose. The Lessor also reserves the right to enter upon the demised premises whenever necessary to repair damage caused by fire or other casualty to the building of which the demised premises is a part, even though the effect of such entry be to render the demised premises or a part thereof untenantable. In either event the rent shall be apportioned and suspended during the time the Lessor is in possession, taking into account the proportion of the demised premises rendered untenantable and the duration of the Lessor's possession. If a dispute arises as to the amount of rent due under this clause, Lessee agrees to pay the full amount claimed by Lessor. Lessee shall, however, have the right to proceed by law to recover the excess payment, if any.

Damage for Interrupted Use

(c) Lessor shall not be liable for any damage, compensation or claim by reason of inconvenience or annoyance arising from the necessity of repairing any portion of the building, the interruption in the use of the premises, or the termination of this lease by reason of the destruction of the premises.

Representation of Condition

13. The Lessor has let the demised premises in their present condition and without any representations on the part of the Lessor, his officers, employees, servants and/or agents. It is understood and agreed that Lessor is under no duty to make repairs or alterations at the time of letting or at any time thereafter.

Miscellaneous Agreements and Conditions

Effect of Repairs or Rentals

14. (a) No contract entered into or that may be subsequently entered into by Lessor with Lessee, relative to any alterations, additions, improvements or repairs, nor the failure of Lessor to make such alterations, additions, improvements or repairs as required by any such contract, nor the making by Lessor or his agents or contractors of such alterations, additions, improvements or repairs shall in any way affect the payment of the rent or said other charges at the time specified in this lease.

Waiver of Custom

(b) It is hereby covenanted and agreed, any law, usage or custom to the contrary notwithstanding, that Lessor shall have the right at all times to enforce the covenants and provisions of this lease in strict accordance with the terms hereof, notwithstanding any conduct or custom on the part of the Lessor in refraining from so doing at any time or times; and further, that the failure of Lessor at any time or times to enforce its rights under said covenants and provisions strictly in accordance with the same shall not be construed as having created a custom in any way or manner contrary to the specific terms, provisions and covenants of this lease or as having in any way or manner modified the same.

Conduct of Lessee

(c) This lease is granted upon the express condition that Lessee and/or the occupants of the premises herein leased, shall not conduct themselves in a manner which the Lessor in his sole opinion may deem improper or objectionable, and that if at any time during the term of this lease or any extension or continuation thereof, Lessee or any occupier of the said premises shall have conducted himself, herself or themselves in a manner which Lessor in his sole opinion deems improper or objectionable, Lessee shall be taken to have broken the covenants and conditions of this lease, and Lessor will be entitled to all of the rights and remedies granted and reserved herein, for the Lessee's failure to observe any of the covenants and conditions of this lease.

Failure of Lessee to Repair

(d) In the event of the failure of Lessee promptly to perform the covenants of Par. #8. (c) hereof, Lessor may go upon the demised premises and perform such covenants, the cost thereof, at the sole option of Lessor, to be charged to Lessee as additional and delinquent rent.

Remedies of Lessor (11-74)

15. If the Lessee

(a) Does not pay in full when due any and all installments of rent and/or any other charge or payment herein reserved, included, or agreed to be treated or collected as rent and/or any other charge, expense, or cost herein agreed to be paid by the Lessee; or

(b) Violates or fails to perform or otherwise breaks any covenant or agreement herein contained; or

(c) Vacates the demised premises or removes or attempts to remove or manifests an intention to remove any goods or property therefrom otherwise than in the ordinary and usual course of business without having first paid and satisfied the Lessor in full for all rent and other charges then due or that may thereafter become due until the expiration of the then current term, above mentioned; or

(d) Becomes embarrassed or insolvent, or makes an assignment for the benefit of creditors, or if a petition in bankruptcy is filed by or against the Lessee or a bill in equity or other proceeding for the appointment of a receiver for the Lessee is filed, or if proceedings for reorganization or for composition with creditors under any State or Federal law be instituted by or against Lessee, or if the real or personal property of the Lessee shall be sold or levied upon by any due process of law, then and in any or either of said events, there shall be deemed to be a breach of this lease, and thereupon ipso facto and without entry or other action by Lessor;

(d1) The rent for the entire unexpired balance of the term of this lease, as well as all other charges, payments, costs and expenses herein agreed to be paid by the Lessee, or at the option of Lessor any part thereof, and also all costs and officers' commissions including watchmen's wages and further including the five percent chargeable by Act of Assembly to the Lessor, shall, in addition to any and all installments of rent already due and payable and in arrears and/or any other charge or payment herein reserved, included or agreed to be treated or collected as rent, and/or any other charge, expense or cost herein agreed to be paid by the Lessee which may be due and payable and in arrears, be taken to be due and payable and in arrears as if by the terms and provisions of this lease, the whole balance of unpaid rent and other charges, payments, taxes, costs and expenses were on that date payable in advance; and if this lease or any part thereof is assigned, or if the premises or any part thereof is sub-let, Lessee hereby irrevocably constitutes and appoints Lessor Lessee's agent to collect the rents due by such assignee or sub-leasee and apply the same to the rent due hereunder without in any way affecting Lessee's obligation to pay any unpaid balance of rent due hereunder; or in the event of any of the foregoing at any time at the option of Lessor;

(d2) This lease and the term hereby created shall determine and become absolutely void without any right on the part of the Lessee to save the forfeiture by payment of any sum due or by other performance of any condition; term or covenant broken; whereupon, Lessor shall be entitled to recover damages for such breach in an amount equal to the amount of rent reserved for the balance of the term of this lease, less the fair rental value of the said demised premises, for the residue of said term.

Further Remedies of Lessor

16. In the event of any default as aforesaid, the Lessor, or anyone acting on Lessor's behalf, at Lessor's option:

(a) May without notice or demand enter the demised premises, breaking open locked doors if necessary to effect entrance, without liability to action for prosecution or damages for such entry or for the matter thereof, for the purpose of distraining or levying and for any other purposes, and take possession of and sell all goods and chattels at auction, on three days notice served in person on the Lessee, or left on the premises, and pay the said Lessor out of the proceeds, and even if the rent be not due and unpaid, should the Lessee at any time remove or attempt to remove goods and chattels from the premises without leaving enough thereon to meet the next periodical payment, Lessee authorizes the Lessor to follow for a period of ninety days after such removal, take possession of and sell at auction, upon like notice, sufficient of such goods to meet the proportion of rent accrued at the time of such removal; and the Lessee hereby releases and discharges the Lessor, and his agents from all claims, actions, suits, damages and penalties, for or by reason or on account of any entry, distraint, levy, appraisement or sale; and/or

(b) May enter the premises, and without demand proceed by distress and sale of the goods there found to levy the rent and/or other charges herein payable as rent, and all costs and officers' commissions, including watchmen's wages and sums chargeable to Lessor, and further including a sum equal to 5% of the amount of the levy as commissions to the constable or other person making the levy, shall be paid by the Lessee, and in such case all costs, officers' commission and other charges shall immediately attach and become part of the claim of Lessor for rent, and any tender of rent without said costs commission and charges made after the issue of a warrant of distress shall not be sufficient to satisfy the claim of the Lessor. Lessee hereby expressly waivers in favor of Lessor the benefit of all laws now made or which may hereafter be made regarding any limitation as to the goods upon which, or the timr within which, distress is to be made after removal of goods, and further relieves the Lessor of the obligations of proving or identifying such goods, it being the purpose and intent of this provision that all goods of Lessee, whether upon the demised premises or not, shall be liable to distress for rent. Lessee waives in favor of Lessor all rights under the Act of Assembly of April 6, 1951, P.L. 69, and all supplements and amendments thereto that have been or may hereafter be passed, and authorizes the sale of any goods distrained for rent at any time after five days from said distraint without any appraisement and/or condemnation thereof. The Lessee further waives the right to issue a Writ of Replevin under the Pennsylvania Rules of Civil Procedure, No. 1071 &c. and Laws of the Commonwealth of Pennsylvania, or under any other law previously enacted and now in force, or which may be hereafter enacted, for the recovery of any articles, household goods, furniture, etc., seized under a distress for rent or levy upon an execution for rent, damages or otherwise; all waivers hereinbefore mentioned are hereby extended to apply to any such action; and/or

(c) May lease said premises or any part or parts thereof to such person or persons as may in Lessor's discretion seem best and the Lessee shall be liable for any loss of rent for the balance of the then current term.

(d) Any re-entry or re-letting by Lessor under the terms hereof shall be without prejudice to Lessor's claim for damages and shall under no circumstances release Lessee from liability for such damages arising out of the breach of any of the covenants, terms and conditions of this lease.

Zoning

17. It is understood and agreed that the Lessor hereof does not warrant or undertake that the Lessee shall be able to obtain a permit under any Zoning Ordinance or Regulation for such use as Lessee intends to make of the said premises, and nothing in this lease contained shall obligate the Lessor to assist Lessee in obtaining said permit; the Lessee further agrees that in the event a permit cannot be obtained by Lessee under any Zoning Ordinance, or Regulation, this lease shall not terminate without Lessor's consent, and the Lessee shall use the premises only in a manner permitted under such Zoning Ordinance or Regulation.

Responsibility of Lessee (11-74)

18. Lessee agrees to be responsible for and to relieve and hereby relieves the Lessor from all liability by reason of any injury or damage to any person or property in the demised premises, whether belonging to the Lessee or any other person, caused by any fire, breakage or leakage in any part or portion of the demised premises, or any part or portion of the building of which the demised premises is a part, or from water, rain or snow that may leak into, issue or flow from any part of the said premises, or of the building of which the demised premises is a part, from the drains, pipes, or plumbing work of the same, or from any place or quarter, whether such breakage, leakage, injury or damage be caused by or result from the negligence of Lessor or his servants or agents or any person or persons whatsoever.

Additional Responsibility of Lessee (11-74)

19. Lessee also agrees to be responsible for and to relieve and hereby relieves Lessor from all liability by reason of any damage or injury to any person or thing which may arise from or be due to the use, misuse or abuse of all or any of the elevators, hatches, openings, stairways, hallways of any kind whatsoever which may exist or hereafter be erected or constructed on the said premises, or from any kind of injury which may arise from any other cause whatsoever on the said premises or the building of which the demised premises is a part, whether such damage, injury, use, misuse or abuse be caused by or result from the negligence of Lessor, his servants or agents or any other person or persons whatsoever.

Confession of Judgment

20. If rent and/or charges hereby reserved as rent shall remain unpaid on any day when the same should be paid Lessee hereby empowers any Prothonotary or attorney of any Court of Record to appear for Lessee in any and all actions which may be brought for rent and/or the charges, payments, costs and expenses reserved as rent, or agreed to be paid by the Lessee and/or to sign for Lessee an agreement for entering in any competent Court an amicable action or actions for the recovery of rent or other charges or expenses, and in said suits or in said amicable action or actions to confess judgment against Lessee for all or any part of the rent specified in this lease and then unpaid including, at Lessor's option, the rent for the entire unexpired balance of the term of this lease, and/or other charges, payments, costs and expenses reserved as rent or agreed to be paid by the Lessee, and for interest and costs together with an attorney's commission of 15%. Such authority shall not be exhausted by one exercise thereof, but judgment may be confessed as aforesaid from time to time as often as any of said rent and/or other charges reserved as rent shall fall due or be in arrears, and such powers may be exercised as well after the expiration of the original term and/or during any extension or renewal of this lease.

Ejectment

21. When this lease shall be determined by condition broken, either during the original term of this lease or any renewal or extension thereof, and also when and as soon as the term hereby created or any extension thereof shall have expired, it shall be lawful for any attorney as attorney for Lessee to file an agreement for entering in any competent Court an amicable action and judgment in ejection against Lessee and all persons claiming under Lessee for the recovery by Lessor of possession of the herein demised premises, for which this lease shall be his sufficient warrant, whereupon, if Lessor so desires, a writ of habere facias possessionem may issue forthwith, without any prior writ or proceedings whatsoever, and provided that if for any reason after such action shall have been commenced the same shall be determined and the possession of the premises hereby demised remain in or be restored to Lessee. Lessor shall have the right upon any subsequent default or defaults, or upon the termination of this lease as hereinbefore set forth, to bring one or more amicable action or actions as hereinbefore set forth to recover possession of the said premises.

Affidavit of Default

22. In any amicable action of ejectment and/or for rent in arrears, Lessor shall first cause to be filed in such action an affidavit made by him or someone acting for him setting forth the facts necessary to authorize the entry of judgment, of which facts such affidavit shall be conclusive evidence, and if a true copy of this lease (and of the truth of the copy such affidavit shall be sufficient evidence) be filed in such action, it shall not be necessary to file the original as a warrant of attorney, any rule of Court, custom or practice to the contrary notwithstanding.

Waivers by Lessee of Errors, Right of Appeal, Stay, Exemption Inquisition

23. Lessee expressly agrees that any judgment, order or decree entered against him by or in any Court or Magistrate by virtue of the powers of attorney contained in this lease, or otherwise, shall be final, and that he will not take an appeal, certiorari, writ of error, exception or objection to the same, or file a motion or rule to strike off or open or to stay execution of the same, and releases to Lessor and to any and all attorneys who may appear for Lessee all errors in the said proceedings, and all liability therefor. Lessee expressly waives the benefits of all laws, now or hereafter in force, exempting any goods on the demised premises, or elsewhere from distraint, levy or sale in any legal proceedings taken by the Lessor to enforce any rights under this lease. Lessee further waives the right of inquisition on any real estate that may be levied upon to collect any amount which may become due under the terms and conditions of this lease, and does hereby voluntarily condemn the same and authorizes the Prothonotary to enter a fieri facias or other process upon Lessee's voluntary condemnation, and further agrees that the said real estate may be sold on a fieri facias or other process. If proceedings shall be commenced by Lessor to recover possession under the Acts of Assembly, either at the end of the term or sooner termination of this lease, or for nonpayment of rent or any other reason, Lessee specifically waives the right to the three months notice and/or the fifteen or thirty days notice required by the Act of April 6, 1951, P.L. 69, and agrees that five days notice shall be sufficient in either or any such case.

Right of Assignee of Lessor

24. The right to enter judgment against Lessee and to enforce all of the other provisions of this lease hereinabove provided for may, at the option of any assignee of this lease, be exercised by any assignee of the Lessor's right, title and interest in this lease in his, her or their own name, notwithstanding the fact that any of all assignments of the said right, title and interest may not be executed and/or witnessed in accordance with the Act of Assembly of May 28, 1715, I Sm. L. 99, and all supplements and amendments thereto that have been or may hereafter be passed and Lessee hereby expressly waives the requirements of said Act of Assembly and any and all laws regulating the manner and/or form in which such assignments shall be executed and witnessed.

Remedies Cumulative

25. All of the remedies hereinbefore given to Lessor and all rights and remedies given to it by law and equity shall be cumulative and concurrent. No determination of this lease or the taking or recovering of the premises shall deprive Lessor of any of its remedies or action against the Lessee for rent due at the time or which, under the terms hereof, would in the future become due as if there has been no determination, or for sums due at the time or which, under the terms hereof, would in the future become due as if there had been no determination, nor shall the bringing of any action for rent or breach of covenant, or the resort to any other remedy herein provided for the recovery of rent be construed as a waiver of the right to obtain possession of the premises.

Subordination

26. This Agreement of Lease and all of its terms, covenants, and provisions are and each of them is subject and subordinate to any lease or other arrangement or right to possession, under which the Lessor is in control of the demised premises, to the rights of the owner or owners of the demised premises and of the land or buildings of which the demised premises are a part to all rights of the Lessor's landlord and to any and all mortgages and other encumbrances now or hereafter placed upon the demised premises or upon the land and/or the buildings containing the same; and Lessee expressly agrees that if Lessor's tenancy, control, or right to possession shall terminate either by expiration, forfeiture or otherwise, then this lease shall thereupon immediately terminate and the Lessee shall, thereupon, give immediate possession and Lessee hereby waives any and all claims for damages or otherwise by reason of such termination as aforesaid.

Condemnation

27. In the event that the premises demised or any part thereof is taken or condemned for a public or quasi-public use, this lease shall, as to the part so taken, terminate as of the date title shall vest in the condemnor, and rent shall abate in proportion to the square feet of leased space taken or condemned or shall cease if the entire premises be so taken. In either event the Lessee waives all claims against the Lessor by reason of the complete or partial taking of the demised premises, and it is agreed that the Lessee shall not be entitled to any notice whatsoever of the partial or complete termination of this lease by reason of the aforesaid.

Termination of Lease

28. It is hereby mutually agreed that either party hereto may determine this lease at the end of said term by giving to the other party prior written notice thereof in accordance with paragraph #1 (l), but in default of such notice, this lease shall continue upon the same terms and conditions in force immediately prior to the expiration or the term hereof as are herein contained for a further period as specified in paragraph #1 (m), and so on from renewal term to renewal term unless or until terminated by either party hereto, giving the other the aforementioned written notice for removal previous to expiration of the then current term; PROVIDED, however, that should this lease be continued for a further period under the terms hereinabove mentioned, any allowance given Lessee on the rent during the original term should not extend beyond such original term, and further provided, however, that if Lessor shall have given such written notice prior to the expiration of any term hereby created, of its intention to change the terms and conditions of this lease, and Lessee shall not within thirty days from such notice notify Lessor of Lessee's intention to vacate the demised premises at the end of the then current term, Lessee shall be considered as Lessee under the terms and conditions mentioned in such notice for a further term as above provided, or for such further term as may be stated in such notice. In the event that Lessee shall give notice, as stipulated in this lease, of intention to vacate the demised premises at the end of the present term, or any renewal or extension thereof, and shall fail or refuse so to vacate the same on the date designated by such notice, then it is expressly agreed that Lessor shall have the option either (a) to disregard the notice so given as having no effect, in which case all the terms and conditions of this lease shall continue thereafter with full force precisely as if such notice had not been given, or (b) Lessor may, at any time within thirty days after the present term or any renewal or extension thereof, as aforesaid, give the said Lessee ten days written

notice of his intention to terminate the said lease; whereupon the Lessee expressly agrees to vacate said premises at the expiration of the said period of ten days specified in said notice. All powers granted to Lessor by this lease may be exercised and all obligations imposed upon Lessee by this lease shall be performed by Lessee as well during any extension of the original term of this lease as during the original term itself.

Inability to give Possession

29. If Lessor is unable to give Lessee possession of the demised premises, as herein provided, by reason of the holding over of a previous occupant, or by reason of any cause beyond the control of the Lessor, the Lessor shall not be liable in damages to the Lessee therefor, and during the period that the Lessor is unable to give possession, all rights and remedies of both parties hereunder shall be suspended.

Additional Rent

30. Lessee agrees to pay as additional rent any and all sums which may become due by reason of the failure of Lessee to comply with any of the covenants of this lease and any and all damages, costs and expenses which the Lessor may suffer or incur by reason of any default of the Lessee or failure on his part to comply with the covenants of this lease, and also any and all damages to the demised premises caused by any act or neglect of the Lessee, his guests, agents, employees or other occupants of the demised premises.

Notices

31. All notices required to be given by Lessor to Lessee shall be sufficiently given by leaving the same upon the demised premises, but notices given by Lessee to Lessor must be given by certified mail, and as against Lessor the only admissable evidence that notice has been given by Lessee shall be a certified return receipt signed by Lessor or his agent.

Right to Enforce

32. The Lessor shall have the right, at all times, to enforce any or all the covenants and provisions of this lease, notwithstanding the failure of the Lessor at any previous time, or times, to enforce his rights under any of the covenants and provisions of this lease.

Definition of Lessor and Lessee

33. The word "Lessor" as used herein, shall include the Owner and the Landlord, whether Person, Firm or Corporation, as well as the Heirs, Executors, Administrators, Successors and Assigns each of whom shall have the same rights, remedies, powers, privileges and obligations as though he, she, it or they had originally signed this lease as Lessor, including the right to proceed in his, her, its, or their own name to enter judgment by confession, or otherwise. The word "Lessee" as used herein, shall include the Tenant, whether Person, Firm or Corporation, as well as the Heirs, Executors, Administrators, Successors and Assigns, each of whom shall have the same rights, remedies, powers, privileges, and shall have no other liabilities, rights, privileges or powers than he, she, it or they would have been under or possessed had he, she, it or they originally signed this lease as Lessee.

Agent

34. It is expressly understood and agreed between the parties hereto that the herein named agent, his salesmen and employees or any officer or partner of agent and any cooperating broker and his salesmen and employees and any officer or partner of the cooperating broker are acting as agent only and will in no case whatsoever be held liable either jointly or severally to either party for the performance of any term of covenant of this agreement or for damages for the nonperformance thereof.

Heirs and Assignees

35. All rights and liabilities herein given to, or imposed upon, or waivers of the respective parties hereto shall extend to and bind the several and respective heirs, executors, administrators, successors and assigns of said parties; and if there shall be more than one Lessee, they shall all be bound jointly and severally by the terms, covenants and agreements herein, and the word "Lessee" shall be deemed and taken to mean each and every person or party mentioned as a Lessee herein, be the same one or more; and if there shall be more than one Lessee, any notice required or permitted by the terms of this lease may be given by or to any one thereof, and shall have the same force and effect as if given by or to all thereof. No rights, however, shall inure to the benefit of any assignee of Lessee unless the assignment of such assignee has been approved by Lessor in writing as aforesaid.

Lease Contains Entire Agreement

36. The Lessor and Lessee hereby agree that this lease sets forth all the promises, agreements, conditions and understandings between the Lessor, or his Agent, and the Lessee relative to the demised premises, and that there are no promises, agreements, conditions or understandings, either oral or written, between them as herein set forth, and any subsequent alteration, amendment, change or addition to this lease shall not be binding upon the Lessor or Lessee unless reduced to writing and signed by them.

Severability (11-74)

37. If any section, subsection, sentence, clause phrase or requirement of this lease is contrary to law or laws subsequently enacted, or should be found contrary to laws during the term or any renewal or extension thereof, the validity of the remaining portions shall not be affected thereby. The parties hereby agree that they would have agreed to each section, subsection, clause sentence, phrase or requirement herein irrespective of the fact that one or more section, subsection sentence, clause, phrase or requirement was contrary to law or during the term or any renewal or extension thereof or are found to be contrary to the law.

Descriptive Heading

38. The descriptive headings used herein are for convenience only and they are not intended to indicate all of the matter in the sections which follow them. Accordingly, they shall have no effect whatsoever in determing the rights or obligations of the parties.

Approval (1-78)

    IN WITNESS WHEREOF, the parties hereto, including to be legally bound hereby, have hereunder set their hands and seals the day and year first above written.

WITNESS AS
TO LESSEE ....   LESSEE .... (SEAL)

WITNESS AS
TO LESSEE ....   LESSEE .... (SEAL)

        LESSEE .... (SEAL)

The Lessor hereby approves this contract on this .... day of .... 19 .... and in consideration of the services rendered in procuring the herein named Lessee and/or collection of rents as agreed and specified in part one of this lease, the Lessor agrees to pay the herein named agent a fee and/or commission in the amount of $ .... for obtaining Lessee together with a commission of ....% for the collection of rents during the term, renewal or extention of this lease or additional lease with the herein named Lessee. Should the Lessee purchase the demised premises from the Lessor during the term of this lease, or during a renewal, extention or any additional lease between said parties for the demised premises, or within a reasonable period of time after the expiration of any such lease, the Lessor agrees to pay to the agent, at the time of settlement, a sales commission of ....% based on the purchase price.

WITNESS AS
TO LESSOR ....   LESSOR .... (SEAL)

        LESSOR .... (SEAL)

WITNESS AS
TO LESSOR ....   AGENT BY ....

The doctrine of caveat emptor as applied to residential leases is abolished, and a warranty of habitability by the landlord will be implied.

A residential lease is deemed to be in the nature of a contract and is to be controlled by principles of contract law. The covenants and warranties of the lease are mutually dependent. The tenant's obligation to pay rent and the landlord's obligation imposed by the implied warranty of habitability to provide and maintain habitable premises are dependent.

To assert the breach of implied warranty of habitability the tenant must prove that notice was given to the landlord of the defect or condition and that the landlord had a reasonable opportunity to make the necessary repairs but failed to do so.

When the landlord materially breaches the habitability warranty, an aggrieved tenant may (a) vacate the premises, (b) abate the rent, (c) repair and deduct the cost of repairs from the rent, or (d) use other traditional contract remedies such as specific performance.

Rent may be abated under the "percentage reduction of use" method of calculating damages for breach of implied warranty whereby the amount of rent owed is reduced by a percentage equal to the percentage by which the use of the premises has been decreased by the breach of warranty.

5. Covenant of quiet enjoyment

The leasehold should insure that the tenant is not interfered with in his or her possession of the property.

6. Dangerous conditions

Depending on the jurisdiction, some degree of care is owed by the landlord to the tenant for defects or unsafe conditions on the premises. Those rights might be summarized to include:

a. Latent defects. Landlord is liable for injuries arising out of the concealed defect if he knew or should have known of same.

b. Joint access of premises. If landlord had access to, and use of the area that contained the defect, then negligence is imputed.

c. Landlord undertakes to repair. Where repairs have been undertaken by the landlord but in a careless manner, negligence will lie with the landlord.

7. Discrimination

Certain provisions adopted by both the federal and state governments serve to protect individuals in the rental market:

a. Federal Fair Housing Act of 1968, 42 USC §3604 et seq. Prohibits refusal to rent a dwelling on the basis of race, color, religion, or national origin.

b. Civil Rights Act of 1966, 42 USC. § 1982. Bars all discrimination, including rental of commercial property, but has no provisions for enforcement except injunction.

c. Equal Rights Amendment enacted in some states.

DISCUSSION QUESTIONS AND PRACTICAL ASSIGNMENTS

1. *Settlement Sheet.* Prepare a settlement sheet reflecting the following basic data and calculate all charges according to your jurisdiction's custom and practice.

Paul F. X. Revere is ecstatic over the fact that he is selling his property for more than he thinks it is worth—$76,000. And he can't believe that John Q. and Abigail Adams want to buy it and move from their beloved village. When they indicated to Paul that the only way they could complete the transaction was through financing, Paul put them in touch with Tory Trust Co., and they got a commitment for $40,000. Now Paul is counting the days until closing, scheduled for June 15, 1982. John Hancock will be the settlement clerk.

It all began back in February when Paul received a $7,600 deposit for his hunting cottage at 11 Beach Avenue. While he didn't think much about it at the time, now he is concerned over how much he will net from the deal. John Hancock prepared a list of items Paul can expect to pay out of the proceeds. The list is as follows:

Mortgage pay off to Patriot National Bank	$14,500
Mortgage cancellation to PNB	25
Mortgage release	12
Termite inspection done by Mid-Atlantic Termite Co.	20
Transfer taxes	760
Disbursement charge to ABC Title Co.	10
Realtor's commission to Colonial Realty Co.	4,560

There will be some further small adjustments in Paul's favor for city taxes ($2 per day) and fuel oil ($55), and Paul can expect to receive over $48,000 from the sale.

John and Abigail were told that Tory Trust expects daily interest from the date of closing until July 1, the due date for the first mortgage payment. Interest on the loan is calculated at $10.25 per day. In addition, they must pay $12 to record the mortgage, one year of hazard insurance, payable to INA, at $200, three months of city property taxes totaling $182.50, and one year of school taxes to the tune of $1,000.

The title company charges are $250 for the work done by Patrick Henry on the title examination. And the attorney for the buyers, T. Jefferson, has submitted a bill for $350. John mentioned that there will also be a $20 endorsement charge, a $30 tax adjustment and a $55 fuel oil adjustment. And the state law requires them to pay for recording the deed ($12) and their share of the transfer tax.

2. *Settlement Sheet: Another Example.* You are a paralegal working with Attorney Jane Smith on a real estate closing. Walter and Anne Sullivan are selling a single-family home at 81 Ballard Drive, Canton, Mass., to Jesse L. Starr and Alexandra L. Starr. The Starrs' attorney has indicated that this clients wish to take title as joint tenants. Atty. Smith is representing Workers' Bank for Savings, which is providing a mortgage loan to the Starrs.

You have been given the following information:

1. The P and S agreement indicates that the sale price is $90,000, and Buyers have made a deposit of $9,000. The broker's fee to A & B Brokers is $5400.
2. The closing will be held at Norfolk Registry of Deeds on November 1, 1980.
3. The cost for recording the deed is $10; the mortgage is $12; and the mortgage discharge is $5.
4. The documentary tax stamp will cost $205.20.
5. Attorney Smith's fee is $500.
6. The municipal lien certificate shows no liens on unpaid charges owed to the town.
7. The municipal lien certificate costs $15.
8. The tax bill for this property for the period from July 1, 1980 to December 31, 1980 is $920.00 ($5/day)
9. The seller's mortgage pay-off figure is $31,745.55 as of the closing date.
10. The Workers' Bank commitment letter to the Starrs indicates the following:
    a. The mortgage loan is in the amount of $60,000 payable over 30 years in monthly installments of $638.36.
    b. The interest rate is 14 percent.
    c. The loan discount fee is 2 points.
    d. The credit report fee is $30.
    e. The loan origination fee is $100.
    f. Payment made 30 days or more late will result in 3 percent late charge.
11. The house has oil heat.
12. The sellers will pay the water bill in full as of the closing date.

Attorney Smith has asked you to prepare the following documents for her to review:

a. Mortgage
b. Note
c. Settlement statement

3. Mortgages and Financing

A. Perform a survey of at least five area banks asking information on the following issues:

1. Rate of fixed mortgage
2. Rate of variables (be specific about different types)

3. Policy on assumption
4. Points on fees charged for a mortgage
5. Any creative financing currently being devised or considered

Compile a chart or a list that outlines the above variables. Devise a permanent form for your own future use, since the above variables will change continuously.

B. Which plan of financing would result in the lowest overall costs, and why? Explain each answer.

1. Purchase money mortgage at 11.5 percent for 20 years.
2. Fixed-rate mortgage at 10 percent for 30 years.
3. Assumable mortgage at 10 percent for 20 years.
4. Balloon mortgage at 5 percent for 5 years.

4. *Surveys.* List five different issues to watch out for when reviewing a survey.

1. _____
2. _____
3. _____
4. _____
5. _____

5. *Preparation of Documents*

A. Draft a mortgage utilizing a copy of the form provided in Exhibit 9.7. Make up all secondary information, but include the following information: $110,000 mortgage, an interest rate of 11 7/8 percent and payable over 30 years. Fill in the rest of the data.

B. Draft a lease, using as models those forms provided in the appendix. Include the following information:

Security deposit	$ 750
Monthly rental	1,000
Term	yearly
Notice to terminate	60 days

All other information can be at your discretion.

6. *Costs of Settlement.* Since settlement is such a costly process, buyers are seeking to economize more and more. Do some comparison shopping on the following three issues by calling two different companies.

Surveys
    Name of Company:_____
             Cost:_____

    Name of Company:_____
             Cost:_____

Insurance (Hazard) $50,000 house with $250 deductible.
    Name of Company:_____
             Cost:_____

    Name of Company:_____
             Cost:_____

Bank: Application Fees
    Name of Bank:_____
             Fee:_____

    Name of Bank:_____
             Fee:_____

Students please note, there is no right answer for this assignment. The comparison shopping is being done for your knowledge and your client's savings.

ENRICHMENT ACTIVITY

Visit a local real estate agency and ask to sit in on a scheduled property settlement. Identify and take note of the role played by each party to the settlement. Based upon your observations, define the paralegal's function or describe in what ways a paralegal's skills would be most useful.

From your county phone directory select at random two or three addresses. Conduct title searches on those properties and determine if there are any liens against each. Outline the procedure that you used to obtain information for the title search, citing each resource consulted. For each resource consulted, cite an available cross-reference.

SUGGESTED READING

BERGER, CURTIS J. *Land Ownership and Use.* Boston: Little, Brown, and Co., 1983.

BERNHARDT, ROGER. *Real Property in a Nutshell.* St Paul: West Publishing Co., 1981.

BOYER, RALPH E. *Survey of the Law of Property.* St. Paul: West Publishing Co., 1981.

COOPER-HILL, JAMES. *Cases and Materials on Mortgages and Real Estate Finance.* Charlottesville, Va.: Michie Co., 1982.

CORLEY, ROBERT NEIL. *Real Estate and the Law.* New York: Random House, 1982.

FRIEDMAN, MILTON R. *Contracts and Conveyances of Real Property.* New York: Practising Law Institute, 1984.

LIFTON, ROBERT K. *Practical Real Estate: Legal, Tax and Business Strategies.* New York: Law and Business, 1979.

NELSON, GRANT S. *Cases and Materials on Real Estate Transfer, Finance and Development, 2d ed.* St Paul: West Publishing Co., 1981.

REILLY, JOHN W. *The Language of Real Estate.* Chicago: Real Estate Education Co., 1982.

WERNER, RAYMOND J. *Real Estate Closings.* New York: Practising Law Institute, 1979.

CHAPTER TEN

ESTATES AND TRUSTS

CHAPTER DESCRIPTION

This chapter covers the requirements and formalities of drafting
and executing wills and trusts, including probating wills, intestacy
law, and administration of wills and estates. Federal estate and U.S.
fiduciary tax returns are discussed as well as state inheritance taxes.

PARALEGAL FUNCTIONS

Wills
   Interview clients.
   Draft will or trust instrument under attorney's supervision.
Estates
   Interview client.
   Gather necessary information for assessing the estate.
   Inventory and value estate assets.
   Prepare probate documents.
   Prepare state death tax returns, when appropriate.
   Prepare federal estate tax return, when appropriate.
   Assist in managing the estate and distributing the estate assets.
   Prepare necessary state or federal income tax returns.
   File tax waivers.

I. INTRODUCTION: THE NATURE OF ESTATES AND THE ROLE OF THE PARALEGAL

Thinking of estates and trusts can conjure up images of crusty tycoons counting money and pondering ways of ruling their worlds from their graves. To be certain, crusty tycoons do require a law firm's time, as they plot and plan the fate of their empires after their demise, but they are not the major element in estate work. Instead, the firm or agency soon discovers that the estate work is family work, some rich families, some poor—all dedicated to dealing in the wisest way with their final accumulations. All people, eventually, must face the reality of death, for it is one of the few things in life in which all individuals are treated equally and that humans cannot change or reverse. Lawyers are playing a major role in meeting the increased demands for estate planning, and accordingly, the paralegal is essential to the task.

At first glance, estates and trusts may appear a boring exercise, where little creativity and imagination is nurtured or supported. Fortunately it is as varied and stimulating as the myriad human familial situations that arise in daily life. The unique needs and requirements of each person, each client, make this field an exercise impossible to pigeonhole or standardize. By the end of this chapter, the student will be capable of:

1. Designing and constructing general will clauses and sections
2. Understanding the nature of trusts, both intervivos and testamentary
3. Discerning the intestate succession schemes adopted by legislatures for those individuals who die without wills (intestate)
4. Skilled interviewing of clients in order to assess estate needs
5. Devising questionnaires, check lists and standardized forms for efficient process of preliminary estate planning
6. Guiding an estate through the requisite steps for estate administration
7. Deciphering the essentials of state and federal estate and inheritance taxes

Be most concerned about the human dimensions of this work—for cold, callous responses or orders, in times like these, (i.e., death or planning thereto) are most frowned upon. At this stage, the lawyer must be a counselor first.

II. WILLS

A. Initial Planning and Preparation

A major function in any firm, and one in which paralegals will increasingly be involved, is the preliminary construction and draftsmanship of wills. Simplicity in drafting wills no longer appears possible, since family relationships are generally more complicated than a generation ago, and the intricacies of taxation boggle the minds of experts every day. More important, the will has become an instrument for the common man and woman, not just respected gentry and those of the elite classes. Today, everyone expects to have a will, and the resulting demand requires increased efficiency in production. What is even more to the point is that most law firms perceive wills as non-money makers, but view them as entry-level activities into the services of their firm. Hence, they are "client getters," so to speak. Good impressions are essential the first time around, and the procedure adopted by the firm must be both congenial and efficient.

Commonly, paralegals are delegated the duty of holding an initial interview with the prospective testator. Telephone contact with the clients is advisable before they ever enter through your office door, so the paralegal can sense the needs of the individuals. A paralegal must be attuned to the problems of family relationships, the personal concerns of human beings, and the difficulties presented by the ownership of certain kinds of assets. More recently, the burdens of income, gift, and estate taxation and the complexities of coping with rules like carryover basis and generation-skipping transfers have added enormously to the lawyer's burden and thus to the paralegal's burden. The fundamental task, however, remains the same. He or she must gather quantities of information, analyze the material, and provide guidance with a diplomatic touch, all with the purpose of realizing the client's objectives.

The client should be forewarned to prepare for the interview. Copies of stockholders' agreements, instruments creating trusts for his benefit, or for members of his family, separation agreements, and the like, have to be assembled. The client should be asked to bring to the first meeting information about his assets, including a general summary of his life insurance and employee benefits. The first meeting will uncover what additional papers should be collected, and the client should be requested to bring the missing papers to the next conference.

Equally demanding is the paralegal's information-gathering function. In essence, the paralegal provides the skeletal though imperative background data so vital in the drafting of wills. Consider the following facts as crucial to will construction:

B. What to Look for in an Estate-Planning Interview

1. Domicile

This is one of the first facts to establish. The law of the domicile will generally cover a number of major points.

a. The law of the domicile governs the rights of the surviving spouse and children.

b. The law of the domicile normally determines the validity of the will, provides the rules of construction and governs the administration of the estate, except for out-of-state real property that the decedent owned directly and not through a corporation.

c. The law of the domicile governs the validity of bequests to charity and the eligibility of the job of executor.

In most cases, domicile is no mystery. The client resides at a specific address, that is his permanent place of residence.

The client's domicile is selected by the client himself as his permanent residence and the client's intentions are backed up by:

a. Registering to vote there

b. Filing federal income tax returns at the proper address

c. Straightening out his state and local tax obligations

d. Making his religious and community ties clear

e. Using his domiciliary address as his home address when traveling

f. Maintaining bank accounts at his principal place of residence and, if feasible, brokerage accounts as well

g. Using the appropriate license plates for his car

h. Taking other similar steps

2. Family history

Was the client ever divorced? The lawyer must know what obligations exist under a separation agreement or court decree in favor of a former spouse and the children of an earlier marriage.

Who are the members of the family?

a. What is needed is a list of names and positions in the family.

b. Ages should be noted so that the lawyer is made aware of minors and can advise his client how best to safeguard their inheritance.

c. The health of each member deserves attention so that the techniques of managing property for infirm or invalid beneficiaries can be considered. A medical problem may require a disproportionate share of the available assets to provide for the afflicted individual.

3. Family assets

It is necessary to get an accurate profile of the family assets. An evaluation of the assets enables the lawyer to estimate the estate taxes and other costs of dying.

The extent of the client's property will show whether the assets are sufficient to sustain the plan he wishes to adopt to provide for his family.

The nature and value of particular assets should show the lawyer whether certain steps are advisable and if sufficient income is likely to be generated to support the client's dependents. The nature of the assets will also reveal special problems, such as potential recapture of depreciation or interests—oil royalties, copyrights, and the like—and they will indicate whether certain assets should be distributed to particular beneficiaries.

4. Registration of assets

The real owner of the assets must be identified—either an individual or joint tenants with right of survivorship.

5. Tax facts

The client's gift tax history is of considerable importance. In weighing the advisability of gifts, all taxable gifts made by the client, at any time in the past, must be taken into account to determine the appropriate gift tax bracket. The paralegal will soon see how essential a standardized process for information gathering is. Various forms and check lists

EXHIBIT 10.1

ESTATE PLANNING INTERVIEW GUIDE

_____
_____
_____
_____

Family Information

	NAME	AGE	HEALTH
Self	_____	_____	_____
Spouse	_____	_____	_____
Children	_____	_____	_____
	_____	_____	_____
	_____	_____	_____
	_____	_____	_____
	_____	_____	_____
	_____	_____	_____
Other	_____	_____	_____
	_____	_____	_____
	_____	_____	_____
	_____	_____	_____

Present Will Information (Please attach present Wills)

List of Property

ASSET	HUSBAND	WIFE	JOINT
Principal Residence (list mortgage, if any)	_____	_____	_____
Summer Residence (list mortgage, if any)	_____	_____	_____
Other Real Estate	_____	_____	_____
Stocks	_____	_____	_____
Mutual Fund Shares	_____	_____	_____
Bonds	_____	_____	_____
Mortgages	_____	_____	_____
Savings Accounts	_____	_____	_____
Checking Accounts	_____	_____	_____
Life Insurance (fill in attached schedule)	_____	_____	_____
Stock Options	_____	_____	_____
Retirement Benefits (fill in attached schedule)	_____	_____	_____
Business Interests	_____	_____	_____
Personal Effects	_____	_____	_____
Interest in Estates or Trusts	_____	_____	_____
Expectancies	_____	_____	_____

Miscellaneous
(Explain)

	_____	_____	_____
	_____	_____	_____
	_____	_____	_____
	_____	_____	_____
	_____	_____	_____
Subtotals	_____	_____	_____
TOTAL	_____	_____	_____

NOTE: Give current market value, date acquired and cost of acquisition.

Life Insurance
(List all Policies)

COMPANY	POLICY NO.	FACE AMOUNT	OWNED BY	BENEFICIARY
_____	_____	_____	_____	_____
_____	_____	_____	_____	_____
_____	_____	_____	_____	_____
_____	_____	_____	_____	_____
_____	_____	_____	_____	_____
_____	_____	_____	_____	_____
_____	_____	_____	_____	_____

Retirement Benefits

TYPE	ESTIMATED VALUE WHICH WOULD PASS TO YOUR ESTATE
Pension Rights	$
Interest in Profit Sharing Plan	$

Comments on any of above assets.

have been provided and will more than adequately cover any estate planning possibility. (See the estate planning interview guide in exhibit 10.1, and the paralegal's checklist for reviewing wills in exhibit 10.2.)

III. GENERAL PRINCIPLES OF DRAFTING WILLS

A. The Role of the Paralegal

Paralegals perform many functions in the construction of wills, but clearly direct draftsmanship is improper. Clients expect legal documents to be drafted by lawyers and no one can hardly blame them. However, as seen thus far, the

EXHIBIT 10.2

A PARALEGAL'S CHECKLIST FOR REVIEWING WILLS

	YES	NO	N/A
I. Exordium			
A. If the testator uses a name other than his legal name, is this indicated?	{ }	{ }	{ }
B. Is the testator's domicile correctly recited?	{ }	{ }	{ }
C. Are all prior wills and codicils revoked?	{ }	{ }	{ }
II. Bequests			
A. Are personal and household effects specifically disposed of?	{ }	{ }	{ }
1. Are bequeathed items clearly and accurately described?	{ }	{ }	{ }
2. Is there casualty insurance on bequeathed items?	{ }	{ }	{ }
3. Is provision made for payment of packing, shipping and storing personal effects where necessary?	{ }	{ }	{ }
4. Is a contingent beneficiary named?	{ }	{ }	{ }
5. If there are more beneficiaries, is there a workable method for dividing bequeathed items?	{ }	{ }	{ }
B. Is there a bequest of life insurance policies on the life of someone other than the testator?	{ }	{ }	{ }
1. Is a contingent beneficiary named?	{ }	{ }	{ }
2. Are the executors to satisfy this bequest as soon as possible after probate?	{ }	{ }	{ }
C. Is there a devise of real property owned by the testator?	{ }	{ }	
1. Is the property clearly and accurately described?	{ }	{ }	
2. Does the devise include casualty insurance covering the property?	{ }	{ }	{ }
3. is it clear whether the beneficiary takes the property free and clear or is subject to any restrictions?	{ }	{ }	{ }
4. Is there a contingent disposition of the property?	{ }	{ }	{ }
D. Is there a specific bequest of a co-operative apartment?	{ }	{ }	
1. Are the stock and proprietary lease clearly and accurately described?	{ }	{ }	{ }
2. Does the bequest include casualty insurance covering the apartment?	{ }	{ }	{ }
3. Is it clear whether the beneficiary takes the apartment free and clear or is it subject to any restrictions?	{ }	{ }	{ }
4. Is there a contingent disposition of the apartment?	{ }	{ }	{ }
E. Does the will exercise any testamentary power granted to the testator by someone else?	{ }	{ }	{ }
1. Is the power exercised with the formalities required in the document granting the power?	{ }	{ }	{ }
2. Is the power exercised within the limits of the rule against perpetuities?	{ }	{ }	{ }
3. Are the appointees within the permitted class?	{ }	{ }	{ }
F. Are there any cash or other general bequests?	{ }	{ }	
1. Is provision made for contingent disposition of those bequests?	{ }	{ }	{ }
2. Are the amounts of those bequests limited to a fixed percentage of the net estate?	{ }	{ }	{ }
3. Is priority of bequests and order of abatement clearly stated in case the testator's assets can't fully satisfy all bequests?	{ }	{ }	{ }
G. Are there any charitable bequests?	{ }	{ }	{ }
1. Are the charitable legatees clearly described?	{ }	{ }	{ }
2. Do the legatees have the legal capacity to accept the bequests?	{ }	{ }	{ }
3. Are the bequests tax deductible?	{ }	{ }	{ }
4. Are the charitable bequests within the maximum limits permitted by local law?	{ }	{ }	{ }
III. Marital Deduction Bequest			
If there is a marital deduction bequest for the testator's wife*:			
A. Is it contingent on her survival?	{ }	{ }	{ }
B. Does the bequest exclude:			
1. non-qualified property	{ }	{ }	{ }
2. income in respect of a decedent?	{ }	{ }	{ }
3. property subject to foreign death taxes?	{ }	{ }	{ }
4. United States of America Treasury Bonds redeemable at par in payment of the Federal estate tax?	{ }	{ }	{ }

*References to "testator's wife" as the surviving spouse are made for convenience only, since men generally predecease their wives, leaving the wives as beneficiaries of their estates.

5. unmatured insurance policies?   { } { } { }
C. Is there a savings clause to limit the trustees' powers so that no part of the marital bequest is disqualified?   { } { } { }
D. Does the bequest compensate for other qualified property passing to the surviving spouse?   { } { } { }
E. If there is a pecuniary formula, is it a fixed dollar amount?   { } { } { }
   1. Are assets to be valued at the date of distribution, or does the will require allocation of a representative proportion of appreciation and depreciation?   { } { } { }
   2. Is income provided from the date of the testator's death?   { } { } { }
F. If there is a fractional formula, is it a true fraction?   { } { } { }

IV. Marital Deduction Trust

If a marital deduction trust is created for the benefit of the testator's wife:

A. Are the trustees to provide her with the maximum enjoyment of trust property accorded by law?   { } { } { }
B. Are the trustees to pay her all trust income?   { } { } { }
   1. Is income payable at least as often as annually?   { } { } { }
   2. Can she require the trustees to convert unproductive assets into productive assets?   { } { } { }
   3. Can the trustees apply income for her benefit?   { } { } { }
C. Can the trustees pay trust principal to the beneficiary?   { } { } { }
   1. Are the trustees given workable standards for principal invasions?   { } { } { }
   2. Are the trustees directed to disregard her other income and resources?   { } { } { }
   3. Can the trustees exhaust trust principal by invading principal for the beneficiary?   { } { } { }
   4. Can the trustees apply principal for her benefit?   { } { } { }
D. Is the beneficiary granted a special lifetime power of appointment over trust principal.   { } { } { }
   1. Has she the right to appoint all trust principal?   { } { } { }
   2. Have the possible appointees been clearly designated?   { } { } { }
   3. Has she the power to direct the trustees to pay from trust principal all gift taxes she incurs by exercising her lifetime power?   { } { } { }
   4. Is there a workable method for computing and paying gift taxes?   { } { } { }
E. Is the beneficiary granted a general power to appoint all trust principal and accrued or undistributed income to anyone in the world, including herself and her estate?   { } { } { }
   1. Is this power exercisable by her alone and in all events?   { } { } { }
   2. Is it exercisable beginning no later than six months after the testator's death?   { } { } { }
F. Are the trustees to pay any death taxes in the beneficiary's own estate resulting from her possession of the power of appointment?   { } { } { }
   1. Are the trustees directed to pay those taxes from unappointed trust assets?   { } { } { }
   2. Is there a workable method for computing and paying her estate taxes?   { } { } { }
G. Is provision made for disposing of all accrued or undistributed income and other unappointed assets remaining in the trust at the beneficiary's death?   { } { } { }
H. If the testator's wife hasn't been granted a general power of appointment, are the trust assets payable to her executors or administrators at her death?   { } { } { }

V. Residuary Estate

A. Does the residuary estate specifically include:
   1. all property owned at the testator's death that isn't effectively disposed of elsewhere in the will?   { } { } { }
   2. future interests?   { } { } { }
   3. after-acquired property?   { } { } { }
   4. foreign property?   { } { } { }
B. Does the residuary estate specifically exclude property over which the testator has a power of appointment?   { } { } { }
C. Is the residuary estate disposed of in all conceivable events including a catastrophe destroying the testator and his entire family?   { } { } { }

VI. Residuary Trusts

If any residuary trusts are created:

A. Are the trustees to pay the beneficiary all trust income { } { } { }
  1. Is income payable at least as often as annually? { } { } { }
  2. Can the trustees apply income? { } { } { }

B. If the trustees are granted discretion to pay income to only one beneficiary:
  1. Are they given workable standards? { } { } { }
  2. Are they to disregard other income and resources? { } { } { }
  3. Can they apply income? { } { } { }
  4. Is undistributed income to be accumulated and added to principal? { } { } { }

C. If the trustees are granted discretion to pay income among two or more beneficiaries:
  1. Are they given workable standards? { } { } { }
  2. Are they to disregard other income and resources? { } { } { }
  3. Can they apply income? { } { } { }
  4. Is undistributed income to be accumulated and added to principal? { } { } { }
  5. Can income be distributed equally or unequally among the beneficiaries? { } { } { }

D. If the trustees are granted discretion to pay principal to only one beneficiary:
  1. Are they given workable standards for principal invasions? { } { } { }
  2. Are they to disregard other income and resources? { } { } { }
  3. Can they exhaust trust principal by invading principal for the beneficiary? { } { } { }
  4. Can they apply principal? { } { } { }

E. If the trustees are granted discretion to pay principal among two or more beneficiaries:
  1. Are they given workable standards for principal invasions? { } { } { }
  2. Are they to disregard other income and resources? { } { } { }
  3. Can they exhaust trust principal by invading principal for the beneficiary? { } { } { }
  4. Can they apply principal? { } { } { }
  5. Can principal be distributed equally or unequally among the beneficiaries? { } { } { }

F. If any beneficiary is granted a special lifetime power of appointment:
  1. Is there a right to appoint all trust principal? { } { } { }
  2. Have the appointees been clearly designated? { } { } { }

G. If any beneficiary is granted a special testamentary power of appointment, have the appointees been clearly designated? { } { } { }

H. If there are fractional distributions at selected ages (such as one-half or one-third), do they equal the entire trust principal? { } { } { }

I. If there is a mandatory payout at a specified age, can the trustees withhold that payout if there is a valid reason for doing so? { } { } { }

J. Is disposition provided for all conceivable events? { } { } { }

K. If there is a potential gift to a beneficiary of another trust, are the assets added to the assets of the other trust? { } { } { }

L. When a trust terminates because of a beneficiary's death, is it clear that the assets go to that beneficiary's issue and then to the issue of the beneficiary's nearest ancestor who has issue before being allocated to the issue of more remote ancestors of the beneficiary? { } { } { }

M. Is it clear that any requirement of survival for receiving distribution is based upon surviving the termination of the trust and not upon surviving the testator? { } { } { }

VII. Statement of Intent

A. Have the trustees been advised of the testator's intention that discretions to distribute income and principal shall be exercised to benefit the immediate beneficiary or beneficiaries of the trusts created? { } { } { }

B. Have the trustees been advised that the administrative and investment powers granted to them should be exercised for the benefit of the immediate beneficiary or beneficiaries of the trusts? { } { } { }

C. Have the trustees been advised that interests of remainderment may be ignored? { } { } { }

D. Have standards for payment of trust income and principal used in the will been clearly explained to the trustees? { } { } { }

E. If the trustees have been granted discretion to hold back funds otherwise mandatorily distributable, have they been told to consider holding back

	YES	NO	N/A

those funds if the beneficiary is in financial, marital, legal, emotional or other trouble serious enough to jeopardize funds paid to him?   { }   { }   { }

F. Are these intentions clearly stated to be non-binding?   { }   { }   { }

VII. Beneficiary Under Disability

If the executors and trustees are granted discretion to retain and manage property of a minor or a person under another disability:

A. Are the executors and trustees authorized to pay or apply income and principal for the benefit of the minor?   { }   { }   { }

B. Are the executors and trustees given workable standards for payment and application of a minor's property?   { }   { }   { }

C. Are the executors and trustees granted discretion to accumulate undistributed income and add it to principal?   { }   { }   { }

D. Is provision made for a contingent disposition of the minor's property if he dies before attaining majority?   { }   { }   { }

E. Can the executor or trustees distribute property to:

   1. a minor or incompetent beneficiary?   { }   { }   { }

   2. a minor's guardian?   { }   { }   { }

   3. a minor's parent?   { }   { }   { }

   4. a custodian for a minor?   { }   { }   { }

   5. a conservator, guardian or committee of an incompetent?   { }   { }   { }

   6. an individual having control, custody or care of a beneficiary?   { }   { }   { }

F. Can the executors and trustees make direct expenditures on behalf of a beneficiary?   { }   { }   { }

G. Are the executors and trustees freed from responsibility for misuse of property after it has been distributed to, or for, a beneficiary?   { }   { }   { }

H. Is majority defined as:

   1. reaching age twenty-one?   { }   { }   { }

   2. reaching the age prescribed by the laws of the jurisdiction in which the will is to be, or was probated?   { }   { }   { }

   3. reaching the age prescribed by the laws of the jurisdiction in which the beneficiary resides?   { }   { }   { }

IX. Taxes and Expenses

A. Is there a tax clause?   { }   { }   { }

B. Are the executors to pay all taxes including taxes on:

   1. property passing under the will?   { }   { }   { }

   2. insurance?   { }   { }   { }

   3. jointly held property?   { }   { }   { }

   4. property subject to a general power of appointment?   { }   { }   { }

   5. all other property includible in the testator's gross estate?   { }   { }   { }

C. Are the executors to pay all funeral expenses, debts and expenses of administration?   { }   { }   { }

D. Are all taxes, expense and debts clearly payable from property other than the marital deduction bequest?   { }   { }   { }

E. If insurance, qualified benefit plans or other assets are payable directly to the trustees, can the executors require the trustees to contribute to the payment of taxes, expenses and debts for payment of which the probate estate is insufficient?   { }   { }   { }

F. Is it clearly stated that proceeds of qualified benefit plans may not be used to pay taxes or expenses, or otherwise used for the benefit of the estate?   { }   { }   { }

X. Vesting of Interests

A. Is there a simultaneous death clause?   { }   { }   { }

   1. Is the testator's wife presumed to have survived him in the event of simultaneous death?   { }   { }   { }

   2. Is there a provision for a contingent disposition in the event of simultaneous death?   { }   { }   { }

B. Can an interest under this will be disclaimed or released?   { }   { }   { }

   1. Is provision made for a method for disclaiming or releasing an interest?   { }   { }   { }

   2. Is there a provision for a contingent disposition of a disclaimed or released interest?   { }   { }   { }

C. Has a spendthrift clause been included to prevent a beneficiary from assigning, selling or otherwise disposing of his interest under this will?   { }   { }   { }

D. If there is any possibility of a trust continuing after the deaths of the testator's wife and children, is there a cut-off clause to prevent a violation of the rule against perpetuities? — YES { } NO { } N/A { }

XI. Appointment of Fiduciaries

A. Does any executor or trustee have the power to name successors? { } { } { }

B. If an executor or trustee fails to exercise a power to name successors, is the vacancy otherwise filled? { } { } { }

C. If a successor is not named, is it clear whether the vacancy is to remain unfilled? { } { } { }

D. Are executors and trustee named? { } { } { }

E. Can a sole individual executor or trustee name an additional person or bank to act with him? { } { } { }

F. Are those serving in a fiduciary capacity authorized to resign? { } { } { }

G. Is a method provided for resignation of an executor or trustee and for the naming of successors? { } { } { }

H. Do the fiduciaries serve without bond? { } { } { }

I. If a bank named has a minimum commission clause, has it been included? { } { } { }

J. Is a guardian of the person and property named for any minors? { } { } { }

K. Are successor guardians named? { } { } { }

L. Does the guardian serve without bond? { } { } { }

XII. Trustee's Powers and Provisions

A. Are the trustees' powers exercisable only in a fiduciary capacity? { } { } { }

B. Do the trustees' powers include the power to:

  1. retain all property originally received without liability for loss? { } { } { }

  2. invest in real or personal property including securities, oil and gas, land, and mortgages without regard to local law limitations? { } { } { }

  3. exchange, alter, construct and deal with real property? { } { } { }

  4. disregard duty to diversify? { } { } { }

  5. abandon or destroy any property which is worthless, dangerous, or subject to confiscatory taxation? { } { } { }

  6. exercise all rights over securities, including granting proxies? { } { } { }

  7. lease property for longer than the period allowable under local law? { } { } { }

  8. sell property at private sale or for credit for any period of time? { } { } { }

  9. exercise options? { } { } { }

  10. form corporations and transfer property to such corporations? { } { } { }

  11. form partnerships and transfer property to such partnerships? { } { } { }

  12. make loans on any terms to beneficiaries? { } { } { }

  13. borrow funds for the benefit of any estate or trust and secure the loan by pledge or mortgage? { } { } { }

  14. maintain bank accounts, safe deposit boxes and brokerage accounts? { } { } { }

  15. make distributions in property? { } { } { }

  16. hold and invest separate trust in consolidated investments? { } { } { }

  17. retain or acquire stock of a corporate trustee? { } { } { }

  18. grant options for longer than the period allowable under local law? { } { } { }

  19. arbitrate, abandon or settle claims of any nature? { } { } { }

  20. remove assets from the state in which the will is admitted to probate? { } { } { }

  21. employ and pay accountants and investment advisers without decreasing commissions? { } { } { }

  22. delegate duties to others, in connection with powers granted in the will? { } { } { }

  23. act despite a conflict of interest? { } { } { }

  24. collect insurance proceeds and elect settlement options? { } { } { }

  25. terminate an uneconomical trust? { } { } { }

  26. execute contracts? { } { } { }

  27. rely upon affidavits, letters or other written instruments believed to be genuine when acting or making distributions? { } { } { }

  28. deal with mineral interests? { } { } { }

  29. deal with farming interests? { } { } { }

  30. deal with patents? { } { } { }

  31. deal with unregistered stock? { } { } { }

  32. deal with closely held business interests? { } { } { }

C. Are the trustees freed from liability for their acts or omissions other than actual fraud, gross negligence or willful misconduct? { } { } { }

D. Is a trustee who is also a beneficiary expressly forbidden from exercising discretion to pay or apply income or principal? { } { } { }

E. Is a trustee who is under a legal obligation to support a beneficiary expressly forbidden to pay or apply income or principal in discharge of that legal obligation? { } { } { }

F. Is a method provided for settlement of disagreements between the trustees? { } { } { }

XIV. Executors' Powers and Provisions

    A. Are the executors granted all of the same powers as are the trustees? { } { } { }

    B. In addition to the powers above, are the executors granted the power to:

        1. join with the testator's wife or her representative in filing income and gift tax returns? { } { } { }

        2. elect the alternate valuation date for estate tax purposes? { } { } { }

        3. claim debts and expenses as income tax deductions? { } { } { }

        4. consent to Subchapter S status for any corporation in which the testator owned stock at his death? { } { } { }

        5. satisfy bequests and make distributions as soon as possible after the testator's death? { } { } { }

        6. refrain from making inventories and accounts of transactions of the testator's estate? { } { } { }

        7. designate an ancillary representative where necessary? { } { } { }

        8. make payment, receive money, take action, make contracts, deeds, or other documents? { } { } { }

    C. Are executors' freed from liability for their acts or omissions other than actual fraud, gross negligence or willful misconduct? { } { } { }

    D. Is a method provided for settlement of disagreements between the executors? { } { } { }

XV. Provisions With Respect to Powers of Appointment

    A. Can the donee of a power of appointment reduce, renounce or release it? { } { } { }

    B. Is it clear that all powers of appointment are discretionary and may or may not be exercised? { } { } { }

    C. Is it clear that all powers of appointment are exclusive and can be exercised to exclude some of the objects of the power in favor of others? { } { } { }

    D. Is it clear that specific reference must be made to exercise a testamentary power? { } { } { }

XVI. Construction Provisions

    A. Does the will clearly provide the meaning of the following terms, if used in the will:

        1. child? { } { } { }

        2. grandchild? { } { } { }

        3. issue? { } { } { }

        4. afterborns? { } { } { }

        5. legitimacy of a child of a female? { } { } { }

        6. legitimacy of a child of a male? { } { } { }

        7. adopted persons? { } { } { }

        8. marriage? { } { } { }

        9. spouse? { } { } { }

        10. wife? { } { } { }

        11. husband? { } { } { }

        12. widow? { } { } { }

        13. widower? { } { } { }

    B. Has the term "trustees" been defined to include all successor trustees and a trustee acting alone? { } { } { }

    C. Has the term "executors" been defined to include all successors including singular, female and neuter executors? { } { } { }

    D. Have "distributees" or "heirs at law" been defined? { } { } { }

XVII. General Appearance

    A. Is the testator's name correctly spelled? { } { } { }

    B. Are other names used in the will (such as names of beneficiaries, banks, corporations) correctly spelled? { } { } { }

    C. Are reference to, and descriptions of, other documents referred to in the will accurate? { } { } { }

    D. Has the will been checked so that:

        1. page numbers are in sequence? { } { } { }

        2. articles, sections, subsections and paragraphs are in sequence? { } { } { }

        3. the first word of a page logically follows the last word of the previous page? { } { } { }

    E. Are all cross-references accurate?

paralegal is a principal player in the initial interview process and equally vital in the collection of information, which will eventually be the content of any given will. Logically, the paralegal must fathom the rudimentary elements in will draftsmanship in order to be of any real assistance.

B. Formalities of Will Drafting

Generally, all states and local jurisdictions do all in their power to validate or uphold wills, since they are hesitant to substitute judicial intentions for the desire of an individual testator. Courts do not like the business of will interpretation, since the author of the instrument is usually not available for consultation. It is therefore essential that attention be given to the formalities in will construction.

1. Capacity to devise a will

☐ What is the age of the testator?
☐ What is the mental and physical condition of the testator?
☐ Is there any duress, coercion, or fraud being employed in its drafting?

2. Execution of the will

☐ Are holographic wills permitted in the jurisdiction?
☐ Is the *writing* sufficient?
☐ Is the signature valid?
☐ How many witnesses are required?
☐ Should the will be self-proving?
☐ Are all witnesses acceptable?
☐ Which law controls the administration of the will?

Generally all jurisdictions address the above questions and seek, at all costs, to uphold the validity of wills. However, failure to review any of the above issues can be devastating to a case of will validity and certainly could establish a prima facie case of legal malpractice.

3. Rules of interpretation and construction

The validity of a will often depends on its provisions and its adherence to statutory rules. Some of those standards include:

a. REVOCATION

Sometimes people think that they have, in fact, revoked a previous will when, in reality, that will is valid and possibly controlling. Be certain not only to ask about previous wills but also to request that they be brought to the law office for destruction.

b. IMPENDING DIVORCE

Most law firms will meet clients who are urgently requesting a will. Their requests are often so emotional that an impending divorce could be the motivation for the request. Check out marital status to insure your client's rights are being amply protected. Most jurisdictions have adopted legislation that revokes a will by operation of law upon the issuance of a divorce decree. Don't plan a will design without assessing the status of marital relations.

c. INCORPORATION BY REFERENCE

If the client wishes to limit the content of his or her will to the document itself, be clear that no other references are permissible. However, a clause can be inserted in the will incorporating other documentation, such as check lists, inventories in safe-deposit boxes, and other secondary materials, an action that legally *incorporates by reference* those documents into the will's overall design.

d. Simultaneous Death

A majority of American jurisdictions have adopted the Uniform Simultaneous Death Act. Section 2-104 of the Uniform Probate Code provides the respected model:

Any person who fails to survive the decedent by 120 hours is deemed to have predeceased the decedent for purposes of homestead allowance, exempt property, and intestate succession and the decedent's heirs are determined accordingly. If the time of death of the decedent or of the person who would otherwise be an heir, or the times of death of both cannot be determined and it cannot be established that the person who would otherwise be an heir, has survived the decedent by 120 hours, it is deemed that the person failed to survive for the required period. This section is not to be applied where its application would result in a taking of intestate estate by the state under Section 2-105.

e. Anti-Lapse Statute

This is a critically important concern every testator should address, particularly in gifts or devises to a class. If A, B, C, D, and E have all been given $100,000 upon the death of the testator, what happens if E dies before the testator does? Does E's portion lapse or does it pass on to E's issue? A preliminary assessment of the testator's wishes is crucial, since the testator may love E very dearly, yet view his or her offspring as less than desirable lineage.

f. Ademption

What if a will's language indicates a specific devise to *"Mr. Rodgers, my beloved friend and cohort, a sum of $5000"*? Will Mr. Rodgers lose out at estate-distribution time because his devise is adeemed, or has been distributed prior to the death of the testator? Under normal *ademption* statutes, Mr. Rodgers would not receive the property or a replacement.

g. Types of Bequests or Devises

A hierarchy of rights exists upon distribution, and some forms of bequests or devises will be paid out or transferred before others, since the testator's intentions clearly evidence his or her other preferences. Description of any property must be (1) sufficiently particular or specific in construction and (2) specific as to possible insurance coverage on that property.

The basic forms of bequests or devises are as follows:

1. Specific bequests of particular property.   e.g., I give and bequest my 100 shares of Ronco Incorporated, valued at $1.00 a share.

2. General bequest of cash.   e.g., I give and bequest $10,000 to my nephew, Fred.

3. Demonstrative bequest.   e.g., I give and bequest $10,000 to be funded with Ronco stock, upon my death, to my friend, Bob Jones.

4. Devise of real property

5. Residuary devise or bequest.

All of the above are common forms of bequests. Will construction and draftsmanship demands an awareness of which language will gain a preference of award in the overall distributive scheme.

h. Marital Deduction

There is a more extensive analysis of how the marital deduction operates in the section on federal taxation. The federal estate system does permit a certain portion of the overall estate value to be exempt from estate taxation. This shelter is known as the marital deduction. A sample clause for inclusion in a will is provided in exhibit 10.3.

i. Elective Share of Surviving Spouse

Virtually all states impose some restrictions on the ability of a spouse to disinherit the other. Historically, the policy of dower and courtesy provided spouses with some protection, but since this general abolition, legislatures have had to provide some remedy for the tremendous injustices that can arise in a disinheritance plot by a spouse. At times, the vindictive, or maybe just cheap, spouse provides so little in remuneration by a bequest that an intelligent spouse can exercise his or her "elective" right to take a different share of the overall estate. Legislation permits the disenchanted spouse to bypass the will's grant or bequest and to receive his or her statutory share, which is usually valued at one-third of the *augmented estate*. The augmented estate is the entire value of the estate reduced by:

Exhibit 10.3

MARITAL DEDUCTION CLAUSE: RESIDUARY CLAUSE

In the event that my wife should survive me, I give devise, and bequeath the residue of my property to _____ (name), _____ (address), as Trustee in trust, to be divided into two separate Trusts, hereinafter referred to as the "Marital Trust" and the "Residuary Trust."

The Marital Trust shall consist of a fractional interest in each and every asset, limited to those assets contained in my residuary estate which qualify for the marital deduction. The fractional share shall be determined as follows: The numerator of the fraction shall be the maximum allowable federal estate marital deduction (as used in determining the federal estate tax payable by reason of my death) minus the value for federal estate tax purposes of all assets in my gross taxable estate which qualify for the marital deduction and which pass or have passed from me to my wife under the other provisions of this Will, or by tenancy by entireties, the proceeds of life insurance, lifetime transfers, or otherwise than under this fractional share bequest of my residuary estate; and the denominator of the fraction shall be the value of my residuary estate. To the extent that assets are included in my residuary estate initially, the value at which such assets are valued in my gross taxable estate shall control; to the extent they are not so included, their value at the time they would have been valued if they had been so included shall control in determining the denominator. For purposes of this paragraph, the words "pass or have passed" shall have the same meaning as such words have under the provisions of the Internal Revenue Code in effect at the time of my death.

The Residuary Trust shall consist of the remaining portion of the residue of my probate estate.

☐ All administrative expenses
☐ Family/homestead allowances
☐ Funeral expenses
☐ Certain transfers by decedent during marriage
☐ Certain gifts exceeding $3,000

Choosing the elective share then becomes a choice of economic wisdom and gain since the reductions, required under the augmented-estate definition, greatly enhance the spouse's financial position.

j. ABATEMENT

What effect will the lifetime distribution of a gift, election of an omitted spouse, pretermitted children, or a general inability to pay the costs of the estate have upon the intentions of the testator?

k. CUSTODY OF THE WILL

Check with your local jurisdiction to see if any filing or registry requirements must be followed once the will is completed.

C. Essential Clauses in Will Design

1. Strategies in construction

A variety of strategies can be used in will design, and depending on individual client needs, wills are highly sophisticated instruments or simple recitations reflecting adherence to statutory requirements and basic rules of construction. Ponder first what your client desires out of the will.

a. TAX BENEFITS

At the federal level, especially since the adoption of TEFRA 1981, the opportunities for savings in estate taxes are quite considerable. Keep in mind the enormous importance of *the marital deduction, trust provisions for both spouse and children* and *charitable bequests or trusts.* Properly constructed wills can save vast sums of money for your client and included in the supplement are a few clauses that take advantage of TEFRA. (See exhibit 10.4 and also the complex will with tax-savings clauses in exhibit 10.5.)

b. HUMAN ISSUES

While no one can rule from the grave, certain will designs give testators a more peaceful feeling about their control

Exhibit 10.4

TAX-SAVING CLAUSE: SAMPLE

I give to my son, JOE, if he survives me, or, if not, to my grandson, STEVE, the amount hereinafter set forth:

IF I DIE IN THE CALENDAR YEAR:	THE AMOUNT OF THIS BEQUEST IS:
1983	$275,000
1984	325,000
1985	400,000
1986	500,000
1987 or later	600,000

All of the rest and residue of my estate I give to my wife, SALLY, if she survives me.

EXHIBIT 10.5

WILL OF

I, _____, of _____
declare that this is my will and revoke all other wills and codicils which I have made.

Article I

I appoint _____, my _____ to be executor of this will. In case _____ cannot serve in this capacity, I appoint _____, of _____, as the second choice to be executor. In addition, I appoint _____ to act as trustee of any trusts created under this will until death, removal or resignation. If any of the above events take place, I appoint _____ to act as trustee.

Article II
Payments of Debts, Taxes and Funeral Arrangements

A. I direct my executor to pay my debts, expenses of my last illness, funeral expenses, and costs of administration, and claims allowed in the administration of my estate from the principal of my residuary estate.

B. I direct my executor to pay out of the principal of my residuary estate all inheritance, transfer, estate and similar taxes (including interest and penalties), assessed or payable by reason of my death on any property or interest in property which is included in my estate for the purpose of computing such taxes. My executor shall not require any recipient of such property or interest in such property to reimburse my estate for taxes paid under this paragraph. I further request that a religious service in the _____ Rite be performed upon my death.

Article III
Tangible Personal Property

A. I give all my tangible personal property not otherwise effectively disposed of, including furniture, furnishings, silver, books, pictures, jewelry and automobiles, and any insurance policies thereon, but not cash on hand or on deposit to, _____ if _____ survives me. If my Wife does not survive me, I give the following tangible personal property to those of my children who survive me, to be divided among them by my executor in as nearly equal portions as may be practical, giving due regard to their personal preferences. If my children fail to agree on the distribution of my tangible personal property within ninety days after my death, that determination shall be made by my executor. If any child of mine is a minor at the time of distribution of property under this Article, my executor may distribute his share to him or for his use to his guardian or to the person with whom he resides, without further responsibility. The receipt of the distributee shall be a sufficient discharge of my executor.

B. Whenever in this instrument I use the words "child" or "children," I intend those words to mean lawful children of the body of the person referred to and persons who have adopted according to law by the person referred to.

Article IV
Distribution of Residuary Estate

A. All my residuary estate, which I define as all real and personal property, wherever situated and wherever acquired by me in which I have any interest at the time of my death, including property in which I have a reversionary interest, or interest in any option to purchase, and all property which is not otherwise effectively disposed of under this will (but excluding any property over which I may have a power of appointment at my death), I give:

1. To _____ if _____ survives me.

---

2. If _____ does not survive me, I give my residuary estate to _____ of _____, to act as trustee of any trusts created under this will, until his death, removal or resignation. If any of the above events take place, I appoint _____ to act as trustee. The trustee, in his discretion, may pay to or use for the benefit of my children so much of the income and principal of the trust as the trustee from time to time determines to be required for their reasonable support, maintenance, health and education, taking into consideration their income from all sources known to the trustee, and may add any excess income to principal at the discretion of the trustee. The trustee may distribute income and principal to or use it for the benefit of one or more of my children, to the exclusion of one or more of them and may exhaust the principal. The trustee should distribute (1/3) one-third the value of the principal, that is their individual proportionate share, to any of my children reaching the age of eighteen (18). The balance of the trust principal will remain intact until the termination date as outlined below. My concern is primarily for the support, maintenance, health and education of my children, rather than for preservation of principal for distribution upon termination of the trust. After there is no living child of mine under the age of twenty-one years, the trustee shall distribute the principal and undistributed income of the trust in equal shares as follows:

    a)   one share to each of my children who is then living, and,

    b)   one share to the then living descendants, collectively, of each deceased child of mine. The trustee shall distribute the shares of the descendants of those of my children who fail to survive me to those descendants, per stirpes.

Article V
General Administration Directions

A. 1. Whenever any principal or income is distributable pursuant to the provisions of this instrument to any beneficiary who is under the age of twenty-one years at the time of distribution, and no other trust has been established under this instrument to hold such property, the share of that beneficiary shall vest in him beneficially, and the trustee may, in its discretion, continue to hold the distribution as a separate trust until that beneficiary reaches twenty-one years of age. The trustee shall use for the beneficiary's benefit, so much of the income and principal of his trust as the trustee determines to be necessary for his reasonable support, maintenance, health and education, taking into consideration his income from all sources.

When the beneficiary reaches the age of twenty-one years the trust shall terminate and the principal and accumulated income of each beneficiary's share shall be distributed to him. If the beneficiary dies before reaching the age twenty-one years, the principal and accumulated income shall be distributed to the executor or administrator of the beneficiary's estate.

2. If the trustee is directed in this instrument to pay income or principal from time to time to any beneficiary who is under legal disability or in the opinion of the trustee incapable of properly managing his affairs when distribution is to be made, the trustee may use such income or principal for his support, maintenance and health.

3. When the trustee has the power under this instrument to use any income or principal for the benefit of any person, the trustee may expend it for the benefit of that person, or pay it directly to that person or for his use to his guardian parent, spouse, or to the person with whom he is residing, without responsibility for its expenditure.

B. Income payable to any beneficiary which is accrued and undistributed at the death of that beneficiary shall be held and accounted for or distributed in the same manner as if it had been received before the beneficiary's death.

C. No interest under this instrument shall be subject to or liable for the beneficiary's anticipation, transfer, assignment, sale, pledge, debt, contract or engagement, or to liability or sequestration under legal or equitable process.

D. Trusts created under this instrument shall terminate not later than twenty-one years after the death of the last survivor of my descendants who are living at my death. At termination, if the trustee is not otherwise able to give effect to the provisions of this instrument, each remaining portion of trust property shall be distributed to the beneficiaries of the then current trust income in the proportions in which they are beneficiaries.

E. If, at any time, a trust created under this instrument shall be of the aggregate principal value of $5,000 or less, the trustee may terminate that trust and distribute the assets in the trustee's possession to the beneficiaries, at that time, of the current income and, if there be more than one beneficiary in the proportions in which they are beneficiaries.

F. This instrument and dispositions under it shall be construed and governed by the Law of _____.

Article VI
Fiduciary Powers

A. In the administration of any property in my estate, whether owned by me at the time of death or subsequently acquired by my executor, my executor shall have the powers as provided in _____ Probate Law as amended from time to time or as similarly provided in other sections of _____ law, to be exercised as the executor, in its discretion, determines to be in the best interests of the beneficiaries. In the administration of any property forming part of any trust established under this instrument, the trustee is authorized and empowered, without court authority, to exercise all powers conferred by law upon trustees or expressed in this instrument as the trustee, in its discretion, determines to be in the best interest of the beneficiaries.

B. 1. The trustee shall have the power to determine the manner of ascertaining income and principal and the allocation and apportionment of receipts and disbursements between income and principal.

2. The trustee is authorized to allocate different kinds of disproportionate shares of property among the beneficiaries or trusts, without regard to the income tax basis of specific property allocated to beneficiaries or trusts, and determine the value of such property.

3. The trustee is authorized to enter into transactions with other fiduciaries including the trustees and executors of other trusts and estates in which any beneficiary under this instrument has any interest, and including itself as fiduciary for other estates and trusts, and in such transactions to purchase property, or make loans or notes secured by property, even though

similar property constitutes a large portion of the trust property and to retain any such property or notes as if they had been an original part of the trust.

    4. The trustee is advised to invest in only conservative, safe, secure markets thereby insuring the longevity of principal.

Article VII
Appointment of a Guardian

    It is my clear intention that upon my death, as well as the death of my spouse, that _____ of _____, be appointed Guardian of my children, _____ or any other children born hereafter. _____ will serve as Guardian until either his death, removal for cause, or resignation. This guardianship should be guided by the following provisions:

    1. The Guardian will provide my children with a _____ upbringing, permitting them to learn the _____ faith, to celebrate _____ holidays and ritutals, and to freely exercise _____ beliefs and ideals.

    2. The Guardian will also give credence and respect to the wishes of each child under this guardianship, especially in matters of school selection, religion and career opportunities and vocational direction.

    3. The Guardian will do all to further and promote the best interests of all my children, and that this guardianship decision is firm and absolute.

Article VIII
Resignation of Trustee

    A. 1. Any trustee may resign by giving written notice, specifying the effective date of its resignation, to the beneficiaries then entitled to the trust income.

    2. If any trustee resigns or is unable or refuses to act, another corporation authorized under the laws of the United States or of any state to administer trusts may be appointed as trustee by a written instrument delivered to it signed by a majority of the beneficiaries then entitled to the trust income. No successor trustee shall be liable for acts, defaults or omissions of prior trustees. Any successor trustee with the written approval of the persons appointing the successor trustee shall accept as correct without examination the accounts rendered by the prior trustee and property delivered by the prior trustee without incurring any liability.

    3. Any successor trustee shall have the title, duties, powers and discretion as the trustee succeeded without the necessity of conveyance or transfer.

    4. The guardian of a beneficiary under legal disability or the parents or guardian of a minor beneficiary, for whose estate no guardian has been appointed, may act for the beneficiary in signing any instrument under this Article.

    B. Any corporate successor to the trust business of the executor or of any corporate trustee named or acting under this instrument shall become executor or trustee in place of its predecessor.

    C. 1. If my executor elects to file joint income tax returns with _____ or consents to treat gifts made by either of us during my life as made one-half by each of us, my executor may, in its discretion, pay out of the principal of my estate the entire amount or any part of the tax due.

    2. My executor shall have the power, in its discretion, to select assets to be sold by my estate for the payment of debts, taxes and pecuniary legacies in a manner that will minimize the recognition by my estate of gain for federal income tax purposes.

    3. I also direct that my executor seek the services of _____ in the administration of this will, if it is at all possible.

    4. My executor shall have the right to exercise any options and elections under the tax laws applicable to my estate, as the executor determines should be made. No compensating adjustments between income and principal, nor with respect to any bequest or devise, shall be made even though the options and elections may affect the interests of the beneficiaries. The action of my executor with respect to options and elections made shall be conclusive and binding upon all beneficiaries. I now sign this will, in the presence of the witnesses whose names appear below, and request that they witness my signature and attest to the due execution of this my will this _____ day of _____, 19_____, at _____.

_____
                              Testator

over the eventual distribution of their estate, especially in light of misgivings about certain individuals in the testator's family. Trusts, incorporated into the will, protect the estate from waste by prodigal sons and daughters and also prevent minors from making their own money decisions. A simple will, with trust provisions, is shown in exhibit 10.5. Also, don't assume that the testator desires all of his or her immediate or nuclear family to share and share alike. Remember, the testator's intentions are what the firm should be honoring.

c. CHARITABLE DEVISES

Certainly, charitable desires are not driven strictly by tax considerations, and it is only predictable that most people, upon their death, wish to give something of their lives to charitable institutions. Stress to clients their perfect right to devise or bequest property to designated charities.

D. Basic Will Provisions

The following list is not intended to be binding, but is intended to be the skeletal framework of every will.

Statement of identification. Provision should contain reference to the full name of the testator, residence, and intention to create a will.

Payment of expenses. Provision should direct payment of all debts and legal, funeral, and administrative expenses, preferably out of the residuary.

Payment of taxes. Provision should cover all state, county, city, and federal estate, fiduciary, and inheritance taxes, again payable from residuary.

Funeral arrangements. As unpleasant as it might seem, clients often desire certain methods of burial, ceremony, or dress at wake or a particular concelebrant. Respect those wishes by outlining them clearly in the will.

Simultaneous death clause. (As noted in prior materials).

Residuary Clause. At some point in the will, as evidenced by the examples in this chapter, some mention must be made as to where the bulk of the estate goes—to a spouse or to all the children. This major bequest will total all estate assets minus expenses and those specific legacies or bequests that will be cited in the will. All that is left over is called the *residuary*. It is common practice to create a trust out of that residuary.

Specific legacies/bequests/devises. Some clause in the will should outline the specific bequests of the testator, such as, "*I give and bequeath my Benson gold-framed watch to my son, Larry.*" Many clients feel emotionally reassured when these specific delineations are present in the document since such language prevents any potential disagreements or misunderstandings amongst the testator's remaining relatives.

Appointment of personal representative. The appointment should be based on a personal choice made realistically in light of the individual chosen and the complexities of administration. Always suggest a secondary choice.

Appointment of trustee.

Appointment of guardian.

Powers of personal representative. A sample set of powers to be included in your will follows:

1. Retain assets owned by the decedent, pending distribution or liquidation, including those in which the representative is personally interested or that are otherwise improper for trust investment.

2. Receive assets from fiduciaries or other sources.

3. Perform, compromise, or refuse performance of the decedent's contracts that continue as obligations of the estate, as he or she may determine under the circumstances. In performing enforceable contracts by the decedent to convey or lease land, the personal representative, among other possible courses of action, may:

   a. Execute and deliver a deed of conveyance for cash payment of all sums remaining due or the purchaser's note for the sum remaining due secured by a mortgage or deed of trust on the land, or

   b. Deliver a deed in escrow with directions that the proceeds, when paid in accordance with the escrow agreement, be paid to the successors of the decedent, as designated in the escrow agreement.

4. Satisfy written charitable pledges, of the decedent, irrespective of whether the pledges constituted binding obligations of the decedent or were properly presented as claims, if in the judgment of the personal representative, the decedent would have wanted the pledges completed under the circumstances.

5. If funds are not needed to meet debts and expenses currently payable and are not immediately distributable, deposit or invest liquid assets of the estate, including monies received from the sale of other assets, in federally insured interest-bearing accounts, readily marketable secured loan arrangements, or other prudent investments that would be reasonable for use by trustees generally.

6. Acquire or dispose of an asset, including land in this or another state, for cash or on credit, at public or private sale, and manage, develop, improve, exchange, partition, change the character of, or abandon an estate asset.

7. Make ordinary or extraordinary repairs or alterations in buildings or other structures, demolish any improvements, raze existing party walls or buildings, or erect new ones.

8. Subdivide, develop or dedicate land to public use, make or obtain the vacation of plats and adjust boundaries, adjust differences in valuation on exchange or partition by giving or receiving considerations, or dedicate easements to public use without consideration.

9. Enter for any purpose into a lease as lessor or lessee, with or without option to purchase or renew, for a term within or extending beyond the period of administration.

10. Enter into a lease or arrangement for exploration and removal of minerals or other natural resources, or enter into a pooling or unitization agreement.

11. Abandon property when, in the opinion of the personal representative, it is valueless or is so encumbered or is in condition that it is of no benefit to the estate.

12. Vote stocks or other securities in person or by general or limited proxy.

13. Pay calls, assessments, and other sums chargeable or accruing against or on account of securities, unless barred by the provisions relating to claims.

14. Hold a security in the name of a nominee or in other form without disclosure of the interest of the estate, but the personal representative is liable for any act of the nominee in connection with the security so held.

15. Insure the assets of the estate against damage, loss, and liability and himself or herself against liability as to third persons.

16. Borrow money with or without security to be repaid from the estate assets or otherwise and advance money for the protection of the estate.

17. Effect a fair and reasonable compromise with any debtor or obligor or extend, renew, or in any manner modify the terms of any obligation owing to the estate. If the personal representative holds a mortgage, pledge or other lien upon property of another person, he or she may, in lieu of foreclosure, accept a conveyance or transfer of encumbered assets from the owner thereof in satisfaction of the indebtedness secured by lien.

18. Pay taxes, assessments, compensation of the personal representative, and other expenses incidental to the administration of the estate.

19. Sell or exercise stock subscription or conversion rights or consent directly or through a committee or other agent to the reorganization, consolidation, merger, dissolution, or liquidation of a corporation or other business enterprise.

20. Allocate items of income or expense to either estate income or principal, as permitted or provided by law.

21. Employ persons, including attorneys, auditors, investment advisors or agents, even if they are associated with the personal representative, to advise or assist the personal representative in the performance of his or her administrative duties, act without independent investigation upon their recommendations, and instead of acting personally, employ one or more agents to perform any act of administration, whether or not discretionary.

22. Prosecute or defend claims or proceedings in any jurisdiction for the protection of the estate and of the personal representative in the performance of his or her duties.

23. Sell, mortgage, or lease any real or personal property of the estate or any interest therein for cash, credit, or part cash and part credit and with or without security for unpaid balances.

24. Continue any unincorporated business or venture in which the decedent was engaged at the time of death (i) in the same business form for a period of not more than four months from the date of appointment of a general personal representative if continuation is a reasonable means of preserving the value of the business, including good will, (ii) in the same business form for any additional period of time that may be approved, by order of the court in a formal proceeding to which the persons interested in the estate are parties, or (iii) throughout the period of administration if the business is incorporated by the personal representative and if none of the probable distributees of the business who are competent adults object to its incorporation and retention in the estate.

25. Incorporate any business or venture in which the decedent was engaged at the time of death.

26. Provide for exoneration of the personal representative from personal liability in any contract entered into on behalf of the estate.

27. Satisfy and settle claims and distribute the estate as provided in this code.

Powers of trustee. See the discussion of trustee in Section V of this chapter

Powers of guardian. This is an important factor often overlooked in will construction. The client must address the issue of his or her children being parentless and if that tragedy should occur, who can best serve in the parents' place? What powers would a testator afford the guardian?

Acknowledgment/signature clauses. Spaces for both testator and all required witnesses must be provided.

Self-proof clause. Saves the time of having witnesses appear before administrative bodies upon application for letters. (See sample in exhibit 10.6.)

Without question, a will can and often does become far more complex, but an adherence to this basic format will more than insure a comprehensive and professional mode of will construction. Review extensively the sample wills provided.

Exhibit 10.6

STATUTORY EXAMPLE OF FORM FOR SELF-PROVED WILL

Self-Proved Will Clause

a. A Will, executed in compliance with Section 4 of this act, may be simultaneously executed, attested and made self-proved, by acknowledgment thereof by the testator and affidavits of the witnesses, each made before an officer authorized, pursuant to _____, to take acknowledgments and proofs of instruments entitled to be recorded under the Laws of this State, in substantially the following form:

I, _____, the Testator, sign my name to this instrument, this _____ day of _____ 19_____, and being duly sworn, do hereby declare to the undersigned authority that I sign and execute this instrument as my Last Will and that I sign it willingly, (or willingly direct another to sign for me), that I execute it as my free and voluntary act, for the purposes therein expressed, and that I am eighteen (18) years of age or older, of sound mind and under no constraint or undue influence.

_____
Testator

We, _____, _____ the witnesses, sign our names to this instrument and being duly sworn, do hereby declare to the undersigned authority that the Testator signs and executes this instrument as his Last Will and he signs it willingly, (or willingly directs another to sign for him), and that each of us, in the presence and hearing of the Testator, hereby signs this Will as witness to the Testator's signing and that to the best of our knowledge, the Testator is eighteen (18) years of age or older, of sound mind and under no constraint or undue influence.

_____
Witness

_____
Witness

The State of: _____
County of: _____
Subscribed, sworn to and acknowledged before me, by _____, _____ and _____, witnesses, this _____ day of _____.

(Signed) _____
(Official Capacity of Officer)

b. A Will, executed in compliance with this act, may, at any time subsequent to its execution, be made self-proved by the acknowledgment thereof by the testator and the affidavits of the witnesses, each made before an officer authorized, pursuant to _____, to take acknowledgments and proofs of instruments entitled to be recorded under the Laws of this State, attached or annexed to the Will, in substantially the following form:

The State of: _____
County of: _____
We, _____, _____ and _____, the Testator and the witnesses, respectively, whose names are signed to the attached or foregoing instrument, being duly sworn, do hereby declare to the undersigned authority that the Testator signed and executed the instrument as his Last Will and that he had signed willingly, (or willingly directed another to sign for him), and that he executed it as his free and voluntary act, for the purposes therein expressed, and that each of the witnesses, in the presence and hearing of the Testator, signed the Will as witness and that to the best of his/her knowledge, the Testator was, at that time, eighteen (18) years of age or older, of sound mind and under no constraint or undue influence.

_____
Testator

_____
Witness

_____
Witness

Subscribed, sworn to and acknowledged before me, by _____, the Testator, and subscribed and sworn to before me, by _____ and _____, witnesses, this _____ day of _____.

(Signed) _____
(Official Capacity of Officer)

IV. INTESTATE SUCCESSION

A. General Comments

Even though wills are becoming more commonplace, the assumption that a will exists is really unfounded and foolhardy. The likelihood of a person's dying "intestate," that is, without a will, is quite high, and as a result, all states have devised methods of estate administration that attempt to serve the needs of what the state thinks are the "normal" family desires. In theory, *intestate succession* is the government's notion as to what the decedent would have wanted if he or she had, in fact, written a will. The method of succession attempts to emulate the typical family preferences; for instance, the spouse of the decedent should have a stronger interest in the eventual estate distribution than cousin Marvin, whom the decedent saw fifty years ago. Plainly, this small example attests as to how critical it is for each individual to have a will because the decedent's preference may really have been for cousin Marvin to get something because the decedent despised his or her spouse and liked the cousin. In short, the decedent who has no will cannot express his or her own intentions, and as a result, the state implies or injects standardized intentions, which generally reflect family habits and patterns of bequests, legacies, and devises. The state is being as fair as it possibly can be in the circumstances.

There are some general trends that can be deduced in all intestate succession schemes:

1. The surviving spouse is generally given the largest share of the intestate estate if there are children and the whole estate if there are no children or parents.

2. Remote relatives are not favored in intestate succession designs, and inheritance is generally limited to grandparents and those descended from grandparents.

3. Most intestate succession patterns adhere to the Uniform Simultaneous Death Act, which requires that an heir must survive the decedent by five days in order to share in the distribution.

4. *Children* are defined to include those adopted.

5. Intrafamily, intervivos gifts are not considered advancements.

B. Property Subject to the Intestate Estate

Any and all property in which the deceased holds a legal and/or equitable interest after death is part of the intestate estate, excluding:

1. Property validly passing by will

2. Jointly held property with rights of survivorship

3. Life insurance/other exempted benefits

4. Intervivos trusts

5. Other contractual obligations entered into by the deceased prior to death

C. Share of the Spouse

Obviously, in the absence of a will the state has to give the highest deference to the spouse of the deceased. Reverse logic indicates that if the decedent desired to exclude his/her spouse from the proceeds of the estate, the decedent would have formally taken those steps. While total exclusion is not possible under the *surviving-spouse rule* or the *elective-share principle*, the decedent, if he or she so chose, could have kept to a minimum the overall value of the distribution to the spouse, by simply reflecting that required by statute.

Accordingly, the intestate succession scheme is designed as follows:

1. If there is no surviving issue or parent of the decedent, the entire intestate estate goes to the surviving spouse.

2. If there is no surviving issue, but the decedent is survived by a parent or parents, the first $50,000 plus one-half of the balance of the intestate estate goes to the surviving spouse.

3. If there are surviving issue, all of whom are issue of the surviving spouse also, the first $50,000 plus one-half of the balance of the intestate estate goes to the surviving spouse.

4. If there are surviving issue, one or more of whom are not issue of the surviving spouse, one-half of the intestate estate goes to the surviving spouse.

D. Share of Remaining Heirs

In imposing its succession scheme, the state is rightfully hesitant when dealing with remote relatives. Hence, it seeks to limit those individuals to those who can assert interest in the value of the estate, and it follows the following criteria when there is *no* surviving spouse.

1. Issue or children

Little questions exists that in the average family, the parents hope to care for both the present and future needs of their children. As a result, the succession scheme treats all children equally if they are all of the same degree of kinship to the decedent. If not of the same degree, then by representation.

2. No surviving spouse or children

The estate then passes to parent(s) of decedent.

3. No parent(s)

The estate passes to the issue of the parents by representation.

4. No issue of parent(s)

a. Half the estate passes to the paternal grandparents, if both survive, or to the surviving paternal grandparent or to the issue of the paternal grandparents, if both are deceased. The issue take equally if they are all of the same degree of kinship to the decedent, but if of unequal degree, those of more remote degree take by representation.

b. The other half passes to the maternal grandparents equally, if both survive, or to the surviving maternal grandparent, or if both are deceased and the decedent is survived by paternal grandparents or grandparent, then to the issue of the maternal grandparents, the issue taking equally if they are all of the same degree of kinship to the decedent; but if of unequal degree, those more remote take by representation.

c. If the decedent is survived by a grandparent or grandparents, only on the paternal side or only on the maternal side and by no issue of the grandparents on the other side, the entire estate passes to the surviving grandparent or grandparents equally.

d. If there is no surviving issue, parent, issue of a parent or grandparent but the decedent is survived by issue of grandparents, the issue take equally, if they are all of the same degree of kinship to the decedent, but if of unequal degree, those of more remote degree take by representation.

If confusion exists as to the dynamics of these provisions, then be assured of normalcy.

For paralegals, who feel this state design is all benevolent, be aware that in the absence of any of the above four scenarios, the value of the estate escheats to the state.

E. Practice Problems: Intestate Succession

a. Determine the interest in each of the following, and complete chart A.

1. Deceased is survived by a spouse, no children, and both parents.
2. Deceased is survived by a spouse, no children, and his father.
3. Deceased is survived by his spouse alone.
4. Deceased is survived by his spouse and three children.
5. Deceased is survived by his spouse, children #1 and #2 and grandchildren #3, #4, and #5.
6. Deceased is survived by only his three children.
7. Deceased is survived by children #1 and #3.
8. Deceased is survived by child #2, grandchildren #1, #3, #4 and #5 and greatgrandchild #1.
9. Deceased is survived by grandchildren #1, #2, #3, #4, and #5.
10. Deceased is survived by child #2 and greatgrandchild #1.

CHART A

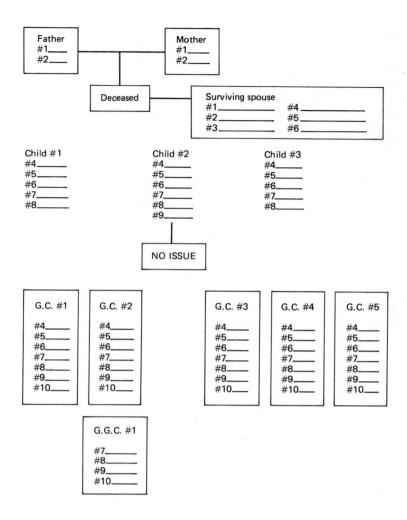

b. Deceased leaves an estate of $1,000,000.

1. Surviving the deceased are his spouse and two children. How much does each receive?

2. The surviving spouse dies intestate ten days later. Based on chart B, who gets what from the surviving spouse's estate?

3. Assuming the facts in question, the spouse, children #1 and 2 and the child of the surviving spouse by a prior marriage die ten days later. Their only asset is that which they got from the deceased, and their heirs are as stated in chart B. Who gets what?

4. Do you think the deceased wanted the grandchild of his surviving spouse to get the same share as his own grandchildren #1 and #2? How about grandchild #3?

CHART B

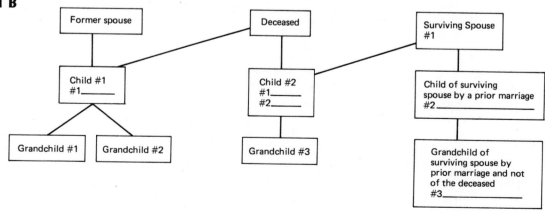

c. Deceased leaves $1,000,000.

    1. Deceased is survived by father, stepmother, brother #1, brother #2, and sister #1. Who gets what?

    2. Deceased is survived by stepmother, brother #1, brother #2, and sister #1. Who gets what?

    3. Deceased is survived by nephew #1, brother #2, nephew #2, and nephew #3. Who gets what?

    4. Deceased is survived by grandnephew #1, grandnephew #2, nephew #2, and nephew #3. Who gets what?

    Note: Common *misunderstandings* are that in question 3 brother #2 gets all and in question 4 all four (grandnephews #1 and #2 and nephews #2 and #3) take the same share.

CHART C

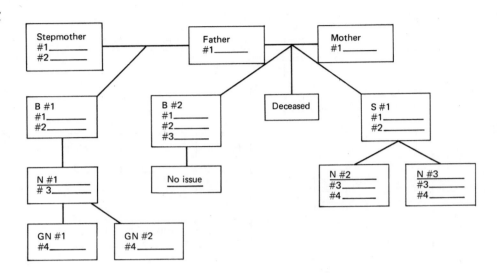

d. Deceased leaves an estate of $1,000,000.

    1. Deceased leaves a paternal uncle, maternal grandmother, and grandnephew. Who gets what?

    2. Deceased leaves his paternal first cousin and grandnephew. Who gets what?

CHART D

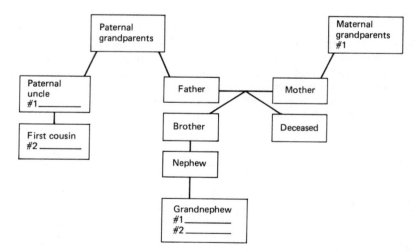

V. TRUSTS

A. Introduction

A trust is a legal relationship usually evidenced by some document in which a donor/settlor turns over the legal title to specific property he or she possesses for the benefit of another (beneficiary). This beneficiary can be the donor/settlor. It's a curious arrangement that requires inherent human trust in another to handle your affairs. Law firms are increasingly involved in handling their client's money as trustees. Naturally, the lawyer-client relationship depends heavily upon trust to be effective at all, and trust relationships tend to emerge.

Understanding trusts also requires a comparative analysis. First, think of gifts, which are unconditional donations with few or no strings attached. Once a gift is made, it's over. There can be no future discussion of a trust or its powers. Second, think of a bailment, whereby a bailee stores, protects, or has custodial control over property for a limited time. While a bailment requires due-care behavior on the part of the bailee, such behavior is not of the same mettle as a settlor-trustee relationship. At best, a bailment is a temporary relationship with a bailee possessing a very limited, specialized property interest, which pales in comparison to the legal exchange of a trust relationship. Lastly, review the principles of agency, and while this last comparison may be getting closer, the agent cannot compare himself or herself to the trustee since the agent has no formal right over any property interest. Thus, the trust relationship is the most solemn of the above, simply because of a real, transferred interest in property. The trustee has legal title.

B. Critical Terms and Definitions

TRUST. A right of property, real or personal, held by one party for the benefit of another

DONOR / GRANTOR SETTLOR One who creates a trust.

TRUSTEE. A person appointed, or required by law, to execute a trust.
TRUST CORPUS. The property that is the subject of the trust.
BENEFICIARY. One for whose benefit a trust is created.
TRUST INSTRUMENT. That document which evidences the trust relationship.
FIDUCIARY. A person holding the character of trustee, in respect to the trust and confidence involved in it, and the scrupulous good faith and candor it requires.

C. Rationales for the Creation of a Trust

1. Asset or financial management

As couples forge dual careers, rear children, and confront the daily complexities and pressures of life, trusts become increasingly popular in the area of financial services. Consider an individual who wishes to go beyond the normal agency or bailment relationship and turn over all legal title to his or her money, both cash and securities and also bonds and other sources of interest. A trust is a perfect instrument; it can be revocable or irrevocable for a term of years. The settlor then also becomes the beneficiary in this scenario and the financial advisor, who may be an attorney or investment counselor, becomes the trustee. Asset management is also a major consideration when the settlor does not feel that the beneficiaries of his or her generosity are capable of handling money because of their age, intellectual acumen, or personal habits.

2. Avoidance of probate

A properly constructed trust can minimize estate administration costs and taxes upon the settlor's death. In particular, an irrevocable trust will generally not be included in the estate of the settlor for federal estate tax if:

a. The settlor does not retain a lifetime income interest or other use or enjoyment of the trust property.
b. The settlor does not retain the right to designate the person or persons, currently or ultimately, to receive the trust income or the trust principal and does not retain other incidents or ownership over the trust property.
c. The settlor does not retain a reversionary interest.
d. The settlor does not retain the right to alter, amend, or revoke the trust.

3. Minimization of tax liability

Depending upon the provisions of the trust, the income earned on the trust property will be taxed to the settlor, will be taxed to the trust, will be taxed to the beneficiaries of the trust, or will be taxed to the trust and to the beneficiaries of the trust. Distributed income will be taxed directly to the recipient beneficiaries. If income is accumulated for future distribution, such income, when distributed to the beneficiaries, may be taxed to the beneficiaries as though that income had been distributed each year in which it was, in fact, being accumulated.

4. Charitable trusts

Aside from tax benefits, many individuals derive maximum satisfaction from creating trusts that serve the needs of hospitals, colleges, charitable organizations, or an indefinite class of individuals who are in need.

5. Any other lawful purpose

Many people have set up trusts for scientific research, educational programs, or cultural contributions.

D. Types of Trusts

1. Testamentary trusts

Trusts are one of the few things human beings can effect both before and after death. A major function of every will is to take care of those loved ones who may or may not be capable of administering their own finances. In particular, a father or mother will always wish to consider a testamentary trust for children under the age of twenty-one, and in certain circumstances, for the purposes of asset management age does not matter at all. The same trust could be used for spouses, charities, and other relationships.

2. Intervivos trusts

Many individuals desire to have their finances managed during their lifetime. Their tax liability can be reduced, and there are other motives for a lawful trust. The term *intervivos* means "between living beings." The advantages of a testamentary trust are many:

□ Client has a lifetime to determine the ability of a trustee.
□ There is no delay in administration at settlor/testator's death.
□ Selection of domicile for the trust.
□ There is no probate administration upon the settlor/testator's death.
□ A trust is not a public document.
□ A trust shifts management responsibilities.
□ A trust provides for care of assets in event of the incapacity of settlor.

Tax advantages also exist, but much of the minimization will depend on whether the trust is *revocable* or *irrevocable*. The creator of a trust must weigh the advantages of a lower tax liability versus the permanancy and inflexibility of an irrevocable trust.

3. Revocable versus irrevocable trusts

As noted thus far, revocability plays a vital role in tax liability of the various parties involved in the trust. The distinction between the two rests with the ability of the settlor/grantor to revoke the existence of the trust and thereby exercise dominion and control over it.

4. Life insurance trusts

Depending upon the type of policy purchased and the method of distribution selected, a life insurance trust is an extremely effective mode of trust initiation and operation. Again, both the courts and the IRS have been looking closely into who really exercises control over the principal and income, and tax preference is generally only given to irrevocable plans.

5. Charitable trusts

A charitable trust is a gift for the benefit of the public, the community, or some indefinite class of persons. These trusts are often for the maintenance, improvement, or enhancement of religious, educational, health, art, scientific, recreational, or governmental operations. Tax advantages are enormous, though highly complex.

6. Honorary trusts

An honorary trust is unique, created for specific noncharitable purposes, such as the care and maintenance of animals or the care of a grave.

7. Section 2503(c) trusts

This form of trust enables a settlor to make a gift to a minor in trust and still obtain the $10,000 annual gift-tax exclusion. The requirements of this type of trust are:

a. A gift to a minor through a section 2503(c) trust will qualify for the annual exclusion (will not be considered a gift of a future interest) if the income and principal may be expended by or on behalf of the beneficiary at any time prior to the beneficiary's becoming twenty-one years of age.

b. Unexpended income and principal must be payable to the beneficiary when he or she reaches twenty-one years of age.

c. If the beneficiary dies, before age twenty-one, the trust corpus must go to the minor's estate or to an appointee under the minor's will.

d. The trust may continue beyond the donee's twenty-first birthday so long as the donee has the ability, after reaching twenty-one years of age, to obtain the property held in the trust by exercising a right of withdrawal.

8. Short-term (Clifford) trusts

Intervivos by nature, the Clifford trust has a limited, though rigorously adhered to, duration: *irrevocable for ten years and one day*. At the expiration of the time period, the trust terminates, and the entire trust corpus is returned to the settlor. This form of trust is a favorite tool of tax planners because:

a. The income is taxed to the trust to the extent it is retained in the trust, and it is taxed to the beneficiaries to the extent the income is paid out or credited to the accounts of individuals during the term of the trust. The income tax saving, of a short-term (Clifford) trust is the difference between the settlor's top bracket and the lower bracket of the trust or its beneficiary. The throwback rule applies unless the beneficiary was under twenty-one years during the period of accumulation.

b. When the trust is created, a gift is made for gift tax purposes and may qualify for the preferential treatment of the gift tax provisions. If the income is or may be accumulated at the trustee's discretion, the gift of the income is considered a gift of a future interest and therefore does not qualify for the $10,000 annual exclusion unless the trust can also comply with the provisions of section 2503(c), or if the beneficiary has a right to withdraw the property.

c. Upon the death of the settlor, the trust is includable in the estate to the extent of his or her reversionary interest in the trust property.

9. Marital trusts

New tax laws that increase the marital deduction and provide for unified credit and a liberal exemption policy have made most ordinary estates free from federal taxation. This trust addresses the needs of the surviving spouse. This marital trust utilizes the unified credit as the trust corpus.

10. Resulting trusts

A resulting trust exists because of the inferred or presumed intent of the property owner and not from an intention that is clearly expressed.

11. Constructive trusts

A constructive trust, artificially created by the courts, prevents one person from taking property from another and enriching himself or herself unjustly. This type of trust is not based on intent of the parties but rather is created by the court.

12. Savings bank, or Totten, trusts

a. A Totten trust comes into existence when one person has deposited his or her money in a bank and directed that the account be entitled "in trust" for another.

b. To determine if a trust truly exists, the courts look to the beneficiary at the time of deposit and the conduct of all parties at the time and after opening of the account.

13. Spendthrift trusts

a. A spendthrift trust is created to provide a fund for the maintenance of another and at the same time secure it against the beneficiary's own improvidence or incapacity for self-protection. Usually the trust prevents the beneficiary from assigning his or her trust interest as collateral to a creditor. It also prevents a creditor from attaching the trust corpus for payment of a debt.

b. Typically, the term *spendthrift* refers to a provision in a trust document, rather than being a type of trust in and of itself.

14. Implied trusts

Legal terminology for both resulting and constructive trusts.

15. Express trusts

a. An express trust comes into being because a person having the power to create it expresses an intent to have the trust arise and goes through the formalities.

b. All of the trusts listed so far are express trusts, except for implied trusts.

16. Generation-skipping trusts

a. A family trust may be continued through a generation-skipping trust, with ultimate distribution to the grandchildren of the grantor.

b. Estate tax consequences:
   i) Tax at the death of the last child to die
   ii) $250,000 exemption in the calculation of a taxable estate

E. Formal Creation of a Trust

As seen thus far, trusts can be created in wills, by implication, by oral assertion, or by other legal documents. The following elements are unique to all of them.

   1. An intention to transfer property to a trustee
   2. A declaration of that intention
   3. Writing under the Statute of Frauds (in some instances, as in trusts involving real property)
   4. Trustee
   5. Settlor/grantor
   6. Corpus
   7. Beneficiary
   8. Lawful purpose

Some sample trusts are included in exhibits 10.7–10.10.

F. Trust Operation and Administration

1. Trustee powers, duties, and obligations

Trustees are generally afforded all powers necessary and convenient to the accomplishment of trust purposes. Their powers must not be under the direct control or supervision of the settlor, since that would contradict the purposes of the trust. Those powers, though, are not always expansive and depend largely on the nature of the trust agreement.

Exhibit 10.7

TRUST AGREEMENT

THIS TRUST AGREEMENT made and executed this _____ day of _____, 1984, by and between _____, currently residing in _____, _____, hereinafter referred to as the "settlor," and _____, hereinafter referred to as the "trustee."

I. Establishment and Continuation of Trust Corpus

The settlor, in consideration of the premises, hereby assigns, transfers, sets over and delivers to the trustee, the property set forth in Schedule A, attached hereto, and has made payable, or will make payable to the trustee, to be held, administered, and disposed of as hereafter set forth in this agreement.

The settlor reserves to herself and any other person the right to deposit with the trustee, or make payable to the trustee, other policies of insurance, and also to assign, transfer, convey, devise, bequeath and deliver to the trustee such other personal property and real estate to be held, administered, and disposed of as hereafter set forth in this agreement.

II. Revocability of the Trust

The settlor reserves and shall have the exclusive right at any time and from time to time during her lifetime by instrument in writing signed by the settlor and delivered to the trustee to modify or alter this agreement, in whole or in part, without the consent of the trustee or any beneficiary, provided that the duties, powers and liabilities of the trustee shall not be changed without her consent; and the settlor reserves and shall have the right during her lifetime, by instrument in writing, signed by the settlor and delivered to the trustee, to cancel and annul this agreement without the consent of the trustee or any beneficiary hereof.

III. Rule Against Perpetuities

If it shall be determined that any provisions of any trust created herein violates any rule against perpetuities or remoteness of vesting now or hereafter in effect in a governing jurisdiction, that portion of the trust herein created shall be administered as herein provided until the termination of the maximum period allowable by law at which time and forthwith such part of the trust shall be distributed in fee simple to the beneficiaries then entitled to receive income therefrom, and for the purpose, it shall be presumed that any beneficiary entitled to receive support or education from the income or principal of any particular fund is entitled to receive income from.

IV. Identification

The settlor is _____ at the time of the execution of this trust, and the settlor has _____ children, _____ AND _____. For the purposes of this agreement, it is my intention that the proceeds of this trust, both principal and interest, be divided equally amongst my children or their issue per stirpes. This intention is a reaffirmation of my will's language.

V. Fiduciary Powers

In addition to any powers granted under applicable law or otherwise, and not in limitation of such powers, but subject to any rights and powers which may be reserved expressly by the settlor in this agreement, the trustee of each trust established hereunder are authorized and empowered to exercise the following powers in their sole and absolute discretion:

a. To hold and retain any or all property, real, personal, or mixed, received from the settlor, the settlor's estate, or from any other source, regardless of any law or rule of court relating to diversification, or non-productivity, for such time as the trustee shall deem best, and to dispose of such property by sale, exchange, or otherwise, as and when they shall deem advisable, notwithstanding this exchange, or otherwise, as and when they shall deem advisable, notwithstanding this provision or any other contained herein, the trustees shall stand without power to sell or otherwise dispose of any interest in a closely held business unless they shall have consulted with all of the adult beneficiaries and the legal representatives of all the minor beneficiaries of this trust, and they shall have agreed to such sale or other disposition by an affirmative vote of a majority of such beneficiaries and representatives.

b. To sell, assign, exchange, transfer, partition and convey, or otherwise dispose of, any property, real, personal, or mixed, which may be included in or may at any time become part of the trust estate, upon such terms and conditions as deemed advisable, at either public or private sales, including options and sales on credit and for the purpose of selling, assigning, exchanging, transferring, partitioning, or conveying the same, to make, execute, acknowledge, and deliver any and all instruments of conveyance, deeds of trust, and assignments in such form and with such warranties and covenants as they may deem expedient and proper, and in the event of any sale, conveyance or other disposition of any of the trust estate, the purchaser shall not be obligated in any way to see to the application of the purchase money or other consideration passing in connection therewith.

c. To invest and reinvest or leave temporarily uninvested any or all of the funds of the trust estate as said trustees in their sole discretion may deem best, including investments in stocks, common and preferred, and common trust funds, without being restricted to those investments expressly approved by statute for investment by fiduciaries, and to change investments from realty to personalty, and vice versa.

d. To lease any or all of the real estate, which may be included in or at any time become a part of the trust estate, upon such terms and conditions deemed advisable, irrespective of whether the term of the lease shall exceed the period permitted by law or the probable period of any trust created hereby, and to review and modify such leases; and for the purpose of leasing said real estate, to make, execute, acknowledge and deliver any and all instruments in such form and with such covenants and warranties as they may deem expedient and proper; and to make any repairs, replacements, and improvements, structural or otherwise, of any property, and to charge the expense thereof in an equitable manner to principal or income, as deemed proper.

e. To vote any stocks, bonds, or other securities held by the trust at any meetings of stockholders, bondholders, or other security holders and to delegate the power so to vote to attorneys in fact or proxies under power of attorney, restricted or unrestricted, and to join in or become a party to any organization, readjustment, voting trust, consideration or exchange, and to deposit securities with any persons, and to pay any fees incurred in connection therewith, and to charge the same to principal or income, as deemed proper, and to exercise all of the rights with regard to such securities as could be done by the absolute owner.

f. To borrow money for any purpose in connection with the administration of any trust created hereby, and to execute promissory notes or other obligations for amounts so borrowed, and to secure the payment of any such amounts by mortgage or pledge of any real or personal property, and to renew or extend the time of payment of any obligation, secured or unsecured, payable to or by any trust created hereby, for such periods of time as deemed advisable.

g. To compromise, adjust, arbitrate, sue or defend, abandon, or otherwise deal with and settle claims, in favor of or against the trust estate as the trustees shall deem best and their decision shall be conclusive. The trustees, however, shall not be required to take any action until indemnified to their satisfaction.

h. To make distributions in cash or in kind, or partly in each, at valuations to be determined by the trustees, whose decision as to values shall be conclusive.

i. To determine in a fair and reasonable manner whether any part of the trust estate, or any addition or any increment thereto be income or principal, or whether any cost, charge, expense, tax, or assessment shall be charged against income and partially against principal.

j. To engage and compensate out of principal or income or both, as equitably determined, agents, accountants, brokers, attorneys-at-law, tax specialists, realtors, clerks, custodians, investment counsel, and other assistants and advisors, to delegate to such persons as discretion deemed proper, and to so do without liability for any neglect, omission, misconduct, or default of any such agent or professional representative, provided he or she was selected and retained with reasonable care.

k. To apportion extraordinary stock and liquidating dividends between the income and principal in such manner as shall fairly take into account the relative interests of the beneficiaries and to determine what constitutes such dividends.

l. To hold and administer the trusts created hereby in one or more consolidated funds, in whole or in part, in which the separate trusts shall have undivided interests.

m. To rely upon any affidavit, certificatee, letter note, telegraph or other paper, or on any telephone conversation, believed by them to be sufficient and to be protected and held harmless in all payments or distributions required to be made hereunder, if made in good faith and without actual notice or knowledge of the changed condition or status of any person receiving payments or other distributions upon a condition.

n. To purchase securities, real estate, or other property from the executor or other personal representative of the settlor's estate, the executor or other personal representative of the settlor's husband's estate, and the trustees of any agreement or declaration executed by the settlor during her lifetime under her last will in case her executors or trustees are in need of cash, liquid assets, or income-producing assets with which to pay taxes, claims, or other estate or trust indebtedness, or in case such executors or trustees are in need of such property to properly exercise and discharge their discretion with respect to distributions to beneficiaries as provided for under such wills, declarations, or agreements. Such purchase may be cash or may be in exchange for other property of this trust, and the trustees shall not be liable in any way for loss resulting to the trust estate by reason of the exercise of this authority.

o. To make loans or advancements to the executor or other personal representative of the settlor's estate, the executor or other personal representative of the settlor's husband estate, and the trustees of any agreement or declaration executed by the settlor during her lifetime or under her last will in case such executors or trustees are in need of cash for any reason. Such loans or advancements may be secured or unsecured, and the trustees shall not be liable in any way for any loss resulting to the trust estate by reason of the exercise of this authority.

p. To do all other acts and things not inconsistent with the provisions of this instrument which they may deem necessary or desirable for the proper management of trusts herein created, in the same manner and to the same extent as an individual might or could do with respect to his or her own property.

VI. Trustee Designation and Terms

_____ shall serve as trustee hereunder, with compensation, until his death, disability, resignation or removal. _____ shall serve as successor trustee in the event of the death, disability, resignation or removal of _____ and shall be entitled to receive as compensation for its services hereunder, commissions computed in accordance with its regularly published fee schedule, applicable to trusts, in effect from time to time.

The trustees named herein shall not be required to provide bond or other security for the faithful performance of their duties hereunder but will provide beneficiary with annual reports on the financial state of the trust.

The trustee, _____ will be compensated for the administration of this trust at an annual fee of _____ plus _____ of the trust's annual profit and increase in volume.

VII. Governing Law Clause (1)

This agreement shall be governed and construed at all times according to the laws of the State of _____.

VIII. Spendthrift Clause

The interest of any beneficiary hereunder, to the extent permitted by law, shall be held and possessed by the trustee in trust upon the condition that it may be paid over by the trustee to a beneficiary only as provided for in this agreement, and that the same shall not be subject to his or her liabilities or creditor or to alienation, assignment, or anticipation by any such beneficiary.

Signature and Notarization

IN WITNESS WHEREOF, the settlor and trustee have hereunto set their hands and seals all as of the day and year first above written.

_____
SETTLOR

_____
TRUSTEE

STATE OF _____
COUNTY OF _____
I _____, a notary public in and for the County aforesaid in the state of _____ hereby certify that _____ whose name is signed to the foregoing writing bearing the date of _____, 1984, has acknowledged the same before me in my County aforesaid.

Given under my hand this _____
day of _____, 1984.

_____
Notary Public

My Commission expires _____

Addendum

SCHEDULE A

1. Proceeds of settlor's settlement payment amounting to $_____.
2. Any other amounts settlor decides to invest in this trust in any given year.

Courts have also held regularly that the powers of trustees are deemed either *imperative, discretionary, express,* or *implied.* Review the sample clauses on trustee powers, in exhibit 10.11. With power also come responsibilities and duties. Since the trustee operates in a fiduciary capacity, he or she must muster every energy to be loyal, reasonable, prudent, accountable, and responsible. In the assessment of these descriptive terms, trustees are not held to herculean standards or penalized because of simple mistakes in judgment. Trustees are judged as ordinary human beings, average in intelligence and in deed. (See exhibit 10.12.)

2. Resignation and removal of trustee

There are generally express provisions in a trust agreement as to how to remove a trustee or how to allow resignation. Resignation is usually a voluntary decision, and no court will by injunction or other remedy force the trustee

Exhibit 10.8

INTERVIVOS TRUST: SAMPLE

THIS TRUST INSTRUMENT made and executed this _____ day of _____, 19_____, by, and between _____, currently residing in _____, _____, hereinafter referred to as the "settlor," and _____, hereinafter referred to as the "trustee."

I. Establishment and Continuation of Trust Corpus

The settlor, in consideration of the premises, hereby assigns, transfers, sets over and delivers to the trustee, the property set forth in Schedule A, attached hereto, and has made payable, or will make payable to the trustee, to be held, administered, and disposed of as hereafter set forth in this agreement.

The settlor reserves to herself and any other person the right to deposit with the trustee, or make payable to the trustee, other policies of insurance, and also to assign, transfer, convey, devise, bequeath and deliver to the trustee such other personal property and real estate to be held, administered, and disposed of as hereafter set forth in this agreement.

Exhibit 10.9

TESTAMENTARY TRUST: RESIDUARY CLAUSE

The rest and residue of my estate, including all property over which I have power of appointment, I give, devise and bequeath to my trustees hereinafter named upon the trusts herein described.

If my wife, _____ (name), is living at my death, I direct them to hold, manage, invest and reinvest the same as two separate trusts, the first to be known as the _____ (name) Trust and the second to be known as the _____ (name) Trust.

The _____ Trust shall consist of that fractional share of my residuary estate which shall be necessary to produce the lowest possible federal estate tax on my estate after taking into account all credits against such tax.

In determining such fraction, my trustees shall take into account and deduct all other property which qualifies for the federal estate tax marital deduction and shall not take into account any deemed increase in my gross estate resulting from the application of the "generation-skipping transfer" provisions of the Internal Revenue Code of 1954, as amended. The final determination in the federal estate tax proceeding in my estate shall control the above determinations.

The _____ Trust shall consist of the balance of my residuary estate after establishing the _____ Trust. If my said wife is not living at my death, the _____ Trust shall consist of my entire residuary estate.

Exhibit 10.10

CHARITABLE TRUST: SAMPLE CLAUSE

Trust Agreement, made this _____ day of _____, 19 _____, between _____, hereinafter called the Donor, and State Bank, a _____ corporation with offices at _____, said Commonwealth, and its corporate successor or successors, hereinafter called the Trustee.

WITNESSETH: That for and in consideration of the covenants and agreements hereinafter contained and the mutual promises of the parties hereto each to the other party given, the parties hereto have covenanted and agreed and hereby do convenant and agree as follows:

A. The Donor hereby assigns, transfers, and delivers to the Trustee, its successors or assigns, the property set forth in the schedule hereto annexed, marked "Schedule A" and made a part hereof as if herein set forth in full, and agrees to execute such further instruments as shall be necessary to vest the Trustee with full title to the property described in said Schedule. The receipt of said property is hereby acknowledged by the Trustee, and the Trustee agrees to hold the said property, and other property into which it or any part thereof from time to time may be converted and any additions which may be made thereto, and all property which may at any time be in the possession of the Trustee as assets hereof, hereinafter sometimes called the Trust Fund, in trust, upon the terms hereinafter set forth.

B. Interest accrued and unpaid upon any securities at, and dividends upon any securities whose record date is subsequent to, the earlier of assignment or delivery of such securities to the Trustee shall become part of the Trust Fund.

C. This Trust is intended to qualify as a charitable remainder unitrust within the meaning of the Internal Revenue Code and the provisions hereof shall be interpreted and the administration thereof shall be carried out with this in mind.

EXHIBIT 10.11

TRUSTEE POWERS: CLAUSES

A.   General Administrative Powers of Trustee

In order to carry out the purposes of the Trust established by this Will, the Trustee, in addition to all other powers granted by this Will or by law, shall have the following powers over the trust estate, subject to any limitations specified elsewhere in this Will:

RETENTION OF ASSETS

(1) To retain any property received by the trust estate for as long as the Trustee considers it advisable.

INVESTMENTS

(2) To invest and reinvest in every kind of property and investment which men of prudence, discretion, and intelligence acquire for their own accounts. Trustee should not invest in any type of account, except those with some form of insurance or governmental guarantees.

MANAGEMENT

(3) To manage, control, repair, and improve all trust Property.

SALES

(4) To sell, for cash or on terms, and to exchange any trust property, but Trustee shall retain the services of _____ as realtor in the exchange of real property.

LEASING AND RELATED RIGHTS

(5) To lease any property for terms within or beyond the duration of the Trust for any purpose which the Trustee in his discretion may deem advisable in accordance with law, with or without an option to purchase, and make such improvements or effect such repairs or replacements to any real estate subject to this Trust, and to insure such real estate against fire or any other risk, and to charge the expense therefor to principal or income or part thereof to each as the Trustee may deem proper, and to develop such property, to subdivide it, dedicate it to public use, or grant easements therein as the Trustee may consider advisable; and any lease or agreement made with respect thereto shall be binding for the full term thereof even though it may extend beyond the duration of the Trust.

BORROWING

(6) To borrow money and to mortgage or pledge or otherwise encumber or hypothecate trust assets as the Trustee may, in his discretion, deem advisable either from himself individually or from others:

DIVISION AND DISTRIBUTION

(7) On any division or distribution of the trust estate, in the discretion of the Trustee, to divide and distribute property of the trust estate in money or in kind, including undivided interest or partly in money and partly in kind, including undivided interest; to exercise such powers, herein conferred, after the termination of the trust estate until final distribution of the trust assets; and to valuate trust property for purposes of determining the amount of the trust principal to be distributed to each beneficiary named herein, which valuation, in the absence of a showing of bad faith, shall be conclusive and binding on all concerned.

B.   Operational Provisions

DETERMINATION OF INCOME AND PRINCIPAL

(1) The Trustee shall determine what is income and what is principal of the Trust established under this Will, and what expenses, costs, taxes, and charges of any kind whatsoever shall be charged against income and what shall be charged against principal in accordance with the applicable law of the _____ of _____ as they now exist and may from time to time be enacted, amended or repealed.

ALTERNATE AND SUCCESSOR TRUSTEES

(2) In the event of the death, resignation, renunciation or inability to act of _____ as the Trustee, then I appoint _____ , as the Trustee in her place and stead with the same powers, rights, discretions, obligations, and immunities.

TRUSTEE'S FEES

(3) The Trustee shall receive a reasonable fee for the ordinary and extraordinary services rendered by him.

WAIVER OF TRUSTEE'S BOND

(4) No bond shall be required of any person appointed in this Will as Trustee.

CHOICE OF LAW

(5) The validity and administration of the Trust established under this Will and all questions relating to the construction or interpretation of the Trust shall be governed by the laws of the State of _____ .

Exhibit 10.12

PRELIMINARY AUDIT STATEMENT

Trust

Auditing Judge: _____ Audit List: _____
(month, year, number)

ORPHANS COURT DIVISION — COURT OF COMMON PLEAS

No. _____ of 19 _____

Estate of _____ , ☐ Deceased, ☐ Settlor

Name of Accountant: _____

Accounting period _____ , 19 _____ to _____ , 19 _____

Current market value of assets as set forth in account (p _____) $ _____

Are questions of law or fact to be presented for determination at the audit? If so, indicate nature on reverse side of page, briefly, and state accountant's position with respect thereto.

A. Trust created by Will:
   1. When did Decedent die? _____   2. Did trustee serve as executor of decedant's estate? _____

B. Trust created by Deed:
   1. Date of Deed? _____   2. Is settlor living? _____

C. In all cases, answer the following questions:
   1. Is any part of corpus to be distributed at this time? _____
   2. Is a request being made to terminate the trust? _____ in whole? _____ in part? _____
   3. Will a trustee or his estate be discharged? _____
   4. Is trustee claiming commissions on principal? _____ If so, state dates and amounts of principal commissions heretofore received: _____ _____ Are commissions based upon agreement executed by testator or settlor? _____
   5. Is trustee claiming special compensation for preparing the account? _____ calculating apportionments? _____ other services (specify)? _____
      (a) What amount is claimed? _____
   6. Is an apportionment involved? _____ by agreement? _____ in dispute? _____
   7. Do minors, unborn persons or other persons under legal disability have any interest, vested or contingent, in this estate (specify)? _____

(a) Is trustee willing to accept confirmation without prejudice? _____

(b) Has a petition been filed for the appointment of a guardian or trustee ad litem? _____ If appointment was made at prior audit, give name _____

8. Do charities have any interest in this estate? _____ vested? _____

contingent? _____ perpetual? _____

(a) Is cy pres doctrine involved? _____

(b) Has notice been given to the Attorney-General? _____

9. Has the accountant complied with the provisions of Rules 63 and *63.1, with respect to notice?

_____

10. Is there any inheritance tax due at this time? _____

_____   _____
(Telephone number)   *Counsel for Accountant*

10-40   NOTE: This statement shall be signed by the attorney who will appear for the accountant at the Audit and shall be submitted
              to the Auditing Judge at least 10 days prior to the Audit: otherwise the case will be continued

to stay on if he or she does not want to. Forcing would not be a policy favorable to efficient and productive trust administration.

Removal is possible and in a revocable trust, strictly within the option of the settlor. The term *for cause* often emerges in removal cases, and before a court will enforce removal, it must be satisfied as to any of these causes:

a. Pursuant to the terms of the trust document.

b. Trustee fails to make and file an accounting.

c. Trustee exhibits habitual drunkenness, neglect of duty, incompetency, and fraudulent conduct.

d. The interest of the trust demands removal.

e. Removal can also be ordered upon the written application of the persons having an interest in the trust, except that no trustee appointed by the will shall be removed upon such written application unless for cause.

VI. PRELIMINARY PROCESS IN ESTATE ADMINISTRATION

A. Human Factors

So often the legal profession acts too much like a business. To be sure, business is fine, but it can also be cold and mechanical. That's one of the frustrations of trying to deal with business—the sense that somehow humanity is lost in the shuffle. By this, it is meant that the law firm forgets to write a sympathy note to a deceased client's family or to make a call to a bereaved client expressing your condolences. The client's family whose estate you may be administering will not forget if you make the gesture. Demonstration of compassion also includes following any special instructions in the will or from the deceased's family on disposition of vital organs or funeral arrangements. Formal preliminary steps in estate administration are covered below.

B. Governmental Documentation

The law firm is responsible for the acquisition of all appropriate governmental documentation that relates to the decedent's benefits. Check for:

Veterans' burial benefits
Veterans' insurance
Vererans' disability
Social Security benefits
  Mother's benefits
  Survivor's benefits

Disability
SSI
Lump-sum death benefits
Black-lung benefits
Railroad retirement benefits

C. Private Benefits

The law firm is responsible for the acquisition of all private benefits payable upon the death of the client. Check for:

Private life insurance
Disability benefits in insurance
Accidental death benefits

Pension funds
Lump-sum distributions
Stocks, securities, or bonds reaching maturity

D. Legal Documentation

The law firm acquires and files all necessary legal documentation relating to the death of the client. It must:

- □ Obtain a taxpayer identification number.
- □ Obtain multiple copies of the death certificate.
- □ Obtain estate tax waivers on joint bank accounts/securities.
- □ Open proper bank accounts in the name of the estate.
- □ Contact all appropriate insurers, especially if the residence will be vacant.
- □ File or secure will (the original or certified copy).

Lastly, make it routine practice to keep in touch with the family of the deceased or their appropriate representatives. Make them feel they are not alone in this time of sadness.

VII. PROCESSES OF PROBATE AND ESTATE ADMINISTRATION

A. Estate Administration Questionnaire: Its Importance

After a few weeks have passed, and the firm can sense that the decedent's family is now ready to initiate the estate process, have the family complete a comprehensive questionnaire. This will enable the firm to collect all the information at once instead of continually pestering the family for every new detail that arises. An excellent form has been included as exhibit 10.13. This form assists the paralegal assigned to the file and also keeps those individuals who are peripherally responsible for the progress of the case aware of the major developments. Again, the paralegal gathers information for the law firm.

B. Distinguishing Informal and Formal Processes in Estate Administration

The philosophy behind state probate and administrative processes in dealing with estates is flexibility in operation with as little procedural rigor as possible. Hence, many states provide both informal and formal probate processes. If a will can be validated in an informal, self-proving way, courts tend to support that tactic. So too, with the general administration of estates. Unless a specific request for "supervised" administration comes forth, the court will grant and support unsupervised or independent administration. These less formal designs assume no contests or protracted litigation. In many respects, the court's role in the administration of estates has become reactive or passive unless some dispute or disagreement emerges that needs a resolution. In essence, the term *formal probate* means litigation, something really exceptional in the majority of American estates.

C. The Role of the Personal Representative, Executor, and/or Administrator in the Administration of Estates

1. Factors in choosing an executor

In preparing wills for clients, the firm must emphasize the importance of the testator's selection of an executor. Because of the complexities involved the choice of an executor should not be taken lightly. It pays to educate the testator

Exhibit 10.13

ESTATE ADMINISTRATION QUESTIONNAIRE

Legend: *Required in every case
**Required if Federal Estate Tax
Return will be filed

*1.   Name of decedent: _____

*2.   Address of decedent: _____

*3.   Social Security Number   _____

*4.   Data re death:

        Date of death: _____

        Place of death: _____

*5.   Location of original will, if any: _____

6.   Residence at time of death   _____
                                                   _____

7.   Date of birth of decedent: _____

8.   Place of birth of decedent: _____

**9.   Date when present domicile
        was established: _____

*10.   Citizenship of decedent: _____

*11.   Nationality of decedent: _____

**12.   Date of marriage to
        surviving spouse: _____

**13.   Matrimonial domicile at
        date of marriage: _____

**14.   Decedent's business or
        occupation or former
        business, etc.   _____

**15.   Length of last illness: _____

**16.   If hospitalized during last
        illness—name and address of
        hospital   _____
                                                   _____

**17.   Name and addresses of
        decedent's physicians: _____
                                                   _____
                                                   _____
                                                   _____

18.   If decedent had nurse or nurses
        during last illness—names and
        addresses of nurses: _____
                                                   _____
                                                   _____
                                                   _____

*19.   Was decedent a veteran—if so,
        give details: _____
                                                   _____
                                                   _____
                                                   _____

20.   Name of cemetery: _____

*21.   Did decedent have a Will—if so,
        when was it executed?   _____

22.   NAMES   ADDRESSES

Personal
Representative: _____   _____

                       _____   _____

Alternate Personal
Representative: _____   _____

                       _____   _____

                       _____   _____

Trustees: _____   _____

                       _____   _____

Alternate
Trustees: _____   _____

                       _____   _____

                       _____   _____

Beneficiaries: _____   _____

                       _____   _____

                       _____   _____

Trust
Beneficiaries: _____   _____

                       _____   _____

                       _____   _____

                       _____   _____

Guardians: _____   _____

                       _____   _____

*23.   Marital status of decedent: _____

*24.   Name and address of
       surviving spouse: _____

                           _____

Surviving children:

                                              MARITAL STATUS
                                              (IF MARRIED,
   NAMES   ADDRESSES   AGES   NAME OF SPOUSE)

_____   _____   ____   _____
_____   _____   ____   _____
_____   _____   ____   _____
_____   _____   ____   _____

        Surviving grandchildren:

_____   _____   ____   _____
_____   _____   ____   _____
_____   _____   ____   _____
_____   _____   ____   _____

        Brothers and sisters:

_____   _____   ____   _____
_____   _____   ____   _____
_____   _____   ____   _____
_____   _____   ____   _____

        Parents, if living:

_____   _____
_____   _____

                        *Assets

25. Safe deposit boxes: NAME OF: Keys with:

_____   _____   _____
_____   _____   _____
_____   _____   _____

26. Automobiles:

YEAR	MAKE	MODEL	SERIAL NUMBER	PRESENT VALUE
_____	_____	_____	_____	_____
_____	_____	_____	_____	_____

27. Bank accounts: (individual)

NAME OF BANK	TYPE OF ACCOUNT	NUMBER OF ACCOUNT	BALANCE ON DEPOSIT
_____	_____	_____	_____
_____	_____	_____	_____
_____	_____	_____	_____
	_____		

28. Bank accounts: (joint)

NAME OF BANK	WHOSE FUNDS USED	NUMBER OF ACCOUNT	BALANCE ON DEPOSIT
_____	_____	_____	_____
_____	_____	_____	_____
_____	_____	_____	_____
	_____		

29. Totten Trust Accounts:

NAME OF BANK	NUMBER OF ACCOUNT	NAME OF BENEFICIARY	BALANCE
_____	_____	_____	_____
_____	_____	_____	_____
_____	_____	_____	_____

30. Trust Accounts held as Trustee:

NAME OF BANK	NUMBER OF ACCOUNT	ESTATE FOR WHICH HELD	BALANCE
_____	_____	_____	_____
_____	_____	_____	_____
	_____		

31. Securities:

NAME OF ISSUING COMPANY	KIND OF SECURITIES	NUMBER	HOW HELD	PLEDGED
_____	_____	_____	_____	_____
_____	_____	_____	_____	_____
	_____			

32. Brokerage Accounts:

NAME OF COMPANY	ADDRESS	SECURITIES HELD IN STREET NAME	CREDIT BALANCE
_____	_____	_____	_____
_____	_____	_____	_____

33. Real Estate: (and mortgages on real estate)

LOCATION	HOW HELD	LIENS ON REALTY	WHEN ACQUIRED	COST OF ACQUISITION PRESENT VALUE
_____	_____	_____	_____	_____
_____	_____	_____	_____	_____
_____	_____	_____	_____	_____

34. Insurance on Decedent's Life:

NAME OF COMPANY	POLICY NUMBER	FACE VALUE	NAME OF BENEFICIARY OR OWNER	CASH SURRENDER VALUE
_____	_____	_____	_____	_____
_____	_____	_____	_____	_____
_____	_____	_____	_____	_____

35. Other Insurance:

NAME OF COMPANY	POLICY NUMBER	TYPE OF INSURANCE	FACE VALUE
_____	_____	_____	_____
_____	_____	_____	_____
_____	_____	_____	_____

36. Pension, Profit-Sharing, Bonus, etc. Plans:

SOURCE	AMOUNT OF BENEFITS	DURATION
_____	_____	_____
_____	_____	_____

37. Deferred Compensation:

SOURCE	AMOUNT OF BENEFITS	DURATION
_____	_____	_____
_____	_____	_____

38. Social Security Benefits: _____

39. Interest in trusts and estates:

SOURCE	KIND OF INTEREST	AMOUNT OR VALUE OF PROPERTY
_____	_____	_____
_____	_____	_____

40. Property held as donee of a power:

SOURCE	KIND OF PROPERTY	AMOUNT OR VALUE OF PROPERTY
_____	_____	_____
_____	_____	_____

41. Property held as custodian:

FOR WHOM HELD	KIND OF PROPERTY	AMOUNT OR VALUE OF PROPERTY
_____	_____	_____
_____	_____	_____

42. Tangible Personal Property:
　　　Furniture: _____
　　　Clothing: _____
　　　Jewelry: _____
　　　Art objects: _____
　　　Machinery: _____
　　　Tools and Equipment: _____
　　　Carpets: _____
　　　Household utensils
　　　and appliances: _____
　　　Animals: _____
　　　Boats: _____
　　　Miscellaneous: _____

43. Claims against:

NAME OF	ADDRESS	KIND OF CLAIM	AMOUNT OR VALUE
_____	_____	_____	_____
_____	_____	_____	_____
_____	_____	_____	_____

44. Business interests of decedent:

NAME OF BUSINESS	ADDRESS	FORM IN WHICH OPERATED	DECEDENT'S INTEREST
_____	_____	_____	_____
_____	_____	_____	_____
_____	_____		

Value of interest _____
_____
_____

45. Employment of decedent prior to death:

NAME OF EMPLOYER	ADDRESS	TYPE OF EMPLOYMENT	PENSION OR OTHER BENEFIT ARRANGEMENT
_____	_____	_____	_____

*Liabilities

NAME OF CREDITOR	TYPE OF LIABILITY	WHEN LIABILITY INCURRED	AMOUNT OF LIABILITY
_____	_____	_____	_____
_____	_____	_____	_____
_____	_____	_____	_____
_____	_____	_____	_____
_____	_____	_____	_____

Tax Information

*   Intervivos gifts in trust: _____
*   Gifts made within three years of death: _____
*   Property received from estates within ten years prior to death: _____
** Had decedent ever filed a federal gift tax return? _____
    Provide details: _____
*   Was decedent a donee of a general power of appointment? _____
    If so, provide details: _____
    _____
    _____

Name and address of person who prepared decedent's tax return: _____
_____

about what is involved, and the firm will be pleasantly surprised at how appreciative clients are when they realize how the role of the executor does not fit the makeup of individuals they assumed to be competent for the duties. In short, it is a big job in which lawyers have to be consulted, investment and real estate people conferred with, and other assorted mundane experiences and relationships considered. Review again the list of powers and rights discussed in chapter 2. Also realize that sometimes the choice of the testator cannot be effected because of the death or illness of the proposed person, personal problems, or simply willful desire not to perform the functions. A renunciation form is usually filed with the registrar and approved in due course. The secondary choice can then take over, or the court can appoint a new representative according to its own statutory preferences. See exhibit 10.14.

Exhibit 10.14

EXECUTOR POWERS: SAMPLE CLAUSES

Executor

(1) I appoint my husband as the Executor of this Will. In the event of his death, resignation, renunciation, or inability to act in that capacity, then I appoint my _____, _____ of _____, as the Executor of this Will in his place and stead. My Executrix or Executor, whether original, substitute, or successor, is referred to herein as my "Executor."

No Bond Required

(2) No bond or other security shall be required of any Executor appointed in this Will.

Compensation of Executor

(3) My Executor shall receive reasonable compensation for services rendered to my estate during administration as determined by the court in which this Will is admitted to probate.

Powers

(4) My Executor shall have, in extension and not in limitation of the powers given by law or by other provision of this Will, the following powers with respect to the settlement and administration of my estate:

Same Powers as Trustee

(a) To exercise with regard to the probate estate all of the powers and authority conferred by this Will on the Trustee over the trust estate.

Employment of Attorneys, Advisors, and Other Agents

(b) To employ as legal counsel, the services of _____ of _____, if at all possible, and to employ investment advisors, accountants, brokers or any other agent deemed necessary.

Distribution of Estate

(c) When paying legacies or dividing or distributing my estate, to make such payments, division, or distribution wholly or partly in kind by allotting and transferring specific securities or other personal or real properties or undivided interests therein as part of the whole or any one or more payments or shares at current values in the manner deemed advisable by my Executor.

All of the above powers may be exercised, except as otherwise provided by law, from time to time in the discretion of my Executor without further court order or license.

---

2. Duties of the personal representative, executor, and/or administrator

a. Retention and Collection of Assets

The firm should immediately make available the estate questionnaire completed long ago by the testator. The comprehensiveness of the report can truly be appreciated at this stage, since every asset, security, bank account, or other interest is listed in detail. Since the representative has to collect those assets, location becomes much easier. When the executor is apprised of the location, he or she can do a far better job of protecting everything. As noted in the preliminary steps to probate, both the attorney and the representative must also:

☐ Check on life insurance proceeds.
☐ Review checking and savings accounts.
☐ Check on Social Security benefits.
☐ Transfer securities into the name of the estate.
☐ Transfer automobile (you will need the title, the registration card and the appropriate state forms).
☐ Be prepared to transfer real property.

The personal representative should also proceed as expeditiously as possible with the settlement and distribution of the decedent's estate and to resolve any questions regarding the estate or its administration. The representative also has a duty to:

- □ Provide regular information to all heirs and devisees.
- □ Assist in the preparation of all inventories, appraisals, and information filings.
- □ Prepare a formal accounting.
- □ Resolve creditors' claims.
- □ Effect final distribution and settlement of the estate.
  (Mention should also be made as to the representative's right to seek and be awarded a commission.)

D. Probate

1. Small estates

One major point that is often misunderstood relates to the sufficiency and size of the estate that qualifies it for the process of probate. Depending on your jurisdiction, the maximum size of an estate that is exempted from the normal estate administration processes ranges from $5,000 to $20,000. Therefore, certain small estates can be informally processed and with little or no expense to the client. Many jurisdictions even exempt a certain portion of the estate from any claim by creditors.

2. Regular estates

Small-estate administrations are a rarity because of the values of the most basic residences in these times. Hence, the majority of estates must be probated, and the action essentially follows these steps:

a. FILING OF A COMPLAINT OR PETITION OF PROBATE FOR A WILL (both formal and informal)

The petition or complaint is presented to the registry or other appropriate official, together with a will and death certificate. Depending on the circumstances, the witnesses may have to attest to the signature in wills lacking a self-proof clause, and the executor may have to be present as well. The end result in this process, whether the probate is formal or informal, is a statement accepting the will as valid.

b. PETITION FOR GRANT OF LETTERS TESTAMENTARY (also known as Letters of Administration)

Once the validity of a will is established, the registrar, court, or other appropriate official will grant letters testamentary upon payment of the required fees. Letters testamentary are official documents giving formal legal powers to the executor, personal representative, or administrator of the will. The executor may also be asked to post bond before he or she begins the task of estate administration. In some jurisdictions, *short certificates* will also be issued that attest formally to the executor's powers. They are usually required by banks, real estate companies, or other legal entities. Be prepared to pay for them, and check with your local jurisdiction as to the cost for each certificate. (See exhibits 10.15 and 10.16.)

c. NOTICE

Within prescribed periods, all interested parties in the estate should be notified of the pending administration. Notice should be sent by certified mail to any corporate, group, or individual beneficiary.

d. TAXES

The death of the client could possibly be near or at the legal filing time for his or her own personal or business taxes. Keep track of those filings to avoid penalties and late charges. Also spend a good deal of time planning appropriate tax strategies. Estate and inheritance taxes were greatly modified under the 1981 Tax Act. (See exhibit 10.2 for a check list of tax considerations in estate administration.)

e. ADVERTISING

Once a grant of letters testamentary has occurred, many jurisdictions require some form of advertisement

Exhibit 10.15

Will

PETITION FOR PROBATE and GRANT OF LETTERS

Estate of .... No. ....

also known as .... To:

.... Register of Wills for the

.... Deceased. County   in the

Social Security No. .... Commonwealth

      The petition of the undersigned respectfully represents that:

      Your petitioner(s) is/are 18 years of age or older and the execut .... named in the last will of the above decedent, dated .... 19 .... and codicil(s) dated ....

....

....

....

(state relevant circumstances, e.g., renunciation, death of executor, etc.)

      Decedent was domiciled at death in Philadelphia County, Pennsylvania, with h ..... last family or principal residence at

....

(list street, number and municipality)

      Decedent, then ..... years of age, died .... , 19 .....

at ....

      Except as follows, decedent did not marry, was not divorced and did not have a child born or adopted after execution of the will offered for probate; was not the victim of a killing and was never adjudicated incompetent: ....

Decedent at death owned property with estimated values as follows:

(If domiciled in Pa.)	All personal property	$	....
(If not domiciled in Pa.)	Personal property in Pennsylvania	$	....
(If not domiciled in Pa.)	Personal property in County	$	....
Value of real estate in Pennsylvania		$	....

situated as follows: ....

....

....

      WHEREFORE, petitioner(s) respectfully request(s) the probate of the last will and codicil(s) presented herewith and the grant of letters .... thereon.

(testamentary, administration e.t.a.; administration d.b.n.c.t.a.)

Signature(s) and Residence(s) of Petitioner(s)

....

....

....

....

OATH OF PERSONAL REPRESENTATIVE

COMMONWEALTH OF   } SS
COUNTY OF

      The petitioner(s) above-named swear(s) or affirm(s) that the statements in the foregoing petition are true and correct to the best of the knowledge and belief of petitioner(s) and that as personal representative(s) of the above decedent petitioner(s) will well and truly administer the estate according to law.

Sworn to or affirmed and subscribed   ....

before me this .... day of   ....

.... 19 ....

....

Deputy Register

Signature(s)

Attorney .... I.D. ....

Address ....

Telephone No.

Exhibit 10.16

PETITION FOR GRANT OF LETTERS OF ADMINISTRATION

Estate of .... No. ....

also known as .... To:

.... Register of Wills for the

.... Deceased. County   in the

Social Security No. .... Commonwealth

The petition of the undersigned respectfully represents that:

Your petitioner(s), who is/are 18 years of age or older, appl .... for letters of administration ....

.... on the estate of the above decedent.
(d.b.n.; pendente lite; durante absentia; durante minoritate)

Decedent was domiciled at death in Philadelphia County, Pennsylvania, with h ..... last family or principal residence

at ....
(list street, number and municipality)

Decedent, then . . . . . years of age, died .... , 19 . . . . . .

at ....

Decedent at death owned property with estimated values as follows:

(If domiciled in Pa.)	All personal property	$ ....
(If not domiciled in Pa.)	Personal property in Pennsylvania	$ ....
(If not domiciled in Pa.)	Personal property in County	$ ....
Value of real estate in Pennsylvania		$ ....

situated as follows: ....

....

....

Petitioner . . . . . . after a proper search ha . . . . . ascertained that decedent left no will and was survived by the following spouse (if any) and heirs:

Name	Relationship	Residence

THEREFORE, petitioner(s) respectfully request(s) the grant of letters of administration in the appropriate form to the undersigned.

Signature(s) and Residence(s) of Petitioner(s)

....

....

....

....

OATH OF PERSONAL REPRESENTATIVE

COMMONWEALTH OF
COUNTY OF   } SS

The petitioner(s) above-named swear(s) or affirm(s) that the statements in the foregoing petition are true and correct to the best of the knowledge and belief of petitioner(s) and that as personal representative(s) of the above decedent petitioner(s) will well and truly administer the estate according to law.

Sworn to or affirmed and subscribed   ....

before me this .... day of   ....

.... 19 ....

Deputy Register   ....

Signature(s)

Exhibit 10.17

Will
Adm.   No. _____ 19 _____   Filed _____

REGISTER OF WILLS

COMMONWEALTH OF   { ss.   # INVENTORY
COUNTY OF

Execut   of the Estate of _____
Administrat
deceased, being duly sworn according to law, depose_____ and say_____ that the items appearing in the following inventory
include all of the personal assets wherever situate and all of the real estate in the Commonwealth of   said
decedent, that the valuation placed opposite each item of said inventory represents its fair value as of the date of the decedent's
death, and that decedent owned no real estate outside of the Commonwealth   except that which appears in a
memorandum at the end of this inventory.

Sworn to and subscribed before me this
_____ day of   _____

_____ A. D. 19 _____   _____

_____

Attorney — (*Name*) _____

        (*Address*) _____
DATE OF DEATH   LAST RESIDENCE   DECEDENTS SOCIAL SECURITY NO.

NOTE: *The Memorandum of real estate outside the Commonwealth of Pennsylvania may, at the election of the personal
representative include the value of each item, but such figures should not be extended into the total of the Inventory. (See
Section 401 (b) of Fiduciaries Act, of 1949.*
NOTE: *This form to be used only in estates of persons dying on or after February 23, 1956.*

identifying the estate to be administered as well as the personal representative, executor, or administrator. Be aware that certain jurisdictions require publication in specific law-related newspapers, and those same jurisdictions sometimes require from one to four publications of the advertisement. Consult the local rules in the appropriate county.

f. Categorization of Assets   (estate or non-estate)

In the interest of tax reduction, the estate must consider which property or interest has the potential to be included or excluded from the overall calculation of estate value. Simply, the lower the value, the lower the tax. The following categories of property can, in most jurisdictions, be excluded from the gross value of an estate:

1. Property, either real or personal, jointly owned, with rights of survivorship; e.g., a personal residence owned as tenants by the entireties
2. U.S. savings bonds
3. Life insurance
4. Pension benefits, if under varied rules of the IRS
5. Some lump-sum distributions
6. TRASOP or ESOP plans, depending on contributions
7. Some intervivos trusts
8. Totten, or savings account, trusts
9. Automobiles, for the purpose of transferring to surviving spouse (check local rules)

In sum, those assets that pass outside of the estate are not includable in the gross valuation of the decedent's estate. A review of the client's original *estate-planning guide* as well as the *administration questionnaire* should highlight potential tax savings.

g. Preparation and Filing of Inventory/Information

The next step in the process of administering an estate is the filing of an *inventory*, which specifically outlines the assets, property, and interests that are includable in the estate. The inventory is generally required within three months or so after the appointment of the representative. The inventory is filed in the county where the letters testamentary were granted and are subsequently reviewed to determine the total value of the estate. The representative or administrator is also required to file supplemental inventories if and when new estate property interests are discovered. From this inventory assessment will come forth various inheritance taxes, which the estate must pay. (See exhibits 10.17 and 10.18 for required forms for filing an inventory.)

h. Handling Claims of Creditors

Within a statutory period, after publication of appointment of the representative and the granting of letters testamentary, creditors must assert their claims or be forever barred. Check local rules for the specific statute of limitations.

The estate recognizes a certain priority or scheme of claims payment when funds are insufficient to meet the demands. As a general recommendation, this order has some support.

1. Cost of administration
2. Funeral expenses
3. Debts and taxes with preference under federal law
4. Reasonable and necessary medical expenses
5. State debts and taxes
6. All other claims

If bona fide claims are filed and the estate possesses sufficient funds to pay those claims, the personal representative has both the duty and power to make payment on those claims.

i. Payment of State and Federal Taxes

This subject matter is covered in the next section.

Exhibit 10.18

FORMAL ACCOUNTING

Account

SUPERIOR COURT—LAW DIVISION
PROBATE PART-

In the Matter of the Estate of   :

 HELEN HART (also known as   :   CIVIL ACTION

 Helen Knowles),   :   ACCOUNT

 deceased.   :

   Plaintiff, Barbara Brown, residing at 601 Fountain Street,   herewith submits this first and final account of her administration as Executrix of the estate of Helen Hart (also known as Helen Knowles) deceased: Plaintiff charges herself as follows:

Eighth Bank & Trust Company, savings account #61388 in name of Helen Hart	$14,803.23
Twelfth National Bank of N.J., savings account #02-312700 in name of Helene Carter	6,934.00
Twelfth National Bank of N.J., savings account #02-311780 in name of Helen Hart	1,831.98
Check from Arthur Advocate, Esq.	222.76
	$23,791.97
Interest on estate savings account in County National Bank	$ 325.78
Interest on account in Twelfth National Bank	18.42
Interest on account in Twelfth National Bank	69.69
	$ 413.89

TOTAL $24,205.86

Plaintiff prays allowance as follows:

1.	Surrogate of Passaic County for accounting fees	$ 91.45
2.	Dr. David Downs, 248 Orange St., .	1,000.00
3.	Jersey Medical Center, Montclair, .	2,000.00
4.	Passaic County Welfare Board (as per judgment entered by the Court on 9/10/)	3,293.00
5.	To Barbara Brown, trustee to open trustee account	100.00
6.	To Barbara Brown, reimbursement for expenses to obtain death certificates and for Surrogate's fees	48.00
7.	To Lawrence Lawyer, reimbursement for Inheritance Tax paid .	39.64
	TOTAL DISBURSED	$ 6,572.09

Statement of Assets

The following is a full statement or list of the investments and assets composing the balance of the estate in accountant's hands setting forth the inventory value or the value when the accountant acquired them and the value as of the day the account is drawn, and also a statement where the investments and assets are deposited or kept and in what name, and a statement of all changes made in the investments and assets since they were acquired or since the date of the last account, together with the dates when the changes were made.

Estate checking account #12 0132 8 in County National Bank	$ 7,532.61
Estate savings account in County Nat'l Bank of N.J.	10,101.16
TOTAL	$17,633.77

STATE OF
PASSAIC COUNTY   )
)ss:
)

     BARBARA BROWN, the above named Executrix, being by me duly sworn according to law, on her oath says that the foregoing account is in all things just and correct, both as to the charge and discharge thereof, according to the best of her knowledge and belief.

Sworn and subscribed this 5th day

of October A.D. 19 ___ before me

                                                  s/
_____
                                           BARBARA BROWN

s/
_____
Myra Master
Notary Public
My Commission Expires July 7, 19

To the Judge of the   County Court, Probate Division:

     The above account having been placed on the files of my office on the _____ day of _____, 19 ____, and being by me audited and stated, is now reported for settlement.

Dated,

_____ 19 ____.

                                   _____
                                             Surrogate

j. Distribution of Estate Proceeds: First and Final Accountings

    Some jurisdictions permit the distribution of estate assets after waiting required periods of time without any formal accounting process. This policy is in keeping with the spirit of flexibility in the administration of estates. A lack of any significant controversy in the smaller estates eliminates the necessity for the formal accounting process, and distribution can readily take place. In the larger estates, a formal accounting is an intelligent step. In some jurisdictions, a *statement of proposed distribution* or a *schedule of distribution* must be filed prior to the audit and eventual formal accounting. After formal approval, the distribution may take place. Note well that the formal accounting must deduct all the expenses of estate from its eventual distribution; otherwise those liabilities will rest with the representative.

k. Discharge of Personal Representative, Executor, or Administrator

    Once the business of the estate is concluded and the final distribution made, a representative may be discharged informally or formally. This process is frequently called a *petition for closing an estate.* Before filing for closing or settlement or requesting discharge, make sure that all matters affecting the estate have been attended to. (See exhibits 10.19 and 10.20.)

l. Other Issues

    No effort has been made to cover every avenue in estate administration, but a brief mention of the following steps is imperative:

    1. Petition for executor's commission. Don't forget to file all appropriate papers to reimburse all expenses and services of the executor. A statutory fee schedule usually exists.

    2. Petition for counsel fee. Most jurisdictions require a filing to insure approval of the fee before payment.

    3. Closing letter from counsel. When all estate matters are complete, a most professional touch can be added by a closing letter to all interested parties in the estate summarizing and clarifying the final distribution. The parties will be appreciative, and as a result more clients may come to the firm because of this courtesy.

VIII. FEDERAL ESTATE TAX: THE ECONOMIC RECOVERY TAX ACT OF 1981

A. Major Features

The amendments fall into three categories:

Exhibit 10.19

DISCHARGE OF REPRESENTATIVE: SAMPLE

IN THE _____ COURT OF _____ COUNTY,

ESTATE OF   )   NO.
)   DOCKET
)

ORDER OF DISCHARGE

On application of _____
                              (name)
independent representative, the representative's verified report having been filed and the court being advised that (a) due notice has been given to or waived by all interested persons entitled thereto, (b) no objection is pending and (c) all acts necessary for the full administration of the estate have been performed according to law:

    IT IS ORDERED that the independent representative is discharged and the estate is closed.

DATE: _____, 19 _____

_____
Judge

Exhibit 10.20

PETITION FOR DISCHARGE

TO THE HONORABLE, THE JUDGES OF THE SAID COURT:

    The petition of _____, respectfully represents:

    1. That he is administrator of the estate of _____ who died _____, 19 ____, letters of administration having been granted _____, 19 ____, by the Register of Wills of _____ County.

    2. That he filed his account in the Register's office _____, 19 ____, and said account was duly adjudicated _____, 19 ____, and confirmed absolutely by your Honorable court.

    3. That the entire estate has been paid and transferred to the parties entitled thereto in accordance with the said adjudication (if schedule of distribution was filed, add: and schedule of distribution approved _____, 19 ____) and no other money or property belonging to the estate has been received by petitioner since the adjudication of the account.

    WHEREFORE, petitioner prays your Honorable Court to discharge him from duties of his appointment.

_____
Petitioner

STATE OF
COUNTY OF _____   ) ss.:
)

_____, being duly sworn according to law, deposes and says that the facts set forth in the foregoing petition are true.

    He further says that the parties who have signed the annexed consents to his discharge are all the parties interested in the estate.

_____

(Jurat)

---

    1. Increase in unified credit
    2. Reduction in top-bracket rates
    3. Unlimited marital deduction

1. Increase in unified credit

    Under prior law, the unified credit was $47,000 for transfers made after 1980. Thus, there was no estate or gift tax liability on taxable transfers up to $175,625. The act increases the credit from $47,000 to $192,800, phased in over a six-year period and based on the following schedule:

TRANSFERS MADE AND DECEDENTS DYING IN	UNIFIED CREDIT	AMOUNT OF TRANSFERS NOT TAXED	LOWEST TAX-BRACKET RATE
1982	$ 62,800	$225,000	32%
1983	79,300	275,000	34
1984	96,300	325,000	34
1985	121,800	400,000	34
1986	155,800	500,000	37
1987 and later	192,800	600,000	37

The filing requirements were amended to conform to the increase in the credit.

2. Reduction in top-bracket

The act phases in a reduction of the top brackets from the current rate of 70 percent down to a maximum rate of 50 percent over a four-year period based on the following schedule:

TRANSFERS MADE AND DECEDENTS DYING IN	TOP-BRACKET RATE	TOP-BRACKET AMOUNT IN EXCESS OF
1982	65%	$4,000,000
1983	60	3,500,000
1984–1987	55	3,000,000
1988 and later	50	2,500,000

3. Unlimited marital deduction

The principal purpose behind the original marital deduction legislation was to allow one spouse to transfer one-half of his or her estate to the other spouse without incurring a gift- or estate-tax liability.

The act eliminates all of the quantitative limitations on the gift and estate tax marital deductions. All qualifying transfers between spouses (including community property) will be allowed to pass free of gift and estate taxes. The primary purpose behind the change appears to be Congress's feeling that a husband and wife represent one economic unit for estate and gift taxes as they do for income taxes.

The act provides a special carryover-basis rule for appreciated property received by the decedent by way of gifts within one year of the decedent's death, where the property passes back to the original donor or donor's spouse. This provision, however, also covers gifts outside the interspousal situation. The new provision applies to property acquired by the decedent after December 31, 1981.

If certain conditions are met, the act will allow life estates transferred to the spouse to qualify for the unlimited marital deduction.

4. Joint interests between spouses

The tax treatment of jointly held property between spouses becomes important only (1) in determining the basis of the property in the hands of the survivor and (2) in determining if certain other provisions apply, such as deferred payments of estate taxes and redemptions to pay estate taxes. It is no longer important in determining how much is to be included in the gross estate.

The act provides that each spouse is to be treated as one-half owner of jointly held property regardless of which spouse paid for the property.

5. Gift tax filing requirements

The unlimited marital deduction has the effect of eliminating the need for the filing of gift tax returns for all qualifying interspousal transfers.

6. Transfers made in contemplation of death

The act eliminates the gift-in-contemplation-of-death rules on most transfers by decedents dying after 1981. Accordingly, gifts made within three years of death will be excluded from the decedent's gross estate. The recipient, however, will be denied a step-up in basis.

7. Gift taxes: Increase in annual exclusion

The amount of exclusion had been $3,000 since 1942 and was intended to reduce the administrative burden for record keeping of small gifts. Because of the increase in price levels since 1942, Congress felt it was necessary to increase the annual exclusion to $20,000. The increase applies generally to gifts after 1981.

8. Transfers for educational and medical expenses

The new law provides an unlimited annual exclusion for qualifying payments made directly to the institution or person furnishing the education or medical service.

9. Other estate and gift tax provisions

1. Simplifies and liberalizes rules for extension of time to pay estate taxes attributable to closely held businesses.
2. Allows an estate and gift tax charitable deduction for donations of works of art that are subject to copyright even though the copyright is not transferred.
3. Allows for valid disclaimers even if they are not recognized under local law.
4. Repeals the provision allowing testamentary tax-free transfers to certain minor children.
5. Extends the transitional rule one year for generation-skipping transfers to include persons dying before 1983 where the trust or will was not amended.
6. Starting with 1982 transfers, gift tax returns are to be filed and taxes paid annually—generally on April 15 following the calendar year in which the gift was made.

B. Specific Transitional Guides

1. Transitional rule

Many existing wills and trusts include maximum marital-deduction-formula clauses under which the amount of property transferred to the surviving spouse is determined by reference to the maximum allowable marital deduction. Because under the old law the maximum estate tax deduction was $250,000 or one-half of the adjusted gross estate, whichever was greater, many individuals may not have intended any greater amount to pass to their surviving spouses, as they might have if the new unlimited marital deduction had been in effect when the marital deduction was computed under a formula clause.

Therefore, the act contains a transitional rule, which provides that the new unlimited marital deduction will not apply to transfers resulting from a will executed or a trust created before the date that is thirty days after the enactment of the act if that will contains a formula marital-deduction clause. The transitional rule applies provided that (1) the decedent died after 1981, (2) the formula clause was not amended before the death of the decedent to refer specifically to the unlimited marital deduction at anytime after the date that was thirty days after the date of the act's enactment, and (3) there is no state law that would construe the formula clause as referring to the unlimited marital deduction.

2. Community property

The act removed the provisions of the law that barred estate and gift tax marital deductions for transfers of community property between spouses. Under the act, such transfers qualify for an estate tax marital deduction for estates of decedents dying after 1981, and for a gift tax marital deduction with respect to gifts made after 1981.

3. Property jointly owned by spouses

Under the old law, one-half of the value of a qualified joint interest in property owned in joint tenancy by a decedent and his or her spouse was includible in the decedent's gross estate. Additionally, a portion of the value of jointly owned property used in a farm or closely held business in which both spouses materially participated was excludable from the decedent's gross estate. If neither of these rules applied, the entire value of the property was includible in the decedent's gross estate, except to the extent that the estate could show contribution of consideration for the property by the other spouse.

The act eliminated these rules. It provides that, in the case of property jointly owned with the right of survivorship by spouses, the estate of the first spouse to die will include one-half of the value of the property regardless of which spouse furnished the consideration for the property. In accord with this new rule the qualified joint-interest requirements were repealed, including the gift tax provisions that governed the creation of such interest. Additionally, the act repealed the rules allowing an exclusion of a portion of the value of jointly owned property used in a farm or other business in which both spouses materially participated.

4. Basis of property acquired from a decedent

Under the old law, the basis of property acquired from a decedent was its fair market value on the date of the decedent's death. However, under the act, this rule does not apply with respect to appreciated property acquired by the decedent as a gift within one year of death if such property passes from the donee-decedent to the original donor or to the donor's spouse. The basis of such property in the hands of the original donor or his spouse is its basis to the decedent immediately prior to death, rather than its fair market value on the date of death. This provision, effective for property acquired after the enactment date of the act by decedents dying after 1981, is intended to prevent individuals from transferring property in contemplation of a donee's death merely to obtain a tax-free step-up in basis upon receipt of the property from the decedent's estate.

IX. FEDERAL ESTATE RETURN

A. General Provisions and Guidelines

1. A return must be filed on form 706 (latest revision January 1985) for the estate of every citizen or resident of the United States whose gross estate exceeds certain threshold values.

2. For anyone dying in 1981 and thereafter, a return is required for all those whose gross estates exceed $175,000.

   a. The threshold amount set forth above has to be adjusted for certain gifts. The applicable threshold amount is to be reduced by the sum of the amount of adjusted taxable gifts made by the decedent after December 31, 1976, plus the aggregate amount allowed as a specific exemption with respect to gifts made by the decedent after September 8, 1976, and prior to January 1, 1977.

3. The estate tax return must be filed within nine months of the date of the decedent's death.

4. In case it is impossible or impracticable for the executor to file a reasonably complete return within nine months of the date of death, the district director or the director of a service center may, upon a showing of good and sufficient cause, grant a reasonable extension of time for filing the return required. Unless the executor is abroad, the extension may not be for more than six months from the date for filing.

5. According to the instructions in form 706, all personal representatives (executors) should verify and sign the return.

6. The federal estate tax shall be paid by the executor. In the event there is no qualified executor or administrator, then any person in actual or constructive possession of any property of the decedent is deemed to be the executor for purposes of paying the federal estate tax. The federal estate tax must be paid at the same time and at the same place designated for filing the federal estate tax return. Extensions for filing the federal estate tax return are not an extension for the payment of the federal estate tax.

7. The executor of an estate is PERSONALLY LIABLE for an unpaid estate tax that results from his or her payment of any debts or the making of any distributions before the entire estate tax has been paid.

8. The executor of an estate is required to file the decedent's income tax return, if said return would be required. The return is due at the same time it would have been due had the individual lived.

B. Alternate Valuation

With the elimination of the carryover-basis provisions, the alternate-valuation-date election (six months after the date of death), is once again a rather straightforward election. It would seem at first glance that the election of the lowest value would seem prudent.

C. Disclaimers

Section 2518 allows an interest that has been disclaimed by a beneficiary to pass without any transfer tax, as though it had never been received by the disclaimant. The qualified disclaimer is a written irrevocable and unqualified refusal to accept a bequest. The disclaimer must be made within nine months after date of death.

Disclaimers are an excellent postmortem estate-planning tool.

D. Generation Skipping

The generation-skipping tax is imposed on property either continuing in trust or passing from trust from one generation to another generation. The tax is designated to impose substantially the same tax as would be imposed if property were transferred by gift or at death. The tax imposed on the generation-skipping transfer is determined by adding the amount of the generation-skipping transfer to other taxable transfers of the deemed transferor. If the deemed transferor is alive at the time of the generation-skipping transfer, then the tax is treated as if it were a gift tax. If the deemed transferor is dead at the time of generation-skipping transfer, the tax is treated like the estate tax.

E. Outline of Form 706

Schedule A

A. REAL ESTATE

1. Any real estate owned by the decedent should be listed. Real estate owned jointly with another should be listed on Schedule E. Each item of real property should be listed separately. The property should be described under the "description" column. The instructions provide that the area and improvements should be listed.

2. Under the description column the basis used for determining "fair market value" should be listed. If based on appraisal, the appraisal should be attached to the return; if by a contract of sale, said contract should be attached.

3. Rents accrued as of the date of death should also be listed.

Schedule B

Schedule B is used to report any interest owned by the decedent at the time of his or her death in stocks and bonds of any type, foreign or domestic, publicly traded securities, government bonds, interest in cooperative apartments, and corporations.

1. Dividends and accrued interest. If the record date for payment of dividends with respect to stock owned by the decedent falls on or before the date of death and payment date falls after, the dividend constitutes part of the gross estate.

2. Interest on bonds accrued till the date of death is also included in gross estate.

3. Example of reporting requirements for Schedule B.

(a) Description of stock should include:

1. Number of shares
2. Whether common or preferred
3. Par value where needed for identification
4. Price per share
5. Exact name of corporation
6. CUSIP number, if available
7. If listed stock, the principal exchange on which sold
8. If not listed, post office address of principal business office and state and date of incorporation

(b) Description of bonds should include:

1. Quantity and denomination
2. Name of obligor
3. CUSIP number, if available
4. Kind of bond
5. Date of maturity
6. Interest rate
7. Interest-due dates
8. The exchange on which listed
9. If not listed, the principal business office

Schedule C

This schedule is used to disclose the decedent's liquid assets.

Schedule D

1. Insurance is includible if the insured possessed any incidental ownership at his or her death, whether exercisable alone or in conjunction with any other person.

2. Insurance is includible if payable to insured's estate or personal representative.

Schedule E

All property of whatever kind or character, whether real estate, personal property, or bank accounts, in which the decedent held at the time of death an interest either as joint tenant with right of survivorship or as a tenant by the entirety must be disclosed under this schedule.

Schedule F

This schedule is used to include all property not included elsewhere, including: "debts due the decedent; interests in business; insurance on the life of another; claims (including the value of the decedent's interest in a claim for refund or income taxes or the amount of the refund actually received); rights; royalties, leaseholds; judgments; reversionary or remainder interests; share in trust funds; household goods and personal effects, including wearing apparel; farm products and growing crops; livestock; farm machinery; automobiles; etc."

Schedule G

Schedule G is designed to obtain disclosure both of antemortem transfers includible in the gross estate and of those not believed to be includible by the executor. In the latter case, the questions asked on Schedule G are designed to elicit sufficient information to give the IRS an opportunity to obtain enough facts to propose includibility.

Disclosure is required of those transfers that include gifts made within three years of death and various types of transfers not completed until decedent's death because of his or her retention of certain interest in or powers over the transferred property or because the transferree can only receive the property by surviving the decedent.

Proper preparation of Schedule G may require extensive questioning of the decedent's family and examination of the decedent's files to assemble the necessary facts with respect to his or her antemortem transfers and to give the executor some basis for judging how much should be disclosed on the schedule and any attachments thereto.

The main portion of Schedule G is divided into two parts. Part A is for giving the description and value of all transfers made by the decedent after December 31, 1976, and within three years of death. The total values on the date of death of these transfers and the gift tax paid by the decedent or the estate for those gifts must be added. Part B then calls for a listing of all other transfers.

Schedule H

Schedule H is designed to obtain disclosure of all general powers of appointment possessed by the decedent at the time of death as well as any such powers that he or she exercised or released (to any extent) and of any trusts not created by the decedent under which he or she possessed any power, beneficial interest, or trusteeship. The purpose of the latter requirements is to give the IRS the opportunity to examine any trust of which the decedent was trustee, to ascertain if he or she had any general powers of appointment.

The instructions for Schedule H require a certified or verified copy of all instruments granting powers of appointment ever possessed by the decedent, together with any instrument by which the power was exercised or released. Copies of these instruments must be filed.

Section 2041 of the IRC includes general powers of appointment in gross estate.

Schedule I

1. Schedule I deals with the inclusion in the gross estate of the value of annuities or other payments receivable by virtue of surviving the decedent.

2. Such annuities or other payments can generally be divided into two groups:

    (a) Those payable under approved employee, self-employed or individual pension or retirement arrangements, and

(b) All others.

3. The general rule for inclusion provides that the gross estate shall include the value of an annuity or other payment (other than life insurance) receivable by a beneficiary by reason of surviving the decedent, under any form of contract or agreement entered into after March 3, 1931, provided that under the same contract or agreement an annuity or other payment was payable to the decedent, or the decedent possessed a right to receive such annuity or payment, either alone or in conjunction with another, for his or her life or for any period not ascertainable without reference to his or her death, or for any period that did not in fact end before his or her death.

Schedule J

FUNERAL EXPENSES

Funeral expenses are deductible for federal *estate tax* purposes. To qualify as a deductible funeral expense, however, the amount deducted must be actually expended and allowable as a claim against property subject to claims.

ADMINISTRATION EXPENSES:

1. IRS authorizes the deduction of administration expenses for federal estate tax purposes.

2. Deductible administration expenses are generally limited to such expenses as are "actually and necessarily" incurred in the administration of the decedent's estate in collecting assets, paying debts, and distributing estate property to the persons entitled thereto. Thus, the item encompasses executor's and attorney's commissions and fees and "miscellaneous" expenses. Generally, any other expense that is actually and necessarily incurred incident to administration in collecting assets, paying debts, and distributing estate property is deductible. Administration expenses can be deducted entirely for income tax purposes or for federal estate tax purposes or partly for one such purpose and partly for the other.

Schedule K

Treasury regulations provide that claims against a decedent's estate are deductible to the extent that they exist at the time of death (whether or not matured) and are enforceable personal obligations of the decedent.

Schedule L

Any expenses incurred in administering property subject to claims are deductible if they would otherwise be allowable as deductions against property subject to claims. To the extent that funeral expenses and claims exceed property subject to claims they must be paid, if they are to be allowed as deductions, before the federal estate tax return is due.

Schedule M

A marital deduction is allowed from the adjusted gross estate of a decedent who was a citizen or resident of the United States at death for the value of any property interest passing from the decedent to the surviving spouse, limited to the greater of 50 percent of his or her adjusted gross estate or $250,000. To obtain this deduction, the executor must establish:

1. That the decedent was survived by his or her spouse. It is not required that the spouse be either a citizen or a resident.
2. That the property interest passed from the decedent to spouse.
3. That the property interest is a deductible interest.
4. The value of the property interest, and
5. The value of the decedent's adjusted gross estate.

The following areas require special attention in the preparation of Schedule M:

1. Disclaimers
2. Election of surviving spouse
3. Will contests and litigations
4. Widow's support allowance
5. Joint and mutual wills
6. Life estate with general power of appointment

7. Transfers subject to an encumbrance
8. Remainder interests
9. Apportionment of death taxes
10. Effect of administration-expense election

Schedule N

Schedule N recognizes a generally accepted responsibility on the part of a decedent to support a minor child and creates a provision analogous to the marital deduction. Only available under estate tax for post 1976 deaths; no gift tax on orphan's deduction.

Where no known parent of the child survives and where decedent does not have a surviving spouse, a maximum estate tax deduction of $5,000 per year for the number of years the child is under the age of twenty-one is granted for an interest in property that is includible in the decedent's gross estate and that "passes or has passed" from the decedent to the child either outright or in a form that, were the property passing to a spouse, would qualify for the marital deduction.

1. The orphan's deduction is unavailable if the child has a surviving parent, even if there has been a divorce.
2. The deduction is unavailable where the child is orphaned but his or her parent was survived by a spouse, even though the latter is merely a stepparent.
3. A relationship created by legal adoption is treated as replacing a blood relationship.

Schedule O

Charitable deductions have always been permitted within the framework of the federal estate tax.

Schedule P

Credit is given for foreign death taxes.

Schedule Q

Credit is given for tax on prior transfers.

F. Description of Gift Tax

The gift tax is an excise tax levied upon transfers of property made without adequate and full consideration. It is levied upon transfers by gift during the decedent's lifetime.

The gift tax is levied during the transferor's lifetime and is cumulative in nature. From 1932 through 1970, the tax was levied annually on a return due on or before April 15 of the year following the end of the calendar year. Starting in 1971, the gift tax has been levied on a calendar-quarter basis on a return due one and one-half months after the end of a quarter. For gifts made after 1976, a gift-tax return is required on a quarterly basis only when taxable gifts for the quarter plus all other taxable gifts for the calendar year for which no return has been filed exceed $25,000.

The value of gifts made during preceding calendar years and calendar quarters determines the rate brackets applicable to the gifts most recently made.

1. Unified rate schedule after 1976

A single unified gift and estate tax rate schedule applies for gifts made, and for the estates of decedents dying, after December 31, 1976. The rates are progressive on the basis of cumulative transfers during lifetime and at death.

2. Unified credit after 1976

For post-1976 gifts and post-1978 estates, a single unified credit is subtracted after the determination of the taxpayer's gift or estate tax liability.

A special transitional rule applies to gifts during the period September 9, 1976, through December 31, 1976. To the extent that use is made of the $30,000 lifetime exemption during this period, the allowable unified credit is reduced by an amount equal to 20 percent of the exemption.

3. Computing the tax on post-1976 gifts

The amount of gift tax payable for any calendar quarter or year, as the case may be, for post-1976 gifts is determined by applying the unified rate schedule to cumulative lifetime taxable gifts and subtracting the taxes payable for prior taxable periods. Gifts made prior to 1977 are taken into account in the computation of post-1976 gifts. In computing the tax payable on post-1976 gifts, the reduction for taxes previously paid is based upon the unified rate schedule. Then, to the extent allowable, the unified credit can be used to offset the gift tax.

4. Annual exclusions

To prevent small gifts from being hampered by tax requirements, the law permits the exclusion each year of the first $3,000 in gifts made to any one donee, provided the gifts are not of future interest.

5. Deductions

Before applying the unified transfer tax rates, the donor may deduct from the value of the gifts he or she is required to report: the first $100,000 of the value of post-1976 transfers to his or her spouse as a "marital deduction;" no deduction is allowed for the second $100,000 of gifts (thereafter, the allowable deduction is 50 percent of transfers in excess of $200,000); transfers for public, charitable, and religious uses; and any items that tend to reduce the net value of the gift.

6. Specific exemption for pre-1977 gifts

In addition to the annual exclusion of $3,000 for gifts to each donee, the donor was entitled to a specific exemption of $30,000 for gifts made prior to 1977. The specific exemption was repealed, starting with gifts made in 1977, and replaced by a unified credit.

7. Rates and computation

For gifts made after December 31, 1970, or for calendar years beginning with 1971, the gift tax generally is computed on a calendar-quarter basis and is reportable on a quarterly return filed on or before the fifteenth day of the second month following the close of the calendar quarter in which a taxable gift is made.

The gift tax for a quarter is determined by computing a tax on the taxable gifts made in that quarter plus taxable gifts made in all prior years and calendar quarters.

8. Cumulative effect of tax

The tax is cumulative in nature. Prior years' and quarters' gifts also push the current quarter's gifts into higher tax brackets.

Starting in 1971, the gift tax for each quarter is determined by computing a tax on the taxable gifts made in that quarter plus taxable gifts made in all prior years beginning with June 6, 1932, and in all prior quarters beginning with the first quarter of calendar 1971. There is then subtracted from the resultant figure a tax computed only on the taxable gifts made in prior years and quarters. The unified transfer rate schedules are used in both of these computations for gifts made after 1976. The difference between the two amounts, as computed above, is the amount of gift tax payable for the quarter less the unified credit to the extent it has not been used in preceding quarters.

Because of the method used to compute gift taxes for a given quarter, it is necessary on the gift tax return not only to determine the amount of taxable gifts for the quarter covered by the return but also to report the amount of taxable gifts determined for all prior calendar quarters and all prior years, beginning with 1932.

9. Computation of gift tax

The gift tax is determined as follows:

a. Compute a tentative tax on the total taxable gifts made by the donor, including:
   (1) The taxable gifts made before 1977
   (2) The taxable gifts made after 1976
   (3) The taxable gifts made in the present quarter

b. Compute a tentative tax on the sum of all taxable gifts made by the donor, excluding the taxable gifts made in the present quarter.

c. Subtract the tax computed in step *b* from the tax computed in step *a*. This result is the gift tax before the available unified credit. The resulting gift tax is reduced by the amount of the unified credit available in the present quarter.

DISCUSSION QUESTIONS AND PRACTICAL EXERCISES

Estate Administration

1. Estate Questionnaire. This assignment requires that the student review the questionnaire in the exhibit 10.12 and make recommendations on the following:
   a. What information appears very hard to collect? Explain (At least three items)
   b. Name at least five outside parties that could assist you in the collection of this information.
2. Collection/Identification of Assets. While not all wills or states require what is formally known as an *inventory*, every state has some mode of asset collection or identification in the estate. Assume the following assets are discovered. Which assets are generally not includible in the inventory?
   a. Life insurance proceeds from testator to wife for $100,000.
   b. Real estate owned by testator and other parties aside from his wife
   c. Pension benefits within IRS guidelines
   d. $5,000 in General Motors stock
   e. Personal residence owned by spouse and testator as tenants by the entireties
3. *Estate-Administration Correspondences.* Draft a sample model letter to be used regularly in your work on the following topics:
   a. Distribution letter to all potential legatees or beneficiaries under the estate
   b. Letter explaining the costs of counsel fees to the estate to all interested legatees or parties under the estate.
   c. Letter explaining the tax system on estates in your jurisdiction.
   d. Letter thanking personal representative, executor, or administrator for a job well done after the estate has been closed.

United States Estate-Tax Return

Ask at your local IRS office for a Federal Estate-Tax form (706). Using the factual situation below, complete that form.

The firm of Peterson and McCune, P.C., 150 Yantic Street, Anytown, Somewhere County, Your State, 11111 will represent the estate of James L. Urban, who died on February 9, 1985. Mr. Urban is survived by his wife, Vanessa, who continues to live in their home at 259 Spring Street, Anytown, Somewhere County, Your State, 11111. Mr. Urban is also survived by two adult sons, Kurt M. Urban, 15 Grieb Road, Anytown, Somewhere County, Your State, and Robert M. Urban, 43 Anthony Terrace, Anytown, Somewhere County, Your State. The Urbans have lived in Anytown for 25 years, having lived in Montego Bay, Long Island, New York, previous to that.

Mr. Urban was a retired law professor. You have a copy of his death certificate (#82-756) issued by the Somewhere County Bureau of Vital Statistics. It indicates that Mr. Urban was born on 4/24/19 and that the cause of death was a heart attack.

The estate is to be administered in Anytown, Your State. After the initial papers are filed, the court assigns #83-416 as the probate number for the estate. The will names Mrs. Urban as executor and requests that no bond be required of her. The will also leaves everything to Mrs. Urban, provided she survives Mr. Urban.

Assets.   Mr. Urban owned or had an interest in the following items:

□ An undivided one-half interest in the real estate where the Urbans lived, described as one-half Lot 7 of Mather's Subdivision, 259 Spring Street. Vanessa owns the other one-half interest as joint tenant with right of survivorship. The real estate was appraised at $140,000 by Sandy McCune, a local real estate broker, and there is an outstanding mortgage in the principal amount of $30,000.
□ 1983 Chevy Nova with a blue book value of $8,500.

□ 1982 Toyota with a blue book value of $6,300.

□ Household goods, personal property, and some tools worth a total of $22,000.

□ Coin collection worth $35,000

□ Stocks and bonds as follows:

400 shares of General Motors common stock, certificate no. N3-21, valued at $36.75 per share. There is an accrued dividend of $1 per share payable on February 15.

200 shares of AT&T common stock, certificate no. NY5 82, valued at $79 per share. No accrued dividends.

□ Bank accounts at the National Bank & Trust Company

Joint checking with Vanessa #4589	$ 568.18
Joint savings with Vanessa #7820	2,452.80
Joint savings with Kurt #5287	10,000.00
Joint savings with Robert #5697	10,000.00
Certificate of deposit #5-487	25,000.00
Certificate of deposit #5-486	40,000.00

□ Life insurance policy no. 11394 in the amount of $200,000 with Northeastern Mutual Insurance Company. The beneficiaries are Kurt and Robert in equal shares.

The plan for administering the estate is as follows:

a) Transfer all jointly held assets immediately

b) Apply for the insurance benefits immediately

c) Transfer the cars to Vanessa immediately

d) Distribute the household and personal goods to Vanessa immediately

e) Cash the two CDs and reinvest them in a bank money market fund in the name of the estate

f) Transfer the real estate and stocks and bonds to Vanessa in December 1982, when the estate is to close

g) File two accountings: September 30, 1982, and December 31, 1982

Vanessa has decided not to take an executor's fee. The attorney's fee has been set at $7,000.

The checkbook for the estate looks like this (withdrawals are in parenthesis):

DATE	DESCRIPTION	AMOUNT
3/15/82	General Motors dividend	$ 400.00
"	#100—Anytown Tax Collector (4th qtr. taxes)	(460.00)
3/16/82	Proceeds of CDs	56,239.12
3/17/82	#101—Anytown Gas & Electric (after death)	(80.00)
"	#102—Court costs	(170.00)
"	#103—Swan Funeral Home	(1,800.00)
"	#104—American Express	(90.00)
"	#105—Anytown Bank & Trust (mortgage)	(300.00)
3/20/82	Service charge	(1.50)
3/29/82	#106—Open money market account	(54,000.00)
4/15/82	#107—1981 federal income tax	(1,100.00)
"	#108—Appraiser's fee—coin collection	(30.00)
"	#109—Appraiser's fee-coin collection	(25.00)
4/20/82	Service charge	(1.50)
5/1/82	#110—Appraiser's fee—house	(250.00)
"	AT&T dividend	125.00
5/5/82	Social Security death benefit	225.00
5/20/82	Service charge	(1.50)
6/15/82	GM dividend	500.00
6/20/82	Service charge	(1.50)
7/20/82	Service charge	(1.50)
8/1/82	AT&T dividend	125.00
8/20/82	Service charge	(1.50)
9/15/82	GM dividend	500.00
"	AT&T interest	500.00
9/19/82	#111—Transfer to money market account	(3,000.00)
9/20/82	Service Charge	(1.50)
10/20/82	Service Charge	(1.50)
11/1/82	AT&T dividend	(125.00)
11/20/82	Service Charge	(1.50)
12/1/82	Transfer from money market account	60,145.50

12/15/82	GM dividend	500.00
12/20/82	Service charge	(1.50)
12/22/82	#112—Attorney fee	(7,000.00)
12/22/82	#113—Final distribution to Vanessa	

The money market fund indicates the following interest earned:

April	$173.00
May	365.00
June	390.00
July	368.00
August	407.00
September	401.00
October	425.00
November	470.00
December	50.00

(NOTE: interest is paid on the last day of the month)

The Urban family have the following Social Security numbers:

James L. Urban	306-91-8432
Vanessa M. Urban	401-18-7631
Kurt M. Urban	434-90-1620
Robert M. Urban	434-86-1287

ENRICHMENT ACTIVITY

Assume that you have just won a million dollar lottery. Make a list of things you would buy with your winnings as well as what investments you would make. Write your own last will and testament based upon your newly created estate. In it establish one charitable trust.

Attend orphans' court for several sessions. Outline the court's procedure in estate probate.

SUGGESTED READING

AKER, J. BROOKE. *Profitable Wills and Estate Practice Under the All-New Tax Law Setup*. Englewood Cliffs, N.J.: Executive Reports Corp., 1982.

AVERILL, LAWRENCE H. *Estate Valuation Handbook*. New York: John Wiley & Sons, 1983.

Basic Will Drafting Techniques. New York: Practising Law Institute, c. 1980.

The Closely Held Business: Financial Planning for the Owners. New York: Practising Law Institute, 1984.

Fundamental Concepts of Estate Planning. New York: Practising Law Institute, 1984.

HOLZMAN, ROBERT S. *Encyclopedia of Estate Planning*. New York: Boardroom Books, 1983.

PINTO, ROBERT J. *Basic Estate Planning*. Newark, N.J.: N.J. Institute for Continuing Legal Education, 1982.

SCHOENBLUM, JEFFREY A. *Multistate and Multinational Estate Planning*. Boston: Little, Brown, & Co., 1982.

SHAFFER, THOMAS L. *The Planning and Drafting of Wills and Trusts*. Mineola, N.Y.: Foundation Press, 1979.

The Use of Trusts in Estate Planning, 1983. New York: Practising Law Institute, 1983.

INDEX